CompTIA Security+™

EXAM GUIDE
Second Edition

ALL · IN · ONE

CompTIA Security+ ™

EXAM GUIDE

Second Edition

Gregory White
Wm. Arthur Conklin
Dwayne Williams
Roger Davis
Chuck Cothren

New York • Chicago • San Francisco • Lisbon
London • Madrid • Mexico City • Milan • New Delhi
San Juan • Seoul • Singapore • Sydney • Toronto

The McGraw·Hill Companies

Cataloging-in-Publication Data is on file with the Library of Congress

CompTIA Security+™ All-in-One Exam Guide, Second Edition

1234567890 DOC DOC 0198

ISBN: Book p/n 978-0-07-160129-0 and CD p/n 978-0-07-160130-6
of set 978-0-07-160127-6

MHID: Book p/n 0-07-160129-5 and CD p/n 0-07-160130-9
of set 0-07-160127-9

Sponsoring Editor	**Technical Editor**	**Production Supervisor**
Tim Green	*Glen Clarke*	*George Anderson*
Editorial Supervisor	**Copy Editor**	**Composition**
Jody McKenzie	*Lisa Theobald*	*EuroDesign - Peter F. Hancik*
Project Editor	**Proofreader**	**Illustration**
LeeAnn Pickrell	*Susie Elkind*	*Lyssa Wald*
Acquisitions Coordinators	**Indexer**	**Art Director, Cover**
Jennifer Housh, Carly Stapleton	*Karin Arrigoni*	*Jeff Weeks*

CompTIA Authorized Quality Curriculum

The logo of the CompTIA Authorized Quality Curriculum (CAQC) program and the status of this or other training material as "Authorized" under the CompTIA Authorized Quality Curriculum program signifies that, in CompTIA's opinion, such training material covers the content of CompTIA's related certification exam.

The contents of this training material were created for the CompTIA Security+ exam covering CompTIA certification objectives that were current as of 2008.

CompTIA has not reviewed or approved the accuracy of the contents of this training material and specifically disclaims any warranties of merchantability or fitness for a particular purpose.

CompTIA makes no guarantee concerning the success of persons using any such "Authorized" or other training material in order to prepare for any CompTIA certification exam.

How to become CompTIA certified:

This training material can help you prepare for and pass a related CompTIA certification exam or exams. In order to achieve CompTIA certification, you must register for and pass a CompTIA certification exam or exams.

In order to become CompTIA certified, you must

1. Select a certification exam provider. For more information please visit http://www.comptia.org/certification/general_information/exam_locations.aspx.

2. Register for and schedule a time to take the CompTIA certification exam(s) at a convenient location.

3. Read and sign the Candidate Agreement, which will be presented at the time of the exam(s). The text of the Candidate Agreement can be found at http://www.comptia.org/certification/general_information/candidate_agreement.aspx.

4. Take and pass the CompTIA certification exam(s).

For more information about CompTIA's certifications, such as its industry acceptance, benefits, or program news, please visit www.comptia.org/certification.

CompTIA is a not-for-profit information technology (IT) trade association. CompTIA's certifications are designed by subject matter experts from across the IT industry. Each CompTIA certification is vendor-neutral, covers multiple technologies, and requires demonstration of skills and knowledge widely sought after by the IT industry.

To contact CompTIA with any questions or comments, please call (1) (630) 678 8300 or email questions@comptia.org.

This book is dedicated to the many security professionals who daily work to ensure the safety of our nation's critical infrastructures. We want to recognize the thousands of dedicated individuals who strive to protect our national assets but who seldom receive praise and often are only noticed when an incident occurs.
To you, we say thank you for a job well done!

ABOUT THE AUTHORS

Dr. Gregory White has been involved in computer and network security since 1986. He spent 19 years on active duty with the United States Air Force and is currently in the Air Force Reserves assigned to the Air Force Information Warfare Center. He obtained his Ph.D. in computer science from Texas A&M University in 1995. His dissertation topic was in the area of computer network intrusion detection, and he continues to conduct research in this area today. He is currently the Director for the Center for Infrastructure Assurance and Security (CIAS) and is an associate professor of information systems at the University of Texas at San Antonio (UTSA). Dr. White has written and presented numerous articles and conference papers on security. He is also the coauthor for three textbooks on computer and network security and has written chapters for two other security books. Dr. White continues to be active in security research. His current research initiatives include efforts in high-speed intrusion detection, infrastructure protection, and methods to calculate a return on investment and the total cost of ownership from security products.

Dr. Wm. Arthur Conklin is an assistant professor in the College of Technology at the University of Houston. Dr. Conklin's research interests lie in software assurance and the application of systems theory to security issues. His dissertation was on the motivating factors for home users in adopting security on their own PCs. He has coauthored four books on information security and has written and presented numerous conference and academic journal papers. A former U.S. Navy officer, he was also previously the Technical Director at the Center for Infrastructure Assurance and Security at the University of Texas at San Antonio.

Chuck Cothren, CISSP, is the president of Globex Security, Inc., and applies a wide array of network security experience to consulting and training. This includes performing controlled penetration testing, network security policies, network intrusion detection systems, firewall configuration and management, and wireless security assessments. He has analyzed security methodologies for Voice over Internet Protocol (VoIP) systems and supervisory control and data acquisition (SCADA) systems. Mr. Cothren was previously employed at The University of Texas Center for Infrastructure Assurance and Security. He has also worked as a consulting department manager, performing vulnerability assessments and other security services for Fortune 100 clients to provide them with vulnerability assessments and other security services. He is coauthor of the book *Voice and Data Security* as well as *Principles of Computer Security.* Mr. Cothren holds a B.S. in Industrial Distribution from Texas A&M University.

Roger L. Davis, CISSP, CISM, CISA, is Program Manager of ERP systems at the Church of Jesus Christ of Latter-day Saints, managing the Church's global financial system in over 140 countries. He has served as president of the Utah chapter of the Information Systems Security Association (ISSA) and various board positions for the Utah chapter of the Information Systems Audit and Control Association (ISACA). He is a retired Air Force lieutenant colonel with 30 years of military and information systems/security experience. Mr. Davis served on the faculty of Brigham Young University and the Air Force Institute of Technology. He coauthored McGraw-Hill's *Principles of Computer Security* and *Voice and Data Security*. He holds a master's degree in computer science from George Washington University, a bachelor's degree in computer science from Brigham Young University, and performed post-graduate studies in electrical engineering and computer science at the University of Colorado.

Dwayne Williams is Associate Director, Special Projects, for the Center for Infrastructure Assurance and Security at the University of Texas at San Antonio and has over 18 years of experience in information systems and network security. Mr. Williams's experience includes six years of commissioned military service as a Communications-Computer Information Systems Officer in the United States Air Force, specializing in network security, corporate information protection, intrusion detection systems, incident response, and VPN technology. Prior to joining the CIAS, he served as Director of Consulting for SecureLogix Corporation, where he directed and provided security assessment and integration services to Fortune 100, government, public utility, oil and gas, financial, and technology clients. Mr. Williams graduated in 1993 from Baylor University with a Bachelor of Arts in Computer Science. Mr. Williams is a Certified Information Systems Security Professional (CISSP) and coauthor of *Voice and Data Security, Security+ Certification,* and *Principles of Computer Security.*

About the Technical Editor

Glen E. Clarke, MCSE/MCSD/MCDBA/MCT/CEH/SCNP/CIWSA/A+/Security+, is an independent trainer and consultant, focusing on network security assessments and educating IT professionals on hacking countermeasures. Mr. Clark spends most of his time delivering certified courses on Windows Server 2003, SQL Server, Exchange Server, Visual Basic .NET, ASP.NET, Ethical Hacking, and Security Analysis. He has authored and technical edited a number of certification titles including *The Network+ Certification Study Guide, 4th Edition.* You can visit Mr. Clark online at http://www.gleneclarke.com or contact him at glenclarke@accesswave.ca.

CONTENTS AT A GLANCE

Part I	Security Concepts	. . . .	1
Chapter 1	General Security Concepts	. . . .	3
Chapter 2	Operational Organizational Security	. . . .	27
Chapter 3	Legal Issues, Privacy, and Ethics	. . . .	53

Part II	Cryptography and Applications	. . . .	75
Chapter 4	Cryptography	. . . .	77
Chapter 5	Public Key Infrastructure	. . . .	109
Chapter 6	Standards and Protocols	. . . .	155

Part III	Security in the Infrastructure	. . . .	183
Chapter 7	Physical Security	. . . .	185
Chapter 8	Infrastructure Security	. . . .	201
Chapter 9	Authentication and Remote Access	. . . .	241
Chapter 10	Wireless Security	. . . .	275

Part IV	Security in Transmissions	. . . .	295
Chapter 11	Intrusion Detection Systems	. . . .	297
Chapter 12	Security Baselines	. . . .	339
Chapter 13	Types of Attacks and Malicious Software	. . . .	391
Chapter 14	E-Mail and Instant Messaging	. . . .	425
Chapter 15	Web Components	. . . .	443

Part V	Operational Security	473
Chapter 16	Disaster Recovery and Business Continuity	475
Chapter 17	Risk Management	493
Chapter 18	Change Management	513
Chapter 19	Privilege Management	529
Chapter 20	Computer Forensics	553

Part VI	Appendixes	567
Appendix A	About the CD	569
Appendix B	OSI Model and Internet Protocols	571
	Glossary	581
	Index	601

CONTENTS

Acknowledgments xxv
Preface xxvii
Introduction xxix

Part I   Security Concepts   I

Chapter 1   General Security Concepts   3
The Security+ Exam   3
Basic Security Terminology   6
    Security Basics   7
    Access Control   16
    Authentication   19
Chapter Review   21
    Quick Tips   21
    Questions   22
    Answers   25

Chapter 2   Operational Organizational Security   27
Policies, Standards, Guidelines, and Procedures   27
The Security Perimeter   28
Logical Access Controls   30
    Access Control Policies   30
Social Engineering   34
    Phishing   35
    Vishing   36
    Shoulder Surfing   36
    Dumpster Diving   37
    Hoaxes   37
Organizational Policies and Procedures   37
    Security Policies   38
    Privacy   43
    Service Level Agreements   44
    Human Resources Policies   44
    Code of Ethics   46
Chapter Review   47
    Questions   47
    Answers   50

Chapter 3   Legal Issues, Privacy, and Ethics 53
               Cybercrime 54
                   Common Internet Crime Schemes 55
                   Sources of Laws 56
                   Computer Trespass 56
                   Significant U.S. Laws 57
                   Payment Card Industry Data Security Standards (PCI DSS) . 59
                   Import/Export Encryption Restrictions 60
                   Digital Signature Laws 63
                   Digital Rights Management 65
               Privacy 66
                   U.S. Privacy Laws 66
                   European Laws 67
               Ethics 68
                   SANS Institute IT Code of Ethics 69
               Chapter Review 71
                   Questions 71
                   Answers 73

Part II   Cryptography and Applications 75

Chapter 4   Cryptography 77
               Algorithms 78
               Hashing 81
                   SHA 82
                   Message Digest 84
                   Hashing Summary 86
               Symmetric Encryption 86
                   DES 87
                   3DES 89
                   AES 90
                   CAST 91
                   RC 91
                   Blowfish 94
                   IDEA 94
                   Symmetric Encryption Summary 95
               Asymmetric Encryption 95
                   RSA 96
                   Diffie-Hellman 97
                   ElGamal 98
                   ECC 98
                   Asymmetric Encryption Summary 99
               Steganography 99

Cryptography Algorithm Use 100
   Confidentiality 100
   Integrity 101
   Nonrepudiation 101
   Authentication 101
   Digital Signatures 102
   Key Escrow 102
   Cryptographic Applications 103
Chapter Review 104
   Questions 104
   Answers 107

Chapter 5 Public Key Infrastructure 109
The Basics of Public Key Infrastructures 109
Certificate Authorities 112
Registration Authorities 113
   Local Registration Authorities 116
Certificate Repositories 116
Trust and Certificate Verification 116
Digital Certificates 120
   Certificate Attributes 121
   Certificate Extensions 123
   Certificate Lifecycles 124
Centralized or Decentralized Infrastructures 130
   Hardware Storage Devices 131
Private Key Protection 132
   Key Recovery 133
   Key Escrow 135
Public Certificate Authorities 136
In-house Certificate Authorities 137
Outsourced Certificate Authorities 138
Tying Different PKIs Together 139
   Trust Models 140
Chapter Review 146
   Questions 147
   Answers 152

Chapter 6 Standards and Protocols 155
PKIX/PKCS 157
   PKIX Standards 158
   PKCS 162
   Why You Need to Know 163
X.509 164
SSL/TLS 165
ISAKMP 167

CMP 168
XKMS 169
S/MIME 171
    IETF S/MIME v3 Specifications 172
PGP 173
    How PGP Works 173
    Where Can You Use PGP? 174
HTTPS 174
IPsec 175
CEP 175
FIPS 175
Common Criteria (CC) 176
WTLS 176
WEP 177
    WEP Security Issues 177
ISO/IEC 27002 (Formerly ISO 17799) 177
Chapter Review 178
    Questions 179
    Answers 181

Part III   Security in the Infrastructure 183

Chapter 7   Physical Security 185
The Security Problem 185
Physical Security Safeguards 188
    Walls and Guards 188
    Policies and Procedures 189
    Access Controls and Monitoring 191
    Environmental Controls 193
    Authentication 194
Chapter Review 197
    Questions 197
    Answers 199

Chapter 8   Infrastructure Security 201
Devices 201
    Workstations 202
    Servers 204
    Network Interface Cards 205
    Hubs 206
    Bridges 206
    Switches 206
    Routers 208
    Firewalls 209

Wireless 212
Modems 214
Telecom/PBX 215
RAS 215
VPN 216
Intrusion Detection Systems 216
Network Access Control 216
Network Monitoring/Diagnostic 217
Mobile Devices 218
Media 219
Coaxial Cable 219
UTP/STP 219
Fiber 221
Unguided Media 222
Security Concerns for Transmission Media 224
Physical Security 224
Removable Media 225
Magnetic Media 225
Optical Media 227
Electronic Media 228
Security Topologies 229
Security Zones 229
Telephony 233
VLANs 233
NAT 235
Tunneling 236
Chapter Review 236
Questions 237
Answers 239

Chapter 9   Authentication and Remote Access 241
The Remote Access Process 241
Identification 242
Authentication 243
Authorization 247
IEEE 802.1x 247
RADIUS 248
RADIUS Authentication 248
RADIUS Authorization 250
RADIUS Accounting 250
DIAMETER 250
TACACS+ 251
TACACS+ Authentication 251
TACACS+ Authorization 253
TACACS+ Accounting 253

L2TP and PPTP	....	254
PPTP	....	254
PPP	....	256
CHAP	....	256
PAP	....	257
EAP	....	257
L2TP	....	257
NT LAN Manager	....	258
Telnet	....	258
SSH	....	258
IEEE 802.11	....	260
VPNs	....	260
IPsec	....	261
Security Associations	....	262
IPsec Configurations	....	262
IPsec Security	....	265
Vulnerabilities	....	268
Chapter Review	....	269
Questions	....	270
Answers	....	272

Chapter 10	**Wireless Security**	....	**275**
	Wireless Networking	....	275
	Mobile Phones	....	276
	Bluetooth	....	279
	802.11	....	281
	Chapter Review	....	289
	Questions	....	289
	Answers	....	292

Part IV	**Security in Transmissions**	....	**295**

Chapter 11	**Intrusion Detection Systems**	....	**297**
	History of Intrusion Detection Systems	....	298
	IDS Overview	....	299
	Host-based IDSs	....	300
	Advantages of HIDSs	....	304
	Disadvantages of HIDSs	....	305
	Active vs. Passive HIDSs	....	306
	Resurgence and Advancement of HIDSs	....	306
	PC-based Malware Protection	....	307
	Antivirus Products	....	307
	Personal Software Firewalls	....	310
	Pop-up Blocker	....	312
	Windows Defender	....	313

Network-based IDSs 315
    Advantages of a NIDS 319
    Disadvantages of a NIDS 319
    Active vs. Passive NIDSs 320
Signatures 320
False Positives and Negatives 322
IDS Models 322
Intrusion Prevention Systems 323
Honeypots and Honeynets 325
Firewalls 327
Proxy Servers 327
Internet Content Filters 328
Protocol Analyzers 329
Network Mappers 331
Anti-spam 331
Chapter Review 333
    Questions 334
    Answers 337

Chapter 12 Security Baselines 339
Overview Baselines 339
Password Selection 340
    Password Policy Guidelines 340
    Selecting a Password 342
    Components of a Good Password 343
    Password Aging 343
Operating System and Network Operating System Hardening 344
    Hardening Microsoft Operating Systems 345
    Hardening UNIX- or Linux-Based Operating Systems 347
Network Hardening 363
    Software Updates 364
    Device Configuration 364
    Ports and Services 366
    Traffic Filtering 368
Application Hardening 370
    Application Patches 371
    Patch Management 371
    Web Servers 374
    Mail Servers 377
    FTP Servers 379
    DNS Servers 379
    File and Print Services 380
    Active Directory 381
Group Policies 382
    Security Templates 384

Chapter Review 385
    Questions 386
    Answers 388

Chapter 13 Types of Attacks and Malicious Software 391
Avenues of Attack 391
    The Steps in an Attack 392
    Minimizing Possible Avenues of Attack 394
Attacking Computer Systems and Networks 394
    Denial-of-Service Attacks 394
    Backdoors and Trapdoors 398
    Null Sessions 398
    Sniffing 399
    Spoofing 400
    Man-in-the-Middle Attacks 403
    Replay Attacks 404
    TCP/IP Hijacking 405
    Attacks on Encryption 405
    Address System Attacks 406
    Password Guessing 407
    Software Exploitation 409
    Malicious Code 409
    War-Dialing and War-Driving 416
    Social Engineering 417
Auditing 417
Chapter Review 418
    Questions 419
    Answers 422

Chapter 14 E-Mail and Instant Messaging 425
Security of E-Mail 425
Malicious Code 426
Hoax E-Mails 428
Unsolicited Commercial E-Mail (Spam) 429
Mail Encryption 431
Instant Messaging 435
Chapter Review 438
    Questions 438
    Answers 441

Chapter 15 Web Components 443
Current Web Components and Concerns 444
Protocols 444
    Encryption (SSL and TLS) 444
    The Web (HTTP and HTTPS) 451
    Directory Services (DAP and LDAP) 452

File Transfer (FTP and SFTP) 454
Vulnerabilities 455
Code-Based Vulnerabilities 455
Buffer Overflows 456
Java and JavaScript 457
ActiveX 459
Securing the Browser 461
CGI 461
Server-Side Scripts 462
Cookies 462
Signed Applets 465
Browser Plug-ins 466
Application-Based Weaknesses 467
Open Vulnerability and Assessment Language (OVAL) 468
Chapter Review 469
Questions 469
Answers 472

Part V   Operational Security 473

Chapter 16   Disaster Recovery and Business Continuity 475
Disaster Recovery 475
Disaster Recovery Plans/Process 476
Backups 478
Utilities 487
Secure Recovery 487
High Availability and Fault Tolerance 488
Chapter Review 488
Questions 489
Answers 491

Chapter 17   Risk Management 493
An Overview of Risk Management 493
Example of Risk Management at the
International Banking Level 494
Key Terms for Understanding Risk Management 494
What Is Risk Management? 495
Business Risks 497
Examples of Business Risks 497
Examples of Technology Risks 498
Risk Management Models 498
General Risk Management Model 499
Software Engineering Institute Model 502
Model Application 502

Qualitatively Assessing Risk 502
Quantitatively Assessing Risk 505
Qualitative vs. Quantitative Risk Assessment 507
Tools 508
Chapter Review 509
    Questions 509
    Answers 511

Chapter 18   Change Management 513
Why Change Management? 514
The Key Concept: Separation (Segregation) of Duties 515
Elements of Change Management 517
Implementing Change Management 519
    The Purpose of a Change Control Board 520
    Code Integrity 522
The Capability Maturity Model Integration 522
Chapter Review 523
    Questions 523
    Answers 526

Chapter 19   Privilege Management 529
User, Group, and Role Management 530
    User 530
    Groups 532
    Role 532
Password Policies 533
    Domain Password Policy 534
Single Sign-On 535
Centralized vs. Decentralized Management 536
    Centralized Management 536
    Decentralized Management 537
    The Decentralized, Centralized Model 538
Auditing (Privilege, Usage, and Escalation) 538
    Privilege Auditing 538
    Usage Auditing 539
    Escalation Auditing 540
Logging and Auditing of Log Files 541
    Common Logs 541
    Periodic Audits of Security Settings 542
Handling Access Control (MAC, DAC, and RBAC) 543
    Mandatory Access Control (MAC) 543
    Discretionary Access Control (DAC) 545
    Role-based Access Control (RBAC) 546
    Rule-based Access Control (RBAC) 546
    Account Expiration 547

Permissions and Rights in Windows Operating Systems 547
Chapter Review 549
    Questions 550
    Answers 552

Chapter 20   Computer Forensics 553
Evidence 554
    Standards for Evidence 554
    Types of Evidence 554
    Three Rules Regarding Evidence 555
Collecting Evidence 555
    Acquiring Evidence 556
    Identifying Evidence 558
    Protecting Evidence 558
    Transporting Evidence 558
    Storing Evidence 558
    Conducting the Investigation 559
Chain of Custody 560
Free Space vs. Slack Space 561
    Free Space 561
    Slack Space 561
Message Digest and Hash 561
Analysis 562
Chapter Review 563
    Questions 564
    Answers 566

Part VI   Appendixes 567

Appendix A   About the CD 569
System Requirements 569
LearnKey Online Training 569
Installing and Running MasterExam 569
    MasterExam 570
Electronic Book 570
Help 570
Removing Installation(s) 570
Technical Support 570
    LearnKey Technical Support 570

Appendix B   OSI Model and Internet Protocols 571
Networking Frameworks and Protocols 571
OSI Model 572
    Application Layer 574
    Presentation Layer 575

Session Layer 575
Transport Layer 575
Network Layer 576
Data-Link Layer 576
Physical Layer 576
Internet Protocols 576
TCP 577
UDP 577
IP 577
Message Encapsulation 578
Review 579

Glossary 581

Index 601

ACKNOWLEDGMENTS

We, the authors of *CompTIA Security+ Certification All-in-One Exam Guide*, have many individuals who we need to acknowledge—individuals without whom this effort would not have been successful.

The list needs to start with those folks at McGraw-Hill who worked tirelessly with the project's multiple authors and contributors and led us successfully through the minefield that is a book schedule and who took our rough chapters and drawings and turned them into a final, professional product we can be proud of. We thank all the good people from the Acquisitions team, Tim Green, Jennifer Housh, and Carly Stapleton; from the Editorial Services team, Jody McKenzie; and from the Illustration and Production team, George Anderson, Peter Hancik, and Lyssa Wald. We also thank the technical editor Glen Clarke; the project editor, LeeAnn Pickrell; the copyeditor, Lisa Theobald; the proofreader, Susie Elkind; and the indexer, Karin Arrigoni for all their attention to detail that made this a finer work after they finished with it.

We also need to acknowledge our current employers who, to our great delight, have seen fit to pay us to work in a career field that we all find exciting and rewarding. There is never a dull moment in security because it is constantly changing.

We would like to thank Art Conklin for herding the cats on this one.

Finally, we would each like to individually thank those people who—on a personal basis—have provided the core support for us individually. Without these special people in our lives, none of us could have put this work together.

I would like to thank my wife, Charlan, for the tremendous support she has always given me. It doesn't matter how many times I have sworn that I'll never get involved with another book project only to return within months to yet another one; through it all, she has remained supportive.

I would also like to publicly thank the United States Air Force, which provided me numerous opportunities since 1986 to learn more about security than I ever knew existed.

To whoever it was who decided to send me as a young captain—fresh from completing my master's degree in artificial intelligence—to my first assignment in computer security: thank you, it has been a great adventure!

—Gregory B. White, Ph.D.

To Susan, my muse and love, for all the time you suffered as I work on books.

—Art Conklin

Special thanks to Josie for all her support.

—Chuck Cothren

Geena, thanks for being my best friend and my greatest support. Anything I am is because of you. Love to my kids and grandkids!

—Roger L. Davis

To my wife and best friend Leah for your love, energy, and support—thank you for always being there. Here's to many more years together.

—Dwayne Williams

PREFACE

Information and computer security has moved from the confines of academia to mainstream America in the last decade. The CodeRed, Nimda, and Slammer attacks were heavily covered in the media and broadcast into the average American's home. It has become increasingly obvious to everybody that something needs to be done in order to secure not only our nation's critical infrastructure but also the businesses we deal with on a daily basis. The question is, "Where do we begin?" What can the average information technology professional do to secure the systems that he or she is hired to maintain? One immediate answer is education and training. If we want to secure our computer systems and networks, we need to know how to do this and what security entails.

Complacency is not an option in today's hostile network environment. While we once considered the insider to be the major threat to corporate networks, and the "script kiddie" to be the standard external threat (often thought of as only a nuisance), the highly interconnected networked world of today is a much different place. The U.S. government identified eight critical infrastructures a few years ago that were thought to be so crucial to the nation's daily operation that if one were to be lost, it would have a catastrophic impact on the nation. To this original set of eight sectors, more have recently been added. A common thread throughout all of these, however, is technology—especially technology related to computers and communication. Thus, if an individual, organization, or nation wanted to cause damage to this nation, it could attack not just with traditional weapons but also with computers through the Internet. It is not surprising to hear that among the other information seized in raids on terrorist organizations, computers and Internet information are usually seized as well. While the insider can certainly still do tremendous damage to an organization, the external threat is again becoming the chief concern among many.

So, where do you, the IT professional seeking more knowledge on security, start your studies? The IT world is overflowing with certifications that can be obtained by those attempting to learn more about their chosen profession. The security sector is no different, and the CompTIA Security+ exam offers a basic level of certification for security. In the pages of this exam guide, you will find not only material that can help you prepare for taking the CompTIA Security+ examination but also the basic information that you will need in order to understand the issues involved in securing your computer systems and networks today. In no way is this exam guide the final source for learning all about protecting your organization's systems, but it serves as a point from which to launch your security studies and career.

One thing is certainly true about this field of study—it never gets boring. It constantly changes as technology itself advances. Something else you will find as you progress in your security studies is that no matter how much technology advances and no matter how many new security devices are developed, at its most basic level, the human is still the weak link in the security chain. If you are looking for an exciting area to delve into, then you have certainly chosen wisely. Security offers a challenging blend of technology and people issues. We, the authors of this exam guide, wish you luck as you embark on an exciting and challenging career path.

—Gregory B. White, Ph.D.

INTRODUCTION

Computer security is becoming increasingly important today as the number of security incidents steadily climbs. Many corporations now spend significant portions of their budget on security hardware, software, services, and personnel. They are spending this money not because it increases sales or enhances the product they provide, but because of the possible consequences should they not take protective actions.

Why Focus on Security?

Security is not something that we want to have to pay for; it would be nice if we didn't have to worry about protecting our data from disclosure, modification, or destruction from unauthorized individuals, but that is not the environment we find ourselves in today. Instead, we have seen the cost of recovering from security incidents steadily rise along with the number of incidents themselves. Since September 11, 2001, this has taken on an even greater sense of urgency as we now face securing our systems not just from attack by disgruntled employees, juvenile hackers, organized crime, or competitors; we now also have to consider the possibility of attacks on our systems from terrorist organizations. If nothing else, the events of September 11, 2001, showed that anybody is a potential target. You do not have to be part of the government or a government contractor; being an American is sufficient reason to make you a target to some, and with the global nature of the Internet, collateral damage from cyber attacks on one organization could have a worldwide impact.

A Growing Need for Security Specialists

In order to protect our computer systems and networks, we will need a significant number of new security professionals trained in the many aspects of computer and network security. This is not an easy task as the systems connected to the Internet become increasingly complex with software whose lines of codes number in the millions. Understanding why this is such a difficult problem to solve is not hard if you consider just how many errors might be present in a piece of software that is several million lines long. When you add the additional factor of how fast software is being developed—from necessity as the market is constantly changing—understanding how errors occur is easy.

Not every "bug" in the software will result in a security hole, but it doesn't take many to have a drastic affect on the Internet community. We can't just blame the vendors for this situation because they are reacting to the demands of government and industry. Most vendors are fairly adept at developing patches for flaws found in their software, and patches are constantly being issued to protect systems from bugs that may introduce security problems. This introduces a whole new problem for managers and administrators—patch management. How important this has become is easily illustrated by how many of the most recent security events have occurred as a result of a security bug that was discovered months prior to the security incident, and for which a patch has been available, but for which the community has not correctly installed the patch, thus making the incident possible. One of the reasons this happens is that many of the individuals responsible for installing the patches are not trained to understand the security implications surrounding the hole or the ramifications of not installing the patch. Many of these individuals simply lack the necessary training.

Because of the need for an increasing number of security professionals who are trained to some minimum level of understanding, certifications such as the Security+ have been developed. Prospective employers want to know that the individual they are considering hiring knows what to do in terms of security. The prospective employee, in turn, wants to have a way to demonstrate his or her level of understanding, which can enhance the candidate's chances of being hired. The community as a whole simply wants more trained security professionals.

Preparing Yourself for the Security+ Exam

CompTIA Security+ Certification All-in-One Exam Guide is designed to help prepare you to take the CompTIA Security+ certification exam. When you pass it, you will demonstrate you have that basic understanding of security that employers are looking for. Passing this certification exam will not be an easy task, for you will need to learn many things to acquire that basic understanding of computer and network security.

How This Book Is Organized

The book is divided into sections and chapters to correspond with the objectives of the exam itself. Some of the chapters are more technical than others—reflecting the nature of the security environment where you will be forced to deal with not only technical details but also other issues such as security policies and procedures as well as training and education. Although many individuals involved in computer and network security have advanced degrees in math, computer science, information systems, or computer or electrical engineering, you do not need this technical background to address security effectively in your organization. You do not need to develop your own cryptographic algorithm; for example, you simply need to be able to understand how cryptography is used along with its strengths and weaknesses. As you progress in your studies, you will learn that many security problems are caused by the human element. The best technology in the world still ends up being placed in an environment where humans have the opportunity to foul things up—and all too often do.

Part I: Security Concepts   The book begins with an introduction of some of the basic elements of security.

Part II: Cryptography and Applications   Cryptography is an important part of security, and this part covers this topic in detail. The purpose is not to make cryptographers out of readers but to instead provide a basic understanding of how cryptography works and what goes into a basic cryptographic scheme. An important subject in cryptography, and one that is essential for the reader to understand, is the creation of public key infrastructures, and this topic is covered as well.

Part III: Security in the Infrastructure   The next part concerns infrastructure issues. In this case, we are not referring to the critical infrastructures identified by the White House several years ago (identifying sectors such as telecommunications, banking and finance, oil and gas, and so forth) but instead the various components that form the backbone of an organization's security structure.

Part IV: Security in Transmissions   This part discusses communications security. This is an important aspect of security because, for years now, we have connected our computers together into a vast array of networks. Various protocols in use today and that the security practitioner needs to be aware of are discussed in this part.

Part V: Operational Security   This part addresses operational and organizational issues. This is where we depart from a discussion of technology again and will instead discuss how security is accomplished in an organization. Because we know that we will not be absolutely successful in our security efforts—attackers are always finding new holes and ways around our security defenses—one of the most important topics we will address is the subject of security incident response and recovery. Also included is a discussion of change management (addressing the subject we alluded to earlier when addressing the problems with patch management), security awareness and training, incident response, and forensics.

Part VI: Appendixes   There are two appendixes in *CompTIA Security+ Certification All-in-One Exam Guide*. Appendix A explains how best to use the CD-ROM included with this book, and Appendix B provides an additional in-depth explanation of the OSI model and Internet protocols, should this information be new to you.

Glossary   Located just before the Index, you will find a useful glossary of security terminology, including many related acronyms and their meaning. We hope that you use the Glossary frequently and find it to be a useful study aid as you work your way through the various topics in this exam guide.

Special Features of the All-in-One Certification Series

To make our exam guides more useful and a pleasure to read, we have designed the All-in-One Certification series to include several conventions.

Icons

To alert you to an important bit of advice, a shortcut, or a pitfall, you'll occasionally see Notes, Tips, Cautions, and Exam Tips peppered throughout the text.

NOTE Notes offer nuggets of especially helpful stuff, background explanations, and information, and terms are defined occasionally.

TIP Tips provide suggestions and nuances to help you learn to finesse your job. Take a tip from us and read the Tips carefully.

CAUTION When you see a Caution, pay special attention. Cautions appear when you have to make a crucial choice or when you are about to undertake something that may have ramifications you might not immediately anticipate. Read them now so you don't have regrets later.

EXAM TIP Exam Tips give you special advice or may provide information specifically related to preparing for the exam itself.

End-of-Chapter Reviews and Chapter Tests

An important part of this book comes at the end of each chapter where you will find a brief review of the high points along with a series of questions followed by the answers to those questions. Each question is in multiple-choice format. The answers provided also include a small discussion explaining why the correct answer actually is the correct answer.

The questions are provided as a study aid to you, the reader and prospective Security+ exam taker. We obviously can't guarantee that if you answer all of our questions correctly you will absolutely pass the certification exam. Instead, what we can guarantee is that the questions will provide you with an idea about how ready you are for the exam.

The CD-ROM

CompTIA Security+ Certification All-in-One Exam Guide also provides you with a CD-ROM of even more test questions and their answers to help you prepare for the certification exam. Read more about the companion CD-ROM in Appendix A.

Onward and Upward

At this point, we hope that you are now excited about the topic of security, even if you weren't in the first place. We wish you luck in your endeavors and welcome you to the exciting field of computer and network security.

PART I

Security Concepts

- **Chapter 1**   General Security Concepts
- **Chapter 2**   Operational Organizational Security
- **Chapter 3**   Legal Issues, Privacy, and Ethics

General Security Concepts

Learn about the Security+ exam
- Learn basic terminology associated with computer and information security
- Discover the basic approaches to computer and information security
- Discover various methods of implementing access controls
- Determine methods used to verify the identity and authenticity of an individual

Why should you be concerned with taking the Security+ exam? The goal of taking the Computing Technology Industry Association (CompTIA) Security+ exam is to prove that you've mastered the worldwide standards for foundation-level security practitioners. With a growing need for trained security professionals, the CompTIA Security+ exam gives you a perfect opportunity to validate your knowledge and understanding of the computer security field. The exam is an appropriate mechanism for many different individuals, including network and system administrators, analysts, programmers, web designers, application developers, and database specialists to show proof of professional achievement in security. The exam's objectives were developed with input and assistance from industry and government agencies, including such notable examples as the Federal Bureau of Investigation (FBI), the National Institute of Standards and Technology (NIST), the U.S. Secret Service, the Information Systems Security Association (ISSA), the Information Systems Audit and Control Association (ISACA), Microsoft Corporation, RSA Security, Motorola, Novell, Sun Microsystems, VeriSign, and Entrust.

The Security+ Exam

The Security+ exam is designed to cover a wide range of security topics—subjects about which a security practitioner would be expected to know. The test includes information from six knowledge domains:

Knowledge Domain	Percent of Exam
Systems Security	21%
Network Infrastructure	20%
Access Control	17%
Assessments & Audits	15%
Cryptography	15%
Organizational Security	12%

The *Systems Security* knowledge domain covers the security threats to computer systems and addresses the mechanisms that systems use to address these threats. A major portion of this domain concerns the factors that go into hardening the operating system as well as the hardware and peripherals. The *Network Infrastructure* domain examines the security threats introduced when computers are connected in local networks and with the Internet. It is also concerned with the various elements of a network as well as the tools and mechanisms put in place to protect networks. Since a major security goal is to prevent unauthorized access to computer systems and the data they process, the third domain examines the many ways that we attempt to control who can access our systems and data. Since security is a difficult goal to obtain, we must constantly examine the ever-changing environment in which our systems operate. The fourth domain, *Assessments & Audits*, covers things individuals can do to check that security mechanisms that have been implemented are adequate and are sufficiently protecting critical data and resources. *Cryptography* has long been part of the basic security foundation of any organization, and an entire domain is devoted to its various aspects. The last domain, *Organizational Security*, takes a look at what an organization should be doing after all the other security mechanisms are in place. This domain covers incident response and disaster recovery, in addition to topics more appropriately addressed at the organizational level.

The exam consists of a series of questions, each designed to have a single best answer or response. The other available choices are designed to provide options that an individual might choose if he or she had an incomplete knowledge or understanding of the security topic represented by the question. The exam questions are chosen from the more detailed objectives listed in the outline shown in Figure 1-1, an excerpt from the 2008 objectives document obtainable from the CompTIA web site at http://certification.comptia.org/resources/objectives.aspx.

The Security+ exam is designed for individuals who have at least two years of networking experience and who have a thorough understanding of TCP/IP with a focus on security. Originally administered only in English, the exam is now offered in testing centers around the world in the English, Japanese, Korean, and German languages. Consult the CompTIA web site at www.comptia.org to determine a location near you.

The exam consists of 100 questions to be completed in 90 minutes. A minimum passing score is considered 764 out of a possible 900 points. Results are available immediately after you complete the exam. An individual who fails to pass the exam the first time will be required to pay the exam fee again to retake the exam, but no mandatory waiting period is required before retaking it the second time. If the individual again fails the exam, a minimum waiting period of 30 days is required for each subsequent retake. For more information on retaking exams, consult CompTIA's retake policy, which can be found on its web site.

This *All-in-One Security + Certification Exam Guide* is designed to assist you in preparing for the Security+ exam. It is organized around the same objectives as the exam and attempts to cover the major areas the exam includes. Using this guide in no way guarantees that you will pass the exam, but it will greatly assist you in preparing to meet the challenges posed by the Security+ exam.

PART I

1.0 Systems Security

    1.1   Differentiate among various systems security threats.

    1.2   Explain the security risks pertaining to system hardware and peripherals.

    1.3   Implement OS hardening practices and procedures to achieve workstation and server security.

    1.4   Carry out the appropriate procedures to establish application security.

    1.5   Implement security applications.

    1.6   Explain the purpose and application of virtualization technology.

2.0 Network Infrastructure

    2.1   Differentiate between the different ports & protocols, their respective threats and mitigation techniques.

    2.2   Distinguish between network design elements and components.

    2.3   Determine the appropriate use of network security tools to facilitate network security.

    2.4   Apply the appropriate network tools to facilitate network security.

    2.5   Explain the vulnerabilities and mitigations associated with network devices.

    2.6   Explain the vulnerabilities and mitigations associated with various transmission media.

    2.7   Explain the vulnerabilities and implement mitigations associated with wireless networking.

3.0 Access Control

    3.1   Identify and apply industry best practices for access control methods.

    3.2   Explain common access control models and the differences between each.

    3.3   Organize users and computers into appropriate security groups and roles while distinguishing between appropriate rights and privileges.

    3.4   Apply appropriate security controls to file and print resources.

    3.5   Compare and implement logical access control methods.

    3.6   Summarize the various authentication models and identify the components of each.

    3.7   Deploy various authentication models and identify the components of each.

    3.8   Explain the difference between identification and authentication (identity proofing).

    3.9   Explain and apply physical access security methods.

Figure 1-1   The CompTIA Security+ objectives

4.0 Assessments & Audits

    4.1   Conduct risk assessments and implement risk mitigation.

    4.2   Carry out vulnerability assessments using common tools.

    4.3   Within the realm of vulnerability assessments, explain the proper use of penetration testing versus vulnerability scanning.

    4.4   Use monitoring tools on systems and networks and detect security-related anomalies.

    4.5   Compare and contrast various types of monitoring methodologies.

    4.6   Execute proper logging procedures and evaluate the results.

    4.7   Conduct periodic audits of system security settings.

5.0 Cryptography

    5.1   Explain general cryptography concepts.

    5.2   Explain basic hashing concepts and map various algorithms to appropriate applications.

    5.3   Explain basic encryption concepts and map various algorithms to appropriate applications.

    5.4   Explain and implement protocols.

    5.5   Explain core concepts of public key cryptography.

    5.6   Implement PKI and certificate management.

6.0 Organizational Security

    6.1   Explain redundancy planning and its components.

    6.2   Implement disaster recovery procedures.

    6.3   Differentiate between and execute appropriate incident response procedures.

    6.4   Identify and explain applicable legislation and organizational policies.

    6.5   Explain the importance of environmental controls.

    6.6   Explain the concept of and how to reduce the risks of social engineering.

Figure 1-1   The CompTIA Security+ objectives *(continued)*

Basic Security Terminology

The term *hacking* is used frequently in the media. A *hacker* was once considered an individual who understood the technical aspects of computer operating systems and networks. Hackers were individuals you turned to when you had a problem and needed extreme technical expertise. Today, as a result of the media use, the term is used more often to refer to individuals who attempt to gain unauthorized access to computer systems or networks. While some would prefer to use the terms *cracker* and *cracking* when referring to this nefarious type of activity, the terminology generally accepted by the public is that of *hacker* and *hacking*. A related term that is sometimes used is *phreaking*, which refers to the "hacking" of computers and systems used by the telephone company.

Security Basics

Computer security is a term that has many meanings and related terms. Computer security entails the methods used to ensure that a system is secure. The ability to control who has access to a computer system and data and what they can do with those resources must be addressed in broad terms of computer security.

Seldom in today's world are computers not connected to other computers in networks. This then introduces the term *network security* to refer to the protection of the multiple computers and other devices that are connected together in a network. Related to these two terms are two others, *information security* and *information assurance*, which place the focus of the security process not on the hardware and software being used but on the data that is processed by them. Assurance also introduces another concept, that of the *availability* of the systems and information when users want them.

Since the late 1990s, much has been published about specific lapses in security that have resulted in the penetration of a computer network or in denying access to or the use of the network. Over the last few years, the general public has become increasingly aware of its dependence on computers and networks and consequently has also become interested in their security.

As a result of this increased attention by the public, several new terms have become commonplace in conversations and print. Terms such as *hacking, virus, TCP/IP, encryption,* and *firewalls* now frequently appear in mainstream news publications and have found their way into casual conversations. What was once the purview of scientists and engineers is now part of our everyday life.

With our increased daily dependence on computers and networks to conduct everything from making purchases at our local grocery store to driving our children to school (any new car these days probably uses a small computer to obtain peak engine performance), ensuring that computers and networks are secure has become of paramount importance. Medical information about each of us is probably stored in a computer somewhere. So is financial information and data relating to the types of purchases we make and store preferences (assuming we have and use a credit card to make purchases). Making sure that this information remains private is a growing concern to the general public, and it is one of the jobs of security to help with the protection of our privacy. Simply stated, computer and network security is essential for us to function effectively and safely in today's highly automated environment.

The "CIA" of Security

Almost from its inception, the goals of computer security have been threefold: confidentiality, integrity, and availability—the "CIA" of security. *Confidentiality* ensures that only those individuals who have the authority to view a piece of information may do so. No unauthorized individual should ever be able to view data to which they are not entitled. *Integrity* is a related concept but deals with the modification of data. Only authorized individuals should be able to change or delete information. The goal of *availability* is to ensure that the data, or the system itself, is available for use when the authorized user wants it.

As a result of the increased use of networks for commerce, two additional security goals have been added to the original three in the CIA of security. *Authentication* deals with ensuring that an individual is who he claims to be. The need for authentication in an online banking transaction, for example, is obvious. Related to this is *nonrepudiation*, which deals with the ability to verify that a message has been sent and received so that the sender (or receiver) cannot refute sending (or receiving) the information.

EXAM TIP Expect questions on these concepts as they are basic to the understanding of what we hope to guarantee in securing our computer systems and networks.

The Operational Model of Security

For many years, the focus of security was on *prevention*. If you could prevent somebody from gaining access to your computer systems and networks, you assumed that they were secure. *Protection* was thus equated with *prevention*. While this basic premise was true, it failed to acknowledge the realities of the networked environment of which our systems are a part. No matter how well you think you can provide prevention, somebody always seems to find a way around the safeguards. When this happens, the system is left unprotected. What is needed is multiple prevention techniques and also technology to alert you when prevention has failed and to provide ways to address the problem. This results in a modification to the original security equation with the addition of two new elements—*detection* and *response*. The security equation thus becomes

Protection = Prevention + (Detection + Response)

This is known as the *operational model of computer security*. Every security technique and technology falls into at least one of the three elements of the equation. Examples of the types of technology and techniques that represent each are depicted in Figure 1-2.

Security Principles

An organization can choose to address the protection of its networks in three ways: ignore security issues, provide host security, and approach security at a network level. The last two, host and network security, have prevention as well as detection and response components.

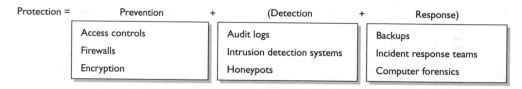

Protection =	Prevention	+	(Detection	+	Response)
	Access controls		Audit logs		Backups
	Firewalls		Intrusion detection systems		Incident response teams
	Encryption		Honeypots		Computer forensics

Figure 1-2 Sample technologies in the operational model of computer security

If an organization decides to ignore security, it has chosen to utilize the minimal amount of security that is provided with its workstations, servers, and devices. No additional security measures will be implemented. Each "out-of-the-box" system has certain security settings that can be configured, and they should be. To protect an entire network, however, requires work in addition to the few protection mechanisms that come with systems by default.

Host Security   *Host security* takes a granular view of security by focusing on protecting each computer and device individually instead of addressing protection of the network as a whole. When host security is implemented, each computer is expected to protect itself. If an organization decides to implement only host security and does not include network security, it will likely introduce or overlook vulnerabilities. Many environments involve different operating systems (Windows, UNIX, Linux, Macintosh), different versions of those operating systems, and different types of installed applications. Each operating system has security configurations that differ from other systems, and different versions of the same operating system can in fact have variations among them. Trying to ensure that every computer is "locked down" to the same degree as every other system in the environment can be overwhelming and often results in an unsuccessful and frustrating effort.

Host security is important and should always be addressed. Security, however, should not stop there, as host security is a complementary process to be combined with network security. If individual host computers have vulnerabilities embodied within them, network security can provide another layer of protection that will hopefully stop intruders getting that far into the environment. Topics covered in this book dealing with host security include bastion hosts, host-based intrusion detection systems (devices designed to determine whether an intruder has penetrated a computer system or network), antivirus software (programs designed to prevent damage caused by various types of malicious software), and hardening of operating systems (methods used to strengthen operating systems and to eliminate possible avenues through which attacks can be launched).

Network Security   In some smaller environments, host security alone might be a viable option, but as systems become connected into networks, security should include the actual network itself. In *network security*, an emphasis is placed on controlling access to internal computers from external entities. This control can be through devices such as routers, firewalls, authentication hardware and software, encryption, and intrusion detection systems (IDSs).

Network environments have a tendency to be unique entities because usually no two networks have exactly the same number of computers, the same applications installed, the same number of users, the exact same configurations, or the same available servers. They will not perform the same functions or have the same overall architecture. Because networks have so many differences, they can be protected and configured in many different ways. This chapter covers some foundational approaches to network and host security. Each approach can be implemented in myriad ways.

Least Privilege

One of the most fundamental approaches to security is *least privilege*. This concept is applicable to many physical environments as well as network and host security. Least privilege means that an object (such as a user, application, or process) should have only the rights and privileges necessary to perform its task, with no additional permissions. Limiting an object's privileges limits the amount of harm that can be caused, thus limiting an organization's exposure to damage. Users may have access to the files on their workstations and a select set of files on a file server, but they have no access to critical data that is held within the database. This rule helps an organization protect its most sensitive resources and helps ensure that whoever is interacting with these resources has a valid reason to do so.

Different operating systems and applications have different ways of implementing rights, permissions, and privileges. Before operating systems are actually configured, an overall plan should be devised and standardized methods developed to ensure that a solid *security baseline* is implemented. For example, a company might want all of the accounting department employees, but no one else, to be able to access employee payroll and profit margin spreadsheets stored on a server. The easiest way to implement this is to develop an Accounting group, put all accounting employees in this group, and assign rights to the group instead of each individual user.

As another example, a company could require implementing a hierarchy of administrators that perform different functions and require specific types of rights. Two people could be tasked with performing backups of individual workstations and servers; thus they do not need administrative permissions with full access to all resources. Three people could be in charge of setting up new user accounts and password management, which means they do not need full, or perhaps any, access to the company's routers and switches. Once these baselines are delineated, indicating what subjects require which rights and permissions, it is much easier to configure settings to provide the least privileges for different subjects.

The concept of least privilege applies to more network security issues than just providing users with specific rights and permissions. When trust relationships are created, they should not be implemented in such a way that everyone trusts each other simply because it is easier to set it up that way. One domain should trust another for very specific reasons, and the implementers should have a full understanding of what the trust relationship allows between two domains. If one domain trusts another, do all of the users automatically become trusted, and can they thus easily access any and all resources on the other domain? Is this a good idea? Can a more secure method provide the same functionality? If a trusted relationship is implemented such that users in one group can access a plotter or printer that is available on only one domain, for example, it might make sense to purchase another plotter so that other more valuable or sensitive resources are not accessible by the entire group.

Another issue that falls under the least privilege concept is the security context in which an application runs. All applications, scripts, and batch files run in the security context of a specific user on an operating system. These objects will execute with specific permissions as if they were a user. The application could be Microsoft Word and be run in the space of a regular user, or it could be a diagnostic program that needs access to more sensitive system files and so must run under an administrative user account, or it could be a program that performs backups and so should operate within the security context of a backup operator. The crux of this issue is that programs should execute only in the security context that is needed for that program to perform its duties successfully. In many environments, people do not really understand how to make programs run under different security contexts, or it just seems easier to have them all run under the administrator account. If attackers can compromise a program or service running under the administrative account, they have effectively elevated their access level and have much more control over the system and many more possibilities to cause damage.

EXAM TIP The concept of least privilege is fundamental to many aspects of security. Remember the basic idea is to give people access only to the data and programs that they need to do their job. Anything beyond that can lead to a potential security problem.

Separation of Duties

Another fundamental approach to security is *separation of duties*. This concept is applicable to physical environments as well as network and host security. Separation of duty ensures that for any given task, more than one individual needs to be involved. The task is broken into different duties, each of which is accomplished by a separate individual. By implementing a task in this manner, no single individual can abuse the system for his or her own gain. This principle has been implemented in the business world, especially financial institutions, for many years. A simple example is a system in which one individual is required to place an order and a separate person is needed to authorize the purchase.

While separation of duties provides a certain level of checks and balances, it is not without its own drawbacks. Chief among these is the cost required to accomplish the task. This cost is manifested in both time and money. More than one individual is required when a single person could accomplish the task, thus potentially increasing the cost of the task. In addition, with more than one individual involved, a certain delay can be expected as the task must proceed through its various steps.

Implicit Deny

What has become the Internet was originally designed as a friendly environment where everybody agreed to abide by the rules implemented in the various protocols. Today, the Internet is no longer the friendly playground of researchers that it once was. This has resulted in different approaches that might at first seem less than friendly but that are required for security purposes. One of these approaches is *implicit deny*.

Frequently in the network world, decisions concerning access must be made. Often a series of rules will be used to determine whether or not to allow access. If a particular situation is not covered by any of the other rules, the implicit deny approach states that access should not be granted. In other words, if no rule would allow access, then access should not be granted. Implicit deny applies to situations involving both authorization and access.

The alternative to implicit deny is to allow access unless a specific rule forbids it. Another example of these two approaches is in programs that monitor and block access to certain web sites. One approach is to provide a list of specific sites that a user is *not* allowed to access. Access to any site not on the list would be implicitly allowed. The opposite approach (the implicit deny approach) would block all access to sites that are not specifically identified as authorized. As you can imagine, depending on the specific application, one or the other approach would be appropriate. Which approach you choose depends on the security objectives and policies of your organization.

 EXAM TIP Implicit deny is another fundamental principle of security and students need to be sure they understand this principle. Similar to least privilege, this principle states if you haven't specifically been allowed access, then access should be denied.

Job Rotation

An interesting approach to enhance security that is gaining increasing attention is through *job rotation*. The benefits of rotating individuals through various jobs in an organization's IT department have been discussed for a while. By rotating through jobs, individuals gain a better perspective of how the various parts of IT can enhance (or hinder) the business. Since security is often a misunderstood aspect of IT, rotating individuals through security positions can result in a much wider understanding of the security problems throughout the organization. It also can have the side benefit of not relying on any one individual too heavily for security expertise. When all security tasks are the domain of one employee, and if that individual were to leave suddenly, security at the organization could suffer. On the other hand, if security tasks were understood by many different individuals, the loss of any one individual would have less of an impact on the organization.

One significant drawback to job rotation is relying on it too heavily. The IT world is very technical and often expertise in any single aspect takes years to develop. This is especially true in the security environment. In addition, the rapidly changing threat environment with new vulnerabilities and exploits routinely being discovered requires a level of understanding that takes considerable time to acquire and maintain.

Layered Security

A bank does not protect the money that it stores only by placing it in a vault. It uses one or more security guards as a first defense to watch for suspicious activities and to secure the facility when the bank is closed. It probably uses monitoring systems to watch various activities that take place in the bank, whether involving customers or employees. The vault is usually located in the center of the facility, and layers of rooms or walls also protect access to the vault. Access control ensures that the people who want to enter the vault have been granted the appropriate authorization before they are allowed access, and the systems, including manual switches, are connected directly to the police station in case a determined bank robber successfully penetrates any one of these layers of protection.

Networks should utilize the same type of *layered security* architecture. No system is 100 percent secure and nothing is foolproof, so no single specific protection mechanism should ever be trusted alone. Every piece of software and every device can be compromised in some way, and every encryption algorithm can be broken by someone with enough time and resources. The goal of security is to make the effort of actually accomplishing a compromise more costly in time and effort than it is worth to a potential attacker.

Consider, for example, the steps an intruder has to take to access critical data held within a company's back-end database. The intruder will first need to penetrate the firewall and use packets and methods that will not be identified and detected by the IDS (more on these devices in Chapter 11). The attacker will have to circumvent an internal router performing packet filtering and possibly penetrate another firewall that is used to separate one internal network from another. From here, the intruder must break the access controls on the database, which means performing a dictionary or brute-force attack to be able to authenticate to the database software. Once the intruder has gotten this far, he still needs to locate the data within the database. This can in turn be complicated by the use of access control lists (ACLs) outlining who can actually view or modify the data. That's a lot of work.

This example illustrates the different layers of security many environments employ. It is important that several different layers are implemented, because if intruders succeed at one layer, you want to be able to stop them at the next. The redundancy of different protection layers assures that no single point of failure can breach the network's security. If a network used only a firewall to protect its assets, an attacker successfully able to penetrate this device would find the rest of the network open and vulnerable. Or, because a firewall usually does not protect against viruses attached to e-mail, a second layer of defense is needed, perhaps in the form of an antivirus program.

Every network environment must have multiple layers of security. These layers can employ a variety of methods such as routers, firewalls, network segments, IDSs, encryption, authentication software, physical security, and traffic control. The layers need to work together in a coordinated manner so that one does not impede another's functionality and introduce a security hole. Security at each layer can be very complex, and putting different layers together can increase the complexity exponentially.

Although having layers of protection in place is very important, it is also important to understand how these different layers interact either by working together or in some cases by working against each other. One example of how different security methods can work against each other occurs when firewalls encounter encrypted network traffic. An organization can use encryption so that an outside customer communicating with a specific web server is assured that sensitive data being exchanged is protected. If this encrypted data is encapsulated within Secure Sockets Layer (SSL) packets and is then sent through a firewall, the firewall will not be able to read the payload information in the individual packets. This could enable the customer, or an outside attacker, to send undetected malicious code or instructions through the SSL connection. Other mechanisms can be introduced in similar situations, such as designing web pages to accept information only in certain formats and having the web server parse through the data for malicious activity. The important piece is to understand the level of protection that each layer provides and how each layer can be affected by activities that occur in other layers.

These layers are usually depicted starting at the top, with more general types of protection, and progress downward through each layer, with increasing granularity at each layer as you get closer to the actual resource, as you can see in Figure 1-3. The top-layer protection mechanism is responsible for looking at an enormous amount of traffic, and it would be overwhelming and cause too much of a performance degradation if each aspect of the packet were inspected here. Instead, each layer usually digs deeper into the packet and looks for specific items. Layers that are closer to the resource have to deal with only a fraction of the traffic that the top-layer security mechanism considers, and thus looking deeper and at more granular aspects of the traffic will not cause as much of a performance hit.

Diversity of Defense

Diversity of defense is a concept that complements the idea of various layers of security; layers are made dissimilar so that even if an attacker knows how to get through a system making up one layer, she might not know how to get through a different type of layer that employs a different system for security.

If, for example, an environment has two firewalls that form a demilitarized zone (a DMZ is the area between the two firewalls that provides an environment where activities can be more closely monitored), one firewall can be placed at the perimeter of the Internet and the DMZ. This firewall will analyze traffic that passes through that specific access point and enforces certain types of restrictions. The other firewall can be placed between the DMZ and the internal network. When applying the diversity of defense concept, you should set up these two firewalls to filter for different types of traffic and provide different types of restrictions. The first firewall, for example, can make sure that no File Transfer Protocol (FTP), Simple Network Management Protocol (SNMP), or Telnet traffic enters the network, but allow Simple Mail Transfer Protocol (SMTP), Secure Shell (SSH), Hypertext Transfer Protocol (HTTP), and SSL traffic through. The

Figure 1-3
Various layers of
security

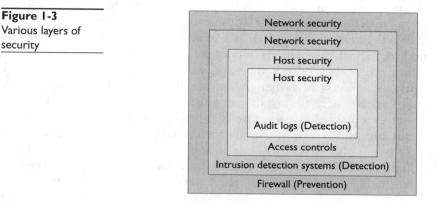

second firewall may not allow SSL or SSH through and can interrogate SMTP and HTTP traffic to make sure that certain types of attacks are not part of that traffic.

Another type of diversity of defense is to use products from different vendors. Every product has its own security vulnerabilities that are usually known to experienced attackers in the community. A Check Point firewall, for example, has different security issues and settings than a Sidewinder firewall; thus, different exploits can be used to crash or compromise them in some fashion. Combining this type of diversity with the preceding example, you might use the Check Point firewall as the first line of defense. If attackers are able to penetrate it, they are less likely to get through the next firewall if it is a Cisco PIX or Sidewinder firewall (or another maker's firewall).

You should consider an obvious trade-off before implementing diversity of security using different vendors' products. This setup usually increases operational complexity, and security and complexity are seldom a good mix. When implementing products from more than one vendor, security staff must know how to configure two different systems, the configuration settings will be totally different, the upgrades and patches will be released at different times and contain different changes, and the overall complexity of maintaining these systems can cause more headaches than security itself. This does not mean that you should not implement diversity of defense by installing products from different vendors, but you should know the implications of this decision.

Security Through Obscurity

With *security through obscurity*, security is considered effective if the environment and protection mechanisms are confusing or supposedly not generally known. Security through obscurity uses the approach of protecting something by hiding it—out of sight, out of mind. Noncomputer examples of this concept include hiding your briefcase or purse if you leave it in the car so that it is not in plain view, hiding a house key under a ceramic frog on your porch, or pushing your favorite ice cream to the back of the freezer so that nobody else will see it. This approach, however, does not provide actual protection of the object. Someone can still steal the purse by breaking into the car, lift the ceramic frog and find the key, or dig through the items in the freezer to find the ice cream. Security through obscurity may make someone work a little harder to accomplish a task, but it does not prevent anyone from eventually succeeding.

Similar approaches occur in computer and network security when attempting to hide certain objects. A network administrator can, for instance, move a service from its default port to a different port so that others will not know how to access it as easily, or a firewall can be configured to hide specific information about the internal network in the hope that potential attackers will not obtain the information for use in an attack on the network.

In most security circles, security through obscurity is considered a poor approach, especially if it is the organization's only approach to security. An organization can use security through obscurity measures to try to hide critical assets, but other security measures should also be employed to provide a higher level of protection. For example, if an administrator moves a service from its default port to a more obscure port, an attacker can still find this service; thus a firewall should be used to restrict access to the service.

Keep It Simple

The terms *security* and *complexity* are often at odds with each other, because the more complex something is, the more difficult it is to understand, and you cannot truly secure something if you do not understand it. Another reason complexity is a problem within security is that it usually allows too many opportunities for something to go wrong. An application with 4000 lines of code has far fewer places for buffer overflows, for example, than an application with 2 million lines of code.

As with any other type of technology, when something goes wrong with security mechanisms, a troubleshooting process is used to identify the problem. If the mechanism is overly complex, identifying the root of the problem can be overwhelming if not impossible. Security is already a very complex issue because many variables are involved, many types of attacks and vulnerabilities are possible, many different types of resources must be secure, and many different ways can be used to secure them. You want your security processes and tools to be as simple and elegant as possible. They should be simple to troubleshoot, simple to use, and simple to administer.

Another application of the principle of keeping things simple concerns the number of services that you allow your system to run. Default installations of computer operating systems often leave many services running. The keep-it-simple principle tells us to eliminate those services that we don't need. This is also a good idea from a security standpoint because it results in fewer applications that can be exploited and fewer services that the administrator is responsible for securing. The general rule of thumb should be to eliminate all nonessential services and protocols. This of course leads to the question, how do you determine whether a service or protocol is essential or not? Ideally, you should know for what your computer system or network is being used, and thus you should be able to identify those elements that are essential and activate only them. For a variety of reasons, this is not as easy as it sounds. Alternatively, a stringent security approach that you can take is to assume that no service is necessary (which is obviously absurd) and activate services and ports only as they are requested. Whatever approach you take, it's a never-ending struggle to try to strike a balance between providing functionality and maintaining security.

Access Control

The term *access control* describes a variety of protection schemes. It sometimes refers to all security features used to prevent unauthorized access to a computer system or network. In this sense, it may be confused with *authentication*. More properly, *access* is the ability of a subject (such as an individual or a process running on a computer system) to interact with an object (such as a file or hardware device). Authentication, on the other hand, deals with verifying the identity of a subject.

To understand the difference, consider the example of an individual attempting to log in to a computer system or network. *Authentication* is the process used to verify to the computer system or network that the individual is who he claims to be. The most common method to do this is through the use of a user ID and password. Once the individual has verified his identity, access controls regulate what the individual can actually do on the system—just because a person is granted entry to the system does not mean that he should have access to all data the system contains.

Consider another example. When you go to your bank to make a withdrawal, the teller at the window will verify that you are indeed who you claim to be by asking you to provide some form of identification with your picture on it, such as your driver's license. You might also have to provide your bank account number. Once the teller verifies your identity, you will have proved that you are a valid (authorized) customer of this bank. This does not, however, mean that you have the ability to view all information that the bank protects—such as your neighbor's account balance. The teller will control what information, and funds, you can access and will grant you access only to information for which you are authorized to see. In this example, your identification and bank account number serve as your method of authentication and the teller serves as the access control mechanism.

In computer systems and networks, access controls can be implemented in several ways. An *access control matrix* provides the simplest framework for illustrating the process and is shown in Table 1-1. In this matrix, the system is keeping track of two processes, two files, and one hardware device. Process 1 can read both File 1 and File 2 but can write only to File 1. Process 1 cannot access Process 2, but Process 2 can execute Process 1. Both processes have the ability to write to the printer.

While simple to understand, the access control matrix is seldom used in computer systems because it is extremely costly in terms of storage space and processing. Imagine the size of an access control matrix for a large network with hundreds of users and thousands of files. The actual mechanics of how access controls are implemented in a system varies, though *access control lists (ACLs)* are common. An ACL is nothing more than a list that contains the subjects that have access rights to a particular object. The list identifies not only the subject but the specific access granted to the subject for the object. Typical types of access include read, write, and execute as indicated in the example access control matrix.

No matter what specific mechanism is used to implement access controls in a computer system or network, the controls should be based on a specific *model* of access. Several different models are discussed in security literature, including discretionary access control (DAC), mandatory access control (MAC), role-based access control (RBAC), and rule-based access control (also RBAC).

	Process 1	Process 2	File 1	File 2	Printer
Process 1	Read, write, execute		Read, write	Read	Write
Process 2	Execute	Read, write, execute	Read, write	Read, write	Write

Table 1-1 An Access Control Matrix

Discretionary Access Control

Both *discretionary access control* and *mandatory access control* are terms originally used by the military to describe two different approaches to controlling an individual's access to a system. As defined by the "Orange Book," a Department of Defense document that at one time was the standard for describing what constituted a trusted computing system, DACs are "a means of restricting access to objects based on the identity of subjects and/or groups to which they belong. The controls are discretionary in the sense that a subject with a certain access permission is capable of passing that permission (perhaps indirectly) on to any other subject." While this might appear to be confusing "government-speak," the principle is rather simple. In systems that employ DACs, the owner of an object can decide which other subjects can have access to the object and what specific access they can have. One common method to accomplish this is the permission bits used in UNIX-based systems. The owner of a file can specify what permissions (read/write/execute) members in the same group can have and also what permissions all others can have. ACLs are also a common mechanism used to implement DAC.

Mandatory Access Control

A less frequently employed system for restricting access is mandatory access control. This system, generally used only in environments in which different levels of security classifications exist, is much more restrictive regarding what a user is allowed to do. Referring to the "Orange Book," a mandatory access control is "a means of restricting access to objects based on the sensitivity (as represented by a label) of the information contained in the objects and the formal authorization (i.e., clearance) of subjects to access information of such sensitivity." In this case, the owner or subject can't determine whether access is to be granted to another subject; it is the job of the operating system to decide.

In MAC, the security mechanism controls access to all objects, and individual subjects cannot change that access. The key here is the label attached to every subject and object. The label will identify the level of classification for that object and the level to which the subject is entitled. Think of military security classifications such as Secret and Top Secret. A file that has been identified as Top Secret (has a label indicating that it is Top Secret) may be viewed only by individuals with a Top Secret clearance. It is up to the access control mechanism to ensure that an individual with only a Secret clearance never gains access to a file labeled as Top Secret. Similarly, a user cleared for Top Secret access will not be allowed by the access control mechanism to change the classification of a file labeled as Top Secret to Secret or to send that Top Secret file to a user cleared only for Secret information. The complexity of such a mechanism can be further understood when you consider today's windowing environment. The access control mechanism will not allow a user to cut a portion of a Top Secret document and paste it into a window containing a document with only a Secret label. It is this separation of differing levels of classified information that results in this sort of mechanism being referred to as *multilevel security*.

Finally, just because a subject has the appropriate level of clearance to view a document, that does not mean that she will be allowed to do so. The concept of "need to know," which is a DAC concept, also exists in MAC mechanisms. "Need to know" means that a person is given access only to information that she needs in order to accomplish her job or mission.

EXAM TIP If trying to remember the difference between MAC and DAC, just remember that MAC is associated with multilevel security.

Role-Based Access Control

ACLs can be cumbersome and can take time to administer properly. Another access control mechanism that has been attracting increased attention is the role-based access control (RBAC). In this scheme, instead of each user being assigned specific access permissions for the objects associated with the computer system or network, each user is assigned a set of roles that he or she may perform. The roles are in turn assigned the access permissions necessary to perform the tasks associated with the role. Users will thus be granted permissions to objects in terms of the specific duties they must perform—not according to a security classification associated with individual objects.

Rule-Based Access Control

The first thing that you might notice is the ambiguity that is introduced with this access control method also using the acronym RBAC. Rule-based access control again uses objects such as ACLs to help determine whether access should be granted or not. In this case, a series of rules are contained in the ACL and the determination of whether to grant access will be made based on these rules. An example of such a rule is one that states that no employee may have access to the payroll file after hours or on weekends. As with MAC, users are not allowed to change the access rules, and administrators are relied on for this. Rule-based access control can actually be used in addition to or as a method of implementing other access control methods. For example, MAC methods can utilize a rule-based approach for implementation.

EXAM TIP Do not become confused between rule-based and role-based access controls, even though they both have the same acronym. The name of each is descriptive of what it entails and will help you distinguish between them.

Authentication

Access controls define what actions a user can perform or what objects a user can access. These controls assume that the identity of the user has already been verified. It is the job of authentication mechanisms to ensure that only valid users are admitted. Described another way, authentication uses some mechanism to prove that you are who you claim to be. Three general methods are used in authentication. To verify your identity, you can provide the following:

- Something you know

- Something you have
- Something you are (something unique about you)

The most common authentication mechanism is to provide something that only you, the valid user, should know. The most frequently used example of this is the common user ID (or username) and password. In theory, since you are not supposed to share your password with anybody else, only you should know your password, and thus by providing it you are proving to the system that you are who you claim to be. In theory, this should be a fairly decent method to provide authentication. Unfortunately, for a variety of reasons, such as the fact that people have a tendency to choose very poor and easily guessed passwords, this technique is not as reliable as it should be. Other authentication mechanisms are consequently always being developed and deployed.

Another method to provide authentication involves the use of something that only valid users should have in their possession. A physical-world example of this would be a simple lock and key. Only those individuals with the correct key will be able to open the lock and thus provide admittance to a house, car, office, or whatever the lock was protecting. A similar method can be used to authenticate users for a computer system or network (though the key may be electronic and may reside on a smart card or similar device). The problem with this technology is that people will lose their keys (or cards), which means they can't log in to the system and somebody else who finds the key can then access the system, even though that person is not authorized. To address this problem, a combination of the something-you-know/something-you-have methods is often used so that the individual with the key can also be required to provide a password or passcode. The key is useless unless you know this code. An example of this is the ATM card most of us carry. The card is associated with a personal identification number (PIN), which only you should know. Knowing the PIN without having the card is useless, just as having the card without knowing the PIN will not give you access to your account.

The third general method to provide authentication involves something that is unique about you. We are used to this concept in our physical world, where people's fingerprints or a sample of their DNA can be used to identify them. This same concept can be used to provide authentication in the computer world. The field of authentication that uses something about you or something that you are is known as *biometrics*. A number of different mechanisms can be used to accomplish this type of authentication, such as a voice or fingerprint, a retinal scan, or hand geometry. All of these methods obviously require some additional hardware in order to operate.

While these three approaches to authentication appear to be easy to understand and in most cases easy to implement, authentication is not to be taken lightly, since it is such an important component of security. Potential attackers are constantly searching for ways to get past the system's authentication mechanism, and some fairly ingenious methods have been employed to do so. Consequently, security professionals are constantly devising new methods, building on these three basic approaches, to provide authentication mechanisms for computer systems and networks. A more in-depth discussion of various authentication schemes is covered in Chapter 9.

Chapter Review

In this chapter, you became acquainted with the objectives that will be tested on the Security+ exam as well as the expected format for the exam. You met with a number of basic security concepts and terms. The operational model of computer security was described and examples provided for each of its components (prevention, detection, and response). The difference between authentication and access control was also discussed. Authentication is the process of providing some sort of verification for who you are to the computer system or network, and access controls are the mechanisms the system uses to decide what you can do once your authenticity has been verified. Authentication generally comes in one of three forms: something you know, something you have, or something you are/something about you. Biometrics is an example of an authentication method, but the most common authentication mechanism is the simple username and password combination. Several approaches to access control were discussed, including discretionary access control, mandatory access control, rule-based access control, and role-based access control.

Quick Tips

- Information assurance and information security place the security focus on the information and not the hardware or software used to process it.

- The original goal of computer and network security was to provide confidentiality, integrity, and availability—the "CIA" of security.

- As a result of the increased reliance on networks for commerce, authentication and nonrepudiation have been added to the original CIA of security.

- The operational model of computer security tells us that protection is provided by prevention, detection, and response.

- Host security focuses on protecting each computer and device individually instead of addressing protection of the network as a whole.

- Least privilege means that an object should have only the necessary rights and privileges to perform its task, with no additional permissions.

- Separation of duties requires that a given task will be broken into different parts that must be accomplished by different individuals. This means that no single individual could accomplish the task without another individual knowing about it.

- Diversity of defense is a concept that complements the idea of various layers of security. It requires that the layers are dissimilar so that if one layer is penetrated, the next layer can't also be penetrated using the same method.

- Access is the ability of a subject to interact with an object. Access controls are devices and methods used to limit which subjects may interact with specific objects.

- Authentication mechanisms ensure that only valid users are provided access to the computer system or network.

- The three general methods used in authentication involve the users providing either something they know, something they have, or something unique about them (something they are).

Questions

To further help you prepare for the Security+ exam, and to test your level of prepared-ness, answer the following questions and then check your answers against the list of correct answers at the end of the chapter.

1. Which access control mechanism provides the owner of an object the opportunity to determine the access control permissions for other subjects?

   A. Mandatory

   B. Role-based

   C. Discretionary

   D. Token-based

2. What is the most common form of authentication used?

   A. Biometrics

   B. Tokens

   C. Access card

   D. Username/password

3. A retinal scan device is an example of what type of authentication mechanism?

   A. Something you know

   B. Something you have

   C. Something about you/something you are

   D. Multifactor authentication

4. Which of the following is true about the security principle of *implicit deny*?

   A. In a given access control situation, if a rule does not specifically allow the access, it is by default denied.

   B. It incorporates both access-control and authentication mechanisms into a single device.

   C. It allows for only one user to an object at a time; all others are denied access.

   D. It bases access decisions on the role of the user, as opposed to using the more common access control list mechanism.

5. From a security standpoint, what are the benefits of *job rotation*?

    A. It keeps employees from becoming bored with mundane tasks that might make it easier for them to make a mistake without noticing.

    B. It provides everybody with a better perspective of the issues surrounding security and lessens the impact of losing any individual employee since others can assume their duties.

    C. It keeps employees from learning too many details related to any one position thus making it more difficult for them to exploit that position.

    D. It ensures that no employee has the opportunity to exploit a specific position for any length of time without risk of being discovered.

6. What was described in the chapter as being essential in order to implement mandatory access controls?

    A. Tokens

    B. Certificates

    C. Labels

    D. Security classifications

7. The CIA of security includes

    A. Confidentiality, integrity, authentication

    B. Certificates, integrity, availability

    C. Confidentiality, inspection, authentication

    D. Confidentiality, integrity, availability

8. *Security through obscurity* is an approach to security that is sometimes used but that is dangerous to rely on. It attempts to do the following:

    A. Protect systems and networks by using confusing URLs to make them difficult to remember or find.

    B. Protect data by relying on attackers not being able to discover the hidden, confusing, or obscure mechanisms being used as opposed to employing any real security practices or devices.

    C. Hide data in plain sight through the use of cryptography.

    D. Make data hard to access by restricting its availability to a select group of users.

9. The fundamental approach to security in which an object has only the necessary rights and privileges to perform its task with no additional permissions is a description of

    A. Layered security

    B. Least privilege

    C. Role-based security

    D. Kerberos

10. Which access control technique discussed relies on a set of rules to determine whether access to an object will be granted or not?

    A. Role-based access control

    B. Object and rule instantiation access control

    C. Rule-based access control

    D. Discretionary access control

11. The security principle that ensures that no critical function can be executed by any single individual (by dividing the function into multiple tasks that can't all be executed by the same individual) is known as

    A. Discretionary access control

    B. Security through obscurity

    C. Separation of duties

    D. Implicit deny

12. The ability of a subject to interact with an object describes

    A. Authentication

    B. Access

    C. Confidentiality

    D. Mutual authentication

13. Information security places the focus of security efforts on

    A. The system hardware

    B. The software

    C. The user

    D. The data

14. In role-based access control, which of the following is true?

    A. The user is responsible for providing both a password and a digital certificate in order to access the system or network.

    B. A set of roles that the user may perform will be assigned to each user, thus controlling what the user can do and what information he or she can access.

    C. The focus is on the confidentiality of the data the system protects and not its integrity.

    D. Authentication and nonrepudiation are the central focus.

15. Using different types of firewalls to protect various internal subnets is an example of

    A. Layered security

    B. Security through obscurity

C. Diversity of defense

D. Implementing least privilege for access control

Answers

1. **C.** Discretionary access control provides the owner of an object the opportunity to determine the access control permissions for other subjects.

2. **D.** Username/password is the single most common authentication mechanism in use today.

3. **C.** A retinal scan is an example of a biometric device, which falls into the category of something about you/something you are.

4. **A.** The basic premise of implicit deny is that an action is allowed only if a specific rule states that it is acceptable, making A the most correct answer.

5. **B.** While both C and D may indeed bear a semblance of truth, they are not the primary reasons given as benefits of rotating employees through jobs in an organization. The reasons discussed included ensuring that no single individual alone can perform security operations, plus the benefit of having more employees understand the issues related to security.

6. **C.** Labels were discussed as being required for both objects and subjects in order to implement mandatory access controls. D is not the correct answer, because mandatory access controls are often used to implement various levels of security classification but security classifications are not needed in order to implement MAC.

7. **D.** Don't forget that even though authentication was described at great length in this chapter, the *A* in the CIA of security represents availability, which refers to the hardware and data being accessible when the user wants it.

8. **B.** Answer B describes the more general definition of this flawed approach, which relies on attackers not being able to discover the mechanisms being used in the belief that if it is confusing or obscure enough, it will remain safe. The problem with this approach is that once the confusing or obscure technique is discovered, the security of the system and data can be compromised. Security must rely on more than just obscurity to be effective. A does at some level describe activity that is similar to the concept of security through obscurity, but it is not the best answer.

9. **B.** This description describes least privilege. Layered security refers to using multiple layers of security (such as at the host and network layers) so that if an intruder penetrates one layer, they still will have to face additional security mechanisms before gaining access to sensitive information.

10. **C.** Rule-based access control relies on a set of rules to determine whether access to an object will be granted or not.

11. **C.** The separation of duties principle ensures that no critical function can be executed by any single individual.

12. **B.** Access is the ability of a subject to interact with an object.

13. **D.** Information security places the focus of the security efforts on the data (information).

14. **B.** In role-based access controls, roles are assigned to the user. Each role will describe what the user can do and the data or information that can be accessed to accomplish that role.

15. **C.** This is an example of diversity of defense. The idea is to provide different types of security and not rely too heavily on any one type of product.

Operational Organizational Security

2

In this chapter, you will

- Learn about the various operational aspects to security in your organization
- Confront social engineering as a means to gain access to computers and networks and determine how your organization should deal with it
- Identify and explain the benefits of organizational security policies
- Describe and compare logical access control methods

To some, the solution to securing an organization's computer systems and network is simply the implementation of various security technologies. Prevention technologies are designed to keep individuals from being able to gain access to systems or data they are not authorized to use. They are intended to prevent unauthorized access. A common prevention technology is the implementation of logical access controls. Although an important element of security, the implementation of any technological solution should be based upon an organizational security policy. In this chapter you will learn about various organizational and operational elements of security. Some of these, such as the establishment of security policies, standards, guidelines, and procedures, are activities that fall in the prevention category of the operational model of computer security. Others, such as the discussion on social engineering, come under the category of detection. All of these components, no matter which part of the operational model they fall under, need to be combined in a cohesive operational security program for your organization.

Policies, Standards, Guidelines, and Procedures

A security program (the total of all technology, processes, procedures, metrics, training, and personnel that are part of the organization's approach to addressing security) should be based on an organization's security policies, procedures, standards, and guidelines that specify what users and administrators should be doing to maintain the security of the systems and network. Collectively, these documents provide the guidance needed to determine how security will be implemented in the organization. Given this guidance, the specific technology and security mechanisms required can be planned for.

Policies are high-level, broad statements of what the organization wants to accomplish. *Standards* are mandatory elements regarding the implementation of a policy. Some standards can be externally driven. Government regulations for banking and financial institutions, for example, require that certain security measures be taken. Other standards may be set by the organization to meet its own security goals. *Guidelines* are recommendations relating to a policy. The key term in this case is *recommendation*— guidelines are not mandatory steps. *Procedures* are the step-by-step instructions on how to implement policies in the organization.

Just as the network itself constantly changes, the policies, standards, guidelines, and procedures should be included in living documents that are periodically evaluated and changed as necessary. The constant monitoring of the network and the periodic review of the relevant documents are part of the process that is the operational model. This operational process consists of four basic steps:

1. Plan (adjust) for security
2. Implement the plans
3. Monitor the implementation
4. Evaluate the effectiveness

In the first step, you develop the policies, procedures, and guidelines that will be implemented and design the security components that will protect your network. Once these are designed and developed, you can implement the plans. Next, you monitor to ensure that both the hardware and the software as well as the policies, procedures, and guidelines are working to secure your systems. Finally, you evaluate the effectiveness of the security measures you have in place. The evaluation step can include a *vulnerability assessment* (an attempt to identify and prioritize the list of vulnerabilities within a system or network) and *penetration test* (a method to check the security of a system by simulating an attack by a malicious individual) of your system to ensure the security is adequate. After evaluating your security posture, you begin again with step one, this time adjusting the security mechanisms you have in place, and then continue with this cyclical process.

The Security Perimeter

The discussion to this point has not mentioned the specific technology used to enforce operational and organizational security or a description of the various components that constitute the organization's security perimeter. If the average administrator were asked to draw a diagram depicting the various components of her network, the diagram would probably look something like Figure 2-1.

This diagram includes the major components typically found in a network. A connection to the Internet generally has some sort of protection attached to it such as a

Figure 2-1
Basic diagram of
an organization's
network

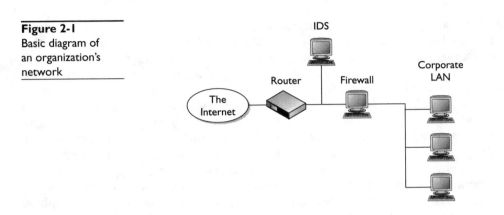

firewall. An intrusion detection system (IDS), also often a part of the security perimeter for the organization, can be on the inside of the firewall, or the outside, or it may in fact be on both sides. The specific location depends on the company and what it seeks to protect against (that is, insider threats or external threats). Beyond this security perimeter is the corporate LAN. Figure 2-1 is obviously a simple depiction—an actual network can have numerous subnets and extranets—but the basic components are present. Unfortunately, if this were the diagram provided by the administrator to show the organization's basic network structure, the administrator would have missed a very important component. A more astute administrator would provide a diagram more like Figure 2-2.

This diagram includes the other important network found in every organization, the telephone network that is connected to the public switched telephone network (PSTN), otherwise known as the phone company. The organization may or may not

Figure 2-2
A more complete
diagram of an
organization's
network

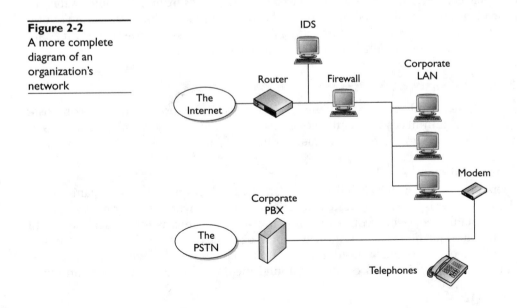

have any authorized modems, but the savvy administrator would realize that because the potential exists for unauthorized modems, the telephone network must be included as a possible source of access for the network. When considering the policies, procedures, and guidelines needed to implement security for the organization, both networks need to be considered.

While Figure 2-2 provides a more comprehensive view of the various components that need to be protected, it is still incomplete. Most experts will agree that the biggest danger to any organization does not come from external attacks but rather from the insider—a disgruntled employee or somebody else who has physical access to the facility. Given physical access to an office, a knowledgeable attacker will quickly be able to find the information he needs to gain access to the organization's computer systems and network. Consequently, every organization also needs security policies, procedures, and guidelines that cover physical security, and every security administrator should be concerned with these as well. While physical security (which can include such things as locks, cameras, guards and entry points, alarm systems, and physical barriers) will probably not fall under the purview of the security administrator, the operational state of the organization's physical security measures is just as important as many of the other network-centric measures.

Logical Access Controls

Access control lists (ACLs) are as important to logical access controls as they are to the control of physical access to the organization and its resources. An ACL is simply a list of the individuals (or groups) that are granted access to a specific resource. It can also include the type of access they have (that is, what actions they can perform on or with the resource). Logical access controls refer to those mechanisms that are used to control who may gain electronic access (access to data or resources from a computer system or network as opposed to physical access to the system itself) to the organization's computer systems and networks. Before setting the system's access controls, you must establish the security policies that the settings will be based upon.

Access Control Policies

As mentioned, policies are statements of what the organization wants to accomplish. The organization needs to identify goals and intentions for many different aspects of security. Each aspect will have associated policies and procedures.

Group Policy

Operating systems such as Windows and Linux allow administrators to organize users into groups. This is used to create categories of users for which similar access policies can be established. Using groups saves the administrator time, as adding a new user will not require that he create a completely new user profile; instead the administrator would determine to which group the new user belongs and then add the user to that group. Examples of groups commonly found include administrator, user, and guest.

Take care when creating groups and assigning users to them so that you do not provide more access than is absolutely required for members of that group. It would be simple to make everybody an administrator—it would cut down on the number of requests users might make of beleaguered administrators, but this is not a wise choice, as it also provides users the ability to modify the system in ways that could impact security. Establishing the correct levels of access for the various groups up front will save you time and eliminate potential problems that might be encountered later on.

Password Policy

Since passwords are the most common authentication mechanism, it is imperative that organizations have a policy addressing them. The list of authorized users will form the basis of the ACL for the computer system or network that the passwords will help control. The *password policy* should address the procedures used for selecting user passwords (specifying what is considered an acceptable password in the organization in terms of the character set and length, for example), the frequency with which they must be changed, and how they will be distributed. Procedures for creating new passwords should an employee forget her old password also need to be addressed, as well as the acceptable handling of passwords (for example, they should not be shared with anybody else, they should not be written down, and so on). It might also be useful to have the policy address the issue of password cracking by administrators, in order to discover weak passwords selected by employees.

Note that the developer of the password policy and associated procedures can go overboard and create an environment that negatively impacts employee productivity and leads to poorer security, not better. If, for example, the frequency with which passwords are changed is too great, users might write them down or forget them. Neither of these is a desirable outcome, as the one makes it possible for an intruder to find a password and gain access to the system, and the other leads to too many people losing productivity as they have to wait for a new password to be created to allow them access again.

EXAM TIP   A password policy is one of the most basic policies that an organization can have. Make sure you understand the basics of what constitutes a good password along with the other issues that surround password creation, expiration, sharing, and use.

Domain Password Policy

Domains are logical groups of computers that share a central directory database. The database contains information about the user accounts and security information for all resources identified within the domain. Each user within the domain is assigned her own unique account (that is, a domain is not a single account shared by multiple users), which is then assigned access to specific resources within the domain. In operating systems that provide domain capabilities, the password policy is set in the root container for the domain and will apply to all users within that domain. Setting a password policy for a domain is similar to setting other password policies in that the same critical elements need to be considered (password length, complexity, life, and so on). If a change to one of these elements is desired for a group of users, a new domain will need to be created. In a Microsoft Windows operating system that employs Active Directory, the domain password policy can be set in the Active Directory Users and Computers menu in the Administrative Tools section of the Control Panel.

Usernames and Passwords

Policies regarding selection of usernames and passwords must weigh usability versus security. At one end of the spectrum is usability, which would dictate that the username be simple and easy to remember, such as the user's first and last name separated by a period or the user's first initial followed by the last name. This makes it easy for the user to remember the user (account) name and makes it easy for other individuals to re-member a user's username (since the username and e-mail name are generally similar). At the same time, however, adhering to a simple policy such as this also makes it easy for a potential attacker to guess a valid account name, which can then be used in an attempt to guess a username/password combination. At the other end of the spectrum is the generation of a completely random series of characters (such as *xzf258*) to be as-signed to a user for a username. Aliases can be used for e-mail so that the more com-mon first name/last name format can still be used for communication with users. The advantage of this random assignment is that it will be more difficult for an attacker to guess a valid username; however, it has the disadvantage of being difficult for the user to remember.

Most operating systems now include a password generation utility that helps users select their passwords. Such utilities use parameters that affect the passwords' complex-ity, which in turn affects the ability for it to be guessed as well as for the user to remem-ber it. Generally, the easier it is to remember the easier it will be to guess. Again, it is possible to generate completely random passwords, but these are difficult for users to remember. Restrictions on password generation can be eased so that the user can select a password that is easier to remember, but some general rules should still be followed. Passwords should contain a mix of uppercase and lowercase characters, special charac-ters, and numbers. They should be at least eight characters in length and they should not be related to the username.

Time of Day Restrictions

Some systems allow for the specification of time of day restrictions in their access con-trol policies. This means that a user's access to the system or specific resources can be restricted to certain times of the day and days of the week. If a user normally accesses certain resources during normal business hours, an attempt to access these resources outside this time period (either at night or on the weekend) might indicate an attacker has gained access to the account. Specifying time of day restrictions can also serve as a mechanism to enforce internal controls of critical or sensitive resources. Obviously, a drawback to enforcing time of day restrictions is that it means that a user can't go to work outside of normal hours in order to "catch up" with work tasks. As with all security policies, usability and security must be balanced in this policy decision.

Account and Password Expiration

Another common restriction that can be enforced in many access control mechanisms is either (or both) an account expiration or password expiration feature. This allows administrators to specify a period of time for which a password or an account will be active. For password expiration, when the expiration date is reached, the user will generally be asked to create a new password. This means that if the password (and thus the account) has been compromised when the expiration date is reached and a new password is set, the attacker will again (hopefully) be locked out of the system. The attacker can't change the password himself since the user would then be locked out and would contact an administrator to have the password reset, thus again locking out the attacker.

The attacker could set a new password, and then attempt to reset it to the original password. This would mean that a new expiration time would be set for the account but would keep the same password and would not lock the user out. This is one reason why a *password history* mechanism should be used. The history is used to keep track of previously used passwords so that they cannot be reused. An account expiration is similar, except that it is generally put in place because a specific account is intended for a specific purpose of limited duration. When an account has expired, it cannot be used unless the expiration deadline is extended.

File and Print Resources

The desire for a collaborative work environment often results in file sharing on servers. In a similar manner, print resources are also often shared so that many users can access high-cost resources. In the past, the potential for security problems associated with shared resources (it was often difficult to isolate who could or could not use the resource if it was opened for sharing) had led to some security administrators simply prohibiting sharing. With some of the more current operating systems, however, sharing can be accomplished with a reasonable balance between it and security. Strict policies regarding sharing need to be established. Some files should not be shared (such as a user's profile folder, for example), so allowing for a blanket sharing of files between users should be avoided. Instead, specific files within folders should be designated and managed through group policies. Similar care should be taken when deciding what print resources should be shared.

Logical Tokens

A *token* is an object that a user must have and present to the system to gain access to some resource or the system itself. Special hardware devices can be used as tokens that need to be inserted into the machine or a special reader, or that can provide some information (such as a one-time code) that must be supplied to the system to obtain access. A problem with all of these methods is that they require that the user have the physical device on hand to gain access. If the user loses the token or forgets it, she will be unable to access the resource.

Considered less secure but not suffering from the same problem is the use of logical or software tokens. These can take the form of a shared secret that only the user and the system know. The user is required to supply the secret when attempting to access the resource. As with passwords, policies should govern how logical tokens are generated, stored, and shared. With a hardware token, a user could give the device to another individual, but only one device is assigned to the user. With a software token, a user could share a token with another individual (along with any other identification information required) and that individual could in turn share it with somebody else. Once shared, there is no real way to control the dissemination of the software token.

Social Engineering

Social engineering is the process of convincing an authorized individual to provide confidential information or access to an unauthorized individual. Social engineering takes advantage of what continually turns out to be the weakest point in our security perimeter—the humans. Kevin Mitnick, a convicted cybercriminal turned security consultant, once stated, "Don't rely on network safeguards and firewalls to protect your information. Look to your most vulnerable spot. You'll usually find that vulnerability lies in your people." In 2000, after being released from jail, Mitnick testified before Congress and spoke on several other occasions about social engineering and how effective it is. He stated that he "rarely had to resort to a technical attack" because of how easily information and access could be obtained through social engineering.

Individuals who are attempting to social engineer some piece of information generally rely on two aspects of human nature. First, most people generally want to help somebody who is requesting help. Second, people generally want to avoid confrontation. The knowledgeable social engineer might call a help desk pretending to be a new employee needing help to log on to the organization's network. By doing so, valuable information can be obtained as to the type of system or network that is being employed. After making this call, a second call may be made that uses the information from the first call to provide background for the second call so that the next individual the attacker attempts to obtain information from will not suspect it is an unauthorized individual asking the questions. This works because people generally assume that somebody is who they claim to be, especially if they have information that would be known by the individual they claim to be.

If the pleasant approach doesn't work, a more aggressive approach can be attempted. People will normally want to avoid unpleasant confrontations and will also not want to get into trouble with their superiors. An attacker, knowing this, may attempt to obtain information by threatening to go to the individual's supervisor or by claiming that he is working for somebody who is high up in the organization's management structure. Because employees want to avoid both a confrontation and a possible reprimand, they might provide the information requested even though they realize that it is against the organization's policies or procedures.

The goal of social engineering is to gradually obtain the pieces of information necessary to make it to the next step. This is done repeatedly until the ultimate goal is reached. If social engineering is such an effective means of gaining unauthorized access to data and information, how can it be stopped? The most effective means is through the training and education of users, administrators, and security personnel. All employees should be instructed in the techniques that attackers might use and trained to recognize when a social engineering attack is being attempted. One important aspect of this training is for employees to recognize the type of information that should be protected and also how seemingly unimportant information can be combined with other pieces of information to potentially divulge sensitive information. This is known as *data aggregation*.

In addition to the direct approach to social engineering, attackers can use other indirect means to obtain the information they are seeking. These include phishing, vishing, shoulder surfing, and dumpster diving and are discussed in the following sections. Again, the first defense against any of these methods to gather information to be used in later attacks is a strong user education and awareness training program.

 EXAM TIP Social engineering attacks can come in many different forms. Taken as a whole, they are the most common attacks facing users. Be sure to understand the differences among the different types of social engineering attacks.

Phishing

Phishing (pronounced "fishing") is a type of social engineering in which an individual attempts to obtain sensitive information from a user by masquerading as a trusted entity in an e-mail or instant message sent to the user. The type of information that the attacker attempts to obtain include usernames, passwords, credit card numbers, or details on the user's bank account. The message sent often encourages the user to go to a web site that appears to be for a reputable entity such as PayPal or eBay, both of which have frequently been used in phishing attempts. The web site the user actually visits will not be owned by the reputable organization, however, and will ask the user to supply information that can be used in a later attack. Often the message sent to the user will tell a story about the user's account having been compromised, and for security purposes they are encouraged to enter their account information to verify the details.

The e-mails and web sites generated by the attackers often appear to be legitimate. A few clues, however, can tip off the user that the e-mail might not be what it claims to be. The e-mail may contain grammatical and typographical errors, for example. Organizations that are used in these phishing attempts (such as eBay and PayPal) are careful about their images and will not send a security-related e-mail to users containing obvious errors. In addition, almost unanimously, organizations tell their users that they will never ask for sensitive information (such as a password or account number) via an e-mail. Despite the increasing media coverage concerning phishing attempts, some

Internet users still fall for them, which results in attackers continuing to use this method to gain the information they are seeking.

Vishing

Vishing is a variation of phishing that uses voice communication technology to obtain the information the attacker is seeking. Vishing takes advantage of the trust that most people place in the telephone network. Users are unaware that attackers can spoof calls from legitimate entities using voice over IP (VoIP) technology. Voice messaging can also be compromised and used in these attempts. Generally, the attackers are hoping to obtain credit card numbers or other information that can be used in identity theft. The user may receive an e-mail asking him to call a number that is answered by a potentially compromised voice message system. Users may also receive a recorded message that appears to come from a legitimate entity. In both cases, the user will be encouraged to respond quickly and provide the sensitive information so that access to an account is not blocked. If a user ever receives a message that claims to be from a reputable entity and is asking for sensitive information, he should not provide it but instead use the Internet or examine a legitimate account statement to find a phone number that can be used to contact the entity. The user can then verify that the message received was legitimate or report the vishing attempt.

Shoulder Surfing

Shoulder surfing does not involve direct contact with the user, but instead involves the attacker directly observing the target entering sensitive information on a form, keypad, or keyboard. The attacker may simply look over the shoulder of the user at work or the attacker can set up a camera or use binoculars to view users entering sensitive data. The attacker can attempt to obtain information such as a PIN at an automated teller machine, an access control entry code at a secure gate or door, or calling card or credit card numbers. Some locations now use a small shield to surround a keypad so that it is difficult to observe somebody entering information. More sophisticated systems can actually scramble the location of the numbers so that the top row at one time includes the numbers 1, 2, and 3 and the next time 4, 8, and 0. While this makes it a bit slower for the user to enter information, it does mean that a person attempting to observe what numbers are pressed will not be able to press the same buttons/pattern since the location of the numbers have changed.

Although methods such as these can help make shoulder surfing more difficult, the best defense is for users to be aware of their surroundings and to not allow individuals to get into a position from which they can observe what the user is entering. A related security comment can be made at this point: It should now be obvious why a person should not use the same PIN for all of their different accounts, gate codes, and so on, since an attacker who learns the PIN for one could then use it for all of the other places requiring a PIN that was also generated by the user.

Dumpster Diving

Dumpster diving is not a uniquely computer security–related activity. It refers to the activity of sifting through an individual's or organization's trash for things that the dumpster diver might find valuable. In the nonsecurity realm, this can be anything from empty aluminum cans to articles of clothing or discarded household items. From a computer security standpoint, the diver is looking for information that can be obtained from listings or printouts, manuals, receipts, or even yellow sticky notes. The information can include credit card or bank account numbers, user IDs or passwords, details about the type of software or hardware platforms that are being used, or even company sensitive information. In most locations, trash is no longer considered private property after it has been discarded (and even where dumpster diving is illegal, little enforcement occurs). An organization should have policies about discarding materials. Sensitive information should be shredded and the organization should consider securing the trash receptacle so that individuals can't forage through it. People should also consider shredding personal or sensitive information that they wish to discard in their own trash. A reasonable quality shredder is inexpensive and well worth the price when compared with the potential loss that could occur as a result of identity theft.

Hoaxes

At first glance, it might seem that a hoax related to security would be considered a nuisance and not a real security issue. This might be the case for some hoaxes, especially those of the urban legend type, but the reality of the situation is that a hoax can be very damaging if it causes users to take some sort of action that weakens security. One real hoax, for example, told the story of a new, highly destructive piece of malicious software. It instructed users to check for the existence of a certain file and to delete it if the file was found. In reality, the file mentioned was an important file that was used by the operating system, and deleting it caused problems the next time the system was booted. The damage caused by users modifying security settings can be serious. As with other forms of social engineering, training and awareness are the best and first line of defense for users. Users should be trained to be suspicious of unusual e-mails and stories and should know who to contact in the organization to verify the validity if they are received.

Organizational Policies and Procedures

Policies are high-level statements created by management that lay out the organization's positions on particular issues. Policies are mandatory but are not specific in their details. Policies are focused on the result, not the methods for achieving that result. *Procedures* are generally step-by-step instructions that prescribe exactly how employees are expected to act in a given situation or to accomplish a specific task. Although standard policies can be described in general terms that will be applicable to all organizations, standards and procedures are often organization-specific and driven by specific organizational policies.

Regarding security, every organization should have several common policies in place in addition to those already discussed relative to access control methods. These policies include acceptable use policies, due care, separation of duties, and policies governing the protection of *personally identifiable information* (PII), and they are addressed in the following sections. Other important policy-related issues covered here include privacy, service level agreements, human resources policies, codes of ethics, and policies governing incident response.

Security Policies

In keeping with the high-level nature of policies, the *security policy* is a high-level statement produced by senior management that outlines what security means to the organization and the organization's goals for security. The main security policy can then be broken down into additional policies that cover specific topics. Statements such as "this organization will exercise the principle of least access in its handling of client information" would be an example of a security policy. The security policy can also describe how security is to be handled from an organizational point of view (such as describing which office and corporate officer or manager oversees the organization's security program).

In addition to policies related to access control, the organization's security policy should include the specific policies described in the next sections. All policies should be reviewed on a regular basis and updated as needed. Generally, policies should be updated less frequently than the procedures that implement them, since the high-level goals will not change as often as the environment in which they must be implemented. All policies should be reviewed by the organization's legal counsel, and a plan should be outlined describing how the organization will ensure that employees will be made aware of the policies. Policies can also be made stronger by including references to the authority who made the policy (whether this policy comes from the CEO or is a department-level policy) and also refer to any laws or regulations that are applicable to the specific policy and environment.

Change Management

The purpose of *change management* is to ensure proper procedures are followed when modifications to the IT infrastructure are made. These modifications can be prompted by a number of different reasons including new legislation, updated versions of software or hardware, implementation of new software or hardware, or improvements to the infrastructure. The term "management" implies that this process should be controlled in some systematic way, and that is indeed the purpose. Changes to the infrastructure can have a detrimental impact on operations. New versions of operating systems or application software can be incompatible with other software or hardware the organization is using. Without a process to manage the change, an organization can suddenly find itself unable to conduct business. A change management process should include various stages including a method to request a change to the infrastructure, a review and approval process for the request, an examination of the consequences of the change, resolution (or mitigation) of any detrimental affects the change might incur, implementation of the change, and documentation of the process as it related to the change.

Classification of Information

A key component of IT security is the protection of the information processed and stored on the computer systems and network. Organizations deal with many different types of information, and they need to recognize that not all information is of equal importance or sensitivity. This prompts a classification of information into various categories, each with its own requirements for its handling. Factors that affect the classification of specific information include its value to the organization (what will be the impact to the organization if it loses this information?), its age, and laws or regulations that govern its protection. The most widely known classification of information is that implemented by the government and military, which classifies information into categories such as *confidential*, *secret*, and *top secret*. Businesses have similar desires to protect information but can use categories such as *publicly releasable*, *proprietary*, *company confidential*, or *for internal use only*. Each policy for a classification of information should describe how it should be protected, who may have access to it, who has the authority to release it and how, and how it should be destroyed. All employees of the organization should be trained in the procedures for handling the information that they are authorized to access. Discretionary and mandatory access control techniques use classifications as a method to identify who may have access to what resources.

Acceptable Use

An *acceptable use policy* (AUP) outlines what the organization considers to be the appropriate use of company resources, such as computer systems, e-mail, Internet, and networks. Organizations should be concerned with the personal uses of organizational assets that do not benefit the company.

The goal of the policy is to ensure employee productivity while limiting organizational liability through inappropriate use of the organization's assets. The policy should clearly delineate what activities are not allowed. Issues such as the use of resources to conduct personal business, installation of hardware or software, remote access to systems and networks, the copying of company-owned software, and the responsibility of users to protect company assets, including data, software, and hardware should be addressed. Statements regarding possible penalties for ignoring any of the policies (such as termination) should also be included.

Related to appropriate use of the organization's computer systems and networks by employees is the appropriate use by the organization. The most important of such issues is whether the organization will consider it appropriate to monitor the employee's use of the systems and network. If monitoring is considered appropriate, the organization should include a statement to this effect in the banner that appears at login. This repeatedly warns employees, and possible intruders, that their actions are subject to monitoring and that any misuse of the system will not be tolerated. Should the organization need to use any information gathered during monitoring in a civil or criminal case, the issue of whether the employee had an expectation of privacy, or whether it was even legal for the organization to be monitoring, is simplified if the organization can point to a statement that is always displayed, stating that use of the system constitutes consent to monitoring. Before any monitoring is conducted, or the actual wording on the warning message is created, the organization's legal counsel should be consulted to determine the appropriate way to address this issue in the particular location.

EXAM TIP   A second very common and also very important policy is the acceptable use policy. Make sure you understand how this policy outlines what is considered acceptable behavior for a computer system's users. This policy often goes hand-in-hand with an organization's Internet usage policy.

Internet Usage Policy   In today's highly connected environment, employee use of access to the Internet is of particular concern. The goal for the *Internet usage policy* is to ensure maximum employee productivity and to limit potential liability to the organization from inappropriate use of the Internet in a workplace. The Internet provides a tremendous temptation for employees to waste hours as they surf the Web for the scores of the important games from the previous night, conduct quick online stock transactions, or read the review of the latest blockbuster movie everyone is talking about. Obviously, every minute they spend conducting this sort of activity is time they are not productively engaged in the organization's business and their jobs. In addition, allowing employees to visit sites that may be considered offensive to others (such as pornographic or hate sites) can open the company to accusations of condoning a hostile work environment and result in legal liability.

The Internet usage policy needs to address what sites employees are allowed to visit and what sites they are not to visit. If the company allows them to surf the Web during non-work hours, the policy needs to clearly spell out the acceptable parameters, in terms of when they are allowed to do this and what sites they are still prohibited from visiting (such as potentially offensive sites). The policy should also describe under what circumstances an employee would be allowed to post something from the organization's network on the Web (on a blog, for example). A necessary addition to this policy would be the procedure for an employee to follow to obtain permission to post the object or message.

E-Mail Usage Policy   Related to the Internet usage policy is the *e-mail usage policy*, which deals with what the company will allow employees to send in terms of e-mail. This policy should spell out whether non-work e-mail traffic is allowed at all or is at least severely restricted. It needs to cover the type of message that would be considered inappropriate to send to other employees (for example, no offensive language, no sex-related or ethnic jokes, no harassment, and so on). The policy should also specify any disclaimers that must be attached to an employee's message sent to an individual outside the company.

Due Care and Due Diligence

Due care and *due diligence* are terms used in the legal and business community to address issues where one party's actions might have caused loss or injury to another's. Basically, the law recognizes the responsibility of an individual or organization to act reasonably relative to another with diligence being the degree of care and caution exercised. Reasonable precautions need to be taken that indicate that the organization is being responsible. In terms of security, it is expected that organizations will take reasonable precautions to protect the information that it maintains on other individuals. Should a person suffer a loss as a result of negligence on the part of an organization in terms of its security, a legal suit can be brought against the organization.

The standard applied—reasonableness—is extremely subjective and will often be determined by a jury. The organization will need to show how it had taken reasonable precautions to protect the information, and despite these precautions, an unforeseen security event occurred that caused the injury to the other party. Since this is so subjective, it is hard to describe what would be considered reasonable, but many sectors have "security best practices" for their industry, which provides a basis for organizations in that sector to start from. If the organization decides not to follow any of the best practices accepted by the industry, it needs to be prepared to justify its reasons in court should an incident occur. If the sector the organization is in has regulatory requirements, explanations on why the mandated security practices were not followed will be much more difficult (and possibly impossible) to justify.

Another element that can help establish due care from a security standpoint is developing and implementing the security policies discussed in this chapter. As the policies outlined become more generally accepted, the level of diligence and care that an organization will be expected to maintain will increase.

Due Process

Due process is concerned with guaranteeing fundamental fairness, justice, and liberty in relation to an individual's legal rights. In the United States, due process is concerned with the guarantee of an individual's rights as outlined by the Constitution and Bill of Rights. Procedural due process is based on the concept of what is "fair." Also of interest is the recognition by courts of a series of rights that are not explicitly specified by the Constitution but that the courts have decided are implicit in the concepts embodied by the Constitution. An example of this is an individual's right to privacy. From an organization's point of view, due process may come into play during an administrative action that adversely affects an employee. Before an employee is terminated, for example, were all of the employee's rights protected? An actual example pertains to the rights of privacy regarding employees' e-mail messages. As the number of cases involving employers examining employee e-mails grows, case law is established and the courts eventually settle on what rights an employee can expect. The best thing an employer can do if faced with this sort of situation is to work closely with HR staff to ensure that appropriate policies are followed and that those policies are in keeping with current laws and regulations.

Separation of Duties

Separation of duties is a principle employed in many organizations to ensure that no single individual has the ability to conduct transactions alone. This means that the level of trust in any one individual is lessened, and the ability for any individual to cause catastrophic damage to the organization is also lessened. An example might be an organization in which one person has the ability to order equipment, but another individual makes the payment. An individual who wants to make an unauthorized purchase for his own personal gain would have to convince another person to go along with the transaction.

Separating duties as a security tool is a good practice, but it is possible to go overboard and break up transactions into too many pieces or require too much oversight. This results in inefficiency and can actually be less secure, since individuals may not scrutinize transactions as thoroughly because they know others will also be reviewing them. The temptation is to hurry something along and assume that somebody else will examine or has examined it.

 EXAM TIP Another aspect of the separation of duties principle is that it spreads responsibilities out over an organization so no single individual becomes the indispensable individual with all of the "keys to the kingdom" or unique knowledge about how to make everything work. If enough tasks have been distributed, assigning a primary and a backup person for each task will ensure that the loss of any one individual will not have a disastrous impact on the organization.

Need to Know and Least Privilege

Two other common security principles are that of *need to know* and *least privilege*. The guiding factor here is that each individual in the organization is supplied with only the absolute minimum amount of information and privileges she needs to perform her work tasks. To obtain access to any piece of information, the individual must have a justified need to know. In addition, she will be granted only the bare minimum number of privileges that are needed to perform her job.

A policy spelling out these two principles as guiding philosophies for the organization should be created. The policy should also address who in the organization can grant access to information or may assign privileges to employees.

Disposal and Destruction

Many potential intruders have learned the value of dumpster diving. Not only should an organization be concerned with paper trash and discarded objects, but it must also be concerned with the information stored on discarded objects such as computers. Several government organizations have been embarrassed when old computers sold to salvagers proved to contain sensitive documents on their hard drives. It is critical for every organization to have a strong *disposal and destruction policy* and related procedures.

Important papers should be shredded, and *important* in this case means anything that might be useful to a potential intruder. It is amazing what intruders can do with what appears to be innocent pieces of information.

Magnetic storage media discarded in the trash (such as disks or tapes) or sold for salvage should have all files deleted, and then the media should be overwritten at least three times with all 1s, all 0s, and then random characters. Commercial products are available to destroy files using this process. It is not sufficient simply to delete all files and leave it at that, since the deletion process affects only the pointers to where the files are stored and doesn't actually get rid of all of the bits in the file. This is why it is possible to "undelete" files and recover them after they have been deleted.

A safer method for destroying files from a storage device is to destroy the data magnetically using a strong magnetic field to *degauss* the media. This effectively destroys all data on the media. Several commercial degaussers can be purchased for this purpose. Another method that can be used on hard drives is to use a file on them (the sort of file you'd find in a hardware store) and actually file off the magnetic material from the surface of the platter. Shredding floppy media is normally sufficient, but simply cutting a floppy into a few pieces is not enough—data has been successfully recovered from floppies that were cut into only a couple of pieces. CDs and DVDs also need to be disposed of appropriately. Many paper shredders now have the ability to shred these forms of storage media. In some highly secure environments, the only acceptable method of disposing of hard drives and other storage devices is the actual physical destruction of the devices.

Privacy

Customers place an enormous amount of trust in organizations to which they provide personal information. These customers expect their information to be kept secure so that unauthorized individuals will not gain access to it and so that authorized users will not use the information in unintended ways. Organizations should have a *privacy policy* that explains what their guiding principles will be in guarding personal data to which they are given access. In many locations, customers have a legal right to expect that their information is kept private, and organizations that violate this trust may find themselves involved in a lawsuit. In certain sectors, such as health care, federal regulations have been created that prescribe stringent security controls on private information.

It is a general practice in most organizations to have a policy that describes explicitly how information provided to the organization will be used (for example, it will not be sold to other organizations). Watchdog organizations monitor the use of individual information by organizations, and businesses can subscribe to services that will vouch for the organization to consumers, stating that the company has agreed to protect and keep private any information supplied to it. The organization is then granted permission to display a seal or certification on its web site where customers can see it. Organizations that misuse the information they promised to protect will find themselves subject to penalties from the watchdog organization.

A special category of private information that is becoming increasingly important today is personally identifiable information (PII). This category of information includes any data that can be used to uniquely identify an individual. This would include an individual's name, address, drivers license number, and other details. With the proliferation of e-commerce on the Internet, this information is used extensively and its protection has become increasingly important. You would not have to look far to find reports in the media of data compromises that have resulted in the loss of information that has led to issues such as identity theft. An organization that collects PII on its employees and customers must make sure that it takes all necessary measures to protect the data from compromise.

Service Level Agreements

Service level agreements (SLAs) are contractual agreements between entities describing specified levels of service that the servicing entity agrees to guarantee for the customer. These agreements clearly lay out expectations in terms of the service provided and support expected, and they also generally include penalties should the described level of service or support not be provided. An organization contracting with a service provider should remember to include in the agreement a section describing the service provider's responsibility in terms of business continuity and disaster recovery. The provider's backup plans and processes for restoring lost data should also be clearly described.

Human Resources Policies

It has been said that the weakest links in the security chain are the humans. Consequently, it is important for organizations to have policies in place relative to its employees. Policies that relate to the hiring of individuals are primarily important. The organization needs to make sure that it hires individuals that can be trusted with the organization's data and that of its clients. Once employees are hired, they should be kept from slipping into the category of "disgruntled employee." Finally, policies must be developed to address the inevitable point in the future when an employee leaves the organization—either on his own or with the "encouragement" of the organization itself. Security issues must be considered at each of these points.

Employee Hiring and Promotions

It is becoming common for organizations to run background checks on prospective employees and check the references they supply. Drug tests, checks for any criminal activity in the past, claimed educational backgrounds, and reported work history are all frequently checked today. For highly sensitive environments, security background checks can also be required. Make sure that your organization hires the most capable and trustworthy employees, and your policies should be designed to ensure this.

After an individual has been hired, your organization needs to minimize the risk that the employee will ignore company rules that could affect security. Periodic reviews by supervisory personnel, additional drug checks, and monitoring of activity during work may all be considered by the organization. If the organization chooses to implement any of these reviews, this must be specified in the organization's policies, and prospective employees should be made aware of these policies before being hired. What an organization can do in terms of monitoring and requiring drug tests, for example, can be severely restricted if not spelled out in advance as terms of employment. New hires should be made aware of all pertinent policies, especially those applying to security, and documents should be signed by them indicating that they have read and understood them.

Occasionally an employee's status will change within the company. If the change can be construed as a negative personnel action (such as a demotion), supervisors should be alerted to watch for changes in behavior that might indicate unauthorized activity is being contemplated or conducted. It is likely that the employee will be upset, and whether he acts on this to the detriment of the company is something that needs to be guarded against. In the case of a demotion, the individual may also lose certain privileges or access rights, and these changes should be made quickly so as to lessen the likelihood that the employee will destroy previously accessible data if he becomes disgruntled and decides to take revenge on the organization. On the other hand, if the employee is promoted, privileges may still change, but the need to make the change to access privileges may not be as urgent, though it should still be accomplished as quickly as possible. If the move is a lateral one, changes may also need to take place, and again they should be accomplished as quickly as possible. The organization's goals in terms of making changes to access privileges should be clearly spelled out in its policies.

Retirement, Separation, or Termination of an Employee

An employee leaving an organization can be either a positive or a negative action. Employees who are retiring by their own choice may announce their planned retirement weeks or even months in advance. Limiting their access to sensitive documents the moment they announce their intention may be the safest thing to do, but it might not be necessary. Each situation should be evaluated individually. Should the situation be a forced retirement, the organization must determine the risk to its data if the employee becomes disgruntled as a result of the action. In this situation, the wisest choice might be to cut off their access quickly and provide them with some additional vacation time. This might seem like an expensive proposition, but the danger to the company of having a disgruntled employee can justify it. Again, each case should be evaluated individually.

When an employee decides to leave a company, generally as a result of a new job offer, continued access to sensitive information should be carefully considered. If the employee is leaving as a result of hard feelings for the company, it might be the wise choice to quickly revoke her access privileges. If she is leaving as a result of a better job offer, you may decide to allow her to gracefully transfer her projects to other employees, but the decision should be considered very carefully, especially if the new company is a competitor.

If the employee is leaving the organization because she is being terminated, you should plan on her becoming disgruntled. While it may not seem the friendliest thing to do, an employee in this situation should immediately have her access privileges to sensitive information and facilities revoked. It is better to give somebody several weeks of paid vacation rather than have a disgruntled employee trash sensitive files to which they have access. Combinations should also be quickly changed once they have been informed of their termination. Access cards, keys, and badges should be collected; the employee should be escorted to her desk and watched as she packs personal belongings; and then she should be escorted from the building.

No matter what the situation, the organization should have policies that describe the intended goals, and procedures should detail the process to be followed for each of the described situations.

 EXAM TIP It is not uncommon for organizations to neglect having a policy that covers the removal of an individual's computer access upon termination. The policy should also include the procedures to reclaim and "clean" a terminated employee's computer system and accounts.

Mandatory Vacations

Organizations have provided vacation time for their employees for many years. Few, however, force employees to take this time if they don't want to. Some employees are given the choice either to "use or lose" their vacation time and if they do not take all of their vacation time they'll lose at least a portion of it. Many arguments can be made as to the benefit of taking time off, but more importantly from a security standpoint, an employee who never takes time off is a potential indicator of nefarious activity. Employees who never take any vacation time could be involved in activity such as fraud or embezzlement and might be afraid that if they leave on vacation, the organization would discover their illicit activities. As a result, requiring employees to use their vacation time through a policy of mandatory vacations can be a security protection mechanism.

Code of Ethics

Numerous professional organizations have established codes of ethics for their members. Each of these describe the expected behavior of their members from a high-level standpoint. Organizations can adopt this idea as well. For organizations, a code of ethics can set the tone for how employees will be expected to act and to conduct business. The code should demand honesty from employees and should require that they perform all activities in a professional manner. The code could also address principles of privacy and confidentiality and state how employees should treat client and organizational data. Conflicts of interest can often cause problems, so this could also be covered in the code of ethics.

By outlining a code of ethics, the organization can encourage an environment that is conducive to integrity and high ethical standards. For additional ideas on possible codes of ethics, check professional organizations such as the Institute for Electrical and Electronics Engineers (IEEE), the Association for Computing Machinery (ACM), or the Information Systems Security Association (ISSA).

Chapter Review

In this chapter, the organizational aspects of computer security were reviewed along with the role that policies, procedures, standards, and guidelines play in it. Taken together, these documents outline the security plan for the organization. Various factors that affect the security of the organization were discussed, including logic access controls and organizational security policies. Social engineering was discussed along with both the direct and indirect methods used. The best defense against all social engineering attacks consists of an active training and awareness program for employees.

Questions

To further help you prepare for the Security+ exam, and to test your level of preparedness, answer the following questions and then check your answers against the list of correct answers at the end of the chapter.

1. Which type of social engineering attack utilizes voice messaging to conduct the attack?

   A. Phishing

   B. War dialing

   C. Vishing

   D. War driving

2. Social engineering attacks work well because the individual who is the target of the attack/attempt

   A. Is often not very intelligent and can't recognize the fact that a social engineering attempt is being attempted.

   B. Often either genuinely wants to help or is trying to avoid a confrontation, depending on the attacker's specific tack.

   C. Is new to the organization and can't tell that the story he is being fed is bogus.

   D. Knows the attacker.

3. From a security standpoint, why should an organization consider a policy of mandatory vacations?

   A. To ensure that employees are not involved in illicit activity that they are attempting to hide.

   B. Because employees who are tired are more prone to making errors.

   C. To provide an opportunity for security personnel to go through their desks and computer systems.

   D. To keep from having lawsuits filed against the organization for adverse working conditions.

4. Select all of the following that are examples of personally identifiable information:

   A. An individual's name

   B. A national identification number

   C. A license plate number

   D. A telephone number

   E. A street address

5. A hoax can still be a security concern because

   A. It may identify a vulnerability that others can then decide to use in an attack.

   B. It shows that an attacker has the contact information for an individual who might be used in a later attack.

   C. It can result in a user performing some action that could lead to a compromise or that might adversely affect the system or network.

   D. A hoax is never a security concern—that is why it is called a hoax.

6. How should CDs and DVDs be disposed of?

   A. By shredding using a paper shredder designed also to shred CDs and DVDs.

   B. By using a commercial grade degausser.

   C. By overwriting the disk with 0s, then 1s, and then a random character.

   D. There is no approved way of disposing of this type of media, so they must be archived in a secure facility.

7. What type of attack consists of looking through an individual's or organization's trash for sensitive information?

   A. Phishing

   B. Vishing

   C. Shoulder surfing

   D. Dumpster diving

8. What type of attack can involve an attacker setting up a camera to record the entries individuals make on keypads used for access control?

   A. Phishing

   B. Shoulder surfing

   C. Dumpster diving

   D. Vishing

9. Which of the following should be included in a password policy?

   A. An explanation of how complex the password should be (i.e., what types of characters a password should be made up of)

   B. The length of time the password will be valid before it expires

   C. A description on how passwords should be distributed and protected

   D. All of the above

10. What is the best method of preventing successful phishing attacks?

    A. Firewalls that can spot and eliminate the phishing e-mails.

    B. Blocking sites where phishing originates.

    C. A viable user training and awareness program.

    D. There is no way to prevent successful phishing attacks.

11. What type of attack uses e-mails with a convincing story to encourage users to provide account or other sensitive information?

    A. Vishing

    B. Shoulder surfing

    C. Dumpster diving

    D. Phishing

12. The reason for providing a group access control policy is

    A. It provides a mechanism for individual users to police the other members of the group.

    B. It provides an easy mechanism to identify common user restrictions for members of the group. This means that individual profiles for each user don't have to be created but instead each is identified as a member of the group with its associated group profile/policies.

    C. It is the only way to identify individual user access restrictions.

    D. It makes it easier for abnormal behaviors to be identified, as a group norm can be established.

13. Which of the following is a high-level, broad statement of what the organization wants to accomplish?

    A. Policy

    B. Procedure

    C. Guideline

    D. Standard

Answers

1. **C.** Vishing is basically a variation of phishing that uses voice communication technology to obtain the information the attacker is seeking. Vishing takes advantage of the trust that most people place in the telephone network. The users are unaware that using Voice over IP (VoIP) technology, attackers can spoof calls from legitimate entities. Voice messaging can be compromised and used in these attempts.

2. **B.** Social engineering works because people generally truly want to help an individual asking for assistance or because they are trying to avoid a confrontation. They also work because people generally want to believe that the individual really is who he claims to be, even if that's not actually the case. The target's intelligence isn't an important factor; anybody can fall prey to an adept social engineer. Being new to an organization can certainly make it easier for an attacker to convince a target that he is entitled to the information requested, but it is not a requirement. Long-time employees can just as easily provide sensitive information to a talented social engineer. The target and attacker generally do not know each other in a social engineering attack, so **D** is not a good answer.

3. **A.** A frequent characteristic of employees who are involved in illicit activities is their reluctance to take a vacation. A prime security reason to require mandatory vacations is to discourage illicit activities in which employees are engaged.

4. **A, B, C, D, E.** All of these are examples of personally identifiable information. Any information that can be used to identify an individual uniquely falls into this category.

5. **C.** A hoax can cause a user to perform some action, such as deleting a file that the operating system needs. Because of this, hoaxes can be considered legitimate security concerns.

6. **A.** Shredders that are designed to destroy CDs and DVDs are common and inexpensive. A degausser is designed for magnetic media, not optical. Writing over with 0s, 1s, and a random character is a method that can be used for other magnetic media but not CDs or DVDs.

7. **D.** This is a description of dumpster diving. From a security standpoint, you should be concerned with an attacker being able to locate information that can help in an attack on the organization. From an individual perspective, you should be concerned about the attacker obtaining information such as bank account or credit card numbers.

8. **B.** This is a description of a shoulder surfing method. Other methods include simply looking over a person's shoulder as she enters code or using binoculars to watch from a distance.

9. **D.** All three of these were mentioned as part of what a password policy should include.

10. **C.** While research is being conducted to support spotting and eliminating phishing e-mails, no effective method is currently available to do this. It may be possible to block some sites that are known to be hostile, but again this is not effective at this time since an e-mail could come from anywhere and its address can be spoofed anyway. There might be some truth to the statement (**D**) that there is no way to prevent successful phishing attacks, because users continue to fall for them. The best way to prevent this is an active and viable user training and awareness program.

11. **D.** This is a description of phishing, which is a type of social engineering attack as are the other options. Vishing employs the use of the telephone network. Shoulder surfing involves the attacker attempting to observe a user entering sensitive information on a form, keypad, or keyboard. Dumpster diving involves the attacker searching through the trash of an organization or individual to find useful and sensitive information.

12. **B.** Groups and domains provide a mechanism to organize users in a logical way. Individuals with similar access restrictions can be placed within the same group or domain. This greatly eases the process of account creation for new employees.

13. **A.** This is the definition of a policy. Procedures are the step-by-step instructions on how to implement policies in an organization.

Legal Issues, Privacy, and Ethics

In this chapter, you will

- Learn about the laws and rules concerning importing and exporting encryption software
- Know the laws that govern computer access and trespass
- Understand the laws that govern encryption and digital rights management
- Learn about the laws that govern digital signatures
- Learn about the laws that govern privacy in various industries with relation to computer security
- Explore ethical issues associated with information security

Computer security is no different from any other subject in our society; as it changes our lives, laws are enacted to enable desired behaviors and prohibit undesired behaviors. The one substantial difference between this aspect of our society and others is that the speed of advancement in the information systems world as driven by business, computer network connectivity, and the Internet is much greater than in the legal system of compromise and law-making. In some cases, laws have been overly restrictive, limiting business options, such as in the area of importing and exporting encryption technology. In other cases, legislation has been slow in coming and this fact has stymied business initiatives, such as in digital signatures. And in some areas, it has been both too fast and too slow, as in the case of privacy laws. One thing is certain: you will never satisfy everyone with a law, but it does delineate the rules of the game.

The cyber-law environment has not been fully defined by the courts. Laws have been enacted, but until they have been fully tested and explored by cases in court, the exact limits are somewhat unknown. This makes some aspects of interpretation more challenging, but the vast majority of the legal environment is known well enough that effective policies can be enacted to navigate this environment properly. Policies and procedures are tools you use to ensure understanding and compliance with laws and regulations affecting cyberspace.

Cybercrime

One of the many ways to examine cybercrime involves studying how the computer is involved in the criminal act. Three types of computer crimes commonly occur: computer-assisted crime, computer-targeted crime, and computer-incidental crime. The differentiating factor is in how the computer is specifically involved from the criminal's point of view. Just as crime is not a new phenomenon, neither are computers, and cybercrime has a history of several decades.

What is new is how computers are involved in criminal activities. The days of simple teenage hacking activities from a bedroom have been replaced by organized crime controlled botnets (groups of computers commandeered by a malicious hacker) and acts designed to attack specific targets. The legal system has been slow to react and law enforcement has been hampered by their own challenges in responding to the new threats posed by high-tech crime.

What comes to mind when most people think about cybercrime is a computer that is targeted and attacked by an intruder. The criminal attempts to benefit from some form of unauthorized activity associated with a computer. In the 1980s and '90s, cybercrime was mainly virus and worm attacks, each exacting some form of damage, yet the gain for the criminal was usually negligible. Enter the 21st century, with new forms of malware, rootkits, and targeted attacks; criminals can now target individual users and their bank accounts. In the current environment it is easy to predict where this form of attack will occur—if money is involved, a criminal will attempt to obtain what he considers his own fair share! A common method of criminal activity is computer-based fraud. Advertising on the Internet is big business, and hence the "new" crime of *click fraud* is now a concern. Click fraud involves a piece of malware that defrauds the advertising revenue counter engine through fraudulent user clicks.

eBay, the leader in the Internet auction space, and its companion PayPal, are frequent targets of fraud. Whether the fraud occurs by fraudulent listing, fraudulent bidding, or outright stealing of merchandise, the results are the same: a crime is committed. As users move toward online banking and stock trading, so moves the criminal element. Malware designed to install a keystroke logger and then watch for bank/brokerage logins is already making the rounds of the Internet. Once the attacker finds the targets, he can begin looting accounts. His risk of getting caught and prosecuted is exceedingly low. Walk into a bank in the United States and rob it, and the odds are better than 95 percent that you will be doing time in federal prison after the FBI hunts you down and slaps the cuffs on your wrists. Do the same crime via a computer, and the odds are even better than the opposite: less than 1 percent of these attackers are caught and prosecuted.

The low risk of being caught is one of the reasons that criminals are turning to computer crime. Just as computers have become easy for ordinary people to use, the trend continues for the criminal element. Today's cyber criminals use computers as tools to steal intellectual property or other valuable data and then subsequently market these materials through underground online forums. Using the computer to physically isolate the criminal from the direct event of the crime has made the investigation and prosecution of these crimes much more challenging for authorities.

The last way computers are involved with criminal activities is through incidental involvement. Back in 1931, the U.S. government used accounting records and tax laws to convict Al Capone of tax evasion. Today, similar records are kept on computers. Computers are also used to traffic child pornography and other illicit activities—these computers act more as storage devices than as actual tools to enable the crime. Because child pornography existed before computers made its distribution easier, the computer is actually incidental to the crime itself.

With the three forms of computer involvement in crimes, coupled with increased criminal involvement, multiplied by the myriad of ways a criminal can use a computer to steal or defraud, added to the indirect connection mediated by the computer and the Internet, computer crime of the 21st century is a complex problem indeed. Technical issues are associated with all the protocols and architectures. A major legal issue is the education of the entire legal system as to the serious nature of computer crimes. All these factors are further complicated by the use of the Internet to separate the criminal and his victim geographically. Imagine this defense: "Your honor, as shown by my client's electronic monitoring bracelet, he was in his apartment in California when this crime occurred. The victim claims that the money was removed from his local bank in New York City. Now, last time I checked, New York City was a long way from Los Angeles, so how could my client have robbed the bank?"

EXAM TIP Computers are involved in three forms of criminal activity: the computer as a tool of the crime, the computer as a victim of a crime, and the computer that is incidental to a crime.

Common Internet Crime Schemes

To find crime, just follow the money. In the United States, the FBI and the National White Collar Crime Center (NW3C) have joined forces in developing the Internet Crime Complaint Center, an online clearinghouse that communicates issues associated with cybercrime. One of the items provided to the online community is a list of common Internet crimes and explanations (www.ic3.gov/crimeschemes.aspx). A separate list offers advice on how to prevent these crimes through individual actions (www.ic3.gov/preventiontips.aspx).

Here's a list of common Internet crimes from the site:

- Auction Fraud
- Auction Fraud—Romania
- Counterfeit Cashier's Check
- Credit Card Fraud
- Debt Elimination
- Parcel Courier Email Scheme
- Employment/Business Opportunities

- Escrow Services Fraud
- Identity Theft
- Internet Extortion
- Investment Fraud
- Lotteries
- Nigerian Letter or "419"
- Phishing/Spoofing
- Ponzi/Pyramid Scheme
- Reshipping
- Spam
- Third Party Receiver of Funds

Sources of Laws

In the United States, three primary sources of laws and regulations affect our lives and govern actions. *Statutory laws* are passed by the legislative branches of government, be it the Congress or a local city council. Another source of laws and regulations are from administrative bodies given power by other legislation. The power of government sponsored agencies, such as the Environmental Protection Agency (EPA), the Federal Aviation Administration (FAA), the Federal Communication Commission (FCC), and others lie in this powerful ability to enforce behaviors through *administrative rule making*. The last source of law in the United States is *common law*, which is based on previous events or precedent. This source of law comes from the judicial branch of government: judges decide on the applicability of laws and regulations.

All three sources have an involvement in computer security. Specific statutory laws, such as the Computer Fraud and Abuse Act, govern behavior. Administratively, the FCC and Federal Trade Commission (FTC) have made their presence felt in the Internet arena with respect to issues such as intellectual property theft and fraud. Common law cases are now working their way through the judicial system, cementing the issues of computers and crimes into the system of precedents and constitutional basis of laws.

 EXAM TIP Three types of laws are commonly associated with cybercrime: statutory law, administrative law, and common law.

Computer Trespass

With the advent of global network connections and the rise of the Internet as a method of connecting computers between homes, businesses, and governments across the globe, a new type of criminal trespass can now be committed. *Computer trespass* is the unauthorized entry into a computer system via any means, including remote network connections. These crimes have introduced a new area of law that has both national and international consequences. For crimes that are committed within a country's borders, national laws apply. For cross-border crimes, international laws and international treaties are the norm. Computer-based trespass can occur even if countries do not share a physical border.

Computer trespass is treated as a crime in many countries. National laws exist in many countries, including the EU, Canada, and the United States. These laws vary by country, but they all have similar provisions defining the unauthorized entry into and use of computer resources for criminal activities. Whether called *computer mischief* as in Canada, or *computer trespass* as in the United States, unauthorized entry and use of computer resources is treated as a crime with significant punishments. With the globalization of the computer network infrastructure, or Internet, issues that cross national boundaries have arisen and will continue to grow in prominence. Some of these issues are dealt with through the application of national laws upon request of another government. In the future, an international treaty may pave the way for closer cooperation.

Convention on Cybercrime

The Convention on Cybercrime is the first international treaty on crimes committed via the Internet and other computer networks. The convention is the product of four years of work by Council of Europe experts, but also by the United States, Canada, Japan, and other countries that are not members of the organization of the member states of the European Council. The current status of the convention is as a draft treaty, ratified by only two members. A total of five members must ratify it to become law.

The main objective of the convention, set out in the preamble, is to pursue a common criminal policy aimed at the protection of society against cybercrime, especially by adopting appropriate legislation and fostering international cooperation. This has become an important issue with the globalization of network communication. The ability to create a virus anywhere in the world and escape prosecution because of lack of local laws has become a global concern.

The convention deals particularly with infringements of copyright, computer-related fraud, child pornography, and violations of network security. It also contains a series of powers and procedures covering, for instance, searches of computer networks and interception. It will be supplemented by an additional protocol making any publication of racist and xenophobic propaganda via computer networks a criminal offense.

Significant U.S. Laws

The United States has been a leader in the development and use of computer technology. As such, it has a longer history with computers and with cybercrime. Because legal systems tend to be reactive and move slowly, this leadership position has translated into a leadership position from a legal perspective as well. The one advantage of this legal leadership position is the concept that once an item is identified and handled by the legal system in one jurisdiction, subsequent adoption in other jurisdictions is typically quicker.

Electronic Communications Privacy Act (ECPA)

The Electronic Communications Privacy Act (ECPA) of 1986 was passed by Congress and signed by President Reagan to address a myriad of legal privacy issues that resulted from the increasing use of computers and other technology specific to telecommunications. Sections of this law address e-mail, cellular communications, workplace privacy, and a host of other issues related to communicating electronically. A major provision was the prohibition against an employer's monitoring an employee's computer usage, including e-mail, unless consent is obtained. Other legal provisions protect electronic communications from wiretap and outside eavesdropping, as users were assumed to have a reasonable expectation of privacy and afforded protection under the Fourth Amendment to the Constitution.

A common practice with respect to computer access today is the use of a warning banner. These banners are typically displayed whenever a network connection occurs and serve four main purposes. First, from a legal standpoint, they establish the level of expected privacy (usually none on a business system) and serve as consent to real-time monitoring from a business standpoint. Real-time monitoring can be conducted for security reasons, business reasons, or technical network performance reasons. The key is that the banner tells users that their connection to the network signals their consent to monitoring. Consent can also be obtained to look at files and records. In the case of government systems, consent is needed to prevent direct application of the Fourth Amendment. And the last reason is that the warning banner can establish the system or network administrator's common authority to consent to a law enforcement search.

Computer Fraud and Abuse Act (1986)

The Computer Fraud and Abuse Act (CFAA) of 1986, amended in 1994, 1996, and in 2001 by the Patriot Act, serves as the current foundation for criminalizing unauthorized access to computer systems. The CFAA makes it a crime to knowingly access a computer or computer system that is a government computer and is a computer involved in interstate or foreign communication, which in today's Internet-connected age can be almost any machine. The act sets financial thresholds, which were lowered by the Patriot Act, but in light of today's investigation costs, these are easily met. The act also makes it a crime to knowingly transmit a program, code, or command that results in damage. Trafficking in passwords or similar access information is also criminalized. This is a wide-sweeping act, but the challenge of proving a case still exists.

Patriot Act

The Patriot Act of 2001, passed in response to the September 11 terrorist attack on the World Trade Center buildings in New York, substantially changed the levels of checks and balances in laws related to privacy in the United States. This law extends the tap and trace provisions of existing wiretap statutes to the Internet and mandated certain technological modifications at ISPs to facilitate electronic wiretaps on the Internet. The act also permitted the Justice Department to proceed with its rollout of the Carnivore program, an eavesdropping program for the Internet. Much controversy exists over Carnivore, but until it's changed, the Patriot Act mandates that ISPs cooperate and facilitate monitoring. The Patriot Act also permits federal law enforcement personnel to investigate computer trespass (intrusions) and enacts civil penalties for trespassers.

Gramm-Leach-Bliley Act (GLB)

In November 1999, President Clinton signed the Gramm-Leach-Bliley Act, a major piece of legislation affecting the financial industry with significant privacy provisions for individuals. The key privacy tenets enacted in GLB included the establishment of an opt-out method for individuals to maintain some control over the use of the information provided in a business transaction with a member of the financial community. GLB is enacted through a series of rules governed by state law, federal law, securities law, and federal rules. These rules cover a wider range of financial institutions, from banks and thrifts, to insurance companies, to securities dealers. Some internal information sharing is required under the Fair Credit Reporting Act (FCRA) between affiliated companies, but GLB ended sharing to external third-party firms.

Sarbanes-Oxley (SOX)

In the wake of several high-profile corporate accounting/financial scandals in the United States, the federal government in 2002 passed sweeping legislation overhauling the financial accounting standards for publically traded firms in the United States. These changes were comprehensive, touching most aspects of business in one way or another. With respect to information security, one of the most prominent changes is Section 404 controls, which specify that all processes associated with the financial reporting of a firm must be controlled and audited on a regular basis. Since the majority of firms use computerized systems, this placed internal auditors into the IT shops, verifying that the systems had adequate controls to ensure the integrity and accuracy of financial reporting. These controls have resulted in controversy over the cost of maintaining these controls versus the risk of not using them.

Section 404 requires firms to establish a control-based framework designed to detect or prevent fraud that would result in misstatement of financials. In simple terms, these controls should detect insider activity that would defraud the firm. This has significant impacts on the internal security controls, because a system administrator with root level access could perform many if not all tasks associated with fraud and would have the ability to alter logs and cover his or her tracks. Likewise, certain levels of power users of financial accounting programs would also have significant capability to alter records.

Payment Card Industry Data Security Standards (PCI DSS)

The payment card industry, including the powerhouses of MasterCard and Visa, designed a private sector initiative to protect payment card information between banks and merchants. This is a voluntary, private sector initiative that is proscriptive in its security guidance. Merchants and vendors can choose not to adopt these measures, but the standard has a steep price for noncompliance; the transaction fee for noncompliant vendors can be significantly higher, fines up to $500,000 can be levied, and in extreme cases the ability to process credit cards can be revoked. The PCI DSS is a set of six control objectives, containing a total of twelve requirements:

1. Build and Maintain a Secure Network

    Requirement 1   Install and maintain a firewall configuration to protect cardholder data

    Requirement 2   Do not use vendor-supplied defaults for system passwords and other security parameters

2. Protect Cardholder Data

    Requirement 3   Protect stored cardholder data

    Requirement 4   Encrypt transmission of cardholder data across open, public networks

3. Maintain a Vulnerability Management Program

    Requirement 5   Use and regularly update anti-virus software

    Requirement 6   Develop and maintain secure systems and applications

4. Implement Strong Access Control Measures

    Requirement 7   Restrict access to cardholder data by business need-to-know

    Requirement 8   Assign a unique ID to each person with computer access

    Requirement 9   Restrict physical access to cardholder data

5. Regularly Monitor and Test Networks

    Requirement 10   Track and monitor all access to network resources and cardholder data

    Requirement 11   Regularly test security systems and processes

6. Maintain an Information Security Policy

    Requirement 12   Maintain a policy that addresses information security for all employees and contractors

Import/Export Encryption Restrictions

Encryption technology has been controlled by governments for a variety of reasons. The level of control varies from outright banning to little or no regulation. The reasons behind the control vary as well, and control over import and export is a vital method of maintaining a level of control over encryption technology in general. The majority of the laws and restrictions are centered on the use of cryptography, which was until recently used mainly for military purposes. The advent of commercial transactions and network communications over public networks such as the Internet has expanded the use of cryptographic methods to include securing of network communications. As is the case in most rapidly changing technologies, the practice moves faster than law. Many countries still have laws that are outmoded in terms of e-commerce and the Internet. Over time, these laws will be changed to serve these new uses in a way consistent with each country's needs.

U.S. Law

Export controls on commercial encryption products are administered by the Bureau of Industry and Security (BIS) in the U.S. Department of Commerce. The responsibility for export control and jurisdiction was transferred from the State Department to the Commerce Department in 1996 and most recently updated on June 6, 2002. Rules governing exports of encryption are found in the Export Administration Regulations (EAR), 15 C.F.R. Parts 730–774. Sections 740.13, 740.17, and 742.15 are the principal references for the export of encryption items.

Needless to say, violation of encryption export regulations is a serious matter and is not an issue to take lightly. Until recently, encryption protection was accorded the same level of attention as the export of weapons for war. With the rise of the Internet, widespread personal computing, and the need for secure connections for e-commerce, this position has relaxed somewhat. The United States updated its encryption export regulations to provide treatment consistent with regulations adopted by the EU, easing export and re-export restrictions among the 15 EU member states and Australia, the Czech Republic, Hungary, Japan, New Zealand, Norway, Poland, and Switzerland. The member nations of the Wassenaar Arrangement agreed to remove key length restrictions on encryption hardware and software that is subject to the certain reasonable levels of encryption strength. This action effectively removed "mass-market" encryption products from the list of dual-use items controlled by the Wassenaar Arrangement.

The U.S. encryption export control policy continues to rest on three principles: review of encryption products prior to sale, streamlined post-export reporting, and license review of certain exports of strong encryption to foreign government end users. The current set of U.S. rules require notification to the BIS for export in all cases, but the restrictions are significantly lessened for mass-market products as defined by all of the following:

- They are generally available to the public by being sold, without restriction, from stock at retail selling points by any of these means:
  - Over-the-counter transactions
  - Mail-order transactions
  - Electronic transactions
  - Telephone call transactions
- The cryptographic functionality cannot easily be changed by the user.
- They are designed for installation by the user without further substantial support by the supplier.

- When necessary, details of the items are accessible and will be provided, upon request, to the appropriate authority in the exporter's country in order to ascertain compliance with export regulations.

Mass-market commodities and software employing a key length greater than 64 bits for the symmetric algorithm must be reviewed in accordance with BIS regulations. Restrictions on exports by U.S. persons to terrorist-supporting states (Cuba, Iran, Iraq, Libya, North Korea, Sudan, or Syria), their nationals, and other sanctioned entities are not changed by this rule.

As you can see, this is a very technical area, with significant rules and significant penalties for infractions. The best rule is that whenever you are faced with a situation involving the export of encryption-containing software, consult an expert and get the appropriate permission, or a statement that permission is not required, first. This is one case where it is better to be safe than sorry.

Non-U.S. Laws

Export control rules for encryption technologies fall under the Wassenaar Arrangement, an international arrangement on export controls for conventional arms and dual-use goods and technologies. The Wassenaar Arrangement has been established in order to contribute to regional and international security and stability, by promoting transparency and greater responsibility in transfers of conventional arms and dual-use goods and technologies, thus preventing destabilizing accumulations. Participating states, of which the United States is one of 33, will seek, through their own national policies and laws, to ensure that transfers of these items do not contribute to the development or enhancement of military capabilities that undermine these goals, and are not diverted to support such capabilities.

Many nations have more restrictive policies than those agreed upon as part of the Wassenaar Arrangement. Australia, New Zealand, United States, France, and Russia go further than is required under Wassenaar and restrict general-purpose cryptographic software as dual-use goods through national laws. The Wassenaar Arrangement has had a significant impact on cryptography export controls, and there seems little doubt that some of the nations represented will seek to use the next round to move toward a more repressive cryptography export control regime based on their own national laws. There are ongoing campaigns to attempt to influence other members of the agreement toward less restrictive rules, and in some cases no rules. These lobbying efforts are based on e-commerce and privacy arguments.

In addition to the export controls on cryptography, significant laws prohibit the use and possession of cryptographic technology. In China, a license from the state is required for cryptographic use. In some other countries, including Russia, Pakistan, Venezuela, and Singapore, tight restrictions apply to cryptographic uses. France relinquished tight state control over the possession of the technology in 1999. One of the driving points behind France's action is the fact that more and more of the Internet technologies have built-in cryptography. Digital rights management, secure USB solutions, digital signatures, and Secure Sockets Layer (SSL)–secured connections are examples of common behind-the-scenes use of cryptographic technologies. In 2007, the United

Kingdom passed a new law mandating that when requested by UK authorities, either police or military, encryption keys must be provided to permit decryption of information associated with terror or criminal investigation. Failure to deliver either the keys or decrypted data can result in an automatic prison sentence of two to five years. Although this seems reasonable, it has been argued that such actions will drive certain financial entities off shore, as the rule applies only to data housed in the UK. As for deterrence, the two-year sentence may be better than a conviction for trafficking in child pornography; hence the law seems not to be as useful as it seems at first glance.

Digital Signature Laws

On October 1, 2000, the Electronic Signatures in Global and National Commerce Act (commonly called the E-Sign law) went into effect in the United States. This law implements a simple principle: a signature, contract, or other record may not be denied legal effect, validity, or enforceability solely because it is in electronic form. Another source of law on digital signatures is the National Conference of Commissioners on Uniform State Laws' Uniform Electronic Transactions Act (UETA), which has been adopted in more than 20 states. A number of states have adopted a nonuniform version of UETA, and the precise relationship between the federal E-Sign law and UETA has yet to be resolved and will most likely be worked out through litigation in the courts over complex technical issues.

Many states have adopted digital signature laws, the first being Utah in 1995. The Utah law, which has been used as a model by several other states, confirms the legal status of digital signatures as valid signatures, provides for use of state-licensed certification authorities, endorses the use of public key encryption technology, and authorizes online databases called repositories, where public keys would be available. The Utah act specifies a negligence standard regarding private encryption keys and places no limit on liability. Thus, if a criminal uses a consumer's private key to commit fraud, the consumer is financially responsible for that fraud, unless the consumer can prove that he or she used reasonable care in safeguarding the private key. Consumers assume a duty of care when they adopt the use of digital signatures for their transactions, not unlike the care required for PINs on debit cards.

From a practical standpoint, the existence of the E-Sign law and UETA have enabled e-commerce transactions to proceed, and the resolution of the technical details via court actions will probably have little effect on consumers. It is worth noting that consumers will have to exercise reasonable care over their signature keys, much as they must over PINs and other private numbers. For the most part, software will handle these issues for the typical user.

Non-U.S. Signature Laws

The United Nations has a mandate to further harmonize international trade. With this in mind, the UN General Assembly adopted the United Nations Commission on International Trade Law (UNCITRAL) Model Law on E-Commerce. To implement specific technical aspects of this model law, more work on electronic signatures was needed. The General Assembly then adopted the United Nations Commission on International

Trade Law (UNCITRAL) Model Law on Electronic Signatures. These model laws have become the basis for many national and international efforts in this area.

Canadian Laws

Canada was an early leader in the use of digital signatures. Singapore, Canada, and the U.S. state of Pennsylvania were the first governments to have digitally signed an inter-state contract. This contract, digitally signed in 1998, concerned the establishment of a Global Learning Consortium between the three governments (source: *Krypto-Digest* Vol. 1 No. 749, June 11, 1998). Canada went on to adopt a national model bill for electronic signatures to promote e-commerce. This bill, the Uniform Electronic Commerce Act (UECA), allows the use of electronic signatures in communications with the government. The law contains general provisions for the equivalence between traditional and electronic signatures (source: *BNA ECLR*, May 27, 1998, p. 700) and is modeled after the UNCITRAL Model Law on E-Commerce (source: *BNA ECLR*, September 13, 2000, p. 918). The UECA is similar to Bill C-54 in authorizing governments to use electronic technology to deliver services and communicate with citizens.

Individual Canadian provinces have passed similar legislation defining digital signature provisions for e-commerce and government use. These laws are modeled after the UNCITRAL Model Law on E-Commerce to enable widespread use of e-commerce transactions. These laws have also modified the methods of interactions between the citizens and the government, enabling electronic communication in addition to previous forms.

European Laws

The European Commission adopted a Communication on Digital Signatures and Encryption: "Towards a European Framework for Digital Signatures and Encryption." This communication states that a common framework at the EU level is urgently needed to stimulate "the free circulation of digital signature related products and services within the Internal market" and "the development of new economic activities linked to electronic commerce" as well as "to facilitate the use of digital signatures across national borders." Community legislation should address common legal requirements for certificate authorities, legal recognition of digital signatures, and international cooperation. This communication was debated, and a common position was presented to the member nations for incorporation into national laws.

On May 4, 2000, the European Parliament and Council approved the common position adopted by the council. In June 2000, the final version Directive 2000/31/EC was adopted. The directive is now being implemented by member states. To implement the articles contained in the directive, member states will have to remove barriers, such as legal form requirements, to electronic contracting, leading to uniform digital signature laws across the EU.

Digital Rights Management

The ability to make flawless copies of digital media has led to another "new" legal issue. For years, the music and video industry has relied on technology to protect its rights with respect to intellectual property. It has been illegal for decades to copy information, such as music and videos, protected by copyright. Even with the law, for years people have made copies of music and videos to share, violating the law. This had not had a significant economic impact in the eyes of the industry, as the copies made were of lesser quality and people would pay for original quality in sufficient numbers to keep the economics of the industry healthy. As such, legal action against piracy was typically limited to large-scale duplication and sale efforts, commonly performed overseas and subsequently shipped to the United States as counterfeit items.

The ability of anyone with a PC to make a perfect copy of digital media has led to industry fears that individual piracy actions could cause major economic issues in the recording industry. To protect the rights of the recording artists and the economic health of the industry as a whole, the music and video recording industry lobbied the U.S. Congress for protection, which was granted under the Digital Millennium Copyright Act (DMCA) on October 20, 1998. This law states the following: "To amend title 17, United States Code, to implement the World Intellectual Property Organization Copyright Treaty and Performances and Phonograms Treaty, and for other purposes." The majority of this law was well crafted, but one section has drawn considerable comment and criticism. A section of the law makes it illegal to develop, produce, and trade any device or mechanism designed to circumvent technological controls used in copy protection.

Although on the surface this seems a reasonable requirement, the methods used in most cases are cryptographic in nature, and this provision had the ability to eliminate and/or severely limit research into encryption and the strengths and weaknesses of specific methods. A provision, Section 1201(g) of DMCA, was included to provide for specific relief and allow exemptions for legitimate research. With this section, the law garnered industry support from several organizations such as the Software & Information Industry Association (SIIA), Recording Industry Association of America (RIAA), and Motion Picture Association of America (MPAA). Based on these inputs, the U.S. Copyright Office issued a report supporting the DMCA in a required report to the Congress. This seemed to settle the issues until the RIAA threatened to sue an academic research team headed by Professor Felten from Princeton University. The issue behind the suit was the potential publication of results demonstrating that several copy protection methods were flawed in their application. This research came in response to an industry-sponsored challenge to break the methods. After breaking the methods developed and published by the industry, Felten and his team prepared to publish their findings. The RIAA objected and threatened a suit under provisions of DMCA. After several years of litigation and support of Felten by the Electronic Freedom Foundation (EFF), the case was eventually resolved in the academic team's favor, although no case law to prevent further industry-led threats was developed.

This might seem a remote issue, but industries have been subsequently using the DMCA to protect their technologically inspired copy protection schemes for such products as laser-toner cartridges and garage-door openers. It is doubtful that the U.S. Congress intended the law to have such effects, yet until these issues are resolved in court, the DMCA may have wide-reaching implications. The act has specific exemptions for research provided four elements are satisfied:

(A) the person lawfully obtained the encrypted copy, phonorecord, performance, or display of the published work;
(B) such act is necessary to conduct such encryption research;
(C) the person made a good faith effort to obtain authorization before the circumvention; and
(D) such act does not constitute infringement under this title or a violation of applicable law other than this section, including section 1030 of title 18 and those provisions of title 18 amended by the Computer Fraud and Abuse Act of 1986.

Additional exemptions are scattered through the law, although many were pasted in during various deliberations on the act and do not make sense when the act is viewed in whole. The effect of these exemptions upon people in the software and technology industry is not clear, and until restrained by case law, the DMCA gives large firms with deep legal pockets a potent weapon to use against parties who disclose flaws in encryption technologies used in various products. Actions have already been initiated against individuals and organizations who have reported security holes in products. This will be an active area of legal contention as the real issues behind digital rights management have yet to be truly resolved.

Privacy

The advent of interconnected computer systems has enabled businesses and governments to share and integrate information. This has led to a resurgence in the importance of privacy laws worldwide. Governments in Europe and the United States have taken different approaches in attempts to control privacy via legislation. Many social and philosophical differences have led to these differences, but as the world becomes interconnected, understanding and resolving them will be important.

Privacy can be defined as the power to control what others know about you and what they can do with this information. In the computer age, personal information forms the basis for many decisions, from credit card transactions to purchase goods, to the ability to buy an airplane ticket and fly domestically. Although it is theoretically possible to live an almost anonymous existence today, the price for doing so is high—from higher prices at the grocery store (no frequent shopper discount), to higher credit costs, to challenges with air travel, opening bank accounts, and seeking employment.

U.S. Privacy Laws

Identity privacy and the establishment of identity theft crimes is governed by the Identity Theft and Assumption Deterrence Act, which makes it a violation of federal law to knowingly use another's identity. The collection of information necessary to do this is also governed by GLB, which makes it illegal for someone to gather identity information on another under false pretenses. In the education area, privacy laws have existed for years. Student records have significant protections under the Family Education Records and Privacy Act of 1974, including significant restrictions on information sharing. These records operate on an opt-in basis, as the student must approve the disclosure of information prior to the actual disclosure.

Health Insurance Portability & Accountability Act (HIPAA)

Medical and health information also has privacy implications, which is why the U.S. Congress enacted the Health Insurance Portability & Accountability Act (HIPAA) of 1996. HIPAA calls for sweeping changes in the way health and medical data is stored, exchanged, and used. From a privacy perspective, significant restrictions of data transfers to ensure privacy are included in HIPAA, including security standards and electronic signature provisions. HIPAA security standards mandate a uniform level of protections regarding all health information that pertains to an individual and is housed or transmitted electronically. The standard mandates safeguards for physical storage, maintenance, transmission, and access to individuals' health information. HIPAA mandates that organizations that use electronic signatures will have to meet standards ensuring information integrity, signer authentication, and nonrepudiation. These standards leave to industry the task of specifying the specific technical solutions and mandate compliance only to significant levels of protection as provided by the rules being released by industry.

Gramm-Leech-Bliley Act (GLB)

In the financial arena, GLB introduced the U.S. consumer to privacy notices, where firms must disclose what they collect, how they protect the information, and with whom they will share it. Annual notices are required as well as the option for consumers to opt out of the data sharing. The primary concept behind U.S. privacy laws in the financial arena is the notion that consumers be allowed to opt-out. This was strengthened in GLB to include specific wording and notifications as well as the appointment of a privacy officer for the firm.

California Senate Bill 1386 (SB 1386)

California Senate Bill 1386 (SB 1386) was a landmark law concerning information disclosures. It mandates that Californians be notified whenever personally identifiable information is lost or disclosed. Since the passage of SB 1386, numerous other states have modeled legislation on this bill, and although national legislation has been blocked by political procedural moves, it will eventually be passed.

European Laws

The EU has developed a comprehensive concept of privacy administered via a set of statutes known as *data protection laws*. These privacy statutes cover all personal data, whether collected and used by government or private firms. These laws are administered by state and national data protection agencies in each country. With the advent of the EU, this common comprehensiveness stands in distinct contrast to the patchwork of laws in the United States.

Privacy laws in Europe are built around the concept that privacy is a fundamental human right that demands protection through government administration. When the EU was formed, many laws were harmonized across the 15 member nations, and data privacy was among those standardized. One important aspect of this harmonization is the Data Protection Directive, adopted by EU members, which has a provision allowing the European Commission to block transfers of personal data to any country outside the EU that has been determined to lack adequate data protection policies. The differences in approach between the U.S. and the EU with respect to data protection led to the EU issuing expressions of concern about the adequacy of data protection in the U.S., a move that could pave the way to the blocking of data transfers. After negotiation, it was determined that U.S. organizations that voluntarily joined an arrangement known as Safe Harbor would be considered adequate in terms of data protection.

Safe Harbor is a mechanism for self-regulation that can be enforced through trade practice law via the FTC. A business joining the Safe Harbor Consortium must make commitments to abide by specific guidelines concerning privacy. Safe Harbor members also agree to be governed by certain self-enforced regulatory mechanisms, backed ultimately by FTC action.

Another major difference between U.S. and European regulation lies in where the right of control is exercised. In European directives, the right of control over privacy is balanced in such a way as to favor consumers. Rather than having to pay to opt-out, as in unlisted phone numbers, consumers have such services for free. Rather than having to opt-out at all, the default privacy setting is deemed to be the highest level of data privacy, and users have to opt-in to share information. This default setting is a cornerstone of the EU Data Protection Directive and is enforced through national laws in all member nations.

Ethics

Ethics has been a subject of study by philosophers for centuries. It might be surprising to note that ethics associated with computer systems has a history dating back to the beginning of the computing age. The first examination of cybercrime occurred in the late 1960s, when the professional conduct of computer professionals was examined with respect to their activities in the workplace. If we consider ethical behavior to be consistent with that of existing social norms, it can be fairly easy to see what is considered right and wrong. But with the globalization of commerce, and the globalization of communications via the Internet, questions are raised on what is the *appropriate* social norm. Cultural issues can have wide-ranging effects on this, and although the idea of an appropriate code of conduct for the world is appealing, is it as yet an unachieved objective.

The issue of globalization has significant local effects. If a user wishes to express free speech via the Internet, is this protected behavior or criminal behavior? Different locales have different sets of laws to deal with items such as free speech, with some recognizing the right, while others prohibit it. With the globalization of business, what are the appropriate controls for intellectual property when some regions support this right, while others do not even recognize intellectual property as something of value, but rather something owned by the collective of society? The challenge in today's business environment is to establish and communicate a code of ethics so that everyone associated with an enterprise can understand the standards of expected performance.

A great source of background information on all things associated with computer security, the SANS Institute, published a set of IT ethical guidelines in April 2004: see www.sans.org/resources/ethics.php?ref=3781.

SANS Institute IT Code of Ethics[1]

Version 1.0 - April 24, 2004
The SANS Institute

I will strive to know myself and be honest about my capability.

- I will strive for technical excellence in the IT profession by maintaining and enhancing my own knowledge and skills. I acknowledge that there are many free resources available on the Internet and affordable books and that the lack of my employer's training budget is not an excuse nor limits my ability to stay current in IT.

- When possible I will demonstrate my performance capability with my skills via projects, leadership, and/or accredited educational programs and will encourage others to do so as well.

- I will not hesitate to seek assistance or guidance when faced with a task beyond my abilities or experience. I will embrace other professionals' advice and learn from their experiences and mistakes. I will treat this as an opportunity to learn new techniques and approaches. When the situation arises that my assistance is called upon, I will respond willingly to share my knowledge with others.

- I will strive to convey any knowledge (specialist or otherwise) that I have gained to others so everyone gains the benefit of each other's knowledge.

- I will teach the willing and empower others with Industry Best Practices (IBP). I will offer my knowledge to show others how to become security professionals in their own right. I will strive to be perceived as and be an honest and trustworthy employee.

- I will not advance private interests at the expense of end users, colleagues, or my employer.

- I will not abuse my power. I will use my technical knowledge, user rights, and permissions only to fulfill my responsibilities to my employer.

- I will avoid and be alert to any circumstances or actions that might lead to conflicts of interest or the perception of conflicts of interest. If such circumstance occurs, I will notify my employer or business partners.

- I will not steal property, time or resources.

- I will reject bribery or kickbacks and will report such illegal activity.

- I will report on the illegal activities of myself and others without respect to the punishments involved. I will not tolerate those who lie, steal, or cheat as a means of success in IT.

I will conduct my business in a manner that assures the IT profession is considered one of integrity and professionalism.

- I will not injure others, their property, reputation, or employment by false or malicious action.

- I will not use availability and access to information for personal gains through corporate espionage.

- I distinguish between advocacy and engineering. I will not present analysis and opinion as fact.

- I will adhere to Industry Best Practices (IBP) for system design, rollout, hardening and testing.

- I am obligated to report all system vulnerabilities that might result in significant damage.

- I respect intellectual property and will be careful to give credit for other's work. I will never steal or misuse copyrighted, patented material, trade secrets or any other intangible asset.

- I will accurately document my setup procedures and any modifications I have done to equipment. This will ensure that others will be informed of procedures and changes I've made.

I respect privacy and confidentiality.

- I respect the privacy of my co-workers' information. I will not peruse or examine their information including data, files, records, or network traffic except as defined by the appointed roles, the organization's acceptable use policy, as approved by Human Resources, and without the permission of the end user.

- I will obtain permission before probing systems on a network for vulnerabilities.

- I respect the right to confidentiality with my employers, clients, and users except as dictated by applicable law. I respect human dignity.

- I treasure and will defend equality, justice and respect for others.
- I will not participate in any form of discrimination, whether due to race, color, national origin, ancestry, sex, sexual orientation, gender/sexual identity or expression, marital status, creed, religion, age, disability, veteran's status, or political ideology.

Chapter Review

From a system administrator's position, complying with cyber-laws is fairly easy. Add warning banners to all systems that enable consent to monitoring as a condition of access. This will protect you and the firm during normal routine operation of the system. Safeguard all personal information obtained in the course of your duties and do not obtain unnecessary information merely because you can get it. With respect to the various privacy statutes that are industry specific—GLB, FCRA, ECPA, FERPA, HIPAA— refer to your own institution's guidelines and policies. When confronted with aspects of the U.S. Patriot Act, refer to your company's general counsel, for although the act may absolve you and the firm of responsibility, this act's implications with respect to existing law are still unknown. And in the event that your system is trespassed upon (hacked), you can get federal law enforcement assistance in investigating and prosecuting the perpetrators.

Questions

To further help you prepare for the Security+ exam, and to test your level of preparedness, answer the following questions and then check your answers against the list of correct answers at the end of the chapter.

1. The VP of IS wants to monitor user actions on the company's intranet. What is the best method of obtaining the proper permissions?

   A. A consent banner displayed upon login

   B. Written permission from a company officer

   C. Nothing, because the system belongs to the company

   D. Written permission from the user

2. Your Social Security number and other associated facts kept by your bank are protected by what law against disclosure?

   A. The Social Security Act of 1934

   B. The Patriot Act of 2001

   C. The Gramm-Leach-Bliley Act

   D. HIPAA

3. Breaking into another computer system in the United States, even if you do not cause any damage, is regulated by what laws?

   A. State law, as the damage is minimal

   B. Federal law under the Identity Theft and Assumption Deterrence Act

   C. Federal law under Electronic Communications Privacy Act (ECPA) of 1986

   D. Federal law under the Patriot Act of 2001

4. Export of encryption programs is regulated by the

   A. U.S. State Department

   B. U.S. Commerce Department

   C. U.S. Department of Defense

   D. National Security Agency

5. For the FBI to install and operate Carnivore on an ISP's network, what is required?

   A. A court order specifying specific items being searched for

   B. An official request from the FBI

   C. An impact statement to assess recoverable costs to the ISP

   D. A written request from an ISP to investigate a computer trespass incident

6. True or false: Digital signatures are equivalent to notarized signatures for all transactions in the United States.

   A. True for all transactions in which both parties agree to use digital signatures

   B. True only for non–real property transactions

   C. True only where governed by specific state statute

   D. False, as the necessary laws have not yet passed

7. The primary factor(s) behind data sharing compliance between U.S. and European companies is/are

   A. Safe Harbor Provision

   B. European Data Privacy Laws

   C. U.S. FTC enforcement actions

   D. All of the above

8. True or false: Writing viruses and releasing them across the Internet is a violation of law.

   A. Always true. All countries have reciprocal agreements under international law.

   B. Partially true. Depends on laws in country of origin.

   C. False. Computer security laws do not cross international boundaries.

 D. Partially true. Depends on the specific countries involved, for the author of the virus and the recipient.

 9. Publication of flaws in encryption used for copy protection is a potential violation of

 A. HIPAA

 B. U.S. Commerce Department regulations

 C. DMCA

 D. National Security Agency regulations

 10. Violation of DMCA can result in

 A. Civil fine

 B. Jail time

 C. Activity subject to legal injunctions

 D. All of the above

Answers

 1. **A.** A consent banner consenting to monitoring resolves issues of monitoring with respect to the Electronic Communications Privacy Act (ECPA) of 1986.

 2. **C.** The Gramm-Leach-Bliley Act governs the sharing of privacy information with respect to financial institutions.

 3. **D.** The Patriot Act of 2001 made computer trespass a felony.

 4. **B.** Export controls on commercial encryption products are administered by the Bureau of Industry and Security (BIS) in the U.S. Department of Commerce.

 5. **B.** The Patriot Act of 2001 mandated ISP compliance with the FBI Carnivore program.

 6. **A.** Electronic digital signatures are considered valid for transactions in the United States since the passing of the Electronic Signatures in Global and National Commerce Act (E-Sign) in 2001.

 7. **D.** All of the above. The primary driver is European data protection laws as enforced on U.S firms by FTC enforcement through the Safe Harbor provision mechanism.

 8. **D.** This is partially true, for not all countries share reciprocal laws. Some common laws and reciprocity issues exist in certain international communities—for example, European Union—so some cross-border legal issues have been resolved.

 9. **C.** This is a potential violation of the Digital Millennium Copyright Act of 1998 unless an exemption provision is met.

10. **D.** All of the above have been attributed to DMCA, including the jailing of a Russian programmer who came to the United States to speak at a security conference. See w2.eff.org/IP/DMCA/?f=20010830_eff_dmca_op-ed.html.

PART II

Cryptography and Applications

- **Chapter 4** Cryptography
- **Chapter 5** Public Key Infrastructure
- **Chapter 6** Standards and Protocols

Cryptography

In this chapter, you will

- Learn about the different types of cryptography
- Learn about the current cryptographic algorithms
- Understand how cryptography is applied for security

Cryptography is the science of *encrypting,* or hiding, information—something people have sought to do since they began using language. Although language allowed them to communicate with one another, people in power attempted to hide information by controlling who was taught to read and write. Eventually, more complicated methods of concealing information by shifting letters around to make the text unreadable were developed.

The Spartans of ancient Greece would write on a ribbon wrapped around a specific gauge cylinder. When the ribbon was unwrapped, it revealed a strange string of letters. The message could be read only when the ribbon was wrapped around the same gauge cylinder. This is an example of a *transposition cipher,* where the same letters are used but the order is changed.

The Romans typically used a different method known as a *shift cipher.* In this case, one letter of the alphabet is shifted a set number of places in the alphabet for another letter. A common modern-day example of this is the ROT13 cipher, in which every letter is rotated 13 positions in the alphabet: *n* is written instead of *a, o* instead of *b,* and so on.

These ciphers were simple to use and also simple to break. Because hiding information was still important, more advanced transposition and substitution ciphers were required. As systems and technology became more complex, ciphers were frequently automated by some mechanical or electromechanical device. A famous example of a modern encryption machine is the German Enigma machine from World War II. This machine used a complex series of substitutions to perform encryption, and interestingly enough it gave rise to extensive research in computers.

Cryptanalysis, the process of analyzing available information in an attempt to return the encrypted message to its original form, required advances in computer technology for complex encryption methods. The birth of the computer made it possible to easily execute the calculations required by more complex encryption algorithms. Today, the computer almost exclusively powers how encryption is performed. Computer technology has also aided cryptanalysis, allowing new methods to be developed, such as linear and differential cryptanalysis. *Differential cryptanalysis* is done by comparing the input plaintext to the output ciphertext to try and determine the key used to encrypt the information. *Linear cryptanalysis* is similar in that it uses both plaintext and ciphertext, but it puts the plaintext through a simplified cipher to try and deduce what the key is likely to be in the full version of the cipher.

This chapter examines the most common symmetric and asymmetric algorithms in use today, as well as some uses of encryption on computer networks.

Algorithms

Every current encryption scheme is based upon an *algorithm,* a step-by-step, recursive computational procedure for solving a problem in a finite number of steps. The cryptographic algorithm—what is commonly called the *encryption algorithm* or *cipher*—is made up of mathematical steps for encrypting and decrypting information. Figure 4-1 shows a diagram of the encryption and decryption process and its parts.

The best algorithms are always public algorithms that have been published for peer review by other cryptographic and mathematical experts. Publication is important, as any flaws in the system can be revealed by others before actual use of the system. Several proprietary algorithms have been reverse-engineered, exposing the confidential data the algorithms try to protect. Examples of this include the decryption of Nikon's proprietary RAW format white balance encryption, and the cracking of the Exxon Mobil SpeedPass RFID encryption. The use of a proprietary system can actually be less secure than using a published system. While proprietary systems are not made available to be tested by potential crackers, public systems are made public for precisely this purpose.

A system that maintains its security after public testing can be reasonably trusted to be secure. A public algorithm can be more secure because good systems rely on the *encryption key* to provide security, not the algorithm itself. The actual steps for encrypting data can be published, because without the key, the protected information cannot be accessed. A *key* is a special piece of data used in both the encryption and decryption processes. The algorithms stay the same in every implementation, but a different key is used for each, which ensures that even if someone knows the algorithm you use to protect your data, he cannot break your security. A classic example of this is the early shift cipher, known as *Caesar's cipher.*

Figure 4-1
Diagram of the encryption and decryption process

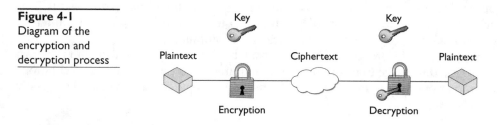

Caesar's cipher uses an algorithm and a key: the algorithm specifies that you offset the alphabet either to the right (forward) or to the left (backward), and the key specifies how many letters the offset should be. For example, if the algorithm specified offsetting the alphabet to the right, and the key was 3, the cipher would substitute an alphabetic letter three to the right for the real letter, so *d* would be used to represent *a*, *f* would be *c*, and so on. In this example, both the algorithm and key are simple, allowing for easy cryptanalysis of the cipher and easy recovery of the plaintext message.

The ease with which shift ciphers were broken led to the development of *substitution ciphers*, which were popular in Elizabethan England and more complex than shift ciphers. They work on the principle of substituting a different letter for every letter: *A* becomes *G*, *B* becomes *D*, and so on. This system permits 26 possible values for every letter in the message, making the cipher many times more complex than a standard shift cipher. Simple analysis of the cipher could be performed to retrieve the key, however. By looking for common letters such as *e* and patterns found in words such as *ing*, you can determine which cipher letter corresponds to which plaintext letter. Making educated guesses about words will eventually allow you to determine the system's key value.

To correct this problem, more complexity had to be added to the system. The *Vigenère cipher* works as a *polyalphabetic substitution cipher* that depends on a password. This is done by setting up a substitution table like this one:

```
A B C D E F G H I J K L M N O P Q R S T U V W X Y Z
B C D E F G H I J K L M N O P Q R S T U V W X Y Z A
C D E F G H I J K L M N O P Q R S T U V W X Y Z A B
D E F G H I J K L M N O P Q R S T U V W X Y Z A B C
E F G H I J K L M N O P Q R S T U V W X Y Z A B C D
F G H I J K L M N O P Q R S T U V W X Y Z A B C D E
G H I J K L M N O P Q R S T U V W X Y Z A B C D E F
H I J K L M N O P Q R S T U V W X Y Z A B C D E F G
I J K L M N O P Q R S T U V W X Y Z A B C D E F G H
J K L M N O P Q R S T U V W X Y Z A B C D E F G H I
K L M N O P Q R S T U V W X Y Z A B C D E F G H I J
L M N O P Q R S T U V W X Y Z A B C D E F G H I J K
M N O P Q R S T U V W X Y Z A B C D E F G H I J K L
N O P Q R S T U V W X Y Z A B C D E F G H I J K L M
O P Q R S T U V W X Y Z A B C D E F G H I J K L M N
P Q R S T U V W X Y Z A B C D E F G H I J K L M N O
Q R S T U V W X Y Z A B C D E F G H I J K L M N O P
R S T U V W X Y Z A B C D E F G H I J K L M N O P Q
S T U V W X Y Z A B C D E F G H I J K L M N O P Q R
T U V W X Y Z A B C D E F G H I J K L M N O P Q R S
U V W X Y Z A B C D E F G H I J K L M N O P Q R S T
V W X Y Z A B C D E F G H I J K L M N O P Q R S T U
W X Y Z A B C D E F G H I J K L M N O P Q R S T U V
X Y Z A B C D E F G H I J K L M N O P Q R S T U V W
Y Z A B C D E F G H I J K L M N O P Q R S T U V W X
Z A B C D E F G H I J K L M N O P Q R S T U V W X Y
```

Then the password is matched up to the text it is meant to encipher. If the password is not long enough, the password is repeated until one character of the password is matched up with each character of the plaintext. For example, if the plaintext is *Sample Message* and the password is *password*, the resulting match is

SAMPLEMESSAGE

PASSWORDPASSW

The cipher letter is determined by use of the grid, matching the plaintext character's row with the password character's column, resulting in a single ciphertext character where the two meet. Consider the first letters *S* and *P*: when plugged into the grid they output a ciphertext character of *H*. This process is repeated for every letter of the message. Once the rest of the letters are processed, the output is *HAEHHSDHHSSYA*.

In this example, the key in the encryption system is the password. It also illustrates that an algorithm can be simple and still provide strong security. If someone knows about the table, she can determine how the encryption was performed, but she still will not know the key to decrypting the message.

The more complex the key, the greater the security of the system. The Vigenère cipher system and systems like it make the algorithms rather simple but the key rather complex, with the best keys being very long and very random data. Key complexity is achieved by giving the key a large number of possible values. The *keyspace* is the size of every possible key value. When an algorithm lists a certain number of bits as a key, it is defining the keyspace. Note that because the keyspace is a numeric value, it is very important to ensure that comparisons are done using similar key types. Comparing a key made of 1-bit (2 possible values) and a key made of 1 letter (26 possible values) would not yield accurate results. Fortunately, the widespread use of computers has made almost all algorithms state their keyspace values in terms of bits.

It is easy to see how key complexity affects an algorithm when you look at some of the encryption algorithms that have been broken. The Data Encryption Standard (DES) uses a 56-bit key, allowing 72,000,000,000,000,000 possible values, but it has been broken by modern computers. The modern implementation of DES, Triple DES (3DES) uses a 128-bit key, or 340,000,000,000,000,000,000,000,000,000,000,000,000 possible values. You can see the difference in the possible values, and why 128 bits is generally accepted as the minimum required to protect sensitive information.

Because the security of the algorithms rely on the key, *key management* is of critical concern. Key management includes anything having to do with the exchange, storage, safeguarding, and revocation of keys. It is most commonly associated with asymmetric encryption, since asymmetric encryption uses both public and private keys. To be used properly for authentication, a key must be current and verified. If you have an old or compromised key, you need a way to check to see that the key has been revoked.

Key management is also important for symmetric encryption, however, as keys must be shared and exchanged easily. They must also be securely stored to provide appropriate confidentiality of the encrypted information. While keys can be stored in many different ways, new PC hardware often includes the Trusted Platform Module (TPM), which provides a hardware-based key storage location that is used by many applications, including the BitLocker drive encryption featured in Microsoft Windows Vista. (More specific information about the management of keys is provided in Chapter 5.)

The same algorithms cannot be used indefinitely; eventually they lose their ability to secure information. When an algorithm is known to be broken, it could be a result of the algorithm being faulty or having been based on poor math—more likely the algorithm has been rendered obsolete by advancing technology. All encryption ciphers other than a "one-time pad" cipher are susceptible to brute-force attacks, in which a cracker attempts every possible key until he gains access. With a very small key, such as a 2-bit key, trying every possible value is a simple matter, with only four possibilities: 00, 01, 10, or 11. 56-bit DES, on the other hand, has 72 quadrillion values, and while that seems like a lot, today's computers can attempt billions of keys every second. This makes brute-forcing a key only a matter of time; large keys are required to make brute-force attacks against the cipher take longer than the effective value of the information that is enciphered by them. *One-time pad* ciphers are interesting, because their keys are equal to the length of the messages they protect, and *completely* random characters *must be used* for the keys. This allows the keyspace to be unlimited, therefore making a brute-force attack practically impossible.

EXAM TIP A one-time pad with a good random key is considered unbreakable. In addition, since keys are never reused, even if a key is broken, no information can be accessed using the key other than the message used by *that* key.

Computers in cryptography and cryptanalysis must handle all this data in bit format. They would have difficulty in using the substitution table shown earlier, so many encryption functions use a logical function to perform the encipherment. This function is typically XOR, which is the bitwise *exclusive OR*. XOR is used because

if $(P \text{ XOR } K) = C$ then $(C \text{ XOR } K) = P$

If P is the plaintext and K is the key, then C is the ciphertext, making a simple symmetric key cipher in the case where the sender and the receiver both have a shared secret (key) to encrypt and decrypt data.

While symmetric encryption is the most common type of encryption, other types of encryption are used, such as public key or asymmetric encryption, and hashing or one-way functions. Each is best suited for particular situations.

Hashing

Hashing functions are commonly used encryption methods. A *hashing function* is a special mathematical function that performs *one-way encryption*, which means that once the algorithm is processed, there is no feasible way to use the ciphertext to retrieve the plaintext that was used to generate it. Also, ideally, there is no feasible way to generate two different plaintexts that compute to the same hash value. Figure 4-2 shows a generic hashing process.

Common uses of hashing functions are storing computer passwords and ensuring message integrity. The idea is that hashing can produce a unique value that corresponds to the data entered, but the hash value is also reproducible by anyone else running the

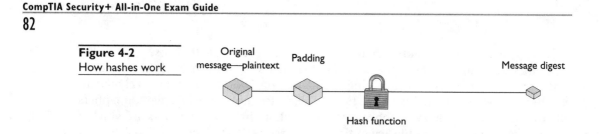

Figure 4-2
How hashes work

Original message—plaintext

Padding

Message digest

Hash function

same algorithm against the data. So you could hash a message to get a message authentication code (MAC), and the computational number of the message would show that no intermediary has modified the message. This process works because hashing methods are typically public, and anyone can hash data using the specified method. It is computationally simple to generate the hash, so it is simple to check the validity or integrity of something by matching the given hash to one that is locally generated.

A hash algorithm can be compromised with what is called a *collision attack*, in which an attacker finds two different messages that hash to the same value. This type of attack is very difficult and requires generating a separate algorithm that will attempt to find a text that will hash to the same value of a known hash. This must occur faster than simply editing characters until you hash to the same value, which is a brute-force type attack. The consequences of a hash function that suffers from collisions is that integrity is lost. If an attacker can make two different inputs purposefully hash to the same value, she might trick people into running malicious code and cause other problems. Two popular hash algorithms are the Secure Hash Algorithm (SHA) series and Message Digest (MD) hash of varying versions (MD2, MD4, MD5).

EXAM TIP The hashing algorithms in common use are MD2, MD4, MD5, and SHA-1, SHA-256, SHA-384, and SHA-512.

Hashing functions are very common, and they play an important role in the way information, such as passwords, is stored securely, and the way in which messages can be signed. By computing a digest of the message, less data needs to be signed by the more complex asymmetric encryption, and this still maintains assurances about message integrity. This is the primary purpose for which the protocols were designed, and their success will allow greater trust in electronic protocols and digital signatures.

SHA

Secure Hash Algorithm (SHA) refers to a set of four hash algorithms designed and published by the National Institute of Standards and Technology (NIST) and the National Security Agency (NSA). These algorithms are included in the SHA standard Federal Information Processing Standards (FIPS) 180-2. Individually, each standard is named SHA-1, SHA-256, SHA-384, and SHA-512. The latter variants are occasionally referred to as SHA-2.

SHA-1

SHA-1, developed in 1993, was designed as the algorithm to be used for secure hashing in the U.S. Digital Signature Standard (DSS). It is modeled on the MD4 algorithm and implements fixes in that algorithm discovered by the NSA. It creates message digests 160 bits long that can be used by the Digital Signature Algorithm (DSA), which can then compute the signature of the message. This is computationally simpler, as the message digest is typically much smaller than the actual message—smaller message, less work.

SHA-1 works, as do all hashing functions, by applying a compression function to the data input. It accepts an input of up to 2^{64} bits or less and then compresses down to a hash of 160 bits. SHA-1 works in block mode, separating the data into words first, and then grouping the words into blocks. The words are 32-bit strings converted to hex; grouped together as 16 words, they make up a 512-bit block. If the data that is input to SHA-1 is not a multiple of 512, the message is padded with zeros and an integer describing the original length of the message.

Once the message has been formatted for processing, the actual hash can be generated. The 512-bit blocks are taken in order—$B_1, B_2, B_3, \ldots, B_n$—until the entire message has been processed. The computation uses 80, 32-bit words labeled $W_0, W_1, W_2, \ldots, W_{79}$ being sent to two, 5-word buffers. The first 5-word buffer's words are labeled A, B, C, D, E, and the second 5-word buffer's words are labeled $H_0, H_1, H_2, H_3,$ and H_4. A single-word buffer, TEMP, also exists. Before processing any blocks, the H_i are initialized as follows:

H_0 = 67452301

H_1 = EFCDAB89

H_2 = 98BADCFE

H_3 = 10325476

H_4 = C3D2E1F0

The first block then gets processed by dividing the first block into 16 words:

W_0 through W_{15}

For t = 16 through 79

$\quad W_t = S^1(W_{t-3} \text{ XOR } W_{t-8} \text{ XOR } W_{t-14} \text{ XOR } W_{t-16})$

Let $A = H_0\ B = H_1\ C = H_2\ D = H_3\ E = H_4$

For t = 0 through 79

Let $\text{TEMP} = S^5(A) + f_t(B,C,D) + E + W_t + K_t;$

$\quad E = D; D = C; C = S^{30}(B); B = A; A = \text{TEMP}$

Let $H_0 = H_0 + A; H_1 = H_1 + B; H_2 = H_2 + C; H_3 = H_3 + D; H_4 = H_4 + E$

After this has been completed for all blocks, the entire message is now represented by the 160-bit string $H_0 H_1 H_2 H_3 H_4$.

At one time, SHA-1 was one of the more secure hash functions, but it has been found vulnerable to a collision attack. Thus, most people are suggesting that implementations of SHA-1 be moved to one of the other SHA versions. These longer versions, SHA-256, SHA-384, and SHA-512, all have longer hash results, making them more difficult to attack successfully. The added security and resistance to attack in SHA-1 does require more processing power to compute the hash.

SHA-256

SHA-256 is similar to SHA-1, in that it will also accept input of less than 2^{64} bits and reduces that input to a hash. This algorithm reduces to 256 bits instead of SHA-1's 160. Defined in FIPS 180-2 in 2002, SHA-256 is listed as an update to the original FIPS 180 that defined SHA. Similar to SHA-1, SHA-256 will accept 2^{64} bits of input and uses 32-bit words and 512-bit blocks. Padding is added until the entire message is a multiple of 512. SHA-256 uses sixty-four 32-bit words, eight working variables, and results in a hash value of eight 32-bit words, hence 256 bits.

SHA-256 is more secure than SHA-1, but the attack basis for SHA-1 can produce collisions in SHA-256 as well since they are similar algorithms. The SHA standard does have two longer versions, however.

SHA-384

SHA-384 is also similar to SHA-1, but it handles larger sets of data. SHA-384 will accept 2128 bits of input, which it pads until it has several blocks of data at 1024-bit blocks. SHA-384 also used 64-bit words instead of SHA-1's 32-bit words. It uses six 64-bit words to produce the 284-bit hash value.

SHA-512

SHA-512 is structurally similar to SHA-384. It will accept the same 2128 input and uses the same 64-bit word size and 1024-bit block size. SHA-512 does differ from SHA-384 in that it uses eight 64-bit words for the final hash, resulting in 512 bits.

Message Digest

Message Digest (MD) is the generic version of one of several algorithms that are designed to create a message digest or hash from data input into the algorithm. MD algorithms work in the same manner as SHA in that they use a secure method to compress the file and generate a computed output of a specified number of bits. They were all developed by Ronald L. Rivest of MIT.

MD2

MD2 was developed in 1989 and is in some ways an early version of the later MD5 algorithm. It takes a data input of any length and produces a hash output of 128 bits. It is different from MD4 and MD5 in that MD2 is optimized for 8-bit machines, whereas the other two are optimized for 32-bit machines. As with SHA, the input data is padded to become a multiple—in this case a multiple of 16 bytes. After padding, a 16-byte checksum is appended to the message. The message is then processed in 16-byte blocks. After initialization, the algorithm invokes a compression function.

The compression function operates as shown here:

$$T = 0$$

For $\quad J = 0$ through 17

For $\quad k = 0$ through 47

$$T = Xk \text{ XOR } St$$

$$Xk = T$$

$$T = (T + J) \bmod 256$$

After the function has been run for every 16 bytes of the message, the output result is a 128-bit digest. The only known attack that is successful against MD2 requires that the checksum not be appended to the message before the hash function is run. Without a checksum, the algorithm can be vulnerable to a collision attack. Some collision attacks are based upon the algorithm's initialization vector (IV).

MD4

MD4 was developed in 1990 and is optimized for 32-bit computers. It is a fast algorithm, but it can be subject to more attacks than more secure algorithms like MD5. Like MD2, it takes a data input of some length and outputs a digest of 128 bits. The message is padded to become a multiple of 512, which is then concatenated with the representation of the message's original length.

As with SHA, the message is then divided into blocks and also into 16 words of 32 bits. All blocks of the message are processed in three distinct rounds. The digest is then computed using a four-word buffer. The final four words remaining after compression are the 128-bit hash.

An extended version of MD4 computes the message in parallel and produces two 128-bit outputs—effectively a 256-bit hash. Even though a longer hash is produced, security has not been improved because of basic flaws in the algorithm. Cryptographer Hans Dobbertin has shown how collisions in MD4 can be found in under a minute using just a PC. This vulnerability to collisions applies to 128-bit MD4 as well as 256-bit MD4. Most people are moving away from MD4 to MD5 or a robust version of SHA.

MD5

MD5 was developed in 1991 and is structured after MD4 but with additional security to overcome the problems in MD4. Therefore, it is very similar to the MD4 algorithm, only slightly slower and more secure.

MD5 creates a 128-bit hash of a message of any length. Like MD4, it segments the message into 512-bit blocks and then into sixteen 32-bit words. First, the original message is padded to be 64 bits short of a multiple of 512 bits. Then a 64-bit representation of the original length of the message is added to the padded value to bring the entire message up to a 512-bit multiple.

After padding is complete, four 32-bit variables, A, B, C, and D, are initialized. A, B, C, and D are copied into a, b, c, and d, and then the main function begins. This has four rounds, each using a different nonlinear function 16 times. These functions operate on three of a, b, c, and d, adding the result to the fourth variable, the fourth variable being a sub-block of the text and a constant, then rotating the result of that addition to the right a variable number of bits, specified by the round of the algorithm. After adding the result of this operation to one of a, b, c, and d, that sum replaces one of a, b, c, and d. After the four rounds are completed, a, b, c, and d are added to A, B, C, and D, and the algorithm moves on to the next block. After all blocks are completed, A, B, C, and D are concatenated to form the final output of 128 bits.

MD5 has been a fairly common integrity standard and was most commonly used as part of the NTLM (NT LAN Manager) challenge response authentication protocol. Recently successful attacks on the algorithm have occurred. Cryptanalysis has displayed weaknesses in the compression function. However, this weakness does not lend itself to an attack on MD5 itself. Czech cryptographer Vlastimil Klíma published work showing that MD5 collisions can be computed in about eight hours on a standard home PC. In November 2007, researchers published the ability to have two entirely different Win32 executables with different functionality but the same MD5 hash. This discovery has obvious implications for the development of malware. The combination of these problems with MD5 has pushed people to adopt a strong SHA version for security reasons.

Hashing Summary

Hashing functions are very common, and they play an important role in the way information, such as passwords, is stored securely and the way in which messages can be signed. By computing a digest of the message, less data needs to be signed by the more complex asymmetric encryption, and this still maintains assurances about message integrity. This is the primary purpose for which the protocols were designed, and their success will allow greater trust in electronic protocols and digital signatures.

Symmetric Encryption

Symmetric encryption is the older and more simple method of encrypting information. The basis of symmetric encryption is that both the sender and the receiver of the message have previously obtained the same key. This is, in fact, the basis for even the oldest ciphers—the Spartans needed the exact same size cylinder, making the cylinder the "key" to the message, and in shift ciphers both parties need to know the direction and amount of shift being performed. All symmetric algorithms are based upon this *shared secret* principle, including the unbreakable one-time pad method.

Figure 4-3 is a simple diagram showing the process that a symmetric algorithm goes through to provide encryption from plaintext to ciphertext. This ciphertext message is, presumably, transmitted to the message recipient who goes through the process to decrypt the message using the same key that was used to encrypt the message. Figure 4-3 shows the keys to the algorithm, which are the same value in the case of symmetric encryption.

Unlike with hash functions, a cryptographic key is involved in symmetric encryption, so there must be a mechanism for *key management*. Managing the cryptographic keys is critically important in symmetric algorithms because the key unlocks the data that is being protected. However, the key also needs to be known or transmitted in a secret way to the party to which you wish to communicate. This key management applies to all things that could happen to a key, securing it on the local computer, securing it on the remote one, protecting it from data corruption, protecting it from loss, as well as probably the most important step, protecting the key while it is transmitted between the two parties. Later in the chapter we will look at public key cryptography, which greatly eases the key management issue, but for symmetric algorithms the most important lesson is to store and send the key only by known secure means.

Some of the more popular symmetric encryption algorithms in use today are DES, 3DES, AES, and IDEA.

 EXAM TIP Common symmetric algorithms are DES, 3DES, AES, IDEA, Blowfish, CAST, RC2, RC4, RC5, and RC6.

DES

DES, the Data Encryption Standard, was developed in response to the National Bureau of Standards (NBS), now known as the National Institute of Standards and Technology (NIST), issuing a request for proposals for a standard cryptographic algorithm in 1973. NBS received a promising response in an algorithm called Lucifer, originally developed by IBM. The NBS and the NSA worked together to analyze the algorithm's security, and eventually DES was adopted as a federal standard in 1976.

NBS specified that the DES standard had to be recertified every five years. While DES passed without a hitch in 1983, the NSA said it would not recertify it in 1987. However, since no alternative was available for many businesses, many complaints ensued, and the NSA and NBS were forced to recertify it. The algorithm was then recertified in 1993. NIST has now certified the Advanced Encryption Standard (AES) to replace DES.

DES is what is known as a *block cipher*; it segments the input data into blocks of a specified size, typically padding the last block to make it a multiple of the block size required. In the case of DES, the block size is 64 bits, which means DES takes a 64-bit input and outputs 64 bits of ciphertext. This process is repeated for all 64-bit blocks in

Figure 4-3
Layout of a
symmetric algorithm

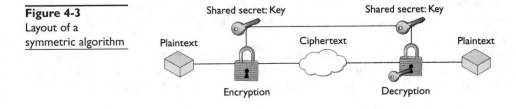

the message. DES uses a key length of 56 bits, and all security rests within the key. The same algorithm and key are used for both encryption and decryption.

At the most basic level, DES performs a substitution and then a permutation (a form of transposition) on the input, based upon the key. This action is called a *round*, and DES performs this 16 times on every 64-bit block. It works in three stages:

1. The algorithm accepts plaintext, P, and performs an initial permutation, IP, on P producing P_0. The block is then broken into left and right halves, the left (L_0) being the first 32 bits of P_0 and the right (R_0) being the last 32 bits of P_0.

2. With L_0 and R_0, 16 rounds are performed until L_{16} and R_{16} are generated.

3. The inverse permutation, IP^{-1}, is applied to $L_{16}R_{16}$ to produce ciphertext C.

The round executes 16 times, and these rounds are where the bulk of the encryption is performed. The individual rounds work with the following computation:

Where i represents the current round,
$$L_i = R_{i-1}$$
$$R_i = L_{i-1} \text{ XOR } f(R_{i-1}, K_i)$$

K_i represents the current round's 48-bit string derived from the 56-bit key, and f represents the diffusion function. This function operates as follows:

1. 48 bits are selected from the 56-bit key.

2. The right half is expanded from 32 bits to 48 bits via an expansion permutation.

3. Those 48 bits are combined via XOR with the 48-key bits.

4. This result is then sent through eight S-boxes, producing 32 new bits, and then it is permuted again.

After all 16 rounds have been completed and the inverse permutation has been completed, the ciphertext is output as 64 bits. Then the algorithm picks up the next 64 bits and starts all over again. This is carried on until the entire message has been encrypted with DES. As mentioned, the same algorithm and key are used to decrypt and encrypt with DES. The only difference is that the sequence of key permutations are used in reverse order.

Over the years that DES has been a cryptographic standard, a lot of cryptanalysis has occurred, and while the algorithm has held up very well, some problems have been encountered. *Weak keys* are keys that are less secure than the majority of keys allowed in the keyspace of the algorithm. In the case of DES, because of the way the initial key is modified to get the subkey, certain keys are weak keys. The weak keys equate in binary to having all 1s or all 0s, or where half the key is all 1s and the other half is all 0s, like those shown in Figure 4-4.

Semi-weak keys, with which two keys will encrypt plaintext to identical ciphertext, also exist, meaning that either key will decrypt the ciphertext. The total number of possibly weak keys is 64, which is very small compared with the 2^{56} possible keys in DES.

Figure 4-4
Weak DES keys

Binary Key

```
0000000 0000000
0000000 FFFFFFF
FFFFFFF 0000000
FFFFFFF FFFFFFF
```

In addition, multiple successful attacks against DES algorithms have used fewer rounds than 16. Any DES with fewer than 16 rounds could be analyzed more efficiently with chosen plaintext than via a brute-force attack using differential cryptanalysis. With 16 rounds and not using a weak key, DES is reasonably secure and amazingly has been for more than two decades. In 1999, a distributed effort consisted of a supercomputer and 100,000 PCs over the Internet to break a 56-bit DES key. By attempting more than 240 billion keys per second, the effort was able to retrieve the key in less than a day. This demonstrates an incredible resistance to cracking a 20-year-old algorithm, but it also demonstrates that more stringent algorithms are needed to protect data today.

3DES

Triple DES (3DES) is a variant of DES. Depending on the specific variant, it uses either two or three keys instead of the single key that DES uses. It also spins through the DES algorithm three times via what's called *multiple encryption*.

Multiple encryption can be performed in several different ways. The simplest method of multiple encryption is just to stack algorithms on top of each other—taking plaintext, encrypting it with DES, then encrypting the first ciphertext with a different key, and then encrypting the second ciphertext with a third key. In reality, this technique is less effective than the technique that 3DES uses, which is to encrypt with one key, then decrypt with a second, and then encrypt with a third, as shown in Figure 4-5.

Figure 4-5
Diagram of 3DES

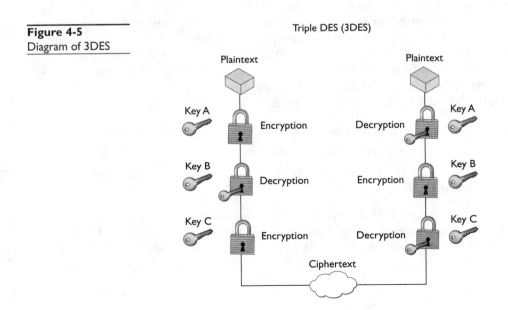

Triple DES (3DES)

This greatly increases the number of attempts needed to retrieve the key and is a significant enhancement of security. The additional security comes with a price, however. It can take up to three times longer to compute 3DES than to compute DES. However, the advances in memory and processing power in today's electronics should make this problem irrelevant in all devices except for very small low-power handhelds.

The only weaknesses of 3DES are those that already exist in DES. Because different keys are used with the same algorithm, affecting a longer key length by adding the first keyspace to the second keyspace and the resulting greater resistance to brute-force attack, 3DES is stronger. 3DES is a good interim step before the new encryption standard, AES, is fully implemented to replace DES.

AES

Because of the advancement of technology and the progress being made in quickly retrieving DES keys, NIST put out a request for proposals for a new Advanced Encryption Standard (AES). It called for a block cipher using symmetric key cryptography and supporting key sizes of 128, 192, and 256 bits. After evaluation, the NIST had five finalists:

- **MARS**   IBM
- **RC6**   RSA
- **Rijndael**   John Daemen and Vincent Rijmen
- **Serpent**   Ross Anderson, Eli Biham, and Lars Knudsen
- **Twofish**   Bruce Schneier, John Kelsey, Doug Whiting, David Wagner, Chris Hall, and Niels Ferguson

In the fall of 2000, NIST picked Rijndael to be the new AES. It was chosen for its overall security as well as its good performance on limited capacity devices. Rijndael's design was influenced by Square, also written by John Daemen and Vincent Rijmen. Like Square, Rijndael is a block cipher separating data input in 128-bit blocks. Rijndael can also be configured to use blocks of 192 or 256 bits, but AES has standardized on 128-bit blocks. AES can have key sizes of 128, 192, and 256 bits, with the size of the key affecting the number of rounds used in the algorithm.

Like DES, AES works in three steps on every block of input data:

1. Add round key, performing an XOR of the block with a subkey.
2. Perform the number of normal rounds required by the key length.
3. Perform a regular round without the mix-column step found in the normal round.

After these steps have been performed, a 128-bit block of plaintext produces a 128-bit block of ciphertext. As mentioned in step 2, AES performs multiple rounds. This is determined by the key size. A key size of 128 bits requires 9 rounds, 192-bit keys will require 11 rounds, and 256-bit keys use 13 rounds. Four steps are performed in every round:

1. *Byte sub.* Each byte is replaced by its S-box substitute.

2. *Shift row.* Bytes are arranged in a rectangle and shifted.

3. *Mix column.* Matrix multiplication is performed based upon the arranged rectangle.

4. *Add round key.* This round's subkey is cored in.

These steps are performed until the final round has been completed, and when the final step has been performed, the ciphertext is output.

The Rijndael algorithm is well thought-out and has suitable key length to provide security for many years to come. While no efficient attacks currently exist against AES, more time and analysis will tell if this standard can last as long as DES has.

CAST

CAST is an encryption algorithm similar to DES in its structure. It was designed by Carlisle Adams and Stafford Tavares. CAST uses a 64-bit block size for 64- and 128-bit key versions, and a 128-bit block size for the 256-bit key version. Like DES, it divides the plaintext block into a left half and a right half. The right half is then put through function *f* and then is XORed with the left half. This value becomes the new right half, and the original right half becomes the new left half. This is repeated for eight rounds for a 64-bit key, and the left and right output is concatenated to form the ciphertext block.

CAST supports longer key lengths than the original 64 bits. Changes to the key length affect the number of rounds: CAST-128 specifies 16 rounds and CAST-256 has 48 rounds. This algorithm in CAST-256 form was submitted for the AES standard but was not chosen. CAST has undergone thorough analysis with only minor weaknesses discovered that are dependent on low numbers of rounds. Currently, no better way is known to break high-round CAST than by brute-forcing the key, meaning that with sufficient key length, CAST should be placed with other trusted algorithms.

RC

RC is a general term for several ciphers all designed by Ron Rivest—RC officially stands for *Rivest Cipher*. RC1, RC2, RC3, RC4, RC5, and RC6 are all ciphers in the series. RC1 and RC3 never made it to release, but RC2, RC4, RC5, and RC6 are all working algorithms.

RC2

RC2 was designed as a DES replacement, and it is a variable-key-size block-mode cipher. The key size can be from 8 bits to 1024 bits with the block size being fixed at 64 bits. RC2 breaks up the input blocks into four 16-bit words and then puts them through 18 rounds of one of two operations. The two operations are mix and mash. The sequence in which the algorithms works is as follows:

1. Initialize the input block to words R_0 through R_3.
2. Expand the key into K_0 through K_{63}.
3. Initialize $j = 0$.
4. Five mix rounds.
5. One mash round.
6. Six mix rounds.
7. One mash round.
8. Five mix rounds.

This outputs 64 bits of ciphertext for 64 bits of plaintext. The individual operations are performed as follows, with *rol* in this description meaning to rotate the word left.

This is the mix operation:

$$Ri = R_i + K_j + (R_{i-1} \& R_{i-2}) + ((\sim R_{i-1}) \& R_{i-1})$$
$$j = j + 1$$
$$R_i = R_i \text{ rol } s_i$$

This is the mash operation:

$$R_i = R_i + K[R_{i-1} \& 63]$$

According to RSA, RC2 is up to three times faster than DES. RSA maintained RC2 as a trade secret for a long time, with the source code eventually being illegally posted on the Internet. The ability of RC2 to accept different key lengths is one of the larger vulnerabilities in the algorithm. Any key length below 64 bits can be easily retrieved by modern computational power.

RC5

RC5 is a block cipher, written in 1994. It has multiple variable elements, numbers of rounds, key sizes, and block sizes. The algorithm starts by separating the input block into two words, A and B.

$$A = A + S_0$$
$$B = B + S_1$$
$$\text{For} \quad i = 1 \quad \text{to} \quad r$$
$$A = ((A \text{ XOR } B) \lll B) + S_{2i}$$
$$B = ((B \text{ XOR } A) \lll A) + S_{2i+1}$$

A and B represent the ciphertext output. This algorithm is relatively new, but if configured to run enough rounds, RC5 seems to provide adequate security for current brute-forcing technology. Rivest recommends using at least 12 rounds. With 12 rounds in the algorithm, cryptanalysis in a linear fashion proves less effective than brute-force against RC5, and differential analysis fails for 15 or more rounds. A newer algorithm is RC6.

RC6

RC6 is based on the design of RC5. It uses a 128-bit block size, separated into four words of 32 bits each. It uses a round count of 20 to provide security, and it has three possible key sizes: 128, 192, and 256 bits. The four words are named A, B, C, and D, and the algorithm works like this:

$$B = B + S_0$$
$$D = D + S_1$$
$$\text{For} \quad i = 1 - 20$$
$$[t = (B * (2B + 1)) <<< 5$$
$$u = (D * (2D + 1)) <<< 5$$
$$A = ((A \text{ XOR } t) <<< u) + S_{2i}$$
$$C = ((C \text{ XOR } u) <<< t) + S_{2i+1}$$
$$(A, B, C, D) = (B, C, D, A)]$$
$$A = A + S_{42}$$
$$C = C + S_{43}$$

The output of A, B, C, and D after 20 rounds is the ciphertext.

RC6 is a modern algorithm that runs well on 32-bit computers. With a sufficient number of rounds, the algorithm makes both linear and differential cryptanalysis infeasible. The available key lengths make brute-force attacks extremely time-consuming. RC6 should provide adequate security for some time to come.

RC4

RC4 was created before RC5 and RC6, but it differs in operation. RC4 is a *stream cipher*, whereas all the symmetric ciphers we have looked at so far have been *block-mode ciphers*. A stream-mode cipher works by enciphering the plaintext in a stream, usually bit by bit. This makes stream ciphers faster than block-mode ciphers. Stream ciphers accomplish this by performing a bitwise XOR with the plaintext stream and a generated key-stream.

RC4 operates in this manner. It was developed in 1987 and remained a trade secret of RSA until it was posted to the Internet in 1994. RC4 can use a key length of 8 to 2048 bits, though the most common versions use 128-bit keys, or if subject to the old export restrictions, 40-bit keys. The key is used to initialize a 256-byte state table. This table is used to generate the pseudo-random stream that is XORed with the plaintext to generate the ciphertext.

The operation is performed as follows:

$$I = 0$$
$$j = 0$$
$$I = (I + 1) \bmod 256$$
$$j = (j + S_i) \bmod 256$$
$$\text{Swap} \quad S_i \quad \text{and} \quad S_j$$
$$t = (S_i + S_j) \bmod 256$$
$$K = S_t$$

K is then XORed with the plaintext. Alternatively, K is XORed with the ciphertext to produce the plaintext.

The algorithm is fast, sometimes ten times faster than DES. The most vulnerable point of the encryption is the possibility of weak keys. One key in 256 can generate bytes closely correlated with key bytes.

Blowfish

Blowfish was designed in 1994 by Bruce Schneier. It is a block-mode cipher using 64-bit blocks and a variable key length from 32 to 448 bits. It was designed to run quickly on 32-bit microprocessors and is optimized for situations with few key changes. Encryption is done by separating the 64-bit input block into two 32-bit words, and then a function is executed every round. Blowfish has 16 rounds. Once the input has been split into left and right words, the following function is performed:

$$
\begin{aligned}
&\text{For} \quad I = 1 - 16 \\
&\qquad X_L = X_L \text{ XOR } P_i \\
&\qquad X_R = F(X_L) \text{ XOR } X_R \\
&\text{Swap} \quad X_L \quad \text{and} \quad X_R \\
&\text{Then, swap} \quad X_L \quad \text{and} \quad X_R \\
&X_R = X_R \text{ XOR } P_{17} \\
&X_L = X_L \text{ XOR } P_{18}
\end{aligned}
$$

The two words are then recombined to form the 64-bit output ciphertext.

The only successful cryptanalysis to date against Blowfish has been against variants that used reduced rounds. There does not seem to be a weakness in the full 16-round version.

IDEA

IDEA (International Data Encryption Algorithm) started out as PES, or Proposed Encryption Cipher, in 1990, and it was modified to improve its resistance to differential cryptanalysis and its name was changed to IDEA in 1992. It is a block-mode cipher using a 64-bit block size and a 128-bit key. The input plaintext is split into four 16-bit segments, A, B, C, and D. The process uses eight rounds with each round performing the following function:

$$
\begin{aligned}
A * S_1 &= X1 \\
B + S_2 &= X_2 \\
C + S_3 &= X_3 \\
D * S_4 &= X_4 \\
X_1 \text{ XOR } X_3 &= X_5 \\
X_2 \text{ XOR } X_4 &= X_6 \\
X_5 * S_5 &= X_7 \\
X_6 + X_7 &= X_8 \\
X8 * S_6 &= X_9
\end{aligned}
$$

$$X_7 + X_9 = X_{10}$$
$$X_1 \text{ XOR } X_9 = X_{11}$$
$$X_3 \text{ XOR } X_9 = X_{12}$$
$$X_2 \text{ XOR } X_{10} = X_{13}$$
$$X_4 \text{ XOR } X_{10} = X_{14}$$
$$X_{11} = A$$
$$X_{13} = B$$
$$X_{12} = C$$
$$X_{14} = D$$

Then the next round starts. After eight rounds are completed, four more steps are done:

$$X_{11} * S_{49} = C_1$$
$$X_{12} + S_{50} = C_2$$
$$X_{13} + S_{51} = C_3$$
$$X_{14} + S_{52} = C_4$$

The output of the last four steps is then concatenated to form the ciphertext.

This algorithm is fairly new, but all current cryptanalysis on full, eight-round IDEA shows that the most efficient attack would be to brute-force the key. The 128-bit key would prevent this attack being accomplished, given current computer technology. The only known issue is that IDEA is susceptible to a weak key—a key that is made of all 0s. This weak key is easy to check for, and the weakness is simple to mitigate.

Symmetric Encryption Summary

Symmetric algorithms are important because they are comparatively fast and have few computational requirements. Their main weakness is that two geographically distant parties both need to have a key that matches exactly. In the past, keys could be much simpler and still be secure, but with today's computational power, simple keys can be brute-forced very quickly. This means that larger and more complex keys must be used and exchanged. This key exchange is difficult because the key cannot be simple, such as a word, but must be shared in a secure manner. It might be easy to exchange a 4-bit key such as *b* in hex, but exchanging the 128-bit key *4b36402c5727472d5571373d22675b4b* is far more difficult to do securely. This exchange of keys is greatly facilitated by our next subject, asymmetric, or public key, cryptography.

Asymmetric Encryption

Asymmetric cryptography is in many ways completely different than symmetric cryptography. While both are used to keep data from being seen by unauthorized users, asymmetric cryptography uses two keys instead of one. It was invented by Whitfield Diffie and Martin Hellman in 1975. Asymmetric cryptography is more commonly known as *public key cryptography*. The system uses a pair of keys: a private key that is kept secret and a public key that can be sent to anyone. The system's security relies upon resistance to deducing one key, given the other, and thus retrieving the plaintext from the ciphertext.

Public key systems typically work by using hard math problems. One of the more common methods is through the difficulty of factoring large numbers. These functions are often called *trapdoor functions,* as they are difficult to process without the key, but easy to process when you have the key—the trapdoor through the function. For example, given a prime number, say 293, and another prime, such as 307, it is an easy function to multiply them together to get 89,951. Given 89,951, it is not simple to find the factors 293 and 307 unless you know one of them already. Computers can easily multiply very large primes with hundreds or thousands of digits but cannot easily factor the product.

The strength of these functions is very important: Because an attacker is likely to have access to the public key, he can run tests of known plaintext and produce ciphertext. This allows instant checking of guesses that are made about the keys of the algorithm. RSA, Diffie-Hellman, Elliptic curve cryptography (ECC), and ElGamal are all popular asymmetric protocols. We will look at all of them and their suitability for different functions.

 EXAM TIP Popular asymmetric encryption algorithms are RSA, Diffie-Hellman, ElGamal, and ECC.

RSA

RSA is one of the first public key cryptosystems ever invented. It can be used for both encryption and digital signatures. RSA is named after its inventors, Ron Rivest, Adi Shamir, and Leonard Adleman, and was first published in 1977.

This algorithm uses the product of two very large prime numbers and works on the principle of difficulty in factoring such large numbers. It's best to choose large prime numbers from 100 to 200 digits in length and that are equal in length. These two primes will be P and Q. Randomly choose an encryption key, E, so that E is greater than 1, E is less than $P * Q$, and E must be odd. E must also be relatively prime to $(P - 1)$ and $(Q - 1)$. Then compute the decryption key D:

$$D = E^{-1} \bmod ((P - 1)(Q - 1))$$

Now that the encryption key and decryption key have been generated, the two prime numbers can be discarded, but they should not be revealed. To encrypt a message, it should be divided into blocks less than the product of P and Q. Then,

$$C_i = M_i^E \bmod (P * Q)$$

C is the output block of ciphertext matching the block length of the input message, M. To decrypt a message take ciphertext, C, and use this function:

$$M_i = C_i^D \bmod (P * Q)$$

The use of the second key retrieves the plaintext of the message.

This is a simple function, but its security has withstood the test of more than 20 years of analysis. Considering the effectiveness of RSA's security and the ability to have two keys, why are symmetric encryption algorithms needed at all? The answer is speed. RSA in software can be 100 times slower than DES, and in hardware it can be even slower.

RSA can be used to perform both regular encryption and digital signatures. Digital signatures try to duplicate the functionality of a physical signature on a document using encryption. Typically RSA and the other public key systems are used in conjunction with symmetric key cryptography. Public key, the slower protocol, is used to exchange the symmetric key (or shared secret), and then the communication uses the faster symmetric key protocol. This process is known as *electronic key exchange*.

Since the security of RSA is based upon the supposed difficulty of factoring large numbers, the main weaknesses are in the implementations of the protocol. Until recently, RSA was a patented algorithm, but it was a de facto standard for many years.

Diffie-Hellman

Diffie-Hellman was created in 1976 by Whitfield Diffie and Martin Hellman. This protocol is one of the most common encryption protocols in use today. It plays a role in the electronic key exchange method of the Secure Sockets Layer (SSL) protocol. It is also used by the SSH and IPsec protocols. Diffie-Hellman is important because it enables the sharing of a secret key between two people who have not contacted each other before.

The protocol, like RSA, uses large prime numbers to work. Two users agree to two numbers, P and G, with P being a sufficiently large prime number and G being the generator. Both users pick a secret number, a and b. Then both users compute their public number:

User 1 $X = Ga \bmod P$, with X being the public number

User 2 $Y = Gb \bmod P$, with Y being the public number

The users then exchange public numbers. User 1 knows P, G, a, X, and Y.

User 1   Computes $Ka = Y^a \bmod P$

User 2   Computes $Kb = X^b \bmod P$

With $Ka = Kb = K$, now both users know the new shared secret K.

This is the basic algorithm, and although there have been methods created to strengthen it, Diffie-Hellman is still in wide use. It remains very effective because of the nature of what it is protecting—a temporary, automatically generated secret key that is good only for a single communication session.

ElGamal

ElGamal can be used for both encryption and digital signatures. Taher ElGamal designed the system in the early 1980s. This system was never patented and is free for use. It is used as the U.S. government standard for digital signatures.

The system is based upon the difficulty of calculating discrete logarithms in a finite field. Three numbers are needed to generate a key pair. User 1 chooses a prime, P, and two random numbers, F and D. F and D should both be less than P. Then you can calculate the public key A:

$$A = D^F \bmod P$$

Then A, D, and P are shared with the second user, with F being the private key. To encrypt a message, M, a random key, k, is chosen that is relatively prime to $P - 1$. Then,

$$C_1 = D^k \bmod P$$
$$C_2 = A^k M \bmod P$$

C_1 and C_2 makes up the ciphertext. Decryption is done by

$$M = C_2 / C_1^F \bmod P$$

ElGamal uses a different function for digital signatures. To sign a message, M, once again choose a random value k that is relatively prime to $P - 1$. Then,

$$C_1 = Dk \bmod P$$
$$C_2 = (M - C_1 * F)/k \;(\bmod P - 1)$$

C_1 concatenated to C_2 is the digital signature.

ElGamal is an effective algorithm and has been in use for some time. It is used primarily for digital signatures. Like all asymmetric cryptography, it is slower than symmetric cryptography.

ECC

Elliptic curve cryptography (ECC) works on the basis of elliptic curves. An elliptic curve is a simple function that is drawn as a gently looping curve on the X,Y plane. They are defined by this equation:

$$y^2 = x^3 + ax^2 + b$$

Elliptic curves work because they have a special property—you can add two points on the curve together and get a third point on the curve.

For cryptography, the elliptic curve works as a public key algorithm. Users agree on an elliptic curve and a fixed curve point. This information is not a shared secret, and these points can be made public without compromising the security of the system. User 1 then chooses a secret random number, K_1, and computes a public key based upon a point on the curve:

$$P_1 = K_1 * F$$

User 2 performs the same function and generates P_2. Now user 1 can send user 2 a message by generating a shared secret:

$$S = K_1 * P_2$$

User 2 can generate the same shared secret independently:

$$S = K_2 * P_1$$

This is true because

$$K_1 * P_2 = K_1 * (K_2 * F) = (K_1 * K_2) * F = K_2 * (K_1 * F) = K_2 * P_1$$

The security of elliptic curve systems has been questioned, mostly because of lack of analysis. However, all public key systems rely on the difficulty of certain math problems. It would take a breakthrough in math for any of the mentioned systems to be weakened dramatically, but research has been done about the problems and has shown that the elliptic curve problem has been more resistant to incremental advances. Again, as with all cryptography algorithms, only time will tell how secure they really are.

Asymmetric Encryption Summary

Asymmetric encryption creates the possibility of digital signatures and also corrects the main weakness of symmetric cryptography. The ability to send messages securely without senders and receivers having had prior contact has become one of the basic concerns with secure communication. Digital signatures will enable faster and more efficient exchange of all kinds of documents, including legal documents. With strong algorithms and good key lengths, security can be assured.

Steganography

Steganography, an offshoot of cryptography technology, gets its meaning from the Greek *steganos* meaning covered. Invisible ink placed on a document hidden by innocuous text is an example of a steganographic message. Another example is a tattoo placed on the top of a person's head, visible only when the person's hair is shaved off.

Hidden writing in the computer age relies on a program to hide data inside other data. The most common application is the concealing of a text message in a picture file. The Internet contains multiple billions of image files, allowing a hidden message to be located almost anywhere without being discovered. The nature of the image files also make a hidden message difficult to detect. While it is most common to hide messages inside images, they can also be hidden in video and audio files.

The advantage to steganography over cryptography is that the messages do not attract attention, and this difficulty in detecting the hidden message provides an additional barrier to analysis. The data that is hidden in a steganographic message is frequently also encrypted, so should it be discovered, the message will remain secure. Steganography has many uses but the most publicized uses are to hide illegal material, often pornography, or allegedly for covert communication by terrorist networks. While there is no direct evidence to support that terrorists use steganography, the techniques have been documented in some of their training materials.

Steganographic encoding can be used in many ways and through many different media. Covering them all is beyond the scope for this book, but we will discuss one of the most common ways to encode into an image file, LSB encoding. LSB, Least Significant Bit, is a method of encoding information into an image while altering the actual visual image as little as possible. A computer image is made up of thousands or millions of pixels, all defined by 1s and 0s. If an image is composed of Red Green Blue (RGB) values, each pixel has an RGB value represented numerically from 0 to 255. For example, 0,0,0 is black, and 255,255,255 is white, which can also be represented as 00000000, 00000000, 00000000 for black and 11111111, 11111111, 11111111 for white. Given a white pixel, editing the least significant bit of the pixel to 11111110, 11111110, 11111110 changes the color. The change in color is undetectable to the human eye, but in a image with a million pixels, this creates a 125KB area in which to store a message.

Cryptography Algorithm Use

The use of cryptographic algorithms grows every day. More and more information becomes digitally encoded and placed online, and all of this data needs to be secured. The best way to do that with current technology is to use encryption. This section considers some of the tasks cryptographic algorithms accomplish and those for which they are best suited. Security is typically defined as a product of five components: confidentiality, integrity, availability, authentication, and nonrepudiation. Encryption addresses four of these five components: confidentiality, integrity, nonrepudiation, and authentication.

Confidentiality

Confidentiality typically comes to mind when the term *security* is brought up. Confidentiality is the ability to keep some piece of data a secret. In the digital world, encryption excels at providing confidentiality.

Confidentiality is used on stored data and on transmitted data. In both cases, symmetric encryption is favored because of its speed and because some asymmetric algorithms can significantly increase the size of the object being encrypted. In the case of a stored item, a public key is typically unnecessary, as the item is being encrypted to protect it from access by others. In the case of transmitted data, public key cryptography is typically used to exchange the secret key, and then symmetric cryptography is used to ensure the confidentiality of the data being sent.

Asymmetric cryptography does protect confidentiality, but its size and speed make it more efficient at protecting the confidentiality of small units for tasks such as electronic key exchange. In all cases, the strength of the algorithms and the length of the keys ensure the secrecy of the data in question.

Integrity

Integrity is better known as *message integrity*, and it is a crucial component of message security. When a message is sent, both the sender and recipient need to know that the message was not altered in transmission. This is especially important for legal contracts—recipients need to know that the contracts have not been altered. Signers also need a way to validate that a contract they sign will not be altered in the future.

Integrity is provided with one-way hash functions and digital signatures. The hash functions compute the message digests, and this guarantees the integrity of the message by allowing easy testing to determine whether any part of the message has been changed. The message now has a computed function (the hash value) to tell the users to resend the message if it was intercepted and interfered with.

This hash value is combined with asymmetric cryptography by taking the message's hash value and encrypting it with the user's private key. This lets anyone with the user's public key decrypt the hash and compare it to the locally computed hash, ensuring not only the integrity of the message but positively identifying the sender.

Nonrepudiation

An item of some confusion, the concept of nonrepudiation is actually fairly simple. Nonrepudiation means that the message sender cannot later deny that she sent the message. This is important in electronic exchanges of data, because of the lack of face-to-face meetings. Nonrepudiation is based upon public key cryptography and the principle of only you knowing your private key. The presence of a message signed by you, using your private key, which nobody else should know, is an example of nonrepudiation. When a third party can check your signature using your public key, that disproves any claim that you were not the one who actually sent the message. Nonrepudiation is tied to asymmetric cryptography and cannot be implemented with symmetric algorithms.

Authentication

Authentication lets you prove you are who you say you are. Authentication is similar to nonrepudiation, except that authentication often occurs as communication begins, not after. Authentication is also typically used in both directions as part of a protocol.

Authentication can be accomplished in a multitude of ways, the most basic being the use of a simple password. Every time you sign in to check your e-mail, you authenticate yourself to the server. This process can grow to need two or three identifying factors, such as a *password*, a *token* (such as a digital certificate), and a *biometric* (such as a fingerprint).

Digital certificates are a form of token. Digital certificates are public encryption keys that have been verified by a trusted third party. When you log in to a secure web site, *one-way* authentication occurs. You want to know that you are logging into the server that you intend to log into, so your browser checks the server's digital certificate. This token is digitally signed by a trusted third party, assuring you that the server is genuine.

This authentication is one way because the server does not need to know that you are who you say you are—it will authenticate your credit card later on. The other option, *two-way* authentication, can work the same way: you send your digital certificate signed by a third party, and the other entity with which you are communicating sends its certificate.

While symmetric encryption can be used as a simple manner of authentication (only the authorized user should know the secret, after all) asymmetric encryption is better suited to show, via digital signatures and certificates, that you are who you say you are.

Digital Signatures

Digital signatures have been touted as the key to truly paperless document flow, and they do have promise for improving the system. Digital signatures are based on both hashing functions and asymmetric cryptography. Both encryption methods play an important role in signing digital documents.

Unprotected digital documents are very easy for anyone to change. If a document is edited after an individual signs it, it is important that any modification can be detected. To protect against document editing, hashing functions are used to create a digest of the message that is unique and easily reproducible by both parties. This ensures that the message integrity is complete.

Protection must also be provided to ensure that the intended party actually did sign the message, and that someone did not edit the message and the hash of the message. This is done by asymmetric encryption. The properties of asymmetric encryption allow anyone to use a person's public key to generate a message that can be read only by that person, as this person is theoretically the only one with access to the private key. In the case of digital signatures, this process works exactly in reverse. When a user can decrypt the hash with the public key of the originator, that user knows that the hash was encrypted by the corresponding private key. This use of asymmetric encryption is a good example of nonrepudiation, because only the signer would have access to the private key. This is how digital signatures work, by using integrity and nonrepudiation to prove not only that the right people signed, but also what they signed.

Key Escrow

The impressive growth of the use of encryption technology has led to new methods for handling keys. Encryption is adept at hiding secrets, and with computer technology being affordable to everyone, criminals and other ill-willed people began using it to conceal communications and business dealings from law enforcement agencies. Because they could not break the encryption, government agencies began asking for key escrow. *Key escrow* is a system by which your private key is kept both by you and by the government. This allows people with a court order to retrieve your private key to gain access to anything encrypted with your public key. The data is essentially encrypted by your key and the government key, giving the government access to your plaintext data.

Key escrow can negatively impact the security provided by encryption, because the government requires a huge complex infrastructure of systems to hold every escrowed key, and the security of those systems is less efficient than the security of your memorizing the key. However, there are two sides to the key escrow coin. Without a practical way to recover a key if or when it is lost or the key holder dies, for example, some important information will be lost forever. Such issues will affect the design and security of encryption technologies for the foreseeable future.

EXAM TIP   Key escrow can solve many problems resulting from an inaccessible key, and the nature of cryptography makes the access of the data impossible without the key.

Cryptographic Applications

A few applications can be used to encrypt data conveniently on your personal computer. (This is by no means a complete list of every application.)

Pretty Good Privacy (PGP) is mentioned in this book because it is a useful protocol suite. Created by Philip Zimmermann in 1991, it passed through several versions that were available for free under a noncommercial license. PGP applications can be plugged into popular e-mail programs to handle the majority of day-to-day encryption tasks using a combination of symmetric and asymmetric encryption protocols. One of the unique features of PGP is its ability to use both symmetric and asymmetric encryption methods, accessing the strengths of each method and avoiding the weaknesses of each as well. Symmetric keys are used for bulk encryption, taking advantage of the speed and efficiency of symmetric encryption. The symmetric keys are passed using asymmetric methods, capitalizing on the flexibility of this method. PGP is now sold as a commercial application with home and corporate versions. Depending on the version, PGP can perform file encryption, whole disk encryption, and public key encryption to protect e-mail.

TrueCrypt is an open source solution for encryption. It is designed for symmetric disk-based encryption of your files. It features AES ciphers and the ability to create a *deniable volume*, encryption stored within encryption so that volume cannot be reliably detected. TrueCrypt can perform file encryption and whole disk encryption. Whole disk encryption encrypts the entire hard drive of a computer, including the operating system.

FreeOTFE is similar to TrueCrypt. It offers "on-the-fly" disk encryption as an open source freely downloadable application. It can encrypt files up to entire disks with several popular ciphers including AES.

GnuPG or Gnu Privacy Guard is an open source implementation of the OpenPGP standard. This command line–based tool is a public key encryption program designed to protect electronic communications such as e-mail. It operates similar to PGP and includes a method for managing public/private keys.

File system encryption is becoming a standard means of protecting data while in storage. Even hard drives are available with built-in AES encryption. Microsoft expanded its encrypting file system (EFS) available since the NT operating system with BitLocker, a boot sector encryption method that protects data on the Vista operating system. Bit-Locker utilizes AES encryption to encrypt every file on the hard drive automatically. All encryption occurs in the background, and decryption occurs seamlessly when data is requested. The decryption key can be stored in the Trusted Platform Module (TPM) or on a USB key.

Chapter Review

Cryptography is in many ways the key to security in many systems. The progression of technology has allowed systems to be built to retrieve the secrets of others. More and more information is being digitized and then stored and sent via computers. Storing and transmitting valuable data and keeping it secure can be best accomplished with encryption.

In this chapter, you have seen the message digest one-way functions for passwords and message integrity checks. You have also examined the symmetric encryption algorithms used for encrypting data at high speeds. Finally, you have learned about the operation of asymmetric cryptography that is used for key management and digital signatures. These are three distinct types of encryption with different purposes.

The material presented in this chapter is based on current algorithms and techniques. When implemented properly, they will improve security; however, they need to be updated as encryption strength decays. Encryption is based on traditionally difficult mathematical problems, and it can keep data secure only for a limited amount of time, as technology for solving those problems improves—for example, encryption that was incredibly effective 50 years ago is now easily broken. However, current encryption methods can provide a reasonable assurance of security.

Questions

To further help you prepare for the Security+ exam, and to test your level of preparedness, answer the following questions and then check your answers against the list of correct answers at the end of the chapter.

1. What is the biggest drawback to symmetric encryption?

    A. It is too easily broken.

    B. It is too slow to be easily used on mobile devices.

    C. It requires a key to be securely shared.

    D. It is available only on UNIX.

2. What is Diffie-Hellman most commonly used for?

    A. Symmetric encryption key exchange

    B. Signing digital contracts

    C. Secure e-mail

    D. Storing encrypted passwords

3. What is AES meant to replace?

    A. IDEA

    B. DES

    C. Diffie-Hellman

    D. MD5

4. What kind of encryption cannot be reversed?

    A. Asymmetric

    B. Hash

    C. Linear cryptanalysis

    D. Authentication

5. What is public key cryptography a more common name for?

    A. Asymmetric encryption

    B. SHA

    C. An algorithm that is no longer secure against cryptanalysis

    D. Authentication

6. How many bits are in a block of the SHA algorithm?

    A. 128

    B. 64

    C. 512

    D. 1024

7. How does elliptical curve cryptography work?

    A. It multiplies two large primes.

    B. It uses the geometry of a curve to calculate three points.

    C. IT shifts the letters of the message in an increasing curve.

    D. It uses graphs instead of keys.

8. A good hash function is resistant to what?

    A. Brute-forcing

    B. Rainbow tables

    C. Interception

    D. Collisions

9. How is 3DES an improvement over normal DES?

    A. It uses public and private keys.

    B. It hashes the message before encryption.

    C. It uses three keys and multiple encryption and/or decryption sets.

    D. It is faster than DES.

10. What is the best kind of key to have?

    A. Easy to remember

    B. Long and random

    C. Long and predictable

    D. Short

11. What makes asymmetric encryption better than symmetric encryption?

    A. It is more secure.

    B. Key management is part of the algorithm.

    C. Anyone with a public key could decrypt the data.

    D. It uses a hash.

12. What kinds of encryption does a digital signature use?

    A. Hashing and asymmetric

    B. Asymmetric and symmetric

    C. Hashing and symmetric

    D. All of the above

13. What does differential cryptanalysis require?

    A. The key

    B. Large amounts of plaintext and ciphertext

    C. Just large amounts of ciphertext

    D. Computers able to guess at key values faster than a billion times per second

14. What is a brute-force attack?

    A. Feeding certain plaintext into the algorithm to deduce the key

    B. Capturing ciphertext with known plaintext values to deduce the key

    C. Sending every key value at the algorithm to find the key

    D. Sending two large men to the key owner's house to retrieve the key

15. What is key escrow?

    A. Printing out your private key

    B. How Diffie-Hellman exchanges keys

    C. When the government keeps a copy of your key

    D. Rijndael

Answers

1. **C.** In symmetric encryption, the key must be securely shared. This can be complicated because long keys are required for good security.

2. **A.** Diffie-Hellman is most commonly used to protect the exchange of keys used to create a connection using symmetric encryption. It is often used in Transport Layer Security (TLS) implementations for protecting secure web pages.

3. **B.** AES, or Advanced Encryption Standard, is designed to replace the old U.S. government standard DES.

4. **B.** Hash functions are one-way and cannot be reversed to provide the original plaintext.

5. **A.** Asymmetric encryption is another name for public key cryptography.

6. **C.** 512 bits make up a block in SHA.

7. **B.** Elliptical curve cryptography uses two points to calculate a third point on the curve.

8. **D.** A good hash algorithm is resistant to collisions, or two different inputs hashing to the same value.

9. **C.** 3DES uses multiple keys and multiple encryption or decryption rounds to improve security over regular DES.

10. **B.** The best encryption key is one that is long and random, to reduce the predictability of the key.

11. **B.** In public key cryptography, only the private keys are secret, so key management is built into the algorithm.

12. **A.** Digital signatures use hashing and asymmetric encryption.

13. **B.** Differential cryptanalysis requires large amounts of plaintext and ciphertext.

14. **C.** Brute-forcing is the attempt to use every possible key to find the correct one.

15. **C.** When the government keeps a copy of your private key, this is typically referred to as key escrow.

Public Key Infrastructure

- Learn the basics of public key infrastructures
- Understand certificate authorities and repositories
- Understand registration authorities
- Understand the relationship between trust and certificate verification
- Understand how to use digital certificates
- Understand centralized and decentralized infrastructures
- Understand public and in-house certificate authorities

Public key infrastructures (PKIs) are becoming a central security foundation for managing identity credentials in many companies. The technology manages the issue of binding public keys and identities across multiple applications. The other approach, without PKIs, is to implement many different security solutions and hope for interoperability and equal levels of protection.

PKIs comprise components that include certificates, registration and certificate authorities, and a standard process for verification. PKI is about managing the sharing of trust and using a third party to vouch for the trustworthiness of a claim of ownership over a credential document, called a *certificate*.

The Basics of Public Key Infrastructures

A PKI provides all the components necessary for different types of users and entities to be able to communicate securely and in a predictable manner. A PKI is made up of hardware, applications, policies, services, programming interfaces, cryptographic algorithms, protocols, users, and utilities. These components work together to allow communication to take place using public key cryptography and asymmetric keys for digital signatures, data encryption, and integrity. (Refer to Chapter 4 if you need a refresher on these concepts.) Although many different applications and protocols can provide the same type of functionality, constructing and implementing a PKI boils down to establishing a level of trust.

If, for example, John and Diane want to communicate securely, John can generate his own public/private key pair and send his public key to Diane, or he can place his public key in a directory that is available to everyone. If Diane receives John's public key, either from him or from a public directory, how does she know it really came from John? Maybe another individual is masquerading as John and replaced John's public key with her own, as shown in Figure 5-1. If this took place, Diane would believe that her messages could be read only by John and that the replies were actually from him. However, she would actually be communicating with Katie. What is needed is a way to verify an individual's identity, to ensure that a person's public key is bound to their identity and thus ensure that the previous scenario (and others) cannot take place.

In PKI environments, entities called *registration authorities* and *certificate authorities* (CAs) provide services similar to those of the Department of Motor Vehicles (DMV). When John goes to register for a driver's license, he has to prove his identity to the DMV by providing his passport, birth certificate, or other identification documentation. If the DMV is satisfied with the proof John provides (and John passes a driving test), the DMV will create a driver's license that can then be used by John to prove his identity. Whenever John needs to identify himself, he can show his driver's license. Although many people may not trust John to identify himself truthfully, they do trust the third party, the DMV.

Figure 5-1
Without PKIs,
individuals could
spoof others'
identities.

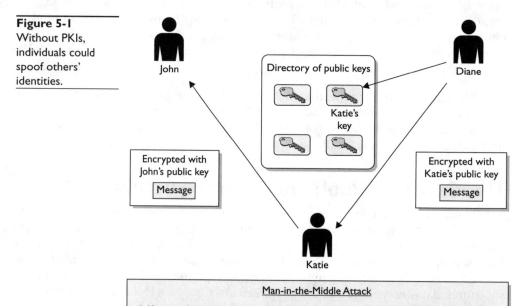

Directory of public keys

Katie's key

Encrypted with John's public key

Message

Encrypted with Katie's public key

Message

John

Diane

Katie

Man-in-the-Middle Attack

1. Katie replaces John's public key with her key in the publicly accessible directory.
2. Diane extracts what she thinks is John's key, but it is in fact Katie's key.
3. Katie can now read messages Diane encrypts and sends to John.
4. After Katie decrypts and reads Diane's message, she encrypts it with John's public key and sends it on to him so he will not be the wiser.

In the PKI context, while some variations exist in specific products, the registration authority will require proof of identity from the individual requesting a certificate and will validate this information. The registration authority will then advise the CA to generate a certificate, which is analogous to a driver's license. The CA will digitally sign the certificate using its private key. The use of the private key ensures to the recipient that the certificate came from the CA. When Diane receives John's certificate and verifies that it was actually digitally signed by a CA that she trusts, she will believe that the certificate is actually John's—not because she trusts John, but because she trusts the entity that is vouching for his identity (the CA).

This is commonly referred to as a *third-party trust model*. Public keys are components of digital certificates, so when Diane verifies the CA's digital signature, this verifies that the certificate is truly John's and that the public key the certificate contains is also John's. This is how John's identity is bound to his public key.

This process allows John to authenticate himself to Diane and others. Using the third-party certificate, John can communicate with her, using public key encryption without prior communication or a preexisting relationship. Once Diane is convinced of the legitimacy of John's public key, she can use it to encrypt and decrypt messages between herself and John, as illustrated in Figure 5-2.

Numerous applications and protocols can generate public/private key pairs and provide functionality similar to what a PKI provides, but no trusted third party is available for both of the communicating parties. For each party to choose to communicate this way without a third party vouching for the other's identity, the two must choose to trust each other and the communication channel they are using. In many situations, it

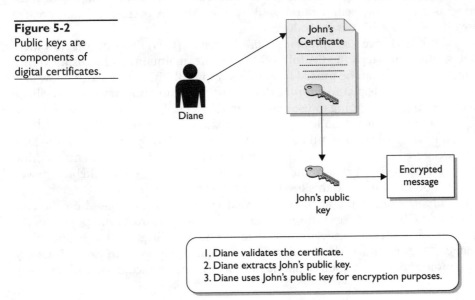

Figure 5-2
Public keys are components of digital certificates.

1. Diane validates the certificate.
2. Diane extracts John's public key.
3. Diane uses John's public key for encryption purposes.

is impractical and dangerous to arbitrarily trust an individual you do not know, and this is when the components of a PKI must fall into place—to provide the necessary level of trust you cannot, or choose not to, provide on your own.

What does the "infrastructure" in "public key infrastructure" really mean? An infrastructure provides a sustaining groundwork upon which other things can be built. So an infrastructure works at a low level to provide a predictable and uniform environment that allows other higher level technologies to work together through uniform access points. The environment that the infrastructure provides allows these higher level applications to communicate with each other and gives them the underlying tools to carry out their tasks.

Certificate Authorities

The CA is the trusted authority that certifies individuals' identities and creates electronic documents indicating that individuals are who they say they are. The electronic document is referred to as a *digital certificate*, and it establishes an association between the subject's identity and a public key. The private key that is paired with the public key in the certificate is stored separately. As noted in Chapter 4, it is important to safeguard the private key, and it typically never leaves the machine or device where it was created.

The CA is more than just a piece of software, however; it is actually made up of the software, hardware, procedures, policies, and people who are involved in validating individuals' identities and generating the certificates. This means that if one of these components is compromised, it can negatively affect the CA overall and can threaten the integrity of the certificates it produces.

Every CA should have a *certification practices statement (CPS)* that outlines how identities are verified; the steps the CA follows to generate, maintain, and transmit certificates; and why the CA can be trusted to fulfill its responsibilities. It describes how keys are secured, what data is placed within a digital certificate, and how revocations will be handled. If a company is going to use and depend on a public CA, the company's security officers, administrators, and legal department should review the CA's entire CPS to ensure that it will properly meet the company's needs, and to make sure that the level of security claimed by the CA is high enough for their use and environment. A critical aspect of a PKI is the trust between the users and the CA, so the CPS should be reviewed and understood to ensure that this level of trust is warranted.

The *certificate server* is the actual service that issues certificates based on the data provided during the initial registration process. The server constructs and populates the digital certificate with the necessary information and combines the user's public key with the resulting certificate. The certificate is then digitally signed with CA's private key. (To learn more about how digital signatures are created and verified, review Chapter 4.)

> ### How Do We Know We Can Actually Trust a CA?
> This question is part of the continuing debate on how much security PKIs actually provide. Overall, people put a lot of faith in a CA. The companies that provide CA services understand this and also understand that their business is based on their reputation. If a CA was compromised or did not follow through on its various responsibilities, word would get out and they would quickly lose customers and business. CAs work to ensure the reputation of their product and services by implementing very secure facilities, methods, procedures, and personnel. But it is up to the company or individual to determine what degree of trust can actually be given and what level of risk is acceptable.

Registration Authorities

The *registration authority (RA)* is the component that accepts a request for a digital certificate and performs the necessary steps of registering and authenticating the person requesting the certificate. The authentication requirements differ depending on the type of certificate being requested.

The types of certificates available can vary between different CAs, but usually at least three different types are available, and they are referred to as *classes*:

- **Class 1**   A Class 1 certificate is usually used to verify an individual's identity through e-mail. A person who receives a Class 1 certificate can use his public/private key pair to digitally sign e-mail and encrypt message contents.

- **Class 2**   A Class 2 certificate can be used for software signing. A software vendor would register for this type of certificate so it could digitally sign its software. This provides integrity for the software after it is developed and released, and it allows the receiver of the software to verify from where the software actually came.

- **Class 3**   A Class 3 certificate can be used by a company to set up its own CA, which will allow it to carry out its own identification verification and generate certificates internally.

Each higher class of certificate can carry out more powerful and critical tasks than the one before it. This is why the different classes have different requirements for proof of identity. If you want to receive a Class 1 certificate, you may only be asked to provide your name, e-mail address, and physical address. For a Class 2 certification, you may need to provide the RA with more data, such as your driver's license, passport, and company information that can be verified. To obtain a Class 3 certificate, you will be asked to provide even more information and most likely will need to go to the RA's office for a face-to-face meeting. Each CA will outline the certification classes it provides and the identification requirements that must be met to acquire each type of certificate.

In most situations, when a user requests a Class 1 certificate, the registration process will require the user to enter specific information into a web-based form. The web page will have a section that accepts the user's public key, or it will step the user through creating a public/private key pair, which will allow the user to choose the size of the keys to be created. Once these steps have been completed, the public key is attached to the certificate registration form and both are forwarded to the RA for processing. The RA is responsible only for the registration process and cannot actually generate a certificate. Once the RA is finished processing the request and verifying the individual's identity, the RA will send the request to the CA. The CA will use the RA-provided information to generate a digital certificate, integrate the necessary data into the certificate fields (user identification information, public key, validity dates, proper use for the key and certificate, and so on), and send a copy of the certificate to the user. These steps are shown in Figure 5-3. The certificate may also be posted to a publicly accessible directory so that others can access it.

Note that a 1:1 correspondence does not necessarily exist between identities and certificates. An entity can have multiple key pairs, using separate public keys for separate purposes. Thus, an entity can have multiple certificates, each attesting to separate public key ownership. It is also possible to have different classes of certificates, again with different keys. This flexibility allows entities total discretion in how they manage

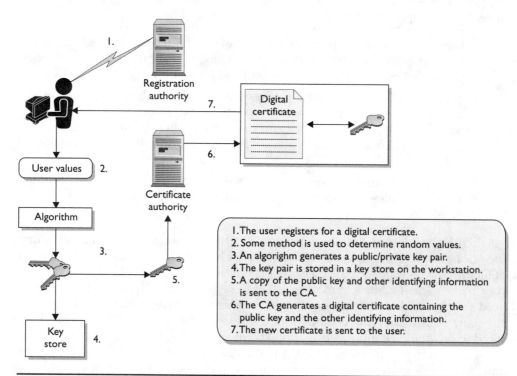

Figure 5-3 Steps for obtaining a digital certificate

their keys, and the PKI manages the complexity by using a unified process that allows key verification through a common interface.

PART II

EXAM TIP The RA verifies the identity of the certificate requestor on behalf of the CA. The CA generates the certificate using information forwarded by the RA.

If an application creates a key store that can be accessed by other applications, it will provide a standardized interface, called the *application programming interface (API)*. In Netscape and UNIX systems, this interface is usually PKCS #11, and in Microsoft applications the interface is Crypto API (CAPI). As an example, Figure 5-4 shows that application A went through the process of registering a certificate and generating a key pair. It created a key store that provides an interface to allow other applications to communicate with it and use the items held within the store.

The local key store is just one location where these items can be held. Often the digital certificate and public key are also stored in a certificate repository (as discussed in the "Certificate Repositories" section of this chapter) so that it is available to a subset of individuals.

Sharing Stores

Different applications from the same vendor may share key stores. Microsoft applications keep a user's keys and certificates in a Registry entry within that particular user's profile. The applications save and retrieve them from this single location, or key store.

Figure 5-4
Some key stores
can be shared by
different applications.

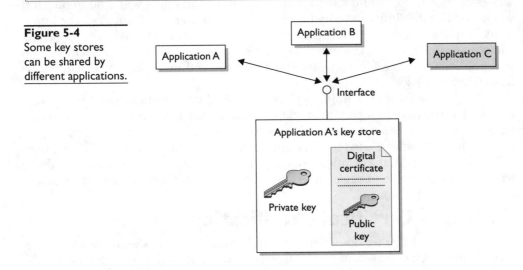

Local Registration Authorities

A *local registration authority (LRA)* performs the same functions as an RA, but the LRA is closer to the end users. This component is usually implemented in companies that have their own internal PKIs and have distributed sites. Each site has users that need RA services, so instead of requiring them to communicate with one central RA, each site can have its own LRA. This reduces the amount of traffic that would be created by several users making requests across wide area network (WAN) lines. The LRA will perform identification, verification, and registration functions. It will then send the request, along with the user's public key, to a centralized CA so that the certificate can be generated. It acts as an interface between the users and the CA. LRAs simplify the RA/CA process for entities that desire certificates only for in-house use.

Certificate Repositories

Once the requestor's identity has been proven, a certificate is registered with the public side of the key pair provided by the requestor. Public keys must be available to anybody who requires them to communicate within a PKI environment. These keys, and their corresponding certificates, are usually held in a publicly available repository. *Repository* is a general term that describes a centralized directory that can be accessed by a subset of individuals. The directories are usually Lightweight Directory Access Protocol (LDAP)–compliant, meaning that they can be accessed and searched via the LDAP.

When an individual initializes communication with another, the sender can send her certificate and public key to the receiver, which will allow the receiver to communicate with the sender using encryption or digital signatures (or both) without needing to track down the necessary public key in a certificate repository. This is equivalent to the sender saying, "If you would like to encrypt any future messages you send to me, or if you would like the ability to verify my digital signature, here are the necessary components." But if a person wants to encrypt the first message sent to the receiver, the sender will need to find the receiver's public key in a certificate repository. (For a refresher on how public and private keys come into play with encryption and digital signatures, refer to Chapter 4.)

A *certificate repository* is a holding place for individuals' certificates and public keys that are participating in a particular PKI environment. The security requirements for repositories themselves are not as high as those needed for actual CAs and for the equipment and software used to carry out CA functions. Since each certificate is digitally signed by the CA, if a certificate stored in the certificate repository is modified, the recipient would be able to detect this change and not accept the certificate as valid.

Trust and Certificate Verification

We need to use a PKI if we do not automatically trust individuals we do not know. Security is about being suspicious and being safe, so we need a third party that we *do* trust to vouch for the other individual before confidence can be instilled and sensitive communication can take place. But what does it mean that we trust a CA, and how can we use this to our advantage?

Distinguished Names

A distinguished name is a label that follows the X.500 standard. This standard defines a naming convention that can be employed so that each subject within an organization has a unique name. An example is {Country = US, Organization = Real Secure, Organizational Unit = R&D, Location = Washington}. CAs use distinguished names to identify the owners of specific certificates.

When a user chooses to trust a CA, she will download that CA's digital certificate and public key, which will be stored on her local computer. Most browsers have a list of CAs configured to be trusted by default, so when a user installs a new web browser, several of the most well-known and most trusted CAs will be trusted without any change of settings. An example of this listing is shown in Figure 5-5.

In the Microsoft CAPI environment, the user can add and remove CAs from this list as needed. In production environments that require a higher degree of protection, this list will be pruned, and possibly the only CAs listed will be the company's *internal* CAs. This ensures that digitally signed software will be automatically installed only if it was signed by the company's CA. Other products, such as Entrust, use centrally controlled policies to determine which CAs are to be trusted instead of expecting the user to make these critical decisions.

A number of steps are involved in checking the validity of a message. Suppose, for example, that Maynard receives a digitally signed message from Joyce, who he does not know or trust. Joyce has also included her digital certificate with her message, which has her public key embedded within it. Before Maynard can be sure of the authenticity of this message, he has some work to do. The steps are illustrated in Figure 5-6.

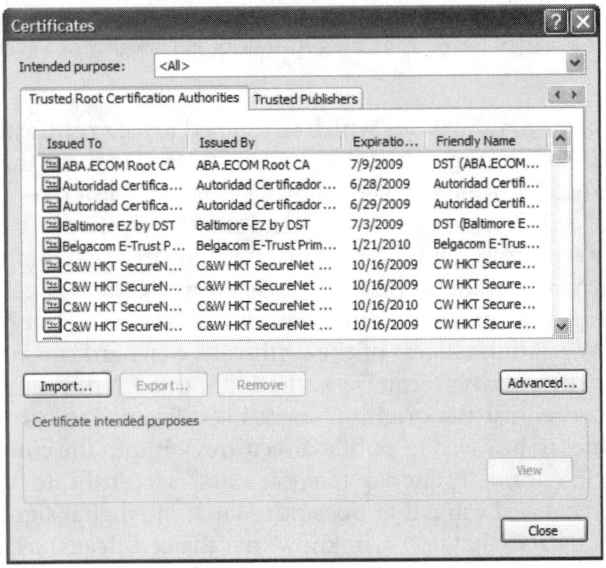

Figure 5-5
Browsers have a long list of CAs configured to be trusted by default.

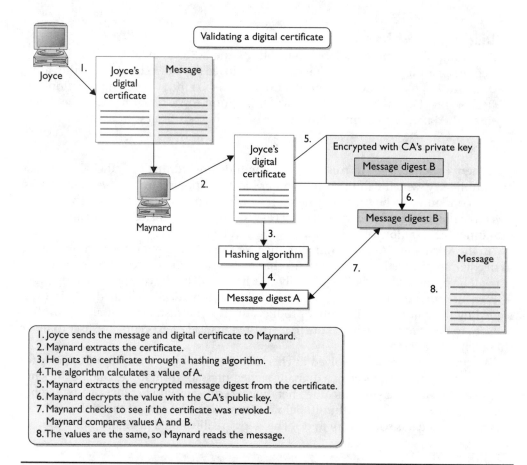

Validating a digital certificate

Joyce

1.

Joyce's digital certificate

Message

Maynard

2.

Joyce's digital certificate

5.

Encrypted with CA's private key

Message digest B

6.

Message digest B

3.

Hashing algorithm

4.

Message digest A

7.

8.

Message

1. Joyce sends the message and digital certificate to Maynard.
2. Maynard extracts the certificate.
3. He puts the certificate through a hashing algorithm.
4. The algorithm calculates a value of A.
5. Maynard extracts the encrypted message digest from the certificate.
6. Maynard decrypts the value with the CA's public key.
7. Maynard checks to see if the certificate was revoked.
   Maynard compares values A and B.
8. The values are the same, so Maynard reads the message.

Figure 5-6   Steps for verifying the authenticity and integrity of a certificate

First, Maynard will see which CA signed Joyce's certificate and compare it to the list of CAs he has configured within his computer. He trusts the CAs in his list and no others. (If the certificate was signed by a CA he does not have in the list, he would not accept the certificate as being valid, and thus he could not be sure that this message was actually sent from Joyce or that the attached key was actually her public key.)

Maynard sees that the CA that signed Joyce's certificate is indeed in his list of trusted CAs, so he now needs to verify that the certificate has not been altered. Using the CA's public key and the digest of the certificate, Maynard can verify the integrity of the certificate. Then Maynard can be assured that this CA did actually create the certificate, so he can now trust the origin of Joyce's certificate. The use of digital signatures allows certificates to be saved in public directories without the concern of them being accidentally or intentionally altered. If a user extracts a certificate from a repository and creates a message digest value that does not match the digital signature embedded within the certificate itself, that user will know that the certificate has been modified by someone other than the CA, and he will know not to accept the validity of the corresponding public key. Similarly, an attacker could not create a new message digest, encrypt it, and embed it within the certificate because he would not have access to the CA's private key.

But Maynard is not done yet. He needs to be sure that the issuing CA has not revoked this certificate. The certificate also has start and stop dates, indicating a time during which the certificate is valid. If the start date hasn't happened yet, or the stop date has been passed, the certificate is not valid. Maynard reviews these dates to make sure the certificate is still deemed valid.

Another step Maynard may go through is to check whether this certificate has been revoked for any reason, so he will refer to a list of revoked certificates to see if Joyce's certificate is listed. The revocation list could be checked directly with the CA that issued the certificate or via a specialized online service that supports the Online Certificate Status Protocol (OCSP). (Certificate revocation and list distribution are explained in the "Certificate Lifecycles" section, later in this chapter.)

To recap, the following steps are required for validating a certificate:

1. Compare the CA that digitally signed the certificate to a list of CAs that have already been loaded into the receiver's computer.

2. Calculate a message digest for the certificate.

3. Use the CA's public key to decrypt the digital signature and recover what is claimed to be the original message digest embedded within the certificate (validating the digital signature).

4. Compare the two resulting message digest values to ensure the integrity of the certificate.

5. Review the identification information within the certificate, such as the e-mail address.

6. Review the validity dates.

7. Check a revocation list to see if the certificate has been revoked.

Maynard now trusts that this certificate is legitimate and that it belongs to Joyce. Now what does he need to do? The certificate holds Joyce's public key, which he needs to validate the digital signature she appended to her message, so Maynard extracts Joyce's public key from her certificate, runs her message through a hashing algorithm, and calculates a message digest value of X. He then uses Joyce's public key to decrypt her digital signature (remember that a digital signature is just a message digest encrypted with a private key). This decryption process provides him with another message digest of value Y. Maynard compares values X and Y, and if they are the same, he is assured that the message has not been modified during transmission. Thus he has confidence in the integrity of the message. But how does Maynard know that the message actually came from Joyce? Because he can decrypt the digital signature using her public key, this indicates that only the associated private key could have been used. There is a miniscule risk that someone could create an identical key pair, but given the enormous keyspace for public keys, this is impractical. The public key can only decrypt something that was encrypted with the related private key, and only the owner of the private key is supposed to have access to it. Maynard can be sure that this message came from Joyce.

After all of this he reads her message, which says, "Hi. How are you?" All of that work just for this message? Maynard's blood pressure would surely go through the roof if he had to do all of this work only to end up with a short and not very useful message. Fortunately, all of this PKI work is performed without user intervention and happens behind the scenes. Maynard didn't have to exert any energy. He simply replies, "Fine. How are you?"

Digital Certificates

A digital certificate binds an individual's identity to a public key, and it contains all the information a receiver needs to be assured of the identity of the public key owner. After an RA verifies an individual's identity, the CA generates the digital certificate, but how does the CA know what type of data to insert into the certificate?

The certificates are created and formatted based on the X.509 standard, which outlines the necessary fields of a certificate and the possible values that can be inserted into the fields. As of this writing, X.509 version 3 is the most current version of the standard. X.509 is a standard of the International Telecommunication Union (www.itu.int). The IETF's Public-Key Infrastructure (X.509), or PKIX, working group has adapted the X.509 standard to the more flexible organization of the Internet, as specified in RFC 3280, and is commonly referred to as PKIX for Public Key Infrastructure (X.509).

The following fields are included within a X.509 digital certificate:

- **Version number**   Identifies the version of the X.509 standard that was followed to create the certificate; indicates the format and fields that can be used.
- **Subject**   Specifies the owner of the certificate.
- **Public key**   Identifies the public key being bound to the certified subject; also identifies the algorithm used to create the private/public key pair.
- **Issuer**   Identifies the CA that generated and digitally signed the certificate.
- **Serial number**   Provides a unique number identifying this one specific certificate issued by a particular CA.
- **Validity**   Specifies the dates through which the certificate is valid for use.
- **Certificate usage**   Specifies the approved use of certificate, which dictates intended use of this public key.
- **Signature algorithm**   Specifies the hashing and digital signature algorithms used to digitally sign the certificate.
- **Extensions**   Allow additional data to be encoded into the certificate to expand the functionality of the certificate. Companies can customize the use of certificates within their environments by using these extensions. X.509 version 3 has extended the extension possibilities.

Figure 5-7 shows the actual values of these different certificate fields for a particular certificate in Internet Explorer. The version of this certificate is V3 (X.509 v3) and the serial number is also listed—this number is unique for each certificate that is created by a specific CA. The CA used the MD5 hashing algorithm to create the message digest value, and it then signed with its private key using the RSA algorithm. The actual CA that issued the certificate is Root SGC Authority, and the valid dates indicate how long this certificate is valid. The subject is MS SGC Authority, which is the entity that registered this certificate and is the entity that is bound to the embedded public key. The actual public key is shown in the lower window and is represented in hexadecimal.

The subject of a certificate is commonly a person, but it does not have to be. The subject can be a network device (router, web server, firewall, and so on), an application, a department, a company, or a person. Each has its own identity that needs to be verified and proven to another entity before secure, trusted communication can be initiated. If a network device is using a certificate for authentication, the certificate may contain the network address of that device. This means that if the certificate has a network address of 10.0.0.1, the receiver will compare this to the address from which it received the certificate to make sure a man-in-the-middle attack is not being attempted.

Certificate Attributes

Four main types of certificates are used:

- End-entity certificates
- CA certificates
- Cross-certification certificates
- Policy certificates

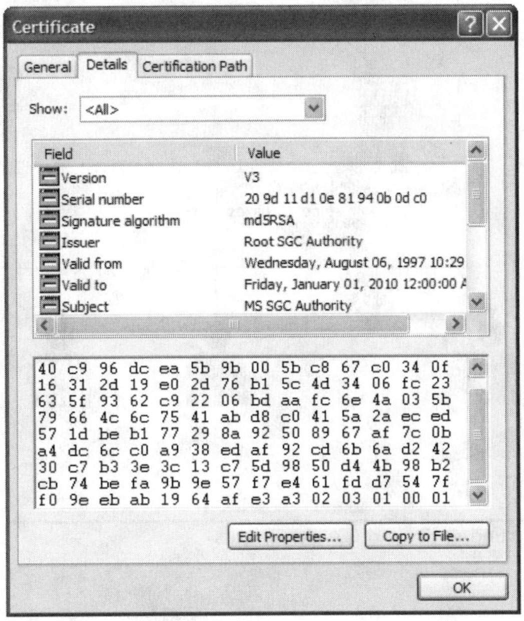

Figure 5-7
Fields within a digital certificate

End-entity certificates are issued by a CA to a specific subject, such as Joyce, the Accounting department, or a firewall, as illustrated in Figure 5-8. An end-entity certificate is the identity document provided by PKI implementations.

A *CA certificate* can be self-signed, in the case of a standalone or root CA, or it can be issued by a superior CA within a hierarchical model. In the model in Figure 5-8, the superior CA gives the authority and allows the subordinate CA to accept certificate requests and generate the individual certificates itself. This may be necessary when a company needs to have multiple internal CAs, and different departments within an organization need to have their own CAs servicing their specific end-entities in their sections. In these situations, a representative from each department requiring a CA registers with the higher trusted CA and requests a Certificate Authority certificate. (Public and private CAs are discussed in the "Public Certificate Authorities" and "In-house Certificate Authorities" sections later in this chapter, as are the different trust models that are available for companies.)

Cross-certificates, or *cross-certification certificates*, are used when independent CAs establish peer-to-peer trust relationships. Simply put, they are a mechanism through which one CA can issue a certificate allowing its users to trust another CA.

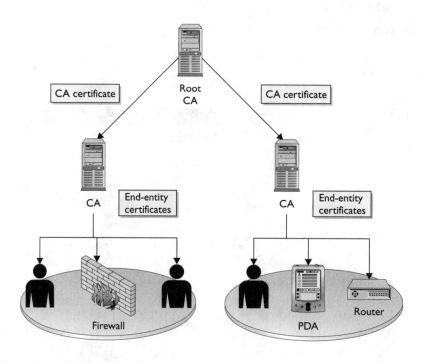

Figure 5-8 End-entity and CA certificates

Within sophisticated CAs used for high-security applications, a mechanism is required to provide centrally controlled policy information to PKI clients. This is often done by placing the policy information in a *policy certificate*.

Certificate Extensions

Certificate extensions allow for further information to be inserted within the certificate, which can be used to provide more functionality in a PKI implementation. Certificate extensions can be standard or private. *Standard certificate extensions* are implemented for every PKI implementation. *Private certificate extensions* are defined for specific organizations (or domains within one organization), and they allow companies to further define different, specific uses for digital certificates to best fit their business needs.

Several different extensions can be implemented, one being *key usage extensions*, which dictate how the public key that is held within the certificate can be used. Remember that public keys can be used for different functions: symmetric key encryption, data encryption, verifying digital signatures, and more. Following are some key examples of certificate extension:

- **DigitalSignature** The key used to verify a digital signature
- **KeyEncipherment** The key used to encrypt other keys used for secure key distribution
- **DataEncipherment** The key used to encrypt data, which cannot be used to encrypt other keys
- **CRLSign** The key used to verify a CA signature on a revocation list
- **KeyCertSign** The key used to verify CA signatures on certificates
- **NonRepudiation** The key used when a nonrepudiation service is being provided

A nonrepudiation service can be provided by a third-party notary. In this situation, the sender's digital signature is verified and then signed by the notary so that the sender cannot later deny signing and sending the message. This is basically the same function performed by a traditional notary using paper—validate the sender's identity and validate the time and date of an item being signed and sent. This is required when the receiver needs to be *really* sure of the sender's identity and wants to be legally protected against possible fraud or forgery.

If a company needs to be sure that accountable nonrepudiation services will be provided, a trusted time source needs to be used, which can be a trusted third party called a *time stamp authority*. Using a trusted time source gives users a higher level of confidence as to *when* specific messages were digitally signed. For example, suppose Barry sends Ron a message and digitally signs it, and Ron later civilly sues Barry over a dispute. This digitally signed message may be submitted by Ron as evidence pertaining to an earlier agreement that Barry now is not fulfilling. If a trusted time source was not used in their PKI environment, Barry could claim that his private key had been compromised before that message was sent. If a trusted time source was implemented, then it could be shown that the message was signed *before* the date on which Barry claims his key was compromised. If a trusted time source is not used, no activity that was carried out within a PKI environment can be truly proven because it is so easy to change system and software time settings.

Critical and Noncritical Extensions

Certificate extensions are considered either *critical* or *noncritical*, which is indicated by a specific flag within the certificate itself. When this flag is set to critical, it means that the extension *must* be understood and processed by the receiver. If the receiver is not configured to understand a particular extension marked as critical, and thus cannot process it properly, the certificate cannot be used for its proposed purpose. If the flag does not indicate that the extension is critical, the certificate can be used for the intended purpose, even if the receiver does not process the appended extension.

So how does this work? When an extension is marked as critical, it means that the CA is certifying the key for only that specific purpose. If Joe receives a certificate with a DigitalSignature key usage extension and the critical flag is set, Joe can use the public key only within that certificate to validate digital signatures, and no more. If the extension was marked as noncritical, the key can be used for purposes outside of those listed in the extensions, so in this case it is up to Joe (and his applications) to decide how the key will be used.

Certificate Lifecycles

Keys and certificates should have lifetime settings that will force the user to register for a new certificate after a certain amount of time. Determining the proper length of these lifetimes is a trade-off: Shorter lifetimes limit the ability of attackers to crack them, but longer lifetimes lower system overhead. More sophisticated PKI implementations perform automated and often transparent key updates to avoid the time and expense of having users register for new certificates when old ones expire.

This means that the certificate and key pair has a lifecycle that must be managed. Certificate management involves administrating and managing each of these phases, including registration, certificate and key generation, renewal, and revocation.

Registration and Generation

A key pair (public and private keys) can be generated locally by an application and stored in a local key store on the user's workstation. The key pair can also be created by a central key-generation server, which will require secure transmission of the keys to the user. The key pair that is created on the centralized server can be stored on the user's workstation or on the user's smart card, which will allow for more flexibility and mobility.

In most modern PKI implementations, users have two key pairs. One key pair is often generated by a central server and used for encryption and key transfers. This allows the corporate PKI to retain a copy of the encryption key pair for recovery, if necessary. The second key pair, a digital signature key pair, is usually generated by the user to make sure that she is the only one with a copy of the private key. Nonrepudiation can be challenged if there is any doubt about someone else obtaining a copy of an individual's signature private key. If the key pair was created on a centralized server, that could weaken the case that the individual was the only one who had a copy of her private key. If a copy of a user's signature private key is stored anywhere other than in her possession, or if there is a possibility of someone obtaining the user's key, then true nonrepudiation cannot be provided.

The act of verifying that an individual indeed has the corresponding private key for a given public key is referred to as *proof of possession*. Not all public/private key pairs can be used for digital signatures, so asking the individual to sign a message and return it to prove that she has the necessary private key will not always work. If a key pair is used for encryption, the RA can send a challenge value to the individual, who, in turn, can use her private key to encrypt that value and return it to the RA. If the RA can successfully decrypt this value with the public key that was provided earlier, the RA can be confident that the individual has the necessary private key and can continue through the rest of the registration phase.

The PKI administrator usually configures the minimum required key size that users must use to have a key generated for the first time, and then for each renewal. In most applications, a drop-down list shows possible algorithms from which to choose, and possible key sizes. The key size should provide the necessary level of security for the current environment. The lifetime of the key should be long enough that continual renewal will not negatively affect productivity, but short enough to ensure that the key cannot be successfully compromised.

Renewal

The certificate itself has its own lifetime, which can be different than the key pair's lifetime. The certificate's lifetime is specified by the validity dates inserted into the digital certificate. These are beginning and ending dates indicating the time period during which the certificate is valid. The certificate cannot be used before the start date, and once the end date is met, the certificate is expired and a new certificate will need to be issued.

A renewal process is different from the registration phase in that the RA assumes that the individual has already successfully completed one registration round. If the certificate has not actually been revoked, the original keys and certificate can be used to provide the necessary authentication information and proof of identity for the renewal phase.

Approaches to Protection
Good key management and proper key replacement intervals protect keys from being compromised through human error. Choosing a large key size makes a brute-force attack more difficult.

The certificate may or may not need to change during the renewal process; this usually depends on why the renewal is taking place. If the certificate just expired and the keys will still be used for the same purpose, a new certificate can be generated with new validity dates. If, however, the key pair functionality needs to be expanded or restricted, new attributes and extensions may need to be integrated into the new certificate. These new functionalities may require more information to be gathered from the individual renewing the certificate, especially if the class changes or the new key uses allow for more powerful abilities.

This renewal process is required when the certificate has fulfilled its lifetime and its end validity date has been met. This situation differs from that of a certificate revocation.

Revocation

A certificate can be revoked when its validity needs to be ended before its actual expiration date is met, and this can occur for many reasons: for example, a user may have lost a laptop or a smart card that stored a private key, an improper software implementation may have been uncovered that directly affected the security of a private key, a user may have fallen victim to a social engineering attack and inadvertently given up a private key, data held within the certificate may no longer apply to the specified individual, or perhaps an employee left a company and should not be identified as a member of an in-house PKI any longer. In the last instance, the certificate, which was bound to the user's key pair, identified the user as an employee of the company, and the administrator would want to ensure that the key pair could not be used in the future to validate this person's affiliation with the company. Revoking the certificate does this.

If any of these things happen, a user's private key has been compromised or should no longer be mapped to the owner's identity. A different individual may have access to that user's private key and could use it to impersonate and authenticate as the original user. If the impersonator used the key to digitally sign a message, the receiver would verify the authenticity of the sender by verifying the signature by using the original user's public key, and the verification would go through perfectly—the receiver would believe it came from the proper sender and not the impersonator. If receivers could look at a list of certificates that had been revoked before verifying the digital signature, however, they would know not to trust the digital signatures on the list. Because of issues associated with the private key being compromised, revocation is permanent and final—once revoked, a certificate cannot be reinstated. If this were allowed and a user revoked his certificate, the unauthorized holder of the private key could use it to restore the certificate validity.

For example, if Joe stole Mike's laptop, which held, among other things, Mike's private key, Joe might be able to use it to impersonate Mike. Suppose Joe writes a message, digitally signs it with Mike's private key, and sends it to Stacy. Stacy communicates with Mike periodically and has his public key, so she uses it to verify the digital signature. It computes properly, so Stacy is assured that this message came from Mike, but in truth it did not. If, before validating any certificate or digital signature, Stacy could check a list of revoked certificates, she might not fall victim to Joe's false message.

The CA provides this type of protection by maintaining a *certificate revocation list (CRL)*, a list of serial numbers of certificates that have been revoked. The CRL also contains a statement indicating why the individual certificates were revoked and a date when the revocation took place. The list usually contains all certificates that have been revoked within the lifetime of the CA. Certificates that have expired are not the same as those that have been revoked. If a certificate has expired, it means that its end validity date was reached.

The CA is the entity that is responsible for the status of the certificates it generates; it needs to be told of a revocation, and it must provide this information to others. The CA is responsible for maintaining CRL and posting it in a publicly available directory.

EXAM TIP The Certificate Revocation List is an essential item to ensure a certificate is still valid. CAs post CRLs in publicly available directories to permit automated checking of certificates against the list before certificate use by a client. A user should never trust a certificate that has not been checked against the appropriate CRL.

What if Stacy wants to get back at Joe for trying to trick her earlier, and she attempts to revoke Joe's certificate herself? If she is successful, Joe's participation in the PKI can be negatively affected because others will not trust his public key. Although we might think Joe may deserve this, we need to have some system in place to make sure people cannot arbitrarily have others' certificates revoked, whether for revenge or for malicious purposes.

When a revocation request is submitted, the individual submitting the request must be authenticated. Otherwise, this could permit a type of denial-of-service attack, in which someone has another person's certificate revoked. The authentication can involve an agreed-upon password that was created during the registration process, but authentication should not be based on the individual proving that he has the corresponding private key, because it may have been stolen, and the CA would be authenticating an imposter.

The CRL's integrity needs to be protected to ensure that attackers cannot modify data pertaining to a revoked certification from the list. If this were allowed to take place, anyone who stole a private key could just delete that key from the CRL and continue to use the private key fraudulently. The integrity of the list also needs to be protected to ensure that bogus data is not added to it. Otherwise, anyone could add another person's certificate to the list and effectively revoke that person's certificate. The only entity that should be able to modify any information on the CRL is the CA.

The mechanism used to protect the integrity of a CRL is a *digital signature*. The CA's revocation service creates a digital signature for the CRL, as shown in Figure 5-9. To validate a certificate, the user accesses to the directory where the CRL is posted, downloads the list, and verifies the CA's digital signature to ensure that the proper authority signed the list and to ensure that the list was not modified in an unauthorized manner. The user then looks through the list to determine whether the serial number of the certificate that he is trying to validate is listed. If the serial number is on the list, the

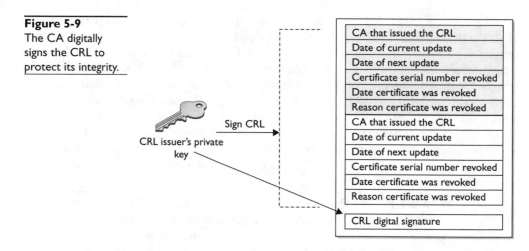

Figure 5-9
The CA digitally
signs the CRL to
protect its integrity.

private key should no longer be trusted, and the public key should no longer be used. This can be a cumbersome process, so it has been automated in several ways that are described in the next section.

One concern is how up-to-date the CRL is—how often is it updated and does it actually reflect *all* the certificates currently revoked? The actual frequency with which the list is updated depends upon the CA and its certification practices statement (CPS). It is important that the list is updated in a timely manner so that anyone using the list has the most current information.

CRL Distribution

CRL files can be requested by individuals who need to verify and validate a newly received certificate, or the files can be periodically pushed down (sent) to all users participating within a specific PKI. This means the CRL can be pulled (downloaded) by individual users when needed or pushed down to all users within the PKI on a timed interval.

The actual CRL file can grow substantially, and transmitting this file and requiring PKI client software on each workstation to save and maintain it can use a lot of resources, so the smaller the CRL is, the better. It is also possible to first push down the full CRL, and after that initial load, the following CRLs pushed down to the users are *delta* CRLs, meaning that they contain only the changes to the original or base CRL. This can greatly reduce the amount of bandwidth consumed when updating CRLs.

In implementations where the CRLs are not pushed down to individual systems, the users' PKI software needs to know where to look for the posted CRL that relates to the certificate it is trying to validate. The certificate might have an extension that points the validating user to the necessary *CRL distribution point*. The network administrator sets up the distribution points, and one or more points can exist for a particular PKI. The distribution point holds one or more lists containing the serial numbers of revoked certificates, and the user's PKI software scans the list(s) for the serial number of the certificate the user is attempting to validate. If the serial number is not present, the user is assured that it has not been revoked. This approach helps point users to the right resource and also reduces the amount of information that needs to be scanned when checking that a certificate has not been revoked.

One last option for checking distributed CRLs is an *online service*. When a client user needs to validate a certificate and ensure that it has not been revoked, he can communicate with an online service that will query the necessary CRLs available within the environment. This service can query the lists for the client instead of pushing down the full CRL to each and every system. So if Joe receives a certificate from Stacy, he can contact an online service and send it the serial number listed in the certificate Stacy sent. The online service would query the necessary revocation lists and respond to Joe indicating whether that serial number was listed as being revoked or not.

One of the protocols used for online revocation services is OCSP, a request and response protocol that obtains the serial number of the certificate that is being validated and reviews revocation lists for the client. The protocol has a responder service that reports the status of the certificate back to the client, indicating whether it has been revoked, it is valid, or its status is unknown. This protocol and service saves the client from having to find, download, and process the right lists.

Suspension

Instead of being revoked, a certificate can be *suspended*, meaning it is temporarily put on hold. If, for example, Bob is taking an extended vacation and wants to ensure that his certificate will not be used during that time, he can make a suspension request to the CA. The CRL would list this certificate and its serial number, and in the field that describes why the certificate is revoked, it would instead indicate a hold state. Once Bob returns to work, he can make a request to the CA to remove his certificate from the list.

Another reason to suspend a certificate is if an administrator is suspicious that a private key might have been compromised. While the issue is under investigation, the certificate can be suspended to ensure that it cannot be used.

Key Destruction

Key pairs and certificates have set *lifetimes*, meaning that they will expire at some specified time. It is important that the certificates and keys are properly destroyed when that time comes, wherever the keys are stored (on users' workstations, centralized key servers, USB token devices, smart cards, and so on).

Authority Revocation Lists

In some PKI implementations, a separate revocation list is maintained for CA keys that have been compromised or should no longer be trusted. This list is known as an *authority revocation list (ARL)*. In the event that a CA's private key is compromised or a cross certification is cancelled, the relevant certificate's serial number is included in the ARL. A client can review an ARL to make sure the CA's public key can still be trusted.

The goal is to make sure that no one can gain access to a key after its lifetime has ended and use this key for malicious purposes. An attacker might use the key to digitally sign or encrypt a message with the hopes of tricking someone else about his identity (this would be an example of a man-in-the-middle attack). Also, if the attacker is performing some type of brute-force attack on your cryptosystem, trying to figure out specific keys that were used for encryption processes, obtaining an old key could give him more insight into how your cryptosystem generates keys. The less information you supply to potential hackers, the better.

Note that in modern PKIs, encryption key pairs usually must be retained long after they expire so that users can decrypt information that was encrypted with the old keys. For example, if Bob encrypts a document using his current key and the keys are updated three months later, Bob's software must maintain a copy of the old key so he can still decrypt the document. In the PKI world, this issue is referred to as *key history maintenance*.

Centralized or Decentralized Infrastructures

Keys used for authentication and encryption within a PKI environment can be generated in a centralized or decentralized manner. In a *decentralized* approach, software on individual computers generates and stores cryptographic keys local to the systems themselves. In a *centralized* infrastructure, the keys are generated and stored on a central server, and the keys are transmitted to the individual systems as needed. You might choose one type over the other for several reasons.

If a company uses an asymmetric algorithm that is resource-intensive to generate the public/private key pair, and if large (and resource-intensive) key sizes are needed, then the individual computers may not have the necessary processing power to produce the keys in an acceptable fashion. In this situation, the company can choose a centralized approach in which a very high-end server with powerful processing abilities is used, probably along with a hardware-based random number generator.

Central key generation and storage offers other benefits as well. For example, it is much easier to back up the keys and implement key recovery procedures with central storage than with a decentralized approach. Implementing a key recovery procedure on each and every computer holding one or more key pairs is difficult, and many applications that generate their own key pairs do not usually interface well with a centralized archive system. This means that if a company chooses to allow its individual users to create and maintain their own key pairs on their separate workstations, no real key recovery procedure can be put in place. This puts the company at risk. If an employee leaves the organization or is unavailable for one reason or another, the company may not be able to access its own business information that was encrypted by that employee.

So a centralized approach seems like the best approach, right? Well, the centralized method has some drawbacks to consider, too. If the keys will be generated on a server, they need to be securely transmitted to the individual clients that require them. This can be more difficult than it sounds. A technology needs to be employed that will send the keys in an encrypted manner, ensure the keys' integrity, and make sure that only the intended user is receiving the key.

Also, the server that centrally stores the keys needs to be highly available and can provide a single point of failure, so some type of fault tolerance or redundancy mechanism may need to be put into place. If that one server goes down, users could not access their keys, which might prevent them from properly authenticating to the network, resources, and applications. Also, since all the keys are in one place, the server is a prime target for an attacker—if the central key server is compromised, the whole environment is compromised.

One other issue pertains to how the keys will actually be used. If a public/private key pair is being generated for digital signatures, and if the company wants to ensure that it can be used to provide *true* authenticity and nonrepudiation, the keys should not be generated at a centralized server. This would introduce doubt that only the one person had access to a specific private key.

If a company uses smart cards to hold users' private keys, each private key often has to be generated on the card itself and cannot be copied for archiving purposes. This is a disadvantage of the centralized approach. In addition, some types of applications have been developed to create their own public/private key pairs and do not allow other keys to be imported and used. This means the keys would have to be created locally by these applications, and keys from a central server could not be used. These are just some of the considerations that need to be evaluated before any decision is made and implementation begins.

Hardware Storage Devices

PKIs can be constructed in software without special cryptographic hardware, and this is perfectly suitable for many environments. But software can be vulnerable to viruses, hackers, and hacking. If a company requires a higher level of protection than a purely software-based solution can provide, several hardware-based solutions are available.

In most situations, hardware key-storage solutions are used only for the most critical and sensitive keys, which are the root and possibly the intermediate CA private keys. If those keys are compromised, the whole security of the PKI is gravely threatened. If a person obtained a root CA private key, she could digitally sign any certificate, and that certificate would be quickly accepted by all entities within the environment. Such an attacker might be able to create a certificate that has extremely high privileges, perhaps allowing her to modify bank account information in a financial institution, and no alerts or warnings would be initiated because the ultimate CA, the root CA, signed it.

Random Number Generators

In most cases, software- and hardware-based generators are actually considered *pseudo-random number generators* because they have a finite number of values to work from. They usually extract these values from their surroundings, which are predictable in nature—the values can come from the system's time or from CPU cycles. If the starting values are predictable, the numbers they generate cannot be truly random. An example of a true random number generator would be a system that collects radiation from a radioactive item. The elements that escape from the radioactive item do so in an unpredictable manner, and the results are used as seed values for key generation.

Private Key Protection

Although a PKI implementation can be complex, with many different components and options, a critical concept common to all PKIs must be understood and enforced: the private key needs to stay private. A digital signature is created solely for the purpose of proving who sent a particular message by using a private key. This rests on the assumption that only one person has access to this private key. If an imposter obtains a user's private key, authenticity and nonrepudiation can no longer be claimed or proven.

When a private key is generated for the first time, it must be stored somewhere for future use. This storage area is referred to as a *key store*, and it is usually created by the application registering for a certificate, such as a web browser, smart card software, or other application. In most implementations, the application will prompt the user for a password, which will be used to create an encryption key that protects the key store. So, for example, if Cheryl used her web browser to register for a certificate, her private key would be generated and stored in the key store. Cheryl would then be prompted for a password, which the software would use to create a key that will encrypt the key store. When Cheryl needs to access this private key later that day, she will be prompted for the same password, which will decrypt the key store and allow her access to her private key.

Unfortunately, many applications do not require that a strong password be created to protect the key store, and in some implementations the user can choose not to provide a password at all. The user still has a private key available, and it is bound to the user's identity, so why is a password even necessary? If, for example, Cheryl decided not to use a password, and another person sat down at her computer, he could use her web browser and her private key and digitally sign a message that contained a nasty virus. If Cheryl's coworker Cliff received this message, he would think it came from Cheryl, open the message, and download the virus. The moral to this story is that users should be required to provide some type of authentication information (password, smart card, PIN, or the like) before being able to use private keys. Otherwise, the keys could be used by other individuals or imposters, and authentication and nonrepudiation would be of no use.

Because a private key is a crucial component of any PKI implementation, the key itself should contain the necessary characteristics and be protected at each stage of its life. The following list sums up the characteristics and requirements of proper private key use:

- The key size should provide the necessary level of protection for the environment.
- The lifetime of the key should correspond with how often it is used and the sensitivity of the data it is protecting.
- The key should be changed and not used past its allowed lifetime.
- Where appropriate, the key should be properly destroyed at the end of its lifetime.
- The key should never be exposed in clear text.

- No copies of the private key should be made if it is being used for digital signatures.

- The key should not be shared.

- The key should be stored securely.

- Authentication should be required before the key can be used.

- The key should be transported securely.

- Software implementations that store and use the key should be evaluated to ensure they provide the necessary level of protection.

If digital signatures will be used for legal purposes, these points and others may need to be audited to ensure that true authenticity and nonrepudiation are provided.

Key Recovery

One individual could have one, two, or many key pairs that are tied to his or her identity. That is because users can have different needs and requirements for public/private key pairs. As mentioned earlier, certificates can have specific attributes and usage requirements dictating how their corresponding keys can and cannot be used. For example, David can have one key pair he uses to encrypt and transmit symmetric keys. He can also have one key pair that allows him to encrypt data and another key pair to perform digital signatures. David can also have a digital signature key pair for his work-related activities and another pair for personal activities, such as e-mailing his friends. These key pairs need to be used only for their intended purposes, and this is enforced through certificate attributes and usage values.

If a company is going to perform and maintain a key recovery system, it will generally back up only the key pair used to encrypt data, not the key pairs that are used to generate digital signatures. The reason that a company archives keys is to ensure that if a person leaves the company, falls off a cliff, or for some reason is unavailable to decrypt important company information, the company can still get to its company-owned data. This is just a matter of the organization protecting itself. A company would not need to be able to recover a key pair that is used for digital signatures, since those keys are to be used only to prove the authenticity of the individual who sent a message. A company would not benefit from having access to those keys and really should not have access to them, since they are tied to one individual for a specific purpose.

CA Private Key

The most sensitive and critical public/private key pairs are those used by CAs to digitally sign certificates. These need to be highly protected because if they were compromised, the trust relationship between the CA and all of the end-entities would be threatened. In high security environments, these keys are often kept in a tamper-proof hardware encryption store, only accessible to individuals with a need to access.

Two systems are important for backing up and restoring cryptographic keys: key archiving and key recovery. The *key archiving system* is a way of backing up keys and securely storing them in a repository; *key recovery* is the process of restoring lost keys to the users or the company.

If keys are backed up and stored in a centralized computer, this system must be tightly controlled, because if it were compromised, an attacker would have access to all keys for the entire infrastructure. Also, it is usually unwise to authorize a single person to be able to recover all the keys within the environment, because that person could use this power for evil purposes instead of just recovering keys when they are needed for legitimate purposes. In security systems, it is best not to fully trust anyone.

 EXAM TIP Key Archiving is the process of storing a set of keys to be used as a backup should something happen to the original set. Key recovery is the process of using the backup keys.

Dual control can be used as part of a system to back up and archive data encryption keys. PKI systems can be configured to allow multiple individuals to be involved in any key recovery process. When a key recovery is required, at least two people can be required to authenticate by the key recovery software before the recovery procedure is performed. This enforces *separation of duties,* which means that one person cannot complete a critical task by himself. Requiring two individuals to recover a lost key together is called *dual control,* which simply means that two people have to be present to carry out a specific task.

This approach to key recovery is referred to as the *m of n authentication,* where *n* number of people can be involved in the key recovery process, but at least *m* (which is a smaller number than *n*) *must* be involved before the task can be completed. The goal is to minimize fraudulent or improper use of access and permissions. A company would not require all possible individuals to be involved in the recovery process, because getting all the people together at the same time could be impossible considering meetings, vacations, sick time, and travel. At least some of all possible individuals must be available to participate, and this is the subset *m* of the number *n*. This form of secret splitting can increase security by requiring multiple people to perform a specific function. Too many people can increase issues associated with availability, too few increases the risk of a small number of people compromising a secret.

 EXAM TIP Secret splitting using m of n authentication schemes can improve security by requiring that multiple people perform critical functions, preventing a single party from compromising a secret.

All key recovery procedures should be highly audited. The audit logs should capture at least what keys were recovered, who was involved in the process, and the time and date. Keys are an integral piece of any encryption cryptosystem and are critical to a PKI environment, so you need to track who does what with them.

Key Escrow

Key recovery and *key escrow* are terms that are often used interchangeably, but they actually describe two different things. *You* should not use them interchangeably after you have read this section.

Key recovery is a process that allows for lost keys to be recovered. *Key escrow* is a process of giving keys to a third party so that they can decrypt and read sensitive information when this need arises. Key escrow almost always pertains to handing over encryption keys to the government, or to another higher authority, so that the keys can be used to collect evidence during investigations. A key pair used in a person's place of work may be required to be escrowed by the employer for obvious reasons. First, the keys are property of the enterprise, issued to the worker for use. Second, the firm may have need for them after an employee leaves the firm.

Several movements, supported by parts of the U.S. government, would require all or many people residing in the United States to hand over copies of the keys they use to encrypt communication channels. The movement in the late '90s behind the Clipper Chip is the most well-known effort to implement this requirement and procedure. It was suggested that all American-made communication devices should have a hardware encryption chip within them. The chip could be used to encrypt data going back and forth between two individuals, but if a government agency decided that they should be able to eavesdrop on this dialog, they would just need to obtain a court order. If the court order was approved, the law enforcement agent would take the order to two escrow agencies, each of which would have a piece of the key that was necessary to decrypt this communication information. The agent would obtain both pieces of the key and combine them, which would allow the agent to listen in on the encrypted communication outlined in the court order.

EXAM TIP   Key escrow, allowing another trusted party to hold a copy of a key, has long been a controversial topic. This essential business process provides continuity should the authorized key holding party leave an organization without disclosing keys. The security of the escrowed key is a concern, and it needs to be managed at the same security level as for the original key.

This was a standard that never saw the light of day because it seemed too "Big Brother" to many American citizens. But the idea was that the encryption keys would be escrowed to two agencies, meaning that each agency would hold one piece of the key. One agency could not hold the whole key, because it could then use this key to wiretap people's conversations illegally. Splitting up the key is an example of separation of duties, put into place to try and prevent fraudulent activities. The current issue of governments demanding access to keys to decrypt information is covered in Chapter 3.

Public Certificate Authorities

An individual or company may decide to rely on a CA that is already established and being used by many other individuals and companies—this would be a *public CA*. A company, on the other hand, may decide that it needs its own CA for internal use, which gives the company more control over the certificate registration and generation process and allows it to configure items specifically for its own needs. This second type of CA is referred to as a *private CA* (or *in-house CA*).

A public CA specializes in verifying individual identities and creating and maintaining their certificates. These companies issue certificates that are not bound to specific companies or intercompany departments. Instead, their services are to be used by a larger and more diversified group of people and organizations. If a company uses a public CA, the company will pay the CA organization for individual certificates and for the service of maintaining these certificates. Some examples of public CAs are VeriSign (including GeoTrust and thawte), Entrust, and Go Daddy.

One advantage of using a public CA is that it is usually well known and easily accessible to many people. Most web browsers have a list of public CAs installed and configured by default, along with their corresponding root certificates. This means that if you install a web browser on your computer, it is already configured to trust certain CAs, even though you might have never heard of them before. So, if you receive a certificate from Bob, and his certificate was digitally signed by a CA listed in your browser, you can automatically trust the CA and can easily walk through the process of verifying Bob's certificate. This has raised some eyebrows among security professionals, however, since trust is installed by default, but the industry has deemed this is a necessary approach that provides users with transparency and increased functionality. Users can remove these CAs from their browser list if they want to have more control over who their system trusts and who it doesn't.

Earlier in the chapter, the different certificate classes and their uses were explained. No global standard defines these classes, the exact requirements for obtaining these different certificates, or their uses. Standards are in place, usually for a particular country or industry, but this means that public CAs can define their own certificate classifications. This is not necessarily a good thing for companies that depend on public CAs, because it does not provide enough control to the company over how it should interpret certificate classifications and how they should be used.

This means another component needs to be carefully developed for companies that use and depend on public CAs, and this component is referred to as the *certificate policy (CP)*. This policy allows the company to decide what certification classes are acceptable and how they will be used within the organization. This is different from the CPS, which explains how the CA verifies entities, generates certificates, and maintains these certificates. The CP is generated and owned by an individual company that uses an external CA, and it allows the company to enforce *its* security decisions and control how certificates are used with its applications.

In-house Certificate Authorities

An *in-house CA* is implemented, maintained, and controlled by the company that implemented it. This type of CA can be used to create certificates for internal employees, devices, applications, partners, and customers. This approach gives the company complete control over how individuals are identified, what certification classifications are created, who can and cannot have access to the CA, and how the certifications can be used.

In-house CAs also provide more flexibility for companies, which often integrate them into current infrastructures and into applications for authentication, encryption, and nonrepudiation purposes. If the CA is going to be used over an extended period of time, this can be a cheaper method of generating and using certificates than having to purchase them through a public CA.

When the decision between an in-house and public CA is made, various factors need to be identified and accounted for. Many companies have embarked upon implementing an in-house PKI environment, which they estimated would be implemented within x number of months and would cost approximately y amount in dollars. Without doing the proper homework, companies might not understand the current environment, might not completely hammer out the intended purpose of the PKI, and might not have enough skilled staff supporting the project; time estimates can double or triple and the required funds and resources can become unacceptable. Several companies have started on a PKI implementation, only to quit halfway through, resulting in wasted time and money, with nothing to show for it except heaps of frustration and many ulcers.

In some situations, it is better for a company to use a public CA, since public CAs already have the necessary equipment, skills, and technologies. In other situations, companies may decide it is a better business decision to take on these efforts themselves. This is not always a strictly monetary decision—a specific level of security might be required. Some companies do not believe that they can trust an outside authority to generate and maintain their users' and company's certificates. In this situation, the scale may tip toward an in-house CA.

Each company is unique, with various goals, security requirements, functionality needs, budgetary restraints, and ideologies. The decision to use a private or in-house CA depends on the expansiveness of the PKI within the organization, how integrated it will be with different business needs and goals, its interoperability with a company's current technologies, the number of individuals who will be participating, and how it will work with outside entities. This could be quite a large undertaking that ties up staff, resources, and funds, so a lot of strategic planning is required, and what will and won't be gained from a PKI should be fully understood before the first dollar is spent on the implementation.

Outsourced Certificate Authorities

The last available option for using PKI components within a company is to outsource different parts of it to a specific service provider. Usually, the more complex parts are outsourced, such as the CA, RA, CRL, and key recovery mechanisms. This occurs if a company does not have the necessary skills to implement and carry out a full PKI environment.

An *outsourced* CA is different from a public CA in that it provides dedicated services, and possibly equipment, to an individual company. A public CA, in contrast, can be used by hundreds or thousands of companies—the CA doesn't maintain specific servers and infrastructures for individual companies.

Although outsourced services might be easier for your company to implement, you need to review several factors before making this type of commitment. You need to determine what level of trust the company is willing to give to the service provider and what level of risk it is willing to accept. Often a PKI and its components serve as large security components within a company's enterprise, and allowing a third party to maintain the PKI can introduce too many risks and liabilities that your company is not willing to undertake. The liabilities the service provider is willing to accept, security precautions and procedures the outsourced CAs provide, and the surrounding legal issues need to be examined before this type of agreement is made.

Some large vertical markets have their own outsourced PKI environments set up because they share similar needs and usually have the same requirements for certification types and uses. This allows several companies within the same market to split the costs of the necessary equipment, and it allows for industry-specific standards to be drawn up and followed. For example, although many medical facilities work differently and have different environments, they have a lot of the same functionality and security needs. If several of them came together, purchased the necessary equipment to provide CA, RA, and CRL functionality, employed one person to maintain it, and then each connected its different sites to the centralized components, both organizations could save a lot of money and resources. In this case, not every facility would need to strategically plan its own full PKI, and each would not need to purchase redundant equipment or employ redundant staff members. Figure 5-10 illustrates how one outsourced service provider can offer different PKI components and services to different companies, and how companies within one vertical market can share the same resources.

A set of standards can be drawn up about how each different facility should integrate its own infrastructure and how they should integrate with the centralized PKI components. This also allows for less complicated intercommunication to take place between the different medical facilities, which will ease information-sharing attempts.

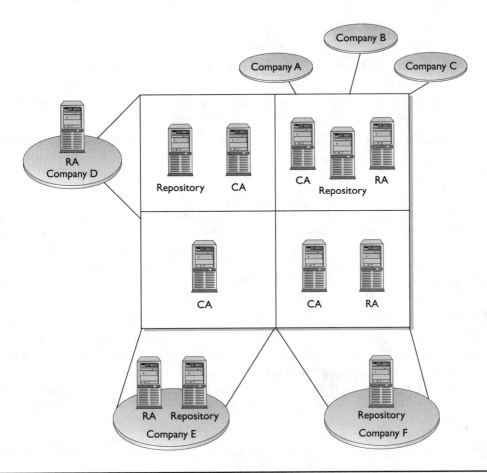

Figure 5-10 A PKI service provider (represented by the four boxes) can offer different PKI components to companies.

Tying Different PKIs Together

In some cases, more than one CA can be needed for a specific PKI to work properly, and several requirements must be met for different PKIs to intercommunicate. Here are some examples:

- A company wants to be able to communicate seamlessly with its suppliers, customers, or business partners via PKI.

- One department within a company has higher security requirements than all other departments and thus needs to configure and control its own CA.

- One department needs to have specially constructed certificates with unique fields and usages.

- Different parts of an organization want to control their own pieces of the network and the CA that is encompassed within it.

- The number of certificates that need to be generated and maintained would overwhelm one CA, so multiple CAs must be deployed.

- The political culture of a company inhibits one department from being able to control elements of another department.

- Enterprises are partitioned geographically, and different sites need their own local CA.

These situations can add much more complexity to the overall infrastructure, inter-communication capabilities, and procedures for certificate generation and validation. To control this complexity properly from the beginning, these requirements need to be understood, addressed, and planned for. Then the necessary trust model needs to be chosen and molded for the company to build upon. Selecting the right trust model will give the company a solid foundation from the beginning, instead of trying to add structure to an inaccurate and inadequate plan later on.

Trust Models

There is more involved in potential scenarios than just having more than one CA—each of the companies or each department of an enterprise can actually represent a trust domain itself. A *trust domain* is a construct of systems, personnel, applications, protocols, technologies, and policies that work together to provide a certain level of protection. All of these components can work together seamlessly within the same trust domain because they are known to the other components within the domain and are trusted to some degree. Different trust domains are usually managed by different groups of administrators, have different security policies, and restrict outsiders from privileged access.

Most trust domains (whether individual companies or departments) are not usually islands cut off from the world—they need to communicate with other less-trusted domains. The trick is to figure out how much two different domains should trust each other, and how to implement and configure an infrastructure that would allow these two domains to communicate in a way that will not allow security compromises or breaches. This can be more difficult than it sounds.

In the nondigital world, it is difficult to figure out who to trust, how to carry out legitimate business functions, and how to ensure that one is not being taken advantage of or lied to. Jump into the digital world and add protocols, services, encryption, CAs, RAs, CRLs, and differing technologies and applications, and the business risks can become overwhelming and confusing. So start with a basic question: What criteria will we use to determine who we trust and to what degree?

One example of trust considered earlier in the chapter is the driver's license issued by the DMV. Suppose, for example, that Bob is buying a lamp from Carol and he wants to pay by check. Since Carol does not know Bob, she does not know if she can trust him or have much faith in his check. But if Bob shows Carol his driver's license, she can compare the name to what appears on the check, and she can choose to accept it. The *trust anchor* (the agreed-upon trusted third party) in this scenario is the DMV, since both Carol and Bob trust it more than they trust each other. Since Bob had to provide documentation to prove his identity to the DMV, that organization trusted him enough to generate a license, and Carol trusts the DMV, so she decides to trust Bob's check.

Consider another example of a trust anchor. If Joe and Stacy need to communicate through e-mail and would like to use encryption and digital signatures, they will not trust each other's certificate alone. But when each receives the other's certificate and sees that they both have been digitally signed by an entity they both do trust—the CA—then they have a deeper level of trust in each other. The trust anchor here is the CA. This is easy enough, but when we need to establish trust anchors between different CAs and PKI environments, it gets a little more complicated.

When two companies need to communicate using their individual PKIs, or if two departments within the same company use different CAs, two separate trust domains are involved. The users and devices from these different trust domains will need to communicate with each other, and they will need to exchange certificates and public keys. This means that trust anchors need to be identified, and a communication channel must be constructed and maintained.

A trust relationship must be established between two issuing authorities (CAs). This happens when one or both of the CAs issue a certificate for the other CA's public key, as shown in Figure 5-11. This means that each CA registers for a certificate and public key from the other CA. Each CA validates the other CA's identification information and generates a certificate containing a public key for that CA to use. This establishes a trust path between the two entities that can then be used when users need to verify other users' certificates that fall within the different trust domains. The trust path can be unidirectional or bidirectional, so either the two CAs trust each other (bidirectional) or only one trusts the other (unidirectional).

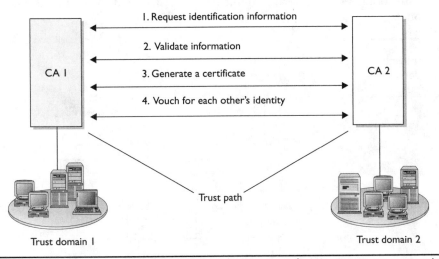

Figure 5-11 A trust relationship can be built between two trust domains to set up a communication channel.

As illustrated in Figure 5-11, all the users and devices in trust domain 1 trust their own CA 1, which is their trust anchor. All users and devices in trust domain 2 have their own trust anchor, CA 2. The two CAs have exchanged certificates and trust each other, but they do not have a common trust anchor between them.

The trust models describe and outline the trust relationships between the different CAs and different environments, which will indicate where the trust paths reside. The trust models and paths need to be thought out before implementation to restrict and control access properly and to ensure that as few trust paths as possible are used. Several different trust models can be used: the hierarchical, peer-to-peer, and hybrid models are discussed in the following sections.

Hierarchical Trust Model

The first type of trust model we'll examine is a basic hierarchical structure that contains a root CA, an intermediate CAs, leaf CAs, and end-entities. The configuration is that of an inverted tree, as shown in Figure 5-12. The root CA is the ultimate trust anchor for all other entities in this infrastructure, and it generates certificates for the intermediate CAs, which in turn generate certificates for the leaf CAs, and the leaf CAs generate certificates for the end-entities (users, network devices, and applications).

Intermediate CAs function to transfer trust between different CAs. These CAs are referred to as *subordinate CAs* as they are subordinate to the CA that they reference. The path of trust is walked up from the subordinate CA to the higher level CA; in essence the subordinate CA is using the higher CA as a reference.

As shown in Figure 5-12, no bidirectional trusts exist—they are all unidirectional trusts as indicated by the one-way arrows. Since no other entity can certify and generate certificates for the root CA, it creates a *self-signed certificate*. This means that the certificate's issuer and subject fields hold the same information, both representing the root CA, and the root CA's public key will be used to verify this certificate when that time comes. This root CA certificate and public key are distributed to all entities within this trust model.

Figure 5-12

The hierarchical trust model outlines trust paths.

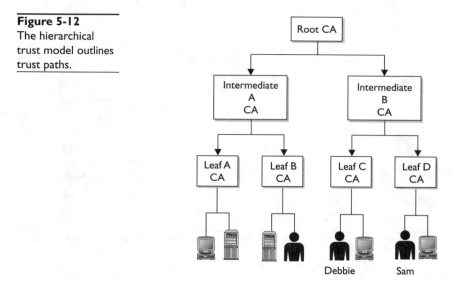

Root CA

If the root CA's private key was ever compromised, all entities within the hierarchical trust model would be drastically affected, because this is their sole trust anchor. The root CA usually has a small amount of interaction with the intermediate CAs and end-entities, and can therefore be taken offline much of the time. This provides a greater degree of protection for the root CA, because when it is offline it is basically inaccessible.

Walking the Certificate Path

When a user in one trust domain needs to communicate with another user in another trust domain, one user will need to validate the other's certificate. This sounds simple enough, but what it really means is that each certificate for each CA, all the way up to a shared trusted anchor, also must be validated. If Debbie needs to validate Sam's certificate, as shown in Figure 5-12, she actually also needs to validate the Leaf D CA and Intermediate B CA certificates, as well as Sam's.

So in Figure 5-12, we have a user, Sam, who digitally signs a message and sends it and his certificate to Debbie. Debbie needs to validate this certificate before she can trust Sam's digital signature. Included in Sam's certificate is an issuer field, which indicates that the certificate was issued by Leaf D CA. Debbie has to obtain Leaf D CA's digital certificate and public key to validate Sam's certificate. Remember that Debbie validates the certificate by verifying its digital signature. The digital signature was created by the certificate issuer using its private key, so Debbie needs to verify the signature using the issuer's public key.

Debbie tracks down Leaf D CA's certificate and public key, but she now needs to verify this CA's certificate, so she looks at the issuer field, which indicates that Leaf D CA's certificate was issued by Intermediate B CA. Debbie now needs to get Intermediate B CA's certificate and public key.

Debbie's client software tracks this down and sees that the issuer for the Intermediate B CA is the root CA, for which she already has a certificate and public key. So Debbie's client software had to follow the *certificate path*, meaning it had to continue to track down and collect certificates until it came upon a self-signed certificate. A self-signed certificate indicates that it was signed by a root CA, and Debbie's software has been configured to trust this entity as her trust anchor, so she can stop there. Figure 5-13 illustrates the steps Debbie's software had to carry out just to be able to verify Sam's certificate.

This type of simplistic trust model works well within an enterprise that easily follows a hierarchical organizational chart, but many companies cannot use this type of trust model because different departments or offices require their own trust anchors. These demands can be derived from direct business needs or from interorganizational politics. This hierarchical model might not be possible when two or more companies need to communicate with each other. Neither company will let the other's CA be the root CA, because each does not necessarily trust the other entity to that degree. In these situations, the CAs will need to work in a peer-to-peer relationship instead of in a hierarchical relationship.

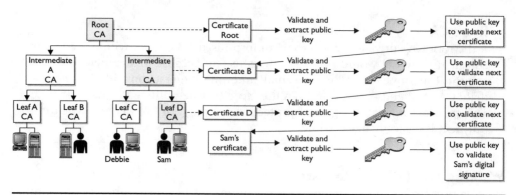

Figure 5-13   Verifying each certificate in a certificate path

Peer-to-Peer Model

In a *peer-to-peer* trust model, one CA is not subordinate to another CA, and no established trusted anchor between the CAs is involved. The end-entities will look to their issuing CA as their trusted anchor, but the different CAs will not have a common anchor.

Figure 5-14 illustrates this type of trust model. The two different CAs will certify the public key for each other, which creates a bidirectional trust. This is referred to as *cross certification*, since the CAs are not receiving their certificates and public keys from a superior CA, but instead they are creating them for each other.

One of the main drawbacks to this model is scalability. Each CA must certify every other CA that is participating, and a bidirectional trust path must be implemented, as shown in Figure 5-15. If one root CA were certifying all the intermediate CAs, scalability would not be as much of an issue. Figure 5-15 represents a fully connected *mesh architecture*, meaning that each CA is directly connected to and has a bidirectional trust relationship with every other CA. As you can see in this illustration, the complexity of this setup can become overwhelming.

Hybrid Trust Model

A company can be complex within itself, and when the need arises to communicate properly with outside partners, suppliers, and customers in an authorized and secured manner, it can make sticking to either the hierarchical or peer-to-peer trust model dif-

Figure 5-14
Cross certification
creates a peer-to-
peer PKI model.

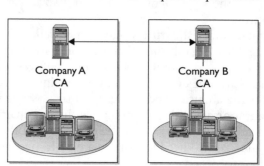

Figure 5-15
Scalability is a
drawback in cross-
certification models.

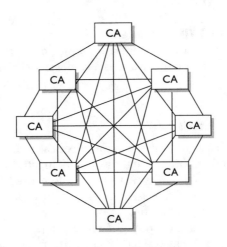

ficult, if not impossible. In many implementations, the different model types have to be combined to provide the necessary communication lines and levels of trust. In a *hybrid* trust model, the two companies have their own internal hierarchical models and are connected through a peer-to-peer model using cross certification.

Another option in this hybrid configuration is to implement a *bridge CA*. Figure 5-16 illustrates the role that a bridge CA could play—it is responsible for issuing cross certificates for all connected CAs and trust domains. The bridge is not considered a root or trust anchor, but merely the entity that generates and maintains the cross certification for the connected environments.

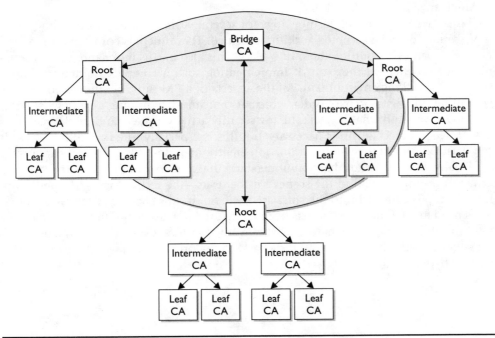

Figure 5-16   A bridge CA can control the cross-certification procedures.

EXAM TIP Three trust models exist: hierarchical, peer-to-peer, and hybrid. Hierarchical trust is like an upside down tree. Peer-to-peer is a lateral series of references, and hybrid is a combination of hierarchical and peer-to-peer trust.

Chapter Review

Public key infrastructures can be complex beasts, as this chapter has shown. They have many different components that must work together seamlessly to provide the expected protection and functionality. A PKI is implemented to provide users and devices with the ability to communicate securely and to provide them with trust anchors, since they do not directly trust each other.

Certificate registration requests are validated by a registration authority (RA), and the certificate is then generated by a certificate authority (CA). The digital certificate binds an individual's identity to the public key that is within the certificate.

Certificates can expire, be revoked, or be suspended. When a user receives a certificate from another user, the other user must be validated, which means that the CA's digital signature that is embedded within the certificate itself must be validated. This can require that the receiving user validate a whole string of certificates and digital signatures, referred to as a *certificate path*. This path must be followed until a self-signed trusted root certificate is reached.

Certificate authorities can be public, private (in-house), or outsourced, depending on a company's needs. Internal PKIs can follow different trust models, which will dictate their trust paths and anchors.

PKIs have been waiting in the wings for several years—waiting for the time when they would finally be accepted and implemented. That time has come, and more and more companies are putting them into place. This also means more and more companies have experienced the pain of implementing such a complex framework into a preexisting working environment. All the aspects of a PKI must be understood before you fill out the first purchase order, which also means determining exactly what a PKI will do for you and what it won't. In any security activity, understanding the reality of any protection mechanism is necessary, but this is especially true for a PKI because it can drastically affect the whole production environment in both good and bad ways.

Finally, it is important that you understand that a majority of these authentication activities take place behind the scenes for the users—the technology and intelligence have been programmed into the software itself. So, in this chapter, when we said that users need to see if their system has been configured to trust a specific CA, or that they need to validate a digital signature or obtain a higher-level CA certificate, the user's *client software* is actually carrying out these tasks. A majority of what was discussed in this chapter happens *transparently* to the users.

Questions

1. When a user wants to participate in a PKI, what component does he or she need to obtain, and how does that happen?

    A. The user submits a certification request to the CA.

    B. The user submits a key pair request to the CRL.

    C. The user submits a certification request to the RA.

    D. The user submits proof of identification to the CA.

2. How does a user validate a digital certificate that is received from another user?

    A. The user will first see whether her system has been configured to trust the CA that digitally signed the other user's certificate and will then validate that CA's digital signature.

    B. The user will calculate a message digest and compare it to the one attached to the message.

    C. The user will first see whether her system has been configured to trust the CA that digitally signed the certificate and then will validate the public key that is embedded within the certificate.

    D. The user will validate the sender's digital signature on the message.

3. What is the purpose of a digital certificate?

    A. It binds a CA to a user's identity.

    B. It binds a CA's identity to the correct RA.

    C. It binds an individual to an RA.

    D. It binds an individual to a public key.

4. What steps does a user take to validate a CA's digital signature on a digital certificate?

    A. The user's software creates a message digest for the digital certificate and decrypts the encrypted message digest included within the digital certificate. If the decryption performs properly and the message digest values are the same, the certificate is validated.

    B. The user's software creates a message digest for the digital signature and encrypts the message digest included within the digital certificate. If the encryption performs properly and the message digest values are the same, the certificate is validated.

    C. The user's software creates a message digest for the digital certificate and decrypts the encrypted message digest included within the digital certificate. If the user can encrypt the message digest properly with the CA's private key and the message digest values are the same, the certificate is validated.

     D. The user's software creates a message digest for the digital signature and encrypts the message digest with its private key. If the decryption performs properly and the message digest values are the same, the certificate is validated.

5. What is a bridge CA, and what is its function?

     A. It is a hierarchical trust model that establishes a root CA, which is the trust anchor for all other CAs.

     B. It is an entity that creates and maintains the CRL for several CAs at one time.

     C. It is a CA that handles the cross-certification certificates for two or more CAs in a peer-to-peer relationship.

     D. It is an entity that validates the user's identity information for the RA before the request goes to the CA.

6. Why would a company implement a key archiving and recovery system within the organization?

     A. To make sure all data encryption keys are available for the company if and when it needs them

     B. To make sure all digital signature keys are available for the company if and when it needs them

     C. To create session keys for users to be able to access when they need to encrypt bulk data

     D. To back up the RA's private key for retrieval purposes

7. Within a PKI environment, where does the majority of the trust actually lie?

     A. All users and devices within an environment trust the RA, which allows them to indirectly trust each other.

     B. All users and devices within an environment trust the CA, which allows them to indirectly trust each other.

     C. All users and devices within an environment trust the CRL, which allows them to indirectly trust each other.

     D. All users and devices within an environment trust the CPS, which allows them to indirectly trust each other.

8. Which of the following properly explains the *m of n control*?

     A. This is the process a user must go through to properly register for a certificate through the RA.

     B. This ensures that a certificate has to be fully validated by a user before he can extract the public key and use it.

     C. This is a control in key recovery to enforce separation of duties.

     D. This is a control in key recovery to ensure that the company cannot recover a user's key without the user's consent.

9. Which of the following is not a valid field that could be present in an X.509 version 3 digital certificate?

   A. Validity dates

   B. Serial number

   C. Extensions

   D. Symmetric key

10. To what does a certificate path pertain?

    A. All of the digital certificates that need to be validated before a received certificate can be fully validated and trusted

    B. All of the digital certificates that need to be validated before a sent certificate can be properly encrypted

    C. All of the digital certificates that need to be validated before a user trusts her own trust anchor

    D. All of the digital certificates that need to be validated before a received certificate can be destroyed

11. Which of the following certificate characteristics was expanded upon with version 3 of the X.509 standard?

    A. Subject

    B. Extensions

    C. Digital signature

    D. Serial number

12. What is a certification practices statement (CPS), and what is its purpose?

    A. A CPS outlines the steps a CA goes through to validate identities and generate certificates. Companies should review this document to ensure that the CA follows the necessary steps the company requires and provides the necessary level of protection.

    B. A CPS outlines the steps a CA goes through to communicate with other CAs in other states. Companies should review this document to ensure that the CA follows the necessary steps the company requires and provides the necessary level of protection.

    C. A CPS outlines the steps a CA goes through to set up an RA at a company's site. Companies should review this document to ensure that the CA follows the necessary steps the company requires and provides the necessary level of protection.

    D. A CPS outlines the steps a CA goes through to become a business within a vertical market. Companies should review this document to ensure that the CA follows the necessary steps the company requires and provides the necessary level of protection.

13. Which of the following properly describes what a public key infrastructure (PKI) actually is?

 A. A protocol written to work with a large subset of algorithms, applications, and protocols

 B. An algorithm that creates public/private key pairs

 C. A framework that outlines specific technologies and algorithms that must be used

 D. A framework that does not specify any technologies, but provides a foundation for confidentiality, integrity, and availability services

14. Once an individual validates another individual's certificate, what is the use of the public key that is extracted from this digital certificate?

 A. The public key is now available to use to create digital signatures.

 B. The user can now encrypt session keys and messages with this public key and can validate the sender's digital signatures.

 C. The public key is now available to encrypt future digital certificates that need to be validated.

 D. The user can now encrypt private keys that need to be transmitted securely.

15. Why would a digital certificate be added to a certificate revocation list (CRL)?

 A. If the public key had become compromised in a public repository

 B. If the private key had become compromised

 C. If a new employee joined the company and received a new certificate

 D. If the certificate expired

16. What is an online CRL service?

 A. End-entities can send a request containing a serial number of a specific certificate to an online CRL service. The online service will query several CRL distribution points and respond with information about whether the certificate is still valid or not.

 B. CAs can send a request containing the expiration date of a specific certificate to an online CRL service. The online service will query several other RAs and respond with information about whether the certificate is still valid or not.

 C. End-entities can send a request containing a public key of a specific certificate to an online CRL service. The online service will query several end-entities and respond with information about whether the certificate is still valid or not.

 D. End-entities can send a request containing a public key of a specific CA to an online CRL service. The online service will query several RA distribution points and respond with information about whether the CA is still trustworthy or not.

17. If an extension is marked as critical, what does this indicate?

    A. If the CA is not programmed to understand and process this extension, the certificate and corresponding keys can be used for their intended purpose.

    B. If the end-entity is programmed to understand and process this extension, the certificate and corresponding keys cannot be used.

    C. If the RA is not programmed to understand and process this extension, communication with the CA is not allowed.

    D. If the end-entity is not programmed to understand and process this extension, the certificate and corresponding keys cannot be used.

18. How can users have faith that the CRL was not modified to present incorrect information?

    A. The CRL is digitally signed by the CA.

    B. The CRL is encrypted by the CA.

    C. The CRL is open for anyone to post certificate information to.

    D. The CRL is accessible only to the CA.

19. When would a certificate be suspended, and where is that information posted?

    A. It would be suspended when an employee leaves the company. It is posted on the CRL.

    B. It would be suspended when an employee changes his or her last name. It is posted on the CA.

    C. It would be suspended when an employee goes on vacation. It is posted on the CRL.

    D. It would be suspended when a private key is compromised. It is posted on the CRL.

20. What does cross certification pertain to in a PKI environment?

    A. When a company uses an outsourced service provider, it needs to modify its CPS to allow for cross certification to take place between the RA and CA.

    B. When two end-entities need to communicate in a PKI, they need to exchange certificates.

    C. When two or more CAs need to trust each other so that their end-entities can communicate, they will create certificates for each other.

    D. A RA needs to perform a cross certification with a user before the certificate registration is terminated.

Answers

1. **C.** The user must submit identification data and a certification request to the registration authority (RA). The RA validates this information and sends the certification request to the certificate authority (CA).

2. **A.** A digital certificate is validated by the receiver by first determining whether her system has been configured to trust the CA that digitally signed the certificate. If this has been configured, the user's software uses the CA's public key and validates the CA's digital signature that is embedded within the certificate.

3. **D.** A digital certificate vouches for an individual's identity and binds that identity to the public key that is embedded within the certificate.

4. **A.** The user's software calculates a message digest for the digital certificate and decrypts the encrypted message digest value included with the certificate, which is the digital signature. The message digest is decrypted using the CA's public key. If the two message digest values match, the user knows that the certificate has not been modified in an unauthorized manner, and since the encrypted message digest can be decrypted properly with the CA's public key, the user is assured that this CA created the certificate.

5. **C.** A bridge CA is set up to handle all of the cross-certification certificates and traffic between different CAs and trust domains. A bridge CA is used instead of requiring all of the CAs to authenticate to each other and create certificates with one another, which would end up in a full mesh configuration.

6. **A.** To protect itself, the company will make backups of the data encryption keys its employees use for encrypting company information. If an employee is no longer available, the company must make sure that it still has access to its own business data. Companies should not need to back up digital signature keys, since they are not used to encrypt data.

7. **B.** The trust anchor for a PKI environment is the CA. All users and devices trust the CA, which allows them to indirectly trust each other. The CA verifies and vouches for each user's and device's identity, so these different entities can have confidence that they are communicating with specific individuals.

8. **C.** The m of n control is the part of the key recovery software that allows a certain number of people to be involved with recovering and reconstructing a lost or corrupted key. A certain number of people (*n*) are allowed to authenticate to the software, which will allow them to participate in the key recovery process. Not all of those people may be available at one time, however, so a larger number of people (*m*) need to be involved with the process. The system should not allow only one person to carry out key recovery, because that person could then use the keys for fraudulent purposes.

9. **D.** The first three values are valid fields that are used in digital certificates. Validity dates indicate how long the certificate is good for, the serial number

is a unique value used to identify individual certificates, and extensions allow companies to expand the use of their certificates. A public key is included in the certificate, which is an asymmetric key, not a symmetric key.

10. **A.** The certificate path is all of the certificates that must be validated before the receiver of a certificate can validate and trust the newly received certificate. When a user receives a certificate, she must obtain the certificate and public key of all of the CAs until she comes to a self-signed certificate, which is the trusted anchor. So the user must validate each of these certificates until the trusted anchor is reached. The path between the receiver and a trusted anchor is referred to as the certificate path. This is a hierarchical model of trust, and each rung of the trust model must be verified before the end user's certificate can be validated and trusted.

11. **B.** The X.509 standard is currently at version 3, which added more extension capabilities to digital certificates and which added more flexibility for companies using PKIs. Companies can define many of these extensions to mean specific things that are necessary for their proprietary or customized environment and software.

12. **A.** The CPS outlines the certificate classes the CA uses and the CA's procedures for verifying end-entity identities, generating certificates, and maintaining the certificates throughout their lifetimes. Any company that will be using a specific CA needs to make sure it is going through these procedures with the level of protection the company would require of itself. The company will be putting a lot of trust in the CA, so the company should do some homework and investigate how the CA actually accomplishes its tasks.

13. **D.** A PKI is a framework that allows several different types of technologies, applications, algorithms, and protocols to be plugged into it. The goal is to provide a foundation that can provide a hierarchical trust model, which will allow end-entities to indirectly trust each other and allow for secure and trusted communications.

14. **B.** Once a receiver validates a digital certificate, the embedded public key can be extracted and used to encrypt symmetric session keys, encrypt messages, and validate the sender's digital signatures.

15. **B.** Certificates are added to a CRL the public/private key pair should no longer be bound to a specific person's identity. This can happen if a private key is compromised, meaning that it was stolen or captured—this would mean someone else could be using the private key instead of the original user, so the CRL is a protection mechanism that will alert others in the PKI of this incident. Certificates can be added to the CRL if an employee leaves the company or is no longer affiliated with the company for one reason or another. Expired certificates are not added to CRLs.

16. **A.** Actually getting the data on the CRLs to end-entities is a huge barrier for many PKI implementations. The environment can have distribution points

set up, which provide centralized places that allow the users' systems to query to see whether a certificate has been revoked or not. Another approach is to push down the CRLs to each end-entity or to use an online service. The online service will do the busy work for the end-entity by querying all the available CRLs and returning a response to the end-entity indicating whether the certificate has been revoked or not.

17. **D.** Digital certificates have extensions that allow companies to expand the use of certificates within their environments. When a CA creates a certificate, it is certifying the key pair to be used for a specific purpose (for digital signatures, data encryption, validating a CA's digital signature, and so on). If a CA adds a critical flag to an extension, it is stating that the key pair can be used only for the reason stated in the extension. If an end-entity receives a certificate with this critical flag set and cannot understand and process the marked extension, the key pair cannot be used at all. The CA is stating, "I will allow the key pair to be used only for this purpose and under these circumstances." If an extension is marked noncritical, the end-entity does not have to be able to understand and process that extension.

18. **A.** The CRL contains all of the certificates that have been revoked. Only the CA can post information to this list. The CA then digitally signs the list to ensure that any modifications will be detected. When an end-entity receives a CRL, it verifies the CA's digital signature, which tells the end-entity whether the list has been modified in an unauthorized manner and guarantees that the correct CA signed the list.

19. **C.** A certificate can be suspended if it needs to be temporarily taken out of production for a period of time. If an employee goes on vacation and wants to make sure no one can use his certificate, he can make a suspension request to the CA, which will post the information to the CRL. The other answers in this question would require the certificate to be revoked, not suspended, and a new certificate would need to be created for the user.

20. **C.** Cross certification means that two or more CAs create certificates for each other. This takes place when two trust domains, each with their own CA, need to be able to communicate—a trusted path needs to be established between these domains. Once the first CA validates the other CA's identity and creates a certificate, it then trusts this other CA, which creates a trusted path between the different PKI environments. The trust can be bidirectional or unidirectional.

Standards and Protocols

- Learn about the standards involved in establishing an interoperable Internet PKI
- Understand interoperability issues with PKI standards
- Discover how the common Internet protocols use and implement the PKI standards

One of the biggest growth industries since the 1990s was the commercial use of the Internet. None of the still steadily growing Internet commerce would be possible without the use of standards and protocols that provide a common, interoperable environment for exchanging information securely. Due to the wide distribution of Internet users and businesses, the most practical solution to date has been the commercial implementation of public key infrastructures (PKIs).

This chapter examines the standards and protocols involved in secure Internet transactions and e-business using a PKI. Although you may use only a portion of the related standards and protocols on a daily basis, you should understand how they interact to provide the services that are critical for security: confidentiality, integrity, authentication, and nonrepudiation.

Chapter 5 introduced the algorithms and techniques used to implement a PKI, but as you probably noticed, there is a lot of room for interpretation. Various organizations have developed and implemented standards and protocols that have been accepted as the basis for secure interaction in a PKI environment. These standards fall into three general categories:

- **Standards that define the PKI**   These standards define the data and data structures exchanged and the means for managing that data to provide the functions of the PKI (certificate issuance, storage, revocation, registration, and management).

- **Standards that define the interface between applications and the underlying PKI**   These standards use the PKI to establish the services required by applications.

- **Other standards**   These standards don't fit neatly in either of the other two categories. They provide bits and pieces that glue everything together; they can address not only the PKI structure and the methods and protocols for using it, but they can also provide an overarching business process environment for PKI implementation (for example, ISO/IEC 27002, Common Criteria, and the Federal Information Processing Standards Publications (FIPS PUBS)). Figure 6-1 shows the relationships between these standards and protocols.

Figure 6-1 conveys the interdependence of the standards and protocols discussed in this chapter. The Internet PKI relies on three main standards for establishing interoperable PKI services: PKI X.509 (PKIX), Public Key Cryptography Standards (PKCS), and X.509. Other protocols and standards help define the management and operation of the PKI and related services—Internet Security Association and Key Management Protocol (ISAKMP) and XML Key Management Specification (XKMS) are both key management protocols, while Certificate Management Protocol (CMP) is used for managing certificates. Wired Equivalent Privacy (WEP) is used to encrypt wireless communications in 802.11 environments to support some of the more application-oriented standards and protocols: Secure/Multipurpose Internet Mail Extensions (S/MIME) for e-mail; Secure Sockets Layer (SSL), Transport Layer Security (TLS), and Wireless Transport Layer Security (WTLS) for secure packet transmission; and IP Security (IPsec) and Point-to-Point Tunneling Protocol (PPTP) to support virtual private networks. ISO/IEC 27002 and FIPS PUBS each address security at the business process, application, protocol, and PKI implementation levels. Finally, Pretty Good Privacy (PGP) provides an alternative method spanning the protocol and application levels.

This chapter examines each standard from the bottom up, starting with building an infrastructure through protocols and applications, and finishing with some of the inherent weaknesses of and potential attacks on a PKI.

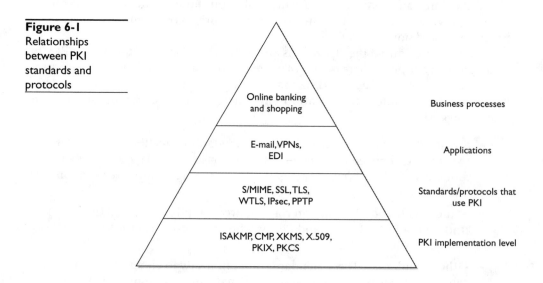

Figure 6-1
Relationships between PKI standards and protocols

PKIX/PKCS

Two main standards have evolved over time to implement PKI on a practical level on the Internet. Both are based on the X.509 certificate standard (discussed shortly in the "X.509" section) and establish complementary standards for implementing PKI. PKIX and PKCS intertwine to define the most commonly used set of standards.

PKIX was produced by the Internet Engineering Task Force (IETF) and defines standards for interactions and operations for four component types: the user (end-entity), certificate authority (CA), registration authority (RA), and the repository for certificates and certificate revocation lists (CRLs). PKCS defines many of the lower level standards for message syntax, cryptographic algorithms, and the like. The PKCS set of standards is a product of RSA Security.

The PKIX working group was formed in 1995 to develop the standards necessary to support PKIs. At the time, the X.509 Public Key Certificate (PKC) format was proposed as the basis for a PKI. X.509 includes information regarding data formats and procedures used for CA-signed PKCs, but it doesn't specify values or formats for many of the fields within the PKC. X.509 v1 (version 1) was originally defined in 1988 as part of the X.500 Directory standard. After being co-opted by the Internet community for implementing certificates for secure Internet communications, X.509's shortcomings became apparent. The current version, X.509 v3, was adopted in 1996. X.509 is very complex, allowing a great deal of flexibility in implementing certificate features. PKIX provides standards for extending and using X.509 v3 certificates and for managing them, enabling interoperability between PKIs following the standards.

PKIX uses the model shown in Figure 6-2 for representing the components and users of a PKI. The user, called an *end-entity*, is not part of the PKI, but end-entities are either users of the PKI certificates, the subject of a certificate (an entity identified by it), or both. The CA is responsible for issuing, storing, and revoking certificates—both PKCs and Attribute Certificates (ACs). The RA is responsible for management activities

Figure 6-2
The PKIX model

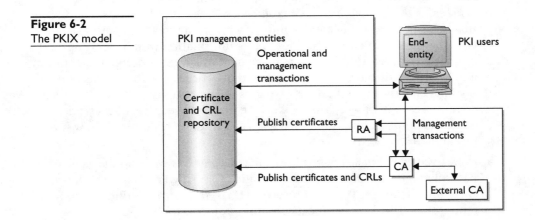

designated by the CA. The RA can, in fact, be a component of the CA rather than a separate component. The final component of the PKIX model is the repository, a system or group of distributed systems that provide certificates and certificate revocation lists to the end-entities.

PKIX Standards

Now that we have looked at how PKIX views the world, let's take a look at what PKIX does. Using X.509 v3, the PKIX working group addresses five major areas:

- *PKIX outlines certificate extensions and content not covered by X.509 v3 and the format of version 2 CRLs, thus providing compatibility standards for sharing certificates and CRLs between CAs and end-entities in different PKIs.* The PKIX profile of the X.509 v3 PKC describes the contents, required extensions, optional extensions, and extensions that need not be implemented. The PKIX profile suggests a range of values for many extensions. In addition, PKIX provides a profile for version 2 CRLs, allowing different PKIs to share revocation information. (For more information on PKIX, see "Internet X.509 Public Key Infrastructure Certificate and CRL Profile" [RFC 5280].)

- *PKIX provides certificate management message formats and protocols, defining the data structures, management messages, and management functions for PKIs.* The working group also addresses the assumptions and restrictions of their protocols. This standard identifies the protocols necessary to support online interactions between entities in the PKIX model. The management protocols support functions for entity registration, initialization of the certificate (possibly key-pair generation), issuance of the certificate, key-pair update, certificate revocation, cross-certification (between CAs), and key-pair recovery if available.

- *PKIX outlines certificate policies and certification practices statements (CPSs), establishing the relationship between policies and CPSs.* A policy is a set of rules that helps determine the applicability of a certificate to an end-entity. For example, a certificate for handling routine information would probably have a policy on creation, storage, and management of key pairs quite different from a policy for certificates used in financial transactions, due to the sensitivity of the financial information. A CPS explains the practices used by a CA to issue certificates. In other words, the CPS is the method used to get the certificate, while the policy defines some characteristics of the certificate and how it will be handled and used.

- *PKIX specifies operational protocols, defining the protocols for certificate handling.* In particular, protocol definitions are specified for using File Transfer Protocol (FTP) and Hypertext Transfer Protocol (HTTP) to retrieve certificates from repositories. These are the most common protocols for applications to use when retrieving certificates.

- *PKIX includes time-stamping and data certification and validation services, which are areas of interest to the PKIX working group, and which will probably grow in use over time.* A time stamp authority (TSA) certifies that a particular entity existed at a particular time. A Data Validation and Certification Server certifies the validity of signed documents, PKCs, and the possession or existence of data. These capabilities support nonrepudiation requirements and are considered building blocks for a nonrepudiation service.

PKCs are the most commonly used certificates, but the PKIX working group has been working on two other types of certificates: Attribute Certificates and Qualified Certificates.

An Attribute Certificate (AC) is used to grant permissions using rule-based, role-based, and rank-based access controls. ACs are used to implement a privilege management infrastructure (PMI). In a PMI, an entity (user, program, system, and so on) is typically identified as a client to a server using a PKC. There are then two possibilities: either the identified client pushes an AC to the server, or the server can query a trusted repository to retrieve the attributes of the client. This situation is modeled in Figure 6-3.

The client push of the AC has the effect of improving performance, but no independent verification of the client's permissions is initiated by the server. The alternative is to have the server pull the information from an AC issuer or a repository. This method is preferable from a security standpoint, because the server or server's domain determines the client's access rights. The pull method has the added benefit of requiring no changes to the client software.

The Qualified Certificate (QC) is based on the term used within the European Commission to identify certificates with specific legislative uses. This concept is generalized in the PKIX QC profile to indicate a certificate used to identify a specific individual (a single human rather than the *entity* of the PKC) with a high level of assurance in a nonrepudiation service.

Table 6-1 summarizes the Internet Requests for Comment (RFCs) that have been produced by the PKIX working group for each of these five areas.

Figure 6-3
The PKIX PMI model

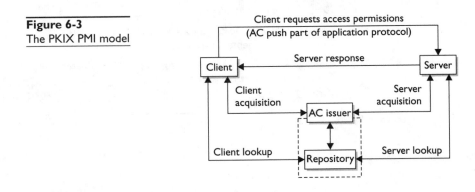

Subject	RFC Number	Title	Notes
Certificates and CRL profiles	RFC 3281	An Internet Attribute Certificate Profile for Authorization	
	RFC 3739	Internet X.509 Public Key Infrastructure: Qualified Certificates Profile	Obsoletes RFC 3039
	RFC 4055	Additional Algorithms and Identifiers for RSA Cryptography for use in the Internet X.509 Public Key Infrastructure Certificate and Certificate Revocation List (CRL) Profile	
	RFC 4476	Attribute Certificate (AC) Policies Extension	
	RFC 5055	Server-based Certificate Validation Protocol (SCVP)	
	RFC 5280	Internet X.509 Public Key Infrastructure Certificate and Certificate Revocation List (CRL) Profile	Obsoletes RFC 4630, RFC 4325, RFC 3280
Certificate management protocols	RFC 2560	X.509 Internet Public Key Infrastructure Online Certificate Status Protocol - OCSP	
	RFC 3709	Internet X.509 Public Key Infrastructure: Logotypes in X.509 certificates	
	RFC 3820	Internet X.509 Public Key Infrastructure Proxy Certificate Profile	
	RFC 4043	Internet X.509 Public Key Infrastructure Permanent Identifier	
	RFC 4059	Internet X.509 Public Key Infrastructure Warranty Certificate Extension	
	RFC 4158	Internet X.509 Public Key Infrastructure: Certification Path Building	
	RFC 4210	Internet X.509 Public Key Infrastructure Certificate Management Protocols	Obsoletes RFC 2510
	RFC 4211	Internet X.509 Public Key Infrastructure Certificate Request Message Format (CRMF)	Obsoletes RFC 2511

Table 6-1 PKIX Subjects and Related RFCs

Subject	RFC Number	Title	Notes
Certificate management protocols	RFC 4386	Internet X.509 Public Key Infrastructure Repository Locator Service	
	RFC 4387	Internet X.509 Public Key Infrastructure Operational Protocols: Certificate Store Access via HTTP	
	RFC 4683	Internet X.509 Public Key Infrastructure Subject Identification Method (SIM)	
	RFC 4985	Internet X.509 Public Key Infrastructure Subject Alternative Name for Expression of Service Name	
	RFC 5272	Certificate Management Messages over CMS	Obsoletes RFC 2797
	RFC 5273	Certificate Management over CMS (CMC): Transport Protocols	
	RFC 5274	Certificate Management Messages over CMS (CMC): Compliance Requirements	
Certificate policies and CPSs	RFC 3647	Internet X.509 Public Key Infrastructure Certificate Policy and Certification Practices Framework	Obsoletes RFC 2527
Operational Protocols	RFC 2528	Internet X.509 Public Key Infrastructure Representation of Key Exchange Algorithm (KEA) Keys in Internet X.509 Public Key Infrastructure Certificates	
	RFC 2585	Internet X.509 Public Key Infrastructure Operational Protocols: FTP and HTTP	
	RFC 3779	X.509 Extensions for IP Addresses and AS Identifiers	
	RFC 4334	Certificate Extensions and Attributes Supporting Authentication in Point-to-Point Protocol (PPP) and Wireless Local Area Networks (WLAN)	Obsoletes RFC 3770
	RFC 5019	The Lightweight Online Certificate Status Protocol (OCSP) Profile for High-Volume Environments	
Time-stamp and data validation	RFC 2875	Diffie-Hellman Proof-of-Possession Algorithms	

Table 6-1   PKIX Subjects and Related RFCs *(continued)*

Subject	RFC Number	Title	Notes
Time-stamp and data validation	RFC 3029	Internet X.509 Public Key Infrastructure Data Validation and Certification Server Protocols	
	RFC 3161	Internet X.509 Public Key Infrastructure Time Stamp Protocols (TSP)	
	RFC 3628	Policy Requirements for Time-Stamping Authorities	
Other PKIX topics	RFC 3279	Algorithms and Identifiers for the Internet X.509 Public Key Infrastructure Certificate and CRI Profile	Updated by RFC 4491
	RFC 3379	Delegated Path Validation and Delegated Path Discovery Protocol Requirements	
	RFC 3874	A 224-bit One-way Hash Function: SHA-224	
	RFC 4491	Using the GOST R 34.10-94, GOST R 34.10-2001 and GOST R 34.11-94 algorithms with the Internet X.509 Public Key Infrastructure Certificate and CRL Profile	Updates RFC 3279

Table 6-1 PKIX Subjects and Related RFCs *(continued)*

Other documents have been produced by the IETF PKIX working group, but those listed in Table 6-1 cover the major implementation details for PKIX. For a complete list of current and pending documents, see the Internet draft for the PKIX working group roadmap (https://datatracker.ietf.org/drafts/draft-ietf-pkix-roadmap/).

PKCS

RSA Laboratories created the Public Key Cryptography Standards (PKCS) to fill some of the gaps in the standards that existed in PKI implementation. As they have with the PKIX standards, PKI developers have adopted many of these standards as a basis for achieving interoperability between different certificate authorities. PKCS is composed of a set of (currently) 13 active standards, with 2 other standards that are no longer active. The standards are referred to as PKCS #1 through PKCS #15, as listed in Table 6-2. The standards combine to establish a common base for services required in a PKI.

Though adopted early in the development of PKIs, some of these standards are being phased out. For example, PKCS #6 is being replaced by X.509 v3 (covered shortly in the "X.509" section) and PKCS #7 and PKCS #10 are used less, as their PKIX counterparts are being adopted.

Standard	Title and Description
PKCS #1	RSA Cryptography Standard: Definition of the RSA encryption standard.
PKCS #2	No longer active; it covered RSA encryption of message digests and was incorporated into PKCS #1.
PKCS #3	Diffie-Hellman Key Agreement Standard: Definition of the Diffie-Hellman key-agreement protocol.
PKCS #4	No longer active; it covered RSA key syntax and was incorporated into PKCS #1.
PKCS #5	Password-Based Cryptography Standard: Definition of a password-based encryption (PBE) method for generating a secret key.
PKCS #6	Extended-Certificate Syntax Standard: Definition of an extended certificate syntax that is being replaced by X.509 v3.
PKCS #7	Cryptographic Message Syntax Standard: Definition of the cryptographic message standard for encoded messages, regardless of encryption algorithm. Commonly replaced with PKIX Cryptographic Message Syntax.
PKCS #8	Private-Key Information Syntax Standard: Definition of a private key information format, used to store private key information.
PKCS #9	Selected Attribute Types: Definition of attribute types used in other PKCS standards.
PKCS #10	Certification Request Syntax Standard: Definition of a syntax for certification requests.
PKCS #11	Cryptographic Token Interface Standard: Definition of a technology-independent programming interface for cryptographic devices (such as smart cards).
PKCS #12	Personal Information Exchange Syntax Standard: Definition of a format for storage and transport of user privates keys, certificates, and other personal information.
PKCS #13	Elliptic Curve Cryptography Standard: Description of methods for encrypting and signing messages using elliptic curve cryptography.
PKCS #14	A standard for pseudo-random number generation.
PKCS #15	Cryptographic Token Information Format Standard: Definition of a format for storing cryptographic information in cryptographic tokens.

Table 6-2   PKCS Standards

Why You Need to Know

If you or your company are planning to use one of the existing certificate servers to support e-commerce, you may not need to know the specifics of these standards (except perhaps for your exam). However, if you plan to implement a private PKI to support secure services within your organization, you will need to understand what standards are out there and how the decision to use a particular PKI implementation (either home grown or commercial) may lead to incompatibilities with other certificate-issuing entities. Your business-to-business requirements must be considered when deciding how to implement a PKI within your organization.

EXAM TIP   All of these standards and protocols are the "vocabulary" of the computer security industry. You should be well versed in all these titles and their purposes and operations.

X.509

What is a certificate? A certificate is merely a data structure that binds a public key to subjects (unique names, DNS entries, or e-mails) and is used to authenticate that a public key indeed belongs to the subject. In the late 1980s, the X.500 OSI Directory Standard was defined by International Organization for Standardization (ISO) and the International Telecommunication Union (ITU). It was developed for implementing a network directory system, and part of this directory standard was the concept of authentication of entities within the directory. X.509 is the portion of the X.500 standard that addresses the structure of certificates used for authentication.

Several versions of the certificates have been created, with version 3 being the current version (as this is being written). Each version has extended the contents of the certificates to include additional information necessary to use certificates in a PKI. The original ITU X.509 definition was published in 1988, was formerly referred to as CCITT X.509, and is sometimes referred to as ISO/IEC/ITU 9594-8. The 1988 certificate format, version 1, was revised in 1993 as the ITU-T X.509 definition when two more fields were added to support directory access control. ITU-T is the Standards Section of the ITU created in 1992.

The 1993, version 2 specification was revised following lessons learned from implementing Internet Privacy Enhanced Mail (PEM). Version 3 added additional optional extensions for more subject identification information, key attribute information, policy information, and certification path constraints. In addition, version 3 allowed additional extensions to be defined in standards or to be defined and registered by organizations or communities. Table 6-3 gives a description of the fields in a X.509 certificate.

Certificates are used to encapsulate the information needed to authenticate an entity. The X.509 specification defines a hierarchical certification structure that relies on a root certification authority that is *self-certifying* (meaning it issues its own certificate). All other certificates can be traced back to such a root through a *path*. A CA issues a certificate to a uniquely identifiable entity (person, corporation, computer, and so on)—issuing a certificate to "John Smith" would cause some real problems if that were all the information the CA had when issuing the certificate. We are saved somewhat by the requirement that the CA determines what identifier is unique (the distinguished name), but when certificates and trust are extended between CAs, the unique identification becomes critical.

Some other extensions to the X.509 certificate have been proposed for use in implementing a PKI. For example, PKIX identified several extensions for use in the certificate policy framework (see RFC 2427). It is essential that you ensure that your PKI ignores extensions that it is not prepared to handle.

Field Name	Field Description
Certificate Signature	X.509 version used for this certificate: Version 1 = 0 Version 2 = 1 Version 3 = 2
Serial Number	A nonnegative integer assigned by the certificate issuer that must be unique to the certificate.
Signature Algorithm Algorithm Parameters (optional)	The algorithm identifier for the algorithm used by the CA to sign the certificate. The optional Parameters field is used to provide the cryptographic algorithm parameters used in generating the signature.
Issuer	Identification for the entity that signed and issued the certificate. This must be a distinguished name within the hierarchy of certificate authorities.
Validity Not valid before time Not valid after time	Validity specifies a period of time during which the certificate is valid using a "not valid before" time and a "not valid after" time (expressed in UTC or in a generalized time).
Subject	The name for the certificate owner.
Subject Public Key Info	This field consists of an encryption algorithm identifier followed by a bit string for the public key.
Issuer Unique ID	Optional for versions 2 and 3—a unique bit-string identifier for the CA that issued the certificate.
Subject Unique ID	Optional for versions 2 and 3—a unique bit-string identifier for the subject of the certificate.
Extensions Extension ID Critical Extension Value	Optional for version 3—the extension area consists of a sequence of extension fields containing an extension identifier, a Boolean field indicating whether the extension is critical, and an octet string representing the value of the extension. Extensions can be defined in standards or defined and registered by organizations or communities.
Thumbprint Algorithm Algorithm Parameters (optional)	This field identifies the algorithm used by the CA to sign this certificate. This field must match the algorithm identified above.
Thumbprint	The signature is the bit-string hash value obtained when the CA signed the certificate. The signature certifies the contents of the certificate, binding the public key to the subject.

Table 6-3 X.509 Certificate Fields

SSL/TLS

Secure Sockets Layer (SSL) and Transport Layer Security (TLS) provide the most common means of interacting with a PKI and certificates. The older SSL protocol was introduced by Netscape as a means of providing secure connections for web transfers using encryption. These two protocols provide secure connections between the client and server for exchanging information. They also provide server authentication (and optionally, client authentication) and confidentiality of information transfers. See Chapter 15 for a detailed explanation.

The IETF established the TLS Working Group in 1996 to develop a standard transport layer security protocol. The working group began with SSL version 3.0 as its basis and released RFC 2246, TLS Protocol Version 1.0, in 1999 as a proposed standard. The working group also published RFC 2712, "Addition of Kerberos Cipher Suites to Transport Layer Security (TLS)," as a proposed standard, and two RFCs on the use of TLS with HTTP. Like its predecessor, TLS is a protocol that ensures privacy between communicating applications and their users on the Internet. When a server and client communicate, TLS ensures that no third party can eavesdrop or tamper with any message.

TLS is composed of two parts: the TLS Record Protocol and the TLS Handshake Protocol. The TLS Record Protocol provides connection security by using supported encryption methods. The TLS Record Protocol can also be used without encryption. The TLS Handshake Protocol allows the server and client to authenticate each other and to negotiate a session encryption algorithm and cryptographic keys before data is exchanged.

Though TLS is based on SSL and is sometimes referred to as SSL, they are not interoperable. However, the TLS protocol does contain a mechanism that allows a TLS implementation to back down to SSL 3.0. The difference between the two is the way they perform key expansion and message authentication computations. TLS uses the MD5 and SHA1 hashing algorithms XORed together to determine the session key. The most recent browser versions support TLS. Though SSL also uses both hashing algorithms, SSL is considered less secure because the way it uses them forces a reliance on MD5 rather than SHA1.

The TLS Record Protocol is a layered protocol. At each layer, messages may include fields for length, description, and content. The Record Protocol takes messages to be transmitted, fragments the data into manageable blocks, optionally compresses the data, applies a message authentication code (MAC) to the data, encrypts it, and transmits the result. Received data is decrypted, verified, decompressed, and reassembled, and then delivered to higher-level clients.

The TLS Handshake Protocol involves the following steps, which are summarized in Figure 6-4:

1. Exchange hello messages to agree on algorithms, exchange random values, and check for session resumption.

2. Exchange the necessary cryptographic parameters to allow the client and server to agree on a pre-master secret.

3. Exchange certificates and cryptographic information to allow the client and server to authenticate themselves.

4. Generate a master secret from the pre-master secret and exchange random values.

5. Provide security parameters to the record layer.

6. Allow the client and server to verify that their peer has calculated the same security parameters and that the handshake occurred without tampering by an attacker.

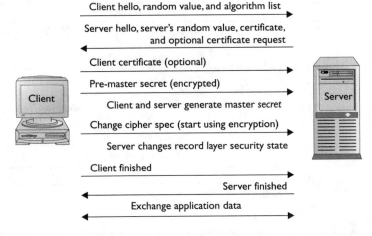

Figure 6-4
TLS Handshake
Protocol

Client hello, random value, and algorithm list

Server hello, server's random value, certificate, and optional certificate request

Client certificate (optional)

Pre-master secret (encrypted)

Client and server generate master secret

Change cipher spec (start using encryption)

Server changes record layer security state

Client finished

Server finished

Exchange application data

Client

Server

Though it has been designed to minimize this risk, TLS still has potential vulnerabilities to a man-in-the-middle attack. A highly skilled and well-placed attacker can force TLS to operate at lower security levels. Regardless, through the use of validated and trusted certificates, a secure cipher suite can be selected for the exchange of data.

Once established, a TLS session remains active as long as data is being exchanged. If sufficient inactive time has elapsed for the secure connection to time out, it can be reinitiated.

ISAKMP

The Internet Security Association and Key Management Protocol (ISAKMP) provides a method for implementing a key exchange protocol and for negotiating a security policy. It defines procedures and packet formats to negotiate, establish, modify, and delete security associates. Because it is a framework, it doesn't define implementation-specific protocols, such as the key exchange protocol or hash functions. Examples of ISAKMP are the Internet Key Exchange (IKE) protocol and IPsec and are used widely throughout the industry.

An important definition for understanding ISAKMP is the term *security association*. A security association (SA) is a relationship in which two or more entities define how they will communicate securely. ISAKMP is intended to support SAs at all layers of the network stack. For this reason, ISAKMP can be implemented on the transport level using TCP or User Datagram Protocol (UDP), or it can be implemented on IP directly.

Negotiation of a SA between servers occurs in two stages. First, the entities agree on how to secure negotiation messages (the ISAKMP SA). Once the entities have secured their negotiation traffic, they then determine the SAs for the protocols used for the remainder of their communications. Figure 6-5 shows the structure of the ISAKMP header. This header is used during both parts of the ISAKMP negotiation.

The initiator cookie is set by the entity requesting the SA, and the responder sets the responder cookie. The payload byte indicates the type of the first payload to be

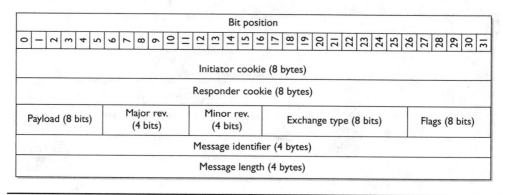

Figure 6-5 ISAKMP header format

encapsulated. Payload types include security associations, proposals, key transforms, key exchanges, vendor identities, and other things. The major and minor revision fields refer to the major version number and minor version number for the ISAKMP. The exchange type helps determine the order of messages and payloads. The flag bits indicate options for the ISAKMP exchange, including whether the payload is encrypted, whether the initiator and responder have "committed" to the SA, and whether the packet is to be authenticated only (and is not encrypted). The final fields of the ISAKMP header indicate the message identifier and a message length. Payloads encapsulated within ISAKMP use a generic header, and each payload has its own header format.

Once the ISAKMP SA is established, multiple protocol SAs can be established using the single ISAKMP SA. This feature is valuable due to the overhead associated with the two-stage negotiation. SAs are valid for specific periods of time, and once the time expires, the SA must be renegotiated. Many resources are also available for specific implementations of ISAKMP within the IPsec protocol.

CMP

The PKIX Certificate Management Protocol (CMP) is specified in RFC 4210. This protocol defines the messages and operations required to provide certificate management services within the PKIX model. Though part of the IETF PKIX effort, CMP provides a framework that works well with other standards, such as PKCS #7 and PKCS #10.

CMP provides for the following certificate operations:

- CA establishment, including creation of the initial CRL and export of the public key for the CA
- Certification of an end-entity, including the following:
  - Initial registration and certification of the end-entity (registration, certificate issuance, and placement of the certificate in a repository)
  - Updates to the key pair for end-entities, required periodically and when a key pair is compromised or keys cannot be recovered

- End-entity certificate updates, required when a certificate expires

- Periodic CA key-pair update, similar to end-entity key-pair updates

- Cross-certification requests, placed by other CAs

- Certificate and CRL publication, performed under the appropriate conditions of certificate issuance and certificate revocation

- Key-pair recovery, a service to restore key-pair information for an end-entity; for example, if a certificate password is lost or the certificate file is lost

- Revocation requests, supporting requests by authorized entities to revoke a certificate

CMP also defines mechanisms for performing these operations, either online or offline using files, e-mail, tokens, or web operations.

XKMS

The XML Key Management Specification defines services to manage PKI operations within the Extensible Markup Language (XML) environment. These services are provided for handling PKI keys and certificates automatically. Developed by the World Wide Web Consortium (W3C), XKMS is intended to simplify integration of PKIs and management of certificates in applications. As well as responding to problems of authentication and verification of electronic signatures, it also allows certificates to be managed, registered, or revoked.

XKMS services reside on a separate server that interacts with an established PKI. The services are accessible via a simple XML protocol. Developers can rely on the XKMS services, making it less complex to interface with the PKI. The services provide for retrieving key information (owner, key value, key issuer, and the like) and key registration and management (such as key registration and revocation).

Retrieval operations rely on the XML signature for the necessary information. Three tiers of service are based on the client requests and application requirements. Tier 0 provides a means of retrieving key information by embedding references to the key within the XML signature. The signature contains an element called a *retrieval method* that indicates ways to resolve the key. In this case, the client sends a request, using the retrieval method, to obtain the desired key information. For example, if the verification key contained a long chain of X.509 v3 certificates, a retrieval method could be included to avoid sending the certificates with the document. The client would use the retrieval method to obtain the chain of certificates. For tier 0, the server indicated in the retrieval method responds directly to the request for the key, possibly bypassing the XKMS server. The tier 0 process is shown in Figure 6-6.

With tier 1 operations, the client forwards the key information portions of the XML signature to the XKMS server, relying on the server to perform the retrieval of the desired key information. The desired information can be local to the XKMS sever, or it can reside on an external PKI system. The XKMS server provides no additional validation of the key information, such as checking to see whether the certificate has been revoked

Figure 6-6
XKMS tier 0
retrieval

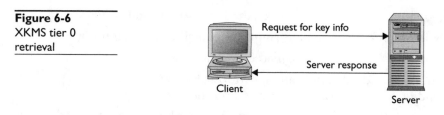

and is still valid. Just as in tier 0, the client performs final validation of the document. Tier 1 is called the *locate service* because it locates the appropriate key information for the client, as shown in Figure 6-7.

Tier 2 is called the *validate service,* and it is illustrated in Figure 6-8. In this case, just as in tier 1, the client relies on the XKMS service to retrieve the relevant key information from the external PKI. The XKMS server also performs a data validation on a portion of the key information provided by the client for this purpose. This validation verifies the binding of the key information with the data indicated by the key information contained in the XML signature.

The primary difference between tier 1 and tier 2 is the level of involvement of the XKMS server. In tier 1, it can serve only as a relay or gateway between the client and the PKI. In tier 2, the XKMS server is actively involved in verifying the relation between the PKI information and the document containing the XML signature.

XKMS relies on the client or underlying communications mechanism to provide for the security of the communications with the XKMS server. The specification suggests using one of three methods for ensuring server authentication, response integrity, and relevance of the response to the request: digitally signed correspondence, a transport layer security protocol (such as SSL, TLS, or WTLS), or a packet layer security protocol (such as IPsec). Obviously, digitally signed correspondence introduces its own issues regarding validation of the signature, which is the purpose of XKMS.

It is possible to define other tiers of service. Tiers 3 and 4, an *assertion service* and an *assertion status service,* respectively, are mentioned in the defining XKMS specification, but they are not defined. The specification states they "could" be defined in other documents.

XKMS also provides services for key registration, key revocation, and key recovery. Authentication for these actions is based on a password or passphrase, which is provided when the keys are registered and when they must be recovered.

Figure 6-7
XKMS tier 1 locate
service

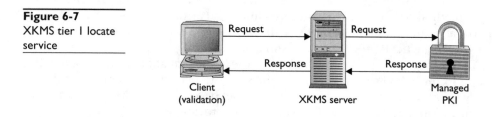

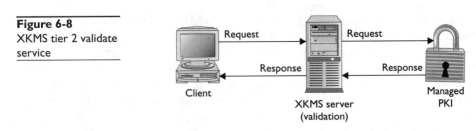

Figure 6-8
XKMS tier 2 validate service

Client

XKMS server
(validation)

Managed
PKI

S/MIME

The Secure/Multipurpose Internet Mail Extensions (S/MIME) message specification is an extension to the MIME standard that provides a way to send and receive signed and encrypted MIME data. RSA Security created the first version of the S/MIME standard, using the RSA encryption algorithm and the PKCS series of standards. The second version dates from 1998 but had a number of serious restrictions, including the restriction to 40-bit Data Encryption Standard (DES). The current version of the IETF standard is dated July 2004 and requires the use of Advanced Encryption Standard (AES).

The changes in the S/MIME standard have been so frequent that the standard has become difficult to implement. Far from having a stable standard for several years that product manufacturers could have time to gain experience with, there have been changes to the encryption algorithms being used. Just as importantly, and not immediately clear from the IETF documents, the standard places reliance upon more than one other standard for it to function. Key among these is the format of a public key certificate as expressed in the X.509 standard.

The S/MIME v2 specifications outline a basic strategy for providing security services for e-mail but lack many security features required by the Department of Defense (DoD) for use by the military. In early 1996, the Internet Mail Consortium (IMC) was formed as a technical trade association pursuing cooperative use and enhancement of Internet e-mail and messaging. An early goal of the IMC was to bring together the DoD (along with its vendor community) and commercial industry in order to devise a standard security protocol acceptable to both. Several existing security protocols were considered, including: MIME Object Security Services (MOSS), Pretty Good Privacy (PGP), and S/MIME v2. After examining these protocols, the group determined that none met the requirements of both the military and commercial communities. Instead of launching into a development of an entirely new set of specifications, however, the group decided that with certain enhancements the S/MIME set of specifications could be used. It also decided that, since the discussion was about a common set of specifications to be used throughout the Internet community, this resulting specification should be brought under the control of the IETF.

Shortly after the decision was made to revise the S/MIME version 2 specifications, the DoD, its vendor community, and commercial industry met to begin development of the enhanced specifications. These new specifications would be known as S/MIME v3. Participants agreed that backward compatibility between S/MIME v3 and v2 should be preserved; otherwise, S/MIME v3–compatible applications would not be able to work with older S/MIME v2–compatible applications.

A minimum set of cryptographic algorithms were mandated so that different implementations of the new S/MIME v3 set of specifications could be interoperable. This minimum set must be implemented in an application for it to be considered S/MIME-compliant. Applications can implement additional cryptographic algorithms to meet their customers' needs, but the minimum set must also be present in the applications for interoperability with other S/MIME applications. Thus, users are not forced to use S/MIME specified algorithms; they can choose their own, but if the application is to be considered S/MIME-compliant, the standard algorithms must also be present.

IETF S/MIME v3 Specifications

Building upon the original work by the IMC organized group, the IETF has worked hard to enhance the S/MIME v3 specifications. The ultimate goal is to have the S/MIME v3 specifications receive recognition as an Internet standard. The current IETF S/MIME v3 set of specifications includes the following:

- Cryptographic Message Syntax (CMS)
- S/MIME v3 message specification
- S/MIME v3 certificate handling specification
- Enhanced security services (ESS) for S/MIME

The CMS defines a standard syntax for transmitting cryptographic information about contents of a protected message. Originally based on the PKCS #7 version 1.5 specification, the CMS specification was enhanced by the IETF S/MIME Working Group to include optional security components. Just as the S/MIME v3 provides backward compatibility with v2, CMS provides backward compatibility with PKCS #7, so applications will be interoperable even if the new components are not implemented in a specific application.

Integrity, authentication, and nonrepudiation security features are provided by using digital signatures using the SignedData syntax described by the CMS. CMS also describes what is known as the EnvelopedData syntax to provide confidentiality of the message's content through the use of encryption. The PKCS #7 specification supports key encryption algorithms, such as RSA. Algorithm independence is promoted through the addition of several fields to the EnvelopedData syntax in CMS, which is the major difference between the PKCS #7 and CMS specifications. The goal was to be able to support specific algorithms such as Diffie-Hellman and the Key Exchange Algorithm (KEA), which is implemented on the Fortezza Crypto Card developed for the DoD. One final significant change to the original specifications is the ability to include X.509 Attribute Certificates in the SignedData and EnvelopedData syntaxes for CMS.

CMS Triple Encapsulated Message

An interesting feature of CMS is the ability to nest security envelopes to provide a combination of security features. As an example, a CMS triple-encapsulated message can be created in which the original content and associated attributes are signed and encapsulated within the inner SignedData object. The inner SignedData is in turn encrypted and encapsulated within an EnvelopedData object. The resulting EnvelopedData object is then also signed and finally encapsulated within a second SignedData object, the outer SignedData object. Usually the inner SignedData object is signed by the original user and the outer SignedData is signed by another entity such as a firewall or a mail list agent providing an additional level of security.

This triple-encapsulation is not required of every CMS object. All that is required is a single SignedData object created by the user to sign a message or an EnvelopedData object if the user desired to encrypt a message.

PGP

Pretty Good Privacy (PGP) is a popular program that is used to encrypt and decrypt e-mail and files. It also provides the ability to digitally sign a message so the receiver can be certain of the sender's identity. Taken together, encrypting and signing a message allows the receiver to be assured of who sent the message and to know that it was not modified during transmission. Public domain versions of PGP have been available for years as well as inexpensive commercial versions. PGP is one of the most widely used programs and is frequently used by both individuals and businesses to ensure data and e-mail privacy. It was developed by Philip R. Zimmermann in 1991 and quickly became a de facto standard for e-mail security.

How PGP Works

PGP uses a variation of the standard public key encryption process. In public key encryption, an individual (here called the *creator*) uses the encryption program to create a pair of keys. One key is known as the *public key* and is designed to be given freely to others. The other key is called the *private key* and is designed to be known only by the creator. Individuals wanting to send a private message to the creator will encrypt the message using the creator's public key. The algorithm is designed such that only the private key can decrypt the message, so only the creator will be able to decrypt it.

This method, known as public key or *asymmetric encryption*, is time consuming. *Symmetric encryption* uses only a single key and is generally faster. It is because of this that PGP is designed the way it is. PGP uses a symmetric encryption algorithm to encrypt the message to be sent. It then encrypts the symmetric key used to encrypt this message with the public key of the intended recipient. Both the encrypted key and message are then sent. The receiver's version of PGP will first decrypt the symmetric key with the private key supplied by the recipient and will then use the resulting decrypted key to decrypt the rest of the message.

PGP can use two different public key algorithms—Rivest-Shamir-Adleman (RSA) and Diffie-Hellman. The RSA version uses the International Data Encryption Algorithm (IDEA) algorithm to generate a short symmetric key to be used to encrypt the message and RSA to encrypt the short IDEA key. The Diffie-Hellman version uses the Carlisle

Adams and Stafford Tavares (CAST) algorithm to encrypt the message and the Diffie-Hellman algorithm to encrypt the CAST key.

To generate a digital signature, PGP takes advantage of another property of public key encryption schemes. Normally, the sender will encrypt using the receiver's public key and the message will be decrypted at the other end using the receiver's private key. The process can be reversed so that the sender encrypts with his own private key. The receiver then decrypts the message with the sender's public key. Since the sender is the only individual who has a key that will correctly be decrypted with the sender's public key, the receiver knows that the message was created by the sender who claims to have sent it. The way PGP accomplishes this task is to generate a hash value from the user's name and other signature information. This hash value is then encrypted with the sender's private key known only by the sender. The receiver uses the sender's public key, which is available to everyone, to decrypt the hash value. If the decrypted hash value matches the hash value sent as the digital signature for the message, then the receiver is assured that the message was sent by the sender who claims to have sent it.

Typically, versions of PGP will contain a user interface that works with common e-mail programs such as Microsoft Outlook. If you want others to be able to send you an encrypted message, you will need to register your public key that was generated by your PGP program with a PGP public-key server. Alternatively, you will have to send your public key to all those who want to send you an encrypted message or post your key to some location from which they can download it, such as your web page. Note that using a public-key server is the better method for all of the reasons of trust described in the discussions of PKIs in Chapter 5.

Where Can You Use PGP?

For many years the U.S. government waged a fight over the exportation of PGP technology, and for many years its exportation was illegal. Today, however, PGP encrypted e-mail can be exchanged with most users outside the United States, and many versions of PGP are available from numerous international sites. Of course, being able to exchange PGP-encrypted e-mail requires that the individuals on both sides of the communication have valid versions of PGP. Interestingly, international versions of PGP are just as secure as domestic versions—a feature that is not true of other encryption products. It should be noted that the freeware versions of PGP are not licensed for commercial purposes.

HTTPS

Most web activity occurs using the Hypertext Transfer Protocol (HTTP), but this protocol is prone to interception. HTTPS uses the Secure Sockets Layer (SSL) to transfer information. Originally developed by Netscape Communications and implemented in its browser, HTTPS has since been incorporated into most common browsers. It uses the open standard SSL to encrypt data at the application layer. In addition, HTTPS uses the standard TCP port 443 for TCP/IP communications rather than the standard port 80 used for HTTP. Early HTTPS implementations made use of the 40-bit RC4 encryption algorithm, but with the relaxation of export restrictions, most implementations now use 128-bit encryption.

IPsec

IPsec is a collection of IP security features designed to introduce security at the network or packet-processing layer in network communication. Other approaches have attempted to incorporate security at higher levels of the TCP/IP suite such as at the level where applications reside. IPsec is designed to be used to provide secure virtual private network capability over the Internet. In essence, IPsec provides a secure version of the IP by introducing authentication and encryption to protect layer 4 protocols. IPsec is optional for IPv4 but is required for IPv6. Obviously, both ends of the communication need to use IPsec for the encryption/decryption process to occur.

IPsec provides two types of security service to ensure authentication and confidentiality for either the data alone (referred to as IPsec *transport mode*) or for both the data and header (referred to as *tunnel mode*). See Chapter 9 for more detail on tunneling and IPsec operation. IPsec introduces several new protocols including the Authentication Header (AH), which basically provides authentication of the sender, and the Encapsulating Security Payload (ESP), which adds encryption of the data to ensure confidentiality. IPsec also provides for payload compression before encryption using the IP Payload Compression Protocol (IPcomp). Frequently, encryption negatively impacts the ability of compression algorithms to fully compress data for transmission. By providing the ability to compress the data before encryption, IPsec addresses this issue.

CEP

Certificate Enrollment Protocol (CEP) was originally developed by VeriSign for Cisco Systems. It was designed to support certificate issuance, distribution, and revocation using existing technologies. Its use has grown in client and CA applications. The operations supported include CA and RA public key distribution, certificate enrollment, certificate revocation, certificate query, and CRL query.

One of the key goals of CEP was to use existing technology whenever possible. It uses both PKCS #7 (Cryptographic Message Syntax Standard) and PKCS #10 (Certification Request Syntax Standard) to define a common message syntax. It supports access to certificates and CRLs using either Lightweight Directory Access Protocol (LDAP) or the CEP-defined certificate query.

FIPS

The Federal Information Processing Standards Publications (FIPS PUBS or simply FIPS) describe various standards for data communication issues. These documents are issued by the U.S. government through the National Institute of Standards and Technology

(NIST), which is tasked with their development. NIST creates these publications when a compelling government need requires a standard for use in areas such as security or system interoperability and no recognized industry standard exists. Three categories of FIPS PUBS are currently maintained by NIST:

- Hardware and software standards/guidelines
- Data standards/guidelines
- Computer security standards/guidelines

These documents require that products sold to the U.S. government comply with one (or more) of the FIPS standards. The standards can be obtained from www.itl.nist .gov/fipspubs.

Common Criteria (CC)

The Common Criteria (CC) are the result of an effort to develop a joint set of security processes and standards that can be used by the international community. The major contributors to the CC are the governments of the United States, Canada, France, Germany, the Netherlands, and the United Kingdom. The CC also provides a listing of laboratories that apply the criteria in testing security products. Products that are evaluated by one of the approved laboratories receive an Evaluation Assurance Level of EAL1 through EAL7 (EAL7 is the highest level), with EAL4, for example, designed for environments requiring a moderate to high level of independently assured security, and EAL1 being designed for environments in which some confidence in the correct operation of the system is required but where the threats to the system are not considered serious. The CC also provide a listing of products by function that have performed at a specific EAL.

WTLS

The Wireless Transport Layer Security (WTLS) protocol is based on the Transport Layer Security (TLS) protocol. WTLS provides reliability and security for wireless communications using the Wireless Application Protocol (WAP). WTLS is necessary due to the limited memory and processing abilities of WAP-enabled phones.

WTLS can be implemented in one of three classes: Class 1 is called *anonymous* authentication but is not designed for practical use. Class 2 is called *server* authentication and is the most common model. The clients and server may authenticate using different means. Class 3 is *server and client* authentication. In Class 3 authentication, the client's and server's WTLS certificates are authenticated. Class 3 is the strongest form of authentication and encryption.

WEP

The Wired Equivalent Privacy (WEP) algorithm is part of the 802.11 standard and is used to protect wireless communications from interception. A secondary function is to prevent access to a wireless network from unauthorized access. WEP relies on a secret key that is shared between a mobile station and an access point. In most installations, a single key is used by all of the mobile stations and access points.

WEP Security Issues

In modern corporate environments, it's common for wireless networks to be created in which systems with 802.11 network interface cards communicate with wireless access points that connect the computer to the corporation's network. WEP is an optional security protocol specified in the 802.11 standard and is designed to address the security needs in this wireless environment. It uses a 24-bit initialization vector as a seed value to begin the security association. This, in itself, is a potential security problem as more than 16 million vectors are possible with 24 bits. At the speeds at which modern networks operate, it does not take long for initialization vectors to repeat. The secret key is only 40 bits in length (for 64-bit encryption; 104 bits for 128-bit encryption), another problem since it does not take too long to brute-force encryption schemes using key lengths this short.

Some vendors provide 128-bit WEP 2 keys in their products to overcome the short encryption key length, but that only increases the complexity in a linear manner and is almost equally vulnerable. In addition, the WEP keys are static. It is up to the system administrator to change WEP keys manually.

One final problem with WEP is that many wireless network implementations do not even come with WEP enabled. Due to the rapid growth of the wireless industry, standards have not been strongly implemented. WPA and WPA2 of the 802.11i standard provide significantly increased wireless security. See Chapter 10 for more details on WPA and WPA2.

ISO/IEC 27002 (Formerly ISO 17799)

ISO/IEC 27002 is a very popular and detailed standard for creating and implementing security policies. ISO/IEC 27002 was formerly ISO 17799, which was based on version 2 of the British Standard 7799 (BS7799) published in May 1999. With the increased emphasis placed on security in both the government and industry over the last few years, many organizations are now training their audit personnel to evaluate their organizations against the ISO/IEC 27002 standard. The standard is divided into 12 sections, each containing more detailed statements describing what is involved for that topic:

- **Risk assessment**
- **Security policy**
- **Organization of information security**

- Asset management

- Human resources security

- **Physical and environmental security**   Protection of the computer facilities

- **Communications and operations management**   Management of technical security controls in systems and networks

- **Access control**   Restriction of access rights to networks, systems, applications, functions, and data

- **Information systems acquisition, development and maintenance**   Building security into applications

- **Information security incident management**   Anticipating and responding appropriately to information security breaches

- **Business continuity management**   Protecting, maintaining, and recovering business-critical processes and systems

- **Compliance**   Ensuring conformance with information security policies, standards, laws, and regulations

Chapter Review

Chapter 5 discussed the various components of a public key infrastructure (PKI). This chapter continued the discussion with the many different standards and protocols that have been implemented to support PKI. Standards and protocols are important because they define the basis for how communication will take place. Without these protocols, two entities may each independently develop its own methods for implementing the various components for a PKI, as described in Chapter 5, and the two will not be compatible. On the Internet, not being compatible and not being able to communicate is not an option.

Three main standards have evolved over time to implement PKI on the Internet. Two are based on a third standard, the X.509 standard, and establish complementary standards for implementing PKI. These two standards are Public Key Infrastructure X.509 (PKIX) and Public Key Cryptography Standards (PKCS). PKIX defines standards for interactions and operations for four component types: the user (end-entity), certificate authority (CA), registration authority (RA), and the repository for certificates and certificate revocation lists (CRLs). PKCS defines many of the lower level standards for message syntax, cryptographic algorithms, and the like.

Other protocols and standards can help define the management and operation of the PKI and related services, such as ISAKMP, XKMS, and CMP. WEP is used to encrypt wireless communications in an 802.11 environment and S/MIME for e-mail; SSL, TLS, and WTLS are used for secure packet transmission; and IPsec and PPTP are used to support virtual private networks.

The Common Criteria (CC) establishes a series of criteria from which security products can be evaluated. The ISO/IEC 27002 standard provides a point from which security policies and practices can be developed in 12 areas. Various types of publications are available from NIST such as those found in the FIPS series.

Questions

1. Which organization created PKCS?

   A. RSA

   B. IEEE

   C. OSI

   D. ISO

2. Which of the following is not part of a public key infrastructure?

   A. Certificates

   B. Certificate revocation list (CRL)

   C. Substitution cipher

   D. Certificate authority (CA)

3. Which of the following is used to grant permissions using rule-based, role-based, and rank-based access controls?

   A. Attribute Certificate

   B. Qualified Certificate

   C. Control Certificate

   D. Operational Certificate

4. Transport Layer Security consists of which two protocols?

   A. TLS Record Protocol and TLS Certificate Protocol

   B. TLS Certificate Protocol and TLS Handshake Protocol

   C. TLS Key Protocol and TLS Handshake Protocol

   D. TLS Record Protocol and TLS Handshake Protocol

5. Which of the following provides connection security by using common encryption methods?

   A. TLS Certificate Protocol

   B. TLS Record Protocol

   C. TLS Layered Protocol

   D. TLS Key Protocol

6. Which of the following provides a method for implementing a key exchange protocol?

   A. EISA

    B. ISA

    C. ISAKMP

    D. ISAKEY

7. A relationship in which two or more entities define how they will communicate securely is known as what?

    A. Security association

    B. Security agreement

    C. Three-way agreement

    D. Three-way handshake

8. The entity requesting an SA sets what?

    A. Initiator cookie

    B. Process ID

    C. Session number

    D. Session ID

9. What protocol is used to establish a CA?

    A. Certificate Management Protocol

    B. Internet Key Exchange Protocol

    C. Secure Sockets Layer

    D. Public Key Infrastructure

10. What is the purpose of XKMS?

    A. Encapsulates session associations over TCP/IP

    B. Extends session associations over many transport protocols

    C. Designed to replace SSL

    D. Defines services to manage heterogeneous PKI operations via XML

11. Which of the following is a secure e-mail standard?

    A. POP3

    B. IMAP

    C. S/MIME

    D. SMTP

12. Secure Sockets Layer uses what port to communicate?

    A. 143

    B. 80

    C. 443

    D. 53

Answers

1. **A.** RSA Laboratories created Public Key Cryptography Standards (PKCS).

2. **C.** The substitution cipher is not a component of PKI. The substitution cipher is an elementary alphabet-based cipher.

3. **A.** An Attribute Certificate (AC) is used to grant permissions using rule-based, role-based, and rank-based access controls.

4. **D.** Transport Layer Security consists of the TLS Record Protocol, which provides security, and the TLS Handshake Protocol, which allows the server and client to authenticate each other.

5. **B.** The TLS Record Protocol provides connection security by using common encryption methods, such as DES.

6. **C.** The Internet Security Association and Key Management Protocol (ISAKMP) provides a method for implementing a key exchange protocol and for negotiating a security policy.

7. **A.** During a security association, the client and the server will list the types of encryption of which they are capable and will choose the most secure encryption standard that they have in common.

8. **A.** The entity requesting a security association will request an initiator cookie.

9. **A.** The Certificate Management Protocol is used to establish a CA.

10. **D.** XML Key Management Specification (XKMS) allows services to manage PKI via XML, which is interoperable across different vendor platforms.

11. **C.** Secure/Multipurpose Internet Mail Extensions (S/MIME) is a secure e-mail standard. Other popular standards include Pretty Good Privacy (PGP) and OpenPGP.

12. **C.** SSL's well-known port is 443. SSL was developed by Netscape.

PART III

Security in the Infrastructure

■ **Chapter 7**   Physical Security
■ **Chapter 8**   Infrastructure Security
■ **Chapter 9**   Remote Access and Authentication
■ **Chapter 10** Infrastructure

Physical Security

- Describe how physical security directly affects computer and network security
- Discuss steps that can be taken to help mitigate risks
- Understand electronic access controls and the principles of convergence

For most American homes, locks are the primary means of achieving physical security, and almost every American locks the doors to his or her home upon leaving the residence. Some go even further and set up intrusion alarm systems in addition to locks. All these precautions are considered necessary because people believe they have something significant inside the house that needs to be protected, such as important possessions and important people.

Physical security is an important topic for businesses dealing with the security of information systems. Businesses are responsible for securing their profitability, which requires a combination of several aspects: They need to secure employees, product inventory, trade secrets, and strategy information. These and other important assets affect the profitability of a company and its future survival. Companies therefore perform many activities to attempt to provide physical security—locking doors, installing alarm systems, using safes, posting security guards, setting access controls, and more.

Most companies today have committed a large amount of effort into network security and information systems security. In this chapter, you will learn about how these two security efforts are linked, and you'll learn several methods by which companies can minimize their exposure to physical security events that can diminish their network security.

The Security Problem

The problem that faces professionals charged with securing a company's network can be stated rather simply: Physical access negates all other security measures. No matter how impenetrable the firewall and intrusion detection system (IDS), if an attacker can find a way to walk up to and touch a server, he can break into it. The more remarkable thing is that gaining physical access to a number of machines is not that difficult.

Consider that most network security measures are, from necessity, directed at protecting a company from the Internet. This fact results in a lot of companies allowing any kind of traffic on the local area network (LAN). So if an attacker attempts to gain access to a server over the Internet and fails, he may be able to gain physical access to the receptionist's machine, and by quickly compromising it, he can use it as a remotely controlled zombie to attack what he is really after. Physically securing information assets doesn't mean just the servers; it means protecting the physical access to all the organization's computers and its entire network infrastructure.

Physical access to a corporation's systems can allow an attacker to perform a number of interesting activities, starting with simply plugging into an open Ethernet jack. The advent of handheld devices with the ability to run operating systems with full networking support has made this attack scenario even more feasible. Prior to handheld devices, the attacker would have to work in a secluded area with dedicated access to the Ethernet for a time. The attacker would sit down with a laptop and run a variety of tools against the network, and working internally typically put the attacker behind the firewall and IDS. Today's capable PDAs can assist these efforts by allowing attackers to place the small device onto the network to act as a *wireless bridge*. The attacker can then use a laptop to attack a network remotely via the bridge from outside the building. If power is available near the Ethernet jack, this type of attack can also be accomplished with an off-the-shelf access point. The attacker's only challenge is finding an Ethernet jack that isn't covered by furniture or some other obstruction.

Another simple attack that can be used when an attacker has physical access is called a *bootdisk*. Before bootable CD-ROMs or DVD-ROMs were available, a boot floppy was used to start the system and prepare the hard drives to load the operating system. Since many machines still have floppy drives, boot floppies can still be used. These floppies can contain a number of programs, but the most typical ones would be NTFS-DOS or a floppy-based Linux distribution that can be used to perform a number of tasks, including mounting the hard drives and performing at least read operations. Once an attacker is able to read a hard drive, the password file can be copied off the machine for offline password cracking attacks. If write access to the drive is obtained, the attacker could alter the password file or place a remote control program to be executed automatically upon the next boot, guaranteeing continued access to the machine.

Bootable CD-ROMs and DVD-ROMs are a danger for the same reason—perhaps even more so, because they can carry a variety of payloads such as malware or even entire operating systems. An operating system designed to run the entire machine from an optical disc without using the hard drive is commonly referred to as a LiveCD. LiveCDs contain a bootable version of an entire operating system, typically a variant of Linux, complete with drivers for most devices. LiveCDs give an attacker a greater array of tools than could be loaded onto a floppy disk. For example, an attacker would likely have access to the hard disk and also to an operational network interface that would allow him to send the drive data over the Internet if properly connected. These bootable operating systems could also be custom built to contain any tool that runs under

Linux, allowing an attacker a standard bootable attack image or a standard bootable forensics image, or something customized for the tools he likes to use.

The use of bootdisks of all types leads to the next area of concern: creating an image of the hard drive for later investigation. Some form of bootable media is often used to load the imaging software.

Drive imaging is the process of copying the entire contents of a hard drive to a single file on a different media. This process is often used by people who perform forensic investigations of computers. Typically, a bootable media is used to start the computer and load the drive imaging software. This software is designed to make a bit-by-bit copy of the hard drive to a file on another media, usually another hard drive or CD-R/DVD-R media. Drive imaging is used in investigations to make an exact copy that can be observed and taken apart, while keeping the original exactly as it was for evidence purposes.

From an attacker's perspective, drive imaging software is useful because it pulls *all* information from a computer's hard drive while still leaving the machine in its original state. The information contains every bit of data that was on this computer: any locally stored documents, locally stored e-mails, and every other piece of information that the hard drive contained. This data could be very valuable if the machine held sensitive information about the company.

Physical access is the most common way of imaging a drive, and the biggest benefit for the attacker is that drive imaging leaves absolutely no trace of the crime. While you can do very little to prevent drive imaging, you can minimize its impact. The use of encryption even for a few important files will provide protection. Full encryption of the drive will protect all files stored on it. Alternatively, placing files on a centralized file server will keep them from being imaged from an individual machine, but if an attacker is able to image the file server, the data will be copied.

EXAM TIP Drive imaging is a threat because all existing access controls to data can be bypassed and all the data once stored on the drive can be read from the image.

An even simpler version of the drive imaging attack is to steal the computer outright. Computer theft typically occurs for monetary gain—the thief later selling his prize. We're concerned with the theft of a computer to obtain the data it holds, however. While physical thievery is not a technical attack, it is often carried in conjunction with a bit of social engineering—for example, the thief might appear to be a legitimate computer repair person and may be allowed to walk out of the building with a laptop or other system in his possession. For anyone who discounts this type of attack, consider this incident: In Australia, two individuals entered a government computer room and managed to walk off with two large servers. They not only escaped with two valuable computers, but they got the data they contained as well.

Many of the methods mentioned so far can be used to perform a denial-of-service (DoS) attack. Physical access to the computers can be much more effective than a network-based DoS. The theft of a computer, using a bootdisk to erase all data on the drives, or simply unplugging computers are all effective DoS attacks. Depending on the company's quality and frequency of backing up critical systems, a DoS attack can have lasting effects.

Physical access can negate almost all the security that the network attempts to provide. Considering this, you must determine the level of physical access that attackers might obtain. Of special consideration are persons with authorized access to the building but who are not authorized users of the systems. Janitorial personnel and others have authorized access to many areas, but they do not have authorized system access. An attacker could pose as one of these individuals or attempt to gain access to the facilities through them.

Physical Security Safeguards

While it is difficult, if not impossible, to be totally secure, many steps can be taken to mitigate the risk to information systems from a physical threat. The following sections discuss policies and procedures as well as access control methods. Then the chapter explores various authentication methods and how they can help protect against physical threats.

Walls and Guards

The primary defense against a majority of physical attacks are the barriers between the assets and a potential attacker—walls and doors. Some organizations also employ full- or part-time private security staff to attempt to protect their assets. These barriers provide the foundation upon which all other security initiatives are based, but the security must be designed carefully, as an attacker has to find only a single gap to gain access.

Walls may have been one of the first inventions of man. Once he learned to use natural obstacles such as mountains to separate him from his enemy, he next learned to build his *own* mountain for the same purpose. Hadrian's Wall in England, the Great Wall of China, and the Berlin Wall are all famous examples of such basic physical defenses. The walls of any building serve the same purpose, but on a smaller scale: they provide barriers to physical access to company assets. In the case of information assets, as a general rule the most valuable assets are contained on company servers. To protect the physical servers, you must look in all directions: Doors and windows should be safeguarded and a minimum number of each should be used in a server room. Less obvious entry points should also be considered: Is a drop ceiling used in the server room? Do the interior walls extend to the actual roof, raised floors, or crawlspaces? Access to the server room should be limited to the people who need access, not to all employees of the organization. If you are going to use a wall to protect an asset, make sure no obvious holes appear in that wall.

 EXAM TIP All entry points to server rooms and wiring closets should be closely controlled and if possible have access logged through an access control system.

Guards provide an excellent security measure, because a visible person has a direct responsibility for security. Other employees expect security guards to behave a certain way with regard to securing the facility. Guards typically monitor entrances and exits and can maintain access logs of who has visited and departed from the building. Everyone who passes through security as a visitor signs the log, which can be useful in tracing who was at what location and why.

Security personnel can be helpful in securing information assets, but proper protection must be provided. Security guards are typically not computer security experts, so they need to be educated about network security as well as physical security involving users. They are the company's eyes and ears for suspicious activity, so the network security department needs to train them to notice suspicious network activity as well. Multiple extensions ringing in sequence during the night, computers rebooting all at once, or strange people parked in the parking lot with laptop computers are all indicators of a network attack that might be missed. Many traditional physical security tools such as access controls and CCTV camera systems are transitioning from closed hardwired systems to Ethernet- and IP-based systems. This transition opens up the devices to network attacks traditionally performed on computers. With physical security systems being implemented using the IP network, everyone in physical security must become smarter about network security.

Policies and Procedures

A policy's effectiveness depends on the culture of an organization, so all of the policies mentioned here should be followed up by functional procedures that are designed to implement them. Physical security *policies and procedures* relate to two distinct areas: those that affect the computers themselves and those that affect users.

To mitigate the risk to computers, physical security needs to be extended to the computers themselves. To combat the threat of bootdisks, the simplest answer is to remove or disable floppy drives from all desktop systems that do not require them. The continued advance of hard drive capacity has pushed file sizes beyond what floppies can typically hold. LANs with constant Internet connectivity have made network services the focus of how files are moved and distributed. These two factors have reduced floppy usage to the point where computer manufacturers are making floppy drives accessory options instead of standard features.

The second boot device to consider is the CD-ROM/DVD-ROM drive. This device can probably also be removed from or disabled on a number of machines. A DVD can not only be used as a boot device, but it can be exploited via the *autorun* feature that some operating systems support. Autorun was designed as a convenience for users, so that when a CD containing an application is inserted, the computer will instantly prompt for input versus having to explore the CD filesystem and find the executable file. Unfortunately, since the autorun file runs an executable, it can be programmed to do anything an attacker wants. If autorun is programmed maliciously, it could run an executable that installs malicious code that could allow an attacker to later gain remote control of the machine.

Disabling autorun is an easy task: In Windows XP, you simply right-click the DVD drive icon and set all media types to No Action. This ability can also be disabled by Active Directory settings. Turning off the autorun feature is an easy step that improves security; however, disabling autorun is only half the solution. Since the optical drive can be used as a boot device, a CD loaded with its own operating system (called a *LiveCD*) could be used to boot the computer with malicious system code. This separate operating system will bypass any passwords on the host machine and can access locally stored files.

Some users will undoubtedly insist on having DVD drives in their machines, but, if possible, the drives should be removed from every machine. If removal is not feasible, particularly on machines that require CD-ROM/DVD use, you can remove the optical drive from the boot sequence in the computer's BIOS.

To prevent an attacker from editing the boot order, *BIOS passwords* should be set. These passwords should be unique to the machine and, if possible, complex, using multiple uppercase and lowercase characters as well as numerics. Considering how often these passwords will be used, it is a good idea to list them all in an encrypted file so that a master passphrase will provide access to them.

As mentioned, floppy drives are being eliminated from manufacturers' machines because of their limited usefulness, but new devices are being adopted in their place, such as *USB devices*. USB ports have greatly expanded users' ability to connect devices to their computers. USB ports automatically recognize a device plugging into the system and usually work without the user needing to add drivers or configure software. This has spawned a legion of USB devices, from MP3 players to CD burners.

The most interesting of these, for security purposes, are the USB flash memory–based storage devices. USB drive keys, which are basically flash memory with a USB interface in a device about the size of your thumb, provide a way to move files easily from computer to computer. When plugged into a USB port, these devices automount and behave like any other drive attached to the computer. Their small size and relatively large capacity, coupled with instant read-write ability, present security problems. They can easily be used by an individual with malicious intent to conceal the removal of files or data from the building or to bring malicious files into the building and onto the company network.

In addition, well-intentioned users could accidentally introduce malicious code from USB devices by using them on an infected home machine and then bringing the infected device to the office, allowing the malware to bypass perimeter protections and possibly infect the organization. If USB devices are allowed, aggressive virus scanning should be implemented throughout the organization. The devices can be disallowed via Active Directory settings or with a Windows registry key entry. They could also be disallowed by unloading and disabling the USB drivers from user's machines, which will stop all USB devices from working—however, doing this can create more trouble if users have USB keyboards and mice. Editing the registry key is probably the most effective solution for users who are not authorized to use these devices. Users who do have authorization for USB drives must be educated about the potential dangers of their use.

EXAM TIP USB devices can be used to inject malicious code onto any machine to which they are attached. They can be used to download malicious code from machine to machine without using the network.

The outright theft of a computer is a simple physical attack. This attack can be mitigated in a number of ways, but the most effective method is to lock up equipment that contains important data. Insurance can cover the loss of the physical equipment, but this can do little to get a business up and running again quickly after a theft. Therefore, special access controls for server rooms, as well as simply locking the racks when maintenance is not being performed, are good ways to secure an area. From a data standpoint, mission-critical or high-value information should be stored on a server only. This can mitigate the risk of a desktop or laptop being stolen for the data it contains. Laptops are popular targets for thieves and should be locked inside a desk when not in use, or special computer lockdown cables can be used to secure them. If desktop towers are used, use computer desks that provide a space in which to lock the computer. All of these measures can improve the physical security of the computers themselves, but most of them can be defeated by attackers if users are not knowledgeable about the security program and do not follow it.

Users are often mentioned as the "weakest link in the security chain," and that can also apply to physical security. Fortunately, in physical security, users are often one of the primary beneficiaries of the security itself. A security program protects a company's information assets, but it also protects the people of the organization. A good security program will provide tangible benefits to employees, helping them to support and reinforce the security program. Users need to be aware of security issues, and they need to be involved in security enforcement. A healthy company culture of security will go a long way toward assisting in this effort. If, for example, workers in the office notice a strange person visiting their work areas, they should challenge the individual's presence—this is especially important if visitor badges are required for entry to the facility. A policy of having a visible badge with the employee's photo on it also assists everyone in recognizing people who do not belong.

Users should be briefed on the proper departments or personnel to contact when they suspect a security violation. Users can perform one of the most simple, yet important, information security tasks: locking a workstation immediately before they step away from it. While a locking screensaver is a good policy, setting it to less than 15 minutes is often counter-productive to active use on the job. An attacker only needs to be lucky enough to catch a machine that has been left alone for 5 minutes.

It is also important to know about workers typically overlooked in the organization. New hires should undergo a background check before being given access to network resources. This policy should also apply to all personnel who will have unescorted physical access to the facility, including janitorial and maintenance workers.

Access Controls and Monitoring

Access control means control of doors and entry points. The design and construction of all types of access control systems as well as the physical barriers to which they are most complementary are fully discussed in other texts. Here, we explore a few important points to help you safeguard the information infrastructure, especially where it meets with the physical access control system. This section talks about layered access systems, as well as electronic door control systems. It also discusses closed circuit television (CCTV) systems and the implications of different CCTV system types.

Locks have been discussed as a primary element of security. Although locks have been used for hundreds of years, their design has not changed much: a metal "token" is used to align pins in a mechanical device. As all mechanical devices have tolerances, it is possible to *sneak-through* these tolerances by "picking" the lock.

As we humans are always trying to build a better mousetrap, high security locks have been designed to defeat attacks; these locks are more sophisticated than a standard home deadbolt system. Typically found in commercial applications that require high security, these locks are produced by two primary manufacturers: Medeco and ASSA. (Medeco's locks, for example, require that the pins in the lock not only be set to a specific depth, but also individually rotated to set direction: left, right, or center.) High-end lock security is more important now that attacks such as "bump keys" are well known and widely available. A bump key is a key cut with all notches to the maximum depth, also known as "all nines." This key uses a technique that has been around a long time, but has recently gained a lot of popularity. The key is inserted into the lock and then sharply struck, bouncing the lock pins up above the shear line and allowing the lock to open.

Layered access is an important concept in security. It is often mentioned in conversations about network security perimeters, but in this chapter it relates to the concept of physical security perimeters. To help prevent an attacker from gaining access to important assets, these assets should be placed inside multiple perimeters. Servers should be placed in a separate secure area, ideally with a separate authentication mechanism. For example, if an organization has an electronic door control system using *contactless access cards*, a combination of the card and a separate PIN code would be required to open the door to the server room. Access to the server room should be limited to staff with a legitimate need to work on the servers. To layer the protection, the area surrounding the server room should also be limited to people who need to work in that area.

Many organizations use electronic access control systems to control the opening of doors. Doorways are electronically controlled via electronic door strikes and magnetic locks. These devices rely on an electronic signal from the control panel to release the mechanism that keeps the door closed. These devices are integrated into an access control system that controls and logs entry into all the doors connected to it, typically through the use of *access tokens*. Security is improved by having a centralized system that can instantly grant or refuse access based upon a token that is given to the user. This kind of system also logs user access, providing nonrepudiation of a specific user's presence in a controlled environment. The system will allow logging of personnel entry, auditing of personnel movements, and real-time monitoring of the access controls.

One caution about these kinds of systems is that they usually work with a software package that runs on a computer, and as such this computer should not be attached to the company network. While attaching it to the network can allow easy administration, the last thing you want is for an attacker to have control of the system that allows physical access to your facility. With this control, an attacker could input the ID of a badge that she owns, allowing full legitimate access to an area the system controls. Another problem with such a system is that it logs only the person who initially used the card to open the door—so no logs exist for doors that are propped open to allow others access, or of people "tailgating" through a door opened with a card. The implementation of a *mantrap* is one way to combat this function. A mantrap comprises two doors closely spaced that require the user to card through one and then the other sequentially. Mantraps make it nearly impossible to trail through a doorway undetected—if you happen to catch the first door, you will be trapped in by the second door.

 EXAM TIP A mantrap door arrangement can prevent unauthorized people from following authorized users through an access controlled door, which is also known as "tailgating."

CCTVs are similar to the door control systems—they can be very effective, but how they are implemented is an important consideration. The use of CCTV cameras for surveillance purposes dates back to at least 1961, when the London Transport train station installed cameras. The development of smaller camera components and lower costs has caused a boon in the CCTV industry since then.

Traditional cameras are analog based and require a video multiplexer to combine all the signals and make multiple views appear on a monitor. IP-based cameras are changing that, as most of them are standalone units viewable through a web browser. These IP-based systems add useful functionality, such as the ability to check on the building from the Internet. This network functionality, however, makes the cameras subject to normal IP-based network attacks. The last thing that anyone would want would be a DoS attack launched at the CCTV system just as a break-in was planned. For this reason, IP-based CCTV cameras should be placed on their own physically separate network that can be accessed only by security personnel. The same physical separation applies to any IP-based camera infrastructure. Older time-lapse tape recorders are slowly being replaced with digital video recorders. While the advance in technology is significant, be careful if and when these devices become IP-enabled, since they will become a security issue, just like everything else that touches the network. If you depend on the CCTV system to protect your organization's assets, carefully consider camera placement and the type of cameras used. Different iris types, focal lengths, and color or infrared capabilities are all options that make one camera superior over another in a specific location.

The issues discussed so far are especially prevalent when physical access control devices are connected to network resources. But no access controls, network or physical, would work without some form of authentication.

Environmental Controls

While the confidentiality of information is important, so is its availability. Sophisticated environmental controls are needed for current data centers. Fire suppression is also an important consideration when dealing with information systems.

Heating ventilating and air conditioning (HVAC) systems are critical for keeping data centers cool, because typical servers put out between 1000 and 2000 BTUs of heat. Enough servers in a confined area will create conditions too hot for the machines to continue to operate. The failure of HVAC systems for any reason is cause for concern. Properly securing these systems is important in helping prevent an attacker from performing a physical DoS attack on your servers.

Fire suppression systems should be specialized for the data center. Standard sprinkler-based systems are not optimal for data centers because water will ruin large electrical infrastructures and most integrated circuit–based devices—that is, computers. Gas-based systems are a good alternative, though they also carry special concerns. Halon was used for many years, and any existing installations may still have it for fire suppression in data centers. Halon displaces oxygen, and any people caught in the gas when the system goes off will need a breathing apparatus to survive. Halon is being replaced with other gas-based suppression systems, such as argon and nitrogen mixing systems or carbon dioxide, but the same danger to people exists, so these systems should be carefully implemented.

Authentication

Authentication is the process by which a user proves that she is who she says she is. Authentication is performed to allow or deny a person access to a physical space. The heart of any access control system is to allow access to authorized users and to make sure access is denied to unauthorized people. Authentication is required because many companies have grown so large that not every employee knows every other employee, so it can be difficult to tell by sight who is supposed to be where. Electronic access control systems were spawned from the need to have more logging and control than provided by the older method of metallic keys. Most electronic systems currently use a token-based card that if passed near a reader, and if you have permission from the system, will unlock the door strike and let you pass into the area. Newer technology attempts to make the authentication process easier and more secure.

The following sections discuss how tokens and biometrics are being used for authentication. It also looks into how multiple-factor authentication can be used for physical access.

Access Tokens

Access tokens are defined as "something you have." An access token is a physical object that identifies specific access rights, and in authentication falls into the "something you have" factor. Your house key, for example, is a basic physical access token that allows you access into your home. Although keys have been used to unlock devices for centuries, they do have several limitations. Keys are paired exclusively with a lock or a set of locks, and they are not easily changed. It is easy to add an authorized user by giving the user a copy of the key, but it is far more difficult to give that user selective access unless that specified area is already set up as a separate key. It is also difficult to take access away from a single key or key holder, which usually requires a rekey of the whole system.

In many businesses, physical access authentication has moved to contactless radio frequency cards and readers. When passed near a card reader, the card sends out a code using radio waves. The reader picks up this code and transmits it to the control panel. The control panel checks the code against the reader from which it is being read and the type of access the card has in its database. The advantages of this kind of token-based system include the fact that any card can be deleted from the system without affecting any other card or the rest of the system. In addition, all doors connected to the system can be segmented in any form or fashion to create multiple access areas, with different permissions for each one. The tokens themselves can also be grouped in multiple ways to provide different access levels to different groups of people. All of the access levels or segmentation of doors can be modified quickly and easily if building space is retasked. Newer technologies are adding capabilities to the standard token-based systems. The advent of *smart cards* (cards that contain integrated circuits) has enabled cryptographic types of authentication.

The primary drawback of token-based authentication is that only the token is being authenticated. Therefore, the theft of the token could grant anyone who possessed the token access to what the system protects. The risk of theft of the token can be offset by the use of *multiple-factor authentication*. One of the ways that people have tried to achieve multiple-factor authentication is to add a biometric factor to the system.

Biometrics

Biometrics use the measurements of certain biological factors to identify one specific person from others. These factors are based on parts of the human body that are unique. The most well-known of these unique biological factors is the fingerprint. However, many others can be used—for instance, the retina or iris of the eye, the geometry of the hand, and the geometry of the face. When these are used for authentication, there is a two part process, enrollment and then authentication. During enrollment, a computer takes the image of the biological factor and reduces it to a numeric value. When the user attempts to authenticate, this feature is scanned by the reader, and the computer compares the numeric value being read to the one stored in the database. If they match, access is allowed. Since these physical factors are unique, theoretically only the actual authorized person would be allowed access.

In the real world, however, the theory behind biometrics breaks down. Tokens that have a digital code work very well because everything remains in the digital realm. A computer checks your code, such as 123, against the database; if the computer finds 123 and that number has access, the computer opens the door. Biometrics, however, take an analog signal, such as a fingerprint or a face, and attempt to digitize it, and it is then matched against the digits in the database. The problem with an analog signal is that it might not encode the exact same way twice. For example, if you came to work with a bandage on your chin, would the face-based biometrics grant you access or deny it?

Engineers who designed these systems understood that if a system was set to exact checking, an encoded biometric might never grant access since it might never scan the biometric exactly the same way twice. Therefore, most systems have tried to allow a certain amount of error in the scan, while not allowing too much. This leads to the concepts of false positives and false negatives. A *false positive* occurs when a biometric is scanned and allows access to someone who is not authorized—for example, two people who have very similar fingerprints might be recognized as the same person by the computer, which grants access to the wrong person. A *false negative* occurs when the system denies access to someone who is actually authorized—for example, a user at the hand geometry scanner forgot to wear a ring he usually wears and the computer doesn't recognize his hand and denies him access. For biometric authentication to work properly, and also be trusted, it must minimize the existence of both false positives and false negatives. To do that, a balance between exacting and error must be created so that the machines allow a little physical variance—but not too much.

Another concern with biometrics is that if someone is able to steal the uniqueness factor that the machine scans—your fingerprint from a glass, for example—and is able to reproduce that factor in a substance that fools the scanner, that person now has your access privileges. This idea is compounded by the fact that it is impossible for you to change your fingerprint if it gets stolen. It is easy to replace a lost or stolen token and delete the missing one from the system, but it is far more difficult to replace a human hand. Another problem with biometrics is that parts of the human body can change. A human face can change, through scarring, weight loss or gain, or surgery. A fingerprint can be changed through damage to the fingers. Eye retinas can be affected by some types of diabetes or pregnancy. All of these changes force the biometric system to allow a higher tolerance for variance in the biometric being read. This has led the way for high-security installations to move toward *multiple-factor authentication.*

Multiple-factor Authentication

Multiple-factor authentication is simply the combination of two or more types of authentication. Three broad categories of authentication can be used: what you are (for example, biometrics), what you have (for instance, tokens), and what you know (passwords and other information). Two-factor authentication combines any two of these before granting access. An example would be a card reader that then turns on a fingerprint scanner—if your fingerprint matches the one on file for the card, you are granted access. Three-factor authentication would combine all three types, such as a smart card reader that asks for a PIN before enabling a retina scanner. If all three correspond to a valid user in the computer database, access is granted.

 EXAM TIP Two-factor authentication combines any two methods, matching items such as a token with a biometric. Three-factor authentication combines any three, such as a passcode, biometric, and a token.

Multiple-factor authentication methods greatly enhance security by making it very difficult for an attacker to obtain all the correct materials for authentication. They also protect against the risk of stolen tokens, as the attacker must have the correct biometric, password, or both. More important, it enhances the security of biometric systems. Multiple-factor authentication does this by protecting against a stolen biometric. Changing the token makes the biometric useless unless the attacker can steal the new token. It also reduces false positives by trying to match the supplied biometric with the one that is associated with the supplied token. This prevents the computer from seeking a match using the entire database of biometrics. Using multiple factors is one of the best ways to ensure proper authentication and access control.

Chapter Review

Physical Security is required to maintain the security of information systems. Any person with malicious intent who gains physical access to a computer system can cause significant damage. If a person can gain physical access, almost no information security safeguard can truly protect valuable information.

You have seen how access controls can provide legitimate access while denying intruders. However, you have also seen how these systems are increasingly computer- and network-based, which can cause a separate path of attack to be generated. Physical access can be compromised through the use of information systems. As the tendency to use the IP network increases for every device in the organization, more and more interlinked systems will require interlinked security requirements. This is the concept of *convergence*, which can apply to security as well as voice, video, and data.

Questions

1. The feature that could allow a CD to load malicious code is called what?

   A. A false negative

   B. A CD-Key

   C. A MBR, or Master Boot Record

   D. Auto-run

2. Why is water not used for fire suppression in data centers?

   A. It would cause a flood.

   B. Water cannot put out an electrical fire.

   C. Water would ruin all the electronic equipment.

   D. Building code prevents it.

3. Which one is not a unique biometric?

   A. Fingerprint

   B. Eye retina

   C. Hand geometry

   D. Shoulder-to-waist geometry

4. Why is physical security so important to good network security?

   A. Because encryption is not involved

    B. Because physical access defeats nearly all network security measures

    C. Because an attacker can steal biometric identities

    D. Authentication

5. How does multiple-factor authentication improve security?

    A. By using biometrics, no other person can authenticate.

    B. It restricts users to smaller spaces.

    C. By using a combination of authentications, it is more difficult for someone to gain illegitimate access.

    D. It denies access to an intruder multiple times.

6. Why is access to an Ethernet jack a risk?

    A. A special plug can be used to short out the entire network.

    B. An attacker can use it to make a door entry card for himself.

    C. Wireless traffic can find its way onto the local area network.

    D. It allows access to the internal network.

7. When a biometric device has a false positive, it has done what?

    A. Generated a positive charge to the system for which compensation is required

    B. Allowed access to a person who is not authorized

    C. Denied access to a person who is authorized

    D. Failed, forcing the door it controls to be propped open

8. Why does an IP-based CCTV system need to be implemented carefully?

    A. Camera resolutions are lower.

    B. They don't record images; they just send them to web pages.

    C. The network cables are more easily cut.

    D. They could be remotely attacked via the network.

9. Which of the following is a very simple physical attack?

    A. Using a custom RFID transmitter to open a door

    B. Accessing an Ethernet jack to attack the network

    C. Outright theft of the computers

    D. Installing a virus on the CCTV system

10. A perfect bit-by-bit copy of a drive is called what?

    A. Drive picture

    B. Drive image

    C. Drive copy

    D. Drive partition

11. What about physical security makes it more acceptable to other employees?

    A. It is more secure.

    B. Computers are not important.

    C. It protects the employees themselves.

    D. It uses encryption.

12. On whom should a company perform background checks?

    A. System administrators only

    B. Contract personnel only

    C. Background checks are not needed outside of the military

    D. All individuals who have unescorted physical access to the facility

13. What is a common threat to token-based access controls?

    A. The key

    B. Demagnetization of the strip

    C. A system crash

    D. Loss or theft of the token

14. Why should security guards get cross-training in network security?

    A. They are the eyes and ears of the corporation when it comes to security.

    B. They are the only people in the building at night.

    C. They are more qualified to know what a security threat is.

    D. They have the authority to detain violators.

15. Why can a USB flash drive be a threat?

    A. They use too much power.

    B. They can bring malicious code past other security mechanisms.

    C. They can be stolen.

    D. They can be encrypted.

Answers

1. D. Auto-run allows CDs to execute code automatically.

2. C. Electronic components would be ruined by a water-based fire-suppression system.

3. D. Shoulder-to-waist geometry is not unique. All the other examples are biometrics that are unique.

4. B. Physical access to a computer system will almost always defeat any security measures put in place on the system.

5. **C.** Multiple-factor authentication gives an attacker several systems to overcome, making the unauthorized access of systems much more difficult.

6. **D.** An exposed Ethernet jack available in a public place can allow access to the internal network, typically bypassing most of the network's security systems.

7. **B.** A false positive means the system granted access to an unauthorized person based on a biometric being *close* to an authorized person's biometric.

8. **D.** Any device attached to the IP network can be attacked using a traditional IP-based attack.

9. **C.** The theft of a computer is a very simple attack that can be carried out surprisingly effectively. This allows an attacker to compromise the stolen machine and its data at his leisure.

10. **B.** A drive image is a perfect copy of a drive that can then be analyzed on another computer.

11. **C.** Physical security protects the people, giving them a vested interest in its support.

12. **D.** All unescorted people entering the facility should be background checked.

13. **D.** The loss or theft of the token is the most common and most serious threat to the system; anyone with a token can access the system.

14. **A.** Security guards are the corporation's eyes and ears and have a direct responsibility for security information.

15. **B.** USB drives have large storage capacities and can carry some types of malicious code past traditional virus filters.

Infrastructure Security

- Learn about the types of network devices used to construct networks
- Discover the types of media used to carry network signals
- Explore the types of storage media used to store information
- Grow acquainted with basic terminology for a series of network functions related to information security
- Explore NAC/NAP methodologies

Infrastructure security begins with the design of the infrastructure itself. The proper use of components improves not only performance but security as well. Network components are not isolated from the computing environment and are an essential aspect of a total computing environment. From the routers, switches, and cables that connect the devices, to the firewalls and gateways that manage communication, from the network design to the protocols employed, all of these items play essential roles in both performance and security.

In the *CIA* of security, the *A* for *availability* is often overlooked. Yet it is availability that has moved computing into this networked framework, and this concept has played a significant role in security. A failure in security can easily lead to a failure in availability and hence a failure of the system to meet user needs.

Security failures can occur in two ways. First, a failure can allow unauthorized users access to resources and data they are not authorized to use, compromising information security. Second, a failure can prevent a user from accessing resources and data the user is authorized to use. This second failure is often overlooked, but it can be as serious as the first. The primary goal of network infrastructure security is to allow all authorized use and deny all unauthorized use of resources.

Devices

A complete network computer solution in today's business environment consists of more than just client computers and servers. *Devices* are needed to connect the clients and servers and to regulate the traffic between them. Devices are also needed to expand this network beyond simple client computers and servers to include yet other devices, such as wireless and handheld systems. Devices come in many forms and with many functions, from hubs and switches, to routers, wireless access points, and special-purpose devices such as virtual private network (VPN) devices. Each device has a specific network function and plays a role in maintaining network infrastructure security.

Workstations

Most users are familiar with the client computers used in the client/server model called *workstation* devices. The workstation is the machine that sits on the desktop and is used every day for sending and reading e-mail, creating spreadsheets, writing reports in a word processing program, and playing games. If a workstation is connected to a network, it is an important part of the security solution for the network. Many threats to information security can start at a workstation, but much can be done in a few simple steps to provide protection from many of these threats.

Workstations are attractive targets for crackers as they are numerous and can serve as entry points into the network and the data that is commonly the target of an attack. Although *safety* is a relative term, following these basic steps will increase workstation security immensely:

- Remove unnecessary protocols such as Telnet, NetBIOS, IPX.
- Remove modems unless needed and authorized.
- Remove all shares that are not necessary.
- Rename the administrator account, securing it with a strong password.
- Remove unnecessary user accounts.
- Install an antivirus program and keep abreast of updates.
- If the floppy drive is not needed, remove or disconnect it.
- Consider disabling USB ports via CMOS to restrict data movement to USB devices.
- If no corporate firewall exists between the machine and the Internet, install a firewall.
- Keep the operating system (OS) patched and up to date.

Antivirus Software for Workstations

Antivirus packages are available from a wide range of vendors. Running a network of computers without this basic level of protection will be an exercise in futility. Even though a virus attack is rare, the time and money you spend cleaning it up will more than equal the cost of antivirus protection. Even more important, once connected by networks, computers can spread a virus from machine to machine with an ease that's even greater than simple floppy disk transfer. One unprotected machine can lead to problems throughout a network as other machines have to use their antivirus software to attempt to clean up a spreading infection.

Even secure networks can fall prey to virus and worm contamination, and infection has been known to come from commercial packages. As important as antivirus software is, it is even more important to keep the virus definitions for the software up to date. Out-of-date definitions can lead to a false sense of security, and many of the most potent virus and worm attacks are the newest ones being developed. The risk associated with a new virus is actually higher than for many of the old ones, which have been eradicated to a great extent by antivirus software.

A virus is a piece of software that must be introduced to the network and then executed on a machine. Workstations are the primary mode of entry for a virus into a network. Although a lot of methods can be used to introduce a virus to a network, the two most common are transfer of an infected file from another networked machine and from e-mail. A lot of work has gone into software to clean e-mail while in transit and at the mail server. But transferred files are a different matter altogether. People bring files from home, from friends, from places unknown and then execute them on a PC for a variety of purposes. It doesn't matter whether it is a funny executable, a game, or even an authorized work application—the virus doesn't care what the original file is, it just uses it to gain access. Even sharing of legitimate work files and applications can introduce viruses.

Once considered by many users to be immune, Apple Macintosh computers had very few examples of malicious software in the wild. This was not due to anything other than a low market share, and hence the devices were ignored by the malware community as a whole. As Mac has increased in market share, so has its exposure, and today a variety of Mac OS X malware steals files and passwords and is even used to take users' pictures with the computer's built-in webcam. All user machines need to install antivirus software in today's environment, because any computer can become a target.

The form of transfer is not an issue either: whether via a USB device, CD/DVD, or FTP doesn't matter. When the transferred file is executed, the virus is propagated. Simple removal of a CD/DVD drive or disabling USB ports will not adequately protect against this threat; nor does training, for users will eventually justify a transfer. The only real defense is an antivirus program that monitors all file movements.

Additional Precautions for Workstations

Personal firewalls are a necessity if a machine has an unprotected interface to the Internet. These are seen less often in commercial networks, as it is more cost effective to connect through a firewall server. With the advent of broadband connections for homes and small offices, this needed device is frequently missed. This can result in penetration of a PC from an outside hacker or a worm infection. Worst of all, the workstation can become part of a larger attack against another network, unknowingly joining forces with other compromised machines in a distributed denial-of-service (DDoS) attack.

The practice of disabling or removing unnecessary devices and software from workstations is also a sensible precaution. If a particular service, device, or account is not needed, disabling or removing it will prevent its unauthorized use by others. Having a standard image of a workstation and duplicating it across a bunch of identical workstations will reduce the workload for maintaining these requirements and reduce total cost of operations. Proper security at the workstation level can increase availability of network resources to users, enabling the business to operate as effectively as possible.

The primary method of controlling the security impact of a workstation on a network is to reduce the available attack surface area. Turning off all services that are not needed or permitted by policy will reduce the number of vulnerabilities. Removing methods of connecting additional devices to a workstation to move data—such as CD/DVD drives and USB ports—assists in controlling the movement of data into and out of the device. User-level controls, such as limiting e-mail attachment options, screening all attachments at the e-mail server level, and reducing network shares to needed shares only, can be used to limit the excessive connectivity that can impact security.

Servers

Servers are the computers in a network that host applications and data for everyone to share. Servers come in many sizes, from small single-CPU boxes that can be less powerful than a workstation, to multiple-CPU monsters, up to and including mainframes. The operating systems used by servers range from Windows Server, to Linux/UNIX, to Multiple Virtual Storage (MVS) and other mainframe operating systems. The OS on a server tends to be more robust than the OS on a workstation system and is designed to service multiple users over a network at the same time. Servers can host a variety of applications, including web servers, databases, e-mail servers, file servers, print servers, and application servers for middleware applications.

The key management issue behind running a secure server setup is to identify the specific needs of a server for its proper operation and enable only items necessary for those functions. Keeping all other services and users off the system improves system throughput and increases security. Reducing the attack surface area associated with a server reduces the vulnerabilities now and in the future as updates are required.

 TIP Specific security needs can vary depending on the server's specific use, but as a minimum, the following are beneficial:

- Remove unnecessary protocols such as Telnet, NetBIOS, Internetwork Packet Exchange (IPX), and File Transfer Protocol (FTP).
- Remove all shares that are not necessary.
- Rename the administrator account, securing it with a strong password.
- Remove unnecessary user accounts.
- Keep the OS patched and up to date.
- Control physical access to servers.

Once a server has been built and is ready to place into operation, the recording of MD5 hash values on all of its crucial files will provide valuable information later in case of a question concerning possible system integrity after a detected intrusion. The use of hash values to detect changes was first developed by Gene Kim and Eugene Spafford at Purdue University in 1992. The concept became the product Tripwire, which is now available in commercial and open source forms. The same basic concept is used by many security packages to detect file level changes.

Antivirus Software for Servers

The need for antivirus protection on servers depends a great deal on the use of the server. Some types of servers, such as e-mail servers, can require extensive antivirus protection because of the services they provide. Other servers (domain controllers and remote access servers, for example) may not require any antivirus software, as they do not allow users to place files on them. File servers will need protection, as will certain types of application servers. There is no general rule, so each server and its role in the network will need to be examined for applicability of antivirus software.

Network Interface Cards

To connect a server or workstation to a network, a device known as a *network interface card (NIC)* is used. A NIC is a card with a connector port for a particular type of network connection, either Ethernet or Token Ring. The most common network type in use for local area networks is the Ethernet protocol, and the most common connector is the RJ-45 connector. Figure 8-1 shows a RJ-45 connector (lower) compared to a standard telephone connector (upper). Additional types of connectors include coaxial cable connectors, frequently used with cable modems and extending from the wall to the cable modem.

The purpose of a NIC is to provide lower level protocol functionality from the OSI (Open System Interconnection) model. A NIC is the physical connection between a computer and the network. As the NIC defines the type of physical layer connection, different NICs are used for different physical protocols. NICs come as single-port and multiport, and most workstations use only a single-port NIC, as only a single network connection is needed. For servers, multiport NICs are used to increase the number of network connections, increasing the data throughput to and from the network.

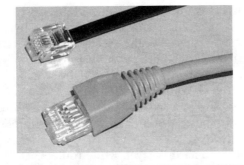

Figure 8-1   Comparison of RJ-45 (lower) and phone connectors (upper)

NICs are serialized with a unique code, referred to as a Media Access Control address (MAC address). These are created by the manufacturer, with a portion being manufacturer and a portion being a serial number, guaranteeing uniqueness. MAC addresses are used in the addressing and delivery of network packets to the correct machine and in a variety of security situations. Unfortunately, these addresses can be changed, or "spoofed," rather easily. In fact, it is common for personal routers to clone a MAC address to allow users to use multiple devices over a network connection that expects a single MAC.

Hubs

Hubs are networking equipment that connect devices using the same protocol at the physical layer of the OSI model. A hub allows multiple machines in an area to be connected together in a star configuration with the hub as the center. This configuration can save significant amounts of cable and is an efficient method of configuring an Ethernet backbone. All connections on a hub share a single *collision domain*, a small cluster in a network where collisions occur. As network traffic increases, it can become limited by collisions. The collision issue has made hubs obsolete in newer, higher performance networks, with low-cost switches and switched Ethernet keeping costs low and usable bandwidth high. Hubs also create a security weakness in that all connected devices see all traffic, enabling sniffing and eavesdropping to occur.

Bridges

Bridges are networking equipment that connect devices using the same protocol at the physical layer of the OSI model. A bridge operates at the data link layer, filtering traffic based on MAC addresses. Bridges can reduce collisions by separating pieces of a network into two separate collision domains, but this only cuts the collision problem in half. Although bridges are useful, a better solution is to use switches for network connections.

Switches

Switches form the basis for connections in most Ethernet-based local area networks (LANs). Although hubs and bridges still exist, in today's high-performance network environment switches have replaced both. A switch has separate collision domains for each port. This means that for each port, two collision domains exist: one from the port to the client on the downstream side and one from the switch to the network upstream. When *full duplex* is employed, collisions are virtually eliminated from the two nodes, host and client. This also acts as a security factor in that a sniffer can see only limited traffic, as opposed to a hub-based system, where a single sniffer can see all of the traffic to and from connected devices.

Switches operate at the data link layer, while routers act at the network layer. For intranets, switches have become what routers are on the Internet—the device of choice for connecting machines. As switches have become the primary network connectivity device, additional functionality has been added to them. A switch is usually a layer 2 device, but layer 3 switches incorporate routing functionality.

Switches can also perform a variety of security functions. Switches work by moving packets from inbound connections to outbound connections. While moving the packets, it is possible to inspect the packet headers and enforce security policies. Port address security based on MAC addresses can determine whether a packet is allowed or blocked from a connection. This is the very function that a firewall uses for its determination, and this same functionality is what allows an 802.1x device to act as an "edge device."

One of the security concerns with switches is that, like routers, they are intelligent network devices and are therefore subject to hijacking by hackers. Should a hacker break into a switch and change its parameters, he might be able to eavesdrop on specific or all communications, virtually undetected. Switches are commonly administered using the Simple Network Management Protocol (SNMP) and Telnet protocol, both of which have a serious weakness in that they send passwords across the network in clear text. A hacker armed with a sniffer that observes maintenance on a switch can capture the administrative password. This allows the hacker to come back to the switch later and configure it as an administrator. An additional problem is that switches are shipped with default passwords, and if these are not changed when the switch is set up, they offer an unlocked door to a hacker. Commercial quality switches have a local serial console port for guaranteed access to the switch for purposes of control. Some products in the marketplace enable an out-of-band network, connecting these serial console ports to enable remote, secure access to programmable network devices.

> **CAUTION** To secure a switch, you should disable all access protocols other than a secure serial line or a secure protocol such as Secure Shell (SSH). Using only secure methods to access a switch will limit the exposure to hackers and malicious users. Maintaining secure network switches is even more important than securing individual boxes, for the span of control to intercept data is much wider on a switch, especially if it's reprogrammed by a hacker.

Virtual Local Area Networks

The other security feature that can be enabled in some switches is the concept of *virtual local area networks (VLANs)*. Cisco defines a VLAN as a "broadcast domain within a switched network," meaning that information is carried in broadcast mode only to devices within a VLAN. Switches that allow multiple VLANs to be defined enable broadcast messages to be segregated into the specific VLANs. If each floor of an office, for example, were to have a single switch and you had accounting functions on two floors, engineering functions on two floors, and sales functions on two floors, then separate VLANs for accounting, engineering, and sales would allow separate broadcast domains for each of these groups, even those that spanned floors. This configuration increases network segregation, increasing throughput and security.

Unused switch ports can be preconfigured into empty VLANs that do not connect to the rest of the network. This significantly increases security against unauthorized network connections. If, for example, a building is wired with network connections in all rooms, including multiple connections for convenience and future expansion, these unused ports become open to the network. One solution is to disconnect the connection at the switch, but this merely moves the network opening into the switch room. The better solution is to disconnect it and disable the port in the switch. This can be accomplished by connecting all unused ports into a VLAN that isolates them from the rest of the network.

Additional aspects of VLANs are explored in the "Security Topologies" section later in this chapter.

Routers

Routers are network traffic management devices used to connect different network segments together. Routers operate at the network layer of the OSI model, routing traffic using the network address (typically an IP address) utilizing routing protocols to determine optimal routing paths across a network. Routers form the backbone of the Internet, moving traffic from network to network, inspecting packets from every communication as they move traffic in optimal paths.

Routers operate by examining each packet, looking at the destination address, and using algorithms and tables to determine where to send the packet next. This process of examining the header to determine the next hop can be done in quick fashion.

Routers use access control lists (ACLs) as a method of deciding whether a packet is allowed to enter the network. With ACLs, it is also possible to examine the source address and determine whether or not to allow a packet to pass. This allows routers equipped with ACLs to drop packets according to rules built in the ACLs. This can be a cumbersome process to set up and maintain, and as the ACL grows in size, routing efficiency can be decreased. It is also possible to configure some routers to act as quasi–application gateways, performing stateful packet inspection and using contents as well as IP addresses to determine whether or not to permit a packet to pass. This can tremendously increase the time for a router to pass traffic and can significantly decrease router throughput. Configuring ACLs and other aspects of setting up routers for this type of use are beyond the scope of this book.

NOTE ACLs can be a significant effort to establish and maintain. Creating them is a straightforward task, but their judicious use will yield security benefits with a limited amount of maintenance. This can be very important in security zones such as a DMZ and at edge devices, blocking undesired outside contact while allowing known inside traffic.

One serious operational security concern regarding routers concerns the access to a router and control of its internal functions. Like a switch, a router can be accessed using SNMP and Telnet and programmed remotely. Because of the geographic separation of routers, this can become a necessity, for many routers in the world of the Internet can be hundreds of miles apart, in separate locked structures. Physical control over a router is absolutely necessary, for if any device, be it server, switch, or router, is physically accessed by a hacker, it should be considered compromised and thus such access must be prevented. As with switches, it is important to ensure that the administrative password is never passed in the clear, only secure mechanisms are used to access the router, and all of the default passwords are reset to strong passwords.

Just like switches, the most assured point of access for router management control is via the serial control interface port. This allows access to the control aspects of the router without having to deal with traffic related issues. For internal company networks, where the geographic dispersion of routers may be limited, third-party solutions to allow out-of-band remote management exist. This allows complete control over the router in a secure fashion, even from a remote location, although additional hardware is required.

Routers are available from numerous vendors and come in sizes big and small. A typical small home office router for use with cable modem/DSL service is shown in Figure 8-2. Larger routers can handle traffic of up to tens of gigabytes per second per channel, using fiber-optic inputs and moving tens of thousands of concurrent Internet connections across the network. These routers can cost hundreds of thousands of dollars and form an essential part of e-commerce infrastructure, enabling large enterprises such as Amazon and eBay to serve many customers concurrently.

Firewalls

A *firewall* can be hardware, software, or a combination whose purpose is to enforce a set of network security policies across network connections. It is much like a wall with a window: the wall serves to keep things out, except those permitted through the window (see Figure 8-3). Network security policies act like the glass in the window; they permit some things to pass, such as light, while blocking others, such as air. The heart of a firewall is the set of security policies that it enforces. Management determines what is allowed in the form of network traffic between devices, and these policies are used to build rule sets for the firewall devices used to filter network traffic across the network.

Security policies are rules that define what traffic is permissible and what traffic is to be blocked or denied. These are not universal rules, and many different sets of rules are created for a single company with multiple connections. A web server connected to the

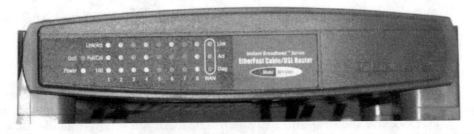

Figure 8-2   A small home office router for cable modem/DSL use

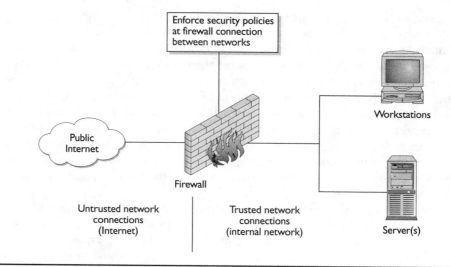

Figure 8-3   How a firewall works

Internet may be configured to allow traffic only on port 80 for HTTP and have all other ports blocked, for example. An e-mail server may have only necessary ports for e-mail open, with others blocked. The network firewall can be programmed to block all traffic to the web server except for port 80 traffic, and to block all traffic bound to the mail server except for port 25. In this fashion, the firewall acts as a security filter, enabling control over network traffic, by machine, by port, and in some cases based on application level detail. A key to setting security policies for firewalls is the same as has been seen for other security policies—the principle of least access. Allow only the necessary access for a function; block or deny all unneeded functionality. How a firm deploys its firewalls determines what is needed for security policies for each firewall.

As will be discussed later, the security topology will determine what network devices are employed at what points in a network. At a minimum, the corporate connection to the Internet should pass through a firewall. This firewall should block all network traffic except that specifically authorized by the firm. This is actually easy to do: Blocking communications on a port is simple—just tell the firewall to close the port. The issue comes in deciding what services are needed and by whom, and thus which ports should be open and which should be closed. This is what makes a security policy useful. The perfect set of network security policies, for a firewall, is one that the end user never sees and that never allows even a single unauthorized packet to enter the network. As with any other perfect item, it will be rare to find the perfect set of security policies for firewalls in an enterprise.

To develop a complete and comprehensive security policy, it is first necessary to have a complete and comprehensive understanding of your network resources and their uses. Once you know how the network will be used, you will have an idea of what to permit. In addition, once you understand what you need to protect, you will have an idea of what to block. Firewalls are designed to block attacks before they reach a target machine. Common targets are web servers, e-mail servers, DNS servers, FTP services, and databases. Each of these has separate functionality, and each has unique vulnerabilities. Once you have decided who should receive what type of traffic and what types should be blocked, you can administer this through the firewall.

How Do Firewalls Work?

Firewalls enforce the established security policies through a variety of mechanisms, including the following:

- Network Address Translation (NAT)
- Basic packet filtering
- Stateful packet filtering
- ACLs
- Application layer proxies

One of the most basic security functions provided by a firewall is NAT, which allows you to mask significant amounts of information from outside of the network. This allows an outside entity to communicate with an entity inside the firewall without truly knowing its address. NAT is a technique used in IPv4 to link private IP addresses to public ones. Private IP addresses are sets of IP addresses that can be used by anyone and by definition are not routable across the Internet. NAT can assist in security by preventing direct access to devices from outside the firm, without first having the address changed at a NAT device. The benefit is less public IP addresses are needed, and from a security point of view the internal address structure is not known to the outside world. If a hacker attacks the source address, he is simply attacking the NAT device, not the actual sender of the packet. NAT is described in detail in the "Security Topologies" section later in this chapter.

NAT was conceived to resolve an address shortage associated with IPv4 and is considered by many to be unnecessary for IPv6. The added security features of enforcing traffic translation and hiding internal network details from direct outside connections will give NAT life well into the IPv6 timeframe.

Basic packet filtering, the next most common firewall technique, involves looking at packets, their ports, protocols, source and destination addresses, and checking that information against the rules configured on the firewall. Telnet and FTP connections may be prohibited from being established to a mail or database server, but they may be allowed for the respective service servers. This is a fairly simple method of filtering based on information in each packet header, such as IP addresses and TCP/UDP ports. Packet filtering will not detect and catch all undesired packets, but it is fast and efficient.

To look at all packets and determine the need for each and its data requires *stateful* packet filtering. Stateful means that the firewall maintains, or knows, the context of a conversation. In many cases, rules depend on the context of a specific communication connection. For instance, traffic from an outside server to an inside server may be allowed if it is requested but blocked if it is not. A common example is a request for a web page. This request is actually a series of requests to multiple servers, each of which can be allowed or blocked. Advanced firewalls employ stateful packet filtering to prevent several types of undesired communications. Should a packet come from outside the network, in an attempt to pretend that it is a response to a message from inside the network, the firewall will have no record of it being requested and can discard it, blocking the undesired external access attempt. As many communications will be transferred to high ports (above 1023), stateful monitoring will enable the system to determine which sets of high communications are permissible and which should be blocked. A disadvantage of stateful monitoring is that it takes significant resources and processing to perform this type of monitoring, and this reduces efficiency and requires more robust and expensive hardware.

 EXAM TIP Firewalls operate by examining packets and selectively denying some based on a set of rules. Firewalls act as gatekeepers or sentries at select network points, segregating traffic and allowing some to pass and blocking others.

Some high-security firewalls also employ application layer proxies. Packets are not allowed to traverse the firewall, but data instead flows up to an application that in turn decides what to do with it. For example, an Simple Mail Transfer Protocol (SMTP) proxy may accept inbound mail from the Internet and forward it to the internal corporate mail server. While proxies provide a high level of security by making it very difficult for an attacker to manipulate the actual packets arriving at the destination, and while they provide the opportunity for an application to interpret the data prior to forwarding it to the destination, they generally are not capable of the same throughput as stateful packet inspection firewalls. The trade-off between performance and speed is a common one and must be evaluated with respect to security needs and performance requirements.

Wireless

Wireless devices bring additional security concerns. There is, by definition, no physical connection to a wireless device; radio waves or infrared carry data, which allows anyone within range access to the data. This means that unless you take specific precautions, you have no control over who can see your data. Placing a wireless device behind a firewall does not do any good, because the firewall stops only physically connected traffic from reaching the device. Outside traffic can come literally from the parking lot directly to the wireless device.

The point of entry from a wireless device to a wired network is performed at a device called a *wireless access point*. Wireless access points can support multiple concurrent devices accessing network resources through the network node they provide. A typical wireless access point is shown here:

A typical wireless access point

Several mechanisms can be used to add wireless functionality to a machine. For PCs, this can be done via an expansion card. For notebooks, a PCMCIA adapter for wireless networks is available from several vendors. For both PCs and notebooks, vendors have introduced USB-based wireless connectors. The following illustration shows one vendor's card—note the extended length used as an antenna. Not all cards have the same configuration, although they all perform the same function: to enable a wireless network connection. The numerous wireless protocols (802.11a, b, g, I, and n) are covered in Chapter 10. Wireless access points and cards must be matched by protocol for proper operation.

A typical PCMCIA wireless network card

NOTE To prevent unauthorized wireless access to the network, configuration of remote access protocols to a wireless access point is common. Forcing authentication and verifying authorization is a seamless method of performing basic network security for connections in this fashion. These protocols are covered in Chapter 10.

Modems

Modems were once a slow method of remote connection that was used to connect client workstations to remote services over standard telephone lines. *Modem* is a shortened form of *modulator/demodulator*, covering the functions actually performed by the device as it converts analog signals to digital and vice versa. To connect a digital computer signal to the analog telephone line required one of these devices. Today, the use of the term has expanded to cover devices connected to special digital telephone lines—DSL modems—and to cable television lines—cable modems. Although these devices are not actually modems in the true sense of the word, the term has stuck through marketing efforts directed to consumers. DSL and cable modems offer broadband high-speed connections and the opportunity for continuous connections to the Internet. Along with these new desirable characteristics come some undesirable ones, however. Although they both provide the same type of service, cable and DSL modems have some differences. A DSL modem provides a direct connection between a subscriber's computer and an Internet connection at the local telephone company's switching station. This private connection offers a degree of security, as it does not involve others sharing the circuit. Cable modems are set up in shared arrangements that theoretically could allow a neighbor to sniff a user's cable modem traffic.

Cable modems were designed to share a party line in the terminal signal area, and the cable modem standard, the Data Over Cable Service Interface Specification (DOCSIS), was designed to accommodate this concept. DOCSIS includes built-in support for security protocols, including authentication and packet filtering. Although this does not guarantee privacy, it prevents ordinary subscribers from seeing others' traffic without using specialized hardware.

Both cable and DSL services are designed for a continuous connection, which brings up the question of IP address life for a client. Although some services originally used a static IP arrangement, virtually all have now adopted the Dynamic Host Configuration Protocol (DHCP) to manage their address space. A static IP has an advantage of being the same and enabling convenient DNS connections for outside users. As cable and DSL services are primarily designed for client services as opposed to host services, this is not a relevant issue. A security issue of a static IP is that it is a stationary target for hackers. The move to DHCP has not significantly lessened this threat, however, for the typical IP lease on a cable modem DHCP is for days. This is still relatively stationary, and some form of firewall protection needs to be employed by the user.

Cable/DSL Security

The modem equipment provided by the subscription service converts the cable or DSL signal into a standard Ethernet signal that can then be connected to a NIC on the client device. This is still just a direct network connection, with no security device separating the two. The most common security device used in cable/DSL connections is a firewall. The firewall needs to be installed between the cable/DSL modem and client computers.

Two common methods exist for this in the marketplace. The first is software on each client device. Numerous software companies offer Internet firewall packages, which can cost under $50. Another solution is the use of a cable/DSL router with a built-in firewall. These are also relatively inexpensive, in the $100 range, and can be combined with software for an additional level of protection. Another advantage to the router solution is that most such routers allow multiple clients to share a common Internet connection, and most can also be enabled with other networking protocols such as VPN. A typical small home office cable modem/DSL router was shown earlier in Figure 8-2. The bottom line is simple: Even if you connect only occasionally and you disconnect between uses, you need a firewall between the client and the Internet connection. Most commercial firewalls for cable/DSL systems come preconfigured for Internet use and require virtually no maintenance other than keeping the system up to date.

Telecom/PBX

Private branch exchanges (PBXs) are an extension of the public telephone network into a business. Although typically considered a separate entity from data systems, they are frequently interconnected and have security requirements as part of this interconnection as well as of their own. PBXs are computer-based switching equipment designed to connect telephones into the local phone system. Basically digital switching systems, they can be compromised from the outside and used by phone hackers (phreakers) to make phone calls at the business' expense. Although this type of hacking has decreased with lower cost long distance, it has not gone away, and as several firms learn every year, voice mail boxes and PBXs can be compromised and the long-distance bills can get very high, very fast.

Another problem with PBXs arises when they are interconnected to the data systems, either by corporate connection or by rogue modems in the hands of users. In either case, a path exists for connection to outside data networks and the Internet. Just as a firewall is needed for security on data connections, one is needed for these connections as well. Telecommunications firewalls are a distinct type of firewall designed to protect both the PBX and the data connections. The functionality of a telecommunications firewall is the same as that of a data firewall: it is there to enforce security policies. Telecommunication security policies can be enforced even to cover hours of phone use to prevent unauthorized long-distance usage through the implementation of access codes and/or restricted service hours.

RAS

Remote Access Service (RAS) is a portion of the Windows OS that allows the connection between a client and a server via a dial-up telephone connection. Although slower than cable/DSL connections, this is still a common method for connecting to a remote network. When a user dials into the computer system, authentication and authorization are performed through a series of remote access protocols, described in Chapter 9. For even greater security, a callback system can be employed, where the server calls back to the client at a set telephone number for the data exchange. RAS can also mean Remote Access Server, a term for a server designed to permit remote users access to a network and to regulate their access. A variety of protocols and methods exist to perform this function; they are described in detail in Chapter 9.

VPN

A virtual private network (VPN) is a construct used to provide a secure communication channel between users across public networks such as the Internet. As described in Chapter 10, a variety of techniques can be employed to instantiate a VPN connection. The use of encryption technologies allows either the data in a packet to be encrypted or the entire packet to be encrypted. If the data is encrypted, the packet header can still be sniffed and observed between source and destination, but the encryption protects the contents of the packet from inspection. If the entire packet is encrypted, it is then placed into another packet and sent via tunnel across the public network. Tunneling can protect even the identity of the communicating parties.

The most common implementation of VPN is via IPsec, a protocol for IP security. IPsec is mandated in IPv6 and is optionally back-fitted into IPv4. IPsec can be implemented in hardware, software, or a combination of both.

Intrusion Detection Systems

Intrusion detection systems (IDSs) are designed to detect, log, and respond to unauthorized network or host use, both in real time and after the fact. IDSs are available from a wide selection of vendors and are an essential part of network security. These systems are implemented in software, but in large systems, dedicated hardware is required as well. IDSs can be divided into two categories: network-based systems and host-based systems. Two primary methods of detection are used: signature-based and anomaly-based. IDSs are covered in detail in Chapter 11.

Network Access Control

Networks comprise connected workstations and servers. Managing security on a network involves managing a wide range of issues, from various connected hardware and the software operating these devices. Assuming that the network is secure, each additional connection involves risk. Managing the endpoints on a case-by-case basis as they connect is a security methodology known as *network access control*. Two main competing methodologies exist: Network Access Protection (NAP) is a Microsoft technology for controlling network access of a computer host, and Network Admission Control (NAC) is Cisco's technology for controlling network admission.

Microsoft's NAP system is based on measuring the system health of the connecting machine, including patch levels of the OS, antivirus protection, and system policies. NAP is first utilized in Windows XP Service Pack 3, Windows Vista, and Windows Server 2008, and it requires additional infrastructure servers to implement the health checks. The system includes enforcement agents that interrogate clients and verify admission criteria. Response options include rejection of the connection request or restriction of admission to a subnet.

Cisco's NAC system is built around an appliance that enforces policies chosen by the network administrator. A series of third-party solutions can interface with the appliance, allowing the verification of a whole host of options including client policy settings, software updates, and client security posture. The use of third-party devices and software makes this an extensible system across a wide range of equipment.

Both the Cisco NAC and Microsoft NAP are in their early stages of implementation. The concept of automated admission checking based on client device characteristics is here to stay, as it provides timely control in the ever-changing network world of today's enterprises.

Network Monitoring/Diagnostic

The computer network itself can be considered a large computer system, with performance and operating issues. Just as a computer needs management, monitoring, and fault resolution, so do networks. SNMP was developed to perform this function across networks. The idea is to enable a central monitoring and control center to maintain, configure, and repair network devices, such as switches and routers, as well as other network services such as firewalls, IDSs, and remote access servers. SNMP has some security limitations, and many vendors have developed software solutions that sit on top of SNMP to provide better security and better management tool suites.

The concept of a network operations center (NOC) comes from the old phone company network days, when central monitoring centers monitored the health of the telephone network and provided interfaces for maintenance and management. This same concept works well with computer networks, and companies with midsize and larger networks employ the same philosophy. The NOC allows operators to observe and interact with the network, using the self-reporting and in some cases self-healing nature of network devices to ensure efficient network operation. Although generally a boring operation under normal conditions, when things start to go wrong, as in the case of a virus or worm attack, the center can become a busy and stressful place as operators attempt to return the system to full efficiency while not interrupting existing traffic.

As networks can be spread out literally around the world, it is not feasible to have a person visit each device for control functions. Software enables controllers at NOCs to measure the actual performance of network devices and make changes to the configuration and operation of devices remotely. The ability to make remote connections with this level of functionality is both a blessing and a security issue. Although this allows efficient network operations management, it also provides an opportunity for unauthorized entry into a network. For this reason, a variety of security controls are used, from secondary networks to VPNs and advanced authentication methods with respect to network control connections.

Network monitoring is an ongoing concern for any significant network. In addition to monitoring traffic flow and efficiency, monitoring of security is necessary. IDSs act merely as alarms, indicating the possibility of a breach associated with a specific set of activities. These indications still need to be investigated and appropriate responses initiated by security personnel. Simple items such as port scans may be ignored by policy, but an actual unauthorized entry into a network router, for instance, would require NOC personnel to take specific actions to limit the potential damage to the system. The coordination of system changes, dynamic network traffic levels, potential security incidents, and maintenance activities is a daunting task requiring numerous personnel working together in any significant network. Software has been developed to help manage the information flow required to support these tasks. Such software can enable remote administration of devices in a standard fashion, so that the control systems can be devised in a hardware vendor–neutral configuration.

SNMP is the main standard embraced by vendors to permit interoperability. Although SNMP has received a lot of security-related attention of late due to various security holes in its implementation, it is still an important part of a security solution associated with network infrastructure. Many useful tools have security issues; the key is to understand the limitations and to use the tools within correct boundaries to limit the risk associated with the vulnerabilities. Blind use of any technology will result in increased risk, and SNMP is no exception. Proper planning, setup, and deployment can limit exposure to vulnerabilities. Continuous auditing and maintenance of systems with the latest patches is a necessary part of operations and is essential to maintaining a secure posture.

Mobile Devices

Mobile devices such as personal digital assistants (PDAs) and mobile phones are the latest devices to join the corporate network. These devices can perform significant business functions, and in the future, more of them will enter the corporate network and more work will be performed with them. These devices add several challenges for network administrators. When they synchronize their data with that on a workstation or server, the opportunity exists for viruses and malicious code to be introduced to the network. This can be a major security gap, as a user may access separate e-mail accounts, one personal, without antivirus protection, the other corporate. Whenever data is moved from one network to another via the PDA, the opportunity to load a virus onto the workstation exists. Although the virus may not affect the PDA or phone, these devices can act as transmission vectors. Currently, at least one vendor offers antivirus protection for PDAs, and similar protection for phones is not far away.

Media

The base of communications between devices is the physical layer of the OSI model. This is the domain of the actual connection between devices, whether by wire, fiber, or radio frequency waves. The physical layer separates the definitions and protocols required to transmit the signal physically between boxes from higher level protocols that deal with the details of the data itself. Four common methods are used to connect equipment at the physical layer:

- Coaxial cable
- Twisted-pair cable
- Fiber-optics
- Wireless

Coaxial Cable

Coaxial cable is familiar to many households as a method of connecting televisions to VCRs or to satellite or cable services. It is used because of its high bandwidth and shielding capabilities. Compared to standard twisted-pair lines such as telephone lines, "coax" is much less prone to outside interference. It is also much more expensive to run, both from a cost-per-foot measure and from a cable-dimension measure. Coax costs much more per foot than standard twisted pair and carries only a single circuit for a large wire diameter.

A coax connector

An original design specification for Ethernet connections, coax was used from machine to machine in early Ethernet implementations. The connectors were easy to use and ensured good connections, and the limited distance of most office LANs did not carry a large cost penalty. The original ThickNet specification for Ethernet called for up to 100 connections over 500 meters at 10 Mbps.

Today, almost all of this older Ethernet specification has been replaced by faster, cheaper twisted-pair alternatives and the only place you're likely to see coax in a data network is from the cable box to the cable modem.

UTP/STP

Twisted-pair wires have all but completely replaced coaxial cables in Ethernet networks. Twisted-pair wires use the same technology used by the phone company for the movement of electrical signals. Single pairs of twisted wires reduce electrical crosstalk and electromagnetic interference. Multiple groups of twisted pairs can then be bundled together in common groups and easily wired between devices.

Twisted pairs come in two types, shielded and unshielded. Shielded twisted-pair (STP) has a foil shield around the pairs to provide extra shielding from electromagnetic interference. Unshielded twisted-pair (UTP) relies on the twist to eliminate interference. UTP has a cost advantage over STP and is usually sufficient for connections, except in very noisy electrical areas.

A typical 8-wire UTP line

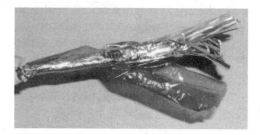

A typical 8-wire STP line

A bundle of UTP wires

Twisted-pair lines are categorized by the level of data transmission they can support. Three current categories are in use:

- Category 3 (Cat 3) minimum for voice and 10 Mbps Ethernet
- Category 5 (Cat 5/Cat5e) for 100 Mbps Fast Ethernet; Cat 5e is an enhanced version of the Cat 5 specification to address Far End Crosstalk
- Category 6 (Cat 6) for Gigabit Ethernet

The standard method for connecting twisted-pair cables is via an 8-pin connector called an RJ-45 connector that looks like a standard phone jack connector but is slightly larger. One nice aspect of twisted-pair cabling is that it's easy to splice and change connectors. Many a network administrator has made Ethernet cables from stock Cat 5 wire, two connectors, and a crimping tool. This ease of connection is also a security issue, as twisted-pair cables are easy to splice into and rogue connections for sniffing could be made without detection in cable runs. Both coax and fiber are much more difficult to splice, with both of these needing a tap to connect, and taps are easier to detect.

Fiber

Fiber-optic cable uses beams of laser light to connect devices over a thin glass wire. The biggest advantage to fiber is its bandwidth, with transmission capabilities into the terabits per second range. Fiber-optic cable is used to make high-speed connections between servers and is the backbone medium of the Internet and large networks. For all of its speed and bandwidth advantages, fiber has one major drawback—cost.

The cost of using fiber is a two-edged sword. It is cheaper when measured by bandwidth to use fiber than competing wired technologies. The length of runs of fiber can be much longer, and the data capacity of fiber is much higher. But connections to a fiber are difficult and expensive and fiber is impossible to splice. Making the precise connection on the end of a fiber-optic line is a highly skilled job and is done by specially trained professionals who maintain a level of proficiency. Once the connector is fitted on the end, several forms of connectors and blocks are used, as shown in the images that follow.

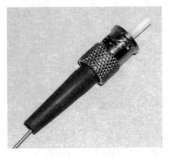

A typical fiber optic fiber and terminator

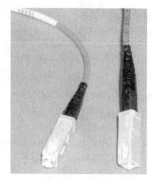

Another type of fiber terminator

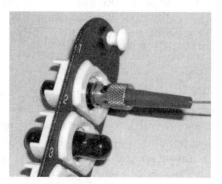

A connector block for fiber optic lines

Splicing fiber-optic is practically impossible; the solution is to add connectors and connect through a repeater. This adds to the security of fiber in that unauthorized connections are all but impossible to make. The high cost of connections to fiber and the higher cost of fiber per foot also make it less attractive for the final mile in public networks where users are connected to the public switching systems. For this reason, cable companies use coax and DSL providers use twisted pair to handle the "last-mile" scenario.

Unguided Media

Electromagnetic waves have been transmitted to convey signals literally since the inception of radio. *Unguided media* is a phrase used to cover all transmission media not guided by wire, fiber, or other constraints; it includes radio frequency (RF), infrared (IR), and microwave methods. Unguided media have one attribute in common: they are unguided and as such can travel to many machines simultaneously. Transmission patterns can be modulated by antennas, but the target machine can be one of many in a reception zone. As such, security principles are even more critical, as they must assume that unauthorized users have access to the signal.

Infrared

Infrared (IR) is a band of electromagnetic energy just beyond the red end of the visible color spectrum. IR has been used in remote control devices for years, and it cannot penetrate walls but instead bounces off them. IR made its debut in computer networking as a wireless method to connect to printers. Now that wireless keyboards, wireless mice, and PDAs exchange data via IR, it seems to be everywhere. IR can also be used to connect devices in a network configuration, but it is slow compared to other wireless technologies. It also suffers from not being able to penetrate solid objects, so stack a few items in front of the transceiver and the signal is lost.

RF/Microwave

The use of radio frequency (RF) waves to carry communication signals goes back to the beginning of the twentieth century. RF waves are a common method of communicating in a wireless world. They use a variety of frequency bands, each with special characteristics. The term *microwave* is used to describe a specific portion of the RF spectrum that is used for communication as well as other tasks, such as cooking.

Point-to-point microwave links have been installed by many network providers to carry communications over long distances and rough terrain. Microwave communications of telephone conversations were the basis for forming the telecommunication company MCI. Many different frequencies are used in the microwave bands for many different purposes. Today, home users can use wireless networking throughout their house and enable laptops to surf the Web while they move around the house. Corporate users are experiencing the same phenomenon, with wireless networking enabling corporate users to check e-mail on laptops while riding a shuttle bus on a business campus. These wireless solutions are covered in detail in Chapter 10.

One key feature of microwave communications is that microwave RF energy can penetrate reasonable amounts of building structure. This allows you to connect network devices in separate rooms, and it can remove the constraints on equipment location imposed by fixed wiring. Another key feature is broadcast capability. By its nature, RF energy is unguided and can be received by multiple users simultaneously. Microwaves allow multiple users access in a limited area, and microwave systems are seeing application as the last mile of the Internet in dense metropolitan areas. Point-to-multipoint microwave devices can deliver data communication to all the business users in a downtown metropolitan area through rooftop antennas, reducing the need for expensive building-to-building cables. Just as microwaves carry cell phone and other data communications, the same technologies offer a method to bridge the last-mile solution.

The "last mile" problem is the connection of individual consumers to a backbone, an expensive proposition because of the sheer number of connections and unshared lines at this point in a network. Again, cost is an issue, as transceiving equipment is expensive, but in densely populated areas, such as apartments and office buildings in metropolitan areas, the user density can help defray individual costs. Speed on commercial microwave links can exceed 10 Gbps, so speed is not a problem for connecting multiple users or for high-bandwidth applications.

Security Concerns for Transmission Media

The primary security concern for a system administrator has to be preventing physical access to a server by an unauthorized individual. Such access will almost always spell disaster, for with direct access and the correct tools, any system can be infiltrated. One of the administrator's next major concerns should be preventing unfettered access to a network connection. Access to switches and routers is almost as bad as direct access to a server, and access to network connections would rank third in terms of worst-case scenarios. Preventing such access is costly, yet the cost of replacing a server because of theft is also costly.

Physical Security

A balanced approach is the most sensible approach when addressing physical security, and this applies to transmission media as well. Keeping network switch rooms secure and cable runs secure seems obvious, but cases of using janitorial closets for this vital business purpose abound. One of the keys to mounting a successful attack on a network is information. Usernames, passwords, server locations—all of these can be obtained if someone has the ability to observe network traffic in a process called *sniffing*. A sniffer can record all the network traffic, and this data can be mined for accounts, passwords, and traffic content, all of which can be useful to an unauthorized user. Many common scenarios exist when unauthorized entry to a network occurs, including these:

- Inserting a node and functionality that is not authorized on the network, such as a sniffer device or unauthorized wireless access point
- Modifying firewall security policies
- Modifying ACLs for firewalls, switches, or routers
- Modifying network devices to echo traffic to an external node

One starting point for many intrusions is the insertion of an unauthorized sniffer into the network, with the fruits of its labors driving the remaining unauthorized activities. The best first effort is to secure the actual network equipment to prevent this type of intrusion.

Network devices and transmission media become targets because they are dispersed throughout an organization, and physical security of many dispersed items can be difficult to manage. This work is not glamorous and has been likened to guarding plumbing. The difference is that in the case of network infrastructure, unauthorized physical access strikes at one of the most vulnerable points and, in many cases, is next to impossible to detect. Locked doors and equipment racks are easy to implement, yet this step is frequently overlooked. Shielding of cable runs, including the use of concrete runs outside buildings to prevent accidental breaches may have high initial costs, but typically pay off in the long run in terms of of reduced downtime. Raised floors, cable runs, closets—there are many places to hide an unauthorized device. Add to this the fact that a large percentage of unauthorized users have a direct connection to the target of the unauthorized use—they are employees, students, or the like. Twisted-pair and coax make it easy for an intruder to tap into a network without notice. A vampire tap is the name given to a spike tap that taps the center conductor of a coax cable. A person with talent can make such a tap without interrupting network traffic, merely by splicing a parallel connection tap. This will allow the information flow to split into two, enabling a second destination.

Although limiting physical access is difficult, it is essential. The least level of skill is still more than sufficient to accomplish unauthorized entry into a network if physical access to the network signals is allowed. This is one factor driving many organizations to use fiber-optics, for these cables are much more difficult to tap. Although many tricks can be employed with switches and VLANs to increase security, it is still essential that you prevent unauthorized contact with the network equipment.

Wireless networks make the intruder's task even easier, as they take the network to the users, authorized or not. A technique called *war-driving* involves using a laptop and software to find wireless networks from outside the premises. A typical use of war-driving is to locate a wireless network with poor (or no) security and obtain free Internet access, but other uses can be more devastating. Methods for securing even the relatively weak Wired Equivalent Privacy (WEP) protocol are not difficult; they are just typically not followed. A simple solution is to place a firewall between the wireless access point and the rest of the network and authenticate users before allowing entry. Home users can do the same thing to prevent neighbors from "sharing" their Internet connections. To ensure that unauthorized traffic does not enter your network through a wireless access point, you must either use a firewall with an authentication system or establish a VPN.

Removable Media

One concept common to all computer users is data storage. Sometimes storage occurs on a file server and sometimes on movable media, allowing it to be transported between machines. Moving storage media represents a security risk from a couple of angles, the first being the potential loss of control over the data on the moving media. Second is the risk of introducing unwanted items, such as a virus or a worm, when the media are attached back to a network. Both of these issues can be remedied through policies and software. The key is to ensure that they are occurring. To describe media-specific issues, the media can be divided into three categories: magnetic, optical, and electronic.

Magnetic Media

Magnetic media store data through the rearrangement of magnetic particles on a non-magnetic substrate. Common forms include hard drives, floppy disks, zip disks, and magnetic tape. Although the specific format can differ, the basic concept is the same. All these devices share some common characteristics: Each has sensitivity to external magnetic fields. Attach a floppy disk to the refrigerator door with a magnet if you want to test the sensitivity. They are also affected by high temperatures as in fires and by exposure to water.

Hard Drives

Hard drives used to require large machines in mainframes. Now they are small enough to attach to PDAs and handheld devices. The concepts remain the same among all of them: a spinning platter rotates the magnetic media beneath heads that read the patterns in the oxide coating. As drives have gotten smaller and rotation speeds increased, the capacities have also grown. Today gigabytes can be stored in a device slightly larger than a bottle cap. Portable hard drives in the 120 to 320GB range are now available and affordable.

One of the latest advances is full drive encryption built into the drive hardware. Using a key that is controlled, through a Trusted Platform Module (TPM) interface for instance, this technology protects the data if the drive itself is lost or stolen. This may not be important if a thief takes the whole PC, but in larger storage environments, drives are placed in separate boxes and remotely accessed. In the specific case of notebook machines, this layer can be tied to smart card interfaces to provide more security. As this is built into the controller, encryption protocols such as Advanced Encryption Standard (AES) and Triple Data Encryption Standard (3DES) can be performed at full drive speed.

Diskettes

Floppy disks were the computer industry's first attempt at portable magnetic media. The movable medium was placed in a protective sleeve, and the drive remained in the machine. Capacities up to 1.4MB were achieved, but the fragility of the device as the size increased, as well as competing media, has rendered floppies almost obsolete. A better alternative, the Zip disk from Iomega Corporation, improved on the floppy with a stronger case and higher capacity (250MB); it has been a common backup and file transfer medium. But even the increased size of 250MB is not large enough for some multimedia files, and recordable optical (CD-R) drives have arrived to fill the gap; they will be discussed shortly.

Tape

Magnetic tape has held a place in computer centers since the beginning of computing. Their primary use has been bulk offline storage and backup. Tape functions well in this role because of its low cost. The disadvantage of tape is its nature as a serial access medium, making it slow to work with for large quantities of data. Several types of magnetic tape are in use today, ranging from quarter inch to digital linear tape (DLT) and digital audio tape (DAT). These cartridges can hold upward of 60GB of compressed data.

Tapes are still a major concern from a security perspective, as they are used to back up many types of computer systems. The physical protection afforded the tapes is of concern, because if a tape is stolen, an unauthorized user could establish a network and recover your data on his system, because it's all stored on the tape. Offsite storage is needed for proper disaster recovery protection, but secure offsite storage and transport is what is really needed. This important issue is frequently overlooked in many facilities. The simple solution to maintain control over the data even when you can't control the tape is through encryption. Backup utilities can secure the backups with encryption, but this option is frequently not used for a variety of reasons. Regardless of the rationale for not encrypting data, once a tape is lost, not using the encryption option becomes a lamented decision.

Optical Media

Optical media involve the use of a laser to read data stored on a physical device. Rather than a magnetic head picking up magnetic marks on a disk, a laser picks up deformities embedded in the media that contain the information. As with magnetic media, optical media can be read-write, although the read-only version is still more common.

CD-R/DVD

The compact disc (CD) took the music industry by storm, and then it took the computer industry by storm as well. A standard CD holds more than 640MB of data, in some cases up to 800 MB. The digital video disc (DVD) can hold almost 4GB of data. These devices operate as optical storage, with little marks burned in them to represent 1's and 0's on a microscopic scale. The most common type of CD is the read-only version, in which the data is written to the disc once and only read afterward. This has become a popular method for distributing computer software, although higher capacity DVDs have begun to replace CDs for program distribution.

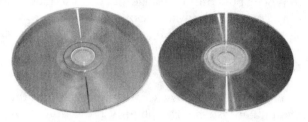

A second-generation device, the recordable compact disc (CD-R), allows users to create their own CDs using a burner device in their PC and special software. Users can now back up data, make their own audio CDs, and use CDs as high-capacity storage. Their relatively low cost has made them economical to use. CDs have a thin layer of aluminum inside the plastic, upon which bumps are burned by the laser when recorded. CD-Rs use a reflective layer, such as gold, upon which a dye is placed that changes upon impact by the recording laser. A newer type, CD-RW, has a different dye that allows discs to be erased and reused. The cost of the media increases from CD, to CD-R, to CD-RW.

DVDs will eventually occupy the same role that CDs have in the recent past, except that they hold more than seven times the data of a CD. This makes full-length movie recording possible on a single disc. The increased capacity comes from finer tolerances and the fact that DVDs can hold data on both sides. A wide range of formats for DVDs include DVD+R, DVD-R, dual layer, and now HD formats, HD-DVD and Blu-ray. This variety is due to competing "standards" and can result in confusion. DVD+R and -R are distinguishable only when recording, and most devices since 2004 should read both. Dual layers add additional space but require appropriate dual-layer–enabled drives. HD-DVD and Blue-ray are competing formats in the high-definition arena, with devices that currently hold 50GB and with research prototypes promising up to 1TB on a disk. In 2008, Toshiba, the leader of the HD-DVD format, announced it was ceasing production, casting doubts onto its future, although this format is also used in gaming systems such as the Xbox 360.

Electronic Media

The latest form of removable media is electronic memory. Electronic circuits of static memory, which can retain data even without power, fill a niche where high density and small size are needed. Originally used in audio devices and digital cameras, these electronic media come in a variety of vendor-specific types, such as smart cards, SmartMedia, flash cards, memory sticks, and CompactFlash devices. Several recent photo-quality color printers have been released with ports to accept the cards directly, meaning that a computer is not required for printing. Computer readers are also available to permit storing data from the card onto hard drives and other media in a computer. The size of storage on these devices ranges from 256MB to 32GB and higher.

PART III

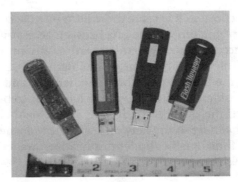

Although they are used primarily for photos and music, these devices could be used to move any digital information from one machine to another. To a machine equipped with a connector port, these devices look like any other file storage location. They can be connected to a system through a special reader or directly via a USB port. In newer PC systems, a USB boot device has replaced the older floppy drive. These devices are small, can hold a significant amount of data—up to 32GB at time of writing—and are easy to move from machine to machine. Another novel interface is a mouse that has a slot for a memory stick. This dual-purpose device conserves space, conserves USB ports, and is easy to use. The memory stick is placed in the mouse, which can then be used normally. The stick is easily removable and transportable. The mouse works with or without the memory stick; it is just a convenient device to use for a portal.

The advent of large capacity USB sticks has enabled users to build entire systems, OSs, and tools onto them to ensure security and veracity of the OS and tools. With the expanding use of virtualization, a user could carry an entire system on a USB stick and boot it using virtually any hardware. The only downside to this form of mobile computing is the slower speed of the USB 2.0 interface, currently limited to 480 Mbps.

Security Topologies

Networks are different than single servers; networks exist as connections of multiple devices. A key characteristic of a network is its layout, or *topology*. A proper network topology takes security into consideration and assists in "building security" into the network. Security-related topologies include separating portions of the network by use and function, strategically designing in points to monitor for IDS systems, building in redundancy, and adding fault-tolerant aspects.

Security Zones

The first aspect of security is a layered defense. Just as a castle has a moat, an outside wall, an inside wall, and even a keep, so, too, does a modern secure network have different layers of protection. Different zones are designed to provide layers of defense, with the outermost layers providing basic protection and the innermost layers providing the highest level of protection. A constant issue is that accessibility tends to be inversely related to level of protection, so it is more difficult to provide complete protection and unfettered access at the same time. Trade-offs between access and security are handled through zones, with successive zones guarded by firewalls enforcing ever-increasingly strict security policies. The outermost zone is the Internet, a free area, beyond any specific controls. Between the inner secure corporate network and the Internet is an area where machines are considered at risk. This zone has come to be called the *DMZ*, after its military counterpart, the demilitarized zone, where neither side has any specific controls. Once inside the inner secure network, separate branches are frequently carved out to provide specific functionality; under this heading, we will discuss intranets, extranets, and virtual LANs (VLANs).

DMZ

The DMZ is a military term for ground separating two opposing forces, by agreement and for the purpose of acting as a buffer between the two sides. A DMZ in a computer network is used in the same way; it acts as a buffer zone between the Internet, where no controls exist, and the inner secure network, where an organization has security policies in place (see Figure 8-4). To demarcate the zones and enforce separation, a firewall is used on each side of the DMZ. The area between these firewalls is accessible from either the inner secure network or the Internet. Figure 8-4 illustrates these zones as caused by firewall placement. The firewalls are specifically designed to prevent access across the DMZ directly, from the Internet to the inner secure network.

Special attention should be paid to the security settings of network devices placed in the DMZ, and they should be considered at all times to be compromised by unauthorized use. A common industry term, *hardened operating system,* applies to machines whose functionality is locked down to preserve security. This approach needs to be applied to the machines in the DMZ, and although it means that their functionality is limited, such precautions ensure that the machines will work properly in a less-secure environment.

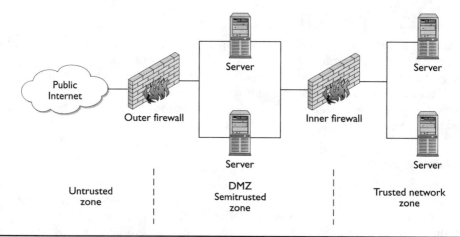

Figure 8-4 The DMZ and zones of trust

Many types of servers belong in this area, including web servers that are serving content to Internet users, as well as remote access servers and external e-mail servers. In general, any server directly accessed from the outside, untrusted Internet zone needs to be in the DMZ. Other servers should not be placed in the DMZ. Domain name servers for your inner trusted network and database servers that house corporate databases should not be accessible from the outside. Application servers, file servers, print servers—all of the standard servers used in the trusted network—should be behind both firewalls, plus routers and switches used to connect these machines.

The idea behind the use of the DMZ topology is to force an outside user to make at least one hop in the DMZ before he can access information inside the trusted network. If the outside user makes a request for a resource from the trusted network, such as a data element from a database via a web page, then this request needs to follow this scenario:

1. A user from the untrusted network (the Internet) requests data via a web page from a web server in the DMZ.

2. The web server in the DMZ requests the data from the application server, which can be in the DMZ or in the inner trusted network.

3. The application server requests the data from the database server in the trusted network.

4. The database server returns the data to the requesting application server.

5. The application server returns the data to the requesting web server.

6. The web server returns the data to the requesting user from the untrusted network.

This separation accomplishes two specific, independent tasks. First, the user is separated from the request for data on a secure network. By having intermediaries do the requesting, this layered approach allows significant security levels to be enforced. Users do not have direct access or control over their requests, and this filtering process can put controls in place. Second, scalability is more easily realized. The multiple-server solution can be made to be very scalable literally to millions of users, without slowing down any particular layer.

 EXAM TIP DMZs act as a buffer zone between unprotected areas of a network (the Internet) and protected areas (sensitive company data stores), allowing for the monitoring and regulation of traffic between these two zones.

Internet

The Internet is a worldwide connection of networks and is used to transport e-mail, files, financial records, remote access—you name it—from one network to another. The Internet is not as a single network, but a series of interconnected networks that allow protocols to operate to enable data to flow across it. This means that even if your network doesn't have direct contact with a resource, as long as a neighbor, or a neighbor's neighbor, and so on, can get there, so can you. This large web allows users almost infinite ability to communicate between systems.

Because everything and everyone can access this interconnected web and it is outside of your control and ability to enforce security policies, the Internet should be considered an untrusted network. A firewall should exist at any connection between your trusted network and the Internet. This is not to imply that the Internet is a bad thing—it is a great resource for all networks and adds significant functionality to our computing environments.

The term World Wide Web (WWW) is frequently used synonymously to represent the Internet, but the WWW is actually just one set of services available via the Internet. WWW is more specifically the Hypertext Transfer Protocol (HTTP)–based services that are made available over the Internet. This can include a variety of actual services and content, including text files, pictures, streaming audio and video, and even viruses and worms.

Intranet

Intranet is a term used to describe a network that has the same functionality as the Internet for users but lies completely inside the trusted area of a network and is under the security control of the system and network administrators. Typically referred to as *campus* or *corporate* networks, intranets are used every day in companies around the world. An intranet allows a developer and a user the full set of protocols—HTTP, FTP, instant messaging, and so on—that is offered on the Internet, but with the added advantage of trust from the network security. Content on intranet web servers is not available over the Internet to untrusted users. This layer of security offers a significant amount of control and regulation, allowing users to fulfill business functionality while ensuring security.

Two methods can be used to make information available to outside users: Duplication of information onto machines in the DMZ can make it available to other users. Proper security checks and controls should be made prior to duplicating the material to ensure security policies concerning specific data availability are being followed. Alternatively, *extranets* can be used to publish material to trusted partners.

Should users inside the intranet require access to information from the Internet, a proxy server can be used to mask the requestor's location. This helps secure the intranet from outside mapping of its actual topology. All Internet requests go to the proxy server. If a request passes filtering requirements, the proxy server, assuming it is also a cache server, looks in its local cache of previously downloaded web pages. If it finds the page in its cache, it returns the page to the requestor without needing to send the request to the Internet. If the page is not in the cache, the proxy server, acting as a client on behalf of the user, uses one of its own IP addresses to request the page from the Internet. When the page is returned, the proxy server relates it to the original request and forwards it on to the user. This masks the user's IP address from the Internet. Proxy servers can perform several functions for a firm; for example, they can monitor traffic requests, eliminating improper requests, such as inappropriate content for work. They can also act as a cache server, cutting down on outside network requests for the same object. Finally, proxy servers protect the identity of internal IP addresses, although this function can also be accomplished through a router or firewall using Network Address Translation (NAT).

Extranet

An *extranet* is an extension of a selected portion of a company's intranet to external partners. This allows a business to share information with customers, suppliers, partners, and other trusted groups while using a common set of Internet protocols to facilitate operations. Extranets can use public networks to extend their reach beyond a company's own internal network, and some form of security, typically VPN, is used to secure this channel. The use of the term *extranet* implies both privacy and security. Privacy is required for many communications, and security is needed to prevent unauthorized use and events from occurring. Both of these functions can be achieved through the use of technologies described in this chapter and other chapters in this book. Proper firewall management, remote access, encryption, authentication, and secure tunnels across public networks are all methods used to ensure privacy and security for extranets.

Telephony

Data and voice communications have coexisted in enterprises for decades. Recent connections inside the enterprise of Voice over IP and traditional PBX solutions increase both functionality and security risks. Specific firewalls to protect against unauthorized traffic over telephony connections are available to counter the increased risk.

VLANs

A local area network (LAN) is a set of devices with similar functionality and similar communication needs, typically co-located and operated off a single switch. This is the lowest level of a network hierarchy and defines the domain for certain protocols at the data link layer for communication. Virtual LANs use a single switch and divide it into multiple broadcast domains and/or multiple network segments, known as *trunking*. This very powerful technique allows significant network flexibility, scalability, and performance.

Trunking

Trunking is the process of spanning a single VLAN across multiple switches. A trunk-based connection between switches allows packets from a single VLAN to travel between switches, as shown in Figure 8-5. Two trunks are shown in the figure: VLAN 10 is implemented with one trunk and VLAN 20 is implemented by the other. Hosts on different VLANs cannot communicate using trunks and are switched across the switch network. Trunks enable network administrators to set up VLANs across multiple switches with minimal effort. With a combination of trunks and VLANs, network administrators can subnet a network by user functionality without regard to host location on the network or the need to recable machines.

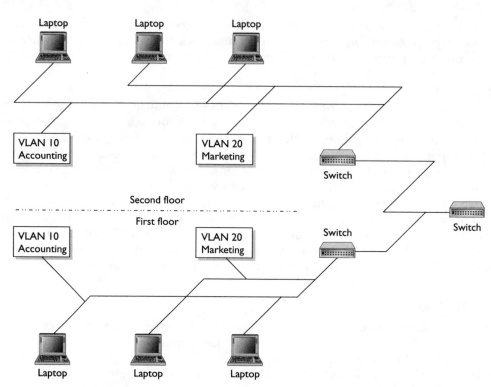

Figure 8-5   VLANs and trunks

Security Implications

VLANs are used to divide a single network into multiple subnets based on functionality. This permit engineering and accounting, for example, to share a switch because of proximity and yet have separate traffic domains. The physical placement of equipment and cables is logically and programmatically separated so adjacent ports on a switch can reference separate subnets. This prevents unauthorized use of physically close devices through separate subnets, but the same equipment. VLANs also allow a network administrator to define a VLAN that has no users and map all of the unused ports to this VLAN. Then if an unauthorized user should gain access to the equipment, he will be unable to use unused ports, as those ports will be securely defined to nothing. Both a purpose and a security strength of VLANs is that systems on separate VLANs cannot directly communicate with each other.

CAUTION   Trunks and VLANs have security implications that need to be heeded so that firewalls and other segmentation devices are not breached through their use. They also require understanding of their use to prevent an unauthorized user from reconfiguring them to gain undetected access to secure portions of a network.

NAT

Network Address Translation (NAT) uses two sets of IP addresses for resources—one for internal use and another for external (Internet) use. NAT was developed as a solution to the rapid depletion of IP addresses in the IPv4 address space; it has since became an Internet standard (see RFC 1631 for details). NAT is used to translate between the two addressing schemes and is typically performed at a firewall or router. This permits enterprises to use the nonroutable private IP address space internally and reduces the number of external IP addresses used across the Internet.

Three sets of IP addresses are defined as nonroutable, which means that addresses will not be routed across the Internet. These addresses are routable internally and routers can be set to route them, but the routers across the Internet are set to discard packets sent to these addresses. This approach enables a separation of internal and external traffic and allows these addresses to be reused by anyone and everyone who wishes to do so. The three address spaces are

- **Class A** 10.0.0.0 – 10.255.255.255
- **Class B** 172.16.0.0 – 172.31.255.255
- **Class C** 192.168.0.0 – 192.168.255.255

The use of these addresses inside a network is unrestricted, and they function like any other IP addresses. When outside—that is, Internet-provided—resources are needed for one of these addresses, NAT is required to produce a valid external IP address for the resource. NAT operates by translating the address when traffic passes the NAT device, such as a firewall. The external addresses used are not externally mappable 1:1 to the internal addresses, for this would defeat the purpose of reuse and address-space conservation. Typically, a pool of external IP addresses is used by the NAT device, with the device keeping track of which internal address is using which external address at any given time. This provides a significant layer of security, as it makes it difficult to map the internal network structure behind a firewall and directly address it from the outside. NAT is one of the methods used for enforcing perimeter security by forcing users to access resources through defined pathways such as firewalls and gateway servers.

Several techniques are used to accomplish NAT. *Static* NAT offers a 1:1 binding of external address to internal address; it is needed for services for which external sources reference internal sources, such as web servers or e-mail servers. For DMZ resources that reference outside resources, addresses can be shared, through *dynamic* NAT, in which a table is constructed and used by the edge device to manage the translation. As the address translation can change over time, the table changes as well. Even finer grained control can be obtained through port address translation (PAT), where actual TCP/UDP ports are translated as well. This will enable a single external IP address to serve two internal IP addresses through the use of ports. Resources that need long-running NAT, but only specific ports—such as a web server on port 80 or e-mail on port 25—can share a single external IP, conserving resources.

Tunneling

Tunneling is a method of packaging packets so that they can traverse a network in a secure, confidential manner. Tunneling involves encapsulating packets within packets, enabling dissimilar protocols to coexist in a single communication stream, as in IP traffic routed over an Asynchronous Transfer Mode (ATM) network. Tunneling also can provide significant measures of security and confidentiality through encryption and encapsulation methods. The best example of this is a VPN that is established over a public network through the use of a tunnel, as shown in Figure 8-6, connecting a firm's Boston office to its New York City (NYC) office.

Assume, for example, that a company has multiple locations and decides to use the public Internet to connect the networks at these locations. To make these connections secure from outside unauthorized use, the company can employ a VPN connection between the different networks. On each network, an edge device, usually a router, connects to another edge device on the other network. Then using IPsec protocols, these routers establish a secure, encrypted path between them. This securely encrypted set of packets cannot be read by outside routers; only the addresses of the edge routers are visible. This arrangement acts as a tunnel across the public Internet and establishes a private connection, secure from outside snooping or use.

Because of ease of use, low-cost hardware, and strong security, tunnels and the Internet are a combination that will see more use in the future. IPsec, VPN, and tunnels will become a major set of tools for users requiring secure network connections across public segments of networks.

Chapter Review

This chapter covered a wide range of topics—from devices, to media, to topologies—and showed you how to use them together to create secure networks. These complementary items can each support the other in an effort to build a secure network structure. Designing a secure network begins with defining a topology and then laying out the necessary components. Separate the pieces using firewalls with clearly defined security policies. Use devices and media to the advantage of the overall network design and implement usable subnets with VLANs. Use encryption and encapsulation to secure communications of public segments to enable extranets and cross-Internet company traffic. Use items such as intrusion detection systems and firewalls to keep unauthor-

Figure 8-6   Tunneling across a public network

ized users out and monitor activity. Taken together, these pieces can make a secure network that is efficient, manageable, and effective.

Questions

To further help you prepare for the Security+ exam, and to test your level of preparedness, answer the following questions and then check your answers against the list of correct answers at the end of the chapter.

1. Switches operate at which layer of the OSI model?

   A. Physical layer

   B. Network layer

   C. Data link layer

   D. Application layer

2. UTP cables are terminated for Ethernet using what type of connector?

   A. A BNC plug

   B. An Ethernet connector

   C. A standard phone jack connector

   D. An RJ-45 connector

3. Coaxial cable carries how many physical channels?

   A. Two

   B. Four

   C. One

   D. None of the above

4. The purpose of a DMZ in a network is to

   A. Provide easy connections to the Internet without an interfering firewall

   B. Allow server farms to be divided into similar functioning entities

   C. Provide a place to lure and capture hackers

   D. Act as a buffer between untrusted and trusted networks

5. Network access control is associated with which of the following?

   A. NAP

   B. IPsec

   C. IPv6

   D. NAT

6. The purpose of twisting the wires in twisted-pair circuits is to

   A. Increase speed

      B. Increase bandwidth

      C. Reduce crosstalk

      D. Allow easier tracing

7. The shielding in STP acts as

      A. A physical barrier strengthening the cable

      B. A way to reduce interference

      C. An amplifier allowing longer connections

      D. None of the above

8. Microsoft NAP permits

      A. Restriction of connections to a restricted subnet only

      B. Checking of a client OS patch level before a network connection is permitted

      C. Denial of a connection based on client policy settings

      D. All of the above

9. One of the greatest concerns addressed by physical security is preventing unauthorized connections having what intent?

      A. Sniffing

      B. Spoofing

      C. Data diddling

      D. Free network access

10. SNMP is a protocol used for which of the following functions?

      A. Secure e-mail

      B. Secure encryption of network packets

      C. Remote access to user workstations

      D. Remote access to network infrastructure

11. Firewalls can use which of the following in their operation?

      A. Stateful packet inspection

      B. Port blocking to deny specific services

      C. NAT to hide internal IP addresses

      D. All of the above

12. SMTP is a protocol used for which of the following functions?

      A. E-mail

      B. Secure encryption of network packets

      C. Remote access to user workstations

D. None of the above

13. Microwave communications are limited by

    A. Speed—the maximum for microwave circuits is 1 Gbps

    B. Cost—microwaves take a lot of energy to generate

    C. Line of sight—microwaves don't propagate over the horizon

    D. Lack of standard operation protocols for widespread use

14. USB-based flash memory is characterized by

    A. Expensive

    B. Low capacity

    C. Slow access

    D. None of the above

15. Mobile devices connected to networks include what?

    A. Smart phones

    B. Laptops

    C. MP3 music devices

    D. All of the above

Answers

1. **C.** Switches operate at layer 2, the data link layer of the OSI model.

2. **D.** The standard connector for UTP in an Ethernet network is the RJ-45 connector. An RJ-45 is larger than a standard phone connector.

3. **C.** A coaxial connector carries one wire, one physical circuit.

4. **D.** A DMZ based topology is designed to manage the different levels of trust between the Internet (untrusted) and the internal network (trusted).

5. **A.** NAP (Network Access Protection) is one form of network access control.

6. **C.** The twist in twisted-pair wires reduces crosstalk between wires.

7. **B.** The shielding on STP is for grounding and reducing interference.

8. **D.** Microsoft Network Access Protection (NAP) enables the checking of a system's health and other policies prior to allowing connection.

9. **A.** Sniffing is the greatest threat, for passwords and accounts can be captured and used later.

10. **D.** The Simple Network Management Protocol is used to control network devices from a central control location.

11. **D.** Firewalls can do all of these things.

12. **A.** SMTP, the Simple Mail Transfer Protocol, is used to move e-mail across a network.

13. **C.** Microwave energy is a line-of-sight transmission medium; hence, towers must not be spaced too far apart or the horizon will block transmissions.

14. **D.** USB-based flash memory is low cost, fast, and high capacity—currently 32GB.

15. **D.** Almost any digital memory–containing device can find its way onto a network.

Authentication and Remote Access

In this chapter, you will
- Learn about the methods and protocols for remote access to networks
- Discover authentication, authorization, and accounting (AAA) protocols
- Be introduced to authentication methods and the security implications in their use
- Cover virtual private networks (VPNs) and their security aspects
- Explore Internet Protocol Security (IPsec) and its use in securing communications

Remote access enables users outside a network to have network access and privileges as if they were inside the network. Being *outside* a network means that the user is working on a machine that is not physically connected to the network and must therefore establish a connection through a remote means, such as dialing in, connecting via the Internet, or connecting through a wireless connection. A user accessing resources from the Internet through an Internet service provider (ISP) is also connecting remotely to the resources via the Internet.

Authentication is the process of establishing a user's identity to enable the granting of permissions. To establish network connections, a variety of methods are used, which depend on network type, the hardware and software employed, and any security requirements. Microsoft Windows has a specific server component called the Remote Access Service (RAS) that is designed to facilitate the management of remote access connections through dial-up modems. Cisco has implemented a variety of remote access methods through its networking hardware and software. UNIX systems also have built-in methods to enable remote access.

The Remote Access Process

The process of connecting by remote access involves two elements: a temporary network connection and a series of protocols to negotiate privileges and commands. The temporary network connection can occur via a dial-up service, the Internet, wireless access, or any other method of connecting to a network. Once the connection is made, the primary issue is authenticating the identity of the user and establishing proper privileges for that user. This is accomplished using a combination of protocols and the operating system on the host machine.

The three steps in the establishment of proper privileges are authentication, authorization, and accounting (AAA). *Authentication* is the matching of user-supplied credentials to previously stored credentials on a host machine, and it usually involves an account username and password. Once the user is authenticated, the authorization step takes place. *Authorization* is the granting of specific permissions based on the privileges held by the account. Does the user have permission to use the network at this time, or is her use restricted? Does the user have access to specific applications, such as mail and FTP, or are some of these restricted? These checks are carried out as part of authorization, and in many cases this is a function of the operating system in conjunction with its established security policies. A last function, *accounting*, is the collection of billing and other detail records. Network access is often a billable function, and a log of how much time, bandwidth, file transfer space, or other resources were used needs to be maintained. Other accounting functions include keeping detailed security logs to maintain an audit trail of tasks being performed. All of these standard functions are part of normal and necessary overhead in maintaining a computer system, and the protocols used in remote access provide the necessary input for these functions.

By using *encryption*, remote access protocols can securely authenticate and authorize a user according to previously established privilege levels. The authorization phase can keep unauthorized users out, but after that, encryption of the communications channel becomes very important in preventing nonauthorized users from breaking in on an authorized session and hijacking an authorized user's credentials. As more and more networks rely on the Internet for connecting remote users, the need for and importance of remote access protocols and secure communication channels will continue to grow.

When a user dials in to the Internet through an ISP, this is similarly a case of remote access—the user is establishing a connection to her ISP's network, and the same security issues apply. The issue of *authentication*, the matching of user-supplied credentials to previously stored credentials on a host machine, is usually done via a user account name and password. Once the user is authenticated, the authorization step takes place.

Access controls define what actions a user can perform or what objects a user is allowed to access. Access controls are built upon the foundation of elements designed to facilitate the matching of a user to a process. These elements are *identification, authentication,* and *authorization*.

Identification

Identification is the process of ascribing a computer ID to a specific user, computer, network device, or computer process. The identification process is typically performed only once, when a user ID is issued to a particular user. User identification enables authentication and authorization to form the basis for accountability. For accountability purposes, user IDs should not be shared, and for security purposes, they should not be descriptive of job function. This practice enables you to trace activities to individual users or computer processes so that they can be held responsible for their actions. Identification usually takes the form of a logon ID or user ID. A required characteristic of such IDs is that they must be unique.

Authentication

Authentication is the process of binding a specific ID to a specific computer connection. Historically, three categories are used to authenticate the identity of a user. Originally published by the U.S. government in one of the Rainbow series manuals on computer security, these categories are

- What users know (such as a password)
- What users have (such as tokens)
- What users are (static biometrics such as fingerprints or iris pattern)

Today, because of technological advances, a new category has emerged, patterned after subconscious behavior:

- What users do (dynamic biometrics such as typing patterns or gait)

These methods can be used individually or in combination. These controls assume that the identification process has been completed and the identity of the user has been verified. It is the job of authentication mechanisms to ensure that only valid users are admitted. Described another way, authentication is using some mechanism to prove that you are who you claimed to be when the identification process was completed.

The most common method of authentication is the use of a password. For greater security, you can add an element from a separate group, such as a smart card token—something a user has in her possession. Passwords are common because they are one of the simplest forms and use memory as a prime component. Because of their simplicity, passwords have become ubiquitous across a wide range of systems.

Another method to provide authentication involves the use of something that only valid users should have in their possession. A physical-world example of this would be a simple lock and key. Only those individuals with the correct key will be able to open the lock and thus gain admittance to a house, car, office, or whatever the lock was protecting. A similar method can be used to authenticate users for a computer system or network (though the key may be electronic and could reside on a smart card or similar device). The problem with this technology, however, is that people do lose their keys (or cards), which means they can't log in to the system and somebody else who finds the key may then be able to access the system, even though they are not authorized. To address this problem, a combination of the something-you-know/something-you-have methods is often used so that the individual with the key can also be required to provide a password or passcode. The key is useless unless you know this code.

The third general method to provide authentication involves something that is unique about you. We are accustomed to this concept in our physical world, where our fingerprints or a sample of our DNA can be used to identify us. This same concept can be used to provide authentication in the computer world. The field of authentication that uses something about you or something that you are is known as *biometrics*. A number of different mechanisms can be used to accomplish this type of authentication, such as a fingerprint, iris scan, retinal scan, or hand geometry. All of these methods obviously require some additional hardware in order to operate. The inclusion of fingerprint readers on laptop computers is becoming common as the additional hardware is becoming cost effective.

While these three approaches to authentication appear to be easy to understand and in most cases easy to implement, authentication is not to be taken lightly, since it is such an important component of security. Potential attackers are constantly searching for ways to get past the system's authentication mechanism, and they have employed some fairly ingenious methods to do so. Consequently, security professionals are constantly devising new methods, building on these three basic approaches, to provide authentication mechanisms for computer systems and networks.

Kerberos

Developed as part of MIT's project Athena, Kerberos is a network authentication protocol designed for a client/server environment. The current version is Kerberos Version 5 release 1.6.3 and is supported by all major operating systems. Kerberos securely passes a symmetric key over an insecure network using the Needham-Schroeder symmetric key protocol. Kerberos is built around the idea of a trusted third party, termed a *key distribution center (KDC)*, which consists of two logically separate parts: an authentication server (AS) and a ticket granting server (TGS). Kerberos communicates via "tickets" that serve to prove the identity of users.

Taking its name from the three-headed dog of Greek mythology, Kerberos is designed to work across the Internet, an inherently insecure environment. Kerberos uses strong encryption so that a client can prove its identity to a server and the server can in turn authenticate itself to the client. A complete Kerberos environment is referred to as a Kerberos *realm*. The Kerberos server contains user IDs and hashed passwords for all users that will have authorizations to realm services. The Kerberos server also has shared secret keys with every server to which it will grant access tickets.

The basis for authentication in a Kerberos environment is the ticket. Tickets are used in a two-step process with the client. The first ticket is a *ticket-granting ticket* issued by the AS to a requesting client. The client can then present this ticket to the Kerberos server with a request for a ticket to access a specific server. This *client-to-server ticket* is used to gain access to a server's service in the realm. Since the entire session can be encrypted, this will eliminate the inherently insecure transmission of items such as a password that can be intercepted on the network. Tickets are time-stamped and have a lifetime, so attempting to reuse a ticket will not be successful.

EXAM TIP Kerberos is a third-party authentication service that uses a series of tickets as tokens for authenticating users. The six steps involved are protected using strong cryptography: 1.) The user presents his credentials and requests a ticket from the Key Distribution Server (KDS). 2.) The KDS verifies credentials and issues a ticket granting ticket (TGT). 3.) The user presents a TGT and request for service to KDS. 4.) KDS verifies authorization and issues a client to server ticket. 5.) The user presents a request and a client to server ticket to the desired service. 6.) If the client to server ticket is valid, service is granted to the client.

To illustrate how the Kerberos authentication service works, think about the common driver's license. You have received a license that you can present to other entities to prove you are who you claim to be. Because other entities trust the state in which the license was issued, they will accept your license as proof of your identity. The state in which the license was issued is analogous to the Kerberos authentication service realm and the license acts as a client to server ticket. It is the trusted entity both sides rely on to provide valid identifications. This analogy is not perfect, because we all probably have heard of individuals who obtained a phony driver's license, but it serves to illustrate the basic idea behind Kerberos.

Certificates

Certificates are a method of establishing authenticity of specific objects such as an individual's public key or downloaded software. A *digital certificate* is generally an attachment to a message and is used to verify that the message did indeed come from the entity it claims to have come from. The digital certificate can also contain a key that can be used to encrypt future communication. For more information on this subject, refer to Chapter 5.

Tokens

A *token* is a hardware device that can be used in a challenge/response authentication process. In this way, it functions as both a something-you-have and something-you-know authentication mechanism. Several variations on this type of device exist, but they all work on the same basic principles. The device has an LCD screen and may or may not have a numeric keypad. Devices without a keypad will display a password (often just a sequence of numbers) that changes at a constant interval, usually about every 60 seconds. When an individual attempts to log in to a system, he enters his own user ID number and then the number that is showing on the LCD. These two numbers are either entered separately or concatenated. The user's own ID number is secret and this prevents someone from using a lost device. The system knows which device the user has and is synchronized with it so that it will know the number that should have been displayed. Since this number is constantly changing, a potential attacker who is able to see the sequence will not be able to use it later, since the code will have changed. Devices with a keypad work in a similar fashion (and may also be designed to function as a simple calculator). The individual who wants to log in to the system will first type his personal identification number into the calculator. He will then attempt to log in. The system will then provide a challenge; the user must enter that challenge into the calculator and press a special function key. The calculator will then determine the correct response and display it. The user provides the response to the system he is attempting to log in to, and the system verifies that this is the correct response. Since each user has a different PIN, two individuals receiving the same challenge will have different responses. The device can also use the date or time as a variable for the response calculation so that the same challenge at different times will yield different responses, even for the same individual.

Multifactor

Multifactor is a term that describes the use of more than one authentication mechanism at the same time. An example of this is the hardware token, which requires both a personal ID number (PIN) or password and the device itself to determine the correct response in order to authenticate to the system. This means that both the something-you-have and something-you-know mechanisms are used as factors in verifying authenticity of the user. Biometrics are also often used in conjunction with a PIN so that they, too, can be used as part of a multifactor authentication scheme, in this case something you are as well as something you know. The purpose of multifactor authentication is to increase the level of security, since more than one mechanism would have to be spoofed in order for an unauthorized individual to gain access to a computer system or network. The most common example of multifactor security is the common ATM card most of us carry in our wallets. The card is associated with a PIN that only the authorized cardholder should know. Knowing the PIN without having the card is useless, just as having the card without knowing the PIN will also not provide you access to your account.

 EXAM TIP The required use of more than one authentication system is known as multifactor authentication. The most common example is the combination of password with a hardware token. For high security, three factors can be used: password, token, and biometric.

Single Sign-on

Single sign-on is a form of authentication that involves the transferring of credentials between systems. As more and more systems are combined in daily use, users are forced to have multiple sets of credentials. A user may have to log in to three, four, five, or even more systems every day just to do her job. Single sign-on allows a user to transfer her credentials, so that logging into one system acts to log her into all of them. This has an advantage of reducing login hassles for the user. It also has a disadvantage of combining the authentication systems in a way such that if one login is compromised, they all are for that user.

Mutual Authentication

Mutual authentication describes a process in which each side of an electronic communication verifies the authenticity of the other. We are accustomed to the idea of having to authenticate ourselves to our ISP before we access the Internet, generally through the use of a user ID/password pair, but how do we actually know that we are really communicating with our ISP and not some other system that has somehow inserted itself into our communication (a man-in-the-middle attack)? Mutual authentication would provide a mechanism for each side of a client/server relationship to verify the authenticity of the other to address this issue.

Authorization

Authorization is the process of permitting or denying access to a specific resource. Once identity is confirmed via authentication, specific actions can be authorized or denied. Many types of authorization schemes are used, but the purpose is the same: determine whether a given user who has been identified has permissions for a particular object or resource being requested. This functionality is frequently part of the operating system and is transparent to users.

The separation of tasks, from identification to authentication to authorization, has several advantages. Many methods can be used to perform each task, and on many systems several methods are concurrently present for each task. Separation of these tasks into individual elements allows combinations of implementations to work together. Any system or resource, be it hardware (router or workstation) or a software component (database system) that requires authorization can use its own authorization method once authentication has occurred. This makes for efficient and consistent application of these principles.

IEEE 802.1x

IEEE 802.1x is an authentication standard that supports communications between a user and an authorization device, such as an edge router. IEEE 802.1x is used by all types of networks, including Ethernet, token ring, and wireless. This standard describes methods used to authenticate a user prior to granting access to an authentication server, such as a RADIUS server. 802.1x acts through an intermediate device, such as an edge switch, enabling ports to carry normal traffic if the connection is properly authenticated. This prevents unauthorized clients from accessing the publicly available ports on a switch, keeping unauthorized users out of a LAN. Until a client has successfully authenticated itself to the device, only Extensible Authentication Protocol over LAN (EAPOL) traffic is passed by the switch.

EAPOL is an encapsulated method of passing EAP messages over 802 frames. EAP is a general protocol that can support multiple methods of authentication, including one-time passwords, Kerberos, public keys, and security device methods such as smart cards. Once a client successfully authenticates itself to the 802.1x device, the switch opens ports for normal traffic. At this point, the client can communicate with the system's AAA method, such as a RADIUS server, and authenticate itself to the network.

RADIUS

Remote Authentication Dial-In User Service (RADIUS) is a protocol that was developed originally by Livingston Enterprises (acquired by Lucent) as an AAA protocol. It was submitted to the Internet Engineering Task Force (IETF) as a series of RFCs: RFC 2058 (RADIUS specification), RFC 2059 (RADIUS accounting standard), and updated RFCs 2865–2869 are now standard protocols. The IETF AAA Working Group has proposed extensions to RADIUS (RFC 2882) and a replacement protocol DIAMETER (Internet Draft DIAMETER Base Protocol).

RADIUS is designed as a connectionless protocol utilizing User Datagram Protocol (UDP) as its transport level protocol. Connection type issues, such as timeouts, are handled by the RADIUS application instead of the transport layer. RADIUS utilizes UDP ports 1812 for authentication and authorization and 1813 for accounting functions (see Table 9-1 in the "Chapter Review" section).

RADIUS is a client/server protocol. The RADIUS client is typically a network access server (NAS). The RADIUS server is a process or daemon running on a UNIX or Windows Server machine. Communications between a RADIUS client and RADIUS server are encrypted using a shared secret that is manually configured into each entity and not shared over a connection. Hence, communications between a RADIUS client (typically a NAS) and a RADIUS server are secure, but the communications between a user (typically a PC) and the RADIUS client are subject to compromise. This is important to note, for if the user's machine (the PC) is not the RADIUS client (the NAS), then communications between the PC and the NAS are typically not encrypted and are passed in the clear.

RADIUS Authentication

The RADIUS protocol is designed to allow a RADIUS server to support a wide variety of methods to authenticate a user. When the server is given a username and password, it can support Point-to-Point Protocol (PPP), Password Authentication Protocol (PAP), Challenge-Handshake Authentication Protocol (CHAP), UNIX login, and other mechanisms, depending on what was established when the server was set up. A user login authentication consists of a query (Access-Request) from the RADIUS client and a corresponding response (Access-Accept or Access-Reject) from the RADIUS server, as you can see in Figure 9-1.

The Access-Request message contains the username, encrypted password, NAS IP address, and port. The message also contains information concerning the type of session the user wants to initiate. Once the RADIUS server receives this information, it searches its database for a match on the username. If a match is not found, either a default profile is loaded or an Access-Reject reply is sent. If the entry is found or the default profile is used, the next phase involves authorization, for in RADIUS, these steps are performed in sequence. Figure 9-1 shows the interaction between a user and the RADIUS client and RADIUS server and the steps taken to make a connection.

1. A user initiates PPP authentication to the NAS.

2. The NAS prompts for

    a. username and password (if PAP), or

    b. challenge (if CHAP).

3. User replies with credentials.

4. RADIUS client sends username and encrypted password to the RADIUS server.

5. RADIUS server responds with Accept, Reject, or Challenge.

6. The RADIUS client acts upon services requested by user.

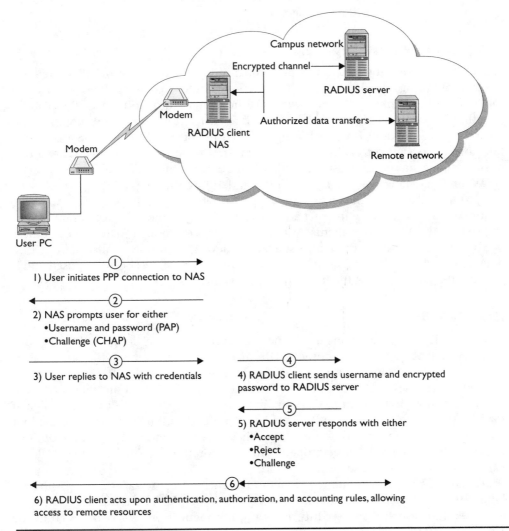

Figure 9-1   RADIUS communication sequence

RADIUS Authorization

In the RADIUS protocol, the authentication and authorization steps are performed together in response to a single Access-Request message, although they are sequential steps (see Figure 9-1). Once an identity has been established, either known or default, the authorization process determines what parameters are returned to the client. Typical authorization parameters include the service type allowed (shell or framed), the protocols allowed, the IP address to assign to the user (static or dynamic), and the access list to apply or static route to place in the NAS routing table. These parameters are all defined in the configuration information on the RADIUS client and server during setup. Using this information, the RADIUS server returns an Access-Accept message with these parameters to the RADIUS client.

RADIUS Accounting

The RADIUS accounting function is performed independently of RADIUS authentication and authorization. The accounting function uses a separate UDP port, 1813 (see Table 9-1 in the "Chapter Review" section). The primary functionality of RADIUS accounting was established to support ISPs in their user accounting, and it supports typical accounting functions for time billing and security logging. The RADIUS accounting functions are designed to allow data to be transmitted at the beginning and end of a session, and it can indicate resource utilization, such as time, bandwidth, and so on.

When RADIUS was first designed in the mid 1990s, the role of ISP NASs was relatively simple. Allowing and denying access to a network and timing usage were the major concerns. Today, the Internet and its access methods have changed dramatically, and so have the AAA requirements. As individual firms extended RADIUS to meet these needs, interoperability became an issue, and a new AAA protocol called DIAMETER, designed to address these issues in a comprehensive fashion, has been proposed and is entering the final stages of the Internet draft/RFC process.

DIAMETER

DIAMETER is a proposed name for the new AAA protocol suite, designated by the IETF to replace the aging RADIUS protocol. DIAMETER operates in much the same way as RADIUS in a client/server configuration, but it improves upon RADIUS, resolving discovered weaknesses. DIAMETER is a TCP-based service and has more extensive capabilities in authentication, authorization, and accounting. DIAMETER is also designed for all types of remote access, not just modem pools. As more and more users adopt broadband and other connection methods, these newer services require more options to determine permissible usage properly and to account for and log the usage. DIAMETER is designed with these needs in mind.

DIAMETER also has an improved method of encrypting message exchanges to prohibit replay and man-in-the-middle attacks. Taken all together, DIAMETER, with its enhanced functionality and security, is an improvement on the proven design of the old RADIUS standard.

TACACS+

The *Terminal Access Controller Access Control System+ (TACACS+)* protocol is the current generation of the TACACS family. Originally TACACS was developed by BBN Planet Corporation for MILNET, an early military network, but it has been enhanced by Cisco and expanded twice. The original BBN TACACS system provided a combination process of authentication and authorization. Cisco extended this to Extended Terminal Access Controller Access Control System (XTACACS), which provided for separate authentication, authorization, and accounting processes. The current generation, TACACS+, has extended attribute control and accounting processes.

One of the fundamental design aspects is the separation of authentication, authorization, and accounting in this protocol. Although there is a straightforward lineage of these protocols from the original TACACS, TACACS+ is a major revision and is not backward-compatible with previous versions of the protocol series.

TACACS+ uses TCP as its transport protocol, typically operating over TCP port 49. This port is used for the login process and is reserved in the assigned numbers RFC, RFC 3232, manifested in a database from IANA. In the IANA specification, both UDP and TCP port 49 are reserved for TACACS login host protocol (see Table 9-1 in the "Chapter Review" section).

TACACS+ is a client/server protocol, with the client typically being a NAS and the server being a daemon process on a UNIX, Linux, or Windows server. This is important to note, for if the user's machine (usually a PC) is not the client (usually a NAS), then communications between PC and NAS are typically not encrypted and are passed in the clear. Communications between a TACACS+ client and TACACS+ server are encrypted using a shared secret that is manually configured into each entity and is not shared over a connection. Hence, communications between a TACACS+ client (typically a NAS) and a TACACS+ server are secure, but the communications between a user (typically a PC) and the TACACS+ client are subject to compromise.

TACACS+ Authentication

TACACS+ allows for arbitrary length and content in the authentication exchange sequence, enabling many different authentication mechanisms to be used with TACACS+ clients. Authentication is optional and is determined as a site-configurable option. When authentication is used, common forms include PPP PAP, PPP CHAP, PPP EAP, token cards, and Kerberos. The authentication process is performed using three different packet types: START, CONTINUE, and REPLY. START and CONTINUE packets originate from the client and are directed to the TACACS+ server. The REPLY packet is used to communicate from the TACACS+ server to the client.

The authentication process is illustrated in Figure 9-2, and it begins with a START message from the client to the server. This message may be in response to an initiation from a PC connected to the TACACS+ client. The START message describes the type of authentication being requested (simple plaintext password, PAP, CHAP, and so on). This START message may also contain additional authentication data, such as username and password. A START message is also sent as a response to a restart request from the server in a REPLY message. A START message always has its sequence number set to 1.

When a TACACS+ server receives a START message, it sends a REPLY message. This REPLY message will indicate whether the authentication is complete or needs to be continued. If the process needs to be continued, the REPLY message also specifies what additional information is needed. The response from a client to a REPLY message requesting additional data is a CONTINUE message. This process continues until the server has all the information needed, and the authentication process concludes with a success or failure.

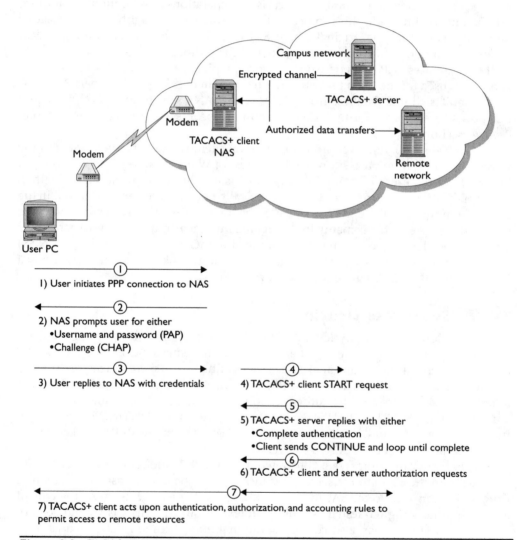

1) User initiates PPP connection to NAS

2) NAS prompts user for either
   •Username and password (PAP)
   •Challenge (CHAP)

3) User replies to NAS with credentials

4) TACACS+ client START request

5) TACACS+ server replies with either
   •Complete authentication
   •Client sends CONTINUE and loop until complete

6) TACACS+ client and server authorization requests

7) TACACS+ client acts upon authentication, authorization, and accounting rules to permit access to remote resources

Figure 9-2 TACAS+ communication sequence

TACACS+ Authorization

Authorization is defined as the action associated with determining permission associated with a user action. This generally occurs after authentication, as shown in Figure 9-3, but this is not a firm requirement. A default state of "unknown user" exists before a user is authenticated, and permissions can be determined for an unknown user. As with authentication, authorization is an optional process and may or may not be part of a site-specific operation. When it is used in conjunction with authentication, the authorization process follows the authentication process and uses the confirmed user identity as input in the decision process.

The authorization process is performed using two message types: REQUEST and RESPONSE. The authorization process is performed using an authorization session consisting of a single pair of REQUEST and RESPONSE messages. The client issues an authorization REQUEST message containing a fixed set of fields that enumerate the authenticity of the user or process requesting permission and a variable set of fields enumerating the services or options for which authorization is being requested.

The RESPONSE message in TACACS+ is not a simple yes or no; it can also include qualifying information, such as a user time limit or IP restrictions. These limitations have important uses, such as enforcing time limits on shell access or IP access list restrictions for specific user accounts.

TACACS+ Accounting

As with the two previous services, accounting is also an optional function of TACACS+. When utilized, it typically follows the other services. Accounting in TACACS+ is defined as the process of recording what a user or process has done. Accounting can serve two important purposes:

- It can be used to account for services being utilized, possibly for billing purposes.
- It can be used for generating security audit trails.

TACACS+ accounting records contain several pieces of information to support these tasks. The accounting process has the information revealed in the authorization and authentication processes, so it can record specific requests by user or process. To support this functionality, TACACS+ has three types of accounting records: START, STOP, and UPDATE. Note that these are record types, not message types as earlier discussed.

START records indicate the time and user or process that began an authorized process. STOP records enumerate the same information concerning the stop times for specific actions. UPDATE records act as intermediary notices that a particular task is still being performed. Together these three message types allow the creation of records that delineate the activity of a user or process on a system.

L2TP and PPTP

Layer Two Tunneling Protocol (L2TP) and Point-to-Point Tunneling Protocol (PPTP) are both OSI layer two tunneling protocols. *Tunneling* is the encapsulation of one packet within another, which allows you to hide the original packet from view or change the nature of the network transport. This can be done for both security and practical reasons.

From a practical perspective, assume that you are using TCP/IP to communicate between two machines. Your message may pass over various networks, such as an Asynchronous Transfer Mode (ATM) network, as it moves from source to destination. As the ATM protocol can neither read nor understand TCP/IP packets, something must be done to make them passable across the network. By encapsulating a packet as the payload in a separate protocol, so it can be carried across a section of a network, a mechanism called a *tunnel* is created. At each end of the tunnel, called the tunnel *endpoints*, the payload packet is read and understood. As it goes into the tunnel, you can envision your packet being placed in an envelope with the address of the appropriate tunnel endpoint on the envelope. When the envelope arrives at the tunnel endpoint, the original message (the tunnel packet's payload) is re-created, read, and sent to its appropriate next stop. The information being tunneled is understood only at the tunnel endpoints; it is not relevant to intermediate tunnel points because it is only a payload.

PPP is a widely used protocol for establishing dial-in connections over serial lines or Integrated Services Digital Network (ISDN) services. PPP has several authentication mechanisms, including PAP, CHAP, and the Extensible Authentication Protocol (EAP). These protocols are used to authenticate the peer device, not a user of the system. PPP is a standardized Internet encapsulation of IP traffic over point-to-point links, such as serial lines. The authentication process is performed only when the link is established.

PPTP

Microsoft led a consortium of networking companies to extend PPP to enable the creation of virtual private networks (VPNs). The result was PPTP, a network protocol that enables the secure transfer of data from a remote PC to a server by creating a VPN across a TCP/IP network. This remote network connection can also span a public switched telephone network (PSTN) and is thus an economical way of connecting remote dial-in users to a corporate data network. The incorporation of PPTP into the Microsoft Windows product line provides a built-in secure method of remote connection using the operating system, and this has given PPTP a large marketplace footprint.

For most PPTP implementations, three computers are involved: the PPTP client, the NAS, and a PPTP server, as shown in Figure 9-3. The connection between the remote client and the network is established in stages, as illustrated in Figure 9-4. First the client makes a PPP connection to a NAS, typically an ISP. Once the PPP connection is established, a second connection is made over the PPP connection to the PPTP server. This second connection creates the VPN connection between the remote client and the PPTP server. This connection acts as a tunnel for future data transfers. Although these diagrams are drawn illustrating a telephone connection, this first link can be virtually

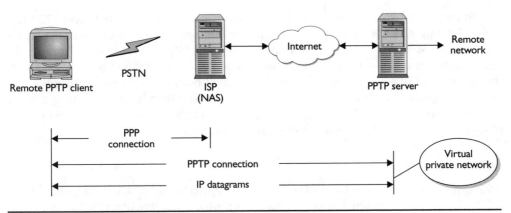

Figure 9-3 PPTP communication diagram

any method. Common in hotels today are wired connections to the Internet. These wired connections to the hotel provided local ISP replaces the phone connection and offers the same services, albeit at a much higher data transfer rate.

As mentioned earlier in this chapter, tunneling is the process of sending packets as data within other packets across a section of a network. This encapsulation enables a network to carry a packet type that it cannot ordinarily route, and it also provides the opportunity to secure the contents of the first packet through encryption. PPTP establishes a tunnel from the remote PPTP client to the PPTP server and enables encryption within this tunnel. This provides a secure method of transport. To do this and still enable routing, an intermediate addressing scheme, Generic Routing Encapsulation (GRE), is used.

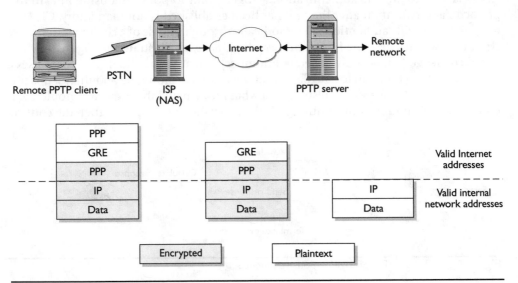

Figure 9-4 PPTP message encapsulation during transmission

To establish the connection, PPTP uses communications across TCP port 1723 (see Table 9-1 in the "Chapter Review" section), so this port must remain open across the network firewalls for PPTP to be initiated. Although PPTP allows the use of any PPP authentication scheme, CHAP is used when encryption is specified to provide an appropriate level of security. For the encryption methodology, Microsoft chose the RSA RC4 cipher, either with a 40-bit or 128-bit session key length, and this is operating-system driven. Microsoft Point-to-Point Encryption (MPPE) is an extension to PPP that enables VPNs to use PPTP as the tunneling protocol.

PPP

PPP is a commonly used data link protocol to connect devices. Defined in RFC 1661, PPP originally was created as an encapsulation protocol to carry IP traffic over point-to-point links. PPP has been extended upon with multiple RFCs to carry a variety of network traffic types over a variety of network types. PPP uses Link Control Protocols (LCP) and Network Control Protocols (NCP) to establish the desired connections over a network.

 EXAM TIP PPP supports three functions: 1) Encapsulate datagrams across serial links; 2) Establish, configure, and test links using LCP; and 3) Establish and configure different network protocols using NCP. PPP supports two authentication protocols: Password Authentication Protocol (PAP) and Challenge Handshake Authentication Protocol (CHAP).

CHAP

CHAP is used to provide authentication across a point-to-point link using PPP. In this protocol, authentication after the link has been established is not mandatory. CHAP is designed to provide authentication periodically through the use of a challenge/response system sometimes described as a *three-way handshake*, as illustrated in Figure 9-5. The initial challenge (a randomly generated number) is sent to the client. The client uses a one-way hashing function to calculate what the response should be and then sends this back. The server compares the response to what it calculated the response should be. If they match, communication continues. If the two values don't match, then the connec-

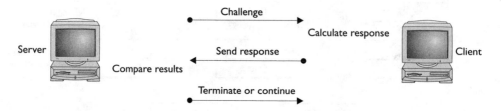

Figure 9-5 The CHAP challenge/response sequence

tion is terminated. This mechanism relies on a shared secret between the two entities so that the correct values can be calculated.

Microsoft has created two versions of CHAP, modified to increase their usability across their product line. MSCHAPv1, defined in RFC 2433, has been deprecated and dropped in Windows Vista. The current standard version 2, RFC 2759, was introduced with Windows 2000.

PAP

PAP authentication involves a two-way handshake in which the username and password are sent across the link in clear text. PAP authentication does not provide any protection against playback and line sniffing. PAP is now a deprecated standard.

EAP

EAP is a universal authentication framework defined by RFC 3748 that is frequently used in wireless networks and point-to-point connections. Although EAP is not limited to wireless and can be used for wired authentication, it is most often used in wireless LANs. EAP is discussed in Chapter 10.

L2TP

L2TP is also an Internet standard and came from the Layer Two Forwarding (L2F) protocol, a Cisco initiative designed to address issues with PPTP. Whereas PPTP is designed around PPP and IP networks, L2F, and hence L2TP, is designed for use across all kinds of networks including ATM and frame relay. Additionally, where PPTP is designed to be implemented in software at the client device, L2TP was conceived as a hardware implementation using a router or a special-purpose appliance. L2TP can be configured in software and is in Microsoft's Routing and Remote Access Service (RRAS) servers, which use L2TP to create a VPN.

L2TP works in much the same way as PPTP, but it opens up several items for expansion. For instance, in L2TP, routers can be enabled to concentrate VPN traffic over higher bandwidth lines, creating hierarchical networks of VPN traffic that can be more efficiently managed across an enterprise. L2TP also has the ability to use IP Security (IPsec) and Data Encryption Standard (DES) as encryption protocols, providing a higher level of data security. L2TP is also designed to work with established AAA services such as RADIUS and TACACS+ to aid in user authentication, authorization, and accounting.

L2TP is established via UDP port 1701, so this is an essential port to leave open across firewalls supporting L2TP traffic. This port is registered with the Internet Assigned Numbers Authority (IANA), as is 1723 for PPTP (see Table 9-1 in the "Chapter Review" section). Microsoft supports L2TP in Windows 2000 and above, but because of the computing power required, most implementations will use specialized hardware (such as a Cisco router).

NT LAN Manager

NT LAN Manager (NTLM) is an authentication protocol designed by Microsoft for use with the Server Message Block (SMB) protocol. SMB is an application-level network protocol primarily used for sharing files and printers on Windows-based networks. NTLM was designed as a replacement for the LANMAN protocol. The current version is NTLMv2, which was introduced with NT 4.0 SP4. Although Microsoft has adopted the Kerberos protocol for authentication, NTLMv2 is still used when

- Authenticating to a server using an IP address
- Authenticating to a server that belongs to a different Active Directory forest
- Authenticating to a server that doesn't belong to a domain
- When no Active Directory domain exists ("workgroup" or "peer-to-peer" connection)

Telnet

One of the methods to grant remote access to a system is through Telnet. Telnet is the standard terminal-emulation protocol within the TCP/IP protocol series, and it is defined in RFC 854. Telnet allows users to log in remotely and access resources as if the user had a local terminal connection. Telnet is an old protocol and offers little security. Information, including account names and passwords, is passed in clear text over the TCP/IP connection.

Telnet makes its connection using TCP port 23. (A list of remote access networking port assignments is provided in Table 9-1 in the "Chapter Review" section.) As Telnet is implemented on most products using TCP/IP, and it is important to control access to Telnet on machines and routers when setting them up. Failure to control access by using firewalls, access lists, and other security methods, or even by disabling the Telnet daemon, is equivalent to leaving an open door for unauthorized users on a system.

SSH

If you are looking for remote access to a system in a secure manner, you could use Secure Shell (SSH), a protocol series designed to facilitate secure network functions across an insecure network. SSH provides direct support for secure remote login, secure file transfer, and secure forwarding of TCP/IP and X Window System traffic. A SSH connection is an encrypted channel, providing for confidentiality and integrity protection.

SSH has its origins all the way back in the beginning of the UNIX operating system. An original component of UNIX, Telnet allowed users to connect between systems. Although Telnet is still used today, it has some drawbacks, as discussed in the preceding section. Some enterprising University of California, Berkeley, students subsequently developed the r- commands, such as rlogin, to permit access based on the user and source system, as opposed to passing passwords. This was not perfect either, however, for when a login was required, it was still passed in the clear. This led to the development of the SSH protocol series designed to eliminate all of the insecurities associated with Telnet, r- commands, and other means of remote access.

SSH opens a secure transport between machines by using an SSH daemon on each end. These daemons initiate contact over TCP port 22 and then communicate over higher ports in a secure mode. One of the strengths of SSH is its support for many different encryption protocols. SSH 1.0 started with RSA algorithms, but at the time they were still under patent, and this led to SSH 2.0 with extended support for Triple DES (3DES) and other encryption methods. Today, SSH can be used with a wide range of encryption protocols, including RSA, 3DES, Blowfish, International Data Encryption Algorithm (IDEA), CAST128, AES256, and others.

The SSH protocol has facilities to encrypt data automatically, provide authentication, and compress data in transit. It can support strong encryption, cryptographic host authentication, and integrity protection. The authentication services are host-based and not user-based. If user authentication is desired in a system, it must be set up separately at a higher level in the OSI model. The protocol is designed to be flexible and simple, and it is designed specifically to minimize the number of round trips between systems. The key exchange, public key, symmetric key, message authentication, and hash algorithms are all negotiated at connection time. Individual data-packet integrity is assured through the use of a message authentication code that is computed from a shared secret, the contents of the packet, and the packet sequence number.

The SSH protocol consists of three major components:

- **Transport layer protocol**   Provides server authentication, confidentiality, integrity, and compression
- **User authentication protocol**   Authenticates the client to the server
- **Connection protocol**   Provides multiplexing of the encrypted tunnel into several logical channels

SSH is very popular in the UNIX environment, and it is actively used as a method of establishing VPNs across public networks. Because all communications between the two machines are encrypted at the OSI application layer by the two SSH daemons, this leads to the ability to build very secure solutions and even solutions that defy the ability of outside services to monitor. As SSH is a standard protocol series with connection parameters established via TCP port 22, different vendors can build differing solutions that can still interoperate. As such, if SSH is enabled on a UNIX platform, it is a built-in method of establishing secure communications with that system from a wide range of client platforms.

Although Windows Server implementations of SSH exist, this has not been a popular protocol in the Windows environment from a server perspective. The development of a wide array of commercial SSH clients for the Windows platform indicates the marketplace strength of interconnection from desktop PCs to UNIX-based servers utilizing this protocol.

PART III

IEEE 802.11

The IEEE 802.11 protocol series covers the use of microwave communications media in networks.designed for wireless LANs. The remainder of this discussion will focus on the 802.11 series because it is in widespread use.

IEEE 802.11is not a single protocol, but an entire series of them, with 802.11b, 802.11a, 802.11g, and 802.11n being common wireless protocols that allow wireless connectivity to a LAN and ad-hoc peer-to-peer wireless networking. Products for these protocols have become common, and they are available at reasonable prices from a variety of vendors. These devices are finding use in corporate networks, metropolitan hot spots, and even home networks. The advantage of wireless communication is simple to understand—the requirement for a physical wire between various machines is eliminated. This provides tremendous ease of setup for a network engineer from a cabling point of view, because no cables need to be connected. This pays off again if a corporation moves employees between desks, because again no wires need to be moved when moving PCs. For laptop users, this means machines and devices can be mobile and remain connected to the network. The details behind wireless authentication is covered in Chapter 10.

VPNs

VPNs are secure *virtual* networks built on top of *physical* networks. Their security lies in the encryption of packet contents between the endpoints that define the VPN network. The physical network upon which a VPN is built is typically a public network, such as the Internet. Because the packet contents between VPN endpoints are encrypted, to an outside observer on the public network, the communication is secure, and depending on how the VPN is set up, security can even extend to the two communicating parties' machines.

Virtual private networking is not a protocol per se, but rather a method of using protocols to achieve a specific objective—secure communications—as shown in Figure 9-6. A user wanting to have a secure communication channel with a server across a public network can set up two intermediary devices, VPN endpoints, to accomplish this task. The user can communicate with his endpoint, and the server can communicate with its endpoint. The two endpoints then communicate across the public network. VPN endpoints can be software solutions, routers, or specific servers set up for specific functionality. This implies that VPN services are set up in advance and are not something negotiated on the fly.

A typical use of VPN services is a user accessing a corporate data network from a home PC across the Internet. The employee will install VPN software from work on a home PC. This software is already configured to communicate with the corporate network's VPN endpoint; it knows the location, the protocols that will be used, and so on. When the home user wants to connect to the corporate network, she connects to the Internet and then starts the VPN software. The user can then log in to the corporate network by using an appropriate authentication and authorization methodology. The

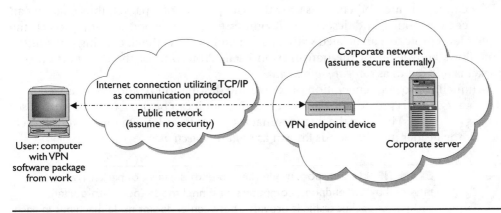

Figure 9-6   VPN service over an Internet connection

sole purpose of the VPN connection is to provide a private connection between the machines, which encrypts any data sent between the home user's PC to the corporate network. Identification, authorization, and all other standard functions are accomplished with the standard mechanisms for the established system.

VPNs can use many different protocols to offer a secure method of communicating between endpoints. Common methods of encryption on VPNs include PPTP, IPsec, SSH, and L2TP, all of which are discussed in this chapter. The key is that both endpoints know the protocol and share a secret. All of this necessary information is established when the VPN is set up. At the time of use, the VPN only acts as a private tunnel between the two points and does not constitute a complete security solution.

IPsec

IPsec is a set of protocols developed by the IETF to securely exchange packets at the network layer (layer 3) of the OSI model (RFC 2401–2412). Although these protocols work only in conjunction with IP networks, once an IPsec connection is established, it is possible to tunnel across other networks at lower levels of the OSI model. The set of security services provided by IPsec occurs at the network layer of the OSI model, so higher layer protocols, such as TCP, UDP, Internet Control Message Protocol (ICMP), Border Gateway Protocol (BGP), and the like, are not functionally altered by the implementation of IPsec services.

The IPsec protocol series has a sweeping array of services it is designed to provide, including but not limited to access control, connectionless integrity, traffic-flow confidentiality, rejection of replayed packets, data security (encryption), and data-origin authentication. IPsec has two defined methods—transport and tunneling—that provide different levels of security. IPsec also has three modes of connection: host-to-server, server-to-server, and host-to-host.

PART III

The transport method encrypts only the data portion of a packet, thus enabling an outsider to see source and destination IP addresses. The transport method protects the higher level protocols associated with a packet and protects the data being transmitted but allows knowledge of the transmission itself. Protection of the data portion of a packet is referred to as *content protection*.

Tunneling provides encryption of source and destination IP addresses, as well as of the data itself. This provides the greatest security, but it can be done only between IPsec servers (or routers) because the final destination needs to be known for delivery. Protection of the header information is known as *context protection*.

EXAM TIP In transport mode (end-to-end), security of packet traffic is provided by the endpoint computers. In tunnel mode (portal-to-portal), security of packet traffic is provided between endpoint node machines in each network and not at the terminal host machines.

It is possible to use both methods at the same time, such as using transport within one's own network to reach an IPsec server, which then tunnels to the target server's network, connecting to an IPsec server there, and then using the transport method from the target network's IPsec server to the target host.

Security Associations

A security association (SA) is a formal manner of describing the necessary and sufficient portions of the IPsec protocol series to achieve a specific level of protection. As many options exist, both communicating parties must agree on the use of the protocols that are available, and this agreement is referred to as a *security association*. SAs exist both for integrity protecting systems and confidentiality protecting systems. In each IPsec implementation, a security association database (SAD) defines parameters associated with each SA. The SA is a one-way (simplex) association, and if two-way communication security is desired, two SAs are used—one for each direction.

EXAM TIP A security association is a logical set of security parameters designed to facilitate the sharing of information between entities.

IPsec Configurations

Four basic configurations can be applied to machine-to-machine connections using IPsec. The simplest is a host-to-host connection between two machines, as shown in Figure 9-7. In this case, the Internet is not a part of the security association between the machines. If bidirectional security is desired, two SAs are used. The SAs are effective from host to host.

The second case places two security devices in the stream, relieving the hosts of the calculation and encapsulation duties. These two gateways have a security association between them. The network is assumed to be secure from each machine to its gateway,

Case 1:
Two SAs from host to host for bidirectional secure communications

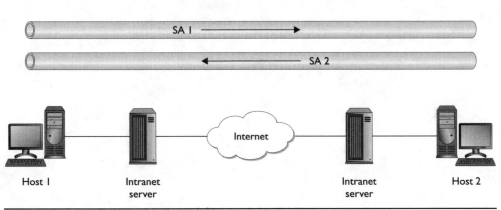

Figure 9-7   A host-to-host connection between two machines

and no IPsec is performed across these hops. Figure 9-8 shows the two security gateways with a tunnel across the Internet, although either tunnel or transport mode could be used.

The third case combines the first two. A separate security association exists between the gateway devices, but a security association also exists between hosts. This could be considered a tunnel inside a tunnel, as shown in Figure 9-9.

Remote users commonly connect through the Internet to an organization's network. The network has a security gateway through which it secures traffic to and from its servers and authorized users. In the last case, illustrated in Figure 9-10, the user establishes a security association with the security gateway and then a separate association with the desired server, if required. This can be done using software on a remote laptop and hardware at the organization's network.

Case 2:
IPsec between machines using gateway security devices

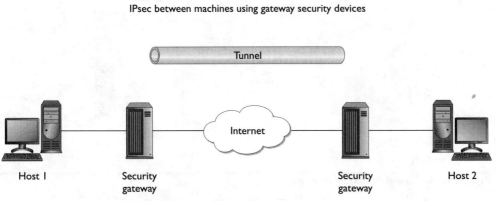

Figure 9-8   Two security gateways with a tunnel across the Internet

Case 3:
Separate IPsec tunnels, host to host and gateway to gateway

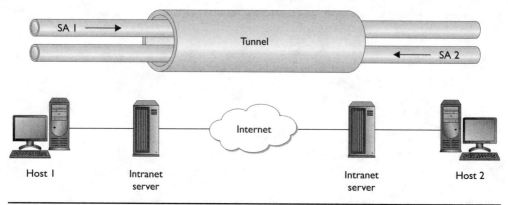

Figure 9-9   A tunnel inside a tunnel

Windows can act as an IPsec server, as can routers and other servers. The primary issue is CPU usage and where the computing power should be implanted. This consideration has led to the rise of IPsec appliances, hardware devices that perform the IPsec function specifically for a series of communications. Depending on the number of connections, network bandwidth, and so on, these devices can be inexpensive for small office or home office use or quite expensive for large enterprise level implementations.

Case 4:
Tunnel from host to gateway
Optional: Two SAs for bidirectional secure communications

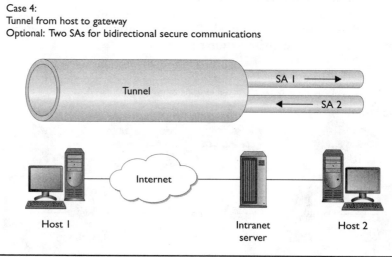

Figure 9-10   Tunnel from host to gateway

IPsec Security

IPsec uses two protocols to provide traffic security:

- Authentication Header (AH)
- Encapsulating Security Payload (ESP)

For key management and exchange, three protocols exist:

- Internet Security Association and Key Management Protocol (ISAKMP)
- Oakley
- Secure Key Exchange Mechanism for Internet (SKEMI)

These key management protocols can be collectively referred to as *Internet Key Management Protocol (IKMP)* or *Internet Key Exchange (IKE)*.

IPsec does not define specific security algorithms, nor does it require specific methods of implementation. IPsec is an open framework that allows vendors to implement existing industry-standard algorithms suited for specific tasks. This flexibility is key in IPsec's ability to offer a wide range of security functions. IPsec allows several security technologies to be combined into a comprehensive solution for network-based confidentiality, integrity, and authentication. IPsec uses the following:

- Diffie-Hellman key exchange between peers on a public network
- Public key signing of Diffie-Hellman key exchanges to guarantee identity and avoid man-in-the-middle attacks
- Bulk encryption algorithms, such as IDEA and 3DES, for encrypting data
- Keyed hash algorithms, such as HMAC, and traditional hash algorithms, such as MD5 and SHA-1, for packet-level authentication
- Digital certificates to act as digital ID cards between parties

To provide traffic security, two header extensions have been defined for IP datagrams. The AH, when added to an IP datagram, ensures the integrity of the data and also the authenticity of the data's origin. By protecting the nonchanging elements in the IP header, the AH protects the IP address, which enables data-origin authentication. The ESP provides security services for the higher level protocol portion of the packet only, not the IP header.

 EXAM TIP IPsec AH protects integrity, but it does not provide privacy. IPsec ESP provides confidentiality, but it does not protect integrity of the packet. To cover both privacy and integrity, both headers can be used at the same time.

AH and ESP can be used separately or in combination, depending on the level and types of security desired. Both also work with the transport and tunnel modes of IPsec protocols. In transport mode, the two communication endpoints are providing security primarily for the upper layer protocols. The cryptographic endpoints, where encryption and decryption occurs, are located at the source and destination of the communication channel. For AH in transport mode, the original IP header is exposed, but its contents are protected via the AH block in the packet, as illustrated in Figure 9-11. For ESP in transport mode, the data contents are protected by encryption, as illustrated in Figure 9-12.

Tunneling is a means of encapsulating packets inside a protocol that is understood only at the entry and exit points of the tunnel. This provides security during transport in the tunnel, because outside observers cannot decipher packet contents or even the identities of the communicating parties. IPsec has a tunnel mode that can be used from server to server across a public network. Although the tunnel endpoints are referred to as *servers*, these devices can be routers, appliances, or servers. In tunnel mode, the tunnel endpoints merely encapsulate the entire packet with new IP headers to indicate the endpoints, and they encrypt the contents of this new packet. The true source and destination information is contained in the inner IP header, which is encrypted in the tunnel. The outer IP header contains the addresses of the endpoints of the tunnel.

As mentioned, AH and ESP can be employed in tunnel mode. When AH is employed in tunnel mode, portions of the outer IP header are given the same header protection that occurs in transport mode, with the entire inner packet receiving protection. This is illustrated in Figure 9-13. ESP affords the same encryption protection to the contents of the tunneled packet, which is the entire packet from the initial sender, as illustrated in Figure 9-14. Together, in tunnel mode, AH and ESP can provide complete protection across the packet, as shown in Figure 9-15. The specific combination of AH and ESP is referred to as a *security association* in IPsec.

In IP version 4 (IPv4), IPsec is an add-on, and its acceptance is vendor driven. It is not a part of the original IP—one of the short-sighted design flaws of the original IP. In IPv6, IPsec is integrated into IP and is native on all packets. Its use is still optional, but its inclusion in the protocol suite will guarantee interoperability across vendor solutions when they are compliant with IPv6 standards.

IPsec uses cryptographic keys in its security process and has both manual and automatic distribution of keys as part of the protocol series. Manual key distribution is included, but it is practical only in small, static environments and does not scale to

Figure 9-11
IPsec use of AH in transport mode

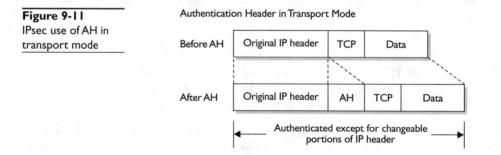

Authentication Header in Transport Mode

Figure 9-12
IPsec use of ESP in transport mode

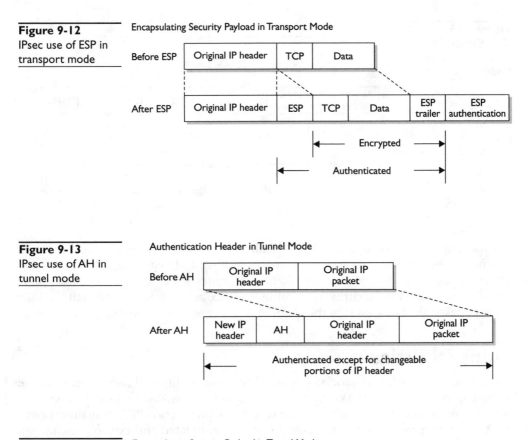

Encapsulating Security Payload in Transport Mode

Before ESP

Original IP header	TCP	Data

After ESP

Original IP header	ESP	TCP	Data	ESP trailer	ESP authentication

Encrypted

Authenticated

Figure 9-13
IPsec use of AH in tunnel mode

Authentication Header in Tunnel Mode

Before AH

Original IP header	Original IP packet

After AH

New IP header	AH	Original IP header	Original IP packet

Authenticated except for changeable portions of IP header

Figure 9-14
IPsec use of ESP in tunnel mode

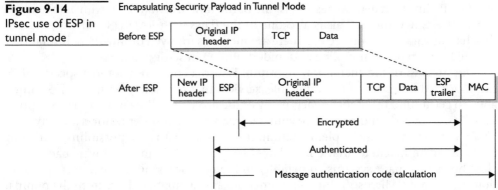

Encapsulating Security Payload in Tunnel Mode

Before ESP

Original IP header	TCP	Data

After ESP

New IP header	ESP	Original IP header	TCP	Data	ESP trailer	MAC

Encrypted

Authenticated

Message authentication code calculation

Figure 9-15
IPsec ESP and AH packet construction in tunnel mode

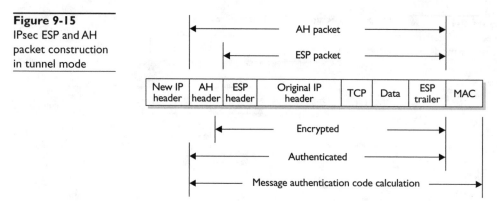

enterprise-level implementations. The default method of key management, IKE, is automated. IKE authenticates each peer involved in IPsec and negotiates the security policy, including the exchange of session keys. IKE creates a secure tunnel between peers and then negotiates the security association for IPsec across this channel. This is done in two phases: the first develops the channel, and the second the security association.

Vulnerabilities

The primary vulnerability associated with all of these methods of remote access is the passing of critical data in the clear. Plaintext passing of passwords provides no security if the password is sniffed, and sniffers are easy to use on a network. Even plaintext passing of user IDs gives away information that can be correlated and possibly used by an attacker. Plaintext credential passing is one of the fundamental flaws with Telnet and is why SSH was developed. This is also one of the flaws with RADIUS and TACACS+, as they have a segment unprotected. There are methods for overcoming these limitations, although they require discipline and understanding in setting up a system.

The strength of the encryption algorithm is also a concern. Should a specific algorithm or method prove to be vulnerable, services that rely solely on it are also vulnerable. To get around this dependency, many of the protocols allow numerous encryption methods, so that should one prove vulnerable, a shift to another restores security.

As with any software implementation, there always exists the possibility that a bug could open the system to attack. Bugs have been corrected in most software packages to close holes that made systems vulnerable, and remote access functionality is no exception. This is not a Microsoft-only phenomenon, as one might believe from the popular press. Critical flaws have been found in almost every product, from open system implementations such as OpenSSH to proprietary systems such as Cisco's IOS. The important issue is not the presence of software bugs, for as software continues to become more complex, this is an unavoidable issue. The true key is vendor responsiveness to fixing the bugs once they are discovered, and the major players, such as Cisco and Microsoft, have been very responsive in this area.

Chapter Review

Many methods can be used to achieve security under remote access conditions, and the number is growing as new protocols are developed to meet the ever-increasing use of remote access. From the beginnings of Telnet, to IPv6 with built-in IPsec, the options are many, but the task is basically the same. Perform the functions of authentication, authorization, and accounting while providing message and data security from outside intervention.

Table 9-1 shows some remote access support solutions.

TCP Port Number	UDP Port Number	Keyword	Protocol
20		FTP-Data	File Transfer (Default Data)
21		FTP	File Transfer Control
22		SSH	Secure Shell Login
23		TELNET	Telnet
25		SMTP	Simple Mail Transfer
37	37	TIME	Time
49	49	TACACS+	TACACS+ login
53	53	DNS	Domain Name Server
65	65	TACACS+	TACACS+ database service
88	88	Kerberos	Kerberos
500	500	ISAKMP	ISAKMP protocol
512		rexec	
513		rlogin	UNIX rlogin
	513	rwho	UNIX Broadcast Naming Service
514		rsh	UNIX rsh and rep
	514	SYSLOG	UNIX system logs
614	614	SSHELL	SSL Shell
	1645	RADIUS	RADIUS: Historical
	1646	RADIUS	RADIUS: Historical
	1701	L2TP	L2TP
1723	1723	PPTP	PPTP
1812	1812	RADIUS	RADIUS authorization
1813	1813	RADIUS-actg	RADIUS accounting

Table 9-1   Common TCP/UDP Remote Access Networking Port Assignments

Some of the remote access solutions have a hardware component (such as L2F and RADIUS), some have software (SSH and PPTP), and some have both (VPN and IPsec), depending on the vendor's implementation and system requirements. Your choice of a remote access solution will depend on several factors, including security requirements, the type of network, the type of clients, required access methods, scalability, existing authentication mechanisms, and cost. Each system has its strengths and weaknesses, and when properly employed, each can be used effectively within its own limitations. There is no best solution at the present time, but as the Internet advances and IPv6 is adopted, IPsec will move up the list into a prime spot and provide a significant number of these required services as part of the TCP/IPv6 protocol suite.

Questions

To further help you prepare for the Security+ exam, and to test your level of preparedness, answer the following questions and then check your answers against the list of correct answers at the end of the chapter.

1. PPP provides for

   A. Network control of printers over a parallel port

   B. Encapsulation of datagrams across serial point-to-point connections

   C. An obsolete layer protocol from before the Internet

   D. A service to establish VPNs across the Internet

2. Authentication is typically based upon what? (Select all that apply.)

   A. Something a user possesses

   B. Something a user knows

   C. Something measured on a user, such as a fingerprint

   D. None of the above

3. Passwords are an example of

   A. Something you have

   B. Something you know

   C. A shared secret

   D. None of the above

4. Which of these protocols is used for carrying authentication, authorization, and configuration (accounting) information between a network access server and a shared authentication server?

   A. IPsec

   B. VPN

   C. SSH

   D. RADIUS

5. On a VPN, traffic is encrypted and decrypted at
   A. Endpoints of the tunnel only
   B. Users' machines
   C. Each device at each hop
   D. The data link layer of access devices

6. What protocol is used for TACACS+?
   A. UDP
   B. NetBIOS
   C. TCP
   D. Proprietary

7. What protocol is used for RADIUS?
   A. UDP
   B. NetBIOS
   C. TCP
   D. Proprietary

8. Which protocols are natively supported by Microsoft Windows XP and Vista for use in securing remote connections?
   A. SSH
   B. PPTP
   C. IPsec
   D. RADIUS

9. What are the foundational elements of an access control system?
   A. Passwords, permissions, cryptography
   B. Shared secrets, authorization, authenticators
   C. Authentication, permissions, user IDs
   D. Identification, authorization, authentication

10. IPsec provides which options as security services?
    A. ESP and AH
    B. ESP and AP
    C. EA and AP
    D. EA and AH

11. Secure Shell uses which port to communicate?
    A. TCP port 80
    B. UDP port 22

C. TCP port 22

D. TCP port 110

12. Elements of Kerberos include which of the following:

    A. Tickets, ticket granting server, ticket authorizing agent

    B. Ticket granting ticket, authentication server, ticket

    C. Services server, Kerberos realm, ticket authenticators

    D. Client to server ticket, authentication server ticket, ticket

13. To establish an PPTP connection across a firewall, you must do which of the following?

    A. Do nothing; PPTP does not need to cross firewalls by design.

    B. Do nothing; PPTP traffic is invisible and tunnels past firewalls.

    C. Open a UDP port of choice and assign to PPTP.

    D. Open TCP port 1723.

14. To establish an L2TP connection across a firewall, you must do which of the following?

    A. Do nothing; L2TP does not cross firewalls by design.

    B. Do nothing; L2TP tunnels past firewalls.

    C. Open a UDP port of choice and assign to L2TP.

    D. Open UDP port 1701.

15. IPsec can provide which of the following types of protection?

    A. Context protection

    B. Content protection

    C. Both context and content protection

    D. Neither context nor content protection

Answers

1. **B.** PPP supports three functions: encapsulate datagrams across serial links; establish, configure, and test links using LCP; and establish and configure different network protocols using NCP.

2. **A, B,** and **C.** Authentication is commonly performed with passwords, something you know; tokens, something you have; and biometrics, such as fingerprints.

3. **B.** Passwords are defined as something you know, and are not to be shared.

4. **D.** RADIUS is a protocol for performing authentication, authorization, and accounting. It involves an information exchange between a network access

server, which desires authentication of specific connections, and a shared authentication server.

5. **A.** A virtual private network (VPN) is a secure communications protocol that encrypts traffic between two endpoints of a tunnel. At each endpoint of the secure VPN tunnel, the traffic is either encrypted or decrypted, depending on whether the traffic is going into or out of the tunnel.

6. **C.** TACACS+ is TCP-based and uses port 49.

7. **A.** RADIUS has been officially assigned UDP ports 1812 for RADIUS Authentication and 1813 for RADIUS Accounting by the Internet Assigned Number Authority (IANA). However, previously, ports 1645–Authentication and 1646–Accounting were used unofficially and became the default ports assigned by many RADIUS client/server implementations of the time. The tradition of using 1645 and 1646 for backward compatibility continues to this day. For this reason, many RADIUS server implementations monitor both sets of UDP ports for RADIUS requests. Microsoft RADIUS servers default to 1812 and 1813, but Cisco devices default to the traditional 1645 and 1646 ports.

8. **B and C.** Both PPTP and IPsec are supported by Microsoft Windows operating systems. IPsec is more resource intensive, but also more versatile, and it allows greater flexibility in connections.

9. **D.** Access control systems need three main components: identification, authorization, and authentication.

10. **A.** IPsec utilizes Encapsulating Security Payload (ESP) and Authentication Headers (AH).

11. **C.** SSH initiates conversations over TCP port 22.

12. **B.** Kerberos works using tickets. A ticket granting ticket is one type of ticket obtained from the authentication server.

13. **D.** PPTP uses TCP port 1723 to establish communications, so this port must be open across a firewall for PPTP to function correctly.

14. **D.** L2TP uses UDP port 1701 to establish communications, so this port must be open across a firewall for L2TP to function correctly.

15. **C.** IPsec can provide both context and content protection by using both ESP and AH.

10

Wireless Security

In this chapter, you will
- Learn about the security implications of wireless networks
- Learn about the security built into different versions of wireless protocols
- Identify the different 802.11 versions and their security controls

Wireless is increasingly the way people access the Internet. Because wireless access is considered a consumer benefit, many businesses add wireless access points to lure customers into their shops. With the rollout of third-generation (3G) cellular networks, people are also increasingly accessing the Internet from their mobile phones.

As wireless use increases, the security of the wireless protocols has become a more important factor in the security of the entire network. As a security professional, you need to understand wireless network applications because of the risks inherent in broadcasting a network signal where anyone can intercept it. Sending unsecured information across public airwaves is tantamount to posting your company's passwords by the front door of the building.

This chapter looks at several current wireless protocols and their security features.

Wireless Networking

Wireless networking is the transmission of packetized data by means of a physical topology that does not use direct physical links. This definition can be narrowed to apply to networks that use radio waves to carry the signals over either public or private bands, instead of using standard network cabling. Although some proprietary applications use point-to-point technology with narrowband radios and highly directional antennas, this technology is not common enough to produce any significant research into its vulnerabilities, and anything that was developed would have limited usefulness. So the chapter focuses on point-to-multipoint systems, the two most common of which are the family of cellular protocols and IEEE 802.11.

The 802.11 protocol has been standardized by the IEEE for wireless local area networks (LANs). Three versions are currently in production—802.11g, 802.11b, and 802.11a. At the time of writing, a fourth standard, 802.11n, remains under development. While the fourth standard is an IEEE draft specification, some manufacturers are already shipping products based on it. The same situation occurred with 802.11g hardware, but as most equipment is backward-compatible, consumers are generally assured of getting something that works. The 802.11n standard is due to be ratified in March 2009, at which time most vendors will release an update to ensure compliance. Cellular phone technology has moved rapidly to embrace data transmission and the Internet. The Wireless Application Protocol (WAP) was one of the pioneers of mobile data applications, but it has been overtaken by a variety of protocols pushing us to third-generation (3G) or fourth-generation (4G) mobile networks.

The 802.11b standard was the first to market, 802.11a followed, and at the time of writing 802.11g products are the most common ones being sold. These chipsets have also commonly been combined into devices that support a/b/g standards. 802.11n is on the horizon, with many manufacturers shipping devices based upon the draft specification.

Bluetooth is a short-range wireless protocol typically used on small devices such as mobile phones. Early versions of these phones also had the Bluetooth on and discoverable as a default, making the compromise of a nearby phone easy. Security research has focused on finding problems with these devices simply because they are so common.

The security world ignored wireless for a long time, and then within the space of a few months, it seemed like everyone was attempting to breach the security of wireless networks and transmissions. One reason that wireless suddenly found itself vulnerable is because wireless targets are so abundant and so unsecured, simply because they are not necessarily attached to crucial infrastructure. The dramatic proliferation of these inexpensive products has made the security ramifications of the protocol astonishing.

No matter what the system, wireless security is a very important topic as more and more applications are designed to use wireless to send data. Wireless is particularly problematic from a security standpoint, because there is no control over the physical layer of the traffic. In most wired LANs, the administrators have physical control over the network and can control to some degree who can actually connect to the physical medium. This prevents large amounts of unauthorized traffic and makes snooping around and listening to the traffic difficult. Wireless does away with the physical limitations. If an attacker can get close enough to the signal's source as it is being broadcast, he can at the very least listen to the access point and clients talking to capture all the packets for examination. Attackers can also try to modify the traffic being sent or try to send their own traffic to disrupt the system. In this chapter, you will learn of the different types of attacks that wireless networks face.

Mobile Phones

When cellular phones first hit the market, security wasn't an issue—if you wanted to keep your phone safe, you'd simply not loan it to people you didn't want making calls. The advance of digital circuitry has added amazing power in smaller and smaller devices, causing security to be an issue as the software becomes more and more complicated. Today's small and inexpensive products have made the wireless market grow by leaps and bounds, as traditional wireless devices such as cellular phones and pagers are replaced by wireless e-mail devices and PDAs.

Almost all current mobile phones have wireless networking features built in. All these devices have generated a demand for additional services. The Wireless Application Protocol (WAP) attempted to satisfy the needs for more data on mobile devices, but it is falling by the wayside as the mobile networks' capabilities increase. The need for more and more bandwidth has pushed carriers to adopt a more IP-centric routing methodology with technologies such as High Speed Packet Access (HSPA) and Evolution Data Optimized (EVDO). Mobile phones have ruthlessly advanced with new technologies and services, causing phones and the carrier networks that support them to be described in generations—1G, 2G, 3G, and 4G. 1G refers to the original analog cellular or AMPS, and 2G refers to the digital network that superseded it. 3G is the mobile networks that are just now being deployed. They allow carriers to offer a wider array of services to the consumer including broadband data service up to 14.4 Mbps and video calling. 4G is the planned move to an entire IP-based network for all services, running voice over IP (VoIP) on your mobile phone.

All of these "gee-whiz" features are nice, but how secure are your bits and bytes going to be when they're traveling across a mobile carrier's network? All the protocols mentioned have their own security implementations—WAP applies its own Wireless Transport Layer Security (WTLS) to attempt to secure data transmissions, but WAP still has issues such as the "WAP gap" (as discussed next). 3G networks have attempted to push a large amount of security down the stack and rely on the encryption designed into the wireless protocol.

EXAM TIP Wireless Application Protocol is a lightweight protocol designed for mobile devices. Wireless Transport Layer Security is a lightweight security protocol designed for WAP.

WAP

WAP was introduced to compensate for the relatively low amount of computing power on handheld devices as well as the generally poor network throughput of cellular networks. It uses the WTLS encryption scheme, which encrypts the plaintext data and then sends it over the airwaves as ciphertext. The originator and the recipient both have keys to decrypt the data and reproduce the plaintext. This method of ensuring confidentiality is very common, and if the encryption is well-designed and implemented, it is difficult for unauthorized users to take captured ciphertext and reproduce the plaintext that created it.

WTLS uses a modified version of the Transport Layer Security (TLS) protocol, formerly known as Secure Sockets Layer (SSL). The WTLS protocol supports several popular bulk encryption algorithms, including Data Encryption Standard (DES), Triple DES (3DES), RC5, and International Data Encryption Algorithm (IDEA). WTLS implements integrity through the use of *message authentication codes (MACs)*. A MAC algorithm generates a one-way hash of the compressed WTLS data. WTLS supports the MD5 and SHA MAC algorithms. The MAC algorithm is also decided during the WTLS handshake. The TLS protocol that WTLS is based on is designed around Internet-based computers, machines that have relatively high processing power, large amounts of memory, and sufficient bandwidth available for Internet applications. The PDAs and other devices that WTLS must accommodate are limited in all these respects. Thus, WTLS has to be able to cope with small amounts of memory and limited processor capacity, as well as long round-trip times that TLS could not handle well. These requirements are the primary reasons that WTLS has security issues.

As the protocol is designed around more capable servers than devices, the WTLS specification can allow connections with little to no security. Clients with low memory or CPU capabilities cannot support encryption, and choosing null or weak encryption greatly reduces confidentiality. Authentication is also optional in the protocol, and omitting authentication reduces security by leaving the connection vulnerable to a man-in-the-middle–type attack. In addition to the general flaws in the protocol's implementation, several known security vulnerabilities exist, including those to the chosen plaintext attack, the PKCS #1 attack, and the alert message truncation attack.

The chosen plaintext attack works on the principle of predictable initialization vectors (IVs). By the nature of the transport medium that it is using, WAP, WTLS needs to support unreliable transport. This forces the IV to be based on data already known to the client, and WTLS uses a linear IV computation. Because the IV is based on the sequence number of the packet and several packets are sent unencrypted, entropy is severely decreased. This lack of entropy in the encrypted data reduces confidentiality.

Now consider the PKCS #1 attack. Public-Key Cryptography Standards (PKCS), used in conjunction with RSA encryption, provides standards for formatting the padding used to generate a correctly formatted block size. When the client receives the block, it will reply to the sender as to the validity of the block. An attacker takes advantage of this by attempting to send multiple guesses at the padding to force a padding error. In vulnerable implementations, WTLS will return error messages providing an Oracle decrypting RSA with roughly 2^{20} chosen ciphertext queries. Alert messages in WTLS are sometimes sent in plaintext and are not authenticated. This fact could allow an attacker to overwrite an encrypted packet from the actual sender with a plaintext alert message, leading to possible disruption of the connection through, for instance, a truncation attack.

 EXAM TIP WAP is a point-to-multipoint protocol, but it can face disruptions or attacks because it aggregates at well-known points: the cellular antenna towers.

Some concern over the so-called *WAP gap* involves confidentiality of information where the two different networks meet, the WAP gateway. WTLS acts as the security protocol for the WAP network, and TLS is the standard for the Internet, so the WAP gateway has to perform translation from one encryption standard to the other. This translation forces all messages to be seen by the WAP gateway in plaintext. This is a weak point in the network design, but from an attacker's perspective, it's a much more difficult target than the WTLS protocol itself. Threats to the WAP gateway can be minimized through careful infrastructure design, such as secure physical location and allowing only outbound traffic from the gateway. A risk of compromise still exists, however, and an attacker would find a WAP gateway an especially appealing target, as plaintext messages are processed through it from all wireless devices, not just a single user. The solution for this is to have end-to-end security layered over anything underlying, in effect creating a VPN from the endpoint to the mobile device, or to standardize on a full implementation of TLS for end-to-end encryption and strong authentication. The limited nature of the devices hampers the ability of the security protocols to operate as intended, compromising any real security to be implemented on WAP networks.

3G Mobile Networks

Our cell phones are one of the most visible indicators of advancing technology. Within recent memory, we were forced to switch from old analog phones to digital models. Currently, they are all becoming "smart" as well, integrating personal digital assistant (PDA) and Internet functions. The networks have been or are being upgraded to 3G, greatly enhancing speed and lowering latency. This has reduced the need for lightweight protocols to handle data transmission, and more standard protocols such as IP can be used. The increased power and memory of the handheld devices also reduce the need for lighter weight encryption protocols. This has caused the protocols used for 3G mobile devices to build in their own encryption protocols. Security will rely on these lower level protocols or standard application-level security protocols used in normal IP traffic.

Several competing data transmission standards exist for 3G networks, such as HSPA and EVDO. However, all the standards include transport layer encryption protocols to secure the voice traffic traveling across the wireless signal as well as the data sent by the device. The cryptographic standard proposed for 3G is known as *KASUMI*. This modified version of the MISTY1 algorithm uses 64-bit blocks and 128-bit keys. Multiple attacks have been launched against this cipher. While the attacks tend to be impractical, this shows that application layer security is needed for secure transmission of data on mobile devices. WAP and WTLS can be used over the lower level protocols, but traditional TLS can also be used.

Bluetooth

Bluetooth was originally developed by Ericsson and known as multi-communicator link; in 1998, Nokia, IBM, Intel, and Toshiba joined Ericsson and adopted the Bluetooth name. This consortium became known as the Bluetooth Special Interest Group (SIG). The SIG now has more than 10,000 member companies and drives the development of the technology and controls the specification to ensure interoperability.

Most people are familiar with Bluetooth as it is part of many mobile phones. This short-range, low-power wireless protocol transmits in the 2.4 GHz band, the same band used for 802.11. The concept for the short-range wireless protocol is to transmit data in personal area networks (PANs). It transmits and receives data from a variety of devices, the most common being mobile phones, laptops, printers, and audio devices. The mobile phone has driven a lot of Bluetooth growth and has even spread Bluetooth into new cars as a mobile phone hands-free kit.

Bluetooth has gone through a few releases. Version 1.1 was the first commercially successful version, with version 1.2 released in 2007 and correcting some of the problems found in 1.1. Version 1.2 allows speeds up to 721 Kbps and improves resistance to interference. Version 1.2 is backward-compatible with version 1.1. Bluetooth 2.0 introduced enhanced data rate (EDR), which allows the transmission of up to 3.0 Mbps.

As soon as Bluetooth got popular, people started trying to find holes in it. Bluetooth features easy configuration of devices to allow communication, with no need for network addresses or ports. Bluetooth uses pairing to establish a trust relationship between devices. To establish that trust, the devices will advertise capabilities and require a passkey. To help maintain security, most devices require the passkey to be entered into both devices; this prevents a default passkey-type attack. The advertisement of services and pairing properties are where some of the security issues start.

 EXAM TIP Bluetooth should always have discoverable mode off unless you're deliberately pairing a device.

Bluejacking is a term used for the sending of unauthorized messages to another Bluetooth device. This involves setting a message as a phonebook contact. Then the attacker sends the message to the possible recipient via Bluetooth. Originally, this involved sending text messages, but more recent phones can send images or audio as well. A popular variant of this is the transmission of "shock" images, featuring disturbing or crude photos. As Bluetooth is a short-range protocol, the attack and victim must be within roughly 10 yards of each other. The victim's phone must also have Bluetooth enabled and must be in discoverable mode. On some early phones, this was the default configuration, and while it makes connecting external devices easier, it also allows attacks against the phone. If Bluetooth is turned off, or if the device is set to nondiscoverable, bluejacking can be avoided.

Bluesnarfing is similar to bluejacking in that it uses the same contact transmission protocol. The difference is that instead of sending an unsolicited message to the victim's phone, the attacker copies off the victim's information, which can include e-mails, contact lists, calendar, and anything else that exists on that device. More recent phones with media capabilities can be snarfed for private photos and videos. Bluesnarfing used to require a laptop with a Bluetooth adapter, making it relatively easy to identify a possible attacker, but bluesnarfing applications are now available for mobile devices. Bloover, a combination of Bluetooth and Hoover, is one such application that runs as a Java applet. The majority of Bluetooth phones need to be discoverable for the bluesnarf attack to work, but it does not necessarily need to be paired. In theory, an attacker can also brute-force the device's unique 48-bit name. A program called RedFang attempts to perform this brute-force attack by sending all possible names and seeing what gets a response. This approach was addressed in Bluetooth 1.2 with an anonymity mode.

Bluebugging is a far more serious attack than either bluejacking or bluesnarfing. In bluebugging, the attacker uses Bluetooth to establish a serial connection to the device. This allows access to the full AT command set—GSM phones use AT commands similar to Hayes compatible modems. This connection allows full control over the phone, including the placing of calls to any number without the phone owner's knowledge. Fortunately, this attack requires pairing of the devices to complete, and phones initially vulnerable to the attack have updated firmware to correct the problem. To accomplish the attack now, the phone owner would need to surrender her phone and allow an attacker to physically establish the connection.

Bluetooth technology is likely to grow due to the popularity of mobile phones. Software and protocol updates have helped to improve the security of the protocol. Almost all phones now keep Bluetooth turned off by default, and they allow you to make the phone discoverable for only a limited amount of time. User education about security risks is also a large factor in avoiding security breaches.

802.11

The 802.11b protocol is an IEEE standard ratified in 1999. The standard launched a range of products that would open the way to a whole new genre of possibilities for attackers and a new series of headaches for security administrators everywhere. 802.11 was a new standard for sending packetized data traffic over radio waves in the unlicensed 2.4 GHz band. This group of IEEE standards is also called Wi-Fi, which is a certification owned by an industry group. A device marked as Wi-Fi certified adheres to the standards of the alliance. As the products matured and became easy to use and affordable, security experts began to deconstruct the limited security that had been built into the standard.

802.11a is the wireless networking standard that supports traffic on the 5 GHz band, allowing faster speeds over shorter ranges. Features of 802.11b and 802.11a were later joined to create 802.11g, an updated standard that allowed the faster speeds of the 5 GHz specification on the 2.4 GHz band. Security problems were discovered in the implementations of these early wireless standards.

Wired Equivalent Privacy (WEP) was a top concern until the adoption of 802.11i-compliant products enhanced the security with Wi-Fi Protected Access (WPA). 802.11n is the latest standard and is still in draft form; it focuses on achieving much higher speeds for wireless networks. The following table offers an overview of each protocol and descriptions of each follow.

802.11 Protocol	Frequency in GHz	Speed in Mbps	Modulation
-	2.4	2	
a	5	54	OFDM
b	2.4	11	DSSS
g	2.4	54	OFDM
n	2.4, 5	248	OFDM
y	3.7	54	OFDM

EXAM TIP The best place for current 802.11 standards and upcoming draft standard information is in the RFCs. You can find them at www.ietf.org/rfc.html.

The 802.11b protocol provides for multiple-rate Ethernet over 2.4 GHz spread-spectrum wireless. It provides transfer rates of 1 Mbps, 2 Mbps, 5.5 Mbps, and 11 Mbps and uses direct-sequence spread spectrum (DSSS). The most common layout is a point-to-multipoint environment with the available bandwidth being shared by all users. Typical range is roughly 100 yards indoors and 300 yards outdoors line of sight. While the wireless transmissions of 802.11 can penetrate some walls and other objects, the best range is offered when both the access point and network client devices have an unobstructed view of each other.

The 802.11a uses a higher band and has higher bandwidth. It operates in the 5 GHz spectrum using orthogonal frequency division multiplexing (OFDM). Supporting rates of up to 54 Mbps, it is the faster brother of 802.11b; however, the higher frequency used by 802.11a shortens the usable range of the devices and makes it incompatible with 802.11b. The chipsets tend to be more expensive for 802.11a, which has slowed adoption of the standard.

802.11g standard uses portions of both of the other standards: It uses the 2.4 GHz band for greater range but uses the OFDM transmission method to achieve the faster 54 Mbps data rates. As it uses the 2.4 GHz band, this standard interoperates with the older 802.11b standard. This allows a 802.11g access point (AP) to give access to both "G" and "B" clients.

The current draft standard, 802.11n, improves on the older standards by greatly increasing speed. It has a data rate of 248 Mbps, gained through the use of wider bands and multiple-input multiple-output processing (MIMO). MIMO uses multiple antennas and can bond separate channels together to increase data throughput.

All these protocols operate in bands that are "unlicensed" by the FCC. This means that people operating this equipment do not have to be certified by the FCC, but it also means that the devices could possibly share the band with other devices, such as cordless phones, closed-circuit TV (CCTV) wireless transceivers, and other similar equipment. This other equipment can cause interference with the 802.11 equipment, possibly causing speed degradation.

The 802.11 protocol designers expected some security concerns and attempted to build provisions into the 802.11 protocol that would ensure adequate security. The 802.11 standard includes attempts at rudimentary authentication and confidentiality controls. Authentication is handled in its most basic form by the 802.11 AP, forcing the clients to perform a handshake when attempting to "associate" to the AP. Association is the process required before the AP will allow the client to talk across the AP to the network. Association occurs only if the client has all the correct parameters needed in the handshake, among them the service set identifier (SSID). This SSID setting should limit access only to the authorized users of the wireless network.

The designers of the standard also attempted to maintain confidentiality by introducing WEP, which uses the RC4 stream cipher to encrypt the data as it is transmitted through the air. WEP has been shown to have an implementation problem that can be exploited to break security.

To understand all the 802.11 security problems, you must first look at some of the reasons it got to be such a prominent a technology.

Wireless networks came along in 2000 and became very popular. For the first time, it was possible to have almost full-speed network connections without having to be tied down to an Ethernet cable. The technology quickly took off, allowing prices to drop into the consumer range. Once the market shifted to focus on customers who were not necessarily technologists, the products also became very easy to install and operate. Default settings were designed to get the novice users up and running without having to alter anything substantial, and products were described as being able to just plug in and work. These developments further enlarged the market for the low-cost, easy-to-use wireless access points. Then attackers realized that instead of attacking machines over the Internet, they could drive around and seek out these APs. Having physical control of an information asset is critical to its security. Physical access to a machine will enable an attacker to bypass *any* security measure that has been placed on that machine.

Typically, access to actual Ethernet segments is protected by physical security measures. This structure allows security administrators to plan for only internal threats to the network and gives them a clear idea of the types and number of machines connected to it. Wireless networking takes the keys to the kingdom and tosses them out the window and into the parking lot. A typical wireless installation broadcasts the network right through the physical controls that are in place. An attacker can drive up and have the same access as if he plugged into an Ethernet jack inside the building—in fact, better access, because 802.11 is a shared medium, allowing sniffers to view all packets being sent to or from the AP and all clients. These APs were also typically behind any security measures the companies had in place, such as firewalls and intrusion detection systems (IDSs). This kind of access into the internal network has caused a large stir among computer security professionals and eventually the media. War-driving, war-flying, war-walking, war-chalking—all of these terms have been used in security article after security article.

Wireless is a popular target for several reasons: the access gained from wireless, the lack of default security, and the wide proliferation of devices. However, other reasons also make it attackable. The first of these is *anonymity*: An attacker can probe your building for wireless access from the street. Then he can log packets to and from the AP without giving any indication that an attempted intrusion is taking place. The attacker will announce his presence only if he attempts to associate to the AP. Even then, an attempted association is recorded only by the MAC address of the wireless card associating to it, and most APs do not have alerting functionality to indicate when users associate to it. This fact gives administrators a very limited view of who is gaining access to the network, if they are even paying attention at all. It gives attackers the ability to seek out and compromise wireless networks with relative impunity. The second reason is the low cost of the equipment needed. A single wireless access card costing less than $100 can give access to any unsecured AP within driving range. Finally, attacking a wireless network is relative easy compared to other target hosts. Windows-based tools for locating and sniffing wireless-based networks have turned anyone who can download files from the Internet and has a wireless card into a potential attacker.

Locating wireless networks was originally termed *war-driving,* an adaptation of the term *war-dialing.* War-dialing comes from the 1983 movie *WarGames;* it is the process of dialing a list of phone numbers looking for computers. *War-drivers* drive around with a wireless locater program recording the number of networks found and their locations. This term has evolved along with *war-flying* and *war-walking,* which mean exactly what you expect. *War-chalking* started with people using chalk on sidewalks to mark some of the wireless networks they find.

The most common tools for an attacker to use are reception-based programs that will listen to the beacon frames output by other wireless devices and programs that will promiscuously capture all traffic. The most widely used of these programs is called NetStumbler, created by Marius Milner and shown in Figure 10-1. This program listens for the beacon frames of APs that are within range of the card attached to the NetStumbler computer. When it receives the frames, it logs all available information about the AP for later analysis. Since it listens only to beacon frames, NetStumbler will display only networks that have the SSID broadcast turned on. If the computer has a GPS unit attached to it, the program also logs the AP's coordinates. This information can be used to return to the AP or to plot maps of APs in a city.

NOTE NetStumbler is a Windows-based application, but programs for other operating systems such as Mac, BSD, Linux, and others work on the same principle.

Once an attacker has located a network, and assuming that he cannot directly connect and start active scanning and penetration of the network, he will use the best attack tool there is: a network sniffer. The network sniffer, when combined with a wireless

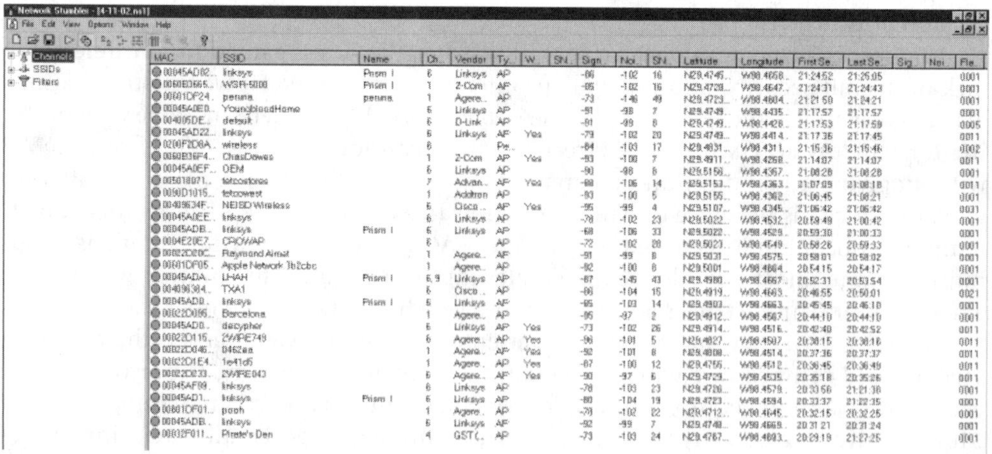

Figure 10-1 NetStumbler on a Windows PC

network card it can support, is a powerful attack tool, as the shared medium of a wireless network exposes all packets to interception and logging. Popular wireless sniffers are Wireshark (formerly Ethereal) and Kismet. Regular sniffers used on wireline Ethernet have also been updated to include support for wireless. Sniffers are also important because they allow you to retrieve the MAC addresses of the nodes of the network. APs can be configured to allow access only to prespecified MAC addresses, and an attacker spoofing the MAC can bypass this feature.

There are specialized sniffer tools designed with a single objective: to crack Wired Equivalent Privacy (WEP) keys. WEP is an encryption protocol that 802.11 uses to attempt to ensure confidentiality of wireless communications. Unfortunately, it has turned out to have several problems. WEP's weaknesses are specifically targeted for attack by the specialized sniffer programs. They work by exploiting weak initialization vectors in the encryption algorithm. To exploit this weakness, an attacker needs a certain number of ciphertext packets; once he has captured enough packets, however, the program can very quickly decipher the encryption key being used. WEPCrack was the first available program to use this flaw to crack WEP keys; however, WEPCrack depends on a dump of actual network packets from another sniffer program. AirSnort is a standalone program that captures its own packets; once it has captured enough ciphertext, it provides the WEP key of the network.

All these tools are used by the wireless attacker to compromise the network. They are also typically used by security professionals when performing wireless site surveys of organizations. The site survey has a simple purpose: To minimize the available wireless signal being sent beyond the physical controls of the organization. By using the sniffer and finding AP beacons, a security official can determine which APs are transmitting into uncontrolled areas. The APs can then be tuned, either by relocation or through the use of directional antennas, to minimize radiation beyond an organization's walls. This type of wireless data emanation is particularly troubling when the AP is located on the internal network. Local users of the network are susceptible to having their entire traffic decoded and analyzed. A proper site survey is an important step in securing a wireless network to avoid sending critical data beyond company walls. Recurring site surveys are important because wireless technology is cheap and typically comes unsecured in its default configuration. If anyone attaches a wireless AP to your network, you want to know about it immediately. If unauthorized wireless is set up, it is known as a *rogue access point*. These can be set up by well-meaning employees or hidden by an attacker with physical access.

802.11b has two tools used primarily for security: one is designed solely for authentication, and the other is designed for authentication and confidentiality. The authentication function is known as the *service set identifier (SSID)*. This unique 32-character identifier is attached to the header of the packet. The SSID is broadcast by default as a network name, but broadcasting this beacon frame can be disabled. Many APs also use a default SSID, for Cisco APs this default is *tsunami*, which can indicate an AP that has not been configured for any security. Renaming the SSID and disabling SSID broadcast are both good ideas; however, because the SSID is part of every frame, these measures should not be considered securing the network. As the SSID is, hopefully, a unique identifier, only people who know the identifier will be able to complete association to the AP. While the SSID is a good idea in theory, it is sent in plaintext in the packets, so in practice SSID offers little security significance—any sniffer can determine the SSID, and some operating systems—Windows XP, for instance—will display a list of SSIDs active in the area and prompt the user to choose which one to connect to. This weakness is magnified by most APs' default settings to transmit beacon frames. The beacon frame's purpose is to announce the wireless network's presence and capabilities so that WLAN cards can attempt to associate to it. This can be disabled in software for many APs, especially the more sophisticated ones. From a security perspective, the beacon frame is damaging because it contains the SSID, and this beacon frame is transmitted at a set interval (ten times per second by default). Since a default AP without any other traffic is sending out its SSID in plaintext ten times a second, you can see why the SSID does not provide true authentication. Scanning programs such as NetStumbler work by capturing the beacon frames and thereby the SSIDs of all APs.

WEP encrypts the data traveling across the network with an RC4 stream cipher, attempting to ensure confidentiality. This synchronous method of encryption ensures some method of authentication. The system depends on the client and the AP having a shared secret key, ensuring that only authorized people with the proper key have access to the wireless network. WEP supports two key lengths, 40 and 104 bits, though these are more typically referred to as 64 and 128 bits. In 802.11a and 802.11g, manufacturers have extended this to 152-bit WEP keys. This is because in all cases, 24 bits of the overall key length are used for the initialization vector.

The IV is the primary reason for the weaknesses in WEP. The IV is sent in the plaintext part of the message, and because the total keyspace is approximately 16 million keys, the same key will be reused. Once the key has been repeated, an attacker has two ciphertexts encrypted with the same key stream. This allows the attacker to examine the ciphertext and retrieve the key. This attack can be improved by examining only packets that have weak IVs, reducing the amount of packets needed to crack the key. Using only weak IV packets, the number of required captured packets is reduced to around four or five million, which can take only a few hours on a fairly busy AP. For a point of reference, this means that equipment with an advertised WEP key of 128 bits can be cracked in less than a day, whereas to crack a normal 128-bit key would take roughly 2,000,000,000,000,000,000 years on a computer able to attempt one trillion keys a second. As mentioned, AirSnort is a modified sniffing program that takes advantage of this weakness to retrieve the WEP keys.

The biggest weakness of WEP is that the IV problem exists regardless of key length, because the IV always remains at 24 bits. Most APs also have the ability to lock access in only to known MAC addresses, providing a limited authentication capability. Given sniffers' capacity to grab all active MAC addresses on the network, this capability is not very effective. An attacker simply configures his wireless cards to a known good MAC address.

EXAM TIP WEP should not be trusted alone to provide confidentiality. If WEP is the only protocol supported by your AP, place it outside the corporate firewall and VPN to add more protection.

After the limited security functions of a wireless network are broken, the network behaves exactly like a regular Ethernet network and is subject to the exact same vulnerabilities. The host machines that are on or attached to the wireless network are as vulnerable as if they and the attacker were physically connected. Being on the network opens up all machines to vulnerability scanners, Trojan horse programs, virus and worm programs, and traffic interception via sniffer programs. Any unpatched vulnerability on any machine accessible from the wireless segment is now open to compromise.

WEP was designed to provide some measure of confidentiality on an 802.11 network similar to what is found on a wired network, but that has not been the case. Accordingly, new standards were developed to improve upon WEP. The 802.11i standard is the IEEE standard for security in wireless networks, also known as Wi-Fi Protected Access (WPA). It uses 802.1X to provide authentication and Advanced Encryption Standard (AES) as the encryption protocol. The 802.11i standard specifies the use of the Temporal Key Integrity Protocol (TKIP) and the Counter Mode with CBC-MAC Protocol (in full, the Counter Mode with Cipher Block Chaining–Message Authentication Codes Protocol, or simply CCMP). These two protocols have different functions, but they both serve to enhance security.

TKIP works by using a shared secret combined with the card's MAC address to generate a new key, which is mixed with the initialization vector to make per-packet keys that encrypt a single packet using the same RC4 cipher used by traditional WEP. This overcomes the WEP key weakness, as a key is used on only one packet. The other advantage to this method is that it can be retrofitted to current hardware with only a software change, unlike AES and 802.1X. CCMP is actually the mode in which the AES cipher is used to provide message integrity. Unlike TKIP, CCMP requires new hardware to perform the AES encryption. The advances of 802.11i have corrected the weaknesses of WEP.

The 802.1X protocol can support a wide variety of authentication methods and also fits well into existing authentication systems such as RADIUS and LDAP. This allows 802.1X to interoperate well with other systems such as VPNs and dial-up RAS. Unlike other authentication methods such as the Point-to-Point Protocol over Ethernet (PP-PoE), 802.1X does not use encapsulation, so the network overhead is much lower. Unfortunately, the protocol is just a framework for providing implementation, so no specifics guarantee strong authentication or key management. Implementations of the protocol vary from vendor to vendor in method of implementation and strength of security, especially when it comes to the difficult test of wireless security.

Three common ways are used to implement 802.1X: EAP-TLS, EAP-TTLS, and EAP-MD5.

EAP-TLS relies on TLS, an attempt to standardize the SSL structure to pass credentials. The standard, developed by Microsoft, uses X.509 certificates and offers dynamic WEP key generation. This means that the organization must have the ability to support the public key infrastructure (PKI) in the form of X.509 digital certificates. Also, per-user, per-session dynamically generated WEP keys help prevent anyone from cracking the WEP keys in use, as each user individually has her own WEP key. Even if a user were logged onto the AP and transmitted enough traffic to allow cracking of the WEP key, access would be gained only to that user's traffic. No other user's data would be compromised, and the attacker could not use the WEP key to connect to the AP. This standard authenticates the client to the AP, but it also authenticates the AP to the client, helping to avoid man-in-the-middle attacks. The main problem with the EAP-TLS protocol is that it is designed to work only with Microsoft's Active Directory and Certificate Services; it will not take certificates from other certificate issuers. Thus a mixed environment would have implementation problems.

EAP-TTLS (the acronym stands for EAP–Tunneled TLS Protocol) is a variant of the EAP-TLS protocol. EAP-TTLS works much the same way as EAP-TLS, with the server authenticating to the client with a certificate, but the protocol tunnels the client side of the authentication, allowing the use of legacy authentication protocols such as Password Authentication Protocol (PAP), Challenge-Handshake Authentication Protocol (CHAP), MS-CHAP, or MS-CHAP-V2. This makes the protocol more versatile while still supporting the enhanced security features such as dynamic WEP key assignment.

EAP-MD5, while it does improve the authentication of the client to the AP, does little else to improve the security of your AP. The protocol works by using the MD5 encryption protocol to hash a user's username and password. This protocol unfortunately provides no way for the AP to authenticate with the client, and it does not provide for dynamic WEP key assignment. In the wireless environment, without strong two-way authentication, it is very easy for an attacker to perform a man-in-the-middle attack. Normally, these type of attacks are difficult to perform, requiring a traffic redirect of some kind, but wireless changes all those rules. By setting up a rogue AP, an attacker can attempt to get clients to connect to it as if it were authorized and then simply authenticate to the real AP, a simple way to have access to the network and the client's credentials. The problem of not dynamically generating WEP keys is that it simply opens up the network to the same lack of confidentiality to which a normal AP is vulnerable. An attacker has to wait only for enough traffic to crack the WEP key, and he can then observe all traffic passing through the network.

Because the security of wireless LANs has been so problematic, many users have simply switched to a layered security approach—that is, they have moved their APs to untrustworthy portions of the network and have forced all clients to authenticate through the firewall to a third-party VPN system. The additional security comes at a price of putting more load on the firewall and VPN infrastructure and possibly adding cumbersome software to the users' devices. While wireless can be set up in a very secure manner in this fashion, it can also be set up poorly. Some systems lack strong authentication of both endpoints, leading to possibilities of a man-in-the-middle attack. Also, even though the data is tunneled through, IP addresses are still sent in the clear, giving an attacker information about what and where your VPN endpoint is.

Another phenomenon of wireless is borne out of its wide availability and low price. All the security measures of the wired and wireless network can be defeated by the rogue AP. Typically added by a well-intentioned employee trying to make their lives more convenient, the AP was purchased at a local retailer. When installed, it works fine, but it typically will have no security installed. Since the IT department doesn't know about it, it is an uncontrolled entry point into the network.

Occasionally an attacker gains physical access to an organization, and will install a rogue AP to maintain network access. In either case, access needs to be removed. The most common way to control rogue AP is some form of wireless scanning to ensure only legitimate wireless is in place at an organization. While complete wireless IDS systems will detect APs, this can also be done with a laptop and free software.

802.11 has enjoyed tremendous growth because of its ease of use and popularity, but that growth is threatened by many organizational rules prohibiting its use due to security measures. As you have seen here, the current state of wireless security is very poor, making attacking wireless a popular activity. With the addition of strong authentication and better encryption protocols, wireless should become both convenient and safe.

Chapter Review

Wireless is a popular protocol that has many benefits but a certain number of risks. Wireless offers local network access to anyone within range. The lack of physical control over the medium necessitates the careful configuration of the security features available. 802.11 has brought inexpensive wireless networking to homes and small businesses. Weak encryption was a problem in early versions of the standard, but current implementations perform better. 3G mobile phones allow you to carry the Internet in your pocket, but it can also allow an attacker to pickpocket your e-mails and contacts through Bluetooth.

Questions

To further help you prepare for the Security+ exam, and to test your level of preparedness, answer the following questions and then check your answers against the list of correct answers at the end of the chapter.

1. What encryption method does WEP use to try to ensure confidentiality of 802.11 networks?

   A. MD5

   B. AES

   C. RC4

   D. Diffie-Hellman

2. How does WTLS ensure integrity?

    A. Sender's address

    B. Message authentication codes

    C. Sequence number

    D. Public key encryption

3. What two key lengths does WEP support?

    A. 1024 and 2048

    B. 104 and 40

    C. 512 and 256

    D. 24 and 32

4. Why does the SSID provide no real means of authentication?

    A. It cannot be changed.

    B. It is only 24 bits.

    C. It is broadcast in every beacon frame.

    D. SSID is not an authentication function.

5. The 802.1X protocol is a new protocol for Ethernet

    A. Authentication

    B. Speed

    C. Wireless

    D. Cabling

6. Why does WTLS have to support shorter key lengths?

    A. WAP doesn't need high security.

    B. The algorithm cannot handle longer key lengths.

    C. Key lengths are not important to security.

    D. WTLS has to support devices with low processor power and limited RAM.

7. Why is 802.11 wireless such a security problem?

    A. It has too powerful a signal.

    B. It provides access to the physical layer of Ethernet without a person needing physical access to the building.

    C. All the programs on wireless are full of bugs that allow buffer overflows.

    D. It draws too much power and the other servers reboot.

8. What protocol is WTLS trying to secure?

    A. WAP

    B. WEP

    C. GSM

    D. SSL

9. Why should wireless have strong two-way authentication?

    A. Because you want to know when an attacker connects to the network.

    B. Because wireless is especially susceptible to a man-in-the-middle attack.

    C. Wireless needs authentication to prevent users from adding their home computers.

    D. Two-way authentication is needed so an administrator can ask the wireless user a set of questions.

10. Why is attacking wireless networks so popular?

    A. There are more wireless networks than wired.

    B. They all run Windows.

    C. It's easy.

    D. It's more difficult and more prestigious than other network attacks.

11. How are the security parameters of WTLS chosen between two endpoints?

    A. Only one option exists for every parameter.

    B. The client dictates all parameters to the server.

    C. The user codes the parameters through DTMF tones.

    D. The WTLS handshake determines what parameters to use.

12. What is bluejacking?

    A. Stealing a person's mobile phone

    B. Sending an unsolicited message via Bluetooth

    C. Breaking a WEP key

    D. Leaving your Bluetooth in discoverable mode

13. How does 802.11n improve network speed?

    A. Wider bandwidth

    B. Higher frequency

    C. Multiple in multiple out

    D. Both A and C

PART III

14. Bluebugging can give an attacker what?

    A. All of your contacts

    B. The ability to send "shock" photos

    C. Total control over a mobile phone

    D. A virus

15. Why is it important to scan your own organization for wireless?

    A. It can detect rogue access points.

    B. It checks the installed encryption.

    C. It finds vulnerable mobile phones.

    D. It checks for wireless coverage.

Answers

1. **C.** WEP uses the RC4 stream cipher.

2. **B.** WTLS uses a message authentication code generated with a one-way hash algorithm.

3. **B.** WEP currently supports 104 and 40, though it is sometimes packaged as 64-bit and 128-bit encryption. The initialization vector takes up 24 bits, leaving the 40- and 104-bit key strings.

4. **C.** The SSID, or service set identifier, attempts to provide an authentication function, but because it is broadcast in every frame, it is trivial for an attacker to break.

5. **A.** Authentication; 802.1X is the new EAP framework for strong authentication over Ethernet networks.

6. **D.** WAP is designed to be used with small mobile devices, usually with low processor power and limited RAM, so it must support lower grade encryption.

7. **B.** The 802.11 protocol provides physical layer access without a person needing to have physical access to the building, thus promoting drive-by and parking lot attacks.

8. **A.** WTLS is an attempt to secure the Wireless Application Protocol, or WAP.

9. **B.** Wireless is not connected to any physical medium, making it especially vulnerable to a man-in-the-middle attack.

10. **C.** Attacking wireless networks is extremely popular because it's easy—the majority of wireless networks have no security installed on them. This allows anyone to connect and have practically full access to the network.

11. **D.** The WTLS handshake lets both endpoints exchange capabilities, and then the parameters are agreed upon.

12. **B.** Bluejacking is a term used for the sending of unauthorized messages to another Bluetooth device.

13. **D.** The "n" protocol uses both wider bandwidth and multiple-input and multiple-output techniques to increase speed several times over the "g" protocol.

14. **C.** Bluebugging give an attacker total control over a mobile phone.

15. **A.** Scanning detects rogue access points.

PART IV

Security in Transmissions

■ **Chapter 11**   Intrusion Detection Systems
■ **Chapter 12**   Security Baselines
■ **Chapter 13**   Types of Attacks and Malicious Software
■ **Chapter 14**   E-Mail and Instant Messaging
■ **Chapter 15**   Web Components

Intrusion Detection Systems

In this chapter, you will

- Understand host-based intrusion detection systems
- Understand PC-based malware protection
- Explore network-based intrusion detection systems
- Explore network traffic shaping and filtering tools
- Learn what honeypots are used for

Ensuring network security can be fairly easily compared to ensuring physical security—the more you want to protect and restrict access to an asset, the more security you need. In the world of physical security, you can use locks, walls, gates, guards, motion sensors, pressure plates, and so on, to protect physical assets. As you add more protective devices, you add "layers" of security that an intruder would have to overcome or breach to obtain access to whatever you are protecting. Correspondingly, in the network and data security arenas, you use protective layers in the form of passwords, firewalls, access lists, file permissions, and Intrusion Detection Systems (IDSs). Most organizations use their own approaches to network security, choosing the layers that make sense for them after they weigh risks, potentials for loss, costs, and manpower requirements.

The foundation for a layered network security approach usually starts with a well-secured system, regardless of the system's function (whether it's a user PC or a corporate e-mail server). A well-secured system uses up-to-date application and operating system patches, well-chosen passwords, the minimum number of services running, and restricted access to available services. On top of that foundation, you can add layers of protective measures such as antivirus products, firewalls, sniffers, and IDSs.

Some of the more complicated and interesting types of network/data security devices are IDSs, which are to the network world what burglar alarms are to the physical world. The main purpose of an IDS is to identify suspicious or malicious activity, note activity that deviates from normal behavior, catalog and classify the activity, and, if possible, respond to the activity. This chapter looks at the history of IDSs and various types of IDSs, considers how they work and the benefits and weaknesses of specific types, and what the future might hold for these systems. You'll also look at some topics complementary to IDSs: malware protection, traffic shaping/filtering, and honeypots.

History of Intrusion Detection Systems

Like much of the network technology we see today, IDSs grew from a need to solve specific problems. Like the Internet itself, the IDS concept came from U.S. Department of Defense–sponsored research. In the early 1970s, the U.S. government and military became increasingly aware of the need to protect the electronic networks that were becoming critical to daily operations. In 1972, James Anderson published a paper for the U.S. Air Force outlining the growing number of computer security problems and the immediate need to secure Air Force systems (James P. Anderson, "Computer Security Technology Planning Study Volume 2," October 1972, http://seclab.cs.ucdavis.edu/projects/history/papers/ande72.pdf). Anderson continued his research and in 1980 published a follow-up paper outlining methods to improve security auditing and surveillance methods ("Computer Security Threat Monitoring and Surveillance," April 15, 1980, http://csrc.nist.gov/publications/history/ande80.pdf). In this paper, Anderson pioneered the concept of using system audit files to detect unauthorized access and misuse. He also suggested the use of automated detection systems, which paved the way for misuse detection on mainframe systems in use at the time.

While Anderson's work got the efforts started, the concept of a real-time, rule-based IDS didn't really exist until Dorothy Denning and Peter Neumann developed the first real-time IDS model, called "The Intrusion Detection Expert System (IDES)," from their research between 1984 and 1986. In 1987, Denning published "An Intrusion-Detection Model," a paper that laid out the model on which most modern IDSs are based (and which appears in *IEEE Transactions on Software Engineering*, Vol. SE-13, No. 2 [February 1987]: 222–232).

With a model and definitions in place, the U.S. government continued to fund research that led to projects such as Discovery, Haystack, Multics Intrusion Detection and Alerting System (MIDAS), and Network Audit Director and Intrusion Reporter (NADIR). Finally, in 1989, Haystack Labs released Stalker, the first commercial IDS. Stalker was host-based and worked by comparing audit data to known patterns of suspicious activity. While the military and government embraced the concept, the commercial world was very slow to adopt IDS products, and it was several years before other commercial products began to emerge.

In the early to mid-1990s, computer systems continued to grow and companies were starting to realize the importance of IDSs; however, the solutions available were host-based and required a great deal of time and money to manage and operate effectively. Focus began to shift away from host-based systems, and network-based IDSs began to emerge. In 1995, WheelGroup was formed in San Antonio, Texas, to develop the first commercial network-based IDS product, called NetRanger. NetRanger was designed to monitor network links and the traffic moving across the links to identify misuse as well as suspicious and malicious activity. NetRanger's release was quickly followed by Internet Security Systems RealSecure in 1996. Several other players followed suit and released their own IDS products, but it wasn't until the networking giant Cisco Systems acquired WheelGroup in February 1998 that IDSs were recognized as a vital part of any network security infrastructure. Figure 11-1 offers a timeline for these developments.

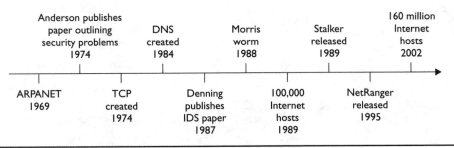

Figure 11-1 History of the Internet and IDS

IDS Overview

As mentioned, an IDS is somewhat like a burglar alarm. It watches the activity going on around it and tries to identify undesirable activity. IDSs are typically divided into two main categories, depending on how they monitor activity:

- **Host-based IDS** Examines activity on an individual system, such as a mail server, web server, or individual PC. It is concerned only with an individual system and usually has no visibility into the activity on the network or systems around it.

- **Network-based IDS** Examines activity on the network itself. It has visibility only into the traffic crossing the network link it is monitoring and typically has no idea of what is happening on individual systems.

 EXAM TIP Know the differences between host-based and network-based IDSs. A host-based IDS runs on a specific system (server or workstation) and looks at all the activity on that host. A network-based IDS sniffs traffic from the network and sees only activity that occurs on the network.

Whether or not it is network- or host-based, an IDS will typically consist of several specialized components working together, as illustrated in Figure 11-2. These components are often logical and software-based rather than physical and will vary slightly from vendor to vendor and product to product. Typically, an IDS will have the following logical components:

- **Traffic collector (or sensor)** This component collects activity/events for the IDS to examine. On a host-based IDS, this could be log files, audit logs, or traffic coming to or leaving a specific system. On a network-based IDS, this is typically a mechanism for copying traffic off the network link—basically functioning as a sniffer. This component is often referred to as a sensor.

- **Analysis engine** This component examines the collected network traffic and compares it to known patterns of suspicious or malicious activity stored in the signature database. The analysis engine is the "brains" of the IDS.

PART IV

Figure 11-2
Logical depiction of
IDS components

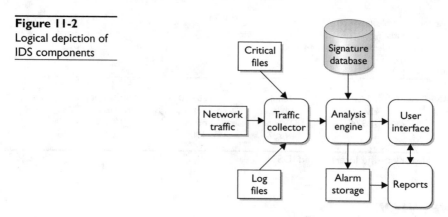

- **Signature database** The signature database is a collection of patterns and definitions of known suspicious or malicious activity.

- **User interface and reporting** This component interfaces with the human element, providing alerts when appropriate and giving the user a means to interact with and operate the IDS.

Most IDSs can be tuned to fit a particular environment. Certain signatures can be turned off, telling the IDS not to look for certain types of traffic. For example, if you are operating in a pure UNIX environment, you may not wish to see Windows-based alarms, as they will not affect your systems. Additionally, the severity of the alarm levels can be adjusted depending on how concerned you are over certain types of traffic. Some IDSs will also allow the user to exclude certain patterns of activity from specific hosts. In other words, you can tell the IDS to ignore the fact that some systems generate traffic that looks like malicious activity, because it really isn't.

Host-based IDSs

The first IDSs were host-based and designed to examine activity only on a specific host. A host-based IDS (HIDS) examines log files, audit trails, and network traffic coming in to or leaving a specific host. HIDSs can operate in *real time*, looking for activity as it occurs, or in *batch mode*, looking for activity on a periodic basis. Host-based systems are typically self-contained, but many of the newer commercial products have been designed to report to and be managed by a central system. Host-based systems also take local system resources to operate. In other words, a HIDS will use up some of the memory and CPU cycles of the system it is protecting. Early versions of HIDSs ran in batch mode, looking for suspicious activity on an hourly or daily basis, and typically looked only for specific events in the system's log files. As processor speeds increased, later versions of HIDSs looked through the log files in real time and even added the ability to examine the data traffic the host was generating and receiving.

Most HIDSs focus on the log files or audit trails generated by the local operating system. On UNIX systems, the examined logs usually include those created by syslog such as messages, kernel logs, and error logs. On Windows systems, the examined logs are typically the three event logs: Application, System, and Security. Some HIDSs can cover specific applications, such as FTP or web services, by examining the logs produced by those specific applications or examining the traffic from the services themselves. Within the log files, the HIDS is looking for certain activities that typify hostile actions or misuse, such as the following:

- Logins at odd hours
- Login authentication failures
- Additions of new user accounts
- Modification or access of critical system files
- Modification or removal of binary files (executables)
- Starting or stopping processes
- Privilege escalation
- Use of certain programs

In general, most HIDSs will operate in a very similar fashion. (Figure 11-3 shows the logical layout of a HIDS.) By considering the function and activity of each component, you can gain some insight into how HIDSs operate.

As on any IDS, the *traffic collector* on a HIDS pulls in the information the other components, such as the analysis engine, need to examine. For most host-based systems, the traffic collector pulls data from information the local system has already generated, such as error messages, log files, and system files. The traffic collector is responsible for reading those files, selecting which items are of interest, and forwarding them to the analysis engine. On some host-based systems, the traffic collector will also examine specific attributes of critical files such as file size, date modified, or checksum.

Figure 11-3
Host-based IDS components

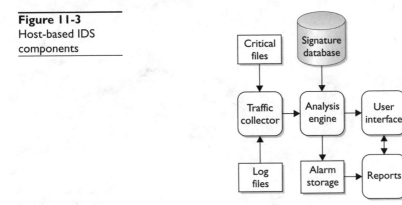

NOTE Critical files are those that are vital to the system's operation or overall functionality. They may be program (or binary) files, files containing user accounts and passwords, or even scripts to start or stop system processes. Any unexpected modifications to these files could mean the system has been compromised or modified by an attacker. By monitoring these files, the IDS can warn users of potentially malicious activity.

Decision Tree

In computer systems, a *tree* is a data structure where each element in the structure is attached to one or more structures directly beneath it (the connections are called *branches*). Structures on the end of a branch without any elements below them are called *leaves*. Trees are most often drawn inverted, with the *root* at the top and all subsequent elements branching down from the root. Trees where each element has no more than two elements below it are called *binary* trees.

In intrusion detection systems, a decision tree is used to help the analysis engine quickly examine traffic patterns. The decision tree helps the analysis engine eliminate signatures that don't apply to the particular traffic being examined so that the fewest number of comparisons can be made. For example, in the following illustration, the sample IDS decision tree shown may contain a section dividing the traffic into three sections based upon origin of the traffic (a log entry for events taken from the system logs, file changes for modifications to critical files, or user actions for something a user has done). When the analysis engine looks at the traffic pattern and starts down the decision tree, it must decide which path to follow. If it is a log entry, the analysis engine can then concentrate on only the signatures that apply to log entries; it does not need to worry about signatures that apply to file changes or user actions. This type of decision tree allows the analysis engine to function much faster, as it does not have to compare traffic to every signature in the database, just the signatures that apply to that particular type of traffic.

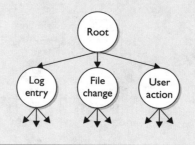

The *analysis engine* is perhaps the most important component of the IDS, as it must decide what activity is "okay" and what activity is "bad." The analysis engine is a sophisticated decision and pattern-matching mechanism—it looks at the information provided by the traffic collector and tries to match it against known patterns of activity stored in the signature database. If the activity matches a known pattern, the analysis engine can react, usually by issuing an alert or alarm. An analysis engine may also be capable of remembering how the activity it is looking at right now compares to traffic it has already seen or may see in the near future so that it can match more complicated, multistep malicious activity patterns. An analysis engine must also be capable of examining traffic patterns as quickly as possible, as the longer it takes to match a malicious pattern, the less time the IDS or human operator has to react to malicious traffic. Most IDS vendors build a "decision tree" into their analysis engines to expedite pattern matching.

The *signature database* is a collection of predefined activity patterns that have already been identified and categorized—patterns that typically indicate suspicious or malicious activity. When the analysis engine has a traffic pattern to examine, it will compare that pattern to the appropriate signatures in the database. The signature database can contain anywhere from a few to a few thousand signatures, depending on the vendor, type of IDS, space available on the system to store signatures, and other factors.

The *user interface* is the visible component of the IDS—the part that humans interact with. The user interface varies widely depending on the product and vendor and could be anything from a detailed GUI to a simple command line. Regardless of the type and complexity, the interface is provided to allow the user to interact with the system: changing parameters, receiving alarms, tuning signatures and response patterns, and so on.

To better understand how a HIDS operates, take a look at examples from a UNIX system and a Windows system.

On a UNIX system, the HIDS is likely going to examine any of a number of system logs—basically large text files containing entries about what is happening on the system. For this example, consider the following lines from the "messages" log on a Red Hat system:

```
Jan 5 18:20:39 jeep su(pam_unix)[32478]: session opened for user bob by (uid=0)
Jan 5 18:20:47 jeep su(pam_unix)[32516]: authentication failure;
   logname= uid=502 euid=0 tty= ruser=bob rhost= user=root
Jan 5 18:20:53 jeep su(pam_unix)[32517]: authentication failure; logname= id=5
02 euid=0 tty= ruser=bob rhost= user=root
Jan 5 18:21:06 jeep su(pam_unix)[32519]: authentication failure; logname= uid=5
02 euid=0 tty= ruser=bob rhost= user=root
```

In the first line, you see a session being opened by a user named *bob*. This usually indicates that whoever owns the account bob has logged into the system. On the next three lines, you see authentication failures as bob tries to become *root*—the superuser account that can do anything on the system. In this case, user bob tries three times to become root and fails on each try. This pattern of activity could mean a number of different things—bob could be an admin who has forgotten the password for the root account, bob could be an admin and someone changed the root password without telling him, bob could be a user attempting to guess the root password, or an attacker could have compromised user bob's account and is now trying to compromise the root account on the system. In any case, our HIDS will work through its decision tree to determine whether an authentication failure in the message log is something it needs to examine. In this instance, when the IDS examines these lines in the log, it will note the fact that three of the lines in the log match one of the patterns it has been told to look for (as determined by information from the decision tree and the signature database), and it will react accordingly, usually by generating an alarm or alert of some type that appears on the user interface or in an e-mail, page, or other form of message.

On a Windows system, the HIDS will likely examine the application logs generated by the operating system. The three logs (application, system, and security) are similar to the logs on a UNIX system, though the Windows logs are not stored as text files and typically require a utility or application to read them. This example uses the security log from a Windows 2000 Professional system:

```
Failure Audit  1/5/2003  6:47:29 PM  Security  Logon/Logoff        529  SYSTEM
Failure Audit  1/5/2003  6:47:27 PM  Security  Logon/Logoff        529  SYSTEM
Failure Audit  1/5/2003  6:47:26 PM  Security  Logon/Logoff        529  SYSTEM
Success Audit  1/5/2003  6:47:13 PM  Security  Privilege Use       578  Administrator
Success Audit  1/5/2003  6:47:12 PM  Security  Privilege Use       577  Administrator
Success Audit  1/5/2003  6:47:12 PM  Security  Privilege Use       577  Administrator
Success Audit  1/5/2003  6:47:06 PM  Security  Account Management  643  SYSTEM
Success Audit  1/5/2003  6:46:59 PM  Security  Account Management  643  SYSTEM
```

In the first three lines of the security log, you see a **Failure Audit** entry for the **Logon/ Logoff** process. This indicates someone has tried to log in to the system three times and has failed each time (much like our UNIX example). You won't see the name of the account until you expand the log entry within the Windows event viewer tool, but for this example, assume it was the Administrator account—the Windows equivalent of the root account. Here again, you see three login failures—if the HIDS has been programmed to look for failed login attempts, it will generate alerts when it examines these log entries.

Advantages of HIDSs

HIDSs have certain advantages that make them a good choice for certain situations:

- *They can be very operating system–specific and have more detailed signatures.* A HIDS can be very specifically designed to run on a certain operating system or to protect certain applications. This narrow focus lets developers concentrate on the specific things that affect the specific environment they are trying to protect. With this type of focus, the developers can avoid generic alarms and develop much more specific, detailed signatures to identify malicious traffic more accurately.

- *They can reduce false positive rates.* When running on a specific system, the IDS process is much more likely to be able to determine whether or not the activity being examined is malicious or not. By more accurately identifying which activity is "bad," the IDS will generate fewer false positives (alarms generated when the traffic matches a pattern but is not actually malicious).

- *They can examine data after it has been decrypted.* With security concerns constantly on the rise, many developers are starting to encrypt their network communications. When designed and implemented in the right manner, a HIDS will be able to examine traffic that is unreadable to a network-based IDS. This particular ability is becoming more important each day as more and more web sites start to encrypt all of their traffic.

- *They can be very application specific.* On a host level, the IDS can be designed, modified, or tuned to work very well on specific applications without having to analyze or even hold signatures for other applications that are not running on that particular system. Signatures can be built for specific versions of web server software, FTP servers, mail servers, or any other application housed on that host.

- *They can determine whether or not an alarm may impact that specific system.* The ability to determine whether or not a particular activity or pattern will really affect the system being protected assists greatly in reducing the number of generated alarms. As the IDS resides on the system, it can verify things such as patch levels, presence of certain files, and system state when it analyzes traffic. By knowing what state the system is in, the IDS can more accurately determine whether an activity is potentially harmful to the system.

Disadvantages of HIDSs

HIDSs also have certain disadvantages that must be weighed into the decision to deploy this type of technology:

- *The IDS must have a process on every system you want to watch.* You must have an IDS process or application installed on every host you want to watch. To watch 100 systems, then, you would need to deploy 100 HIDSs.

- *The IDS can have a high cost of ownership and maintenance.* Depending on the specific vendor and application, a HIDS can be fairly costly in terms of time and manpower to maintain. Unless some type of central that allows you to maintain remote processes, administrators must maintain each IDS process individually. Even with a central console, with a HIDS, there will be a high number of processes to maintain, software to update, and parameters to tune.

- *The IDS uses local system resources.* To function, the HIDS must use CPU cycles and memory from the system it is trying to protect. Whatever resources the IDS uses are no longer available for the system to perform its other functions. This becomes extremely important on applications such as high-volume web servers where fewer resources usually means fewer visitors served and the need for more systems to handle expected traffic.

- *The IDS has a very focused view and cannot relate to activity around it.* The HIDS has a limited view of the world, as it can see activity only on the host it is protecting. It has little to no visibility into traffic around it on the network or events taking place on other hosts. Consequently, a HIDS can tell you only if the system it is running on is under attack.

- *The IDS, if logged locally, could be compromised or disabled.* When an IDS generates alarms, it will typically store the alarm information in a file or database of some sort. If the HIDS stores its generated alarm traffic on the local system, an attacker that is successful in breaking into the system may be able to modify or delete those alarms. This makes it difficult for security personnel to discover the intruder and conduct any type of post-incident investigation. A capable intruder may even be able to turn off the IDS process completely.

Active vs. Passive HIDSs

Most IDSs can be distinguished by how they examine the activity around them and whether or not they interact with that activity. This is certainly true for HIDSs. On a *passive* system, the IDS is exactly that—it simply watches the activity, analyzes it, and generates alarms. It does not interact with the activity itself in any way, and it does not modify the defensive posture of the system to react to the traffic. A passive IDS is similar to a simple motion sensor—it generates an alarm when it matches a pattern much as the motion sensor generates an alarm when it sees movement.

An *active* IDS will contain all the same components and capabilities of the passive IDS with one critical exception—the active IDS can *react* to the activity it is analyzing. These reactions can range from something simple, such as running a script to turn a process on or off, to something as complex as modifying file permissions, terminating the offending processes, logging off specific users, and reconfiguring local capabilities to prevent specific users from logging in for the next 12 hours.

Resurgence and Advancement of HIDSs

The past few years have seen a strong resurgence in the use of HIDS. With the great advances in processer power, the introduction of multi-core processors, and the increased capacity of hard drives and memory systems, some of the traditional barriers to running a HIDS have been overcome. Combine that with the widespread adoption of always-on broadband connections and a rise in the use of telecommuting, and a greater overall awareness of the need for computer security and solutions such as HIDS start to become an attractive and sometimes effective solution for business and home users alike.

The latest generation of HIDS have introduced new capabilities designed to stop attacks by preventing them from ever executing or accessing protected files in the first place, rather than relying on a specific signature set that only matches known attacks. The more advanced host-based offerings, which most vendors refer to as host-based intrusion prevention systems (IPS), combine the following elements into a single package:

- **Integrated system firewall** The firewall component checks all network traffic passing into and out of the host. Users can set rules for what types of traffic they want to allow into or out of their system.

- **Behavioral- and signature-based IDS** This hybrid approach uses signatures to match well-known attacks and generic patterns for catching "zero-day" or unknown attacks for which no signatures exist.

- **Application control** This allows administrators to control how applications are used on the system and whether or not new applications can be installed. Controlling the addition, deletion, or modification of existing software can be a good way to control a system's baseline and prevent malware from being installed.

- **Enterprise management** Some host-based products are installed with an "agent" that allows them to be managed by and report back to a central server. This type of integrated remote management capability is essential in any large scale deployment of host-based IDS/IPS.

- **Malware detection and prevention** Some HIDSs/HIPSs include scanning and prevention capabilities that address spyware, malware, rootkits, and other malicious software.

PC-based Malware Protection

In the early days of PC use, threats were limited: most home users were not connected to the Internet 24/7 through broadband connections, and the most common threat was a virus passed from computer to computer via an infected floppy disk. But things have changed dramatically over the last decade and current threats pose a much greater risk than ever before. According to SANS Internet Storm Center, the average survival time of an unpatched Windows PC on the Internet is less than 60 minutes (http://isc.sans.org/survivaltime.html). This is the estimated time before an automated probe finds the system, penetrates it, and compromises it. Automated probes from botnets and worms are not the only threats roaming the Internet—viruses and malware spread by e-mail, phishing, infected web sites that execute code on your system when you visit them, adware, spyware, and so on. Fortunately, as the threats increase in complexity and capability, so do the products designed to stop them.

Antivirus Products

Antivirus products attempt to identify, neutralize, or remove malicious programs, macros, and files. These products were initially designed to detect and remove computer viruses, though many of the antivirus products are now bundled with additional security products and features. At the present time, there is no real consensus regarding the first antivirus product. The first edition of Polish antivirus software *mks_vir* was released in 1987, and the first publicly-known neutralization of a PC virus was performed by

European Bernt Fix (also known as Bernd) early in the same year. By 1990, software giants McAfee and Norton both had established commercial antivirus products.

Although antivirus products have had nearly two decades to refine their capabilities, the purpose of the antivirus products remain the same: to detect and eliminate computer viruses and malware. Most antivirus products combine the following approaches when scanning for viruses:

- **Signature-based scanning**   Much like an IDS, the antivirus products scan programs, files, macros, e-mails, and other data for known worms, viruses, and malware. The antivirus product contains a virus dictionary with thousands of known virus signatures that must be frequently updated, as new viruses are discovered daily. This approach will catch known viruses but is limited by the virus dictionary—what it does not know about it cannot catch.

- **Heuristic scanning (or analysis)**   Heuristic scanning does not rely on a virus dictionary. Instead, it looks for suspicious behavior—anything that does not fit into a "normal" pattern of behavior for the operating system and applications running on the system being protected.

As signature-based scanning is a familiar concept, let's examine heuristic scanning in more detail. Heuristic scanning typically looks for commands or instructions that are not normally found in application programs, such as attempts to access a reserved memory register. Most antivirus products use either a weight-based or rule-based system in their heuristic scanning (more effective products use a combination of both techniques). A weight-based system rates every suspicious behavior based on the degree of threat associated with that behavior. If the set threshold is passed based on a single behavior or combination of behaviors, the antivirus product will treat the process, application, macro, and so on, performing those behaviors as a threat to the system. A rules-based system compares activity to a set of rules meant to detect and identify malicious software. If part of the software matches a rule or a process, application, macro, and so on, and performs a behavior that matches a rule, the antivirus software will treat that as a threat to the local system.

Some heuristic products are very advanced and contain capabilities for examining memory usage and addressing, a parser for examining executable code, a logic flow analyzer, and a disassembler/emulator so they can "guess" what the code is designed to do and whether or not it is malicious.

As with IDS/IPS products, encryption poses a problem for antivirus products: anything that cannot be read cannot be matched against current virus dictionaries or activity patterns. To combat the use of encryption in malware and viruses, many heuristic scanners look for encryption and decryption loops. As malware is usually designed to run alone and unattended, if it uses encryption, it must contain all the instructions to encrypt and decrypt itself as needed. Heuristic scanners look for instructions such as the initialization of a pointer with a valid memory address, manipulation of a counter, or a branch condition based on a counter value. While these actions don't always indicate the presence of an encryption/decryption loop, if the heuristic engine can find a loop it might be able to decrypt the software in a protected memory space, such as an emulator, and evaluate the software in more detail. Many viruses share common encryption/decryption routines that helps antivirus developers.

Current antivirus products are highly configurable and most offerings will have the following capabilities:

- **Automated updates** Perhaps the most important feature of a good antivirus solution is its ability to keep itself up to date by automatically downloading the latest virus signatures on a frequent basis. This usually requires that the system be connected to the Internet in some fashion and updates should be performed on a daily (or more frequent) basis.

- **Automated scanning** Most antivirus products allow for the scheduling of automated scans when the antivirus product will examine the local system for infected files. These automated scans can typically be scheduled for specific days and times, and the scanning parameters can be configured to specify what drives, directories, and types of files are scanned.

- **Media scanning** Removable media is still a common method for virus and malware propagation, and most antivirus products can be configured to automatically scan CDs, USB drives, memory sticks, or any other type of removable media as soon as they are connected to or accessed by the local system.

- **Manual scanning** Many antivirus products allow the user to scan drives, files, or directories "on demand."

- **E-mail scanning** E-mail is still a major method of virus and malware propagation. Many antivirus products give users the ability to scan both incoming and outgoing messages as well as any attachments.

- **Resolution** When the antivirus product detects an infected file or application, it can typically perform one of several actions. The antivirus product may quarantine the file, making it inaccessible; it may try and repair the file by removing the infection or offending code; or it may delete the infected file. Most antivirus products allow the user to specify the desired action, and some allow for an escalation in actions such as cleaning the infected file if possible and quarantining the file if it cannot be cleaned.

Antivirus solutions are typically installed on individual systems (desktops and servers), but network-based antivirus capabilities are also available in many commercial gateway products. These gateway products often combine firewall, IDS/IPS, and antivirus capabilities into a single integrated platform. Most organizations will also employ antivirus solutions on e-mail servers, as that continues to be a very popular propagation method for viruses.

While the installation of a good antivirus product is still considered a necessary best practice, there is growing concern about the effectiveness of antivirus products against developing threats. Early viruses often exhibited destructive behaviors; were poorly written, modified files; and were less concerned with hiding their presence than they were with propagation. We are seeing an emergence of viruses and malware created by professionals, sometimes financed by criminal organizations, that go to great lengths to hide their presence. These viruses and malware are often used to steal sensitive information or turn the infected PC into part of a larger botnet for use in spamming or attack operations.

Personal Software Firewalls

Personal firewalls are host-based protective mechanisms that monitor and control traffic passing into and out of a single system. Designed for the end user, software firewalls often have a configurable security policy that allows the user to determine what traffic is "good" and allowed to pass and what traffic is "bad" and is blocked. Software firewalls are extremely commonplace—so much so that most modern operating systems come with some type personal firewall included.

For example, with the introduction of the Windows XP Professional operating system, Microsoft included a utility called the Internet Connection Firewall. Though disabled by default and hidden in the network configuration screens where most users would never find it, the Internet Connection Firewall did give users some direct control over the network traffic passing through their systems. When Service Pack 2 was launched, Microsoft renamed the Internet Connection Firewall the Windows Firewall (see Figure 11-4) and enabled it by default (Vista also enables the Windows firewall by default). The Windows firewall is fairly configurable; it can be set up to block all traffic, make exceptions for traffic you want to allow, and log rejected traffic for later analysis.

With the introduction of the Vista operating system, Microsoft modified the Windows Firewall to make it more capable and configurable. More options were added to allow for more granular control of network traffic as well as the ability to detect when certain components are not behaving as expected. For example, if your MS Outlook client suddenly attempts to connect to a remote web server, the Windows Firewall can detect this as a deviation from normal behavior and block the unwanted traffic.

UNIX-based operating systems have had built-in software-based firewalls (see Figure 11-5) for a number of years including TCP wrappers, ipchains, and iptables.

TCP Wrappers is a simple program that limits inbound network connections based on port number, domain, or IP address and is managed with two text files called hosts.allow and hosts.deny. If the inbound connection is coming from a trusted IP address and destined for a port to which it is allowed to connect, then the connection is allowed.

Ipchains is a more advanced, rule-based software firewall that allows for traffic filtering, Network Address Translation (NAT), and redirection. Three configurable "chains" are used for handling network traffic: input, output, and forward. The input chain contains rules for traffic that is coming into the local system. The output chain contains rules for traffic that is leaving the local system. The forward chain contains rules for traffic that was received by the local system but is not destined for the local system. Iptables is the latest evolution of ipchains and is designed to work with Linux kernels 2.4 and 2.6. Iptables uses the same three chains for policy rules and traffic handling as ipchains, but with iptables each packet is processed only by the appropriate chain. Under

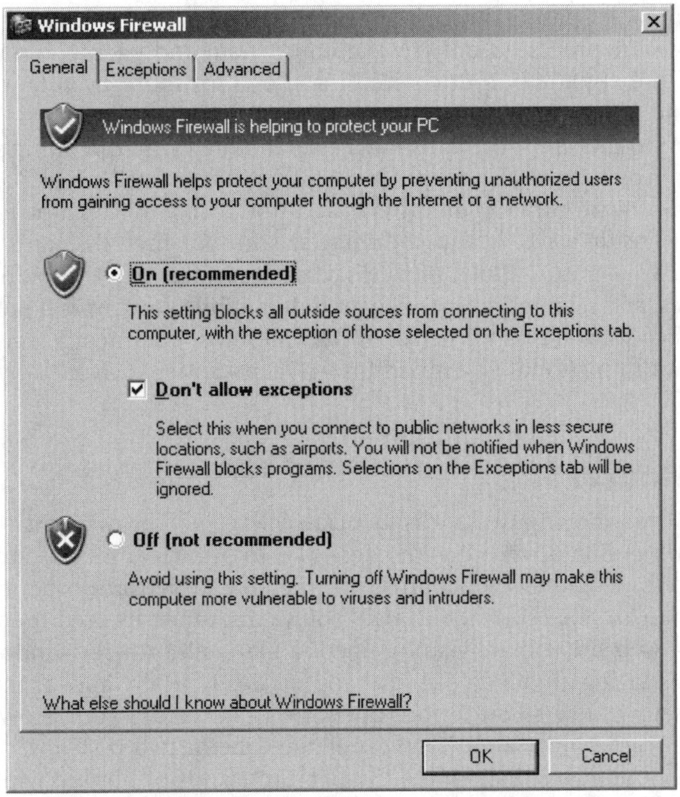

Figure 11-4 Windows Firewall is enabled by default in SP2 and Vista.

Figure 11-5 UNIX firewall

ipchains, each packet passes through all three chains for processing. With iptables, incoming packets are processed only by the input chain and packets leaving the system are processed only by the output chain. This allows for more granular control of network traffic and enhances performance.

In addition to the "free" firewalls that come bundled with operating systems, many commercial personal firewall packages are available. Programs such as ZoneAlarm from Check Point Software provide or bundle additional capabilities not found in some bundled software firewalls. Many commercial software firewalls limit inbound and outbound network traffic, block pop-ups, detect adware, block cookies, block malicious processes, and scan instant messenger traffic. While you can still purchase or even download a free software-based personal firewall, most commercial vendors are bundling the firewall functionality with additional capabilities such as antivirus and anti-spyware.

Pop-up Blocker

One of the most annoying nuisances associated with web browsing is the pop-up ad. Pop-up ads are online advertisements designed to attract web traffic to specific web sites, capture e-mail addresses, advertise a product, and perform other tasks. If you've spent more than an hour surfing the web, you've undoubtedly seen them. They're created when the web site you are visiting opens a new web browser window for the sole purpose of displaying an advertisement. Pop-up ads typically appear in front of your current browser window to catch your attention (and disrupt your browsing). Pop-up ads can range from mildly annoying, generating one or two pop-ups, to system crippling if a malicious web site attempts to open thousands of pop-up windows on your system.

Similar to the pop-up ad is the pop-under ad that opens up behind your current browser window. You won't see these ads until your current window is closed, and they are considered by some to be less annoying than pop-ups. Another form of pop-up is the hover ad that uses Dynamic HTML to appear as a floating window superimposed over your browser window. Dynamic HTML can be very CPU-intensive and can have a significant impact on the performance of older systems.

To some users, pop-up ads are as undesirable as spam, and many web browsers now allow users to restrict or prevent pop-ups either built into the web browser or available as an add-on. Internet Explorer contains a built-in Pop-up Blocker (shown in Figure 11-6 and available from the Tools menu in Internet Explorer 7).

Firefox also contains a built-in pop-up blocker (available by choosing Tools | Options and then selecting the Content tab). Popular add-ons such as the Google and Yahoo! toolbars also contain pop-up blockers. If these freely available options are not enough for your needs, many commercial security suites from McAfee, Symantec, and Check Point contain pop-up blocking capabilities as well. Users must be careful when selecting a pop-up blocker, as some unscrupulous developers have created adware products disguised as free pop-up blockers or other security tools.

Pop-ups ads can be generated in a number of ways, including JavaScript and Adobe Flash, and an effective pop-up blocker must be able to deal with the many methods

Figure 11-6 Pop-up Blocker in IE 7

used to create pop-ups. When a pop-up is created, users typically can click a close or cancel button inside the pop-up or close the new window using a method available through the operating system, such as closing the window from the taskbar in Windows. With the advanced features available to them in a web development environment, some unscrupulous developers program the close or cancel buttons in their pop-ups to launch new pop-ups, redirect the user, run commands on the local system, or even load software.

Windows Defender

As part of its ongoing efforts to help secure its PC operating systems, Microsoft created and released a free utility called Windows Defender in February 2006. The stated purpose of Windows Defender is to protect your computer from spyware and other unwanted software (http://www.microsoft.com/athome/security/spyware/software/default.mspx). Windows Defender is standard with all versions of the Vista operating system and is available via free download for Windows XP Service Pack 2 or later in both 32- and 64-bit versions. It has the following capabilities:

- **Spyware detection and removal** Windows Defender is designed to find and remove spyware and other unwanted programs that display pop-ups, modify browser or Internet settings, or steal personal information from your PC.

- **Scheduled scanning** You can schedule when you want your system to be scanned or you can run scans on demand.

- **Automatic updates**   Updates to the product can be automatically downloaded and installed without user interaction.

- **Real-time protection**   Processes are monitored in real time to stop spyware and malware when they first launch, attempt to install themselves, or attempt to access your PC.

- **Software Explorer**   One of the more interesting capabilities within Windows Defender is the ability to examine the various programs running on your computer. Windows Defender allows you to look at programs that run automatically on startup, are currently running on your PC, or are accessing network connections on your PC. Windows Defender provides you with details such as the publisher of the software, when it was installed on your PC, whether or not the software is "good" or considered to be known malware, the file size, publication date, and other information.

- **Configurable responses**   Windows Defender (see Figure 11-7) lets you choose what actions you want to take in response to detected threats; you can automatically disable the software, quarantine it, attempt to uninstall it, and perform other tasks.

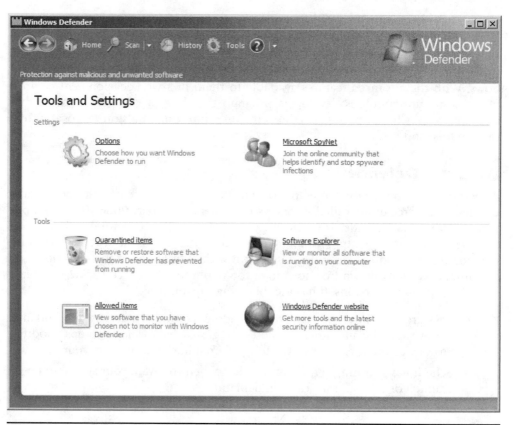

Figure 11-7   Windows Defender configuration options

Network-based IDSs

Network-based IDSs (NIDS) came along a few years after host-based systems. After running host-based systems for a while, many organizations grew tired of the time, energy, and expense involved with managing the first generation of these systems. The desire for a "better way" grew along with the amount of interconnectivity between systems and consequently the amount of malicious activity coming across the networks themselves. This fueled development of a new breed of IDS designed to focus on the source for a great deal of the malicious traffic—the network itself.

The NIDS integrated very well into the concept of *perimeter security*. More and more companies began to operate their computer security like a castle or military base with attention and effort focused on securing and controlling the ways in and out—the idea being that if you could restrict and control access at the perimeter, you didn't have to worry as much about activity inside the organization. Even though the idea of a security perimeter is somewhat flawed (many security incidents originate inside the perimeter), it caught on very quickly, as it was easy to understand and devices such as firewalls, bastion hosts, and routers were available to define and secure that perimeter. The best way to secure the perimeter from outside attack is to reject all traffic from external entities, but as this is impossible and impractical to do, security personnel needed a way to let traffic in but still be able to determine whether or not the traffic was malicious. This is the problem that NIDS developers were trying to solve.

As its name suggests, a NIDS focuses on network traffic—the bits and bytes traveling along the cables and wires that interconnect the systems. A NIDS must examine the network traffic as it passes by and be able to analyze traffic according to protocol, type, amount, source, destination, content, traffic already seen, and other factors. This analysis must happen quickly, and the NIDS must be able to handle traffic at whatever speed the network operates to be effective.

NIDSs are typically deployed so that they can monitor traffic in and out of an organization's major links: connections to the Internet, remote offices, partners, and so on. Like host-based systems, NIDSs look for certain activities that typify hostile actions or misuse, such as the following:

- Denial-of-service attacks
- Port scans or sweeps
- Malicious content in the data payload of a packet or packets
- Vulnerability scanning
- Trojans, viruses, or worms
- Tunneling
- Brute-force attacks

In general, most NIDSs operate in a fairly similar fashion. Figure 11-8 shows the logical layout of a NIDS. By considering the function and activity of each component, you can gain some insight into how NIDS operate.

Figure 11-8
Network IDS
components

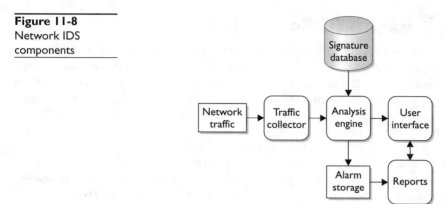

As you can see, the logical components of a NIDS are very similar to those of the host-based system. In the simplest form, a NIDS has the same major components: traffic collector, analysis engine, reports, and a user interface.

In a NIDS, the *traffic collector* is specifically designed to pull traffic from the network. This component usually behaves in much the same way as a network traffic sniffer—it simply pulls every packet it can see off the network to which it is connected. In a NIDS, the traffic collector will logically attach itself to a network interface card (NIC) and instruct the NIC to accept every packet it can. A NIC that accepts and processes every packet regardless of the packet's origin and destination is said to be in *promiscuous mode*.

The *analysis engine* in a NIDS serves the same function as its host-based counterpart, with some substantial differences. The network analysis engine must be able to collect packets and examine them individually or, if necessary, reassemble them into an entire traffic session. The patterns and signatures being matched are far more complicated than host-based signatures, so the analysis engine must be able to remember what traffic preceded the traffic currently being analyzed so that it can determine whether or not that traffic fits into a larger pattern of malicious activity. Additionally, the network-based analysis engine must be able to keep up with the flow of traffic on the network, rebuilding network sessions and matching patterns in real time.

The NIDS *signature database* is usually much larger than that of a host-based system. When examining network patterns, the IDS must be able to recognize traffic targeted at many different applications and operating systems as well as traffic from a wide variety of threats (worms, assessment tools, attack tools, and so on). Some of the signatures themselves can be quite large, as the NIDS must look at network traffic occurring in a specific order over a period of time to match a particular malicious pattern.

Using the lessons learned from the early host-based systems, NIDS developers modified the logical component design somewhat to distribute the user interface and reporting functions. As many companies had more than one network link, they would need an IDS capable of handling multiple links in many different locations. The early IDS vendors solved this dilemma by dividing the components and assigning them to separate entities. The traffic collection, analysis engine, and signature database were bundled into a single entity usually called a *sensor* or *appliance*. The sensors would report to and be controlled by a central system or master console. This central system, shown in Figure 11-9, consolidated alarms and provided the user interface and reporting functions that allowed users in one location to manage, maintain, and monitor sensors deployed in a variety of remote locations.

By creating separate entities designed to work together, the network IDS developers were able to build a more capable and flexible system. With encrypted communications, network sensors could be placed around both local and remote perimeters and still be monitored and managed securely from a central location. Placement of the sensors very quickly became an issue for most security personnel, as the sensors obviously had to have visibility of the network traffic in order to analyze it. Because most organizations with network-based IDSs also had firewalls, location of the IDS relative to the firewall had to be considered as well. Placed before the firewall, as shown in Figure 11-10, the IDS will see all traffic coming in from the Internet, including attacks against the firewall itself. This includes traffic that the firewall stops and does not permit into the corporate network. With this type of deployment, the network IDS sensor will generate a large number of alarms (including alarms for traffic that the firewall would stop) that tends to overwhelm the human operators managing the system.

Placed after the firewall, as shown in Figure 11-11, the NIDS sensor sees and analyzes the traffic that is being passed through the firewall and into the corporate network. While this does not allow the NIDS to see attacks against the firewall, it generally results in far fewer alarms and is the most popular placement for NIDS sensors.

PART IV

Figure 11-9
Distributed network
IDS components

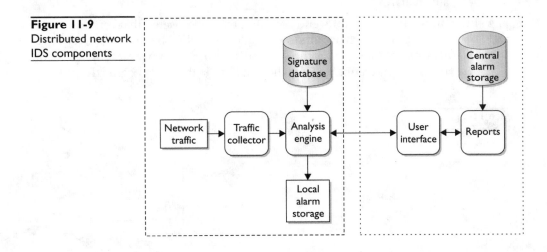

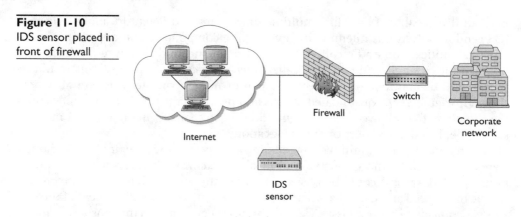

Figure 11-10
IDS sensor placed in front of firewall

As you already know, NIDSs examine the network traffic for suspicious or malicious activity. Here are two examples to illustrate the operation of a NIDS:

- **Port scan** A port scan is a reconnaissance activity a potential attacker will use to find out information about the systems he wants to attack. Using any of a number of tools, the attacker will attempt to connect to various services (Web, FTP, SMTP, and so on) to see if they exist on the intended target. In normal network traffic, a single user might connect to the FTP service provided on a single system. During a port scan, an attacker may attempt to connect to the FTP service on every system. As the attacker's traffic passes by the IDS, this pattern of attempting to connect to different services on different systems will be noticed. When the IDS compares the activity to its signature database, it will very likely match this traffic against the port scanning signature and generate an alarm.

- **Ping of death** Toward the end of 1996, it was discovered that certain operating systems, such as Windows, could be crashed by sending a very large Internet Control Message Protocol (ICMP) echo request packet to that system. The vulnerable operating systems did not handle the packet correctly and

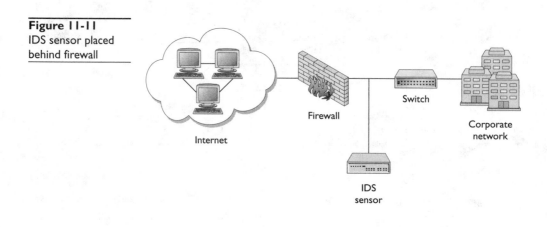

Figure 11-11
IDS sensor placed behind firewall

would subsequently reboot or lock up after receiving the packets. This is a fairly simple traffic pattern for a NIDS to identify, as it simply has to look for ICMP packets over a certain size.

Advantages of a NIDS

A NIDS has certain advantages that make it a good choice for certain situations:

- *It takes fewer systems to provide IDS coverage.* With a few well-placed NIDS sensors, you can monitor all the network traffic going in and out of your organization. Fewer sensors usually equates to less overhead and maintenance, meaning you can protect the same number of systems at a lower cost.

- *Deployment, maintenance, and upgrade costs are usually lower.* The fewer systems that have to be managed and maintained to provide IDS coverage, the lower the cost to operate the IDS. Upgrading and maintaining a few sensors is usually much cheaper than upgrading and maintaining hundreds of host-based processes.

- *A NIDS has visibility into all network traffic and can correlate attacks among multiple systems.* Well-placed NIDS sensors can see the "big picture" when it comes to network-based attacks. The network sensors can tell you whether attacks are widespread and unorganized or focused and concentrated on specific systems.

Disadvantages of a NIDS

A NIDS has certain disadvantages:

- *It is ineffective when traffic is encrypted.* When network traffic is encrypted from application to application or system to system, a NIDS sensor will not be able to examine that traffic. With the increasing popularity of encrypted traffic, this is becoming a bigger problem for effective IDS operations.

- *It can't see traffic that does not cross it.* The IDS sensor can examine only traffic crossing the network link it is monitoring. With most IDS sensors being placed on perimeter links, traffic traversing the internal network is never seen.

- *It must be able to handle high volumes of traffic.* As network speeds continue to increase, the network sensors must be able to keep pace and examine the traffic as quickly as it can pass the network. When NIDSs were introduced, 10 Mbps networks were the norm. Now 100 Mbps and even 1 Gbps networks are commonplace. This increase in traffic speeds means IDS sensors must be faster and more powerful than ever before.

- *It doesn't know about activity on the hosts themselves.* NIDSs focus on network traffic. Activity that occurs on the hosts themselves will not be seen by a NIDS.

PART IV

Active vs. Passive NIDSs

Most NIDSs can be distinguished by how they examine the traffic and whether or not they interact with that traffic. On a *passive* system, the IDS simply watches the traffic, analyzes it, and generates alarms. It does not interact with the traffic itself in any way, and it does not modify the defensive posture of the system to react to the traffic. A passive IDS is very similar to a simple motion sensor—it generates an alarm when it matches a pattern much as the motion sensor generates an alarm when it sees movement. An *active* IDS will contain all the same components and capabilities of the passive IDS with one critical addition—the active IDS can *react* to the traffic it is analyzing. These reactions can range from something simple, such as sending a TCP reset message to interrupt a potential attack and disconnect a session, to something complex, such as dynamically modifying firewall rules to reject all traffic from specific source IP addresses for the next 24 hours.

The most common defensive ability for an active IDS is to send a TCP reset message. Within TCP, the reset message (RST) essentially tells both sides of the connection to drop the session and stop communicating immediately. While this mechanism was originally developed to cover situations such as systems accidentally receiving communications intended for other systems, the reset message works fairly well for IDSs—with one serious drawback: a reset message affects only the current session. Nothing prevents the attacker from coming back and trying again and again. Despite the "temporariness" of this solution, sending a reset message is usually the only defensive measure implemented on IDS deployments, as the fear of blocking legitimate traffic and disrupting business processes, even for a few moments, often outweighs the perceived benefit of discouraging potential intruders.

Signatures

As you have probably deduced from the discussion so far, one of the critical elements of any good IDS is the signature set—the set of patterns the IDS uses to determine whether or not activity is potentially hostile. Signatures can be very simple or remarkably complicated, depending on the activity they are trying to highlight. In general, signatures can be divided into two main groups, depending on what the signature is looking for: context-based and context-based.

Content-based signatures are generally the simplest. They are designed to examine the content of such things as network packets or log entries. Content-based signatures are typically easy to build and look for simple things, such as a certain string of characters or a certain flag set in a TCP packet. Here are some example content-based signatures:

- *Matching the characters* /etc/passwd *in a Telnet session.* On a UNIX system, the names of valid user accounts (and sometimes the passwords for those user accounts) are stored in a file called *passwd* located in the *etc* directory.

- *Matching a TCP packet with the synchronize, reset, and urgent flags all set within the same packet.* This combination of flags is impossible to generate under normal conditions, and the presence of all of these flags in the same packet would indicate this packet was likely created by a potential attacker for a specific purpose, such as to crash the targeted system.

- *Matching the characters* to: decode *in the header of an e-mail message.* On certain older versions of sendmail, sending an e-mail message to "decode" would cause the system to execute the contents of the e-mail.

Context-based signatures are generally more complicated, as they are designed to match large patterns of activity and examine how certain types of activity fit into the other activities going on around them. Context signatures generally address the question How does this event compare to other events that have already happened or might happen in the near future? Context-based signatures are more difficult to analyze and take more resources to match, as the IDS must be able to "remember" past events to match certain context signatures. Here are some examples of context-based signatures:

- *Match a potential intruder scanning for open web servers on a specific network.* A potential intruder may use a port scanner to look for any systems accepting connections on port 80. To match this signature, the IDS must analyze all attempted connections to port 80 and then be able to determine which connection attempts are coming from the same source but are going to multiple, different destinations.

- *Identify a Nessus scan.* Nessus is an open-source vulnerability scanner that allows security administrators (and potential attackers) to quickly examine systems for vulnerabilities. Depending on the tests chosen, Nessus will typically perform the tests in a certain order, one after the other. To be able to determine the presence of a Nessus scan, the IDS must know which tests Nessus runs as well as the typical order in which the tests are run.

- *Identify a ping flood attack.* A single ICMP packet on its own is generally regarded as harmless, certainly not worthy of an IDS signature. Yet thousands of ICMP packets coming to a single system in a short period of time can have a devastating effect on the receiving system. By flooding a system with thousands of valid ICMP packets, an attacker can keep a target system so busy it doesn't have time to do anything else—a very effective denial-of-service attack. To identify a ping flood, the IDS must recognize each ICMP packet and keep track of how many ICMP packets different systems have received in the recent past.

 EXAM TIP   Know the differences between content-based and context-based signatures. Content-based signatures match specific content such as a certain string or series of characters (matching the string */etc/passwd* in an FTP session). Context-based signatures match a pattern of activity based on the other activity around it (such as a port scan).

To function, the IDS must have a decent signature base with examples of known, undesirable activity that it can use when analyzing traffic or events. Any time an IDS matches current events against a signature, the IDS could be considered successful, as it

PART IV

has correctly matched the current event against a known signature and reacted accordingly (usually with an alarm or alert of some type).

False Positives and Negatives

Viewed in its simplest form, an IDS is really just looking at activity (be it host-based or network-based) and matching it against a predefined set of patterns. When it matches an activity to a specific pattern, the IDS cannot know the true intent behind that activity—whether or not it is benign or hostile—and therefore it can react only as it has been programmed to do. In most cases, this means generating an alert that must then be analyzed by a human who tries to determine the intent of the traffic from whatever information is available. When an IDS matches a pattern and generates an alarm for benign traffic, meaning the traffic was not hostile and not a threat, this is called a *false positive*. In other words, the IDS matched a pattern and raised an alarm when it didn't really need to do so. Keep in mind that the IDS can only match patterns and has no ability to determine intent behind the activity, so in some ways this is an unfair label. Technically, the IDS is functioning correctly by matching the pattern, but from a human standpoint this is not information the analyst needed to see, as it does not constitute a threat and does not require intervention.

An IDS is also limited by its signature set—it can match only activity for which it has stored patterns. Hostile activity that does not match an IDS signature and therefore goes undetected is called a *false negative*. In this case, the IDS is not generating any alarms, even though it should be, giving a false sense of security.

IDS Models

In addition to being divided along the host and network lines, IDSs are often classified according to the detection model they use: anomaly or misuse. For an IDS, a model is a method for examining behavior so that the IDS can determine whether that behavior is "not normal" or in violation of established policies.

An *anomaly* detection model is the more complicated of the two. In this model, the IDS must know what "normal" behavior on the host or network being protected really is. Once the "normal" behavior baseline is established, the IDS can then go to work identifying deviations from the norm, which are further scrutinized to determine whether that activity is malicious. Building the profile of normal activity is usually done by the IDS, with some input from security administrators, and can take days to months. The IDS must be flexible and capable enough to account for things such as new systems, new users, movement of information resources, and other factors, but be sensitive enough to detect a single user illegally switching from one account to another at 3 A.M. on a Saturday.

Anomaly detection was developed to make the system capable of dealing with variations in traffic and better able to determine which activity patterns were malicious. A perfectly functioning anomaly-based system would be able to ignore patterns from legitimate hosts and users but still identify those patterns as suspicious should they come from a potential attacker. Unfortunately, most anomaly-based systems suffer from extremely high false positives, especially during the "break-in" period while the IDS is learning the network. On the other hand, an anomaly-based system is not restricted to a specific signature set and is far more likely to identify a new exploit or attack tool that would go unnoticed by a traditional IDS.

 EXAM TIP Anomaly detection looks for things that are out of the ordinary, such as a user logging in when he's not supposed to or unusually high network traffic into and out of a workstation.

A *misuse* detection model is a little simpler to implement, and therefore it's the more popular of the two models. In a misuse model, the IDS looks for suspicious activity or activity that violates specific policies and then reacts as it has been programmed to do. This reaction can be an alarm, e-mail, router reconfiguration, or TCP reset message. Technically, misuse is the more efficient model, as it takes fewer resources to operate, does not need to learn what "normal" behavior is, and will generate an alarm whenever a pattern is successfully matched. However, the misuse model's greatest weakness is its reliance on a predefined signature base—any activity, malicious or otherwise, that the misuse-based IDS does not have a signature for will go undetected. Despite that drawback and because it is easier and cheaper to implement, most commercial IDS products are based on the misuse detection model.

Intrusion Prevention Systems

An intrusion prevention system (IPS) monitors network traffic for malicious or unwanted behavior and can block, reject, or redirect that traffic in real time. Sound familiar? It should: While many vendors will argue that an IPS is a different animal from an IDS, the truth is that most IPS are merely expansions of existing IDS capabilities. As a core function, an IPS must be able to monitor for and detect potentially malicious network traffic, which is essentially the same function as an IDS. However, an IPS does not stop at merely monitoring traffic—it must be able to block, reject, or redirect that traffic in real time to be considered a true IPS. It must be able to stop or prevent malicious traffic from having an impact. To qualify as an IDS a system just needs to see and classify the traffic as malicious. To qualify as an IPS, the system must be able to do something about that traffic. In reality, most products that are called IDSs, including the first commercially available IDS, NetRanger, can interact with and stop malicious traffic, so the distinction between the two is often blurred. The term *intrusion prevention system* was originally coined by Andew Plato in marketing literature developed for NetworkICE, a company that was purchased by ISS and which is now part of IBM.

Like IDSs, most IPSs have an internal signature base to compare network traffic against known "bad" traffic patterns. IPSs can perform content-based inspections, looking inside network packets for unique packets, data values, or patterns that match known malicious patterns. Some IPSs can perform protocol inspection, in which the IPS decodes traffic and analyzes it as it would appear to the server receiving it. For

PART IV

example, many IPSs can do HTTP protocol inspection, so they can examine incoming and outgoing HTTP traffic and process it as an HTTP server would. The advantage here is that the IPS can detect and defeat popular evasion techniques such as encoding URLs as the IPS "sees" the traffic in the same way the web server would when it receives and decodes it. The IPS can also detect activity that is abnormal or potentially malicious for that protocol, such as passing an extremely large value (over 10,000 characters) to a login field on a web page.

Unlike a traditional IDS, an IPS must sit in line to be able to interact effectively with the network traffic. Most IPSs can operate in "stealth mode" and do not require an IP address for the connections they are monitoring. When an IPS detects malicious traffic, it can drop the offending packets, reset incoming or established connections, generate alerts, quarantine traffic to/from specific IP addresses, or even block traffic from offending IP addresses on a temporary or permanent basis. As they are sitting in line, most IPSs can also offer *rate-based monitoring* to detect and mitigate denial-of-service attacks. With rate-based monitoring, the IPS can watch the amount of traffic traversing the network. If the IPS sees too much traffic coming into or going out from a specific system or set of systems, the IPS can intervene and throttle down the traffic to a lower and more acceptable level. Many IPSs perform this function by "learning" what are "normal" network traffic patterns with regard to number of connections per second, amount of packets per connection, packets coming from or going to specific ports, and so on, and comparing current traffic rates for network traffic (TCP, UDP, ARP, ICMP, and so on) to those established norms. When a traffic pattern reaches a threshold or varies dramatically from those norms, the IPS can react and intervene as needed.

Like a traditional IDS, the IPS has a potential weakness when dealing with encrypted traffic. Traffic that is encrypted will typically pass by the IPS untouched (provided it does not trigger any non-content–related alarms such as rate-based alarms). To counter this problem, some IPS vendors are including the ability to decrypt Secure Sockets Layer (SSL) sessions for further inspection. To do this, some IPS solutions will store copies of any protected web servers' private keys on the sensor itself. When the IPS sees a session initiation request, it monitors the initial transactions between the server and the client. By using the server's stored private keys, the IPS will be able to determine the session keys negotiated during the SSL session initiation. With the session keys, the IPS can decrypt all future packets passed between server and client during that web session. This gives the IPS the ability to perform content inspection on SSL-encrypted traffic.

You will often see IPS (and IDS) advertised and marketed by their wire speed or amount of traffic they can process without dropping packets or interrupting the flow of network traffic. The term *wire speed* refers to the theoretical maximum transmission rate of a cable or other medium and is based on a number of factors, including the properties of the cable itself and the connection protocol in use (in other words, how much data can be pushed through under ideal conditions). In reality, a network will never reach its hypothetical maximum transmission rate due to errors, collisions, retransmissions, and other factors; therefore, a 1 Gbps network is not actually capable of passing an actual 1 Gbps of network traffic, even if all the components are rated to handle 1 Gbps. When used in a marketing sense, wire speed is the maximum throughput rate networking or security device equipment can process without impacting that network traffic. For example, a 1 Gbps IPS should be able to process, analyze, and protect 1 Gbps of network traffic without impacting traffic flow. IPS vendors will often quote their products' capacity as the combined throughput possible through all available ports on the IPS sensor—a 10 Gbps sensor may have 12-gigabit Ethernet ports but is capable of handling only 10 Gbps of network traffic.

Honeypots and Honeynets

As is often the case, one of the best tools for information security personnel has always been knowledge. To secure and defend a network and the information systems on that network properly, security personnel need to know what they are up against. What types of attacks are being used? What tools and techniques are popular at the moment? How effective is a certain technique? What sort of impact will this tool have on my network? Often this sort of information is passed through white papers, conferences, mailing lists, or even word of mouth. In some cases, the tool developers themselves provide much of the information in the interest of promoting better security for everyone.

Information is also gathered through examination and forensic analysis, often after a major incident has already occurred and information systems are already damaged. One of the most effective techniques for collecting this type of information is to observe activity first-hand—watching an attacker as she probes, navigates, and exploits his way through a network. To accomplish this without exposing critical information systems, security researchers often use something called a *honeypot*.

A honeypot, sometimes called a *digital sandbox*, is an artificial environment where attackers can be contained and observed without putting real systems at risk. A good honeypot appears to an attacker to be a real network consisting of application servers, user systems, network traffic, and so on, but in most cases it's actually made up of one or a few systems running specialized software to simulate the user and network traffic common to most targeted networks. Figure 11-12 illustrates a simple honeypot layout in which a single system is placed on the network to deliberately attract attention from potential attackers.

Figure 11-12 shows the security researcher's view of the honeypot, while Figure 11-13 shows the attacker's view. The security administrator knows that the honeypot, in this

Figure 11-12
Logical depiction of a honeypot

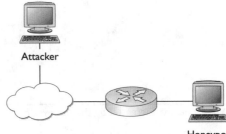

Attacker

Honeypot system

case, actually consists of a single system running software designed to react to probes, reconnaissance attempts, and exploits as if it were an entire network of systems. When the attacker connects to the honeypot, she is presented with an entire "virtual" network of servers and PCs running a variety of applications. In most cases, the honeypot will appear to be running versions of applications that are known to be vulnerable to specific exploits. All this is designed to provide the attacker with an enticing, hopefully irresistible, target.

Any time an attacker has been lured into probing or attacking the virtual network, the honeypot records the activity for later analysis: what the attacker does, which systems and applications she concentrates on, what tools are run, how long the attacker stays, and so on. All this information is collected and analyzed in the hopes that it will allow security personnel to better understand and protect against the threats to their systems.

There are many honeypots in use, specializing in everything from wireless to denial-of-service attacks; most are run by research, government, or law enforcement organizations. Why aren't more businesses running honeypots? Quite simply, the time and cost are prohibitive. Honeypots take a lot of time and effort to manage and maintain and even more effort to sort, analyze, and classify the traffic the honeypot collects. Unless they are developing security tools, most companies focus their limited security efforts on preventing attacks, and in many cases, companies aren't even that concerned with detecting attacks as long as the attacks are blocked, are unsuccessful, and don't affect business operations. Even though honeypots can serve as a valuable resource by luring attackers away from production systems and allowing defenders to identify and thwart potential attackers before they cause any serious damage, the costs and efforts involved deter many companies from using honeypots.

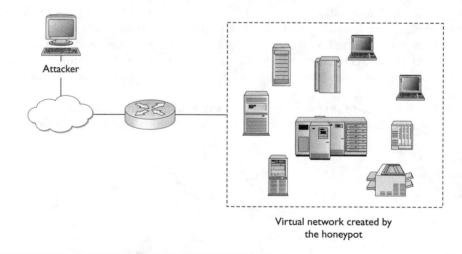

Virtual network created by
the honeypot

Figure 11-13   Virtual network created by the honeypot

EXAM TIP   A honeypot is a system designed to attract potential attackers by pretending to be one or more systems with open network services.

A *honeynet* is a collection of two or more honeypots. Larger, very diverse network environments can deploy multiple honeypots (thus forming a honeynet) when a single honeypot device does not provide enough coverage. Honeynets are often integrated into an organization-wide IDS/IPS as the honeynet can provide relevant information about potential attackers.

Firewalls

Arguably one of the first and most important network security tools is the firewall. A *firewall* is a device that is configured to permit or deny network traffic based on an established policy or rule set. In their simplest form, firewalls are like network traffic cops; they determine which packets are allowed to pass into or out of the network perimeter. The term *firewall* was borrowed from the construction field, in which a fire wall is literally a wall meant to confine a fire or prevent a fire's spread within or between buildings. In the network security world, a firewall stops the malicious and untrusted traffic (the fire) of the Internet from spreading into your network. Firewalls control traffic flow between zones of network traffic; for example, between the Internet (a zone with no trust) and an internal network (a zone with high trust). (Personal software firewalls were already discussed in this chapter; for more discussion on network firewalls refer to Chapter 8.)

Proxy Servers

Though not strictly a security tool, a *proxy server* can be used to filter out undesirable traffic and prevent employees from accessing potentially hostile web sites. A proxy server takes requests from a client system and forwards it to the destination server on behalf of the client. Proxy servers can be completely transparent (these are usually called *gateways* or *tunneling proxies*), or a proxy server can modify the client request before sending it on or even serve the client's request without needing to contact the destination server. Several major categories of proxy servers are in use:

- **Anonymizing proxy**   An anonymizing proxy is designed to hide information about the requesting system and make a user's web browsing experience "anonymous." This type of proxy service is often used by individuals concerned with the amount of personal information being transferred across the Internet and the use of tracking cookies and other mechanisms to track browsing activity.

- **Caching proxy**   This type of proxy keeps local copies of popular client requests and is often used in large organizations to reduce bandwidth usage and increase performance. When a request is made, the proxy server first checks to see whether it has a current copy of the requested content in the

PART IV

cache; if it does, it services the client request immediately without having to contact the destination server. If the content is old or the caching proxy does not have a copy of the requested content, the request is forwarded to the destination server.

- **Content filtering proxy**   Content filtering proxies examine each client request and compare it to an established acceptable use policy. Requests can usually be filtered in a variety of ways including the requested URL, destination system, or domain name or by keywords in the content itself. Content filtering proxies typically support user-level authentication so access can be controlled and monitored and activity through the proxy can be logged and analyzed. This type of proxy is very popular in schools, corporate environments, and government networks.

- **Open proxy**   An open proxy is essentially a proxy that is available to any Internet user and often has some anonymizing capabilities as well. This type of proxy has been the subject of some controversy with advocates for Internet privacy and freedom on one side of the argument, and law enforcement, corporations, and government entities on the other side. As open proxies are often used to circumvent corporate proxies, many corporations attempt to block the use of open proxies by their employees.

- **Reverse proxy**   A reverse proxy is typically installed on the server side of a network connection, often in front of a group of web servers. The reverse proxy intercepts all incoming web requests and can perform a number of functions including traffic filtering, SSL decryption, serving of common static content such as graphics, and performing load balancing.

- **Web proxy**   A web proxy is solely designed to handle web traffic and is sometimes called a *web cache*. Most web proxies are essentially specialized caching proxies.

Deploying a proxy solution within a network environment is usually done by either setting up the proxy and requiring all client systems to configure their browsers to use the proxy or by deploying an intercepting proxy that actively intercepts all requests without requiring client-side configuration.

From a security perspective, proxies are most useful in their ability to control and filter outbound requests. By limiting the types of content and web sites employees can access from corporate systems, many administrators hope to avoid loss of corporate data, hijacked systems, and infections from malicious web sites. Administrators also use proxies to enforce corporate acceptable use policies and track use of corporate resources.

Internet Content Filters

With the dramatic proliferation of Internet traffic and the push to provide Internet access to every desktop, many corporations have implemented content-filtering systems to protect them from employees' viewing of inappropriate or illegal content at the workplace and the subsequent complications that occur when such viewing takes place. Internet content filtering is also popular in schools, libraries, homes, government offices, and any other environment where there is a need to limit or restrict access to undesirable content. In addition to filtering undesirable content, such as pornography, some content filters can also filter out malicious activity such as browser hijacking attempts or cross-site–scripting attacks. In many cases, content filtering is performed with or as a part of a proxy solution as the content requests can be filtered and serviced by the same device. Content can be filtered in a variety of ways, including via the requested URL, the destination system, the domain name, by keywords in the content itself, and by type of file requested.

Content filtering systems face many challenges, because the ever-changing Internet makes it difficult to maintain lists of undesirable sites (sometime called black lists); terms used on a medical site can also be used on a pornographic site, making keyword filtering challenging; and determined users are always seeking ways to bypass proxy filters. To help administrators, most commercial content-filtering solutions provide an update service, much like IDS or antivirus products, that update keywords and undesirable sites automatically.

Protocol Analyzers

A *protocol analyzer* (also known as a *packet sniffer, network analyzer,* or *network sniffer*) is a piece of software or an integrated software/hardware system that can capture and decode network traffic. Protocol analyzers have been popular with system administrators and security professionals for decades because they are such versatile and useful tools for a network environment. From a security perspective, protocol analyzers can be used for a number of activities, such as the following:

- Detecting intrusions or undesirable traffic (IDS/IPS must have some type of capture and decode ability to be able to look for suspicious/malicious traffic)
- Capturing traffic during incident response or incident handling
- Looking for evidence of botnets, Trojans, and infected systems
- Looking for unusual traffic or traffic exceeding certain thresholds
- Testing encryption between systems or applications

From a network administration perspective, protocol analyzers can be used for activities such as these:

- Analyzing network problems
- Detecting misconfigured applications or misbehaving applications
- Gathering and reporting network usage and traffic statistics
- Debugging client/server communications

Regardless of the intended use, a protocol analyzer must be able to see network traffic in order to capture and decode it. A software-based protocol analyzer must be able to place the NIC it is going to use to monitor network traffic in *promiscuous mode* (sometimes called *promisc mode*). Promiscuous mode tells the NIC to process every network packet it sees regardless of the intended destination. Normally, a NIC will process only *broadcast* packets (that are going to everyone on that subnet) and packets with the NIC's Media Access Control (MAC) address as the destination address inside the packet. As a sniffer, the analyzer must process every packet crossing the wire, so the ability to place a NIC into promiscuous mode is critical.

 EXAM TIP A sniffer must use a NIC placed in promiscuous (promisc) mode or it will not see all the network traffic coming into the NIC.

With older networking technologies, such as hubs, it was easier to operate a protocol analyzer, as the hub broadcast every packet across every interface regardless of the destination. With switches becoming the standard for networking equipment, placing a protocol analyzer became more difficult.

To accommodate protocol analyzers, IDS, and IPS devices, most switch manufacturers support *port mirroring* or a *Switched Port Analyzer (SPAN)* port. Depending on the manufacturer and the hardware, a mirrored port will see all the traffic passing through the switch or through a specific VLAN(s), or all the traffic passing through other specific switch ports. The network traffic is essentially copied (or mirrored) to a specific port, which can then support a protocol analyzer.

Another option for traffic capture is to use a *network tap*, a hardware device that can be placed in-line on a network connection and that will copy traffic passing through the tap to a second set of interfaces on the tap. Network taps are often used to sniff traffic passing between devices at the network perimeter, such as the traffic passing between a router and a firewall. Many common network taps work by bridging a network connection and passing incoming traffic out one tap port (A) and outgoing traffic out another tap port (B), as shown in Figure 11-14.

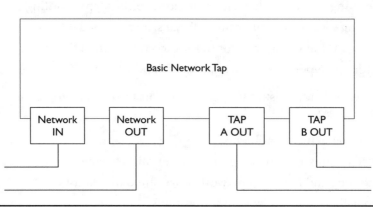

Figure 11-14 A basic network tap

A popular open-source protocol analyzer is Wireshark (www.wireshark.org/). Available for both UNIX and Windows operating systems, Wireshark is a GUI-based protocol analyzer that allows users to capture and decode network traffic on any available network interface in the system on which the software is running (including wireless interfaces). Wireshark has some interesting features, including the ability to "follow the TCP stream," which allows the user to select a single TCP packet and then see all the other packets involved in that TCP conversation.

Network Mappers

One of the biggest challenges in securing a network can be simply knowing what is connected to that network at any given point in time. For most organizations, the "network" is a constantly changing entity. While servers may remain fairly constant, user workstations, laptops, printers, and network-capable peripherals may connect to and then disconnect from the network on a daily basis, making the network at 3 AM look quite different than the network at 10 AM. To help identify devices connected to the network, many administrators use networking mapping tools.

Network mappers are tools designed to identify what devices are connected to a given network and, where possible, the operating system in use on that device. Most network mapping tools are "active" in that they generate traffic and then listen for responses to determine what devices are connected to the network. These tools typically use the ICMP or SNMP protocol for discovery and some of the more advanced tools will create a "map" of discovered devices showing their connectivity to the network in relation to other network devices. A few network mapping tools have the ability to perform device discovery passively by examining all the network traffic in an organization and noting each unique IP address and MAC address in the traffic stream.

Anti-spam

The bane of users and system administrators everywhere, *spam* is essentially unsolicited or undesired bulk electronic messages. While typically applied to e-mail, spam can be transmitted via text message to phones and mobile devices, as postings to Internet forums, and by other means. If you've ever used an e-mail account, chances are you've received spam.

From a productivity and security standpoint, spam costs businesses and users billions of dollars each year, and it is such a widespread problem that the U.S. Congress passed the CAN-SPAM Act of 2003 to empower the Federal Trade Commission to enforce the act and the Department of Justice to enforce criminal sanctions against spammers. The act establishes requirements for those who send commercial e-mail, spells out penalties for spammers and companies whose products are advertised in spam if they violate the law, and gives consumers the right to ask e-mailers to stop spamming them. Despite all our best efforts, however, spam just keeps coming; as the technologies and techniques developed to stop the spam get more advanced and complex, so do the tools and techniques used to send out the unsolicited messages.

Here are a few of the more popular methods used to fight the spam epidemic; most of these techniques are used to filter e-mail but could be applied to other mediums as well:

- **Blacklisting**   Blacklisting is essentially noting which domains and source addresses have a reputation for sending spam and rejecting messages coming from those domains and source addresses. This is basically a permanent "ignore" or "call block" type capability. Several organizations and a few commercial companies provide lists of known spammers.

- **Content or keyword filtering**   Similar to Internet content filtering, this method filters e-mail messages for undesirable content or indications of spam. Much like content filtering of web content, filtering e-mail based on something like keywords can cause unexpected results, as certain terms can be used in both legitimate and spam e-mail. Most content-filtering techniques use regular expression matching for keyword filtering.

- **Trusted servers**   The opposite of blacklisting, a trusted server list includes SMTP servers that are being "trusted" not to forward spam.

- **Delay-based filtering**   Some Simple Mail Transfer Protocol (SMTP) servers are configured to insert a deliberate pause between the opening of a connection and the sending of the SMTP server's welcome banner. Some spam-generating programs do not wait for that greeting banner, and any system that immediately starts sending data as soon as the connection is opened is treated as a spam generator and dropped by the SMTP server.

- **PTR and reverse DNS checks**   Some e-mail filters check the origin domain of an e-mail sender. If the reverse checks show the mail is coming from a dial-up user, home-based broadband, a dynamically assigned address, or has a generic or missing domain, then the filter rejects it as these are common sources of spam messages.

- **Callback verification**   As many spam messages use forged "from" addresses, some filters attempt to validate the "from" address of incoming e-mail. The receiving server can contact the sending server in an attempt to validate the sending address, but this is not always effective as spoofed addresses are sometimes valid e-mail addresses that can be verified.

- **Statistical content filtering**   Statistical filtering is much like a document classification system. Users mark received messages as either spam or legitimate mail and the filtering system learns from the user's input. The more messages that are seen and classified as spam, the better the filtering software should get at intercepting incoming spam. Spammers counteract many filtering technologies by inserting random words and characters into the messages, making it difficult for content filters to identify patterns common to spam.

- **Rule-based filtering**   Rule-based filtering is a simple technique that merely looks for matches in certain fields or keywords. For example, a rule-based filtering system may look for any message with the words "get rich" in the subject line of the incoming message. Many popular e-mail clients have the ability to implement rule-based filtering.

- **Egress filtering**   Some organizations perform spam filtering on e-mail leaving their organization as well, and this is called egress filtering. The same types of anti-spam techniques can be used to validate and filter outgoing e-mail in an effort to combat spam.

- **Hybrid filtering**   Most commercial anti-spam methods use hybrid filtering, or a combination of several different techniques to fight spam. For example, a filtering solution may take each incoming message and match it against known spammers, then against a rule-based filter, then a content filter, and finally against a statistical based filter. If the message passes all filtering stages, it will be treated as a legitimate message; otherwise, it is rejected as spam.

Much spam filtering is done at the network or SMTP server level. It's more efficient to scan all incoming and outgoing messages with a centralized solution than it is to deploy individual solutions on user desktops throughout the organization. E-mail is essentially a proxied service by default: messages generally come into and go out of an organization's mail server. (Users don't typically connect to remote SMTP servers to send and receive messages, but they can.) Anti-spam solutions are available in the form of software that is loaded on the SMTP server itself or on a secondary server that processes messages either before they reach the SMTP server or after the messages are processed by the SMTP server. Anti-spam solutions are also available in appliance form, where the software and hardware are a single integrated solution. Many centralized anti-spam methods allow individual users to customize spam filtering for their specific inbox, specifying their own filter rules and criteria for evaluating inbound e-mail.

The central issue with spam is that, despite all the effort placed into building effective spam filtering programs, spammers continue to create new methods for flooding inboxes. Spam filtering solutions are good but are far from perfect and continue to fight the constant challenge of allowing in legitimate messages while keeping the spam out. The lack of central control over Internet traffic also makes anti-spam efforts more difficult. Different countries have different laws and regulations governing e-mail, which range from draconian to nonexistent. For the foreseeable future, spam will continue to be a burden to administrators and users alike.

Chapter Review

Intrusion detection is a mechanism for detecting unexpected or unauthorized activity on computer systems. IDSs can be host-based, examining only the activity applicable to a specific system, or network-based, examining network traffic for a large number of systems. IDSs match patterns known as *signatures* that can be content or context-based. Some IDSs are model-based and alert an administrator when activity does not match normal patterns (anomaly based) or when it matches known suspicious or malicious patterns (misuse detection). Newer versions of IDSs include prevention capabilities that will automatically block suspicious or malicious traffic before it reaches its intended destination, and many vendors call these Intrusion Prevention Systems (IPSs).

Firewalls are security devices that protect an organization's network perimeter by filtering traffic coming into the organization based on an established policy. They can be simple packet filtering devices or can have more advanced application layer filtering capabilities. Personal software firewalls are software packages that help protect individual systems by controlling network traffic coming into and out of that individual system.

Antivirus technologies scan network traffic, e-mail, files, and removable media for malicious code. Available in software and appliance form, they provide a necessary line of defense against the massive amount of malicious code roaming the Internet.

Proxies service client requests by forwarding requests from users to other servers. Proxies can be used to help filter and manage network traffic, particularly web browsing. Proxies are often combined with a content-filtering capability that administrators can use to block access to malicious or inappropriate content. Many organizations and users also employ pop-up blockers, mechanisms that prevent the annoying ads that appear in new browser windows as you visit certain web pages.

Protocol analyzers, often called sniffers, are tools that capture and decode network traffic. Analyzers must be able to see and capture network traffic to be effective, and many switch vendors support network analysis through the use of mirroring or span ports. Network traffic can also be viewed using network taps, a device for replicating network traffic passing across a physical link.

Honeypots are specialized forms of intrusion detection that involve setting up simulated hosts and services for attackers to target. Honeypots are based on the concept of luring attackers away from legitimate systems by presenting more tempting or interesting systems that, in most cases, appear to be easy targets. By monitoring activity within the honeypot, security personnel are better able to identify potential attackers along with their tools and capabilities.

Questions

1. What are the three types of event logs generated by Windows NT and 2000 systems?

   A. Event, Process, and Security

   B. Application, User, and Security

   C. User, Event, and Security

   D. Application, System, and Security

2. What are the two main types of intrusion detection systems?

   A. Network-based and host-based

   B. Signature-based and event-based

   C. Active and reactive

   D. Intelligent and passive

3. The first commercial, network-based IDS product was

   A. Stalker

   B. NetRanger

   C. IDES

   D. RealSecure

4. What are the two main types of IDS signatures?

   A. Network-based and file-based

   B. Context-based and content-based

   C. Active and reactive

   D. None of the above

5. A passive, host-based IDS

   A. Runs on the local system

   B. Does not interact with the traffic around it

   C. Can look at system event and error logs

   D. All of the above

6. Which of the following is *not* a capability of network-based IDS?

   A. Can detect denial-of-service attacks

   B. Can decrypt and read encrypted traffic

   C. Can decode UDP and TCP packets

   D. Can be tuned to a particular network environment

7. An active IDS can

   A. Respond to attacks with TCP resets

   B. Monitor for malicious activity

   C. A and B

   D. None of the above

8. Honeypots are used to

   A. Attract attackers by simulating systems with open network services

   B. Monitor network usage by employees

   C. Process alarms from other IDSs

   D. Attract customers to e-commerce sites

9. Egress filtering is used to detect SPAM that is

   A. Coming into an organization

   B. Sent from known spammers outside your organization

    C. Leaving an organization

    D. Sent to mailing lists in your organization

10. Preventative intrusion detection systems

    A. Are cheaper

    B. Are designed to stop malicious activity from occurring

    C. Can only monitor activity

    D. Were the first types of IDS

11. Which of the following is not a type of proxy?

    A. Reverse

    B. Web

    C. Open

    D. Simultaneous

12. IPS stands for

    A. Intrusion processing system

    B. Intrusion prevention sensor

    C. Intrusion prevention system

    D. Interactive protection system

13. A protocol analyzer can be used to

    A. Troubleshoot network problems

    B. Collect network traffic statistics

    C. Monitor for suspicious traffic

    D. All of the above

14. True or False: Windows Defender is available with every version of the Windows operating system.

    A. True

    B. False

15. Heuristic scanning looks for

    A. Normal network traffic patterns

    B. Viruses and spam only

    C. Firewall policy violations

    D. Commands or instructions that are not normally found in application programs

Answers

1. **D.** The three main types of event logs generated by Windows NT and 2000 systems are Application, System, and Security.

2. **A.** The two main types of intrusion detection systems are network-based and host-based. Network-based systems monitor network connections for suspicious traffic. Host-based systems reside on an individual system and monitor that system for suspicious or malicious activity.

3. **B.** The first commercial network-based IDS product was NetRanger, released by Wheelgroup in 1995.

4. **B.** The two main types of IDS signatures are context-based and content-based. Context-based signatures examine traffic and how that traffic fits into the other traffic around it. A port scan is a good example of a context-based signature. A content-based signature looks at what is inside the traffic, such as the contents of a specific packet.

5. **D.** A passive, host-based IDS runs on the local system, cannot interfere with traffic or activity on that system, and would have access to local system logs.

6. **B.** A network-based IDS typically cannot decrypt and read encrypted traffic. This is one of the principle weaknesses of network-based intrusion detection systems.

7. **C.** An active IDS can perform all the functions of a passive IDS (monitoring, alerting, reporting, and so on) with the added ability of responding to suspected attacks with capabilities such as sending TCP reset messages to the source and destination IP addresses.

8. **A.** Honeypots are designed to attract attackers by providing what appear to be easy, inviting targets. The honeypot collects and records the activity of attackers and their tools.

9. **C.** Egress filtering is performed to detect and stop SPAM from leaving your organization. Mail is checked as it leaves your organization.

10. **B.** Preventative intrusion detection systems are designed to "prevent" malicious actions from having any impact on the targeted system or network. For example, a host-based preventative IDS may intercept an attacker's buffer overflow attempt and prevent it from executing. By stopping the attack, the IDS prevents the attacker from affecting the system.

11. **D.** Reverse, Web, and Open are all types of proxies discussed in the chapter. Simultaneous is not a type of known proxy.

12. **C.** IPS stands for intrusion prevention system.

13. **D.** A protocol analyzer is a very flexible tool and can be used for network traffic analysis, statistics collection, and monitoring and identification of suspicious or malicious traffic.

14. **B.** False. Windows Defender is available for Windows XP, Vista, Windows Server 2003, and Windows Server 2008.

15. **D.** Heuristic scanning typically looks for commands or instructions that are not normally found in application programs.

Security Baselines

In this chapter, you will
- Learn about hardening operating systems
- Understand hardening network devices
- Discuss patch management
- Explore hardening applications
- Learn about group policies

Computers are such an integral part of everything we do today that it is difficult to imagine life without them. Operating systems, network devices, and applications all work together on millions of computers to process, transmit, and store the billions of pieces of information exchanged every day. Everything from cars to credit cards require computers to operate.

The many uses for systems and operating systems require flexible components that allow users to design, configure, and implement the systems they need. Yet it is this very flexibility that causes some of the biggest weaknesses in computer systems. Computer and operating system developers often build and deliver systems in "default" modes that do little to secure the system from external attacks. From the view of the developer, this is the most efficient mode of delivery, as there is no way they could anticipate what every user in every situation will need. From the user's view, however, this means a good deal of effort must be put into protecting and securing the system before it is ever placed into service. The process of securing and preparing a system for the production environment is called *hardening*. Unfortunately, many users don't understand the steps necessary to secure their systems effectively, resulting in hundreds of compromised systems every day.

 EXAM TIP System hardening is the process of preparing and securing a system and involves the removal of all unnecessary software and network services.

Overview Baselines

To secure systems effectively and consistently, you must take a structured and logical approach. This starts with an examination of the system's intended functions and capabilities to determine what processes and applications will be housed on the system. As a best practice, anything that is not required for operations should be removed or disabled on the system; then all the appropriate patches, hotfixes, and settings are applied to protect and secure it.

This process of establishing a system's security state is called *baselining,* and the resulting product is a security *baseline* that allows the system to run safely and securely. Once the process has been completed for a particular hardware and software combination, any similar systems can be configured with the same baseline and achieve the same level and depth of security and protection. Uniform baselines are critical in large-scale operations, as maintaining separate configurations and security levels for hundreds or thousands of systems is far too costly.

Password Selection

Password selection is one of those critical activities that is often neglected as part of a good security baseline. The heart of the problem is that most systems today are protected only by a simple user ID and password. If an attacker discovers the right user ID and password combination—either by hand or by using any of the numerous, freely available brute-force attack tools—they are in, and they have completely bypassed all the normal steps taken to secure the system. Worse still, on a server system supporting multiple users, the attacker only has to guess one correct user ID and password combination to gain access.

This basic security challenge exists for every topic we examine in this chapter, from operating systems to applications. Selecting a good password for all user accounts is critical to protecting information systems. What makes a good password? One that is still relatively easy to remember but still difficult to guess? Unfortunately, no magic answer covers all situations, but if you follow some basic guidelines and principles in choosing passwords, you can ensure that the passwords used on your system will protect your assets.

Password Policy Guidelines

A username and password is arguably the most popular security mechanism in use today. Unfortunately, it's also the most poorly configured, neglected, and easily circumvented system. The first step in addressing the password issue is to create an effective and manageable *password policy* that both system administrators and users can work with. In creating a policy, you should examine your business and security needs carefully. What level of risk is acceptable? How secure does the system need to be? How often should users change their passwords? Should you ever lock accounts? What guidelines should users use when selecting passwords? Your list of questions will vary greatly, but the key is to spend time identifying your concerns and addressing them specifically in your password policy.

Once you have created your password policy, spread the word. Make sure every user gets a copy. Post it on your company intranet. Have new users read a copy of the policy before you create an account for them. Periodically send out e-mail reminders highlighting items in the password policy. Make announcements at company gatherings. The method is not important—the goal is simply to ensure that every single user understands the policy—and follows it.

Once you have taught everyone about the policy, you must enforce it to make it effective. Set a minimum number of characters to use for passwords, and never accept a shorter password. Implement password aging and prompt users to change passwords on a regular basis. Do not accept passwords based on dictionary words. Do not allow users to use the same password over and over. Many operating systems have built-in utilities or add-ons that allow administrators to enforce good password selection, force password aging, and prevent password reuse. Here are some useful references for different operating systems:

- **Microsoft Windows** PASSFILT.DLL, introduced in Windows NT 4.0, Service Pack 2, forces users to follow specific conventions when creating new passwords: http://support.microsoft.com/support/kb/articles/q161/9/90.asp. Newer versions of Microsoft operating systems, including XP, 2003, Vista, and 2008, all have built-in capabilities to create and enforce password complexity requirements.

- **Linux**
  - **Npasswd** This replacement for passwd provides intelligent password screening to help users select a more secure password: www.utexas.edu/cc/unix/software/npasswd/.
  - **PAM (Pluggable Authentication Modules)** This provides a common authentication scheme that can be used for a variety of applications and allows administrators to set parameters such as minimum password length. Google "PAM" along with your favorite flavor of Linux for more information.

- **Solaris**
  - **PAM** Solaris also has an implementation of this common authentication scheme: www.sun.com/solaris/pam/.

Take the time to audit your own password files by running some of the popular password cracking utilities against them. In a large organization with many user accounts (more than a thousand), this will take some time and computing power, but it is well worth the effort. Perform these audits as often as you can—monthly, every other month, or every quarter. If you find accounts with easily cracked passwords, have the users review the password policy and change their passwords immediately.

Remember that many publicly available password-cracking tools are out there, and any account you crack easily can be cracked by someone else. The following are some popular password-cracking utilities:

- **Cain & Abel for Windows** www.oxid.it/cain.html
- **John the Ripper (UNIX and DOS)** www.openwall.com/
- **Crack (UNIX)** http://packetstormsecurity.nl/Crackers/crack/

Most password auditing/cracking tools can examine a password file using any or all of the following techniques:

- **Dictionary attack**   Uses a list of words as potential passwords. The tool reads each word from the list, encrypts it, and then attempts to match the encrypted result against the passwords in the password file. If the encrypted result matches a password from the password file, tool records the user ID and the matching password. This attack method is named after the practice of using entire dictionaries as the input list; many dictionary and specialized dictionary files are available for use in cracking/auditing efforts.

- **Hybrid attack**   Uses a word list and performs character substitutions or character additions on those words. For example, the tool might add numbers to the beginning or end of a word or substitute the number 3 for the letter *e*. This method takes longer than a straight dictionary attack using the same word list, because multiple modifications are made to each word in the list.

- **Brute force**   The user defines the character set to use (A–Z, a–z, 0–9, and so on) and the minimum and maximum length of the password string. Then the tool proceeds to guess every possible combination of characters using the defined character set and password length (*a*, then *aa*, then *aaa*, and so on). This method takes a substantial amount of time and processing power.

Another password auditing/cracking method that is gaining in popularity are rainbow tables. A *rainbow table* is a lookup table of precomputed password strings (usually called *hashes*). Using a lookup table of precomputed hashes can reduce the time and processing power required to audit/crack some password files as the attacker does not need to compute the hash on the fly—he can simply read the already encrypted hash from the rainbow table and match it against the password file. Not all auditing/cracking tools can make use of rainbow tables.

Selecting a Password

The many different methods of selecting a password range from random generation to one-time use. Each method has its own advantages and weaknesses, but typically when security increases, usability tends to decrease. For example, random generation tends to produce secure passwords composed of random letters (no dictionary words, and a mix of uppercase and lowercase letters with usually one or two numbers) that are very difficult to guess and will defeat most password-cracking utilities. Unfortunately, randomly generated passwords tend to be difficult to remember, and users often write down these passwords, usually in a location close to the machine, thus defeating the purpose of the password. The best compromise between security and usability lies in teaching users how to select their own secure password based on an easy-to-remember *passphrase*.

A password based on a passphrase can be formed in many ways: using the first letter of each word in a sentence; using the first letter from the first word, second letter from the second word, and so on; combining words; or replacing letters with other characters. Here are some passphrase examples and the resulting passwords:

- Use the first letter of each word in the following sentence:
  Sentence   I love to drive my 1969 Mustang!
  Password   Iltdm69M!
- Combining words and replacing letters with characters:
  Sentence   Bad to the Bone
  Password   Bad2theB1

Passphrases can be almost anything—lines from your favorite movie, lyrics from your favorite song, or something you make up on the spot. Use any method you choose, but the end result should be a difficult-to-guess, easy-to-remember password.

Components of a Good Password

By using the passphrase method, users should be able to create their own easy-to-remember passwords. However, since a password is meant to protect access and resources from intruders, it should not be easy for someone else to guess or obtain using password-cracking utilities, such as John the Ripper or Crack. To make a password more difficult to guess or obtain, it should meet the following guidelines:

- Should be at least eight characters long (some operating systems require longer passwords by default)
- Should have at least three of the following four elements:
  - One or more uppercase letters (A–Z)
  - One or more lowercase letters (a–z)
  - One or more numerals (0–9)
  - One or more special characters or punctuation marks (!@#$%^&*,.:;?)
- Should not consist of dictionary words
- Should never be the same as the user's login name or contain the login name
- Should not consist of the user's first or last name, family member's name, birth date, pet name, or any other item that is easily identified with the user

Password Aging

Given enough time and computing power, virtually any password can be cracked by simply testing all possible passwords using the brute-force method. If the same password is used forever, an attacker will, in most cases, eventually be able to get the password and access the user's account. Changing passwords on a regular basis helps protect against brute-force attacks, because when the password is changed, the attacker must restart the attack from the beginning. If the password is changed often enough, an attacker will never be able to cycle through all the possible combinations before the password is changed again.

Because almost any password can be cracked eventually, it is also important to prevent users from "recycling" passwords (using the same password over and over). Changing passwords frequently can also reduce the potential damage to the system and access an attacker has should a password be compromised. If an attacker gains access to a user account and the password is changed, the attacker may lose access to that account and have to start all over in an attempt to crack the new password. Many operating systems have options allowing system administrators to enforce password aging and prevent password reuse. Consider using the following guidelines:

- Have users change their passwords every 60 to 90 days (very secure facilities may want to change passwords every 30 to 45 days).

- Have the system "remember" each user's last five to ten passwords, and do not allow the user to use those passwords again.

Operating System and Network Operating System Hardening

The operating system (OS) of a computer is the basic software that handles things such as input, output, display, memory management, and all the other highly detailed tasks required to support the user environment and associated applications. Most users are familiar with the Microsoft family of operating systems: Windows 95, Windows 98, Windows NT, Windows 2000, Windows ME, Windows XP, Vista, Windows 2003, and Windows 2008. Indeed, the vast majority of home and business PCs run some version of a Microsoft OS. Other users may be familiar with Mac OS, Solaris, or one of the many varieties of UNIX.

A network operating system (NOS) includes additional functions and capabilities to assist in connecting computers and devices, such as printers, to a local area network (LAN). Some of the more common network OSs include Novell's Netware and Sparta-Com's LANtastic. For most modern OSs, including Windows, Solaris, and Linux, the terms *operating system* and *network operating system* are used interchangeably as they perform all the basic functions and provide enhanced capabilities for connecting to LANs.

OS developers and manufacturers all share a common problem: They cannot anticipate the many different configurations and variations that the user community will require from their products. So rather than spending countless hours and funds attempting to meet every need, manufacturers provide "default" installations for their products that usually contain the base operating system and some more commonly desirable options, such as drivers, utilities, and enhancements. As the OS could be used for any of a variety of purposes, and could be placed in any number of logical locations (local LAN, DMZ, WAN, and so on), the manufacturer typically does little to nothing regarding security. The manufacturer may provide some recommendations or simplified tools and settings to facilitate securing the system, but, in general, end users are responsible for securing their own systems. This usually involves removing unnecessary applications and utilities, disabling unneeded services, setting appropriate permissions on files, and updating the OS and application code to the latest version.

This process of securing an OS is called *hardening,* and it is intended to make the system more resistant to attack, much like armor or steel is hardened to make it less susceptible to breakage or damage. Each OS has its own approach to security, and while the process of hardening is generally the same, each OS requires that different steps be taken to secure it.

Hardening Microsoft Operating Systems

For this book, Windows XP, Vista, 2003, and 2008 are the focus of the discussion. Older Microsoft OSs, such as Windows 3.11, 95, 98, and ME were designed with little in the way of security capabilities, and not much can be done to harden those systems.

Hardening Windows 2003

In response to the public outcry demanding better security in its products, Microsoft created the Trustworthy Computing Initiative (TCI) in 2002. To produce more secure products, Microsoft adopted a "secure by design, secure by default" motto to product development, attempted to re-educate its entire development staff, and started creating freely available security resources for administrators. The first OS to benefit from the TCI was Windows 2003 Serve: fewer features were installed by default, administrators could pick and choose what functionality they needed on the server more easily, and Microsoft produced a series of hardening guides tailored to various server roles (domain controller, web server, DNS server, and so on). For example, Microsoft's *Windows Server 2003 Security Guide* provides specific recommendations on how to secure a Windows 2003 server in various operating environments. This guide is freely available for download from Microsoft at www.microsoft.com/technet/security/prodtech/windowsserver2003/w2003hg/sgch00.mspx.

In its own efforts to secure the Windows Server 2003 OS, Microsoft made some extensive modifications and added some new capabilities:

- *Internet Information Services (IIS) 6 gained the ability to isolate individual web applications into self-contained web service processes.* This prevents one application from disrupting all web services or other web applications running on the server. In addition, third-party application code runs in isolated worker processes within IIS, which by default use a lower-privileged Network Service logon account. This makes it possible to restrict a web site or application to its root directory through access control lists (ACLs).

- *By default, 19 services running under Windows 2000 were disabled in Windows Server 2003.* For example, IIS 6 must be installed by administrators: it is not part of the "default" installation as it was in Windows 2000 Server.

- *Two new service accounts with lower privilege levels were introduced.* The Network Service account can be used to run IIS processes, and the Local Service account can be used to run a service such as Secure Shell (SSH). These lower privilege accounts help isolate processes and prevent a compromise in one service from escalating into a system-level compromise.

- *The Security Configuration Wizard (SCW) was introduced.* This tool allows administrators to configure their servers with the minimal amount of functionality required. The SCW also allows administrators to run lockdown tests to ensure their security policies are achieving the desired affect.

- *The Software Restriction Policy (SRP) was introduced.* This tool gives administrators a policy-driven mechanism to identify software and control its ability to execute.

- *Enhanced audit capabilities were provided.* These allow auditing of specific users, enhanced logon/logoff auditing with IP address tracking, and operations based auditing.

- *Network Access Quarantine Control was introduced.* This allows administrators to prevent computers from connecting to the network until their configuration has been reviewed and deemed "safe."

Hardening Windows 2008

Microsoft claims that its Windows 2008 OS is its "most secure server" to date. Building on the changes it made to the Windows 2003 and Vista OSs, Microsoft attempted to add more defense-in-depth protections to the newest server OS. As with the 2003 OS, Microsoft has a free hardening guide for the 2008 OS available at http://www .microsoft.com/downloads/details.aspx?FamilyID=fb8b981f-227c-4af6-a44b-b115696a80ac&displaylang=en.

Here are some of the new security capabilities in Windows 2008:

- *Bitlocker allows for encryption of all data on a server including any data volumes.* This capability is also available in certain versions of Vista.

- *Role-based installation of functions and capabilities to minimize the server's footprint.* For example, if a server is going to be a web server, it does not need DNS or SMTP software and those features are no longer installed by default.

- *Network Access Protection (NAP) controls access to network resources based on a client computer's identity and compliance with corporate governance policy.* NAP allows network administrators to define granular levels of network access based on client identity, group membership, and the degree to which that client is compliant with corporate policies. NAP can also bring clients up-to-compliance with corporate policies. Suppose, for example, that a sales manager connects her laptop to the corporate network. NAP can be used to examine the laptop and see if it is fully patched and running a company approved antivirus product with updated signatures. If the laptop does not meet those standards, network access for that laptop can be restricted until the laptop is brought back into compliance with corporate standards.

- *Read-only domain controllers can be created and deployed in high-risk locations, but they can't be modified to add new users, change access levels, and so on.*

- *More granular password policies that allow for different password policies on a group or user basis.*

- *Web sites or web applications can be administered within IIS 7.*

Hardening UNIX- or Linux-Based Operating Systems

As a general rule, any OS can be made relatively secure, but by default UNIX systems tend to be more secure than default installations of Windows systems. However, that does not mean that UNIX systems are *completely* secure by default and don't need additional security configuration. UNIX systems, like Windows systems, need to be carefully examined, modified, and baselined to provide secure operations.

Depending on the skill and knowledge of the system administrator, securing UNIX systems can be more challenging than securing Windows systems, because UNIX is so powerful and flexible and so much control is placed in the hands of the administrator. Unlike Windows, no single UNIX manufacturer provides specific guidelines and step-by-step checklists for securing the systems. Instead, many general and version-specific guidelines must be adapted and applied to a specific version of UNIX to complete the baselining process. This section examines some of the common guidelines for a sampling of the more popular versions of UNIX.

General UNIX Baselines

General UNIX baselining is the same as baselining for Windows OSs: disable unnecessary services, restrict permissions on files and directories, remove unnecessary software, apply patches, remove unnecessary users, and apply password guidelines. Some versions of UNIX provide GUI-based tools for these tasks, while others require administrators to edit configuration files manually. In most cases, anything that can be accomplished through a GUI interface can be accomplished from the command line or by manually editing configuration files.

Like Windows systems, UNIX systems are easiest to secure and baseline if they are providing a single service or performing a single function, such as acting as a Simple Mail Transfer Protocol (SMTP) or web server. Prior to any installing or baselining being performed, the purpose of the system should be defined and all required capabilities and functions should be identified. One nice advantage of UNIX systems is that you typically have complete control over what does or does not get installed on the system. During the installation process, the administrator can select which services and applications are placed on the system, offering an opportunity to not install services and applications that will not be required. However, this assumes that the administrator knows and understands the purpose of this system, which is not always the case. In other cases, the function of the system itself may have changed.

Regardless of the installation decisions, the administrator may need to remove applications or components that are no longer needed. With UNIX systems, no "add/remove program" wizard is usually available, unlike Windows, but you will often encounter package managers that help you remove unneeded components and applications automatically. On some UNIX versions, though, you must manually delete the files associated with the applications or services you want to remove.

Services on a UNIX system can be controlled through a number of different mechanisms. As the root user, an administrator can start and stop services manually from the command line or through a GUI tool. The OS can also stop and start services automatically through configuration files (usually contained in the /etc directory). (Note that UNIX systems vary a good deal in this regard, as some use a super-server process such as inetd while others have individual configuration files for each network service.) Unlike Windows, UNIX systems can also have different *run levels*, in which the system can be configured to bring up different services depending on the run level selected.

On a running UNIX system, you can see which processes, applications, and services are running by using the process status, or **ps**, command, as shown in Figure 12-1. To stop a running service, an administrator can identify the service by its unique *process identifier (PID)* and then use the **kill** command to stop the service. For example, if you wanted to stop the klogd service in Figure 12-1, you would use the command **kill 743**. To prevent this service from starting again when the system is rebooted, you would have to modify the appropriate run levels to remove this service or modify the configuration files that control this service.

Accounts on a UNIX system can also be controlled via GUIs in some cases and command-line interfaces in others. On most popular UNIX versions, the user information can be found in the passwd file located in the /etc directory. By manually editing this file, you can add, delete, or modify user accounts on the system. By examining this file, an administrator can see which user accounts exist on the system and then determine which accounts to remove or disable. On most UNIX systems, if you remove the user account from the passwd file, you must manually remove any files that belong to

```
C:\WINNT\System32\telnet.exe                                            _ □ ×
UID          PID    PPID   C STIME TTY          TIME CMD
root           1      0    0 May13 ?        00:00:04 init
root           2      1    0 May13 ?        00:00:00 [keventd]
root           3      1    0 May13 ?        00:00:00 [kapmd]
root           4      1    0 May13 ?        00:00:00 [ksoftirqd_CPU0]
root           5      1    0 May13 ?        00:00:24 [kswapd]
root           6      1    0 May13 ?        00:00:05 [bdflush]
root           7      1    0 May13 ?        00:00:00 [kupdated]
root           8      1    0 May13 ?        00:00:00 [mdrecoveryd]
root          16      1    0 May13 ?        00:00:04 [kjournald]
root          95      1    0 May13 ?        00:00:00 [khubd]
root         223      1    0 May13 ?        00:00:00 [kjournald]
root         224      1    0 May13 ?        00:00:13 [kjournald]
root         225      1    0 May13 ?        00:00:00 [kjournald]
root         739      1    0 May13 ?        00:00:01 syslogd -m 0
root         744      1    0 May13 ?        00:00:00 klogd -x
rpc          764      1    0 May13 ?        00:00:00 portmap
rpcuser      792      1    0 May13 ?        00:00:00 rpc.statd
root         904      1    0 May13 ?        00:00:00 /usr/sbin/apmd -p 10 -w 5 -W -P
root         959      1    0 May13 ?        00:00:00 /usr/sbin/sshd
root         992      1    0 May13 ?        00:00:00 xinetd -stayalive -reuse -pidfil
root        1020      1    0 May13 ?        00:00:00 sendmail: accepting connections
root        1039      1    0 May13 ?        00:00:00 gpm -t ps/2 -m /dev/mouse
--More--
```

Figure 12-1   Running the ps command on a UNIX system

that user, including home directories. Most modern UNIX versions store the actual password associated with a user account in a *shadow file* located in the /etc directory. The shadow file contains the actual password hashes for each user account and is readable only by the root user (or a process with root-level permissions).

How you patch a UNIX system depends a great deal on the UNIX version in use and the patch being applied. In some cases, a patch will consist of a series of manual steps requiring the administrator to replace files, change permissions, and alter directories. In other cases, the patches are executable scripts or utilities that perform the patch actions automatically. Some UNIX versions, such as Red Hat and Solaris, have built-in utilities that handle the patching process. In those cases, the administrator downloads a specifically formatted file that the patching utility then processes to perform any modifications or updates that need to be made.

To better illustrate UNIX baselines, we will examine two popular UNIX-based operating systems: Solaris and Red Hat Linux.

Solaris   The Solaris OS, developed and distributed by Sun Microsystems, has been an extremely popular choice in high-performance and high-availability environments. As a commercial OS, Solaris is typically bundled with a hardware platform from Sun, but it can be purchased separately and is even available for Intel-based processor platforms (Solaris x86). For more secure environments, a specially hardened version called Trusted Solaris is available, though this is typically used only by the government, military, and banking communities.

Baselining a Solaris system is fairly simple. Once the system's purpose is defined, installation is typically done through a graphical interface that allows the administrator to select which applications and services should be loaded on the system. On a running Solaris system, patches and services can be added or removed using the **pkgadd** command, which adds binary packages, and the **pkgrm** command, which removes binary packages.

The binary packages themselves are unusable in the format in which they are downloaded or delivered on removable media. The pkg utilities take care of interpreting the package's software control files to determine where to install or remove files or directories. Any package handled by the Solaris system is stored in a package information database, so administrators can easily obtain a list of currently installed software. Software can also be installed or removed using the Admintool shown in Figure 12-2.

Obtaining a list of running services on a Solaris system is much the same as on all UNIX systems. You can use the **ps** command to view running processes, and you can examine the Internet servers configuration file, called inetd.conf in Solaris. The inetd. conf file, located in the /etc directory, contains a list of services controlled by the Internet services daemon, simply called *inetd*. On Solaris and many other UNIX variants, inetd listens for incoming connections on the TCP and UDP ports associated with each of the services listed in its configuration file, inetd.conf. When a connection request is received, inetd will launch the program or process associated with that service, if necessary, and pass the connection request to the appropriate service. To prevent unwanted services from running and processing requests, administrators can edit inetd.conf and either comment out or remove the lines for the services they want to disable. On most

Figure 12-2
The Solaris
Admintool is used
to add or remove
software.

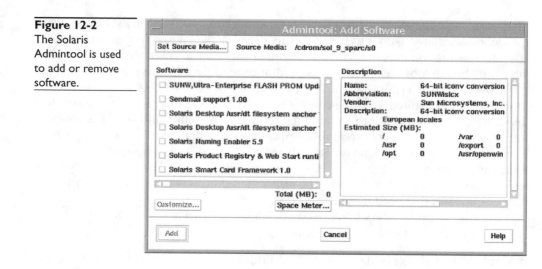

UNIX systems, you can simply add the # character to the beginning of each line you want to comment out.

In addition to disabling or removing unnecessary network services, Solaris allows administrators to use local security mechanisms called *TCP wrappers* that provide additional layers of security for network services. TCP wrappers are essentially filters that compare incoming connection requests to lists of authorized and unauthorized connections. If a connection is authorized, it is permitted to reach the network service it is attempting to contact. If a connection is unauthorized, it is dropped by the TCP wrappers. These functions are controlled by two files: hosts.allow and hosts.deny. The hosts.allow file contains a list of IP addresses or subnets that are allowed to connect to a specific service, such as **10.0.0.0: FTP**, which would allow any address in the 10.X.X.X network to connect to the FTP service on the local machine. In more secure installations, the hosts.allow file is populated, and the entry **ALL: ALL** is placed in the hosts.deny file. This type of configuration will reject any inbound connections to the local system unless they are specifically authorized by the hosts.allow file.

TIP TCP wrappers can be a great additional layer of protection for UNIX systems. When creating a security baseline for UNIX systems, be sure to consider the use of TCP wrappers.

Securing access to files and directories in Solaris is done in the same manner as in most UNIX variants. Each file and directory has a list of associated permissions for the owner of the file or directory, the group of users to which the owner of the file or directory belongs, and anyone else (often called the "world"). The permissions are listed in owner-group-world order and consist of three values for each grouping: read, write, and execute. The logical representation looks like this: **rwx rwx rwx**. Read (**r**) allows for viewing of the file or listing of the directory. Write (**w**) allows for modification of the file or directory. Execute (**x**) allows the file, usually an executable or script, to be run. If you want a file to have read, write, and execute permissions for the owner, read and write permissions for the group, and no permissions for the world, the permissions could be logically represented as shown here:

Owner	Group	World
rwx	**rw-**	**---**

In Solaris, you can use the **chmod** command to modify the permissions associated with a file or directory. Similarly, the **chown** command allows you to modify the ownership of a file or directory, and **chgrp** allows you to change the group ownership of a file or directory. To secure a Solaris system adequately, you should ensure that all configuration and system files have appropriately restrictive permissions—you don't want any user on the system to be able to modify inted.conf without appropriate access. To assist you in securing files and directories, many different resources are available on Sun's web site, as well as on security-related web sites.

A crucial step in baselining a Solaris system is to ensure that all the latest patches and fixes are in place. Patches for Solaris systems are typically distributed from Sun and are available from Sun's web site but can also be obtained on CD, floppy, or tape in some cases. Once obtained, patches must be processed, and Solaris provides several tools to assist administrators in managing and maintaining patches: **patchadd**, **patchrm**, **smpatch**, and **pkgparam**. The **patchadd** command can be used to add patches to the system as well as obtain information about what patches are currently installed on the system. The **patchrm** command can be used to remove installed patches from the system. The **smpatch** command is used to process signed patches. The **pkgparam** command shows patches installed for a specific software package. In addition to the command-line tools, Solaris provides a GUI-based management console, called the Solaris Management Console, that provides the same level of functionality. The Solaris Management Console is shown in Figure 12-3.

In spite of the security efforts identified so far, a Solaris system can still be easily compromised if the user base is not effectively managed and maintained. The keys to protecting accounts and system access are to remove or disable unused accounts and to ensure that all accounts are secured with a good, strong password. In Solaris, user accounts are maintained in the passwd file, and groups are maintained in the groups file, both of which are located in the /etc directory. Three main methods are used for maintaining users and groups on a Solaris system: manually editing the required configuration files, using command-line interface tools such as **useradd**, and using the management console. Each method can be used interchangeably, offering a level of flexibility not found on Windows systems. Removing unused user accounts can be accomplished through any of these methods—the end result is the same.

The second step to managing your user base effectively is to ensure that users select good passwords. On Solaris systems, passwords are generally stored in a separate shadow file that contains the encrypted password for each account on the system; it must therefore be guarded and protected appropriately. An administrator can use any of a

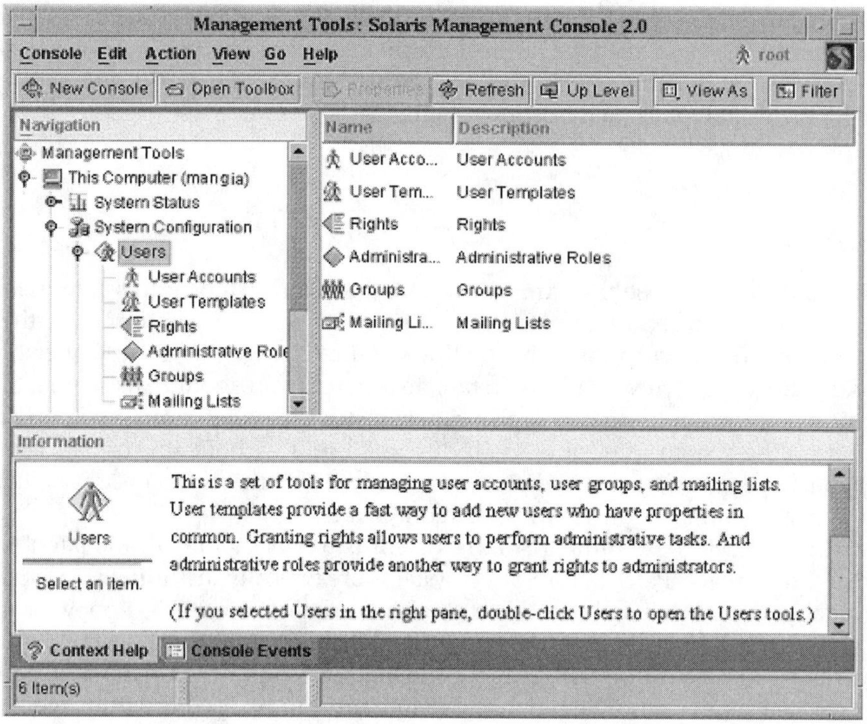

Figure 12-3 Solaris Management Console

number of popular password-cracking programs to check the user passwords to ensure that they are not easily guessed or based on a simple dictionary word. Additionally, Solaris already imposes some restrictions on what is considered a "suitable" password for users. In most implementations, a password must be at least six characters long, must contain at least two letters and one number or symbol, must not be the same as the login ID, and must be different than the user's previous password. If these are not strict enough guidelines, the administrator can alter these parameters by using the **passwd** command and the appropriate option flag or by modifying the parameters in /etc/default/passwd. Solaris also supports Pluggable Authentication Modules (PAM), a mechanism for providing interoperation and secure access to a variety of services on different platforms.

Linux Linux is a rather unique OS that is UNIX-based, very powerful, open source, can be obtained for free, and is available in many different distributions from several vendors. Linux was initially conceived and written by Linus Torvalds in 1991. His concept of creating a lightweight, flexible, and free OS gave rise to an entirely new OS that is very popular and is installed on millions of computers around the world. Due to its open nature, the entire source-code base for the OS is available to anyone who wants to examine it, modify it, or recompile it for specific uses. Linux is a favored OS among security professionals, system administrators, and other highly technical users who enjoy the flexibility and power that Linux provides.

While most versions of Linux can be obtained for free simply by downloading them from the Internet (including major commercial distributions), you can also purchase commercial versions of the Linux OS from vendors, such as Red Hat, Slackware, SuSE, and Debian, who have built a business out of providing custom versions of Linux along with support and training. Red Hat is arguably the most popular of these commercial Linux distributions, and it is used as the example for the rest of this section. Regardless of which Linux version you prefer, baselining a Linux system follows the same guidelines as any other UNIX system: disable unnecessary services, restrict permissions on files and directories, remove unnecessary software, apply patches, remove unnecessary users, and apply password guidelines.

Services under Linux are normally controlled by their own configuration files or by xinetd, the extended Internet services daemon and a secure version of the inetd super-server daemon. Instead of starting all Internet services, such as FTP servers, at system startup, Linux uses xinetd (or sometimes inetd) to listen for incoming connections. Xinetd listens to all the appropriate ports (those that match the services in its configuration files), and when a connection request comes in, xinetd starts the appropriate server and hands over the connection request. This "master process" approach makes it fairly simple to disable unwanted services—all the configuration information for each server is located in /etc/xinetd.d with a configuration file for each process, as shown in Figure 12-4.

Inside each configuration file are the options to be used when starting the service, the location where the server binary is located, and the disable flag. By changing the value of the disable flag to "yes," you can disable any process controlled by xinetd. Figure 12-5 shows the configuration file for the Telnet service on a Red Hat Linux system. Services in Red Hat Linux can also be configured via a GUI-based utility, as shown in

```
[root@Jeep xinetd.d]# ls -la
total 64
drwxr-xr-x    2 root     root         4096 Feb 16 17:54
drwxr-xr-x   62 root     root         4096 Apr  5 15:18
-rw-r--r--    1 root     root          563 Nov 19 11:00 chargen
-rw-r--r--    1 root     root          580 Nov 19 11:00 chargen-udp
-rw-r--r--    1 root     root          419 Nov 19 11:00 daytime
-rw-r--r--    1 root     root          438 Nov 19 11:00 daytime-udp
-rw-r--r--    1 root     root          341 Nov 19 11:00 echo
-rw-r--r--    1 root     root          360 Nov 19 11:00 echo-udp
-rw-r--r--    1 root     root          312 Nov 19 11:00 servers
-rw-r--r--    1 root     root          314 Nov 19 11:00 services
-rw-r--r--    1 root     root          392 Apr  7  2002 sgi_fam
-rw-r--r--    1 root     root          363 Nov 20 11:24 swat
-rw-r--r--    1 root     root          304 Feb 16 16:54 telnet
-rw-r--r--    1 root     root          497 Nov 19 11:00 time
-rw-r--r--    1 root     root          518 Nov 19 11:00 time-udp
-rw-r--r--    1 root     root          329 Feb 16 16:55 wu-ftpd
[root@Jeep xinetd.d]# _
```

Figure 12-4   Listing of server configuration files for xinetd

```
[root@Jeep xinetd.d]# more telnet
# default: on
# description: The telnet server serves telnet sessions; it uses \
#             unencrypted username/password pairs for authentication.
service telnet
{
        flags           = REUSE
        socket_type     = stream
        wait            = no
        user            = root
        server          = /usr/sbin/in.telnetd
        log_on_failure  += USERID
        disable         = no
}

[root@Jeep xinetd.d]#
```

Figure 12-5   Telnet service configuration file under Red Hat Linux

Figure 12-6. Regardless of the method chosen, the end result should be the same—all unnecessary services should be removed or disabled.

Permissions under Linux are the same as for other UNIX-based OSs. Permissions can be set for owner, group, and others (or world). Permissions are based on the same read-write-execute principle and can be adjusted using the **chmod** command. Individual and group ownership information can be changed using **chown** and **chgrp**, respec-

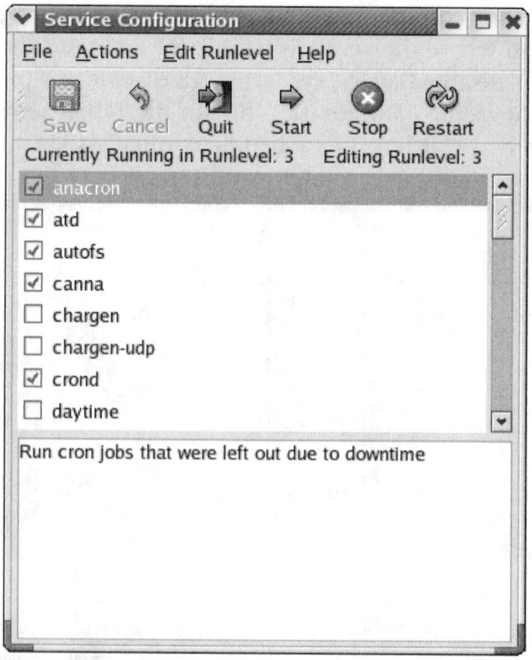

Figure 12-6
Red Hat Linux's
GUI-based service
configuration

tively. As with other baselining exercises, permissions should be as restrictive as functionally possible, giving read-only access when possible and write or execute access when necessary.

Adding and removing software under Linux is typically done through a package manager. In Red Hat Linux, the package manager is called Red Hat Package Manager, or rpm for short. Using rpm, you can add, modify, update, or remove software packages from your system. Using the **rpm -qa** command will show you a list of all the software packages installed on your Red Hat system. You can remove any packages you do not want to leave installed using the **rpm -e** command. As with most things under Linux, a GUI-based utility is available to accomplish this same task. The GUI-based Package Management utility is shown in Figure 12-7.

Patching and keeping a Red Hat Linux system up-to-date is a fairly simple exercise, as well. Red Hat has provided an Update Agent that, once configured, will examine your system, obtain the list of available updates from Red Hat, and, if desired, install those updates on your system. As with any other OS, you must maintain the patch level of your Red Hat system. For more information on the Red Hat Update Agent, see the "Updates (a.k.a. Hotfixes, Service Packs, and Patches)" section later in this chapter.

Managing and maintaining user accounts under Linux can be accomplished with either the command line or a GUI. Unlike some other OSs, only one default account for Linux systems has privileged access—the root or superuser account. (Other default

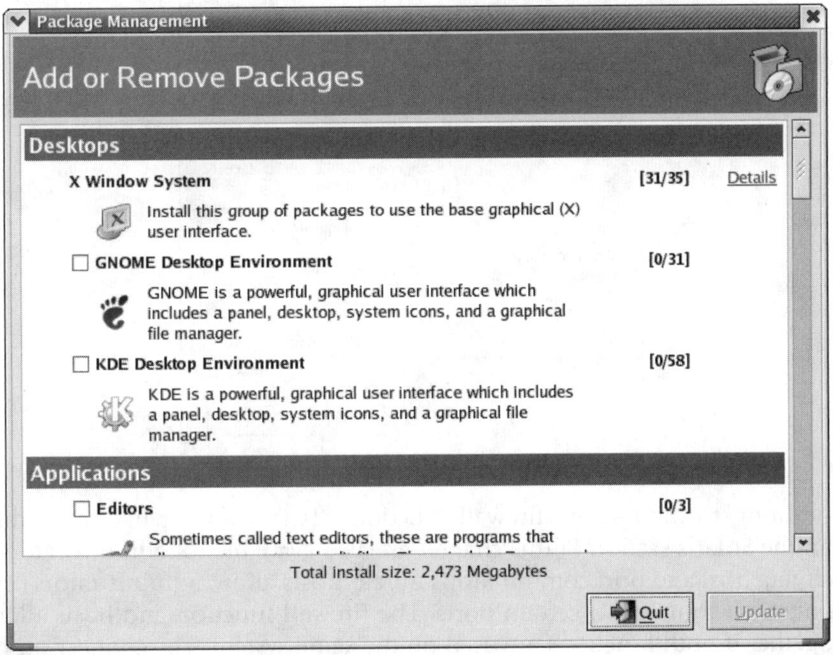

Figure 12-7   Red Hat Package Management utility

accounts exist, such as system or operator, but quite often those accounts are automatically configured so that no user can ever log in using that account.) The root account has complete and total control over the system and should therefore be protected with an exceptionally strong password. Many administrators configure their systems to prevent anyone from logging in directly as root; instead, they must log in with their own personal accounts and switch to the root account using the **su** command. Adding user accounts can be done with the **useradd** command, and unwanted user accounts can be removed using the **userdel** command. In addition, you can manually edit /etc/passwd to add or remove user accounts. User accounts can also be managed via a GUI, as shown in Figure 12-8.

For increased local security, Red Hat also provides a built-in firewall function that can be managed either via the command line or through a GUI, as shown in the following illustration. To protect network access to the local system, administrators can control to which ports external users may connect, such as mail, FTP, or web. Administrators can choose a security level, from high, medium, off, and a customized option, where they can individually select to which ports on which interfaces external users may connect.

In addition to the built-in firewall functions, TCP wrappers like those discussed earlier in the Solaris section of this chapter are also available for administrators to use. By specifying host and port combinations in /etc/hosts.allow, administrators can allow certain hosts to connect on certain ports. The firewall function and hosts.allow must work together if both functions are used on the same system. The connection must be allowed by both utilities or it will be dropped.

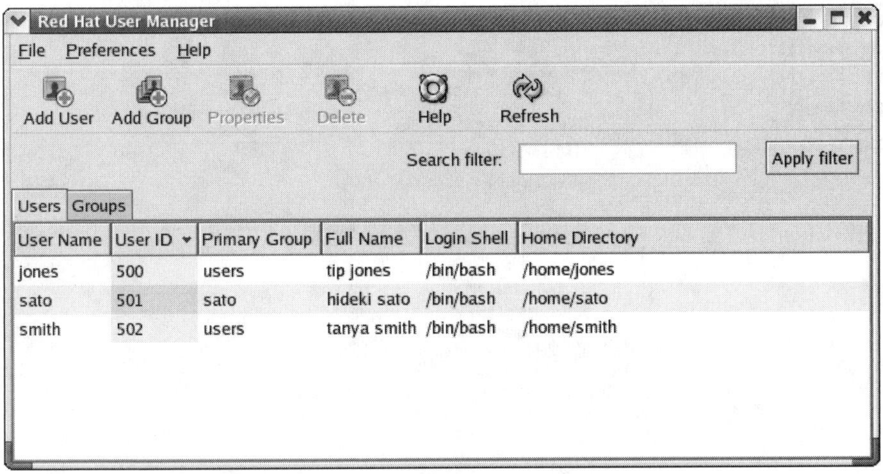

Figure 12-8   Managing user accounts with the Red Hat User Manager

Mac OS

Apple's latest version of its operating system is essentially a new variant of the UNIX operating system. While this brings a new level of power, flexibility, and stability to Mac users everywhere, it also brings a new level of security concerns. Traditionally, the Mac OS was largely ignored by the hacker community—the deployment was relatively small, largely being restricted to individual users or departments, and more difficult to obtain information. With the migration to a UNIX-based OS, Mac users should anticipate a sharp increase in unwanted attention and scrutiny from potential attackers.

Because it is a UNIX-based OS, the same rough guidelines for all UNIX systems apply to Mac OS X. As with Solaris, Linux, and all the other UNIX variants, each workstation can become an instant server by installing the right application or enabling a specific service. As with other UNIX variants, it is important with Mac OS X that unnecessary services, such as web, mail, FTP, and so on, are disabled unless they are going to be properly configured and secured. Mac OS services can be manually controlled by editing the appropriate files, as with other UNIX variants, but one of Apple's strengths (or weaknesses, depending on how you look at it) is providing user interfaces that greatly simplify tasks for their user base. For example, within Mac OS X, Apple has provided Services, Firewall, and Internet tabs under the Sharing window. As Figure 12-9 shows, certain services can be turned on or off simply by clicking the box next to the appropriate service.

The Firewall tab similarly provides users with the ability to restrict incoming connections to the system, again by simply clicking the box next to the service a user wants to allow to reach a computer, as shown in Figure 12-10.

For Mac OS X users, the task of identifying and disabling unwanted services is relatively simple compared to those for other OSs. Apple has conveniently located the

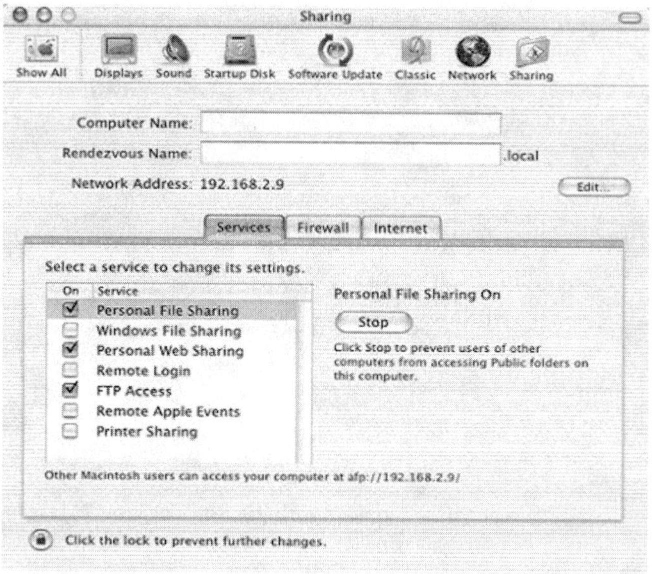

Figure 12-9
Turning services
on and off in the
Services tab in
Mac OS X

services and the firewall functions together and has reduced the administration tasks to selecting the appropriate check boxes.

File permissions in Mac OS X are nearly identical to those in any other UNIX variant and are based on separate read, write, and execute permissions for owner, group, and

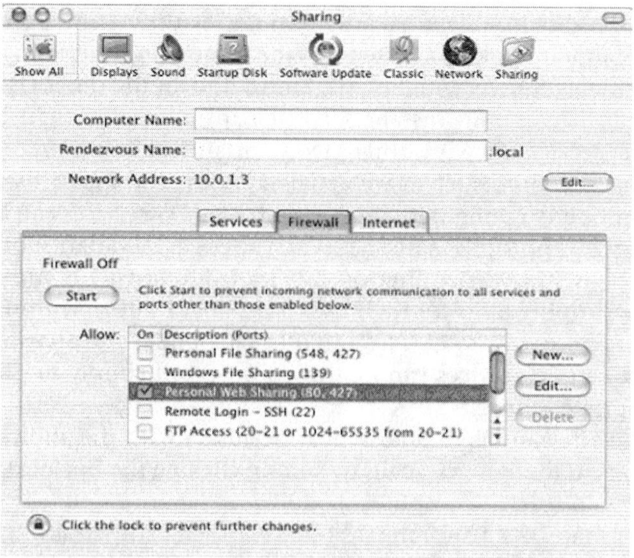

Figure 12-10
Turning the firewall
settings on and off
in the Firewall tab in
Mac OS X

world. While these permissions can be adjusted manually from a command-line interface, with the standard **chown**, **chmod**, and **chgrp** commands, Apple again provides some nice interface capabilities for viewing and managing file and directory permissions. By selecting the properties of any given file or folder, the user can view and modify the permissions for that file or folder, as shown in Figure 12-11. Note that the GUI follows the same user-group-world pattern of permissions as other UNIX variants, though Apple uses the term *others* as opposed to *world*.

This GUI allows users to restrict access to sensitive files and directories quickly and effectively. By default, Mac OS X limits a user's ability to access or modify certain areas of the file system, including those areas containing system binaries. However, these restrictions can be circumvented by a user with the appropriate permissions or by certain third-party applications.

Removing unwanted or unnecessary programs in Mac OS X is usually done through the program's own uninstaller utility or by simply using the Finder to locate and then delete the folder containing the program and associated utilities. Like Windows, Mac OS X maps certain file extensions to specific programs, so deleting a program that handles specific extension types may require that an administrator clear up associated extensions.

Like most UNIX-based OSs, Mac OS X is a multiuser platform. As part of the baselining effort, the active user accounts should be examined to ensure they have the right level of access, permissions, group memberships, and so on. In addition, any accounts that are not used should be removed from the system completely. To access the user

PART IV

Figure 12-11
Setting file permissions in Mac OS X

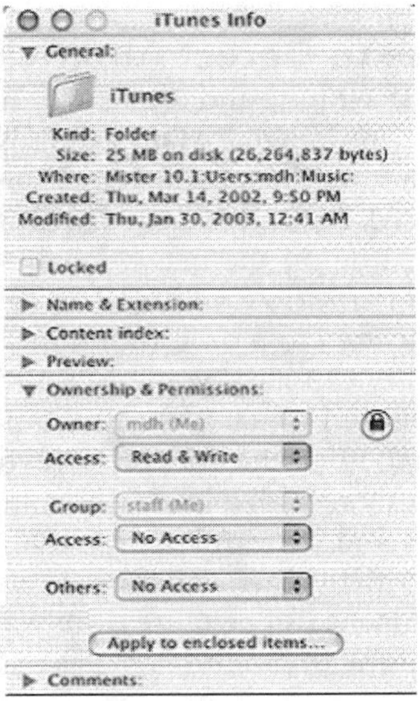

accounts under Mac OS X, select the Users icons under System Preferences—this should display the Users window, shown here.

As you can see, adding, editing, and deleting users is simply a matter of selecting the user account and clicking the correct button on the right side of the window.

Mac OS X also permits administrators to lock accounts so they can be modified only by users with administrative-level privileges. Those who are familiar with UNIX OSs may notice something odd about Mac OS X—no root account is enabled by default. The root account does exist and can be enabled, but for "security reasons," it is not enabled by default.

Using Baselines to Detect Anomalies

One advantage to developing and implementing baselines is the ability to detect when something doesn't "look right." Many administrators use system monitors or similar tools that tell them how "busy" a system is—what processes are running, how much memory is being used, how many active network connections exist, the CPU load, and so on. The same is true on the network side where administrators will use network monitors to look at traffic flow, volume, source addresses, and so on. While these types of tools are typically used to monitor for things like network congestion or impending hardware failure, they can also be used to detect security-related anomalies. If something looks "out of the ordinary," such as a network server that is using three times more memory than it normally does or a network traffic volume that is ten times higher than any previously recorded level, this could indicate an attack or successful compromise. If profiles and performance baselines are developed for "normal" network traffic and system activity, then "abnormal" activity, which is often associated with a security-related anomaly, can be more readily identified using the same tools administrators are already using to monitor systems and networks.

Updates (a.k.a. Hotfixes, Service Packs, and Patches)

Operating systems are large and complex mixes of interrelated software modules written by dozens or even thousands of separate individuals. With the push toward GUI-based functionality and enhanced capabilities that has occurred over the past several years, OSs have continued to grow and expand. Windows 2003 contains approximately 50 million lines of code, and though it may be one of the largest OS programs in that respect, other modern OSs are not far behind. As OSs continue to grow and introduce new functions, the potential for problems with the code grows as well. It is almost impossible for an OS vendor to test its product on every possible platform under every possible circumstance, so functionality and security issues do arise after an OS has been released.

To the average user or system administrator, this means a fairly constant stream of updates designed to correct problems, replace sections of code, or even add new features to an installed OS. Vendors typically follow a hierarchy for software updates:

- **Hotfix** This term refers to a (usually) small software update designed to address a specific problem, such as a buffer overflow in an application that exposes the system to attacks. Hotfixes are typically developed in reaction to a discovered problem and are produced and released rather quickly.

- **Patch** This term refers to a more formal, larger software update that can address several or many software problems. Patches often contain enhancements or additional capabilities as well as fixes for known bugs. Patches are usually developed over a longer period of time.

- **Service pack** This refers to a large collection of patches and hotfixes that are rolled into a single, rather large package. Service packs are designed to bring a system up to the latest known good level all at once, rather than requiring the user or system administrator to download dozens or hundreds of updates separately.

Every OS, from Linux to Solaris to Windows, requires software updates, and each has different methods of assisting users in keeping their systems up to date. Microsoft, for example, typically makes updates available for download from its web site. While most administrators or technically proficient users may prefer to identify and download updates individually, Microsoft recognizes that nontechnical users prefer a simpler approach, which is built into it Internet Explorer browser. By selecting Windows Update from the Tools menu in Internet Explorer, users will be taken to the Microsoft web site. By selecting "Scan For Updates," users can allow their systems to be examined for needed or required updates. The web site will identify which updates the user's system needs and provide the user with the option to download and install the required updates. While this typically requires admin or power-user level access, it does simplify the update process for most users.

In addition to a web-based update utility, Microsoft also provides an automated update functionality that will, once configured, locate any required updates, download them to your system, and even install the updates if that is your preference. Figure 12-12 shows the Automatic Updates window, which can be found in the Control Panel. Note that both the web-based updates and automatic updates require active Internet connections to retrieve information and updates from Microsoft.

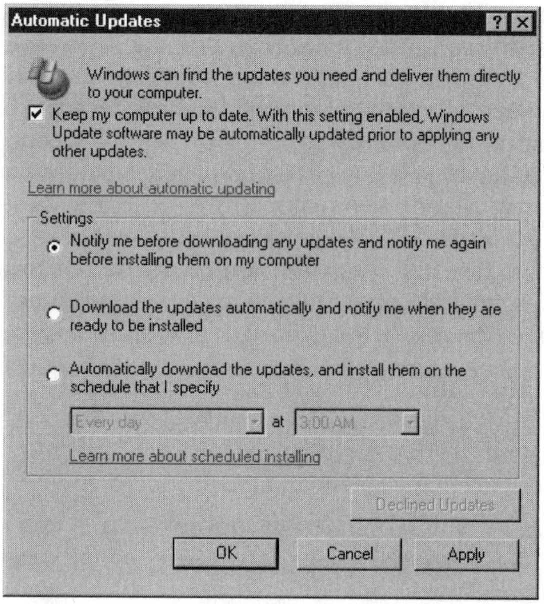

Figure 12-12
Setting up
Microsoft's
Automatic
Updates utility in
Windows 2000

Microsoft is not alone in providing utilities to assist users in keeping their systems up-to-date and secure. The latest versions of Red Hat Linux contain a utility called the Red Hat Update Agent, which does essentially the same thing. By registering your system and user profile with Red Hat, you can obtain a customized list of updates for your specific system. By customizing your system profile, as shown in Figure 12-13, you can even tell the Red Hat Update Agent to look for updates on specific packages only.

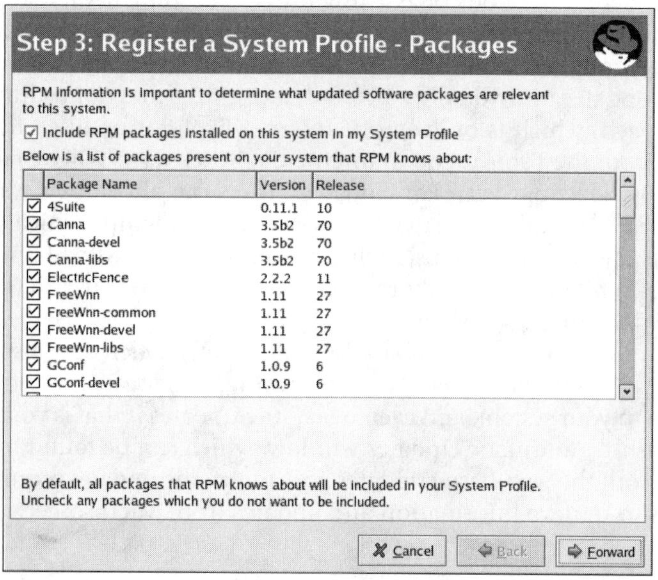

Figure 12-13
Registering a system
with the Red Hat
Update Agent

Once the profile has been built, the Update Agent contacts the Red Hat update server to obtain information on available updates for the packages selected in the profile. Once a list of updates is obtained, the Update Agent allows the user to select which updates to download and install, as shown in Figure 12-14. This lets users selectively download and install updates at their convenience. An active Internet connection is required to use the Red Hat Update Agent.

Regardless of the method used to update the OS, it is critically important that you keep systems up to date. New security advisories are issued every day, and while a buffer overflow may be a "potential" problem today, it will almost certainly become a "definite" problem in the near future. Much like the steps taken to baseline and initially secure an OS, keeping every system patched and up to date is critical to protecting the system and the information it contains.

Network Hardening

While considering the baseline security of systems, you must consider the role the network connection plays in the overall security profile. The tremendous growth of the Internet and the affordability of multiple PCs and Ethernet networking have resulted in almost every computer to be attached to some kind of network, and once computers are attached to a network, they are open to access from any other user on that network. Proper controls over network access must be established on computers by controlling the services that are running and the ports that are opened for network access. In addition to servers and workstations, however, network devices must also be examined: routers, switches, and modems, as well as other various components.

Today's network infrastructure components are similar to other computing devices on the network—they have dedicated hardware that runs an OS, typically with one or

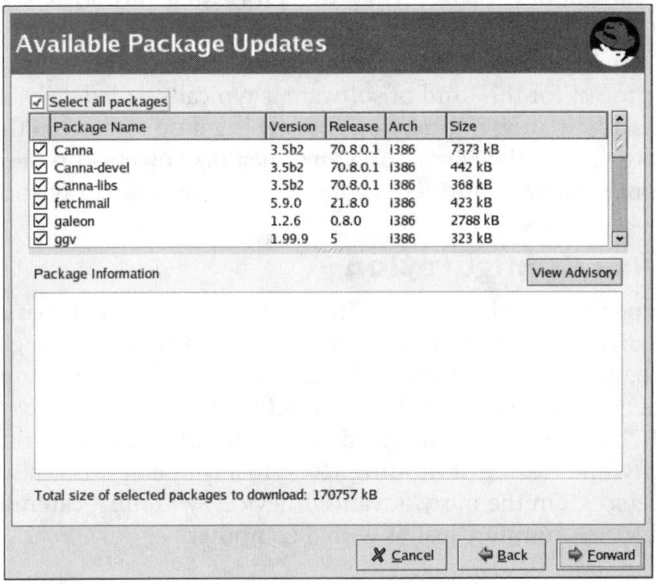

Figure 12-14
Selecting from available updates in the Red Hat Update Agent

Available Package Updates

☑ Select all packages

Package Name	Version	Release	Arch	Size
☑ Canna	3.5b2	70.8.0.1	i386	7373 kB
☑ Canna-devel	3.5b2	70.8.0.1	i386	442 kB
☑ Canna-libs	3.5b2	70.8.0.1	i386	368 kB
☑ fetchmail	5.9.0	21.8.0	i386	423 kB
☑ galeon	1.2.6	0.8.0	i386	2788 kB
☑ ggv	1.99.9	5	i386	323 kB

Package Information   View Advisory

Total size of selected packages to download: 170757 kB

✗ Cancel   ⇦ Back   ⇨ Forward

more open ports for direct connection to the OS, as well as ports supporting various network services. Any flaws in the coding of the OS can be exploited to gain access as with any "regular" computer. These network devices should be configured with very strict parameters to maintain network security. Like normal computer OSs that need to be patched and updated, the software that runs network infrastructure components needs to be updated regularly. Finally, an outer layer of security should be added by implementing appropriate firewall rules and router ACLs.

Software Updates

Maintaining current vendor patch levels for your software is one of the most important things you can do to maintain security. This is also true for the infrastructure that runs the network. While some equipment is unmanaged and typically has no network presence and few security risks, any managed equipment that is responding on network ports will have some software or firmware controlling it. This software or firmware needs to be updated on a regular basis.

The most common device that connects people to the Internet is the network router. Dozens of brands of routers are available on the market, but Cisco Systems products dominate. The popular Internetwork Operating System (IOS) runs on more than 70 of Cisco's devices and is installed countless times at countless locations. Its popularity has fueled research into vulnerabilities in the code, and over the past few years quite a few vulnerabilities have been reported. These vulnerabilities can take many forms as routers send and receive several different kinds of traffic, from the standard Telnet remote terminal, to routing information in the form of Routing Information Protocol (RIP) or Open Shortest Path First (OSPF) packets, to Simple Network Management Protocol (SNMP) packets. This highlights the need to update the IOS software on a regular basis.

Cisco's IOS also runs on many of its Ethernet switching products. Like routers, these have capabilities for receiving and processing protocols such as Telnet and SNMP. Smaller network components do not usually run large software suites and typically have smaller software loaded on internal Nonvolatile RAM (NVRAM). While the update process for this kind of software is typically called a *firmware update*, this does not change the security implications of keeping it up to date. In the case of a corporate network with several devices, someone must take ownership of updating the devices, and updates must be performed regularly according to security and administration policies.

Device Configuration

As important as it is to keep software up to date, properly configuring network devices is equally, if not more, important. Many network devices, such as routers and switches, now have advanced remote management capabilities with multiple open ports accepting network connections. Proper configuration is necessary to keep these devices secure. Choosing a good password is very important in maintaining external and internal security, and closing or limiting access to any open ports is also a good step for securing the devices. On the more advanced devices, you must carefully consider what services the device is running, just as with a computer.

In many cases, a network device's primary protection method is a password. Good passwords are one of the most effective security tools, because a good password can be resistant to several forms of attack. This resistance makes an attacker use simple brute-forcing methods, taking tremendous amounts of time and generating a large amount of network traffic, both increasing the likelihood of the attacker's efforts being detected. Unfortunately, good passwords are often hard to remember, so weaker passwords are usually used.

To recognize the impact on security that a bad password can have, consider the fact that a typical brute-force program can try every word in the unabridged English dictionary in less than a day, but it would take several thousand years to attempt to brute-force an eight-character password. This is based upon using not only the standard 26-character alphabet, but also adding capitalization for 26 more characters, numeric digits for 10 more, and special characters, adding another 32 different characters. This totals 95 different characters that can be used, giving 6,704,780,954,517,120, or 6 quadrillion different possibilities for a one- to eight-character password. This is in stark contrast to the estimated 2 million words in the English language, or the 217 billion possibilities provided by simple lowercase alphabetic characters.

The best kinds of passwords bear no resemblance to actual words, such as "AvhB42^&nFh." However, although such passwords provide greater security, they are difficult to remember, leading users to choose passwords that are based on regular dictionary words. While this is a concern for any password on any system, it is of greater concern on network infrastructure equipment, because many pieces of network equipment require only password authentication for access—typically, no username is required.

One of the password-related issues that many administrators overlook is SNMP, which was developed in 1988 and has been implemented on a huge variety of network devices. Its wide implementation is directly related to its simplicity and extensibility. Since every manufacturer can add objects to the Management Information Base (MIB), one manufacturer can add functionality without interfering with any other manufacturer's portion of the MIB tree. This feature of the protocol lets manufacturers make SNMP very powerful for configuration and monitoring purposes. The downside is that many devices have SNMP turned on by default. Network administrators not using SNMP will often forget to disable SNMP or will forget to change the well-known default passwords—typically "public" for read-only access and "private" for read/write access. With the SNMP service active and using a default password, an attacker can retrieve a great deal of interesting information from a network device, as well as altering any SNMP-capable settings. If SNMP is employed, well-thought-out passwords should be used, as well as a schedule for password updates.

 EXAM TIP The use of the word "public" as a public SNMP community string is an extremely well-known vulnerability. Any system using an SNMP community string of "public" should be changed immediately.

Keep in mind that SNMP passwords are often passed in the clear, so it should never be treated as a trusted protocol. The SNMP service should also be limited only to connections from the management station's IP address. If SNMP is not used, the service should be disabled, if possible. Otherwise, the ports for SNMP should not be accessible from anywhere on the external or internal network.

As with any system, security is largely dependent on proper configuration of the system itself. A router can be secured with proper configuration just as easily as it can be left unsecured through poor configuration. Good passwords and knowledge of what services the devices are running is important to maintaining the security of those devices.

Ports and Services

A part of configuration that deserves its own section is the configuration of ports and services. For any networked machine, you need to take care to establish which ports and services are running and then conduct regular audits to ensure that only the authorized ports and services are open.

The advent and growth of networks permit almost any machine to be electronically connected to any other machine. This is a danger, as many machines are designed around a principle of trusting any other system on their local network. Many machines have default configurations that offer a wide variety of services to the network, resulting in a large number of open ports. The overarching rule of security is to give an attacker as little information or opportunity as possible, whether the attacker is inside or outside your network. While not all ports can be dangerous, they can provide information, so it is best to open only ports that are necessary to run the services that the machine provides. By limiting the number of open ports, you reduce not only the possible avenues an attacker can use to compromise a machine, but also the amount of information that an attacker can retrieve about the system.

Table 12-1 shows an example output from a very popular port scanning program called nmap. This tool checks remote systems for open services and reports back which services are open and accepting connections and which ports are closed and not accepting connections. In this example, nmap has scanned for open services on 1013 different ports—any port not listed in Table 12-1 is closed.

Table 12-1 shows interesting ports on localhost (127.0.0.1). The 1013 ports scanned but not shown are in a closed state. Many ports are left open by default on Windows systems, such as 135 epmap, 139 netbios-ssn, and 445 microsoft-ds.

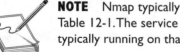

NOTE Nmap typically lists open services as "number/protocol," as shown in Table 12-1. The service name is a "best guess" by nmap based on the service typically running on that specific port.

Typically, most servers are used to provide one or two services, the most prevalent service on Internet servers being web and secure web, or 80/tcp and 443/tcp, respectively. Having web servers that also run Telnet, SMTP, or Post Office Protocol 3(POP3) provides multiple paths for an attacker who is attempting to compromise the system. It also requires more administration, as every service that is running needs to have its patch level kept up to date to ensure security. Figure 12-15 shows the output of a **netstat -a** command on a workstation running Windows 2000 Professional.

Port	State	Service
Table 12-1 Open Ports and Services on a Typical UNIX Machine		
21/tcp	open	ftp
22/tcp	open	ssh
23/tcp	open	telnet
25/tcp	open	smtp
80/tcp	open	http
110/tcp	open	pop
111/tc0p	open	pop
113/tcp	open	ident
143/tcp	open	imap2
512/tcp	open	exec
513/tcp	open	login
514/tcp	open	shell
587/tcp	open	unknown
783/tcp	open	unknown
940/tcp	open	unknown
946/tcp	open	unknown
7256/tcp	open	smtp-stats

TIP To list open or listening ports on most machines, use the command **netstat -l** (UNIX) or **netstat -a** (Windows) (shown in Figure 12-15).

```
C:\WINNT\System32\cmd.exe                                          _ □ ×

Active Connections

  Proto  Local Address          Foreign Address        State
  TCP    piii:epmap             piii:0                 LISTENING
  TCP    piii:microsoft-ds      piii:0                 LISTENING
  TCP    piii:1025              piii:0                 LISTENING
  TCP    piii:1030              piii:0                 LISTENING
  TCP    piii:1114              piii:0                 LISTENING
  TCP    piii:2446              piii:0                 LISTENING
  TCP    piii:2711              piii:0                 LISTENING
  TCP    piii:netbios-ssn       piii:0                 LISTENING
  TCP    piii:1103              piii:0                 LISTENING
  TCP    piii:1103              TANK:netbios-ssn       ESTABLISHED
  TCP    piii:1114              192.168.1.33:telnet    ESTABLISHED
  TCP    piii:2608              piii:0                 LISTENING
  TCP    piii:4659              piii:0                 LISTENING
  UDP    piii:epmap             *:*
  UDP    piii:microsoft-ds      *:*
  UDP    piii:1026              *:*
  UDP    piii:netbios-ns        *:*
  UDP    piii:netbios-dgm       *:*
  UDP    piii:isakmp            *:*

C:\>
```

Figure 12-15   Output from netstat -a command on Windows 2000

Once the running services are known, you should shut off the unused ones by editing the inetd.conf file found in /etc on most UNIX systems, or by erasing the software that is providing the service (such as by completely removing sendmail from the system). In Windows XP or 2003, the service must be stopped and set to Disable in the Services Control Panel. Netstat can be rerun multiple times while editing the configuration files to ensure that all unnecessary services are shut down.

Any networked computer is typically going to have open ports and services, but many networked devices are being delivered with advanced remote management capabilities and have their own open ports and services. The most common are remote terminal services, such as Telnet 23/tcp, SSH 22/tcp, embedded web services on HTTP 80/tcp or HTTPS 443/tcp, and SNMP services on 161/udp. These types of services are more difficult to disable on network equipment, but this is sometimes possible. In Cisco's IOS, the command **no snmp-server** in config mode will disable the server service and close the port. Contact the vendor of your network equipment for information on disabling unnecessary services or limiting access to network services.

Some equipment will simply not allow you to disable the running service, but you can almost always find another way to restrict access. Quite often, the most effective method is to perform filtering on the equipment itself using ACLs.

Traffic Filtering

Filtering is one of the most common tools used in security. If something is trying to get in that you don't want to get in, you filter it. This is accomplished in a variety of ways, but they all consist of the same basic elements: rules that accept traffic and rules that deny traffic. These rules are typically arranged into sequential lists that the device steps through, one by one, as it receives traffic and attempts to find a match between rule and traffic. If this methodology looks familiar, that's because it is also how many brands of firewalls handle network traffic. While routers and other network devices typically make poor firewalls, they do have filtering capabilities that can be used to help secure the network as well as the routers and network devices themselves.

Filtering, while always following the same basic principle, is accomplished in many ways on different types of equipment. One of the most common places to perform at least rudimentary filtering for your network is at the border routers. In Cisco's IOS, these filters are referred to as access control lists (ACLs). Routers were originally built for the forwarding of traffic between networks, and current routers are optimized for that task. Traffic filtering was later added as a convenience, so ACLs can assist in the control of traffic across the network, but they will not turn a router into a true firewall.

ACLs, like the majority of filtering rules, work on the principle of pattern matching. Every packet that the router accepts is examined for a match between the packet and the rules in the ACL. The rules are processed in sequential order, meaning that the packet is compared against the first rule, then the second, then the third, and so on, until a match is found or the packet has been compared to every rule. At very high data rates, or for very long lists of rules, this can become computationally intensive. This large drain on resources is the primary reason to avoid using a router as a firewall, but using ACLs to drop known rogue traffic at the borders to the network makes good sense.

A typical access-list entry would look something like this:

```
Access-List 201 deny icmp any 192.168.1.0 255.255.255.0
```

This will drop ICMP traffic from anywhere to the 192.168.1.0 network. These ACL entries must follow a specific syntax. The first component is an access-list number, in this case 201. The next part of the rule is the action that the rule will take—permit or deny, if the traffic matches this particular rule. The type of traffic that the rule applies to is next, and while it is ICMP in this case, it can be set to any particular type of traffic you want to allow or deny. The next required component is the source address and network mask (which determines what octets need to be matched in the source IP address). This can be a single address, a list of addresses, or it can be set to all 0's or a wildcard to signify all addresses. In this case, "any" is used as an abbreviation of the all 0's address. The last component is the destination address and mask. This follows the same format as the source address and mask, and it can also be a single address, a list of addresses, or all addresses.

While Cisco dominates the router market, other manufacturers do produce similar products. These products generally follow a similar format for their filtering rules, possibly with different syntax; however, they generally have statements involving traffic type, source, destination, and the action to be performed on the traffic. The versatility of ACLs allows a lot of filtering power, but filtering on a router should be used primarily to drop large blocks of the Internet that are known to not have contact with your organization, or to drop entire types of traffic from the entire Internet. This allows the firewall to handle the more complex rules for traffic filtering.

The next piece of equipment that should handle traffic after it passes through the router is the firewall. This is where the most complex filtering is performed, but it is typically still done with ACL-like statements. However, while the configuration is similar, take care when using firewalls, as they typically bridge public networks and private ones—if an attacker breaches the firewall, she will have a great deal of access to all the networks that the firewall is in contact with.

Firewalls should have all their open ports and services restricted to a very limited number of source addresses, typically the authorized control stations. Once traffic has been allowed inside the firewall, it can also be filtered on the host itself, as both Windows 2003 and most variants of UNIX support traffic filtering natively. Almost any other OS can have traffic filtering added as an application. Windows 2003 provides traffic filtering on a per-port basis, and many versions of UNIX support traffic filtering to the point that they are well suited to be firewalls. The IPFIREWALL (IPFW), ipchains, and iptables are all programs that implement the same filtering concept, which is once again based on access control statements formed into lists. Ipchains and iptables both have multiple lists allowing further specialization of inbound and outbound traffic on each interface. The statements that make up the lists follow the same format of list, action, type of traffic, source, and destination.

Many UNIX flavors allow you to perform filtering within certain applications. The TCP Wrapper program sits between inetd (the UNIX Internet superserver described in the Solaris and Linux sections of this chapter) and the individual services. When a request comes in, inetd starts TCP Wrapper, and it will allow authorized connections to the associated daemon when that specific service, such as FTP or Telnet, is needed by an authorized connection. Some newer versions of inetd now contain TCP Wrapper–like functionality.

Filtering rules for TCP Wrapper are typically contained in two separate files: /etc/hosts.allow and /etc/hosts.deny. These files enumerate the hosts allowed to connect to certain services, as well as those that are denied access to certain services. These files are processed from top to bottom until a matching rule is found, but they work only on source address and service. The rules in the files are formatted as *SERVICE:SOURCE*, so an example hosts.allow might read as follows:

```
telnetd: ALL
ftpd: 192.168.1.
sendmail: localhost
```

Note that this example specifies <BF102>ALL<MF255> for the Telnet service, which means any source IP address can attempt to connect to it, 192.168.1. for the FTP service, so only source addresses starting with 192.168.1. will be allowed to connect to it. It also specifies **localhost** for the sendmail service, which means that only the system itself will be allowed to connect to the sendmail service.

Any traffic that matches a rule in the hosts.allow file is allowed to connect to the system. The hosts.deny file has the same format, but it denies traffic that matches its rules. This functionality can be very useful for protecting not only against external threats, but also against internal threats, because you are locking down services only to the machines authorized to make use of them. TCP Wrapper checks hosts.allow first and then hosts.deny—any traffic permitted by hosts.allow will be allowed in regardless of any rules contained in hosts.deny. This allows administrators to specify connections in hosts.allow and then place a generic "deny all" statement in hosts.deny to reject anything not specifically allowed in the hosts.allow file.

Network hardening is, on first glance, a fairly simple task: Disallow any traffic that is unauthorized by filtering it at all possible junctures in the network, and keep all software up to date on any devices that have contact with the network. Actually accomplishing that task is much more complex and maintenance-oriented. The tools for controlling traffic are ACLs, traffic filters such as TCP Wrapper, and closing all unnecessary ports by properly configuring them. Vendor patches and firmware updates should be installed regularly. As always, any open services should be configured with maximum authentication and good passwords. Taking these steps will not completely solve the problem of security, but it will ensure that an attack is as difficult as it can be.

Application Hardening

Perhaps as important as OS and network hardening is *application hardening*—securing an application against local and Internet-based attacks. Hardening applications is fairly similar to hardening operating systems—you remove the functions or components you don't need, restrict access where you can, and make sure the application is kept up to date with patches. In most cases, the last step in that list is the most important for maintaining application security. After all, you need to make applications accessible to users or they serve no purpose. As most problems with applications tend to be buffer overflows in legitimate user input fields, patching the application is often the only way to secure it from attack.

Application Patches

As obvious as this seems, application patches are most likely going to come from the vendor that sells the application. After all, who else has access to the source code? In some cases, such as with Microsoft's IIS, this is the same company that sold the OS that the application runs on. In other cases, such as Apache, the vendor is OS independent and provides an application with versions for many different OSs.

Application patches are likely to come in three varieties: hotfixes, patches, and upgrades. As for OSs, *hotfixes* are usually small sections of code designed to fix a specific problem. For example, a hotfix may address a buffer overflow in the login routine for an application. *Patches* are usually collections of fixes, they tend to be much larger, and they are usually released on a periodic basis or whenever enough problems have been addressed to warrant a patch release. *Upgrades* are another popular method of patching applications, and they tend to be received with a more positive spin than patches. Even the term *upgrade* has a positive connotation—you are moving up to a better, more functional, and more secure application. For this reason, many vendors release "upgrades" that consist mainly of fixes rather than new or enhanced functionality.

Application patches can come in a variety of forms. They can be downloaded from the vendor's web site or FTP site, or they can be received on a CD. In many cases, a patch is a small binary application that, when run, automatically replaces defective application binaries with updated ones. The patch may also change settings or modify configuration files. In other cases, the patch will be a zipped archive of files with a set of instructions that require the user or administrator to replace defective applications with the updated ones manually. Some advanced applications will have automatic update routines that update the application automatically in much the same fashion as an OS.

Patch Management

In the early days of network computing things were easy—fewer applications, vendor patches came out annually or quarterly, and access was restricted to authorized individuals. Updates were few and easy to handle. Now application and OS updates are pushed constantly as vendors struggle to provide new capabilities, fix problems, and address vulnerabilities. Microsoft has created "Patch Tuesday" in an effort to condense the update cycle and reduce the effort required to maintain its products. As the number of patches continues to rise, many organizations struggle to keep up with patches, which should be applied immediately, which are compatible with the current configuration, which will not affect current business operations, and so on. To help cope with this flood of patches, many organizations have adopted *patch management*, the process of planning, testing, and deploying patches in a controlled manner.

Patch management is a disciplined approach to the acquisition, testing, and implementation of OS and application patches and requires a fair amount of resources to implement properly. To implement patch management effectively, you must first have a good inventory of the software used in your environment, including all OSs and applications. Then you must set up a process to monitor for updates to those software packages. Many vendors provide the ability to update their products automatically or automatically check for updates and inform the user when updates are available. For example, Microsoft's Automatic Updates, shown in Figure 12-16, allows the user to configure for completely automatic updates on a scheduled basis, download new updates but let the user choose when to install them, or notify the user when updates are available. Some vendors provide notification of patches and some vendors provide a service that will alert you when patches that apply to your environment are available.

Keeping track of patch availability is merely the first step; in many environments, patches must be analyzed and tested. Does the patch apply to the software you are running? Does the patch address a vulnerability or critical issue that must be addressed immediately? What is the impact of applying that patch or group of patches? Will it break something else if you apply this patch? To address these issues, some organizations use development or test platforms where patches are carefully analyzed and tested

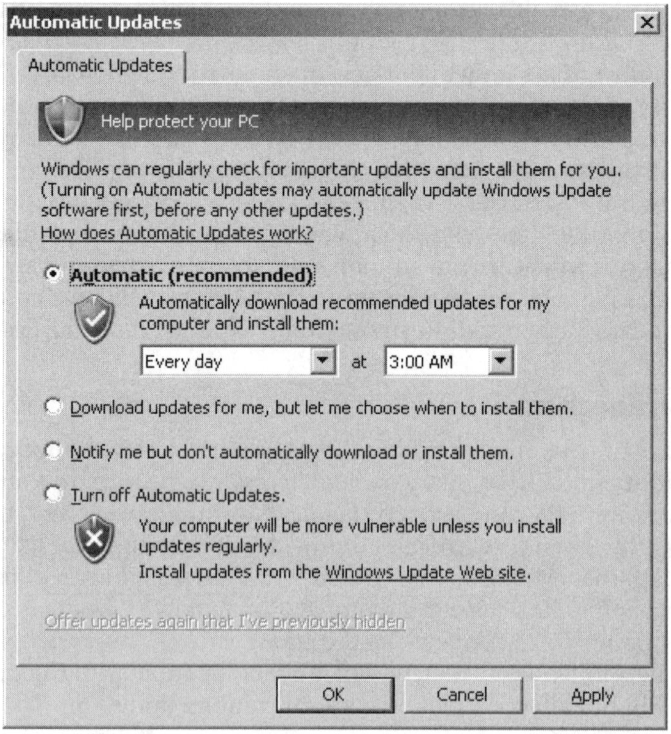

Figure 12-16   Microsoft's Windows Automatic Update utility

before being placed into a production environment. While patches are generally "good," they are not always exhaustively tested, some patches have been known to "break" other products or functions within the product being patched, and some patches have introduced new vulnerabilities while attempting to address an existing vulnerability. The extent of analysis and testing varies widely from organization to organization. Testing and analysis will also vary depending on the application or OS and the extent of the patch.

Once a patch has been analyzed and tested, administrators have to determine when to apply the patch. As many patches require a restart of applications or services or even a reboot of the entire system, most operational environments apply patches only at specific times to reduce downtime and possible impact and to ensure administrators are available if something goes wrong. Many organizations will also have a rollback plan that allows them to recover the systems back to a known good configuration prior to the patch should the patch have unexpected or undesirable effects. Some organizations require extensive coordination and approval of patches prior to implementation, and some institute "lockout" dates where no patching or system changes (with few exceptions) can be made to ensure business operations are not disrupted. For example, an e-commerce site might have a lockout between the Thanksgiving and Christmas holidays to ensure the site is always available to holiday shoppers.

With any environment, but especially with larger environments, it can be a challenge to track the update status of every desktop and server in the organization. Documenting and maintaining patch status can be a challenge. However, with a disciplined approach, training, policies, and procedures, even the largest environments can be managed. To assist in their patch management efforts, many organizations use a patch-management product that automates many of the mundane and manpower-intensive tasks associated with patch management. For example, many patch-management products provide the following:

- Ability to inventory applications and operating systems in use
- Notification of patches that apply to your environment
- Periodic or continual scanning of systems to validate patch status and indentify missing patches
- Ability to select which patches to apply and to which systems to apply them
- Ability to push patches to systems on an on-demand or scheduled basis
- Ability to report patch success or failure
- Ability to report patch status on any or all systems in the environment

Patch-management solutions can also be useful to satisfy audit or compliance requirements, as they can show a structured approach to patch management, show when and how systems are patched, and provide a detailed accounting of patch status within the organization.

Microsoft provides a free patch-management product called Windows Server Update Services (WSUS). Using the WSUS product, administrators can manage updates for any compatible Windows-based system in their organization. The WSUS product can be configured to download patches automatically from Microsoft based on a variety of factors (such as OS, product family, criticality, and so on). When updates are downloaded, the administrator can determine whether or not to push out the patches and when to apply them to the systems in their environment. The WSUS product can also help administrators track patch status on their systems, which is a useful and necessary feature.

Web Servers

Without a doubt, the most common Internet server-side application in use is the *web server*. Web servers are designed to provide content and functionality to remote users through a standard web browser. Web servers are used to deliver news, sell just about every product ever created, conduct auctions, and show pictures of someone's wedding or new baby. Due to their popularity and prolific use, web servers have become extremely popular targets for attackers. Web sites are defaced, and the original content is replaced with something the owner did not intend to display. E-commerce sites are attacked, and credit card numbers and user information is stolen.

Vendors have made setting up a web server remarkably easy, and this is one of the reasons for their enormous popularity. Unfortunately, vendors don't always provide good security configurations as part of the default installation. Fortunately, hardening a web server is not that difficult, as will be illustrated with examples of the two most popular web servers: IIS and Apache.

Microsoft's Internet Information Server

Microsoft IIS is one of the most popular web server applications in use today. IIS comes as a standard package with the Windows 2000/2003 Server OSs and can be loaded at install time or added to the configuration of a running system (with Windows 2003, you must select to install IIS as it is not installed by default). Due to its widespread use, IIS is a very popular target, and new vulnerabilities and exploits are released on a weekly or daily basis.

The first step in securing an IIS server is to remove all sample files (less of an issue on IIS 6 and 7 as by default they should not install sample materials). To assist users in setting up their new web servers, Microsoft provides a number of sample files that users can examine and use as references when constructing their web sites. Unfortunately, these sample applications tend to be full of vulnerabilities and holes and should therefore never be present on a production web server. To remove IIS sample applications, remove the virtual and physical directories where the samples exist. For more information on the location of the sample files, refer to the following table:

Sample Name	Virtual Directory	Location
IIS Samples	\IISSamples	C:\Inetpub\IISsamples
IIS Documentation	IISHelp	C:\Winnt\Help\IIShelp
Data Access	\MSADC	C:\Program files\Common files\System\MSadc

Next, you should set up the appropriate permissions for the web server's files and directories. In IIS you can do this using ACLs, which are essentially the same file permissions discussed in the context of OS hardening. As web servers are usually designed to give the public at large access, the key is to limit the user's ability to browse or navigate outside the intended path. This will typically involve removing permissions for the "everyone" group from certain files and directories. In most cases, you should never allow the "everyone" group to have write and execute privileges to the same directory. For that matter, in most cases you will not want to allow users to have write permissions for any of the web server's directories. Microsoft has provided some suggested ACL settings that are outlined in the following table:

File Type	ACL
Common Gateway Interface (CGI) files (exe, dll, cmd, pl)	Everyone (execute) Administrators (full control) System (full control)
Script files (asp)	Everyone (execute) Administrators (full control) System (full control)
Include files (inc, shtm, shtml)	Everyone (execute) Administrators (full control) System (full control)
Static content (txt, gif, jpg, html)	Everyone (read-only) Administrators (full control) System (full control)

Patching is also an extremely important part of the process of securing an IIS server. Since IIS is almost an integral part of the Windows Server OS, the service packs for the OS often contain patches and fixes for IIS. Microsoft also releases security bulletins to address each specific vulnerability that is discovered. Within each security bulletin there are links to the patch or hotfix that will mitigate or remove the reported vulnerability or manual steps an administrator can perform until a formal patch is released.

IIS is such a popular target that it is often difficult for an administrator to keep pace with all the discovered vulnerabilities and patches required to keep it up to date and secure from attack. To ease the burden somewhat, Microsoft has developed two tools specifically designed to help secure IIS servers: the URLScan and IIS LockDown tools. URLScan is a monitoring utility and preprocessor that examines all incoming URLs and rejects any requests for files, directories, or services outside the intended scope of the web site. The IIS LockDown tool asks the administrator a series of questions to determine which features are needed. Based on the answers, IIS LockDown can deny write permissions for anonymous accounts, disable WebDAV, remove dynamic script type associations, restore default security settings, and back up the IIS Metabase and ACLs.

EXAM TIP The IIS LockDown tool is used on older versions of IIS (4 and 5 —versions 6 and 7 already meet or exceed the security settings implemented by the LockDown tool). The tool sets appropriate permissions and removes unnecessary features, capabilities, and extensions.

Securing newer versions of IIS (6 and 7) is easier as Microsoft has already taken some steps to address the issues affecting earlier versions of the product. For example, under IIS 6, dynamic content must be enabled, the server process runs under a low-privilege account, and administrators must explicitly allow any dynamic extensions they want to serve on their web site. IIS 7 installs even fewer default features, adds the ability to restrict access to URLs based on roles and authenticated users, and has expanded URL filtering capabilities.

Apache

The Apache HTTP server from the Apache Software Foundation is the most popular web server in use today. Its Internet presence is greater than all the other web server versions combined. In 1995, a group of individuals known as the Apache Group joined to develop the Apache HTTP server. By 1999, the web server software and associated projects had become so popular that the organization grew into the Apache Software Foundation, a nonprofit corporation. According to the Apache.org web site, "The Apache HTTP Server Project is an effort to develop and maintain an open-source HTTP server for modern operating systems including UNIX and Windows NT. The goal of this project is to provide a secure, efficient and extensible server that provides HTTP services in sync with the current HTTP standards." This statement highlights two of the keys to Apache's popularity: the software is open source, and it is available for virtually every popular OS.

The first step in securing an Apache web server is to secure the host OS. Because Apache is available for most popular OSs, outlining the possible security issues here could be a large task and would depend heavily on the OS chosen. For the sake of brevity, we'll just say that a secure host OS is one that is patched, has strong passwords for all user accounts, has no unnecessary services or software, has strong file and directory permissions, and has auditing enabled.

Once the host OS has been taken care of, you will need to create an unprivileged account that will run the Apache server. This account, typically called "httpd" or "apache," is given the minimum permissions necessary to run the server software. Additional security measures include locking the account so it can never be used to log in to the system and assigning it to a special group where it is the only member. You essentially end up creating a user account that is able to run only the web server software and nothing more—this is fairly close to the ideal for Internet-visible services. By running the Apache software under an unprivileged account, you reduce the risk of potential compromise.

How you install the Apache software depends on whether you choose a precompiled binary or choose to compile it from the source code yourself. Regardless of the method you choose for installation, it is essential that you delete unneeded files and directories immediately after installation. Any source code files, samples, cgi-bin scripts,

HTML pages, or documentation files that you don't absolutely need should be removed from the system. Like IIS, some of Apache's vulnerabilities have been in sample files and scripts that should not be placed on a production web server.

Locking down file and directory permissions is also important when securing an Apache server. In most cases, you are going to restrict access to web server configuration files to highly privileged users only, such as the root user. Files used for development or for maintaining the site itself are usually restricted to the web server development or maintenance team. The unprivileged user that was created to run the server is typically given read access to the web site content, and in some cases read and execute permission on any scripts required to support web site functionality. By restricting permissions and access to files and directories in this manner, you can help prevent web site visitors from wandering off the intended path or gaining access to files they should not see.

Patching an Apache server is just as critical as patching or maintaining any other application. New vulnerabilities are discovered on a frequent basis, and in some cases the only defense is either to disable functionality or implement the patch to correct the issue. No specific tools are available to ensure that your version of Apache is up to date, so the best defense is to regularly visit the main Apache web site at www.apache.org for more information.

Mail Servers

Electronic mail is such an integral part of business and, for many of us, our daily lives that it is hard to imagine getting by without it. It has literally changed the way the world communicates and is so popular that millions of mail servers are spread across the Internet sending billions of messages each day. As with so many things, increased popularity, use, and presence on the Internet also bring an increase in attention from potential attackers. Mail servers have become very popular targets, which makes securing them a constant challenge for administrators.

Securing a mail server typically means removing or disabling unwanted functionality and ensuring the software is patched. Earlier versions of mail server packages often contained bugs or even backdoors, such as the **wiz** command that gave potential attackers complete access to the host system. As mail server software matured, attacks started to focus on three areas: reconnaissance, relaying, and buffer overflows.

Reconnaissance, or *information discovery*, on a mail server is rather simple. The attacker's goal is to pull information from the system without having to authenticate or provide any information in return. Reconnaissance usually involves an attacker attempting to discover the names and addresses of valid user accounts, which are used later for other purposes. The two most common techniques use the **vrfy** and **expn** commands. When an attacker connects to a mail server, usually by telnetting to port 25 on the target system, the attacker can enter commands and interact with the mail server itself. The **vrfy** command was initially designed to allow servers to verify e-mail addresses. For example, **vrfy jones** may yield a result of jones@sample.com. This tells the attacker that the account jones does exist and gives the correct e-mail address for that account. The **expn** command expands an alias list into the full list of e-mail addresses belonging to that list. For example, **expn all-users** would provide a list of every e-mail address belonging to the mailing list called all-users, if that mailing list existed. As you can see, while neither of these commands causes any direct harm, they do provide some useful information. For that reason, most administrators disable the **vrfy** and **expn** functions on their mail servers.

Relaying occurs when a mail server handles a message and neither the sender nor the recipient is a local user. Essentially, an attacker can take advantage of the mail server to send out e-mail on her behalf, even though she is not a legitimate user of that system. Spammers—those parties responsible for filling your e-mail inbox with unwanted junk messages promising to make you rich beyond your wildest dreams—actively seek out open mail relays so they can take advantage of someone else's resources to do their dirty work. Attackers also seek out open relays and leverage them to launch e-mail attacks, flooding recipients with so many messages that their mailbox fills up or their mail server crashes. Preventing your mail server from becoming an open relay usually involves ensuring only authenticated users are allowed to send outgoing mail. Many mail server software packages, such as sendmail, now provide relay-prevention capabilities as part of the default install. In most cases, you can also specify which systems, by system and domain name or IP address, are allowed to send mail through the server.

 EXAM TIP   The relay function should be disabled on ALL mail servers.

Buffer overflows continue to be the greatest danger to mail server security. A buffer overflow is a rather simple attack—you find a place where the server is accepting input, and you provide more input than the server is expecting to receive. Depending on the "extra" input provided and the software being attacked, a buffer overflow can do anything from crashing the server to giving the attacker remote access to the system. These continue to be extremely popular attacks, and the most effective way to prevent them is to ensure your mail server software is kept patched and up to date.

Microsoft's Exchange

Microsoft's mail server implementation is called Exchange, and, like other Microsoft products, it has its share of vulnerabilities. By default, **vrfy** and **expn** are disabled in later versions of Exchange, but they can be enabled if required by modifying certain Registry settings. Service packs and patches for later versions of Exchange also provide anti-relay capabilities that can be configured through the Routing tab of the Internet Mail Service Properties.

Microsoft also provides a tool called the Microsoft Baseline Security Analyzer (MBSA), designed to scan Exchange, along with other applications and the OS itself, for vulnerabilities, incorrect settings, and missing patches to ensure that the software is up to date and patched appropriately. Running this tool on a regular basis will help ensure your Exchange system is patched against the latest vulnerabilities.

Microsoft also offers several useful guides, such as "Securing Exchange Server 2007 Client Access," to assist administrators in securing Exchange servers.

Sendmail

Sendmail was the initial mail server software, and it is still extremely popular. It is available as a completely free, open source product or as a fully licensed commercial product.

By default, recent versions of sendmail disable the **expn** and **vrfy** functions, but they can be disabled in earlier versions by adding **PrivacyOptions=noexpn novrfy** to the sendmail.cf configuration file. Relaying is also restricted by default in recent versions, though an administrator can allow relaying for specific IPs or domains by modifying the relay-domains configuration file. Buffer overflows have been a frequent problem for sendmail—as usual, the best defense is to ensure your sendmail software is patched and up to date. For more information on sendmail, refer to www.sendmail.org.

FTP Servers

The File Transfer Protocol (FTP) allows users to access remotely stored files, and the applications that provide FTP services are very popular. Users can typically download files from FTP sites and, in certain cases, may even be allowed to upload files to the server. FTP is most commonly used as a distribution method for application updates, device drivers, free software—anything that needs to be made available to a large group of people.

FTP servers are typically configured as read-only services, meaning that you can download files from the server but you cannot upload files or modify anything on the server itself. The most interesting dilemma concerning FTP servers is the use of anonymous access. In many cases, this is exactly what the system has been designed to do—permit thousands of remote users to download files and information anonymously. So in some cases, anonymous is the expected condition, assuming all related security precautions have been taken. Anonymous access to FTP servers becomes a problem only when the administrator does not mean to provide anonymous access or does not properly secure the FTP service. This typically involves setting the appropriate permissions, having the FTP process run by a nonprivileged user, and not allowing users to upload or modify files. Some FTP servers are meant as an upload and download service for authorized users only—in those cases, anonymous access should be completely removed.

Like many other Internet services, buffer overflows have been a consistent problem for FTP servers. Ensuring your FTP server software is up to date and patched is the best defense against buffer overflows. If you are not providing anonymous FTP services, you may also wish to restrict which external IP addresses are allowed to connect to the FTP service.

DNS Servers

Domain Name Service (DNS) is an integral part of making the Internet work. Human beings are not good at remembering long strings or numbers such as IP addresses, but we are pretty good at remembering names such as cnn.com, yahoo.com, or amazon.com. To navigate the Internet, your computer will need to know the IP address of your destination system, and DNS provides the translation from name to IP address that makes it all possible.

DNS services are built as a hierarchical structure with many systems, called *nameservers*, working together to resolve names into IP addresses. When you request a name resolution, your system queries a local nameserver. If the nameserver does not know how to perform the translation (doesn't know the name-to-IP address translation), it asks the next nameserver up in that chain. This continues until the answer is found and is passed back down to your system. At the top of the DNS tree are 13 root nameservers that provide the definitive answers for all DNS queries.

The most popular DNS server implementation is Berkeley Internet Name Domain (BIND). BIND is an open-source, free server package that can be downloaded and run on a variety of OSs. The two most common types of attacks against DNS servers are reconnaissance attacks and buffer overflows.

Reconnaissance attacks against DNS servers usually consist of an attacker attempting a zone transfer. A *zone transfer* occurs whenever a DNS server provides all the information it knows about an entire zone, which usually corresponds to an entire domain name. This information typically includes all the names and IP addresses of systems in that zone—a very useful set of information for a potential attacker. Zone transfers also have a legitimate use, as they can update zone information between nameservers. To protect against zone transfers, some organizations employ a split DNS architecture by using one nameserver to handle internal name queries and another server to handle external name queries. The two nameservers are never connected and never share information—the internal server is visible only from inside the network, and the external server knows nothing about the internal organization. Other organizations block all inbound connections on TCP port 53—the port used for zone transfers. You can also specify on your nameserver which external systems are allowed to execute zone transfers.

 EXAM TIP   Zone transfers should be limited only to those DNS servers that need access to the entire zone information for update and replication purposes. If the zone transfer capability is not needed, it should be disabled completely.

Buffer overflows are best defeated by ensuring the DNS software is patched and up to date. BIND, due to its popularity and widespread use, has been an extremely popular target in the last few years, and new vulnerabilities are introduced on a fairly regular basis. For the latest version and patches, see the main BIND web site at www.isc.org/products/BIND.

File and Print Services

Securing file and print services boils down to a matter of permissions and ensuring legitimate users have access while unauthorized users do not. Network print services should be configured so that they receive print jobs from authorized, authenticated users. Users should, in most cases, be allowed to stop, pause, or delete their own print jobs. Only administrators should be able to control or modify the entire print queue or the printer itself.

In a similar manner, securing file services is usually a matter of permissions. Users should be given full control over their own files, read access to public resources that should not be modified, and possibly read and write access to group folders. In most cases, file services are extensions of the OS itself, but some specialized file-service applications, such as Network File System (NFS), are specifically designed to provide network access to stored data and files. NFS, a service that has a long history of security problems, has made advancements in recent versions, including better authentication methods, encryption, and public key infrastructure (PKI) support.

Active Directory

The old adage "the network is the system" comes much closer to reality with systems such as Microsoft's Active Directory services. Active Directory allows single login access to multiple applications, data sources, and systems, and it includes advanced encryption capabilities, such as Kerberos and PKI.

Active Directory is built around a database, called a *schema*, containing information about network objects, such as domains, servers, workstations, printers, groups, and users. Each object is placed into a domain, which can then be used to control which users may access which objects. Each domain has its own security policies, administrative control, privileges, and relationships to other domains.

Domains are organized into a hierarchical structure called a *forest*, with the forest root domain being at the top of the tree. Branching off the main domain are trees containing *parent* and *child* domains. Every child domain has a two-way trust with its parent, which, by virtue of design, extends to every other child domain under that parent. Under this concept, when a user authenticates successfully into one child domain, all the other child domains under the same parent will accept the authentication as well, due to the two-way trust system. While the other child domains may accept the authentication information, access to resources is still controlled by the access controls for each specific child domain. So while a child domain may recognize you as an authenticated user from another child domain, it may not grant you access to its resources, due to local access controls.

Another key feature of Active Directory is *delegation*—the ability to selectively push administrative control to users in each domain. While enterprise-level administrative accounts exist only in the root domain, local admin accounts can exist in child domains. This means that you can have a high level admin in the central office grant local authority to add users, configure printers, and so on, to local admins in remote offices. This type of selective, localized administrative control can be very useful in large, distributed organizations.

Each object in Active Directory also has an ACL to determine who can view the object, what attributes they can read, and what actions each user can perform on the object. Access controls can be inherited or passed down from a parent to a child. For example, administrators can set permissions on a specific folder and specify that every subfolder or file in that folder receive the same permissions.

Active Directory also maintains a global catalog that contains a subset of information on all the objects in the Active Directory database. The global catalog is used for many functions within Active Directory, including user identification and e-mail addresses. The global catalog must be available and queryable for Active Directory to function properly. To update and query Active Directory, Microsoft uses the Lightweight Directory Access Protocol (LDAP). Every object in Active Directory has a unique name for use in LDAP queries and updates. Unfortunately, LDAP is not, by default, an encrypted protocol, meaning that anyone on the network could intercept and examine LDAP queries and updates.

The key to securing Active Directory is carefully planning and using appropriate permissions. While the granular control and enhanced capabilities of Active Directory could lead to more secure systems, its complexity can also lead to administrators overwriting each other's changes or accidentally granting access to unauthorized individuals. Microsoft provides some very good Active Directory resources on its web site.

Group Policies

Microsoft defines a *group policy* as "an infrastructure used to deliver and apply one or more desired configurations or policy settings to a set of targeted users and computers within an Active Directory environment. This infrastructure consists of a Group Policy engine and multiple client-side extensions (CSEs) responsible for writing specific policy settings on target client computers." Introduced with the NT operating system, group polices are a great way to manage and configure systems centrally in an Active Directory environment. Group policies can also be used to manage users, making these policies valuable tools in any large environment.

Within the Windows environment, group policies can be used to refine, set, or modify a system's Registry settings, auditing and security policies, user environments, logon/logoff scripts, and so on. Policy settings are stored in *group policy objects (GPOs)* and are referenced internally by the OS using a *globally unique identifier (GUID)*. A single policy can be linked to a single user, a group of users, a group of machines, or an entire organizational unit, which makes updating common settings on large groups of users or systems much easier. Users and systems can have more than one GPO assigned and active, which can create conflicts between policies that must then be resolved at an attribute level. Group policies can also overwrite local policy settings. Group policies should not be confused with local policies. *Local* policies are created and applied to a specific system (locally), are not user specific (you can't have local policy X for user A and local policy Y for user B), and are overwritten by GPOs.

Creating GPOs is usually done through either the Group Policy Object Editor, shown in Figure 12-17, or the Group Policy Management Console (GPMC). The GPMC is a more powerful GUI-based tool that can summarize GPO settings, simplify security filtering settings, backup/clone/restore/edit GPOs, and perform other tasks. After creating a GPO, administrators will associate it with the desired targets. After association, group policies operate on a *pull model*. At a semi-random interval, the Group Policy client will collect and apply any policies associated to the system and the currently logged on user.

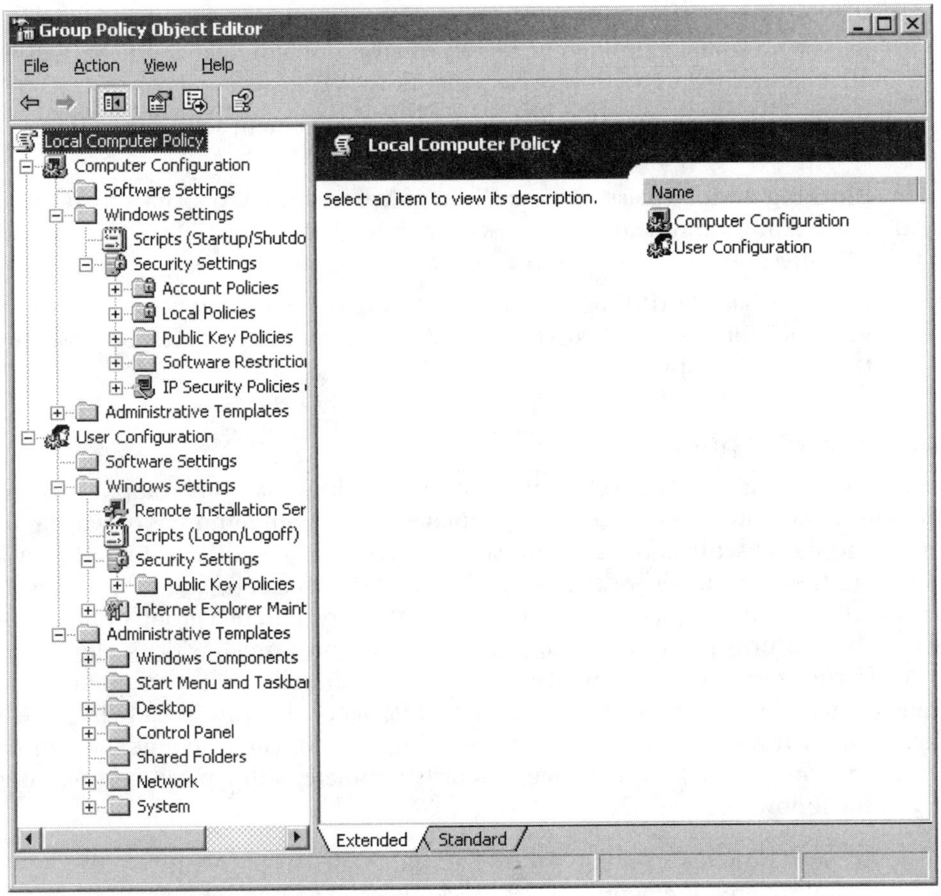

Figure 12-17 Group Policy Object Editor

With the most recent implementation of group policies, Microsoft has added some interesting and effective new capabilities:

- **Network location awareness** Systems are now "aware" of which network they are connected to and can apply different GPOs as needed. For example, a system can have a very restrictive GPO when connected to a public network and a less restrictive GPO when connected to an internal trusted network.

- **Ability to process without ICMP** Older group policy processes would occasionally time out or fail completely if the targeted system did not respond to ICMP packets. Current implementations in Vista do not rely on ICMP during the GPO update process.

- **VPN compatibility**   As a side benefit of Network Location Awareness, mobile users who connect through VPNs can receive a GPO update in the background after connecting to the corporate network via VPN.

- **Power management**   Under Vista, power management settings can be configured using GPOs.

- **Blocking device access**   Under Vista, policy settings have been added that allow administrators to restrict user access to USB drives, CD-RW drives, DVD-RW drives, and other removable media.

- **Location-based printing**   Users can be assigned to various printers based on their location. As mobile users move, their printer locations can be updated to the closest local printer.

Security Templates

A *security template* is simply a collection of security settings that can be applied to a system. Within the Windows OSs, security templates can contain hundreds of settings that control or modify settings on a system such as password length, auditing of user actions, or restrictions on network access. Security templates can be standalone files that are applied manually to each system, but they can also be part of a group policy, allowing common security settings to be applied to systems on a much wider scale.

When creating a security template, all settings are initially "not configured," which means the template will make no changes to whatever settings are already in place. By selecting the settings he wants to modify, an administrator can fine tune the template to create a more (or less) secure system. Security templates will typically configure settings in the following areas:

- **Account policies**   Settings for user accounts such as password length, complexity requirements, account lockouts, and so on

- **Event log settings**   Settings that apply to the three main audit logs within Windows (Application, System, and Security), such as log file size, retention of older entries, and so on

- **File permissions**   Settings that apply to files and folders such as permission inheritance, locking permissions, and so on

- **Registry permissions**   Settings that control who can access the Registry and how it can be accessed

- **Restricted groups**   Settings that control who should be allowed to join or be part of certain groups—if the user is not already a member of a group as defined in the policy, you will not be able to add that user to the corresponding group on the local system.

- **System services**   Settings for services that run on the system such as startup mode, whether or not users can stop/start the service, and so on

- **User rights**   Settings that control what a user can and cannot do on the system

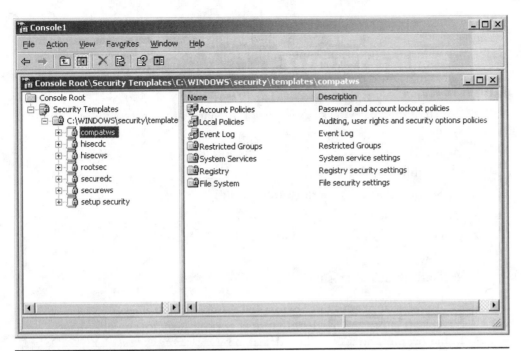

Figure 12-18 MMC with Security Templates snap-in

You can create and/or modify security templates on your local system through the Microsoft Management Console (if you have the Security Templates snap-in installed). Microsoft includes a series of predefined security templates (usually stored in \WINDOWS \security\templates) that will appear under Security Templates in your MMC window. These templates range from minimal to maximal security and can all be applied as-is or modified as needed. You can also create a completely new security template and then customize each of the settings to your specifications. Figure 12-18 shows the MMC with the Security Templates snap-in enabled.

Chapter Review

Security baselines are critical to protecting information systems, particularly those allowing connections from external users. Hardening is the process by which operating systems, network resources, and applications are secured against possible attacks. Securing operating systems consists of removing or disabling unnecessary services, restricting permissions on files and directories, removing unnecessary software (or not installing it in the first place), applying the latest patches, removing unnecessary user accounts, and ensuring strong password guidelines are in place. Securing network resources consists of disabling unnecessary functions, restricting access to ports and services, ensuring strong passwords are used, and ensuring the code on the network devices is patched and up to date. Securing applications depends heavily on the application involved but typically consists of removing samples and default materials, preventing reconnaissance attempts, and ensuring the software is patched and up to date. Group policies are a method for managing the settings and configurations of many different users and systems.

Questions

1. Which of the following steps is part of the hardening process for operating systems?

   A. Removing unnecessary applications and utilities

   B. Disabling unneeded services

   C. Setting appropriate permissions on files

   D. All of the above

2. Group policies can be applied to

   A. Users and systems

   B. Only to the local system

   C. Only to users

   D. Only to systems

3. Buffer overflow attacks are best defeated by

   A. Removing sample files

   B. Selecting strong passwords

   C. Setting appropriate permissions on files

   D. Installing the latest patches

4. Which of the following is a disciplined approach to the acquisition, testing, and implementation of operating system and application updates?

   A. Security templates

   B. Patch management

   C. System hardening

   D. System baselining

5. Traffic filtering is used to

   A. Scan incoming web requests for malformed code

   B. Restrict access to ports and services

   C. Prevent buffer overflows

   D. Optimize the flow of time-sensitive traffic

6. File permissions under UNIX consist of what three types?

   A. Modify, read, and execute

   B. Full control, read-only, and run

    C. Write, read, and open

    D. Read, write, and execute

7. The **netstat** command

    A. Lists active network connections

    B. Provides the status of all hardware interfaces

    C. Shows open files and directories

    D. All of the above

8. Security templates can be used to configure settings in the following areas:

    A. Restricted Groups, User Rights, and Memory Usage

    B. User Rights, System Services, and Disk Usage

    C. System Services, Registry Permissions, and Restricted Groups

    D. Disk Usage, File Permissions, and Bandwidth Usage

9. The inetd daemon

    A. Listens for incoming connections

    B. Starts the appropriate service when required

    C. Runs at system startup

    D. All of the above

10. To provide an immediate solution addressing a specific vulnerability, a vendor may release

    A. A hotfix

    B. A service pack

    C. A patch

    D. None of the above

11. Network Access Quarantine Control allows administrators to

    A. Block malicious or suspicious traffic on wireless connections

    B. Prevent computers from connecting to the network until their configuration has been reviewed and deemed "safe"

    C. Filter out viruses, malware, and Trojans

    D. Restrict traffic from systems using non-Microsoft operating systems

12. Password security consists of

    A. Selecting a password with at least eight characters, at least one change in case, and at least one number or nonalphanumeric character

    B. Storing the password in your wallet or purse

    C. Using the same password on every system

    D. Changing passwords at least once a year

13. TCP wrappers

    A. Verify checksums on every packet entering or leaving the system

    B. Help prioritize network traffic for optimal throughput

    C. Help restrict access to the local system

    D. None of the above

14. Ensuring software is patched and up to date is important for

    A. Operating systems

    B. Network devices

    C. Applications

    D. All of the above

15. Security templates are

    A. A collection of security settings

    B. A method of managing patches

    C. Application-specific security features

    D. Available only on domain controllers

Answers

1. **D.** All of the steps mentioned (removing unnecessary applications, disabling unnecessary services, and setting appropriate permissions on files) are part of the hardening process. Leaving out any of these steps could result in an insecure system.

2. **A.** Group policies can be applied to both users and systems.

3. **D.** The best defense against buffer overflows is to apply the appropriate patches or fixes that eliminate the buffer overflow condition.

4. **B.** Patch management is a disciplined approach to the acquisition, testing, and implementation of operating system and application updates.

5. **B.** Traffic filtering is used to restrict access to ports and services. This helps control who has access to network services and which services they may access.

6. **D.** File permissions under UNIX consist of read, write, and execute.

7. **A.** The **netstat** (network statistics) command lists information about active network connections.

8. **C.** Security templates can be used to configure settings in all of the following areas: Account Policies, Event Log settings, File Permissions, Registry Permissions, Restricted Groups, System Services, and User Rights.

9. **D.** The Internet superserver daemon, inetd, performs all of the functions listed. This helps prevent other services from using system resources until they need to do so.

10. **A.** Immediate solutions designed to address a specific vulnerability are usually called hotfixes. Patches and service packs tend to be larger, they are released on a slower timetable, and they often contain fixes for many different problems.

11. **B.** Network Access Quarantine Control enables administrators to prevent computers from connecting to the network until their configuration has been reviewed and deemed "safe." This capability can help prevent the spread of viruses and malware.

12. **A.** Password security consists of selecting a password with at least eight characters, at least one change in case, and at least one number or nonalphanumeric character.

13. **C.** TCP wrappers help restrict access to the local system by controlling what systems are allowed to connect to what services. This functionality is typically implemented in the hosts.allow and hosts.deny files on a specific system.

14. **D.** Ensuring software is patched and up to date is important for *every* piece of software and network equipment.

15. **A.** Security templates are a collection of security settings that can be applied to systems to increase their security posture.

Types of Attacks and Malicious Software

In this chapter, you will

- Learn about various types of computer and network attacks, including denial-of-service, spoofing, hijacking, and password guessing
- Understand the different types of malicious software that exist, including viruses, worms, Trojan horses, logic bombs, and time bombs
- Explore how social engineering can be used as a means to gain access to computers and networks
- Discover the importance of auditing and what should be audited

Attacks can be made against virtually any layer or level of software, from network protocols to applications. When an attacker finds a vulnerability in a system, he exploits the weakness to attack the system. The effect of an attack depends on the attacker's intent and can result in a wide range of effects, from minor to severe. An attack on a system might not be visible on that system because the attack is actually occurring on a different system, and the data the attacker will manipulate on the second system is obtained by attacking the first system.

Avenues of Attack

A computer system is attacked for two general reasons: it is specifically targeted by the attacker, or it is a target of opportunity. In the first case, the attacker has chosen the target not because of the hardware or software the organization is running but for another reason, such as a political reason. For example, an individual in one country might attack a government system in another country to gather secret information. Or the attacker might target an organization as part of a "hacktivist" attack—the attacker could deface the web site of a company that sells fur coats because the attacker believes using animals in this way is unethical, for example. Perpetrating some sort of electronic fraud is another reason a specific system might be targeted for attack. Whatever the reason, an attack of this nature is usually begun before the hardware and software of the organization is known.

The second type of attack, an attack against a target of opportunity, is launched against a site that has hardware or software that is vulnerable to a specific exploit. The attacker, in this case, is not targeting the organization; he has instead learned of a specific vulnerability and is simply looking for an organization with this vulnerability that he can exploit. This is not to say that an attacker might not be targeting a given sector and looking for a target of opportunity in that sector. For example, an attacker may want to obtain credit card or other personal information and can search for any exploitable company that stores credit card information on its system to accomplish the attack.

Targeted attacks are more difficult and take more time and effort than attacks on a target of opportunity. The latter simply relies on the fact that with any piece of widely distributed software, somebody in the organization will not have patched the system as they should have. Defense against attacks begins with elimination of vulnerabilities exploited by the target of opportunity avenue, as they are also used in targeted attacks.

The Steps in an Attack

Attackers are like bank robbers in the sense that they undergo an organized process when performing an attack. The steps an attacker takes in attempting to penetrate a targeted network are similar to those that a security consultant performs during a penetration test. The following outlines the common steps of the hacking process:

1. Reconnaissance (also known as profiling)
2. Scanning
3. Researching vulnerability
4. Performing the attack

Reconnaissance

The attacker can gather as much information about the organization as possible via several means, including studying the organization's own web site, looking for postings on news groups, or consulting resources such as the Securities and Exchange Commission's (SEC's) Filings & Forms (EDGAR) web site (www.sec.gov/edgar.shtml). A number of different financial reports are available through the EDGAR site that can provide information about an organization that can prove useful for an attack, especially for social engineering attacks. The attacker wants information about IP addresses, phone numbers, names of important individuals, and what networks the organization maintains. The attacker can also use tools such as Whois.Net (www.whois.net) to link IP addresses to registrants.

Scanning

The next step begins the technical part of an attack that determines what target systems are available and active. This is often done using a *ping sweep*, which simply sends a ping (an Internet Control Message Protocol echo request) to the target machine. If the machine responds, the attacker knows it is reachable. His next step is often to perform a *port scan* to help identify which ports are open, which indicates which services may be running on the target machine. The program nmap is the de facto standard for ping sweeping and port scanning. Running nmap with the **–sv** option will perform a *banner grab* in an attempt to determine the version of the software behind open ports. An alternative GUI program for Windows is SuperScan (www.snapfiles.com/get/superscan.html).

 NOTE Windows XP Service Pack 2 has removed raw socket access (access to sockets that grant access to packets) and this slows down programs attempting to perform fast and massive sweeps. This effect can be somewhat mitigated by issuing the following command prior to starting the scanning/sweep program: **net stop SharedAccess**.

Determining which operating system is running on the target machine, as well as any specific application programs, occurs after the attacker determines which services are available. Various techniques can be used to send specifically formatted packets to the ports on a target system to view the response. This response will often provide clues as to which operating system and specific applications are running on the target system. Then the attacker should have a list of possible target machines, the operating system running on them, and some specific applications or services to target.

Researching Vulnerability

After the hacker has a list of software running on the systems, he will start researching the Internet for vulnerabilities associated with that software. Numerous web sites provide information on vulnerabilities in specific application programs and operating systems. This information is valuable to administrators who need to know what problems exist and how to patch them.

In addition to information about specific vulnerabilities, some sites also provide tools that can be used to exploit the vulnerabilities. An attacker can search for known vulnerabilities and tools to exploit them, download the information and tools, then use them against a site. If the administrator for the targeted system has not installed the correct patch, the attack may be successful; if the patch has been installed, the attacker will move on to the next possible vulnerability. If the administrator has installed all the appropriate patches so that all known vulnerabilities have been addressed, the attacker may have to resort to a brute-force attack, which involves calculating user ID and password combinations. Unfortunately, this type of attack, which could be easily prevented, sometimes proves successful.

Performing the Attack

Now the attacker is ready to execute an attack, which could have many different results—the system could crash, information could be stolen off the system, or a web site could be defaced. Hackers often install a backdoor and build their own user accounts with administrative privileges so that even when you do patch the system, they can still gain access.

This discussion of attack steps is by no means complete. A system can be attacked in many different ways. The driving force behind the type of attack is the attacker's objective;

if activism can be accomplished by a web site defacement, he may consider this a sufficient attack. If the target is more sinister, such as intellectual property theft or identity theft, data theft may be the hacker's object and hence guide his attack.

Minimizing Possible Avenues of Attack

By understanding the steps an attacker can take, you can limit the exposure of your system and minimize the possible avenues an attacker can exploit. Your first step to minimize possible attacks is to ensure that all patches for the operating system and applications are installed. Many security problems, such as viruses and worms, exploit known vulnerabilities for which patches actually exist. These attacks are successful only because administrators have not taken the appropriate actions to protect their systems.

The next step is to limit the services that are running on the system. As mentioned in earlier chapters, limiting the number of services to those that are absolutely necessary provides two safeguards: it limits the possible avenues of attack (the possible services for which a vulnerability may exist and be exploited), and it reduces the number of services the administrator has to worry about patching in the first place.

Another step is to limit public disclosure of private information about your organization and its computing resources. Since the attacker is after this information, don't make it easy to obtain.

Attacking Computer Systems and Networks

Although hackers and viruses receive the most attention in the news (due to the volume of these forms of attack), they are not the only methods used to attack computer systems and networks. This chapter addresses many different ways computers and networks are attacked on a daily basis. Each type of attack threatens at least one of the three security requirements mentioned in Chapter 1: confidentiality, integrity, and availability (the CIA of security). Attacks are thus attempts by unauthorized individuals to access or modify information, to deceive the system so that an unauthorized individual can take over an authorized session, or to disrupt service to authorized users.

From a high-level standpoint, attacks on computer systems and networks can be grouped into two broad categories: attacks on specific software (such as an application or the operating system) and attacks on a specific protocol or service. Attacks on a specific application or operating system are generally possible because of an oversight in the code (and possibly in the testing of that code) or because of a flaw, or bug, in the code (again indicating a lack of thorough testing). Attacks on specific protocols or services are attempts either to take advantage of a specific feature of the protocol or service or use the protocol or service in a manner for which it was not intended. This section discusses various forms of attacks of which security professionals need to be aware.

Denial-of-Service Attacks

Denial-of-service (DoS) attacks can exploit a known vulnerability in a specific application or operating system, or they can attack features (or weaknesses) in specific protocols or services. In a DoS attack, the attacker attempts to deny authorized users access either to specific information or to the computer system or network itself. This can be accomplished by crashing the system—taking it offline—or by sending so many requests that the machine is overwhelmed.

The purpose of a DoS attack can be simply to prevent access to the target system, or the attack can be used in conjunction with other actions to gain unauthorized access to a computer or network. For example, a *SYN flooding* attack can be used to prevent service to a system temporarily in order to take advantage of a trusted relationship that exists between that system and another.

SYN flooding is an example of a DoS attack that takes advantage of the way TCP/IP networks were designed to function, and it can be used to illustrate the basic principles of any DoS attack. SYN flooding uses the TCP three-way handshake that establishes a connection between two systems. Under normal circumstances, the first system sends a SYN packet to the system with which it wants to communicate. The second system responds with a SYN/ACK if it is able to accept the request. When the initial system receives the SYN/ACK from the second system, it responds with an ACK packet, and communication can then proceed. This process is shown in Figure 13-1.

NOTE A SYN/ACK is actually the SYN packet sent to the first system, combined with an ACK flag acknowledging the first system's SYN packet.

In a SYN flooding attack, the attacker sends fake communication requests to the targeted system. Each of these requests will be answered by the target system, which then waits for the third part of the handshake. Since the requests are fake (a nonexistent IP address is used in the requests, so the target system is responding to a system that doesn't exist), the target will wait for responses that never come, as shown in Figure 13-2. The target system will drop these connections after a specific time-out period, but if the attacker sends requests faster than the time-out period eliminates them, the system will quickly be filled with requests. The number of connections a system can support is finite, so when more requests come in than can be processed, the system will soon be reserving all its connections for fake requests. At this point, any further requests are simply dropped (ignored), and legitimate users who want to connect to the target system will not be able to do so, because use of the system has been denied to them.

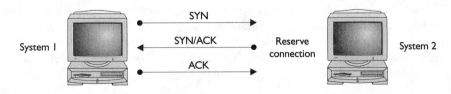

Figure 13-1 The TCP three-way handshake

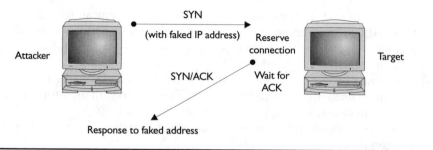

Figure 13-2 A SYN flooding DoS attack

Another simple DoS attack is the infamous ping of death (POD), and it illustrates the other type of attack—one targeted at a specific application or operating system, as opposed to SYN flooding, which targets a protocol. In the POD attack, the attacker sends an Internet Control Message Protocol (ICMP) ping packet equal to, or exceeding, 64KB (which is to say, greater than $64 \times 1024 = 65,536$ bytes). This type of packet should not occur naturally (there is no reason for a ping packet to be larger than 64KB). Certain systems are not able to handle this size of packet, and the system will hang or crash.

DoS attacks are conducted using a single attacking system. A DoS attack employing multiple attacking systems is known as a distributed denial-of-service (DDoS) attack. The goal of a DDoS attack is also to deny the use of or access to a specific service or system. DDoS attacks were made famous in 2000 with the highly publicized attacks on eBay, CNN, Amazon, and Yahoo!.

In a DDoS attack, service is denied by overwhelming the target with traffic from many different systems. A network of attack agents (sometimes called *zombies*) is created by the attacker, and upon receiving the attack command from the attacker, the attack agents commence sending a specific type of traffic against the target. If the attack network is large enough, even ordinary web traffic can quickly overwhelm the largest of sites, such as those targeted in 2000.

Creating a DDoS network is no simple task. The attack agents are not willing agents—they are systems that have been compromised and on which the DDoS attack software has been installed. To compromise these agents, the attacker has to have gained unauthorized access to the system or tricked authorized users to run a program that installed the attack software. The creation of the attack network may in fact be a multi-step process in which the attacker first compromises a few systems that are then used as *handlers* or *masters*, which in turn compromise other systems. Once the network has been created, the agents wait for an attack message that will include data on the specific target before launching the attack. One important aspect of a DDoS attack is that with just a few messages to the agents, the attacker can have a flood of messages sent against the targeted system. Figure 13-3 illustrates a DDoS network with agents and handlers.

How can you stop or mitigate the effects of a DoS or DDoS attack? One important precaution is to ensure that you have applied the latest patches and upgrades to your

Figure 13-3
DDoS attacks

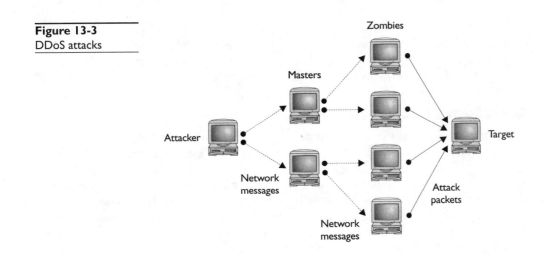

systems and the applications running on them. Once a specific vulnerability is discovered, it does not take long before multiple exploits are written to take advantage of it. Generally you will have a small window of opportunity in which to patch your system between the time the vulnerability is discovered and the time exploits become widely available. A vulnerability can also be discovered by hackers, and exploits provide the first clues that a system has been compromised. Attackers can also reverse-engineer patches to learn what vulnerabilities have been patched, allowing them to attack unpatched systems.

Another approach involves changing the time-out option for TCP connections so that attacks such as the SYN flooding attack are more difficult to perform, because unused connections are dropped more quickly.

For DDoS attacks, much has been written about distributing your own workload across several systems so that any attack against your system would have to target several hosts to be completely successful. While this is true, if large enough DDoS networks are created (with tens of thousands of zombies, for example), any network, no matter how much the load is distributed, can be successfully attacked. Such an approach also involves additional costs to your organization to establish this distributed environment. Addressing the problem in this manner is actually an attempt to mitigate the effect of the attack, rather than preventing or stopping an attack.

To prevent a DDoS attack, you must either be able to intercept or block the attack messages or keep the DDoS network from being established in the first place. Tools have been developed that will scan your systems, searching for sleeping zombies waiting for an attack signal. Many of the current Antivirus/spyware security suite tools will detect known zombie type infections. The problem with this type of prevention approach, however, is that it is not something you can do to prevent an attack on your network—it is something you can do to keep your network from being used to attack other networks or systems. You have to rely on the community of network administrators to test their own systems to prevent attacks on yours.

A final option you should consider that will address several forms of DoS and DDoS attacks is to block ICMP packets at your border, since many attacks rely on ICMP. Carefully consider this approach before implementing it, however, because it will also prevent the use of some possibly useful troubleshooting tools.

Backdoors and Trapdoors

Backdoors were originally (and sometimes still are) nothing more than methods used by software developers to ensure that they could gain access to an application even if something were to happen in the future to prevent normal access methods. An example would be a hard-coded password that could be used to gain access to the program in the event that administrators forgot their own system password. The obvious problem with this sort of backdoor (also sometimes referred to as a *trapdoor*) is that, since it is hard-coded, it cannot be removed. Should an attacker learn of the backdoor, all systems running that software would be vulnerable to attack.

The term *backdoor* is also, and more commonly, used to refer to programs that attackers install after gaining unauthorized access to a system to ensure that they can continue to have unrestricted access to the system, even if their initial access method is discovered and blocked. Backdoors can also be installed by authorized individuals inadvertently, should they run software that contains a Trojan horse (more on this later in this chapter). Common backdoors include NetBus and Back Orifice. Both of these, if running on your system, can allow an attacker remote access to your system—access that allows them to perform any function on your system. A variation on the backdoor is the *rootkit*, and they are established not to gain root access but rather to ensure continued root access.

Null Sessions

Microsoft Windows systems prior to XP and Server 2003 exhibited a vulnerability in their Server Message Block system that allowed users to establish null sessions. A null session is a connection to a Windows interprocess communications share (IPC$). There is good news and bad news associated with this vulnerability. The good news is that Windows XP, Server 2003, and beyond are not susceptible to this vulnerability by default. The bad news is that the millions of previous version machines are vulnerable and patching will not solve the problem. This vulnerability can be used to glean many useful pieces of information from a machine, including user IDs, share names, registry settings, and security settings. A wide range of tools and malware use this vulnerability to achieve their aim.

To harden an affected system from the null session vulnerability requires a bit of work. The seemingly obvious path of upgrading systems to XP and beyond is not a perfect solution, for they too can be tweaked by a malicious user to become susceptible to null sessions. Although there are registry settings to restrict anonymous connections, these will not limit all types; the best method is to limit access to TCP ports 139 and 445 to only trusted users.

Sniffing

The group of protocols that make up the TCP/IP suite was designed to work in a friendly environment where everybody who connected to the network used the protocols as they were designed. The abuse of this friendly assumption is illustrated by network-traffic sniffing programs, sometimes referred to as *sniffers*.

A network sniffer is a software or hardware device that is used to observe traffic as it passes through a network on shared broadcast media. The device can be used to view all traffic, or it can target a specific protocol, service, or even string of characters (looking for logins, for example). Normally, the network device that connects a computer to a network is designed to ignore all traffic that is not destined for that computer. Network sniffers ignore this friendly agreement and observe all traffic on the network, whether destined for that computer or others, as shown in Figure 13-4. A network card that is listening to all network traffic and not just its own is said to be in "promiscuous mode." Some network sniffers are designed not just to observe all traffic but to modify traffic as well.

Network sniffers can be used by network administrators for monitoring network performance. They can be used to perform traffic analysis, for example, to determine what type of traffic is most commonly carried on the network and to determine which segments are most active. They can also be used for network bandwidth analysis and to troubleshoot certain problems (such as duplicate MAC addresses).

Network sniffers can also be used by attackers to gather information that can be used in penetration attempts. Information such as an authorized username and password can be viewed and recorded for later use. The contents of e-mail messages can also

Figure 13-4
Network sniffers listen to all network traffic.

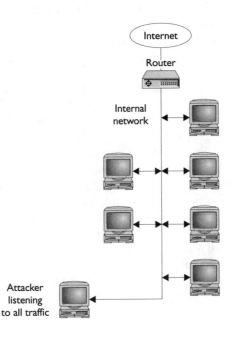

PART VI

be viewed as the messages travel across the network. It should be obvious that administrators and security professionals will not want unauthorized network sniffers on their networks because of the security and privacy concerns they introduce. Fortunately, for network sniffers to be most effective, they need to be on the internal network, which generally means that the chances for outsiders to use them against you is extremely limited. This is another reason that physical security is an important part of information security in today's environment.

Spoofing

Spoofing is nothing more than making data look like it has come from a different source. This is possible in TCP/IP because of the friendly assumptions behind the protocols. When the protocols were developed, it was assumed that individuals who had access to the network layer would be privileged users who could be trusted.

When a packet is sent from one system to another, it includes not only the destination IP address and port but the source IP address as well. You are supposed to fill in the source with your own address, but nothing stops you from filling in another system's address. This is one of the several forms of spoofing.

Spoofing E-Mail

In e-mail spoofing, a message is sent with a From address that differs from that of the sending system. This can be easily accomplished in several different ways using several programs. To demonstrate how simple it is to spoof an e-mail address, you can Telnet to port 25 (the port associated with e-mail) on a mail server. From there, you can fill in any address for the From and To sections of the message, whether or not the addresses are yours and whether they actually exist or not.

You can use several methods to determine whether an e-mail message was probably not sent by the source it claims to have been sent from, but most users do not question their e-mail and will accept where it appears to have originated. A variation on e-mail spoofing, though it is not technically spoofing, is for the attacker to acquire a URL similar to the URL they want to spoof so that e-mail sent from their system appears to have come from the official site—until you read the address carefully. For example, if attackers want to spoof XYZ Corporation, which owns XYZ.com, the attackers might gain access to the URL XYZ.Corp.com. An individual receiving a message from the spoofed corporation site would not normally suspect it to be a spoof but would take it to be official. This same method can be, and has been, used to spoof web sites. The most famous example of this is probably www.whitehouse.com. The www.whitehouse. gov site is the official site for the White House. The www.whitehouse.com URL takes you to a pornographic site. In this case, nobody is likely to take the pornographic site to be the official government site, and it was not intended to be taken that way. If, however, the attackers made their spoofed site appear similar to the official one, they could easily convince many potential viewers that they were at the official site.

IP Address Spoofing

IP is designed to work so that the originators of any IP packet include their own IP address in the From portion of the packet. While this is the intent, nothing prevents a system from inserting a different address in the From portion of the packet. This is known as *IP address spoofing*. An IP address can be spoofed for several reasons. In a specific DoS attack known as a *smurf* attack, the attacker sends a spoofed packet to the broadcast address for a network, which distributes the packet to all systems on that network. In the smurf attack, the packet sent by the attacker to the broadcast address is an echo request with the From address forged so that it appears that another system (the target system) has made the echo request. The normal response of a system to an echo request is an echo reply, and it is used in the ping utility to let a user know whether a remote system is reachable and is responding. In the smurf attack, the request is sent to all systems on the network, so all will respond with an echo reply to the target system, as shown in Figure 13-5. The attacker has sent one packet and has been able to generate as many as 254 responses aimed at the target. Should the attacker send several of these spoofed requests, or send them to several different networks, the target can quickly become overwhelmed with the volume of echo replies it receives.

 EXAM TIP A smurf attack allows an attacker to use a network structure to send large volumes of packets to a victim. By sending ICMP requests to a broadcast IP address, with the victim as the source address, the multitudes of replies will flood the victim system.

Spoofing and Trusted Relationships

Spoofing can also take advantage of a *trusted relationship* between two systems. If two systems are configured to accept the authentication accomplished by each other, an individual logged on to one system might not be forced to go through an authentication process again to access the other system. An attacker can take advantage of this arrangement by sending a packet to one system that appears to have come from a

Figure 13-5
Smurfing used in a
Smurf DoS attack

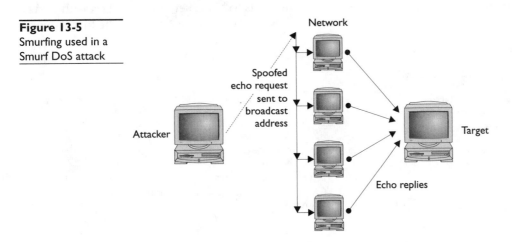

PART VI

trusted system. Since the trusted relationship is in place, the targeted system may perform the requested task without authentication.

Since a reply will often be sent once a packet is received, the system that is being impersonated could interfere with the attack, since it would receive an acknowledgement for a request it never made. The attacker will often initially launch a DoS attack (such as a SYN flooding attack) to temporarily take out the spoofed system for the period of time that the attacker is exploiting the trusted relationship. Once the attack is completed, the DoS attack on the spoofed system would be terminated and possibly, apart from having a temporarily nonresponsive system, the administrators for the systems may never notice that the attack occurred. Figure 13-6 illustrates a spoofing attack that includes a SYN flooding attack.

Because of this type of attack, administrators are encouraged to strictly limit any trusted relationships between hosts. Firewalls should also be configured to discard any packets from outside of the firewall that have From addresses indicating they originated from inside the network (a situation that should not occur normally and that indicates spoofing is being attempted).

Spoofing and Sequence Numbers

How complicated the spoofing is depends heavily on several factors, including whether the traffic is encrypted and where the attacker is located relative to the target. Spoofing attacks from inside a network, for example, are much easier to perform than attacks from outside of the network, because the inside attacker can observe the traffic to and from the target and can do a better job of formulating the necessary packets.

Formulating the packets is more complicated for external attackers because a sequence number is associated with TCP packets. A sequence number is a 32-bit number established by the host that is incremented for each packet sent. Packets are not guaranteed to be received in order, and the sequence number can be used to help reorder packets as they are received and to refer to packets that may have been lost in transmission.

In the TCP three-way handshake, two sets of sequence numbers are created, as shown in Figure 13-7. The first system chooses a sequence number to send with the original SYN packet. The system receiving this SYN packet acknowledges with a SYN/ACK. It sends an acknowledgement number back, which is based on the first sequence

Figure 13-6
Spoofing to take advantage of a trusted relationship

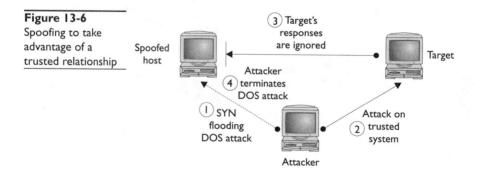

Figure 13-7
Three-way
handshake with
sequence numbers

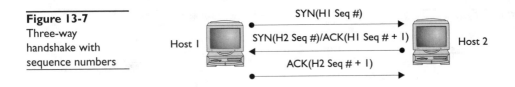

number plus one (that is, it increments the sequence number sent to it by one). It then also creates its own sequence number and sends that along with it. The original system receives the SYN/ACK with the new sequence number. It increments the sequence number by one and uses it as the acknowledgement number in the ACK packet with which it responds.

The difference in the difficulty of attempting a spoofing attack from inside a network and from outside involves determining the sequence number. If the attacker is inside of the network and can observe the traffic with which the target host responds, the attacker can easily see the sequence number the system creates and can respond with the correct sequence number. If the attacker is external to the network and the sequence number the target system generates is not observed, it is next to impossible for the attacker to provide the final ACK with the correct sequence number. So the attacker has to guess what the sequence number might be.

Sequence numbers are somewhat predictable. Sequence numbers for each session are not started from the same number, so that different packets from different concurrent connections will not have the same sequence numbers. Instead, the sequence number for each new connection is incremented by some large number to keep the numbers from being the same. The sequence number may also be incremented by some large number every second (or some other time period). An external attacker has to determine what values are used for these increments. The attacker can do this by attempting connections at various time intervals to observe how the sequence numbers are incremented. Once the pattern is determined, the attacker can attempt a legitimate connection to determine the current value, and then immediately attempt the spoofed connection. The spoofed connection sequence number should be the legitimate connection incremented by the determined value or values.

Sequence numbers are also important in session hijacking, which is discussed in the "TCP/IP Hijacking" section of this chapter.

Man-in-the-Middle Attacks

A man-in-the-middle attack, as the name implies, generally occurs when attackers are able to place themselves in the middle of two other hosts that are communicating. Ideally, this is done by ensuring that all communication going to or from the target host is routed through the attacker's host (which can be accomplished if the attacker can compromise the router for the target host). The attacker can then observe all traffic before relaying it and can actually modify or block traffic. To the target host, it appears that communication is occurring normally, since all expected replies are received. Figure 13-8 illustrates this type of attack.

PART VI

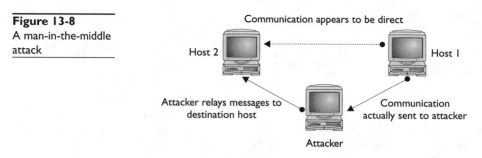

Figure 13-8
A man-in-the-middle attack

Communication appears to be direct

Host 2

Host 1

Attacker relays messages to destination host

Communication actually sent to attacker

Attacker

The amount of information that can be obtained in a man-in-the-middle attack will obviously be limited if the communication is encrypted. Even in this case, however, sensitive information can still be obtained, since knowing what communication is being conducted, and between which individuals, may in fact provide information that is valuable in certain circumstances.

Man-in-the-Middle Attacks on Encrypted Traffic

The term "man-in-the-middle attack" is sometimes used to refer to a more specific type of attack—one in which the encrypted traffic issue is addressed. Public-key encryption, discussed in detail in Chapter 5, requires the use of two keys: your public key, which anybody can use to encrypt or "lock" your message, and your private key, which only you know and which is used to "unlock" or decrypt a message locked with your public key.

If you wanted to communicate securely with your friend Bob, you might ask him for his public key so you could encrypt your messages to him. You, in turn, would supply Bob with your public key. An attacker can conduct a man-in-the-middle attack by intercepting your request for Bob's public key and the sending of your public key to him. The attacker would replace your public key with her public key, and she would send this on to Bob. The attacker's public key would also be sent to you by the attacker instead of Bob's public key. Now when either you or Bob encrypt a message, it will be encrypted using the attacker's public key. The attacker can now intercept it, decrypt it, and then send it on by re-encrypting it with the appropriate key for either you or Bob. Each of you thinks you are transmitting messages securely, but in reality your communication has been compromised. Well-designed cryptographic products use techniques such as mutual authentication to avoid this problem.

Replay Attacks

A *replay attack* occurs when the attacker captures a portion of a communication between two parties and retransmits it at a later time. For example, an attacker might replay a series of commands and codes used in a financial transaction to cause the transaction to be conducted multiple times. Generally replay attacks are associated with attempts to circumvent authentication mechanisms, such as the capturing and reuse of a certificate or ticket.

The best way to prevent replay attacks is with encryption, cryptographic authentication, and time stamps. If a portion of the certificate or ticket includes a date/time stamp or an expiration date/time, and this portion is also encrypted as part of the ticket or certificate, replaying it at a later time will prove useless, since it will be rejected as having expired.

 EXAM TIP The best method for defending against replay attacks is through the use of encryption and short time frames for legal transactions. Encryption can protect the contents from being understood, and a short time frame for a transaction prevents subsequent use.

TCP/IP Hijacking

TCP/IP hijacking and *session hijacking* are terms used to refer to the process of taking control of an already existing session between a client and a server. The advantage to an attacker of hijacking over attempting to penetrate a computer system or network is that the attacker doesn't have to circumvent any authentication mechanisms, since the user has already authenticated and established the session. Once the user has completed the authentication sequence, the attacker can then usurp the session and carry on as if the attacker, and not the user, had authenticated with the system. To prevent the user from noticing anything unusual, the attacker can decide to attack the user's system and perform a DoS attack on it, taking it down so that the user, and the system, will not notice the extra traffic that is taking place.

Hijack attacks generally are used against web and Telnet sessions. Sequence numbers as they apply to spoofing also apply to session hijacking, since the hijacker will need to provide the correct sequence number to continue the appropriate sessions.

Attacks on Encryption

Cryptography is the art of "secret writing," and *encryption* is the process of transforming *plaintext* into an unreadable format known as *ciphertext* using a specific technique or algorithm. Most encryption techniques use some form of key in the encryption process. The key is used in a mathematical process to scramble the original message to arrive at the unreadable ciphertext. Another key (sometimes the same one and sometimes a different one) is used to decrypt or unscramble the ciphertext to re-create the original plaintext. The length of the key often directly relates to the strength of the encryption.

Cryptanalysis is the process of attempting to break a cryptographic system—it is an attack on the specific method used to encrypt the plaintext. Cryptographic systems can be compromised in various ways. Encryption is discussed in detail in Chapter 4.

Weak Keys

Certain encryption algorithms may have specific keys that yield poor, or easily decrypted, ciphertext. Imagine an encryption algorithm that consisted solely of a single XOR function (an exclusive OR function where two bits are compared and a 1 is returned if either of the original bits, but not both, is a 1), where the key was repeatedly used to XOR with the plaintext. A key where all bits are 0's, for example, would result in ciphertext that is the same as the original plaintext. This would obviously be a weak key for this encryption algorithm. In fact, any key with long strings of 0's would yield portions of the ciphertext that were the same as the plaintext. In this simple example, many keys could be considered weak.

Encryption algorithms used in computer systems and networks are much more complicated than a simple, single XOR function, but some algorithms have still been found to have weak keys that make cryptanalysis easier.

Exhaustive Search of Key Space

Even if the specific algorithm used to encrypt a message is complicated and has not been shown to have weak keys, the key length will still play a significant role in how easy it is to attack the method of encryption. Generally speaking, the longer a key, the harder it will be to attack. Thus, a 40-bit encryption scheme will be easier to attack using a brute-force technique (which tests all possible keys, one by one) than a 256-bit based scheme. This is easily demonstrated by imagining a scheme that employed a 2-bit key. Even if the resulting ciphertext were completely unreadable, performing a brute-force attack until one key is found that can decrypt the ciphertext would not take long, since only four keys are possible. Every bit that is added to the length of a key doubles the number of keys that have to be tested in a brute-force attack on the encryption. It is easy to understand why a scheme utilizing a 40-bit key would be much easier to attack than a scheme that utilized a 256-bit key.

The bottom line is simple: an exhaustive search of the keyspace will decrypt the message. The strength of the encryption method is related to the sheer size of the keyspace, which with modern algorithms is large enough to provide significant time constraints when using this method to break an encrypted message. Algorithmic complexity is also an issue with respect to brute force, and you cannot immediately compare different key lengths from different algorithms and assume relative strength.

Indirect Attacks

One of the most common ways of attacking an encryption system is to find weaknesses in mechanisms surrounding the cryptography. Examples include poor random number generators, unprotected key exchanges, keys stored on hard drives without sufficient protection, and other general programmatic errors, such as buffer overflows. In attacks that target these types of weaknesses, it is not the cryptographic algorithm itself that is being attacked, but rather the implementation of that algorithm in the real world.

Address System Attacks

Addresses control many aspects of a computer system. IP addresses can be manipulated, as shown previously, and the other address schemes can be manipulated as well. In the summer of 2008, much was made of a serious domain name system (DNS) vulnerability that required the simultaneous patching of systems by over 80 vendors. This coordinated effort closed a technical loophole in the domain name resolution infra-structure that allowed hijacking and man-in-the-middle attacks on the DNS system worldwide.

The DNS system has been the target of other attacks. One attack, DNS kiting, is an economic attack against the terms of using a new DNS entry. New DNS purchases are allowed a five day "test period" during which the name can be relinquished for no fee. Creative users learned to register a name, use it for less than five days, relinquish the name, and then get the name and begin all over, repeating this cycle many times using a name without paying for it. Typical registration versus permanent entry ratios of 15:1 occurred in February 2007. GoDaddy reported that out of 55.1 million requests only 3.6 million were not canceled. Another twist on this scheme is the concept of domain name front running, where a registrar places a name on five-day hold after someone searches for it, and then offers it for sale at a higher price. In January 2008, Network Solutions was accused of violating the trust as a registrar by forcing people to purchase names from them after they engaged in domain name tasting.

Another attack on DNS is through the concept of DNS poisoning. DNS poisoning is the unauthorized changing of DNS tables on a machine. When an IP address needs to be resolved, a check against the local cache is performed first. If the address is present, this alleviates the need to ask an outside DNS resource. If the local cache is tampered with, this can result in the hijacking of information as the computer will connect to the wrong site.

Local MAC addresses can also be poisoned in the same manner, although this is called ARP poisoning, which can cause miscommunications locally. Poisoning attacks can be used to steal information, establish man-in-the-middle attacks, and even create DoS opportunities.

Password Guessing

The most common form of authentication is the user ID and password combination. While it is not inherently a poor mechanism for authentication, the combination can be attacked in several ways. All too often, these attacks yield favorable results for the attacker not as a result of a weakness in the scheme but usually due to the user not following good password procedures.

Poor Password Choices

The least technical of the various password-attack techniques consists of the attacker simply attempting to guess the password of an authorized user of the system or net-work. It is surprising how often this simple method works, and the reason it does is because people are notorious for picking poor passwords. Users need to select a pass-word that they can remember, so they create simple passwords, such as their birthday, their mother's maiden name, the name of their spouse or one of their children, or even simply their user ID itself. All it takes is for the attacker to obtain a valid user ID (often a simple matter, because organizations tend to use an individual's names in some com-bination—first letter of their first name combined with their last name, for example) and a little bit of information about the user before guessing can begin. Organizations sometimes make it even easier for attackers to obtain this sort of information by posting the names of their "management team" and other individuals, sometimes with short biographies, on their web sites.

Even if the person doesn't use some personal detail as her password, she may still get lucky, since many people use a common word for their password. Attackers can obtain lists of common passwords—a number of them exist on the Internet. Words such as "password" and "secret" have often been used as passwords. Names of favorite sports teams also often find their way onto lists of commonly used passwords.

Dictionary Attack

Another method of determining passwords is to use a password-cracking program that uses a list of dictionary of words to try to guess the password. The words can be used by themselves, or two or more smaller words can be combined to form a single possible password. A number of commercial and public-domain password-cracking programs employ a variety of methods to crack passwords, including using variations on the user ID.

The programs often permit the attacker to create various rules that tell the program how to combine words to form new possible passwords. Users commonly substitute certain numbers for specific letters. If the user wanted to use the word *secret* for a password, for example, the letter *e* could be replaced with the number *3*, yielding *s3cr3t*. This password will not be found in the dictionary, so a pure dictionary attack would not crack it, but the password is still easy for the user to remember. If a rule were created that tried all words in the dictionary and then tried the same words substituting the number *3* for the letter *e*, however, the password would be cracked.

Rules can also be defined so that the cracking program will substitute special characters for other characters or combine words. The ability of the attacker to crack passwords is directly related to the method the user employs to create the password in the first place, as well as the dictionary and rules used.

Brute-Force Attack

If the user has selected a password that is not found in a dictionary, even if various numbers or special characters are substituted for letters, the only way the password can be cracked is for an attacker to attempt a brute-force attack, in which the password-cracking program attempts all possible password combinations.

The length of the password and the size of the set of possible characters in the password will greatly affect the time a brute-force attack will take. A few years ago, this method of attack was very time consuming, since it took considerable time to generate all possible combinations. With the increase in computer speed, however, generating password combinations is much faster, making it more feasible to launch brute-force attacks against certain computer systems and networks.

A brute-force attack on a password can take place at two levels: It can attack a system where the attacker is attempting to guess the password at a login prompt, or it can attack against the list of password hashes contained in a password file. The first attack can be made more difficult if the account locks after a few failed login attempts. The second attack can be thwarted if the password file is securely maintained so that others cannot obtain a copy of it.

Hybrid Attack

A hybrid password attack is a system that combines the preceding methods. Most cracking tools have this option built in, first attempting a dictionary attack, and then moving to brute-force methods.

Birthday Attack

The *birthday attack* is a special type of brute-force attack that gets its name from something known as the *birthday paradox*, which states that in a group of at least 23 people, the chance that two individuals will have the same birthday is greater than 50 percent. Mathematically, we can use the equation $1.25k^{1/2}$ (with k equaling the size of the set of possible values), and in the birthday paradox, k would be equal to 365 (the number of possible birthdays). This same phenomenon applies to passwords, with k (number of passwords) being quite a bit larger.

Software Exploitation

An attack that takes advantage of bugs or weaknesses in software is referred to as *software exploitation*. These weaknesses can be the result of poor design, poor testing, or poor coding practices. They can also result from what are sometimes called "features." An example of this might be a debugging feature, which when used during debugging might allow unauthenticated individuals to execute programs on a system. If this feature remains in the program in when the final version of the software is shipped, it creates a weakness that is just waiting to be exploited.

Buffer Overflow Attack

A common weakness that has often been exploited is a buffer overflow. A buffer overflow occurs when a program is provided more data for input than it was designed to handle. For example, what would happen if a program that asks for a 7- to 10-character phone number instead receives a string of 150 characters? Many programs will provide some error checking to ensure that this will not cause a problem. Some programs, however, cannot handle this error, and the extra characters continue to fill memory, overwriting other portions of the program. This can result in a number of problems, including causing the program to abort or the system to crash. Under certain circumstances, the program can execute a command supplied by the attacker. Buffer overflows typically inherit the level of privilege enjoyed by the program being exploited. This is why programs that use root level access are so dangerous when exploited with a buffer overflow, as the code that will execute does so at root level access.

Malicious Code

Malicious code refers to software that has been designed for some nefarious purpose. Such software can be designed to cause damage to a system, such as by deleting all files, or it can be designed to create a backdoor in the system to grant access to unauthorized individuals. Generally the installation of malicious code is done so that it is not obvious to the authorized users. Several different types of malicious software can be used, such as viruses, Trojan horses, logic bombs, spyware, and worms, and they differ in the ways they are installed and their purposes.

Viruses

The best-known type of malicious code is the virus. Much has been written about viruses as a result of several high-profile security events that involved them. A virus is a piece of malicious code that replicates by attaching itself to another piece of executable code. When the other executable code is run, the virus also executes and has the opportunity to infect other files and perform any other nefarious actions it was designed to do. The specific way that a virus infects other files, and the type of files it infects, depends on the type of virus. The first viruses created were of two types—boot sector or program viruses.

Boot Sector Virus   A boot sector virus infects the boot sector portion of either a floppy disk or a hard drive (years ago, not all computers had hard drives, and many booted from a floppy). When a computer is first turned on, a small portion of the operating system is initially loaded from hardware. This small operating system then attempts to load the rest of the operating system from a specific location (sector) on either the floppy or the hard drive. A boot sector virus infects this portion of the drive.

An example of this type of virus was the Stoned virus, which moved the true Master Boot Record (MBR) from the first to the seventh sector of the first cylinder and replaced the original MBR with the virus code. When the system was turned on, the virus was first executed, which had a one-in-seven chance of displaying a message stating the computer was "stoned"; otherwise, it would not announce itself and would instead attempt to infect other boot sectors. This virus was rather tame in comparison to other viruses of its time, which were often designed to delete the entire hard drive after a period of time in which they would attempt to spread.

Program Virus   A second type of virus is the program virus, which attaches itself to executable files—typically files ending in .exe or .com on Windows-based systems. The virus is attached in such a way that it is executed before the program executes. Most program viruses also hide a nefarious purpose, such as deleting the hard drive data, which is triggered by a specific event, such as a date or after a certain number of other files are infected. Like other types of viruses, program viruses are often not detected until after they execute their malicious payload. One method that has been used to detect this sort of virus before it has an opportunity to damage a system is to calculate checksums for commonly used programs or utilities. Should the checksum for an executable ever change, it is quite likely that it is due to a virus infection.

Macro Virus   In the late 1990s, another type of virus appeared that now accounts for the majority of viruses. As systems and operating systems became more powerful, the boot sector virus, which once accounted for most reported infections, became less common. Systems no longer commonly booted from floppies, which were the main method for boot sector viruses to spread. Instead, the proliferation of software that included macro-programming languages resulted in a new breed of virus—the macro virus.

The Concept virus was the first known example of this new breed. It appeared to be created to demonstrate the possibility of attaching a virus to a document file, something that had been thought to be impossible before the introduction of software that included powerful macro language capabilities. By this time, however, Microsoft Word documents could include segments of code written in a derivative of Visual Basic. Further development of other applications that allowed macro capability, and enhanced versions of the original macro language, had the side effect of allowing the proliferation of viruses that took advantage of this capability.

This type of virus is so common today that it is considered a security best practice to advise users never to open a document attached to an e-mail if it seems at all suspicious. Many organizations now routinely have their mail servers eliminate any attachments containing Visual Basic macros.

Avoiding Virus Infection Always being cautious about executing programs or opening documents sent to you is a good security practice. "If you don't know where it came from or where it has been, don't open or run it" should be the basic mantra for all computer users. Another security best practice for protecting against virus infection is to install and run an antivirus program. Since these programs are designed to protect against known viruses, it is also important to maintain an up-to-date listing of virus signatures for your antivirus software. Antivirus software vendors provide this information, and administrators should stay on top of the latest updates to the list of known viruses.

Two advances in virus writing have made it more difficult for antivirus software to detect viruses. These advances are the introduction of *stealth virus* techniques and *polymorphic viruses*. A stealthy virus employs techniques to help evade being detected by antivirus software that uses checksums or other techniques. Polymorphic viruses also attempt to evade detection, but they do so by changing the virus itself (the virus "evolves"). Because the virus changes, signatures for that virus may no longer be valid, and the virus may escape detection by antivirus software.

Virus Hoaxes Viruses have caused so much damage to systems that many Internet users have become extremely cautious anytime a rumor of a new virus is heard. Many users will not connect to the Internet when they hear about a virus outbreak, just to be sure their machines don't get infected. This has given rise to virus hoaxes, in which word is spread about a new virus and the extreme danger it poses. It may warn users to not read certain files or connect to the Internet.

A good example of a virus hoax was the Good Times virus warning, which has been copied repeatedly and can still be seen in various forms today. It caused widespread panic as users read about this extremely dangerous virus, which could actually cause the processor to overheat (from being put into an "nth complexity infinite binary loop") and be destroyed. Many folks saw through this hoax, but many less experienced users did not, and they passed the warning along to all of their friends.

Hoaxes can actually be even more destructive than just wasting time and bandwidth. Some hoaxes warning of a dangerous virus have included instructions to delete certain files if they're found on the user's system. Unfortunately for those who follow the advice, the files may actually be part of the operating system, and deleting them could keep the system from booting properly. This suggests another good piece of security advice: ensure the authenticity and accuracy of any virus report before following somebody's advice. Antivirus software vendors are a good source of factual data for this sort of threat as well. (See www.symantec.com/business/security_response/threatexplorer/risks/hoaxes.jsp or http://vil.mcafee.com/hoax.asp for examples of hoaxes.)

Trojan Horses

A Trojan horse, or simply *Trojan*, is a piece of software that appears to do one thing (and may, in fact, actually do that thing) but hides some other functionality. The analogy to the famous story of antiquity is very accurate. In the original case, the object appeared to be a large wooden horse, and in fact it was. At the same time, it hid something much more sinister and dangerous to the occupants of the city of Troy. As long as the horse was left outside the city walls, it could cause no damage to the inhabitants. It had to be taken in by the inhabitants, and it was inside that the hidden purpose was activated. A computer Trojan works in much the same way. Unlike a virus, which reproduces by attaching itself to other files or programs, a Trojan is a standalone program that must be copied and installed by the user—it must be "brought inside" the system by an authorized user. The challenge for the attacker is enticing the user to copy and run the program. This generally means that the program must be disguised as something that the user would want to run—a special utility or game, for example. Once it has been copied and is inside the system, the Trojan will perform its hidden purpose with the user often still unaware of its true nature.

A good example of a Trojan is Back Orifice (BO), originally created in 1999 and now offered in several versions. BO can be attached to a number of types of programs. Once it is attached, and once an infected file is run, BO will create a way for unauthorized individuals to take over the system remotely, as if they were sitting at the console. BO is designed to work with Windows-based systems. Many Trojans communicate to the outside through a port that the Trojan opens, and this is one of the ways Trojans can be detected.

The single best method to prevent the introduction of a Trojan to your system is never to run software if you are unsure of its origin, security, and integrity. A virus-checking program may also be useful in detecting and preventing the installation of known Trojans.

Spyware

Spyware is software that "spies" on users, recording and reporting on their activities. Typically installed without user knowledge, spyware can perform a wide range of activities. It can record keystrokes (commonly called *keylogging*) when the user logs onto specific web sites. It can monitor how a user applies a specific piece of software, that is, monitor attempts to cheat at games. Many spyware uses seem innocuous at first, but the unauthorized monitoring of a system can be abused very easily. In other cases, the spyware is specifically designed to steal information. Many states have passed legislation banning the unapproved installation of software, but spyware can circumvent this issue through complex and confusing end-user license agreements.

Logic Bombs

Logic bombs, unlike viruses and Trojans, are a type of malicious software that is deliberately installed, generally by an authorized user. A logic bomb is a piece of code that sits dormant for a period of time until some event invokes its malicious payload. An example of a logic bomb might be a program that is set to load and run automatically, and that periodically checks an organization's payroll or personnel database for a specific employee. If the employee is not found, the malicious payload executes, deleting vital corporate files.

If the event is a specific date or time, the program will often be referred to as a *time bomb*. In one famous example of a time bomb, a disgruntled employee left a time bomb in place just prior to being fired from his job. Two weeks later, thousands of client records were deleted. Police were eventually able to track the malicious code to the disgruntled ex-employee, who was prosecuted for his actions. He had hoped that the two weeks that had passed since his dismissal would have caused investigators to assume he could not have been the individual who had caused the deletion of the records.

Logic bombs are difficult to detect because they are often installed by authorized users and, in particular, have been installed by administrators who are also often responsible for security. This demonstrates the need for a separation of duties and a periodic review of all programs and services that are running on a system. It also illustrates the need to maintain an active backup program so that if your organization loses critical files to this sort of malicious code, it loses only transactions that occurred since the most recent backup and no permanent loss of data results.

Rootkits

Rootkits are a form of malware that is specifically designed to modify the operation of the operating system in some fashion to facilitate nonstandard functionality. The history of rootkits goes back to the beginning of the UNIX operating system, where they were sets of modified administrative tools. Originally designed to allow a program to take greater control over operating system function when it fails or becomes unresponsive, the technique has evolved and is used in a variety of ways. One high-profile case occurred at Sony BMG Corporation, when rootkit technology was used to provide copy protection technology on some of the company's CDs. Two major issues led to this being a complete debacle for Sony: first, the software modified systems without the user's approval; and second, the software opened a security hole on Windows-based systems, creating an exploitable vulnerability at the rootkit level. This led the Sony case to be labeled as *malware*, which is the most common use of rootkits.

A rootkit can do many things—in fact, it can do virtually anything that the operating system does. Rootkits modify the operating system kernel and supporting functions, changing the nature of the system's operation. Rootkits are designed to avoid, either by subversion or evasion, the security functions of the operating system to avoid detection. Rootkits act as a form of malware that can change thread priorities to boost an application's performance, perform keylogging, act as a sniffer, hide other files from other applications, or create backdoors in the authentication system. The use of rootkit functionality to hide other processes and files enables an attacker to use a portion of a computer without the user or other applications knowing what is happening. This hides exploit code from antivirus and antispyware programs, acting as a cloak of invisibility.

Rootkits can load before the operating system loads, acting as a virtualization layer, as in SubVirt and Blue Pill. Rootkits can exist in firmware, and these have been demonstrated in both video cards and PCI expansion cards. Rootkits can exist as loadable library modules, effectively changing portions of the operating system outside the kernel. Further information on specific rootkits in the wild can be found at www.antirootkit.com.

EXAM TIP   Five types of rootkits exist: firmware, virtual, kernel, library, and application level.

Once a rootkit is detected, it needs to be removed and cleaned up. Because of rootkits' invasive nature, and the fact that many aspects of rootkits are not easily detectable, most system administrators don't even attempt to clean up or remove a rootkit. It is far easier to use a previously captured clean system image and reimage the machine than attempt to determine the depth and breadth of the damage and attempt to fix individual files.

Worms

It was once easy to distinguish between a worm and a virus. Recently, with the introduction of new breeds of sophisticated malicious code, the distinction has blurred. Worms are pieces of code that attempt to penetrate networks and computer systems. Once a penetration occurs, the worm will create a new copy of itself on the penetrated system. Reproduction of a worm thus does not rely on the attachment of the virus to another piece of code or to a file, which is the definition of a virus.

Viruses were generally thought of as a system-based problem, and worms were network-based. If the malicious code is sent throughout a network, it may subsequently be called a worm. The important distinction, however, is whether the code has to attach itself to something else (a virus) or if it can "survive" on its own (a worm).

Some recent examples of worms that have had high profiles include the Sobig worm of 2003, the SQL Slammer worm of 2003, the 2001 attacks of Code Red and Nimba, and the 2005 Zotob worm that took down CNN Live. Nimba was particularly impressive in that it used five different methods to spread; via e-mail, via open network shares, from browsing infected web sites, using directory traversal vulnerability of Microsoft IIS 4.0/5.0, and most impressively through the use of backdoors left by Code Red II and sadmind worms.

The Morris Worm   The most famous example of a worm was the Morris worm in 1988. Also sometimes referred to as the Internet worm, because of its effect on the early Internet, the worm was able to insert itself into so many systems connected to the Internet that it has been repeatedly credited with "bringing the Internet to its knees" for several days. This worm provided the impetus for the creation of what was once called the Computer Emergency Response Team Coordination Center, now the CERT Coordination Center (CERT/CC), located at Carnegie Mellon University.

The Morris worm was created by graduate student Robert Morris. It utilized several known vulnerabilities to gain access to a new system, and it also relied on password guessing to obtain access to accounts. Once a system was penetrated, a small bootstrap program was inserted into the new system and executed. This program then downloaded the rest of the worm to the new system. The worm had some stealth characteristics to make it harder to determine what it was doing, and it suffered from one major miscalculation. The worm would not be loaded if a copy of it was already found on the new system, but it was designed to ignore this check periodically, reportedly to ensure that the worm could not be easily eliminated. The problem with this plan was that interconnected systems were constantly being reinfected. Eventually the systems were running so many copies of the worm that the system response time ground to a stop. It took a concerted effort by many individuals to eliminate the worm. While the Morris worm carried no malicious payload, it is entirely possible for worms to do so.

Samy Worm (The MySpace Worm)   MySpace is a popular social networking site with a feature that allows people to list other users as friends. In 2005, a clever MySpace user looking to expand his friends list created the first self-propagating cross-site scripting (XSS) worm. In less than a day, the worm had gone viral and user Samy had amassed more than 1 million friends on the popular online community. The worm's code, now posted at http://namb.la/popular/tech.html, used a fairly sophisticated JavaScript. Fortunately the script was written for fun and didn't try to take advantage of unpatched security holes in Internet Explorer to create a massive MySpace botnet. MySpace was taken down as the worm replicated too efficiently, eventually surpassing several thousand replications per second.

Protection Against Worms   How you protect your system against worms depends on the type of worm. Those attached and propagated through e-mail can be avoided by following the same guidelines about not opening files and not running attachments unless you are absolutely sure of their origin and integrity. Protecting against the Morris type of Internet worm involves securing systems and networks against penetration in the same way you would protect your systems against human attackers. Install patches, eliminate unused and unnecessary services, enforce good password security, and use firewalls and intrusion detection systems. More sophisticated attacks, such as the Samy worm, are almost impossible to avoid.

Application-Level Attacks

Attacks against a system can occur at the network level, at the operating system level, at the application level, or at the user level (social engineering). Early attack patterns were against the network, but most of today's attacks are aimed at the applications. This is primarily because this is where the objective of most attacks resides; in the infamous words of bank robber Willie Sutton, "because that's where the money is." In fact, many of today's attacks on systems are combinations of using vulnerabilities in networks, operating systems, and applications, all means to an end to obtain the desired objective of an attack, which is usually some form of data.

Application level attacks take advantage of several facts associated with computer applications. First, most applications are large programs written by groups of programmers and by their nature have errors in design and coding that create vulnerabilities. For a list of typical vulnerabilities, see the Common Vulnerability and Exposures (CVE) list maintained by Mitre, http://cve.mitre.org. Second, even when vulnerabilities are discovered and patched by software vendors, end users are slow to apply patches, as evidenced by the SQL Slammer incident in January 2003. The vulnerability exploited was a buffer overflow, and the vendor supplied a patch six months prior to the outbreak, yet the worm still spread quickly due to the multitude of unpatched systems. A more complete examination of common application vulnerabilities is presented in Chapter 15.

War-Dialing and War-Driving

War-dialing is the term used to describe an attacker's attempt to discover unprotected modem connections to computer systems and networks. The term's origin is the 1983 movie *War Games,* in which the star has his machine systematically call a sequence of phone numbers in an attempt to find a computer connected to a modem. In the case of the movie, the intent was to find a machine with games the attacker could play, though obviously an attacker could have other purposes once access is obtained.

War-dialing is surprisingly successful, mostly because of *rogue modems*—unauthorized modems attached to computers on a network by authorized users. Generally the reason for attaching the modem is not malicious—an individual may simply want to be able to go home and then connect to the organization's network to continue working. The problem, however, is that if a user can connect, so can an attacker. If the authorized user has not implemented any security protection, this means of access could be totally open. This is often the case. Most organizations enact strict policies against connecting unauthorized modems, but it is difficult to enforce this kind of policy. Recently, new technology has been developed to address this common backdoor into corporate networks. Telephone firewalls have been created, which block any unauthorized modem connections into an organization. These devices make it impossible for an unauthorized modem connection to be established and can also enforce strict access policies on any authorized modems.

Another avenue of attack on computer systems and networks has seen a tremendous increase over the last few years because of the increase in the use of wireless networks. Wireless networks have some obvious advantages—they free employees from the cable connection to a port on their wall, allowing them to move throughout the building with their laptops and still be connected. An employee could, for example, leave her desk with her laptop and move to a conference room where she could then make a presentation, all without ever having to disconnect her machine from the wall or find a connection in the conference room.

The problem with wireless networks is that it is difficult to limit access to them. Since no physical connection exists, the distance that a user can go and still remain connected is a function of the wireless network itself and where the various components of the network are placed. To ensure access throughout a facility, stations are often placed at numerous locations, some of which may actually provide access to areas outside of the organization to ensure that the farthest offices in the organization can be reached. Frequently, access extends into adjacent offices or into the parking lot or street. Attackers can locate these access areas that fall outside of the organization and attempt to gain unauthorized access.

The term *war-driving* has been used to refer to the activity in which attackers wander throughout an area (often in a car) with a computer with wireless capability, searching for wireless networks they can access. Some security measures can limit an attacker's ability to succeed at this activity, but, just as in war-dialing, the individuals who set up the wireless networks don't always activate these security mechanisms.

Social Engineering

Social engineering relies on lies and misrepresentation, which an attacker uses to trick an authorized user into providing information or access the attacker would not normally be entitled to. The attacker might, for example, contact a system administrator pretending to be an authorized user, asking to have a password reset. Another common ploy is to pose as a representative from a vendor needing temporary access to perform some emergency maintenance. Social engineering also applies to physical access. Simple techniques include impersonating pizza or flower delivery personnel to gain physical access to a facility.

Attackers know that, due to poor security practices, if they can gain physical access to an office, the chances are good that, given a little unsupervised time, a user ID and password pair might be found on a notepad or sticky note. Unsupervised access might not even be required, depending on the quality of the security practices of the organization. (One of the authors of this book was once considering opening an account at a bank near his home. As he sat down at the desk across from the bank employee taking his information, the author noticed one of the infamous little yellow notes attached to the computer monitor the employee was using. The note read "password for July is julyjuly." It probably isn't too hard to guess what August's password might be. Unfortunately, this is all too often the state of security practices in most organizations. With that in mind, it is easy to see how social engineering might work and might provide all the information an attacker needs to gain unauthorized access to a system or network.

Auditing

Auditing, in the financial community, is done to verify the accuracy and integrity of financial records. Many standards have been established in the financial community about how to record and report a company's financial status correctly. In the computer security world, auditing serves a similar function. It is a process of assessing the security state of an organization compared against an established standard.

The important elements here are the standards. Organizations from different communities may have widely different standards, and any audit will need to consider the appropriate elements for the specific community. Audits differ from security or vulnerability assessments in that assessments measure the security posture of the organization but may do so without any mandated standards against which to compare them. In a security assessment, general security "best practices" can be used, but they may lack the regulatory teeth that standards often provide. Penetration tests can also be encountered—these tests are conducted against an organization to determine whether any holes in the organization's security can be found. The goal of the penetration test is to penetrate the security rather than measuring it against some standard. Penetration tests are often viewed as *white-hat hacking* in that the methods used often mirror those that attackers (often called *black hats*) might use.

You should conduct some form of security audit or assessment on a regular basis. Your organization might spend quite a bit on security, and it is important to measure how effective the efforts have been. In certain communities, audits can be regulated on a periodic basis with very specific standards that must be measured against. Even if your organization is not part of such a community, periodic assessments are important.

Many particulars can be evaluated during an assessment, but at a minimum, the security perimeter (with all of its components, including host-based security) should be examined, as well as the organization's policies, procedures, and guidelines governing security. Employee training is another aspect that should be studied, since employees are the targets of social engineering and password-guessing attacks.

Security audits, assessments, and penetration tests are a big business, and a number of organizations can perform them for you. The costs of these varies widely depending on the extent of the tests you want, the background of the company you are contracting with, and the size of the organization to be tested.

Chapter Review

In attempting to attack a computer system or network, an attacker follows several general steps. These include gathering as much information about the target as possible, obtaining information about potential vulnerabilities that might exist in the operating system or applications running on the target system, and finally using tools to attempt to exploit those vulnerabilities. An administrator can make this process more difficult for the attacker by limiting the amount of information that can be obtained about the organization, by limiting the services offered, and by installing all appropriate patches for the remaining services.

Attackers can access computer systems and networks in a number of different ways. These vary from the non-technical social engineering attacks, where attackers attempt to lie and misrepresent themselves to authorized users in order to obtain key information, to DDoS attacks, which can incorporate thousands of penetrated systems in an attack on a targeted system or network.

In addition to guarding against human attackers, you must try to prevent various forms of malicious software from attacking your system. Security auditing and assessments can be used to measure an organization's current security posture. It is important that you understand the various types of attacks that could affect your organization to plan how you will address them, should they occur.

Questions

To further help you prepare for the Security+ exam, and to test your level of preparedness, answer the following questions and then check your answers against the list of correct answers at the end of the chapter.

1. A SYN flood is an example of what type of attack?

   A. Malicious code

   B. Denial-of-service

   C. Man-in-the-middle

   D. Spoofing

2. An attack in which the attacker simply listens for all traffic being transmitted across a network, in the hope of viewing something such as a user ID and password combination, is known as

   A. A man-in-the-middle attack

   B. A denial-of service-attack

   C. A sniffing attack

   D. A backdoor attack

3. Which attack takes advantage of a trusted relationship that exists between two systems?

   A. Spoofing

   B. Password guessing

   C. Sniffing

   D. Brute-force

4. In what type of attack does an attacker resend the series of commands and codes used in a financial transaction to cause the transaction to be conducted multiple times?

   A. Spoofing

   B. Man-in-the-middle

   C. Replay

   D. Backdoor

5. The trick in both spoofing and TCP/IP hijacking is in trying to

A. Provide the correct authentication token.

B. Find two systems between which a trusted relationship exists.

C. Guess a password or brute-force a password to gain initial access to the system or network.

D. Maintain the correct sequence numbers for the response packets.

6. Rootkits are challenging security problems because

A. They can be invisible to the operating system and end user.

B. Their true functionality can be cloaked, preventing analysis.

C. They can do virtually anything an operating system can do.

D. All of the above.

7. The ability of an attacker to crack passwords is directly related to the method the user employed to create the password in the first place, as well as

A. The length of the password

B. The size of the character set used in generating the password

C. The speed of the machine cracking the password

D. The dictionary and rules used by the cracking program

8. A piece of malicious code that must attach itself to another file to replicate itself is known as

A. A worm

B. A virus

C. A logic bomb

D. A Trojan

9. A piece of malicious code that appears to be designed to do one thing (and may in fact do that thing) but that hides some other payload (often malicious) is known as

A. A worm

B. A virus

C. A logic bomb

D. A Trojan

10. An attack in which an attacker attempts to lie and misrepresent himself in order to gain access to information that can be useful in an attack is known as

A. Social science

B. White-hat hacking

C. Social engineering

D. Social manipulation

11. The first step in an attack on a computer system consists of

    A. Gathering as much information about the target system as possible

    B. Obtaining as much information about the organization in which the target lies as possible

    C. Searching for possible exploits that can be used against known vulnerabilities

    D. Searching for specific vulnerabilities that may exist in the target's operating system or software applications

12. The best way to minimize possible avenues of attack for your system is to

    A. Install a firewall and check the logs daily.

    B. Monitor your intrusion detection system for possible attacks.

    C. Limit the information that can be obtained on your organization and the services that are run by your Internet-visible systems.

    D. Ensure that all patches have been applied for the services that are offered by your system.

13. A war-driving attack is an attempt to exploit what technology?

    A. Fiber-optic networks whose cables often run along roads and bridges

    B. Cellular telephones

    C. The public switched telephone network (PSTN)

    D. Wireless networks

14. How can you protect against worms of the type that Robert Morris unleashed on the Internet?

    A. Follow the same procedures you'd use to secure your system from a human attacker.

    B. Install antivirus software.

    C. Ensure that no executable attachments to e-mails are executed unless their integrity has been verified.

    D. Monitor for changes to utilities and other system software.

15. Malicious code that is set to execute its payload on a specific date or at a specific time is known as

    A. A logic bomb

    B. A Trojan horse

    C. A virus

    D. A time bomb

PART VI

Answers

1. **B.** A SYN flood attack involves launching a large number of SYN packets at a system. In TCP, the response to this is a SYN/ACK, and the system then waits for an ACK to complete the three-way handshake. If no ACK is received, the system will wait until a time-out occurs, and then it will release the connection. If enough SYN packets are received (requesting that communication be set up) the system can fill up and not process any more requests. This is a type of DoS attack.

2. **C.** Sniffing consists of a person simply listening to all traffic on a network. It takes advantage of the friendly nature of the network, in which systems are only supposed to grab and examine packets that are destined to them. Sniffing looks at all packets traveling across the network.

3. **A.** One form of spoofing attack attempts to take advantage of the trusted relationship that may exist between two systems. This trusted relationship could mean that users on one system will not be required to authenticate themselves when accessing the other system; the second system trusts the first to have performed any necessary authentication. If packets are formed that claim to have come from one of the trusted systems, the target can be fooled into performing actions as if an authorized user had sent them.

4. **C.** This is the description of a replay attack.

5. **D.** Getting the correct sequence number is the tricky part of any attempt to spoof or take over a session. This is made easy if the attacker can observe (sniff) the network traffic. If, however, the attacker is external to the network, the task is much more complicated.

6. **D.** Rootkits have almost unlimited power over an infected system. They can cloak themselves from detection and hide their true nature.

7. **D.** This is a tricky question. All of the answers have a bearing on the ability of the attacker to crack the password, but, as discussed in the text, the dictionary and rule set used will make or break the attempt (unless an attacker *wants* to try a brute-force attack, which is generally his last option). The size of the password will certainly have a bearing, but the difference between brute-forcing a 13-character password and a 14-character password is not important—neither will be accomplished in the lifetime of the attacker. The same can be said of the size of the character set used to generate the password. The more characters that are available, the larger the number of passwords that must be tried in order to brute-force it—but attackers try to stay away from using brute-force attacks. The speed of the machine will have some bearing, but speed will make little difference if the attacker uses a brute-force attack, since he still won't crack it in time to take advantage of it. If the

attacker can pick a good dictionary and rule set, he can probably crack the password (remember that users have a tendency to select poor passwords).

8. **B.** This answer defines a virus. This is the distinguishing aspect of a virus that separates it from other forms of malicious code, especially worms.

9. **D.** This describes a Trojan (or Trojan horse). A virus that is attached to another file and that appears to be that file may also hide a malicious payload, but the description provided is traditionally used to describe a Trojan.

10. **C.** This is a description of social engineering. The term *white-hat hacking* is often used to refer to authorized penetration tests on a network.

11. **B.** The first step is generally acknowledged to be to gather as much information about the organization as possible. This information can then be used in social engineering attacks that can result in the revelation of even more information, or even access to the system. If access can be obtained without having to run any exploits, the attacker's chance of discovery is minimized. The second step is to gather information about the specific systems and networks—details on the actual hardware and software that is being used. It is not until both of these steps have been accomplished that possible vulnerabilities and tools to exploit them can be determined. This sequence may differ if the attacker is not targeting a specific system, but is instead looking for systems that are vulnerable to a specific exploit. In this case, the attacker would probably be searching for a vulnerability first, and then for a tool that exploits it, and he may never even consider the organization that is being targeted.

12. **C.** To minimize the avenues of attack, you need to limit the information that can be obtained and the number of services you offer. The more services that are available, the greater the number of possible avenues that can be exploited. It is important to install patches, but this doesn't minimize the avenues; it protects specific avenues from attack. The use of firewalls and intrusion detection systems is important, but monitoring them doesn't aid in minimizing the avenues of attack (though a properly administered firewall can help to limit the exposure of your network).

13. **D.** War-driving is an attempt to locate wireless networks whose access area extends into publicly accessible space.

14. **A.** The Morris worm used the same type of techniques to penetrate the systems that human attackers use. Therefore, if you protect the system against one, you are protecting it against the other. Installing an antivirus package and not allowing executable attachments to e-mail to be executed are good ideas, but they address the other type of worm, not the Morris type of Internet worm. Monitoring the system for changes to utilities and other system software is

also a good idea, but it is reactive in nature and discovering these changes means the individual or worm has already penetrated your system. Your goal should be to try to prevent this in the first place.

15. **D.** This defines a time bomb. The more general term *logic bomb* is sometimes used, but this term generally refers to a piece of software that is set to execute when some specified event occurs. When that event is a date or time, we often refer to the malicious code as a time bomb.

CHAPTER 14

E-Mail and Instant Messaging

In this chapter, you will

- Learn about security issues associated with e-mail
- Understand some of the security practices for e-mail
- Learn about the security issues of instant messaging protocols

E-mail is the most popular application on the Internet. It is also by far the most popular application on intracompany networks. Roughly 12 million e-mails were sent each day in 2001, meaning that about 4.38 billion e-mails were sent in that year. In 2000, 569 million e-mail inboxes existed in the world. A Pew report from 2007 states that 91 percent of U.S. Internet users use e-mail. Several sources indicate that in 2007, more than a billion active e-mail accounts sent more than 150 billion e-mail messages every day, or more than 50 trillion e-mails a year.

Security of E-Mail

E-mail started with mailbox programs on early time-sharing machines, allowing researchers to leave messages for others using the same machine. The first intermachine e-mail was sent in 1972, and a new era in person-to-person communication was launched. E-mail proliferated, but it remained unsecured, only partly because most e-mail is sent in plaintext, providing no privacy in its default form. Current e-mail is not much different from its earlier versions; it's still a simple way to send a relatively short text message to another user. Users' dependence on e-mail has grown with the number of people accessing the Internet.

Viruses started as simple self-replicating programs that spread via the transfer of floppy disks, but e-mail gave virus files a passport to travel. Sending themselves to every user that they possibly can, viruses have achieved record-breaking infection rates. Trojan horse programs are also often sent through the e-mail, with computer owners as accomplices, compromising hundreds of machines every day. These programs seem to be innocuous, but if you install the malicious code, you become the installer of the program that compromises your machine.

The e-mail hoax has become another regular occurrence; Internet-based urban legends are spread through e-mail, with users forwarding them in seemingly endless loops around the globe. And, of course, people still haven't found a good way to block ubiquitous spam e-mails, despite the remarkable advance of every other technology.

E-mail security is ultimately the responsibility of users themselves, because they are the ones who will actually be sending and receiving the messages. However, security administrators can give users the tools they need to fight malware, spam, and hoaxes. Secure/Multipurpose Internet Mail Extensions (S/MIME) and Pretty Good Privacy (PGP) are two popular methods used for encrypting e-mail. Server-based and desktop-based virus protection can help against malicious code, and spam filters attempt to block all unsolicited commercial e-mail. E-mail users need to be educated about security as well, however, because the popularity and functionality of e-mail is only going to increase with time.

Instant messaging (IM), while not part of the e-mail system, is similar to e-mail in many respects, particularly in the sense that it is commonly plaintext and can transmit files. IM's handling of files opens the protocol to virus exploitation just like e-mail. IM has experienced a boom in popularity in the last few years, so we will look at some popular IM programs in this chapter.

Malicious Code

Viruses and worms are popular programs because they make themselves popular. When viruses were constrained only to one computer, they attempted to spread by attaching themselves to every executable program that they could find. This worked out very well for the viruses, because they could piggyback onto a floppy disk with a program that was being transferred to another computer. The virus would infect the next computer, and the next computer after that. While often successful, virus propagation was slow, and floppies could be scanned for viruses.

The advent of computer networks was a computer virus writer's dream, allowing viruses to attempt to infect every network share to which the computer was attached. This extended the virus's reach from a set of machines that might share a floppy disk to every machine on the network. Because the e-mail protocol permits users to attach files to e-mail messages, viruses can travel by e-mail from one local network to another, anywhere on the Internet. This changed the nature of virus programs, since they once were localized but now could spread virtually everywhere. E-mail gave the virus a global reach.

Viruses spread by e-mail further and faster than ever before, but viruses also evolved. This evolution started with viruses that were scripted to send themselves to other users, and this type of virus was known as a *worm*. A worm uses its code to automate the infection process. For example, when a worm program is executed, the code may seek out the user's e-mail address book and mail itself to as many people as the worm's programming dictates. This method of transmission depends on the user actually executing the worm file. Some worms use multiple methods of attack. They not only send multiple infected e-mails, but they also scan hosts on the Internet looking for a specific vulnerability. Upon finding the vulnerability, the worm infects the remote host and, with a new launching point, starts the process all over again.

Viruses and worms are a danger not only to the individual user's machine, but also to network security, because they can introduce all kinds of malicious traffic to other machines. This can cause not only loss of data, but it can sometimes send data out to other users. The Sircam worm, for example, attached random files from the infected user's hard drive to the e-mails the worm sent out.

Worms can also carry Trojan horse payloads, as can any e-mail message. A Trojan horse program seems to be safe but actually has a sinister hidden purpose. For example, an executable game program or an executable self-playing movie could be a Trojan. These programs will run and do what they claim, but they typically also install some other program, such as a remote control package such as SubSeven or Back Orifice. These programs allow an attacker to remotely control an infected machine. Once control is achieved, the attacker can use the machine to perform a number of tasks, such as using it in distributed denial-of-service (DDoS) attacks, using it as a launching point to compromise other machines, or using it as a remote place to store some extra files.

While the distribution of malicious code in e-mail is tied to the files that are attached to the e-mail messages, in the past a user actually had to execute the attached file. The original system of e-mail used plaintext to send messages, but the advent of the World Wide Web changed this. Hypertext Markup Language (HTML) was created to allow plaintext to represent complex page designs in a standardized way. HTML was soon adopted by e-mail programs so users could use different fonts and colors and embed pictures in their e-mails. E-mail programs then grew more advanced and, like web browsers, were designed to automatically open files attached to e-mails.

When active content was designed for the web, in the form of Java and ActiveX scripts, these scripts were interpreted and run by the web browser. E-mail programs also would run these scripts, and that's when the trouble began. Some e-mail programs, most notably Microsoft Outlook, use a preview pane, which allows users to read e-mails without opening them in the full screen. Unfortunately, this preview still activates all the content in the e-mail message, and because Outlook supports Visual Basic scripting, it is vulnerable to e-mail worms. A user doesn't need to run the program or even open the e-mail to activate the worm—simply previewing the e-mail in the preview pane can launch the malicious content. This form of automatic execution was the primary reason for the spread of the ILOVEYOU worm.

All malware is a security threat, with the several different types having different countermeasures. The antivirus systems that we have used for years have progressed to try and stop all forms of malicious software, but they are not a panacea. Worm prevention also relies on patch management of the operating system and applications. Viruses are user-launched, and since one of the most common transfer methods for viruses is through e-mail, the people using the e-mail system create the front line of defense against viruses. In addition to antivirus scanning of the user's system, and possibly an e-mail virus filter, users need to be educated about the dangers of viruses.

Although the great majority of users are now aware of viruses and the damage they can cause, more education may be needed to instruct them on the specific things that need to be addressed when a virus is received via e-mail. These can vary from organization to organization and from e-mail software to e-mail software; however, some useful examples of good practices involve examining all e-mails for a known source as well as a known destination, especially if the e-mails have attachments. Strange files or unexpected attachments should always be checked before execution. Users also need to know that some viruses can be executed simply by opening the e-mail or viewing it in the preview pane. Education and proper administration is also useful in configuring the e-mail software to be as virus resistant as possible—turning off scripting support and the preview pane are good examples. Many organizations outline specific user responsibilities for e-mail, similar to network acceptable use policies. Some examples include using e-mail resources responsibly, avoiding the installation of untrusted programs, and the use of localized antivirus scanning programs.

Another protection is to carefully create virus scanning procedures. If possible, perform virus scans on every e-mail as it comes into the company's e-mail server. Some users will also attempt to retrieve e-mail offsite from a normal Internet service provider (ISP) account, which can bypass the server-based virus protection, so every machine should also be protected with a host-based virus protection program that scans all files on a regular basis and performs checks of files upon their execution. While these steps will not eliminate the security risks of malicious code in e-mail, it will limit infection and help to keep the problem to manageable levels.

Hoax E-Mails

An interesting offshoot of e-mail viruses is the phenomenon of e-mail hoaxes. If you've had an Internet e-mail address for more than a couple of months, you've probably received at least one of these—the Neiman-Marcus cookie recipe sent to you because someone was charged $250, the "famous" commencement speech by Kurt Vonnegut, and the young dying boy whose last wish was to make it into the record books by receiving the most get well cards ever. These are the most famous of the e-mail hoaxes, though many others exist.

E-mail hoaxes are mostly a nuisance, but they do cost everyone, not only in the time wasted by receiving and reading the e-mails, but also in the Internet bandwidth and server processing time they take up. E-mail hoaxes are global urban legends, perpetually traveling from one e-mail account to the next, and most have a common theme of some story you must tell ten other people about right away for good luck or some virus that will harm your friends unless you tell them immediately. Hoaxes are similar to chain letters, but instead of promising a reward, the story in the e-mail is typically what produces the action. Whether it's a call for sympathy from a dying boy, or an overly expensive recipe sent to the masses in the name of justice, all hoaxes prompt action of some sort, and this call for action is probably what keeps them going. Hoaxes have been circling the Internet for many, many years, and many web sites are dedicated to debunking them.

The power of the e-mail hoax is actually quite amazing. The Neiman-Marcus story, in which someone gets charged $250 for a chocolate chip cookie recipe, thinking that she is only being charged $2.50, used to have a fatal flaw: Neiman-Marcus did not sell chocolate chip cookies (but it does now simply because of the hoax). The Kurt Vonnegut hoax was convincing enough to fool his wife, and the dying boy, who is now 20, still receives cards in the mail. The power of these hoaxes probably means that they will never be stopped, though they might be slowed down. The most important thing to do in this case is educate e-mail users: They should be familiar with a hoax or two before they go online, and they should know how to search the Internet for hoax information. Users need to apply the same common sense on the Internet that they would in real life: If it sounds too outlandish to be true, it probably isn't. The goal of education about hoaxes should be to change user behavior to delete the hoax e-mail and not send it on.

Unsolicited Commercial E-Mail (Spam)

Every Internet user has received spam, and usually on a daily basis. Spam refers to unsolicited commercial e-mail whose purpose is the same as the junk mail you get in your physical mailbox—it tries to persuade you to buy something. The term *spam* comes from a skit on Monty Python's Flying Circus, where two people are in a restaurant that only serves the infamous potted meat product. This concept of the repetition of unwanted things is the key to e-mail spam.

The first spam e-mail was sent in 1978 by a DEC employee. However, the first spam that really captured everyone's attention was in 1994, when two lawyers posted a commercial message to every Usenet newsgroup. This was the origin of using the Internet to send one message to as many recipients as possible via an automated program. Commercial e-mail programs have taken over, resulting in the variety of spam that most users receive in their inboxes every day. In 2000, AOL estimated that nearly 30 percent of e-mail sent to its systems was spam, accounting for nearly 24 million messages a day (according to *The Industry Standard*, www.thestandard.com/article/0,1902,15586,00. html). Botnet researchers have reported that 1 million–plus infected machines send more than 100 billion spam e-mails every day.

The appeal to the people generating the spam is the extremely low cost per advertising impression. The senders of spam e-mail can generally send the messages for less than a cent apiece. This is much less expensive than more traditional direct mail or print advertisements, and this low cost will ensure the continued growth of spam e-mail unless something is done about it. The amount of spam being transmitted has been large enough to trigger state and federal legislators to consider action, but no effective laws have been passed as of this writing. This has forced most people to seek out technical solutions to the spam problem.

The front line of the war against spam mail is filtering. Almost all e-mail providers filter spam at some level; however bandwidth is still used to send the spam, and the recipient e-mail server still has to process the message. To reduce spam, it must be fought on several fronts. The first thing to be done is educate users about spam. A good way for users to fight spam is to be cautious about where on the Internet they post their e-mail address. However, you can't keep e-mail addresses secret just to avoid spam, so one of the steps that the majority of system administrators running Internet e-mail servers have taken to reduce spam, and which is also a good e-mail security principle, is to shut down mail relaying. Port scanning occurs across all hosts all the time, typically with a single host scanning large subnets for a single port, and some of these people could be attempting to send spam e-mail. When they scan for TCP port 25, they are looking for Simple Mail Transfer Protocol (SMTP) servers, and once they find a host that is an open relay, they can use that host to send as many commercial e-mails as possible. The reason that they look for an open relay is that spammers typically do not want the e-mails traced back to them. Mail relaying is similar to dropping a letter off at a post office instead of letting the postal carrier pick it up at your mailbox. On the Internet, that consists of sending e-mail from a separate IP address, making it more difficult for the mail to be traced back to you. SMTP server software is typically configured to accept mail only from specific hosts or domains, and a mail server that will accept mail from anyone is called an *open relay*. All SMTP software can and should be configured to accept only mail from known hosts, or to known mailboxes; this closes down mail relaying and helps to reduce spam.

Since it may not be possible to close all mail relays, and because some spammers will mail from their own mail servers, software must be used to combat spam at the recipient's end. Span can be filtered at two places: at the host itself or at the server. Filtering spam at the host level is done by the e-mail client software and is usually employs basic pattern matching, focusing on the sender, subject, or text of the e-mail. This fairly effective system uses an inordinate amount of bandwidth and processing power on the host computer, however. These problems can be solved by filtering spam at the mail server level.

The server-based approach can be beneficial, because other methods of filtering spam can be used at the server: pattern matching is still used, but SMTP software can also use the *Realtime Blackhole List (RBL)*. This list is maintained in real time specifically for blocking spam mail. Started in 1997, this service is so popular that many programs, such as sendmail, Postfix, and Eudora Internet Mail Server, include support for it by default. In addition to the RBL, multiple Domain Name Service (DNS)–based blacklist services can assist filtering based upon DNS sources of mail. Commercial packages can block spam at the server level using both methods mentioned, maintaining their own blacklists and pattern-matching algorithms.

Many additional techniques exist for server-based spam filtering—enough to fill an entire book on the subject. One technique is to use a *challenge/response system*: once an e-mail is received by a "new" contact, a challenge is sent back to the originating address to confirm the contact. Since spammers send e-mails in bulk, the response mechanism is too cumbersome and they will not respond. Another technique is known as *greylisting*. When an e-mail is received it is bounced as a temporary rejection. SMTP servers that are RFC-compliant will wait a configurable amount of time and attempt retransmission of the message. Obviously, spammers will not retry sending of any messages, so spam is reduced. All these techniques have advantages and disadvantages, and most people will run some combination of techniques to attempt to filter as much spam as possible while not rejecting legitimate messages.

A side benefit of filtering spam at the receiving server is reduced e-mail. In enterprises, performing backups of information is a significant task. Backups are size-dependent, both in cost and time, and reducing e-mail by eliminating spam can have significant impacts on e-mail backups. Spam reduction will also have a significant impact on the e-discovery process as it reduces the quantity of material that needs to be searched.

Microsoft offers another server-based solution to spam called the Sender ID Framework (SIDF). Sender ID attempts to authenticate messages by checking the sender's domain name against a list of IP addresses authorized to send e-mail by the domain name listed. This list is maintained in a text (TXT) record published by the DNS called a *Sender Policy Framework (SPF)* record. So when a mail server receives an e-mail, it will check the sender's domain name in the DNS; if the outbound server's IP matches, the message gets a "pass" rating by the SIDF. This is similar to the idea that routers should drop any outbound port 25 traffic that does not come from known e-mail servers on the subnet managed by the router. However, the SIDF system handles the authentication of the e-mail server when it is received, not when it is sent. This system still allows wasted bandwidth from the sender of the message to the receiver, and since bandwidth is increasingly a metered service, this means the cost of spam is still paid by the recipient.

These methods will take care of 90 percent of the junk mail clogging our networks, but they cannot stop it entirely. Better control of port 25 traffic is required to slow the tide of spam hitting our inboxes. This would stop spammers using remote open relays and hopefully prevent many users from running unauthorized e-mail servers of their own. Because of the low cost of generating spam, until serious action is taken, or spam is somehow made unprofitable, it will remain with us.

Mail Encryption

The e-mail concerns discussed so far in this chapter are all global issues involving security, but e-mail suffers from a more important security problem—the lack of confidentiality, or, as it is sometimes referred to, privacy. As with many Internet applications, e-mail has always been a plaintext protocol. When many people first got onto the Internet, they heard a standard lecture about not sending anything through e-mail that you wouldn't want posted on a public bulletin board. Part of the reason for this was that e-mail is sent with the clear text of the message exposed to anyone who is sniffing the network. Any attacker at a choke point in the network could read all e-mail passing through that network segment.

Some tools can be used to solve this problem by encrypting the e-mail's content. The first method is S/MIME and the second is PGP.

S/MIME is a *secure* implementation of the MIME (Multipurpose Internet Mail Extensions) protocol specification. MIME was created to allow Internet e-mail to support new and more creative features. The original e-mail RFC specified only text e-mail, so any nontext data had to be handled by a new specification—MIME. MIME handles audio files, images, applications, and multipart e-mails. MIME allows e-mail to handle multiple types of content in a message, including file transfers. Every time you send a file as an e-mail attachment, you are using MIME. S/MIME takes this content and specifies a framework for encrypting the message as a MIME attachment.

S/MIME was developed by RSA Data Security and uses the X.509 format for certificates. The specification supports both 40-bit RC2 and 3DES for symmetric encryption. The protocol can affect the message in one of two ways: the host mail program can encode the message with S/MIME, or the server can act as the processing agent, encrypting all messages between servers.

The host-based operation starts when the user clicks Send; the mail agent will then encode the message using the generated symmetric key. Then the symmetric key is encoded with the remote user's public key for confidentiality or signed with the local user's private key for authentication/nonrepudiation. This enables the remote user to decode the symmetric key and then decrypt the actual content of the message. Of course, all of this is handled by the user's mail program, requiring the user simply to tell the program to decode the message. If the message is signed by the sender, it will be signed with the sender's public key, guaranteeing the source of the message. The reason that both symmetric and asymmetric encryption are used in the mail is to increase the speed of encryption and decryption. As encryption is based on difficult mathematical problems, it takes time to encrypt and decrypt. To speed this up, the more difficult process, asymmetric encryption, is used only to encrypt a relatively small amount of data, the symmetric key. The symmetric key is then used to encrypt the rest of the message.

The S/MIME process of encrypting e-mails provides integrity, privacy, and, if the message is signed, authentication. Several popular e-mail programs support S/MIME, including the popular Microsoft products, Outlook and Outlook Express. They both manage S/MIME keys and functions through the Security screen, shown in Figure 14-1. This figure shows the different settings that can be used to encrypt messages and use X.509 digital certificates. This allows interoperability with web certificates, and trusted authorities are available to issue the certificates. Trusted authorities are needed to ensure the senders are who they claim to be, an important part of authentication. In Outlook Express, the window is more simplistic (see Figure 14-2), but the same functions of key management and secure e-mail operation are available.

While S/MIME is a good and versatile protocol for securing e-mail, its implementation can be problematic. S/MIME allows the user to select low strength (40-bit) encryption, which means a user can send a message that is thought to be secure but that can be more easily decoded than messages sent with 3DES encryption. Also, as with any protocol, bugs can exist in the software itself. Just because an application is designed for security does not mean that it, itself, is secure. (In October 2002, for example, a buffer overrun was found in Outlook Express's S/MIME error handling.) Despite its potential flaws, however, S/MIME is a tremendous leap in security over regular e-mail.

Pretty Good Privacy (PGP) implements e-mail security in a similar fashion to S/MIME, but PGP uses completely different protocols. The basic framework is the same: The user sends the e-mail, and the mail agent applies encryption as specified in the mail program's programming. The content is encrypted with the generated symmetric key, and that key is encrypted with the public key of the recipient of the e-mail for confidentiality. The sender can also choose to sign the mail with a private key, allowing the recipient

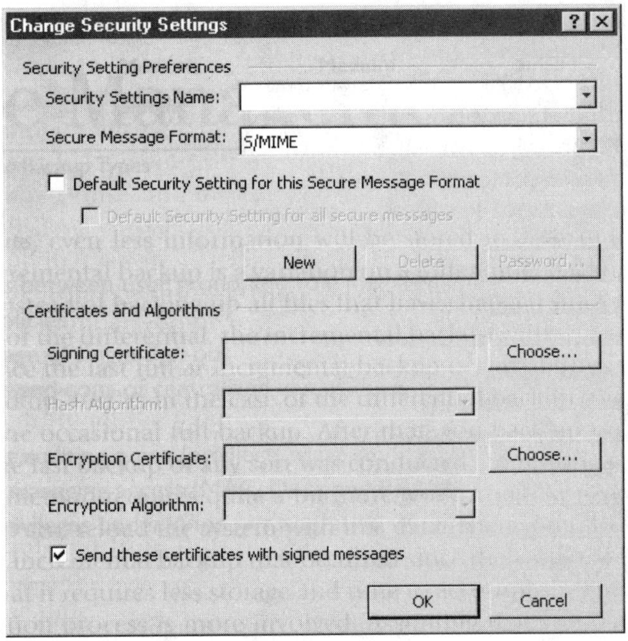

Figure 14-1
S/MIME options in
Outlook

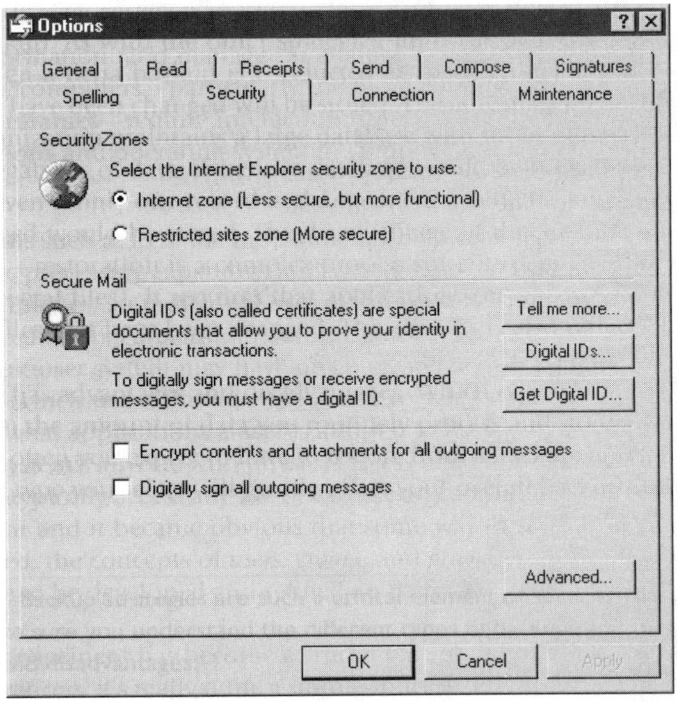

Figure 14-2
S/MIME options in
Outlook Express

to authenticate the sender. Currently PGP supports public key infrastructure (PKI) provided by multiple vendors, including X.509 certificates, Lightweight Directory Access Protocol (LDAP) key sources such as Microsoft's Active Directory, and Novell's NDS, now called eDirectory

In Figure 14-3, you can see how PGP manages keys locally in its own software. This is where a user stores not only local keys, but also any keys that were received from other users. A free key server is available for storing PGP public keys. PGP can generate its own keys using either Diffie-Hellman or RSA, and it can then transmit the public keys to the PGP LDAP server so other PGP users can search for and locate your public key to communicate with you. This key server is convenient, as each person using PGP for communications does not have to implement a server to handle key management. For the actual encryption of the e-mail content itself, PGP supports International Data Encryption Algorithm (IDEA), 3DES, and Carlisle Adams and Stafford Tavares (CAST) for symmetric encryption. PGP provides pretty good security against brute-force attacks by using a 3DES key length of 168 bits, an IDEA key length of 128 bits, and a CAST key length of 128 bits. All of these algorithms are difficult to brute-force with existing hardware, requiring well over a million years to break the code. While this is not a promise of future security against brute-force attacks, the security is reasonable today.

PGP has plug-ins for many popular e-mail programs, including Outlook, Outlook Express, and Qualcomm's Eudora. These plug-ins handle the encryption and decryption behind the scenes, and all that the user must do is enter the encryption key's passphrase to ensure that they are the owner of the key. In Figure 14-4, you can see the string of encrypted text that makes up the MIME attachment. This text includes the encrypted content of the message and the encrypted symmetric key. You can also see that the program does not decrypt the message upon receipt; it waits until instructed to decrypt it. PGP also stores encrypted messages in the encrypted format, as does S/MIME. This is important, since it provides end-to-end security for the message.

Like S/MIME, PGP is not problem-free. You must be diligent about keeping the software up-to-date and fully patched, because vulnerabilities are occasionally found.

Figure 14-3
PGP key
management

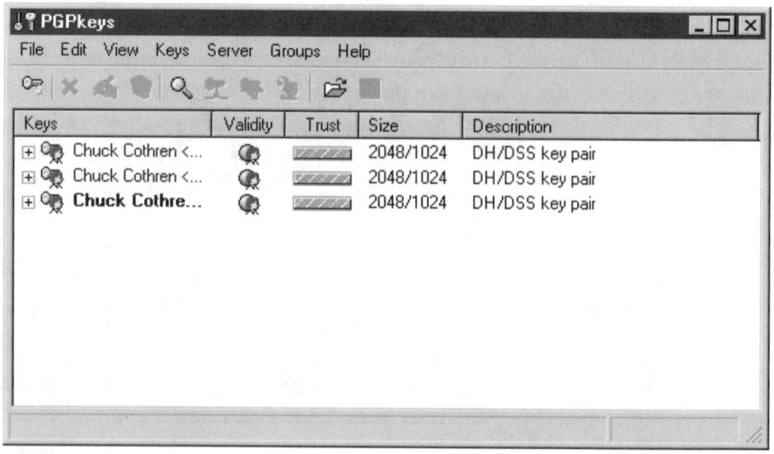

Keys	Validity	Trust	Size	Description
Chuck Cothren <...			2048/1024	DH/DSS key pair
Chuck Cothren <...			2048/1024	DH/DSS key pair
Chuck Cothre...			2048/1024	DH/DSS key pair

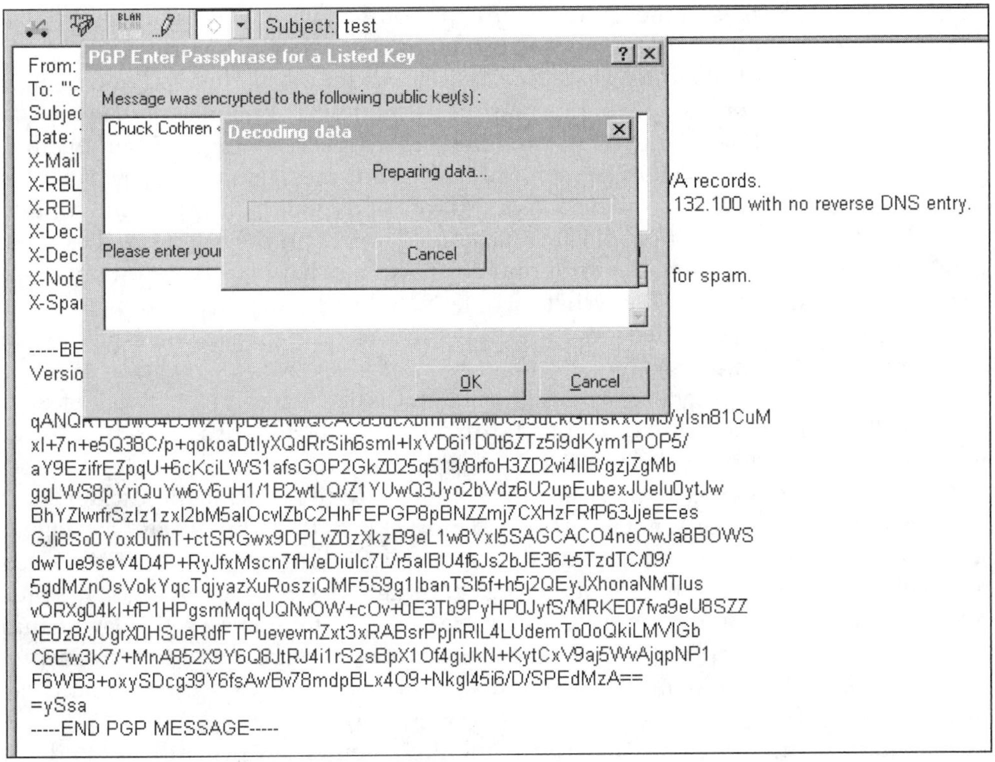

Figure 14-4 Decoding a PGP-encoded message in Eudora

For example, a buffer overflow was found in the way PGP was handled in Outlook, causing the overwriting of heap memory and leading to possible malicious code execution. There is also a lot of discussion about the way PGP handles key recovery, or key escrow. PGP uses what's called *Additional Decryption Key (ADK)*, which is basically an additional public key stacked upon the original public key. ADK, in theory, would give the proper organization a private key that would be used to retrieve the secret messages. In practice, the ADK is not always controlled by a properly authorized organization, and the danger exists for someone to add an ADK and then distribute it to the world. This creates a situation in which other users will be sending messages that they believe can be read only by the first party, but that can actually be read by the third party who modified the key. These are just examples of the current vulnerabilities in the product, showing that PGP is just a tool, not the ultimate answer to security.

Instant Messaging

Instant messaging is another technology that has seen widespread acceptance in recent years. With the growth of the Internet pulling customers away from AOL, one of the largest dial-up providers in the United States, the company had to look at new ways of providing content. It started AIM, or AOL Instant Messenger, which was conceived as a way to find people of like interests online, and it was modeled after earlier chat programs. With GUI features and enhanced ease of use, it quickly became popular enough for AOL to release to regular users of the Internet. With several competing programs, AIM was feeding the tremendous growth of the instant messaging segment. The programs had to appeal to a wide variety of users, so ease of use was paramount, and security was not a priority. Now that people are accustomed to instant messaging applications, they see the benefit of using them not only for personal chatting on the Internet, but also for legitimate business use. When people install these applications, they unwittingly expose the corporate network to security breaches. Instant messages traverse the Internet in plaintext and also cross third-party servers—be it MSN, Google, or AOL.

Instant messaging programs are designed to attach to a server, or a network of servers, and allow you to talk with other people on the same network of servers in near real time. The nature of this type of communication opens several holes in a system's security. First, the program has to attach to a server, typically announcing the IP address of the originating client. This is not a problem in most applications, but instant messaging identifies a specific user associated with the IP address, making attacks more likely. Also associated with this fact is that for other users to be able to send you messages, the program is forced to announce your presence on the server. So now a user is displaying that his or her computer is on and is possibly broadcasting the source IP address to anyone who is looking. This problem is compounded by the tendency for people to run these programs in the background so that they don't miss any messages.

Popular instant messaging clients were not implemented with security in mind. All support sending files as attachments, few currently support encryption, and they do not have a virus scanner built into the file-sharing utility. File sharing in any form must be a carefully handled application to prevent the spread of viruses and other malicious code. Chat programs produce security risks because the sharing is done ad hoc between end users, administrators have no control over the quality of the files being sent, and there is no monitoring of the original sources of those files. The only authentication for the files is the human interaction between the two users in question. This kind of vulnerability coupled with a social engineering attack can produce dramatic enough results for Computer Emergency Response Team (CERT) to issue an incident note (CERT Incident Note IN-2002-03: Social Engineering Attacks via IRC and Instant Messaging). This personal type of authentication was abused, tricking people into downloading and executing backdoor or Trojan horse programs.

A user can also be persuaded autonomously to download and run a file via IM. Several worms exist that attempt, via IM, to get users to download and run the payload. W32.pipeline uses AIM to install a rootkit. Goner, running via ICQ, asks users to download a screen saver. Choke, spreading via MSN, attempts to get users to download a game; if the game is downloaded, the worm will attempt to spread to any user the infected user chats with. These worms and others all depend on user interaction to run the payload. This file sharing mechanism bypasses all the server-side virus protection that is part of most organizations' e-mail infrastructure. This pushes more of the responsibility for malware protection onto the local users' antivirus system. This can be problematic with users who do not regularly update their systems or who fail to perform regular antivirus scans.

One of the largest problems with IM programs is the lack of support for encryption. AIM, ICQ, MSN Messenger, and Yahoo Messenger all currently do not natively support encryption of the text messages traveling between users. However, some third-party programs will add encryption as a plug-in. The lack of encryption was not a significant concern while these programs were still used primarily for personal communication, but with businesses moving to adopt the systems, people are not aware of the infrastructure difference between IM and e-mail. Intracompany e-mail never leaves the company's network, but an intracompany instant message typically will do so unless the organization purchases a product and operates an internal IM server. This can and does expose large amounts of confidential business information to anyone who is physically in a spot to monitor and has the desire to capture the traffic.

If you think about how often client information is sent in e-mail between two people at a company, you start to see the danger that sending it via IM creates. IM is an application that is typically installed by the end user, without the knowledge of the administrator. These types of rogue applications have always been a danger to a network's security, but administrators have typically been able to control them by eliminating the applications' ports through the firewall.

Some instant messaging applications have even been programmed for use as *rogue apps*. In the event that they can't reach a server on the default ports, they begin to scan all ports looking for one that is allowed out of the firewall. As these applications can connect on any port, including common ones such as 23 Telnet and 80 HTTP, they are very hard to control. These types of security risks go above and beyond the routine security holes generated in IM software that arise as in any other piece of software, through coding errors.

IM applications work only in a networked environment and therefore are forced to accept traffic as well as send it, giving attackers a way to exploit flaws in the code of the program. AIM has encountered two buffer overflow problems that allow a remote attacker to gain control of the user's computer. These flaws, which have been patched, are just the beginning—with the proliferation of these applications, many more bugs are out there waiting to be exploited.

You can improve the security of IM now, however, and new programs will offer improved security features. Businesses that use IM should use a local IM server. Keeping messages within the perimeter of the organization goes a long way toward ensuring that confidential information does not get out. Microsoft Exchange 2000 provided a built-in IM server, and this capability was later moved into the company's Live Communications Server. This server can act as an internal IM server, routing employee-to-employee IMs within the organization, and it also provides presence management, so the system will know what device you are available to communicate with. This capability has now been renamed Office Communications Server 2007, with IM, presence, and voice and video capabilities. It supports Live Meeting clients and the Microsoft Office Communicator clients.

Trillian is a third-party chat client program that works with multiple chat networks; its most significant feature is that it can encrypt the chat messages, on AIM and ICQ networks, that the client sends to the server. While this does not help with file-sharing problems, it will provide confidentiality in one direction. To protect the method of file exchange, the clients will have to be changed to integrate a virus scanner. These solutions and others should be applied widely to ensure that IM will occur securely.

Instant messaging is an application that can increase productivity by saving communication time, but it's not without risks. The protocol sends messages in plaintext and thus fails to preserve their confidentiality. It also allows for sharing of files between clients, allowing a backdoor access method for files. There are some methods to minimize security risks, but more development efforts are required before IM is ready to be implemented in a secure fashion. The best ways in which to protect yourself on an IM network are similar to those for almost all Internet applications: Avoid communication with unknown persons, avoid running any program you are unsure of, and do not write anything you wouldn't want posted with your name on it.

Chapter Review

E-mail is one of the oldest and most popular applications on the Internet. Security was not a primary concern when it was created, and many extensions to the protocol, while greatly increasing the functionality to users, have increased security problems. The MIME extensions allowed file attachments and HTML mail, which allowed the e-mail transfer of viruses and Trojan programs. E-mail software that is capable of interpreting HTML also opened the door for self-installing e-mail worms. E-mail also offers simple annoyances, such as unwanted commercial spam and the hoax e-mails that never seem to die out. Worst of all is the complete lack of privacy and weak authentication inherent in e-mail. S/MIME and PGP attempt to reduce some of the limitations of e-mail, providing privacy, integrity, and authentication. Instant messaging is a newer protocol, but it carries similar risks for malicious software. Both e-mail and IM share the weakness of being a clear text protocol subject to interception. Both protocols need to be implemented with care to maintain security.

Questions

1. What is spam?
    A. Unsolicited commercial e-mail
    B. A Usenet archive
    C. A computer virus
    D. An encryption algorithm
2. How does the Realtime Blackhole List help fight spam?
    A. It is a universal Internet receptacle for spam.
    B. It maintains current signatures of all available spam for download.

    C. It takes all spam and returns it to the sender.

    D. It maintains a list of spam sources against which e-mail servers can check messages.

3. How many bits are needed in a symmetric encryption algorithm to give decent protection from brute-force attacks?

    A. 24 bits

    B. 40 bits

    C. 56 bits

    D. 128 bits

4. How do some instant messaging programs cause problems for intrusion detection systems?

    A. They can scan for open ports trying to find a server.

    B. They force the IDS to decode your conversations.

    C. They force the IDS to shut down.

    D. They run on Windows PCs.

5. What makes e-mail hoaxes popular enough to keep the same story floating around for years?

    A. They are written by award-winning authors.

    B. The story prompts action on the reader's part.

    C. The story will grant the user good luck only if he or she forwards it on.

    D. The hoax e-mail forwards itself.

6. What is greylisting?

    A. E-mail messages are temporarily rejected so that the sender is forced to resend.

    B. E-mail messages are run through a strong set of filters before delivery.

    C. E-mail messages are sent through special secure servers.

    D. E-mail is sent directly from the local host to the remote host, bypassing servers entirely.

7. Why do PGP and S/MIME need public key cryptography?

    A. Public keys are necessary to determine whether the e-mail is encrypted.

    B. The public key is necessary to encrypt the symmetric key.

    C. The public key unlocks the password to the e-mail.

    D. The public key is useless and gives a false sense of privacy.

8. What symmetric encryption protocols does S/MIME support?

    A. AES and RC4

PART IV

    B. IDEA and 3DES

    C. 3DES and RC2

    D. RC4 and IDEA

9. Why is HTML e-mail dangerous?

    A. It can't be read by some e-mail clients.

    B. It sends the content of your e-mails to web pages.

    C. It can allow launching of malicious code from the preview pane.

    D. It is the only way spam can be sent.

10. What is a Trojan horse program?

    A. A program that encrypts e-mail for security

    B. A program that appears legitimate but is actually malicious code

    C. A program that runs only on a single computer

    D. A program that self-compiles before it runs

11. Why is S/MIME sometimes considered unsecured?

    A. It doesn't actually encrypt the e-mail.

    B. It can send unsigned e-mails.

    C. It uses inferior Triple DES encryption.

    D. It can be used with only 40-bit ciphers.

12. If they are both text protocols, why is instant messaging traffic riskier than e-mail?

    A. More viruses are coded for IM.

    B. IM has no business purpose.

    C. IM traffic has to travel outside of the organization to a server.

    D. Emoticons.

13. What makes spam so popular as an advertising medium?

    A. Its low cost per impression

    B. Its high rate of return

    C. Its ability to canvass multiple countries

    D. Its quality of workmanship

14. What is one of the popular Trojan horse payloads?

    A. Word processor

    B. Web server

    C. Remote control programs

15. What is a potential security problem with key escrow?

    A. The key gets lost.

    B. Someone could add a key to your encryption and then distribute the key.

    C. The key could contain a Trojan horse.

    D. Key escrow requires 40-bit keys.

Answers

1. **A.** Spam is unsolicited commercial e-mail.

2. **D.** The Realtime Blackhole List is a list of sources known to send spam, and e-mail servers can use it to perform checks against the source of e-mail. If the source matches, often the e-mail is simply dropped from the server.

3. **D.** 128 bits is the current requirement to provide decent security from brute-force attacks against the key.

4. **A.** Some instant messaging programs can look like an internal port scan when trying to find a server, causing the IDS to alert you even when an actual attack is not occurring.

5. **B.** Hoax e-mails work by prompting action on the user's part. Typically the action is to forward the e-mail to everyone the reader knows, sometimes to right some moral injustice.

6. **A.** Greylisting is a temporary rejection of e-mail to force the remote server to resend the message. Since spammers will not follow the RFC specifications, they will not perform resending.

7. **B.** The public key is used to encrypt the symmetric key, which is then used to encrypt the message contents, because encrypting the entire message would take too much processing power.

8. **C.** S/MIME supports 3DES and RC2.

9. **C.** HTML e-mail can carry embedded instructions to download or run scripts that can be launched from the preview pane in some e-mail programs, without requiring that the user actively launch the attached program.

10. **B.** A Trojan horse program looks like a legitimate game or video but actually carries malicious code.

11. **D.** S/MIME currently supports a 40-bit cipher to perform the symmetric encryption, and this is considered unsecured by some, as 128 bits should be the minimum on symmetric keys.

12. **C.** IM protocols require the traffic travel to the hosting server, so two users in an organization are sending the traffic to an outside server and back when communicating via IM.

13. **A.** Spam is popular simply because of its low cost. Spam can be sent to thousands of people for less than a cent per reader.

14. **C.** Remote control programs, such as SubSeven and Back Orifice, are popular Trojan horse programs because they give the attacker access to all the resources of the machine.

15. **B.** Because key escrow involves adding an additional private key to your original private key in the encryption routine, if an attacker is able to add a key without your knowledge, he can secretly decode all your messages.

Web Components

In this chapter, you will

- Learn about the SSL/TLS protocol suite
- Study web applications, plug-ins, and associated security issues
- Understand secure file transfer options
- Discover directory usage for data retrieval
- Study scripting and other Internet functions that present security concerns
- Learn the use of cookies to maintain parameters between web pages
- Examine web-based application security issues

The World Wide Web was invented by Tim Berners-Lee to give physicists a convenient method of exchanging information. What began in 1990 as a physics tool in the European Laboratory for Particle Physics (CERN) has grown into a complex system that is used by millions of computer users for tasks from e-commerce, to e-mail, chatting, games, and even the original intended use—file and information sharing. Before the WWW, plenty of methods were used to perform these tasks, and they were already widespread in use. File Transfer Protocol (FTP) was used to move files, and Telnet allowed users access to other machines. What was missing was the common architecture brought by Berners-Lee: First, a common addressing scheme, built around the concept of a Uniform Resource Locator (URL); second was the concept of linking documents to other documents by URLs through the Hypertext Markup Language (HTML).

Although these elements might seem minor, they formed a base that spread like wildfire. Berners-Lee developed two programs to demonstrate the usefulness of his vision: a web server to serve documents to users and a web browser to retrieve documents for users. Both of these key elements contributed to the spread of this new technological innovation. The success of these components led to network after network being connected together in a "network of networks" known today as the Internet. Much of this interconnection was developed and funded through grants from the U.S. government to further technological and economic growth.

What enabled the WWW's explosive growth into the PC market were the application programs, called browsers, that were developed to use these common elements and allow users ease of access to the new world of connected resources. Browsers became graphically based, and as more users began to use them, a market for more services via the WWW channel was born. Out of this market, standards emerged to provide the required levels of security necessary as the user base and functionality of the WWW expanded.

Current Web Components and Concerns

The usefulness of the WWW is due not just to browsers, but also to web components that enable services for end users through their browser interfaces. These components use a wide range of protocols and services to deliver the desired content to end users. From a security perspective, they offer users an easy-to-use, secure method of conducting data transfers over the Internet. Many protocols have been developed to deliver this content, although for most users, the browser handles the details.

From a systems point of view, many security concerns have arisen, but they can be grouped into three main tasks:

- Securing a server that delivers content to users over the web
- Securing the transport of information between users and servers over the web
- Securing the user's computer from attack over a web connection

This chapter will present the components used on the WWW to request and deliver information securely over the Internet.

Protocols

When two people communicate, several things must happen for the communication to be effective: They must use a language that both parties understand, and they must correctly use the language—that is, structure and syntax—to express their thoughts. The mode of communication is a separate entity entirely, for the previous statements are important in both spoken and written forms of communication. The same requirements are present with respect to computer communications and they are addressed through *protocols*. Protocols refer to agreed upon sets of rules that allow different vendors to produce hardware and software that can interoperate with hardware and software developed by other vendors. Because of the worldwide nature of the Internet, protocols are very important and form the basis by which all the separate parts can work together. The specific instantiation of protocols is done through hardware and software components. The majority of this chapter will concentrate on protocols related to the Internet as instantiated by software components.

Encryption (SSL and TLS)

Secure Sockets Layer (SSL) is a general-purpose protocol developed by Netscape for managing the encryption of information being transmitted over the Internet. It began as a competitive feature to drive sales of Netscape's web server product, which could then send information securely to end users. This early vision of securing the transmission channel between the web server and the browser became an Internet standard. Today, SSL is almost ubiquitous with respect to e-commerce—all browsers support it as do web servers, and virtually all sensitive financial traffic from e-commerce web sites uses this method to protect information in transit between web servers and browsers.

The Internet Engineering Task Force (IETF) embraced SSL in 1996 through a series of RFCs and named the group Transport Layer Security (TLS). Starting with SSL 3.0, in 1999 the IETF issued RFC 2246, "TLS Protocol Version 1.0," followed by RFC 2712, which added Kerberos authentication, and then RFCs 2817 and 2818, which extended TLS to HTTP version 1.1 (HTTP/1.1). Although SSL has been through several versions, TLS begins with an equivalency to SSL 3.0, so today SSL and TLS are essentially the same although not interchangeable.

SSL/TLS is a series of functions that exist in the OSI (Open System Interconnection) model between the application layer and the transport and network layers. The goal of TCP is to send an unauthenticated error-free stream of information between two computers. SSL/TLS adds message integrity and authentication functionality to TCP through the use of cryptographic methods. Because cryptographic methods are an ever-evolving field, and because both parties must agree on an implementation method, SSL/TLS has embraced an open, extensible, and adaptable method to allow flexibility and strength. When two programs initiate an SSL/TLS connection, one of their first tasks is to compare available protocols and agree on an appropriate common cryptographic protocol for use in this particular communication. As SSL/TLS can use separate algorithms and methods for encryption, authentication, and data integrity, each of these is negotiated and determined depending upon need at the beginning of a communication. Currently the browsers from Mozilla (Firefox) and Microsoft (Internet Explorer 7) allow fairly extensive SSL/TLS setup options, as illustrated in Figure 15-1 (Internet Explorer 7), Figure 15-2 (Firefox), and Figure 15-3 (Firefox).

How SSL/TLS Works

SSL/TLS uses a wide range of cryptographic protocols. To use these protocols effectively between a client and a server, an agreement must be reached on which protocol to use via the SSL handshake process. The process begins with a client request for a secure connection and a server's response. The questions asked and answered are which protocol and which cryptographic algorithm will be used. For the client and server to communicate, both sides must agree on a commonly held protocol (SSL v1, v2, v3, or TLS v1). Commonly available cryptographic algorithms include Diffie-Hellman and RSA. The next step is to exchange certificates and keys as necessary to enable authentication. Authentication was a one-way process for SSL v1 and v2 with only the server providing authentication. In SSL v3/TLS, mutual authentication of both client and server is possible. The certificate exchange is via X.509 certificates, and public key cryptography is used to establish authentication. Once authentication is established, the channel is secured with symmetric key cryptographic methods and hashes, typically RC4 or 3DES for symmetric key and MD5 or SHA-1 for the hash functions.

PART IV

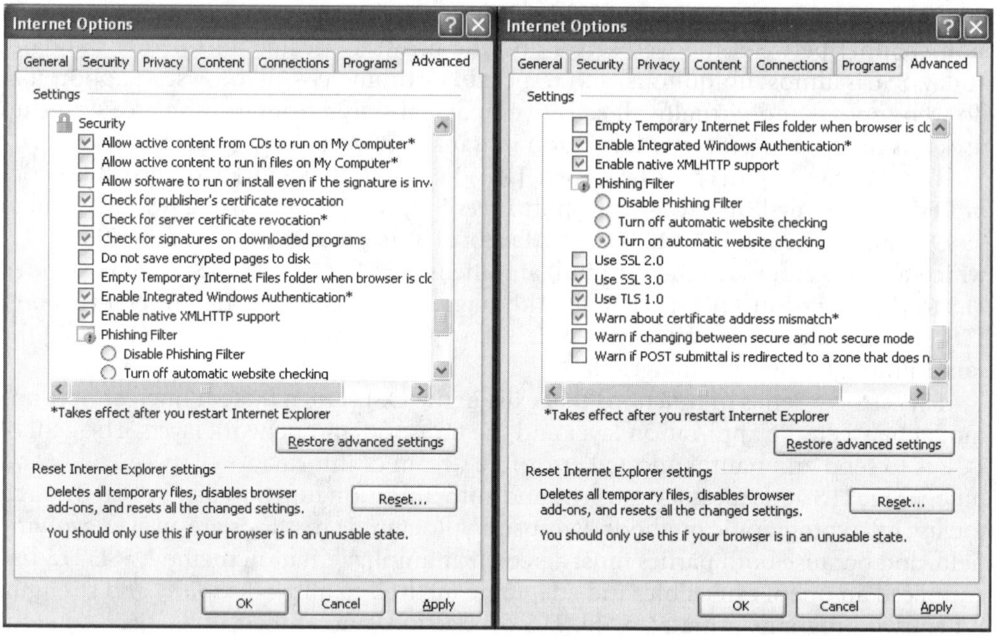

Figure 15-1   Internet Explorer 7 security options

Figure 15-2
Firefox SSL security
options

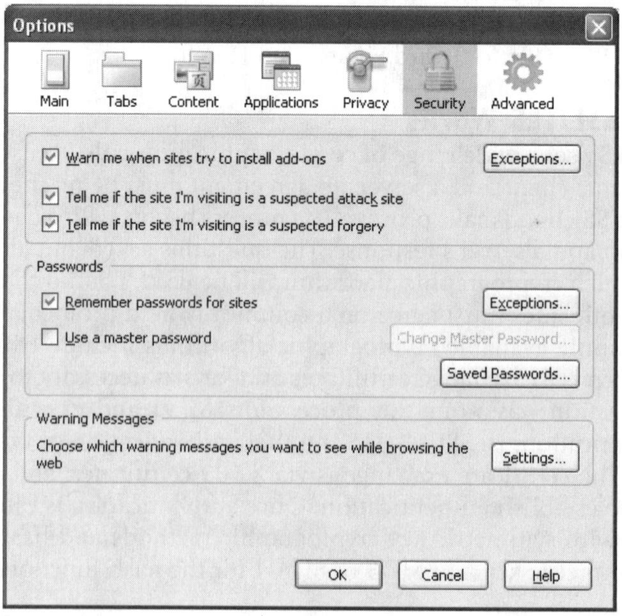

Figure 15-3
Firefox SSL cipher
options

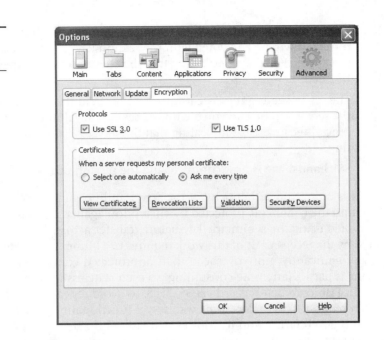

The following steps establish an SSL/TLS secured channel (SSL handshake):

1. The client sends to the server the client's SSL version number, cipher settings, and session-specific data.

2. The server sends to the client the server's SSL version number, cipher settings, session-specific data, and its own certificate. If the resource requested requires client authentication, the server requests the client's certificate.

3. The client authenticates the server using the information it has received. If the server cannot be authenticated, the user is warned of the problem and informed that an encrypted and authenticated connection should not be trusted.

4. The client encrypts a seed value with the server's public key and sends it to the server. If the server requested client authentication, the client also sends another piece of signed data that is unique to this handshake and known by both the client and server.

5. If the server requested client authentication, the server attempts to authenticate the client. If the client cannot be authenticated, the session ends.

6. If the client is successfully authenticated, the server uses its private key to decrypt the secret, and then performs the required series of steps (which the client also performs) to generate a master secret. The steps depend on the cryptographic method used for key exchange.

7. Both the client and the server use the master secret to generate the session key, which is the symmetric key used to encrypt and decrypt information exchanged during the SSL session.

PART IV

8. The client sends a message informing the server that future messages from the client will be encrypted with the session key. It then sends a separate (encrypted) message indicating that the client portion of the handshake is finished.

9. The server sends a message informing the client that future messages from the server will be encrypted with the session key. It then sends a separate (encrypted) message indicating that the server portion of the handshake is finished.

10. SSL handshake is now complete and the session can begin.

At this point, the authenticity of the server and possibly the client has been established, and the channel is protected by encryption against eavesdropping. Each packet is encrypted using the symmetric key before transfer across the network, and then decrypted by the receiver. All of this work requires CPU time; hence, SSL/TLS connections require significantly more overhead than unprotected connections. Establishing connections is particularly time-consuming, so even stateless web connections are held in a stateful fashion when secured via SSL/TLS, to avoid repeating the handshake process for each request. This makes some web server functionality more difficult, such as implementing web farms, and it requires that either an SSL/TLS appliance is used before the web server to maintain state or the SSL/TLS state information be maintained in a directory type service accessible by all of the web farm servers. Either method requires additional infrastructure and equipment. However, to enable secure e-commerce and other private data transactions over the Internet, this is a cost-effective method to establish a specific level of necessary security.

A certificate is merely a standard set of formatted data that represents the authenticity of the public key associated with the signer. The use of certificates allows a third party to act as notary in the electronic world. A person using a notary assumes the notary is honest, and states have regulations and notaries have insurance to protect against fraud. The same idea is true with certificates, although the legal system has not caught up to the electronic age, nor has the business of liability insurance. Still, certificates provide a method of proving who someone is, provided you trust the issuer. If the issuer is a third party of stature, such as VeriSign or AT&T, you can rest your faith upon that authenticity. If the issuer is a large firm such as Microsoft, you can probably trust it since you are downloading its code. If the issuer is Bob's Certificate Shack—well, unless you know Bob, you may have cause for concern. Certificates do not vouch for code security, they only say that the person or entity that is signing them is actually the person or entity they claim to be.

The use of certificates could present a lot of data and complication to a user. Fortunately, browsers have incorporated much of this desired functionality into a seamless operation. Once you have decided always to accept code from XYZ Corporation, subsequent certificate checks are handled by the browser. The ability to manipulate certificate settings is under the Options menus in both Internet Explorer (Figures 15-4 and 15-5) and Mozilla Firefox (Figures 15-6 and 15-7).

Figure 15-4
Internet Explorer
certificate
management options

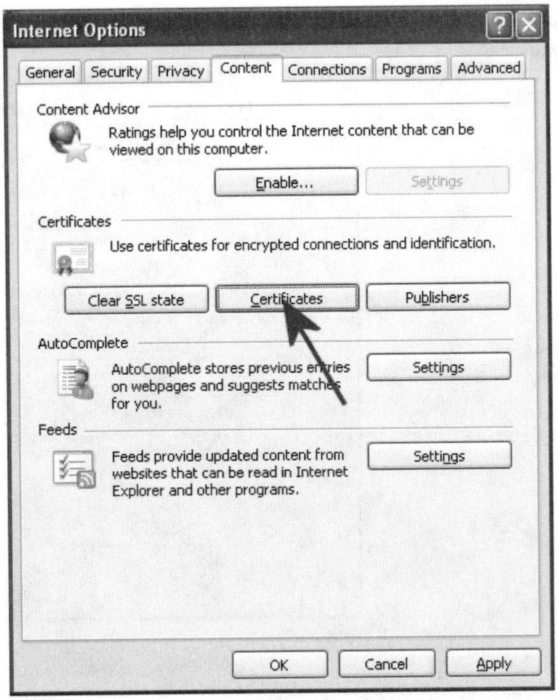

Figure 15-5
Internet Explorer
certificate store

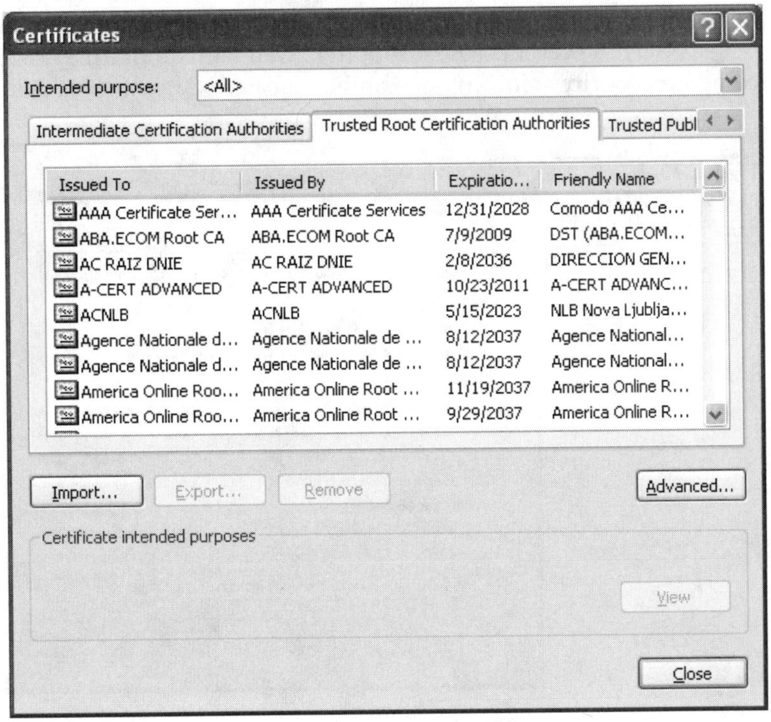

Figure 15-6
Firefox certificate
options

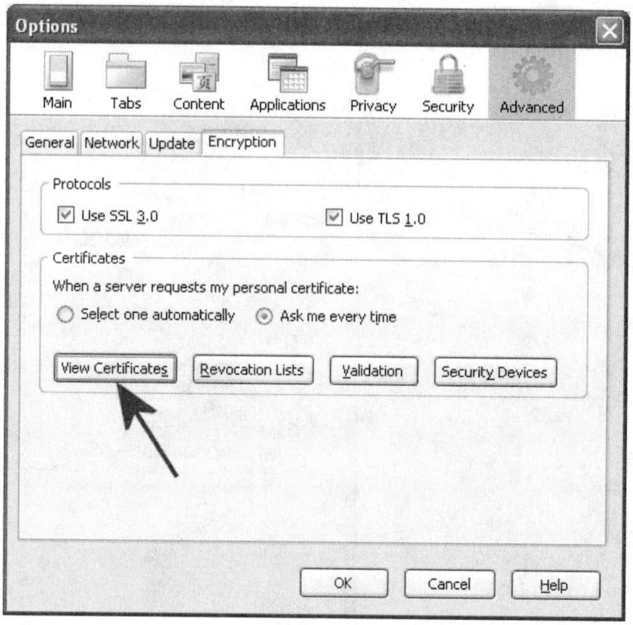

SSL/TLS is specifically designed to provide protection from man-in-the-middle attacks. By authenticating the server end of the connection, SSL/TLS prevents the initial hijacking of a session. By encrypting all of the conversations between the client and the server, SSL/TLS prevents eavesdropping. Even with all of this, however, SSL/TLS is not a complete security solution and can be defeated. Once a communication is in the SSL/

Figure 15-7
Firefox certificate
store

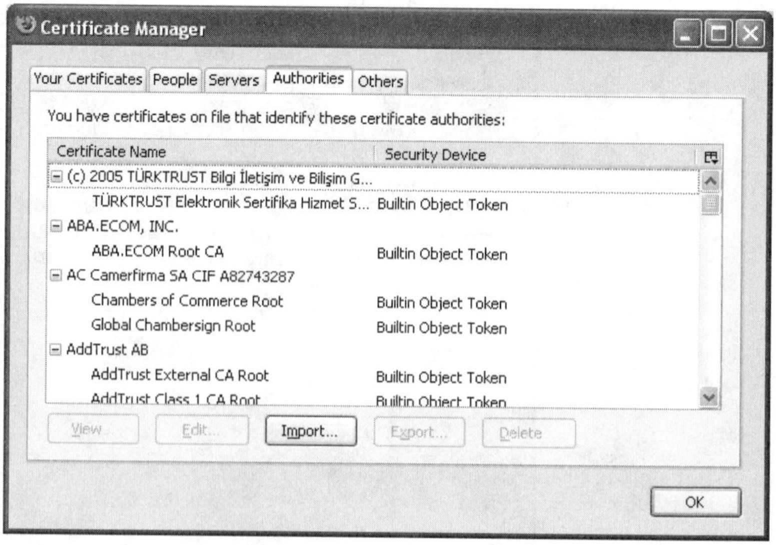

TLS channel, it is very difficult to defeat the protocol. Before data enters the secured channel, however, defeat is possible. A Trojan program that copies keystrokes and echoes them to another TCP/IP address in parallel with the intended communication can defeat SSL/TLS, for example, provided that the Trojan program copies the data prior to SSL/TLS encapsulation. This type of attack has occurred and has been used to steal passwords and other sensitive material from users, performing the theft as the user actually types in the data.

The Web (HTTP and HTTPS)

HTTP is used for the transfer of hyperlinked data over the Internet, from web servers to browsers. When a user types a URL such as http://www.example.com into a browser, the http:// portion indicates that the desired method of data transfer is HTTP. Although it was initially created just for HTML pages, today many protocols deliver content over this connection protocol. HTTP traffic takes place over TCP port 80 by default, and this port is typically left open on firewalls because of the extensive use of HTTP.

One of the primary drivers behind the development of SSL/TLS was the desire to hide the complexities of cryptography from end users. When using an SSL/TLS-enabled browser, this can be done simply by requesting a secure connection from a web server instead of nonsecure connection. With respect to HTTP connections, this is as simple as using https:// in place of http://.

When a browser is SSL/TLS-aware, the entry of an SSL/TLS-based protocol will cause the browser to perform the necessary negotiations with the web server to establish the required level of security. Once these negotiations have been completed and the session is secured by a session key, a closed padlock icon is displayed in the lower right of the screen to indicate that the session is secure. If the protocol is *https:*, your connection is secure; if it is *http:*, then the connection is carried by plaintext for anyone to see. Figure 15-8 shows a secure connection in Internet Explorer 7, and Figure 15-9 shows the equivalent in Firefox. As the tiny padlock placed in the lower-right corner of the screen could have been missed, Microsoft moved it to an obvious position next to the URL in Internet Explorer 7. Another new security feature that begins with Internet Explorer 7 and Firefox 3 is the use of high assurance SSL, a combination of an extended validation SSL certificate and a high security browser. If a high security browser, Internet Explorer 7 or Firefox 3 and beyond, establish a connection with a vendor that has registered with a certificate authority for an extended validation SSL certificate, then the URL box will be colored green and the box next to it will display the registered entity and additional validation information when clicked. These improvements were in response to phishing

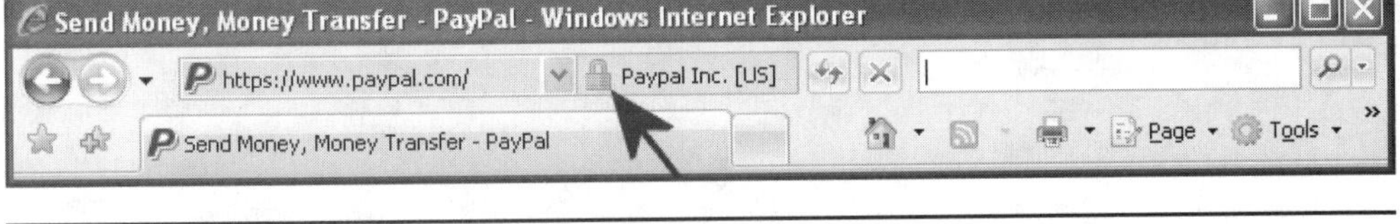

Figure 15-8   High assurance notification in Internet Explorer 7

Figure 15-9 High assurance notification in Firefox

sites and online fraud, and although they require additional costs and registration on the part of the vendors, this is a modest up-front cost to help reduce fraud and provide confidence to customers.

One important note on SSL certificate-based security is the concept of single- versus dual-sided authentication. The vast majority of SSL connections are single-sided, meaning that only the identity of the server side is vouched for via a certificate. The client is typically not identified by certificate, mainly because of the number of clients and corresponding PKI issues. A single-sided SSL secured conversation can be attacked using a man-in-the-middle attack by capturing all the traffic and relaying responses. Dual-sided SSL would prevent this attack mechanism, yet the management of every client needing to obtain and maintain a certificate makes this practically infeasible with the current PKI available to most end users.

The objective of enabling cryptographic methods in this fashion is to make it easy for end users to use these protocols. SSL/TLS is designed to be *protocol agnostic*. Although designed to run on top of TCP/IP, it can operate on top of other lower level protocols, such as X.25. SSL/TLS requires a reliable lower level protocol, so it is not designed and cannot properly function on top of a nonreliable protocol such as the User Datagram Protocol (UDP). Even with this limitation, SSL/TLS has been used to secure many common TCP/IP-based services, as shown in Table 15-1.

Directory Services (DAP and LDAP)

A *directory* is a data storage mechanism similar to a database, but it has several distinct differences designed to provide efficient data retrieval services compared to standard database mechanisms. A directory is designed and optimized for reading data, offering very fast search and retrieval operations. The types of information stored in a directory tend to be descriptive attribute data. A directory offers a static view of data that can be changed without a complex update transaction. The data is hierarchically described in a treelike structure, and a network interface for reading is typical. Common uses of directories include e-mail address lists, domain server data, and resource maps of network resources.

Protocol	TCP Port	Use
HTTPS	443	SSL/TSL secured HTTP traffic
SSMTP	465	SSL/TLS secured SMTP for mail sending
SPOP3 (Secure POP3)	995	SSL/TLS secured POP3 for mail receiving
sNEWS	563	SSL/TLS secured Usenet news
SSL - LDAP	636	SSL/TLS secured LDAP services

Table 15-1 SSL/TLS Protected Services

To enable interoperability, the X.500 standard was created as a standard for directory services. The primary method for accessing an X.500 directory is through the Directory Access Protocol (DAP), a heavyweight protocol that is difficult to implement completely, especially on PCs and more constrained platforms. This led to the Lightweight Directory Access Protocol (LDAP), which contains the most commonly used functionality. LDAP can interface with X.500 services, and, most importantly, LDAP can be used over TCP with significantly less computing resources than a full X.500 implementation. LDAP offers all of the functionality most directories need and is easier and more economical to implement, hence LDAP has become the Internet standard for directory services. LDAP standards are governed by two separate entities depending upon use: The International Telecommunication Union (ITU) governs the X.500 standard, and LDAP is governed for Internet use by the IETF. Many RFCs apply to LDAP functionality, but some of the most important are RFCs 2251 through 2256 and RFCs 2829 and 2830.

SSL/TLS LDAP

LDAP over TCP is a plaintext protocol, meaning data is passed in the clear and is susceptible to eavesdropping. Encryption can be used to remedy this problem, and the application of SSL/TLS-based service will protect directory queries and replies from eavesdroppers. SSL/TLS provides several important functions to LDAP services. It can establish the identity of a data source through the use of certificates, and it can also provide for the integrity and confidentiality of the data being presented from an LDAP source. As LDAP and SSL/TLS are two separate independent protocols, interoperability is more a function of correct setup than anything else. To achieve LDAP over SSL/TLS, the typical setup is to establish an SSL/TLS connection and then open an LDAP connection over the protected channel. To do this requires that both the client and the server be enabled for SSL/TLS. In the case of the client, most browsers are already enabled. In the case of an LDAP server, this specific function must be enabled by a system administrator. As this setup initially is complicated, it's definitely a task for a competent system administrator.

Once an LDAP server is set up to function over an SSL/TLS connection, it operates as it always has. The LDAP server responds to specific queries with the data returned from a node in the search. The SSL/TLS functionality operates to secure the channel of communication, and it is transparent to the data flow from the user's perspective. From the outside, SSL/TLS prevents observation of the data request and response, ensuring confidentiality.

File Transfer (FTP and SFTP)

One of the original intended uses of the Internet was to transfer files from one machine to another in a simple, secure, and reliable fashion, which was needed by scientific researchers. Today, file transfers represent downloads of music content, reports, and other data sets from other computer systems to a PC-based client. Until 1995, the majority of Internet traffic was file transfers. With all of this need, a protocol was necessary so that two computers could agree on how to send and receive data. As such, FTP is one of the older protocols.

FTP

FTP is an application-level protocol that operates over a wide range of lower level protocols. FTP is embedded in most operating systems and provides a method of transferring files from a sender to a receiver. Most FTP implementations are designed to operate both ways, sending and receiving, and can enable remote file operations over a TCP/IP connection. FTP clients are used to initiate transactions and FTP servers are used to respond to transaction requests. The actual request can be either to upload (send data from client to server) or download (send data from server to client).

Clients for FTP on a PC can range from an application program to the command line ftp program in Windows/DOS to most browsers. To open an FTP data store in a browser, you can enter **ftp://url** in the browser's address field to indicate that you want to see the data associated with the URL via an FTP session—the browser handles the details. File transfers via FTP can be either binary or in text mode, but in either case, they are in plaintext across the network.

Blind FTP (Anonymous FTP)

To access resources on a computer, an account must be used to allow the operating-system–level authorization function to work. In the case of an FTP server, you may not wish to control who gets the information, so a standard account called *anonymous* exists. This allows unlimited public access to the files and is commonly used when you want to have unlimited distribution. On a server, access permissions can be established to allow only downloading or only uploading or both, depending on the system's function. As FTP can be used to allow anyone access to upload files to a server, it is considered a security risk and is commonly implemented on specialized servers isolated from other critical functions. As FTP servers can present a security risk, they are typically not permitted on workstations and are disabled on servers without need for this functionality.

SFTP

FTP operates in a plaintext mode, so an eavesdropper can observe the data being passed. If confidential transfer is required, Secure FTP (SFTP) utilizes both the Secure Shell (SSH) protocol and FTP to accomplish this task. SFTP is an application program that encodes both the commands and the data being passed and requires SFTP to be on both the client and the server. SFTP is not interoperable with standard FTP—the encrypted commands cannot be read by the standard FTP server program. To establish SFTP data transfers, the server must be enabled with the SFTP program, and then clients can access the server provided they have the correct credentials. One of the first SFTP operations is the same as that of FTP: an identification function that uses a username and an authorization function that uses a password. There is no anonymous SFTP account by definition, so access is established and controlled from the server using standard access control lists (ACLs), IDs, and passwords.

Vulnerabilities

Modern encryption technology can provide significant levels of privacy, up to military-grade secrecy. The use of protocols such as SSL/TLS provide a convenient method for end users to use cryptography without having to understand how it works. This can result in complacency—the impression that once SSL/TLS is enabled, the user is safe, but this is not necessarily the case. If a Trojan program is recording keystrokes and sending the information to another unauthorized user, for example, SSL/TLS cannot prevent the security breach. If the user is connecting to an untrustworthy site, the mere fact that the connection is secure does not prevent the other site from running a scam. Using SSL/TLS and other encryption methods will not guard against your credit card information being "lost" by a company with which you do business, as in the egghead.com credit card hack of 2000. In December 2000, egghead.com's credit card database was hacked, and as many as 3.7 million credit card numbers were exposed. Other similar stories include 55,000 credit card records being compromised by creditcards.com in 2000 and more than 300,000 records being compromised by the CD Universe hack in 1999.

The key to understanding what is protected and where it is protected requires an understanding of what these protocols can and cannot do. The SSL/TLS suite can protect data in transit, but not on either end in storage. It can authenticate users and servers, provided that the certificate mechanisms are established and used by both parties. Properly set up and used, SSL/TLS can provide a very secure method of authentication, followed by confidentiality in data transfers and data integrity checking. But again, all of this occurs during transit, and the protection ends once the data is stored.

Code-Based Vulnerabilities

The ability to connect many machines together to transfer data is what makes the Internet so functional for so many users. Browsers enable much of this functionality, and as the types of data have grown on the Internet, browser functionality has grown as well.

But not all functions can be anticipated or included in each browser release, so the idea of extending browser functions through plug-ins became a standard. Browsers can perform many types of data transfer, and in some cases, additional helper programs, or plug-ins, can increase functionality for specific types of data transfers. In other cases, separate application programs may be called by a browser to handle the data being transferred. Common examples of these plug-ins and programs include Shockwave plug-ins, RealOne player (both plug-in and standalone application), Windows Media Player, and Adobe Acrobat (both plug-in and standalone). The richness that enables the desired functionality of the Internet has also spawned some additional types of interfaces in the form of ActiveX components and Java applets.

In essence, all of these are pieces of code that can be written by third parties, distributed via the Internet, and run on your PC. If the code does what the user wants, the user is happy. But the opportunity exists for these applications or plug-ins to include malicious code that performs actions not desired by the end user. Malicious code designed to operate within a web browser environment is a major tool for computer crackers to use to obtain unauthorized access to computer systems. Whether delivered by HTML-based e-mail, by getting a user to visit a web site, or even delivery via an ad server, the result is the same: malware performs malicious tasks in the browser environment.

Buffer Overflows

One of the most common exploits used to hack into software is the *buffer overflow.* The buffer overflow is a result of poor coding practices on the part of software programmers—when any program reads input into a buffer (an area of memory) and does not validate the input for correct length, the potential for a buffer overflow exists. The buffer overflow vulnerability occurs when an application can accept more input than it has assigned storage space and the input data overwrites other program areas. The exploit concept is simple: A cracker writes an executable program that performs some action on the target machine and appends this code fragment to a legitimate response to a program on the target machine. When the target machine reads through the too-long response, a buffer overflow condition causes the original program to fail. The extra malicious code fragment is now in the machine's memory, awaiting execution. If the cracker executed it correctly, the program will skip into the cracker's code, running it instead of crashing.

Buffer overflows have been shown to be exploitable in a wide range of programs, from UNIX, to Windows, to applications such as Internet Explorer, Netscape Communicator, and many more. Historically, more than 50 percent of the security incidents by type are due to buffer-overflow exploits. It is one of the most common hacks used, and the primary defense users have is to keep their machines up-to-date with patches from software manufacturers. Unfortunately, patching has not proven to be a very effective method of protection. Many people don't keep up-to-date with the patches, as demonstrated by the Slammer worm attack, which took place almost six months after Microsoft had released a patch specifically for the vulnerability. Even with the patch widely available, both in a hotfix and in a service pack, many SQL servers had not received the patch and were affected by this worm, which used a buffer overflow to propagate.

Java and JavaScript

Java is a computer language invented by Sun Microsystems as an alternative to Microsoft's development languages. Designed to be platform-independent and based on C, Java offered a low learning curve and a way of implementing programs across an enterprise, independent of platform. Although platform independence never fully materialized, and the pace of Java language development was slowed by Sun, Java has found itself to be a leader in object-oriented programming languages.

Java, and its close cousin JavaScript, operates through an interpreter called a Java Virtual Machine (JVM) on each platform that interprets the Java code, and this JVM enables the program's functionality for the specific platform. This reliance on an interpretive step has led to performance issues, and Java is still plagued by poor performance when compared to most other languages. Security was one of the touted advantages of Java, but in reality, security is not a built-in function but an afterthought and is implemented independent of the language core. This all being said, properly coded Java can operate at reasonable rates, and when properly designed can act in a secure fashion. These facts have led to the wide dependence on Java for much of the server-side coding for e-commerce and other web-enabled functionality. Servers can add CPUs to address speed concerns, and the low learning curve has proven cost efficient for enterprises.

Java was initially designed to be used in trusted environments, and when it moved to the Internet for general use, safety became one of its much-hyped benefits. Java has many safety features, such as type checking and garbage collection, that actually improve a program's ability to run safely on a machine and not cause operating system–level failures. This isolates the user from many common forms of operating system faults that can end in the "blue screen of death" in a Windows environment, where the operating system crashes and forces a reboot of the system. Safety is not security, however, and although safe, a malicious Java program can still cause significant damage to a system.

The primary mode of a computer program is to interact with the operating system and perform functional tasks for a user, such as getting and displaying data, manipulating data, storing data, and so on. Although these functions can seem benign, when enabled across the web they can have some unintended consequences. The ability to read data from a hard drive and display it on the screen is essential for many programs, but when the program is downloaded and run from the Internet and the data is, without the knowledge of the user, sent across the Internet to an unauthorized user, this enables a program to spy on a user and steal data. Writing data to the hard drive can also cause deletions if the program doesn't write the data where the user expects. Sun recognized these dangers and envisioned three different security policies for Java that would be implemented via the browser and JVM, providing different levels of security. The first policy is not to run Java programs at all. The second restricts Java program functionality when the program is not run directly from the system's hard drive—programs being directly executed from the Internet have severe restrictions that block disk access and force other security-related functions to be performed. The last policy runs any and all Java programs as presented.

Most browsers adopted the second security policy, restricting Java functionality on a client unless the program was loaded directly from the client's hard drive. Although this solved many problems initially, it also severely limited functionality. Today, browsers allow much more specific granularity on security for Java, based on security zones and user settings.

JavaScript is a form of Java designed to be operated within a browser instance. The primary purpose of JavaScript is to enable features such as validation of forms before they are submitted to the server. Enterprising programmers found many other uses for JavaScript, such as manipulating the browser history files, now prohibited by design. JavaScript actually runs within the browser and the code is executed by the browser itself. This has led to compatibility problems, and not just between vendors, such as Microsoft and Mozilla, but between browser versions. Security settings in Internet Explorer are done by a series of zones, allowing differing level of control over .Net functionality, ActiveX functionality, and Java functionality (see Figure 15-10). Unfortunately, these settings can be changed by a Trojan program, altering the browser without alerting the user and lowering the security settings. In Firefox, using the NoScript add-in is a solution to this, but the reduced functionality leads to other issues, as shown in Figure 15-11, and requires more diligent user intervention.

Although JavaScript was designed not to be able to access files or network resources directly, except through the browser functions, it has not proven to be as secure as de-

Figure 15-10
Security settings in
Internet Explorer 7

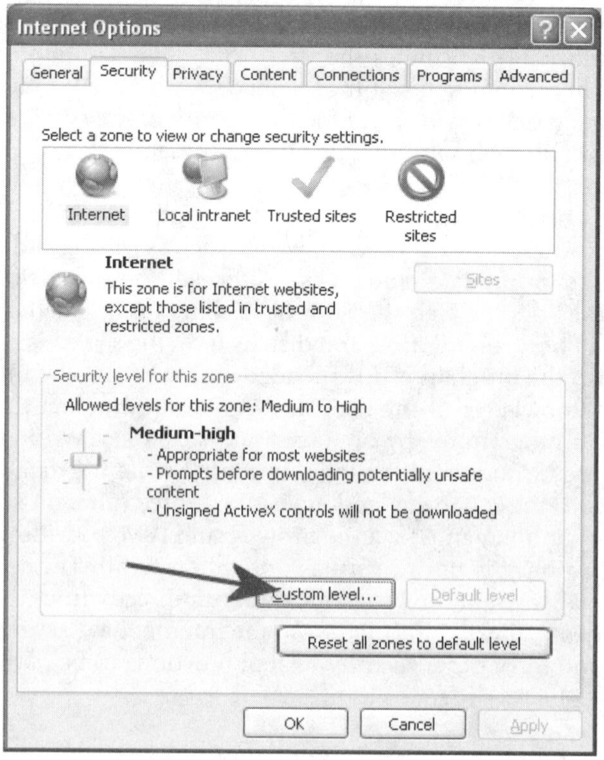

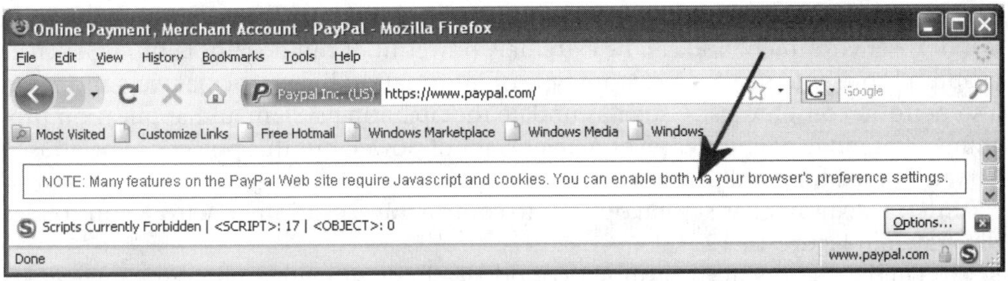

Figure 15-1i   Security setting functionality issues

sired. This fault traces back to a similar fault in the Java language, where security was added on, without the benefit of a comprehensive security model. So, although designers put thought and common sense into the design, the lack of a comprehensive security model left some security holes. For instance, a form could submit itself via e-mail to an undisclosed recipient, either eavesdropping, spamming, or causing other problems—imagine your machine sending death threat e-mails to high-level government officials from a rogue JavaScript implementation.

Further, most browsers do not have a mechanism to halt a running script short of aborting the browser instance, and even this may not be possible if the browser has stopped responding to commands. Malicious JavaScripts can do many things, including opening two new windows every time you close one, each with the code to open two more. There is no way out of this one, short of killing the browser process from the operating system. JavaScripts can also trick users into thinking they are communicating with one entity, when in fact they are communicating with another. For example, a window may open asking whether you want to download and execute the new update from "http://www.microsoft.com..../update.exe," and what is covered by the ellipsis (…) is actually "www.microsoft.com.attacker.org/"—the user assumes this is a Microsoft address that is cut short by space restrictions on the display.

As a browser scripting language, JavaScript is here to stay. Its widespread popularity for developing applets such as animated clocks, mortgage calculators, simple games, and the like will overcome its buggy nature and poor level of security. Similarly, Java as a development language is also here to stay, although it may never live up to its initial hype and will continue to have security issues. Both of these technologies boast many skilled developers, low learning curves (because of their heritage in the C language), and popularity in computer science courses. When viewed as a total package, the marketplace has decided that the benefits outweigh the drawbacks, and these two technologies will be a cornerstone for much Internet programming development.

ActiveX

ActiveX is the name given to a broad collection of APIs, protocols, and programs developed by Microsoft to download and execute code automatically over an Internet-based channel. The code is bundled together into an ActiveX control with an .ocx extension.

These controls are referenced in HTML using the **<object>** tag. ActiveX is a tool for the Windows environment and can be extremely powerful. It can do simple things, such as enable a browser to display a custom type of information in a particular way, and it can also perform complex tasks, such as update the operating system and application programs. This range of abilities gives ActiveX a lot of power, but this power can be abused as well as used for good purposes.

Internet Explorer has several options to control the execution of ActiveX controls, as illustrated in Figure 15-12.

To enable security and consumer confidence in downloaded programs such as ActiveX controls, Microsoft developed Authenticode, a system that uses digital signatures and allows Windows users to determine who produced a specific piece of code and whether or not the code has been altered. As in the case of Java, safety and security are different things, and Authenticode promotes neither in reality. Authenticode provides limited accountability at the time of download and guarantees that the code has not been changed since the time of signing. Authenticode does not identify whether a piece of code will cause damage to a system, nor does it regulate how code is used, so a perfectly safe ActiveX control under one set of circumstances may be malicious if used improperly. As with a notary's signature, recourse is very limited—if code is signed by a terrorist organization and the code ruins your machine, all Authenticode did was make it seem legitimate. It is still incumbent upon the users to know from whom they are getting code and to determine whether or not they trust that organization.

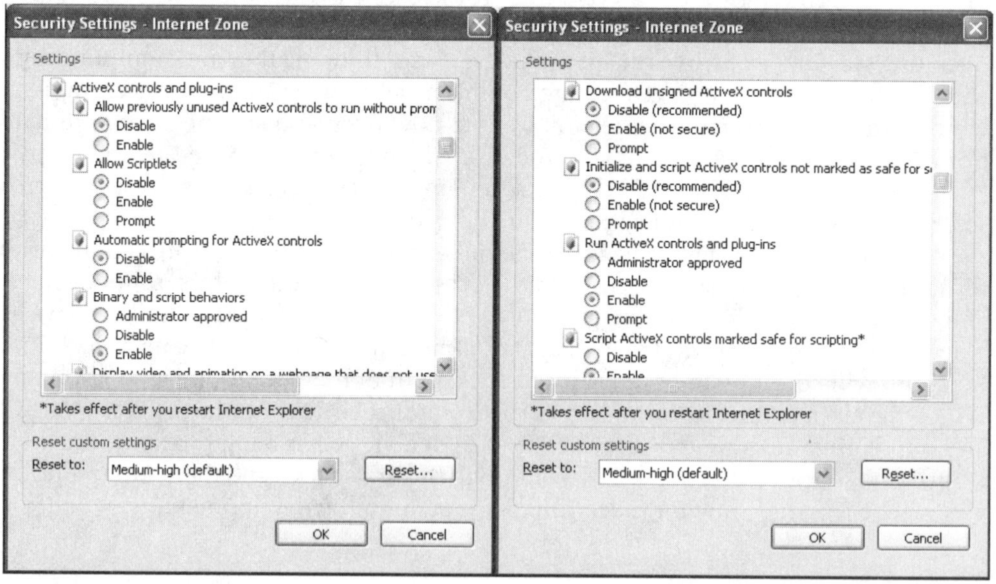

Figure 15-12 ActiveX security settings in Internet Explorer 7

EXAM TIP ActiveX technology can be used to create complex application logic that is then embedded into other container objects such as a web browser. ActiveX components have very significant capabilities and thus malicious ActiveX objects can be very dangerous. Authenticode is a means of signing an ActiveX control so that a user can judge trust based on the control's creator.

Critics of Authenticode and other code-signing techniques are not against code signing, for this is a universally recognized good thing. What the critics argue is that code signing is not a panacea for security issues and that marketing it as doing more than it really does is irresponsible. Understanding the nuances of security is important in today's highly technical world, and leaving the explanations to marketing departments is not the ideal solution.

Securing the Browser

A great deal of debate concerns the relative security issue of browser extensions versus the rich user interaction that they provide. There is no doubt that the richness of the environment offered by ActiveX adds to the user experience. But as is the case in most coding situations, added features means weaker security, all other things being constant. If nothing else, a constant development budget must spend some portion of its time on secure development practices, time that some developers and marketers would prefer to spend on new features. Although no browser is 100 percent safe, the use of Firefox coupled with the NoScript plug-in comes the closest to fitting the bill. Firefox will not execute ActiveX, so that threat vector is removed. The NoScript plug-in allows the user to determine from which domains to trust scripts. The use of NoScript puts the onus back on the user as to which domain scripts they choose to trust, and although it's not perfect from a security perspective, this at least allows a measure of control over what code you want to run on your machine.

CGI

The Common Gateway Interface (CGI) was the original method for having a web server execute a program outside the web server process, yet on the same server. The intent was to pass information via environment variables to an independent program, execute the program, and return the results to the web server for display. Web servers are presentation and display engines, and they provide less than stellar results when used for other purposes. For example, a web server instance can have numerous independent connections, and a program failure that results in a process bounce can affect multiple users if it is run within the web server process. Separating any time-consuming and more risky programming cores, such as database lookups and manipulation, complex calculations, and other tasks, into separate processes was and still is a prudent idea.

CGI offers many advantages to web-based programs. The programs can be written in a number of languages, although Perl is a favorite. These scripted programs embrace the full functionality of a server, allowing access to databases, UNIX commands, other programs, and so on. This provides a wide range of functionality to the web environment.

With this unrestrained capability, however, come security issues. Poorly written scripts can cause unintended consequences at runtime.

The problem with poorly written scripts is that they are not always obvious. Sometimes scripts appear to be fine, but unexpected user inputs can have unintended consequences. The addition of extra elements on a command line, for example, can result in dramatically different outputs. The use of the Perl backquote function, for example, allows a user to programmatically encode user input to a UNIX shell, and this works properly given proper user input, but if the user appends & /bin/ls -l to a proper input, this could generate a directory listing of the cgi-bin directory, which in turn gives away script names for future exploitation attempts. Permitting users to execute other programs in such an uncontrolled fashion led many ISPs to prohibit the use of CGI scripts unless they were specifically approved by the ISP. This led to considerable overhead and code checking to ensure clean code and validated user inputs.

A variety of books have been written on how to write secure code, and CGI has benefited. Properly coded, CGI offers no more and no less risk than any other properly coded solution. CGI's loss was that it was first and was abused first, and many developers learned by making mistakes early on CGI. On UNIX systems, CGI offers the ultimate in programmable diversity and capability, and now that security standard practices have been learned and put to use, the system is experiencing new popularity.

Server-Side Scripts

CGI has been replaced in many web sites through newer server-side scripting technologies such as Java, Active Server Pages (ASP), ASP.Net, and PHP. All these technologies operate in much the same fashion as CGI: they allow programs to be run outside the web server and to return data to the web server to be served to end users via a web page. Each of these newer technologies has advantages and disadvantages, but all of them have stronger security models than CGI. With these security models comes reduced functionality and, as each is based on a different language, the learning curves are steeper. Still, the need for adherence to programming fundamentals exists in these technologies—code must be well designed and well written to avoid the same vulnerabilities that exist in all forms of code. Buffer overflows are still an issue. Changing languages or technologies does not eliminate the basic security problems associated with incorporating open-ended user input into code. Understanding and qualifying user responses before blindly using them programmatically is essential to the security of a system.

Cookies

Cookies are small chunks of ASCII text passed within an HTTP stream to store data temporarily in a web browser instance. Invented by Netscape, cookies pass back and forth between web server and browser and act as a mechanism to maintain state in a stateless world. *State* is a term that describes the dependence on previous actions. By definition, HTTP traffic served by a web server is *stateless*—each request is completely independent of all previous requests, and the server has no memory of previous requests. This dramatically simplifies the function of a web server, but it also significantly complicates the task of providing anything but the most basic functionality in a site. Cookies were developed to bridge this gap. Cookies are passed along with HTTP data through a Set-Cookie message in the header portion of an HTTP message.

A cookie is actually a series of name-value pairs that is stored in memory during a browser instance. The specification for cookies established several specific name-value pairs for defined purposes. Additional name-value pairs may be defined at will by a developer. The specified set of name-value pairs include the following:

- **Expires** This field specifies when the cookie expires. If no value exists, the cookie is good only during the current browser session and will not be persisted to the user's hard drive. Should a value be given, the cookie will be written to the user's machine and persisted until this datetime value occurs.

- **Domain** This name-value pair specifies the domain where the cookie is used. Cookies were designed as memory-resident objects, but as the user or data can cause a browser to move between domains, say from comedy.net to jokes.org, some mechanism needs to tell the browser which cookies belong to which domains.

- **Path** This name-value pair further resolves the applicability of the cookie into a specific path within a domain. If path = /directory, the cookie will be sent only for requests within /directory on the given domain. This allows a level of granular control over the information being passed between the browser and server, and it limits unnecessary data exchanges.

- **Secure** The presence of the keyword [secure] in a cookie indicates that it is to be used only when connected in an SSL/TLS session. This does not indicate any other form of security, as cookies are stored in plaintext on the client machine. In fact, one browser-based security issue was the ability to read another site's cookies from the browser cache and determine the values by using a script.

Cookie management on a browser is normally an invisible process, but both Internet Explorer and Firefox have methods for users to examine and manipulate cookies on the client side. Firefox users can examine, delete, and block individual cookies through the interface shown in Figure 15-13.

Internet Explorer has a much simpler interface, with just a Delete Cookies option in the browser (Figure 15-14). Additional cookie manipulation is done through the file processing system, because cookies are stored as individual files, as shown in Figure 15-15. This combination allows easier bulk manipulation, a useful option, as cookies can become quite numerous in short order.

So what good are cookies? Disable cookies in your browser and go to some common sites that you visit, and you'll quickly learn the usefulness of cookies. Cookies store a variety of information, from customer IDs, to data about previous visits. Because cookies are stored on a user's machine in a form that will allow simple manipulation, they must always be considered suspect and are not suitable for use as a security mechanism. They can, however, allow the browser to provide crucial pieces of information

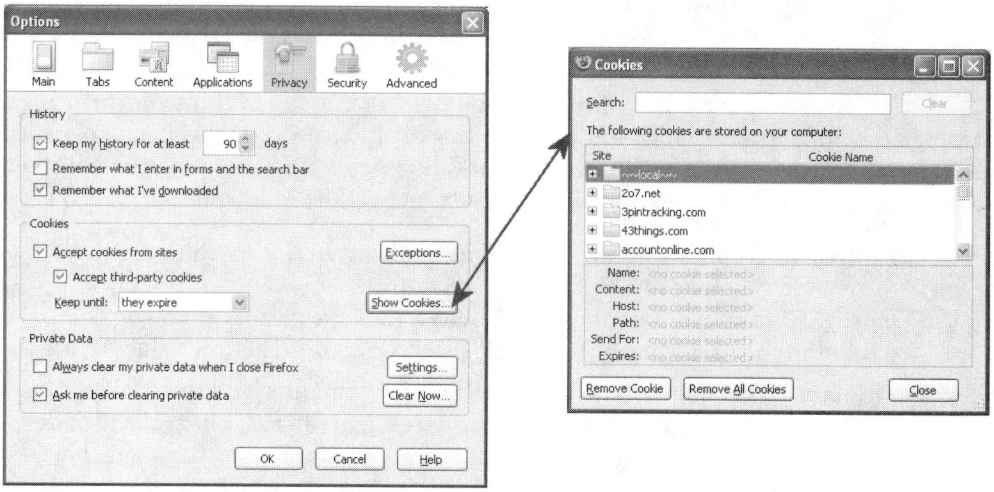

Figure 15-13 Firefox cookie management

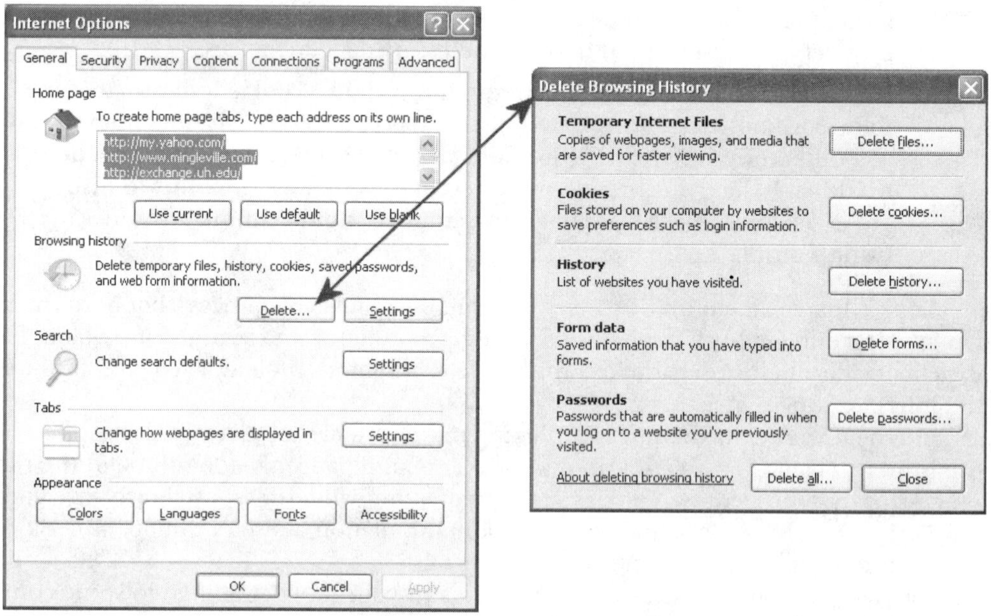

Figure 15-14 Internet Explorer 7 cookie management

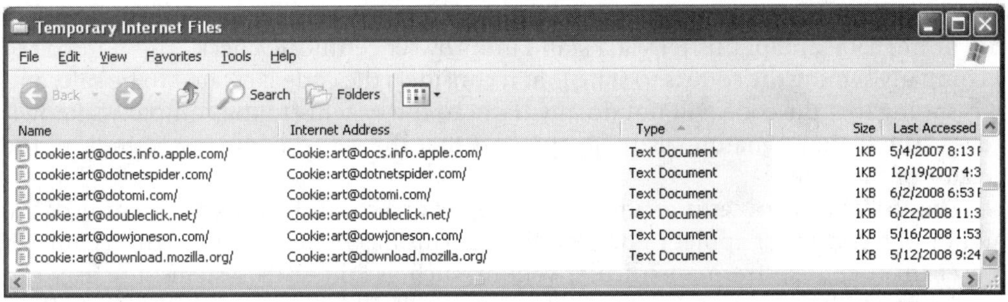

Figure 15-15 Internet Explorer 7 cookie store

to a web server. Advertisers can use them to control which ads you are shown, based on previous ads you have viewed, and regardless of ad location by site. Specific sites can use cookies to pass state information between pages, enabling functionality at the user's desired levels. Cookies can also remember your ZIP code for a weather site, your ID for a stock tracker site, the items in your shopping cart—these are all typical cookie uses. In the end analysis, cookies are a part of daily web experience, here to stay and useful if not used improperly (such as to store security data and to provide ID and authentication).

Disabling Cookies

If the user disables cookies in a browser, this type of information will not be available for the web server to use. IETF RFC 2109 describes the HTTP state-management system (cookies) and specifies several specific cookie functions to be enabled in browsers, specifically

- The ability to turn on and off cookie usage
- An indicator as to whether cookies are in use
- A means of specifying cookie domain values and lifetimes

Several of these functions have already been discussed, but to surf cookie-free requires more than a simple step. Telling a browser to stop accepting cookies is a setup option available through an OPTIONS menu, but this has no effect on cookies already received and stored on the system. To prevent the browser from sending cookies already received, the user must delete the cookies from the system. This bulk operation is easily performed, and then the browser can run cookie-free. Several third-party tools enable even a finer granularity of cookie control.

Signed Applets

Code signing was an attempt to bring the security of shrink-wrapped software to software downloaded from the Internet. Code signing works by adding a digital signature and a digital certificate to a program file to demonstrate file integrity and authenticity. The certificate identifies the author, and the digital signature contains a hash value that covers code, certificate, and signature to prove integrity, and this establishes the integrity of the code and publisher via a standard browser certificate check. The purpose of a company signing the code is to state that it considers the code it created to be safe, and it is stating that the code will not do any harm to the system (to the company's knowledge). The digital signature also tells the user that the stated company is, indeed, the creator of the code.

The ability to use a certificate to sign an applet or a control allows the identity of the author of a control or applet to be established. This has many benefits. For instance, if a user trusts content from a particular vendor, such as Sun Microsystems, the user can trust controls that are signed by Sun Microsystems. This signing of a piece of code does not do anything other than identify the code's manufacturer and guarantee that the code has not been modified since it was signed.

A signed applet can be hijacked as easily as a graphic or any other file. The two ways an attacker could hijack a signed control are by inline access or copying the file in its entirety and republishing it. *Inlining* is using an embedded control from another site with or without the other site's permission. Republishing a signed control is done much like stealing a GIF or JPEG image—a copy of the file is maintained on the unauthorized site and served from there instead of from the original location. If a signed control cannot be modified, why be concerned with these thefts, apart from the issue of intellectual property? The primary security concern comes from how the control is used. A cracker may be able to use a control in an unintended fashion, resulting in file loss or buffer overflow—conditions that weaken a system and can allow exploitation of other vulnerabilities. A common programming activity is cleaning up installation files from a computer's hard drive after successfully installing a software package. If a signed control is used for this task and permission has already been granted, then improperly using the control could result in the wrong set of files being deleted. The control will still function as designed, but the issue becomes who it is used by and how. These are concerns not addressed simply by signing a control or applet.

Browser Plug-ins

The addition of browser scripting and ActiveX components allows a browser to change how it handles data, tremendously increasing its functionality as a user interface. But all data types and all desired functionality cannot be offered through these programming technologies. Plug-ins are used to fill these gaps.

Plug-ins are small application programs that increase a browser's ability to handle new data types and add new functionality. Sometimes these plug-ins are in the form of ActiveX components, which is the form Microsoft chose for its Office plug-in, which enables a browser to manipulate various Office files, such as pivot tables from Excel, over the web. Adobe has developed Acrobat Reader, a plug-in that enables a browser to read and display Portable Document Format (PDF) files directly in a browser. PDF files offer platform independence for printed documents and are usable across a wide array of platforms—they are a compact way to provide printed information.

Dynamic data such as movies and music can be manipulated by a wide variety of plug-ins, and one of the most popular comes from Real Networks. RealOne Player can operate both as a standalone program or run video and audio files in a web page. QuickTime from Apple Computer provides the same type of functionality, and not just for Apple computers, but for Windows PCs as well. Microsoft has responded with its own viewer technology, the Windows Media Player, which also acts as a standalone application in addition to enhancing browser capabilities.

Two strikingly different plug-ins that few computers are without are the Flash and Shockwave plug-ins. These plug-ins from Macromedia can provide developers with the ability to develop striking graphic and cartoon animations that greatly enhance the look and feel of a web experience. The combination of a development environment for developers and plug-in–enabled browsers that can display the content has caused these technologies to see widespread use. The result is a tremendous increase in visual richness in web communications, and this, in turn, has made the web more popular and has increased usage in various demographic segments.

Until recently, these plug-ins have had a remarkable safety record. As Flash-based content has grown more popular, crackers have examined the Flash plug-ins and software, determined vulnerabilities, and developed exploit code to use against the Flash protocol. Adobe, the current owner of the Macromedia, has patched the issue, but as more and more third-party plug-ins become popular, expect data losses to occur as crackers investigate the more popular plug-ins and protocols for vulnerabilities.

Application-Based Weaknesses

Web browsers are not the only aspect of software being abused by crackers. The application software written to run on servers and serve up the content for users is also a target. Web Application Security is a fairly hot topic in security, as it has become a prime target for professional crackers. Criminal hackers typically are after some form of financial reward, whether from stolen data, stolen identity, or some form of extortion. Attacking web-based applications has proven to be a lucrative venture for several reasons. First, the target is a rich environment as company after company has developed a customer facing web presence, often including custom-coded functionality that permits customer access to back-end systems for legitimate business purposes. Second, building these custom applications to high levels of security is a difficult if not impossible feat, especially given the corporate pressure on delivery time and cost.

The same programmatic errors that plague operating systems, such as buffer overflows, can cause havoc with web-based systems. But web-based systems have a new history of rich customer interactions, including the collection of information from the customer and dynamically using customer supplied information to modify the user experience. This makes the customer a part of the application, and when proper controls are not in place, errors such as the Samy worm from MySpace can occur. A series of different types of errors are commonly observed in the deployment of web applications, and these have been categorized into six logical groupings of vulnerabilities: authentication, authorization, logical attacks, information disclosure, command execution, and client-side attacks. A total of 24 different types of vulnerabilities have been classified by the Web Application Security Consortium (WASC), an international organization that establishes best practices for web-application security. This list is sure to grow as different methods of attack are developed by the hacker community.

The changing nature of the web-based vulnerabilities is demonstrated by the changing of the top-ten list of web application vulnerabilities maintained by The Open Web Application Security Project (OWASP). OWASP is a worldwide free and open community focused on improving the security of application software and has published a series of top-ten vulnerability lists highlighting the current state of the art and threat environment facing web application developers. OWASP maintains a web site with significant resources to help firms build better software and eliminate these common and pervasive problems at www.owasp.org. The true challenge in this area is not just about coding, but developing an understanding of the nature of web applications and the difficulty of using user-supplied inputs for crucial aspects in a rich user experience–based web application. The errors in the top-ten list have plagued some of the largest sites and those with arguably the best talent, including Amazon, eBay, MySpace, and Google.

Open Vulnerability and Assessment Language (OVAL)

The Mitre Corporation, a government-funded research group (www.mitre.org), has done extensive research into software vulnerabilities. To enable collaboration among the many different parties involved in software development and maintenance, they have developed a taxonomy of vulnerabilities—the *Common Vulnerability Enumeration (CVE)*. This is just one of the many related enumerations that they have developed in an effort to make machine-readable data exchanges to facilitate system management across large enterprises. The CVE led efforts such as the development of the *Open Vulnerability and Assessment Language (OVAL)*. OVAL is comprised of two main elements, an XML-based machine readable language for describing vulnerabilities and a repository; see oval.mitre.org for more information.

In addition to the CVE and OVAL efforts, Mitre has developed a wide range of enumerations and standards designed to ease the automation of security management at the lowest levels across an enterprise. Additional efforts include

- Attack Patterns (CAPEC)
- Checklist Language (XCCDF)
- Security Content Automation (SCAP)
- Configurations (CCE)
- Platforms (CPE)
- Software Weakness Types (CWE)
- Log Format (CEE)
- Reporting (CRF)

Additional information can be obtained from the Mitre Corporation web site for Making Security Measurable at measurablesecurity.mitre.org.

Chapter Review

This chapter covered a lot of web technologies that have been developed in response to challenges presented by the massive interconnectivity and data sharing available across the Internet and the World Wide Web. The need for an easy way to handle the complexities of encryption and decryption led to the development of the SSL protocol series and then the TLS series. This session-layer protocol allows for the addition of authentication and data integrity checking for all activities that occur at lower levels, including TCP/IP functionality. SSL/TLS provides seamless integration through SSL/TLS-aware software, alleviating the user from tedious setups and data manipulation.

The WWW has become a major forum for data exchange, and with this widespread application of computing came the need to retrieve attribute information rapidly from data stores for identifying users, resources, and other hierarchical data structures. Directory technologies were thus born from database technologies, providing methods to accomplish these narrowly defined data storage and retrieval tasks. FTP, a longtime protocol used on the Internet, continues to thrive and also has a secure form, the SSH-enabled SFTP.

One of the new possibilities enabled by the Internet's high degree of interconnectivity is downloadable application code that operates in a browser environment. Developers are using web browsers as user interfaces. Standard functionality and user familiarity make web browsers a good choice for many application interfaces. To enable this extensible use, browsers are now designed to be extended via plug-ins and scripting functions. These extensions offer much in the way of functionality and also introduce new levels of security concerns. Java applets, JavaScript, and ActiveX technologies are some of the examples of new methods that enable developers to write browser-based applications. For more complex work, server-side implementations also exist, such as CGI and server-side scripts.

Cookies aren't just for snacking anymore; they have spread with the Internet and act as tiny data stores on computers everywhere. These small text files are essential little pieces of code that help to maintain state between web pages and web applications, and they can significantly enhance functionality for browser-based applications. As with any technology that offers to increase functionality, cookies also introduce security concerns that need to be understood and managed appropriately.

Questions

1. A cookie is

   A. A piece of data in a database that enhances web browser capability

   B. A small text file used in some HTTP exchanges

   C. A segment of script to enhance a web page

   D. A favorite snack of web developers, so they named a program after it

2. The use of certificates in SSL is similar to

   A. A receipt proving purchase

    B. Having a notary notarize a signature

    C. A historical record of a program's lineage

    D. None of the above

3. SSL can be used to secure

    A. POP3 traffic

    B. HTTP traffic

    C. SMTP traffic

    D. All of the above

4. SFTP uses which method to secure its transmissions?

    A. IPsec

    B. VPN

    C. SSH

    D. SSL

5. Security for JavaScript is established by whom?

    A. The developer at the time of code development.

    B. The user at the time of code usage.

    C. The user through browser preferences.

    D. Security for JavaScript is not necessary—the Java language is secure by design.

6. ActiveX can be used for which of the following purposes?

    A. Add functionality to a browser

    B. Update the operating system

    C. Both A and B

    D. Neither A nor B

7. CGI has a weakness in its implementation because

    A. It offers almost unlimited operating system access and functionality on a UNIX box.

    B. It is limited to Windows operating systems only.

    C. It is difficult to program in.

    D. It has a proprietary interface.

8. The keyword [secure] in a cookie

    A. Causes the system to encrypt its contents

    B. Prevents it from passing over HTTP connections

    C. Tells the browser that the cookie is a security upgrade

    D. None of the above

9. Code signing is used to

    A. Allow authors to take artistic credit for their hard work

    B. Provide a method to demonstrate code integrity

    C. Guarantee code functionality

    D. Prevent copyright infringement by code copying

10. SSL provides which of the following functionality?

    A. Data integrity services

    B. Authentication services

    C. Data confidentiality services

    D. All of the above

11. SSL uses which port to carry HTTPS traffic?

    A. TCP port 80

    B. UDP port 443

    C. TCP port 443

    D. TCP port 8080

12. High security browsers can use what to validate SSL credentials for a user?

    A. AES encrypted links to a root server

    B. An extended validation SSL certificate

    C. MD-5 hashing to ensure integrity

    D. SSL v. 3.0

13. To establish an SSL connection for e-mail and HTTP across a firewall, you must

    A. Open TCP ports 80, 25, 443, and 223

    B. Open TCP ports 443, 465, and 995

    C. Open a TCP port of choice and assign it to all SSL traffic

    D. Do nothing; SSL tunnels past firewalls

14. Directories are characterized by

    A. Being optimized for read-only data

    B. Being optimized for attribute type data

    C. More functionality than a simple database

    D. Better security model than a database

15. To prevent the use of cookies in a browser, a user must

    A. Tell the browser to disable cookies via a setup option.

    B. Delete all existing cookies.

    C. All of the above.

    D. The user need do nothing—by design, cookies are necessary and cannot be totally disabled.

Answers

1. **B.** Cookies are small pieces of ASCII text used in HTTP transfers to exchange data between client and server.

2. **B.** A certificate acts as an electronic notary, providing a method of determining authenticity through a third party.

3. **D.** SSL can be used to secure all of the above—SPOP3 is POP3 secured, HTTPS is secure HTTP, and SSMTP is secure SMTP.

4. **C.** SFTP uses SSH to enable secure file transfers.

5. **C.** JavaScript security is ultimately the responsibility of the end user, and the options exist in browsers to select various security levels or even disable it altogether.

6. **C.** ActiveX can be used to create all kinds of software and modifications to existing software. ActiveX is technology that can be used to create complex application logic that is then embedded into other container objects such as a web browser.

7. **A.** Unlimited access to operating system functionality makes many CGI scripts security hazards to the system, and special care is required in their design and implementation.

8. **B.** Cookies with the **[secure]** tag are only passed by browsers over HTTPS connections.

9. **B.** Code signing includes data integrity checking through a hash value.

10. **D.** SSL provides all of the above.

11. **C.** HTTPS traffic is connection oriented (TCP) and carried over port 443 by default.

12. **B.** Extended validation SSL certificate is signed by the CA to prove authenticity.

13. **B.** HTTP uses 443, SSMTP uses 465, and SPOP3 uses 995.

14. **B.** Directories are used primarily for reading attribute type data to support fast lookups and searches.

15. **C.** The user must do both **A** and **B**. **A** will prevent future cookies from interacting, but **B** is necessary to stop cookies already downloaded from being passed back to the server on subsequent visits.

PART V

Operational Security

■ **Chapter 16** Disaster Recovery and Business Continuity
■ **Chapter 17** Risk Management
■ **Chapter 18** Change Management
■ **Chapter 19** Privilege Management
■ **Chapter 20** Computer Forensics

Disaster Recovery and Business Continuity

In this chapter, you will

- Learn about the various ways backups are conducted and stored
- Discover different strategies for alternative site processing
- Understand the various components of a business continuity plan
- Understand how policies and procedures play a daily role in addressing the security needs of an organization

Much of this book focuses on avoiding the loss of confidentiality or integrity due to a security breach. The issue of availability is also discussed in terms of specific events, such as denial-of-service and distributed denial-of-service attacks. In reality, however, many things can disrupt the operations of your organization, and you need to be prepared to address them.

Disaster Recovery

Many types of disasters, whether natural or caused by people, can stop your organization's operations for some length of time. Such disasters are unlike the threats to your computer systems and networks, because the events that cause the disruption are not specifically aimed at your organization. This is not to say that those other threats won't disrupt operations—they can, and industrial espionage, hacking, disgruntled employees, and insider threats all must be considered. The purpose of this chapter is to point out additional events that you may not have previously considered.

The amount of time your organization's operations are disrupted depends in part on how prepared it is for a disaster and what plans are in place to mitigate the effects of a disaster. Any of these events could cause a disruption in operations:

fire	flood	tornado	hurricane
electrical storm	earthquake	political unrest/riot	blizzard
gas leak/explosion	chemical spill	terrorism	war

Fortunately, these types of events do not happen very often. It is more likely that business operations will be interrupted due to employee error (such as accidental corruption of a database, or unplugging a system to plug in a vacuum cleaner—an event that has occurred at more than one organization). A good disaster recovery plan will prepare your organization for any type of organizational disruption.

Disaster Recovery Plans/Process

No matter what event you're worried about—whether natural or not, targeted at your organization or not—you can make preparations to lessen the impact on your organization and the length of time that your organization will be out of operation. A *disaster recovery plan (DRP)* is critical for effective disaster recovery efforts. A DRP defines the data and resources necessary and the steps required to restore critical organizational processes.

Consider what your organization needs to perform its mission. This information provides the beginning of a DRP, since it tells you what needs to be restored quickly. When considering resources, don't forget to include both the *physical resources* (such as computer hardware and software) and *personnel* (somebody must know how to run the systems that process your critical data).

To begin creating your DRP, first identify all critical functions for your organization, and then answer the following questions for each of these critical functions:

- Who is responsible for the operation of this function?
- What do these individuals need to perform the function?
- When should this function be accomplished relative to other functions?
- Where will this function be performed?
- How is this function performed (what is the process)?
- Why is this function so important or critical to the organization?

By answering these questions, you can create an initial draft of your organization's DRP. The name often used to describe the document created by addressing these questions is a *business impact assessment (BIA)*. This plan, of course, will need to be approved by management, and it is essential that they buy into the plan—otherwise your efforts will more than likely fail. That old adage, "Those who fail to plan, plan to fail" certainly applies in this situation.

It is important in a good DRP to include the processes and procedures needed to restore your organization so that it is functioning again and to ensure continued operation. What specific steps will be required to restore operations? These processes should be documented, and, where possible and feasible, they should be reviewed and *exercised* on a periodic basis. Having a plan with step-by-step procedures that nobody knows how to follow does nothing to ensure the continued operation of the organization. Exercising your disaster recovery plans and processes in a *disaster recovery exercise* before a disaster occurs provides you with the opportunity to discover flaws or weaknesses in the plan when there is still time to modify and correct them. It also provides an opportunity for key figures in the plan to practice what they will be expected to accomplish.

NOTE The restoration process can be as simple as restoring a single critical system that may have experienced a hardware failure up to the restoration of all company functions in the event of a catastrophe such as a natural disaster. The DRP should take into account these different levels of recovery.

EXAM TIP Disaster recovery exercises are an often overlooked aspect of security. Many organizations do not believe that they have the time to spend on such events but the question to ask is whether they can afford to not conduct these exercises as they ensure that the organization has a viable plan to recover from a disaster and to ensure continued operation should a disaster occur. Make sure you understand what is involved in these critical tests of your organization's plans.

Categories of Business Functions

In developing your BIA and DRP, you may find it useful to categorize the various functions your organization performs. This categorization is based on how critical or important the function is to business operation. Those functions that are the most critical will be restored first, and your DRP should reflect this. One possible categorization scheme might be to divide functions into the following categories:

- **Critical**   The function is absolutely essential for operations. Without the function, the basic mission of the organization cannot occur.

- **Necessary for normal processing**   The function is required for normal processing, but the organization can live without it for a short period of time (such as for less than 30 days).

- **Desirable**   The function is not needed for normal processing but enhances the organization's ability to conduct its mission efficiently.

- **Optional**   The function is nice to have but does not affect the operation of the organization.

An important aspect of this categorization scheme is understanding how long the organization can survive without the specific function. This information will help you place the function in the appropriate category. If the function is needed immediately, it is *critical*. If you can live without it for at most 30 days before its loss significantly impacts your organization, it falls into the *necessary for normal processing* category. If you can live without the function for more than 30 days, but it is a function that will eventually need to be accomplished when normal operations are restored, it falls into the *desirable* category (this implies some subsequent catch-up processing will need to be accomplished). If the function is not needed, and no subsequent processing will be

PART V

required to restore this function, it falls into the *optional* category. If the function doesn't fall into any of these categories because it doesn't really affect the operation of your organization, it falls into a category not mentioned yet—the *get rid of it* category. You may want to consider eliminating this function, since it might not be serving any useful purpose.

Business Continuity Plans

Another term that is often used when discussing the issue of continued organizational operations is *business continuity plan (BCP)*. You might wonder what the difference is between a DRP and a BCP—after all, isn't the purpose of the DRP the continued operation of the organization or business? In reality, these two terms are sometimes used synonymously, and for many organizations there may be no major difference in the two. There are, however, slight differences between a BCP and a DRP, one of which is the *focus*.

The focus of business continuity planning is the continued operation of the business or organization. The focus of a disaster recovery plan is on the recovery and rebuilding of the organization after a disaster has occurred. The DRP is part of the larger BCP since business continuity is always an issue. In a DRP, the protection of human life should be addressed and is a major focus of the document. Evacuation plans and system shutdown procedures should be addressed. The safety of employees should be a theme throughout a DRP. In the rest of the BCP, on the other hand, you may not see the same level of emphasis placed on protection of employees. The focus of the BCP are the critical systems the organization needs in order to operate.

Another way to look at these is that the BCP will be used to ensure that your operations continue in the face of whatever event has occurred that has caused a disruption in operations. If a disaster has occurred and has destroyed all or part of your facility, the DRP portion of the BCP will address the building or acquisition of a new facility. The DRP can also include details related to the long-term recovery of the organization.

However you view these two plans, an organization that is not able to restore business functions quickly after an operational interruption is an organization that will most likely suffer an unrecoverable loss and may cease to exist.

 EXAM TIP The terms DRP and BCP are often used synonymously by many but there are subtle differences between them. Study this section carefully to ensure that you can discriminate between the two terms.

Backups

Backups are important in any BCP, not only because of the possibility of a disaster but also because hardware and storage media will periodically fail, resulting in loss or corruption of critical data. An organization might also find backups critical when security measures have failed and an individual has gained access to important information that may have become corrupted or at the very least can't be trusted. Data backup is thus a critical element in BCPs, as well as in normal operation. You must consider several factors in an organization's data backup strategy:

- How frequently should backups be conducted?
- How extensive do the backups need to be?
- What is the process for conducting backups?
- Who is responsible for ensuring backups are created?
- Where will the backups be stored?
- How long will backups be kept?
- How many copies will be maintained?

Keep in mind that the purpose of a backup is to provide valid, uncorrupted data in the event of corruption or loss of the original file or media where the data was stored. Depending on the type of organization, legal requirements for conducting backups can also affect how it is accomplished.

What Needs to Be Backed Up

Backups commonly comprise the data that an organization relies on to conduct its daily operations. While this is certainly true, a good backup plan will consider more than just data; it will include any application programs needed to process the data and the operating system and utilities that the hardware platform requires to run the applications. Obviously, the application programs and operating system will change much less frequently than the data itself, so the frequency with which these items need to be backed up is considerably different. This should be reflected in the organization's backup plan and strategy.

The BCP should also address other items related to backups, such as personnel, equipment, and electrical power. Somebody needs to understand the operation of the critical hardware and software used by the organization. If the disaster that destroyed the original copy of the data and the original systems also results in the loss of the only person who knows how to process the data, having backup data will not be enough to restore normal operations for the organization. Similarly, if the data requires specific software to be run on a very specific hardware platform, then having the data without the application program or required hardware will also not be sufficient. As you can see, a BCP is an involved document that must consider many different factors and possibilities.

Strategies for Backups

The process for creating a backup copy of data and software requires more thought than simply stating "copy all required files." The size of the resulting backup must be considered, as well as the time required to perform the backup. Both of these will affect details such as how frequently the backup will occur and the type of storage media that will be used. Other considerations include who will be responsible for conducting the backup, where the backups will be stored, and how long they should be maintained. Short-term storage for accidentally deleted files that users need to have restored should probably be close at hand. Longer-term storage for backups that may be several months or years old should be in a different facility.

It should be evident by now that even something that sounds as simple as maintaining backup copies of essential data requires careful consideration and planning. In addition, as with your disaster recovery plans, which should be tested and exercised on a periodic basis, your backup process and plans also need to be exercised and tested. You can imagine the frustration experienced when an organization that has been consistently creating backups suddenly needs them but finds that a mistake has been made and the backups are unusable. By periodically exercising your recovery plans, you can test to make sure that restoration from your backups is possible and that your plans are sufficient, your process is working, and that your personnel have the necessary tools and knowledge to be able to restore your systems in the event it is really needed.

Types of Backups The amount of data that will be backed up and the time it takes to accomplish the backup have direct bearing on the type of backup that will be performed. Four basic types of backups, the amount of space required for each, and the ease of restoration using each strategy are outlined in Table 16-1.

The values for each of the strategies in Table 16-1 vary depending on your specific environment. The more files are changed between backups, the more these strategies will look alike. What each strategy entails bears further explanation.

The easiest type of backup to understand is the *full backup*, in which all files and software are backed up onto the storage media and an archive bit is cleared. Restoration from a full backup is similarly straightforward—you must restore all the files onto the system. This process can take a considerable amount of time. Consider the size of even the average home PC today, for which storage is measured in tens and hundreds of gigabytes. Backing up this amount of data, or more, takes time.

In a *differential backup*, only files and software that have changed since the last full backup was completed are backed up. This also implies that periodically a full backup needs to be accomplished. The frequency of the full backup versus the interim differential backups depends on your organization and is part of your defined strategy. Restoration from a differential backup requires two steps: the last full backup first needs to be loaded, and then the differential backup can be applied to update the files that have been changed since the full backup was conducted. Although the differential backup process can take time, the amount of time required is much less than that of a full backup, and this is one of the advantages of this method. Obviously, if a lot of time has passed between differential backups, or if your environment results in most files changing frequently, then the differential backup does not differ much from a full backup. It should also be obvious that to accomplish the differential backup, the system has to have a method of determining which files have been changed since a given point in time. The archive bit is used for this purpose.

	Full	Differential	Incremental	Delta
Amount of space	Large	Medium	Medium	Small
Restoration	Simple	Simple	Involved	Complex

Table 16-1   Characteristics of Backup Types

With *incremental backups*, even less information will be stored in each individual backup increment. The incremental backup is a variation on a differential backup, with the difference being that instead of backing up all files that have changed since the last full backup, as in the case of the differential, the incremental backup will back up only files that have changed since the last full *or* incremental backup occurred, thus requiring fewer files to be backed up. Just as in the case of the differential backup, the incremental backup relies on the occasional full backup. After that, you back up only files that have changed since the last backup of any sort was conducted. To restore a system using this type of backup method requires quite a bit more work. You first need to go back to the last full backup and reload the system with this data. Then you have to update the system with every incremental backup that occurred since then. The advantage of this type of backup is that it requires less storage and time to accomplish. The disadvantage is that the restoration process is more involved. Assuming that you don't frequently have to conduct a complete restoration of your system, however, the incremental backup is a valid technique.

Finally, the goal of the *delta backup* is to save as little information as possible each time you perform a backup. As with the other strategies, an occasional full backup is required. After that, when a delta backup is conducted at specific intervals, only the portions of the files that have been changed will be stored. The advantage of this is easy to illustrate. If your organization maintains a large database with thousands of records and several hundred megabytes of data, the entire database would be backed up in the previous backup types even if only one record is changed. For a delta backup, only the actual record that changed would be stored. The disadvantage of this method should also be readily apparent—restoration is a complex process since it requires more than just loading a file (or several files). It requires that application software be run to update the records in the files that have been changed. This process is also called a *transactional backup*.

Each type of backup has advantages and disadvantages. Which type is best for your organization depends on the amount of data you routinely process and store, how frequently it changes, how often you expect to have to restore from a backup, and a number of other factors. The type you select will greatly affect your overall backup strategy, plans, and processes.

 EXAM TIP   Backup strategies are such a critical element of security that you need to make sure you understand the different types of backups and their advantages and disadvantages.

PART V

Backup Frequency and Retention The type of backup strategy an organization employs is often affected by how frequently the organization conducts the backup activity. The usefulness of a backup is directly related to how many changes have occurred since the backup was created, and this is obviously affected by how often backups are created. The longer it has been since the backup was created, the more changes will likely have occurred. There is no easy answer, however, to how frequently an organization should perform backups. Every organization should consider how long it can survive without current data from which to operate. It can then determine how long it will take to restore from backups using various methods, and decide how frequently backups need to occur. This sounds simple, but it is a serious, complex decision to make.

Related to the frequency question is the issue of how long backups should be maintained. Is it sufficient to maintain a single backup from which to restore data? Security professionals will tell you no; multiple backups should be maintained for a variety of reasons. If the reason for restoring from the backup is the discovery of an intruder in the system, it is important to restore the system to its pre-intrusion state. If the intruder has been in the system for several months before being discovered, and backups are taken weekly, it will not be possible to restore to a pre-intrusion state if only one backup is maintained. This would mean that all data and system files would be suspect and may not be reliable. If multiple backups were maintained, at various intervals, it is easier to return to a point before the intrusion (or before the security or operational event that is necessitating the restoration) occurred.

Several strategies or approaches to backup retention include the common and easy-to-remember "rule of three," in which the three most recent backups are kept. When a new backup is created, the oldest backup is overwritten. Another strategy is to keep the most recent copy of backups for various time intervals. For example, you might keep the latest daily, weekly, monthly, quarterly, and yearly backups. Note that in certain environments, regulatory issues may prescribe a specific frequency and retention period, so it is important to know these requirements when determining how often you will create a backup and how long you will keep it.

If you are not in an environment for which regulatory issues dictate the frequency and retention for backups, your goal will be to optimize the frequency. In determining the optimal backup frequency, two major costs need to be considered: the cost of the backup strategy you choose and the cost of recovery if you do not implement this backup strategy (if no backups were created). You must also factor into the equation the probability that the backup will be needed on any given day. The two figures to consider then are

(probability the backup is needed) × *(cost of restoring with no backup)*

(probability the backup isn't needed) × *(cost of the backup strategy)*

For example, if the probability of a backup being needed is 10 percent, and the cost of restoring with no backup is $100,000, then the first equation would yield a figure of $10,000. This can be compared with the alternative which would be a 90 percent chance the backup is not needed multiplied by the cost of implementing our backup strategy (of taking and maintaining the backups) which is, say, $10,000 annually. The second equation yields a figure of $9000. The first of these two figures can be considered the probable loss you can expect if your organization has no backup. The second figure can be considered the price you are willing to pay (spend) to ensure that you can restore, should a problem occur (think of this as backup insurance—the cost of an insurance policy that may never be used but that you are willing to pay for, just in case). In our example, the cost of maintaining the backup is less than the cost of not having backups, so the former would be the better choice. While conceptually this is an easy tradeoff to understand, in reality it is often difficult to accurately determine the probability of a backup being needed. Fortunately, the figures for the potential loss if there is no backup is generally so much greater than the cost of maintaining a backup that a mistake in judging the probability will not matter—it just makes too much sense to maintain backups.

To optimize your backup strategy, you need to determine the correct balance between these two figures. Obviously, you don't want to spend more in your backup strategy than you face losing should you not have a backup plan at all. When working with these two calculations, you have to remember that this is a cost-avoidance exercise. The organization is not going to increase revenues with its backup strategy. Your goal is to minimize the potential loss due to some catastrophic event by creating a backup strategy that will address your organization's needs.

When calculating the cost of the backup strategy, consider the following elements:

- The cost of the backup media required for a single backup
- The storage costs for the backup media and the retention policy
- The labor costs associated with performing a single backup
- The frequency with which backups are created

All these considerations can be used to arrive at an annual cost for implementing your chosen backup strategy, and this figure can then be used as previously described.

Storage of Backups   An important element to factor into the cost of the backup strategy is the expense of storing the backups. A simple backup storage strategy might be to store all your backups together for quick and easy recovery actions. This is not, however, a good idea. Suppose the catastrophe that necessitated the restoration of backed-up data was a fire that destroyed the computer system on which the data was processed? In this case, any backups that were stored in the same facility could also be lost in the same fire.

The solution is to keep copies of backups in separate locations. The most recent copy could be stored locally, as it is the most likely to be needed. Other copies can be kept at other locations. Depending on the level of security desired, the storage facility itself could be reinforced against possible threats in your area (such as tornados or floods). Another more recent advance is online backup services. A number of third-party companies offer high-speed connections for storing data in a separate facility on a frequent basis. Transmitting the backup data via network connections alleviates some other concerns with physical movement of more traditional storage media—such as the care during transportation (tapes do not fare well in direct sunlight, for example) or the time that it takes to transport the tape data.

Issues with Long-Term Storage of Backups   Depending on the media used for an organization's backups, degradation of the media is a distinct possibility and needs to be considered. Magnetic media degrade over time (measured in years). In addition, tapes can be used a limited number of times before the surface begins to flake off. Magnetic media should be rotated and tested to ensure that it is still usable.

Another consideration is advances in technology. The media you used to store your data two years ago may now be considered obsolete (5.25-inch floppy drives, for example). Software applications also evolve, and the media may be present but may not be compatible with current versions of the software. Both hardware and software versions associated with the data at creation can become obsolete, yet they might be needed to recover the information.

Another issue is security related. If the file you stored was encrypted for security purposes, does anyone in the company remember the password to decrypt the file to restore the data?

Alternative Sites   Related to the location of backup storage is where the restoration services will be located. If the organization has suffered physical damage to its facility, having offsite data storage is only part of the solution. This data will need to be processed somewhere, which means that computing facilities similar to those used in normal operations are required. This problem can be approached in a number of ways, including hot sites, warm sites, cold sites, and mobile backup sites.

A *hot site* is a fully configured environment similar to the normal operating environment that can be operational immediately or within a few hours depending on its configuration and the needs of the organization. A *warm site* is partially configured, usually having the peripherals and software but perhaps not the more expensive main processing computer. It is designed to be operational within a few days. A *cold site* will have the basic environmental controls necessary to operate but few of the computing components necessary for processing. Getting a cold site operational may take weeks. Mobile backup sites are generally trailers with the required computers and electrical power that can be driven to a location within hours of a disaster and set up to commence processing immediately.

Shared alternate sites may also be considered. These sites can be designed to handle the needs of different organizations in the event of an emergency. The hope is that the disaster will affect only one organization at a time. The benefit of this method is that the cost of the site can be shared among organizations. Two similar organizations located close to each should not share the same alternate site as there is a greater chance that they would both need it at the same time.

All these options can come with considerable price tags, which makes another option, *mutual aid agreements*, a possible alternative. With mutual aid agreements, similar organizations agree to assume the processing for the other party in the event that a disaster occurs. The obvious assumption here is that both organizations will not be affected by the same disaster and that both have similar processing environments. If these two assumptions are correct, a mutual aid agreement should be considered.

 EXAM TIP Just like the different backup strategies, the need to have a facility to conduct recovery operations is a critical element of any organization's recovery plans and you should understand the differences among the different types of alternative sites.

RAID A relatively new approach to increasing reliability in disk storage is *Redundant Array of Inexpensive Disks*, now known as *Redundant Array of Independent Disks (RAID)*. RAID takes data that is normally stored on a single disk and spreads it out among several others. If any single disk is lost, the data can be recovered from the other disks where the data also resides. With the price of disk storage decreasing, this approach has become increasingly popular to the point that many individual users even have RAID arrays for their home systems. RAID can also increase the speed of data recovery as multiple drives can be busy retrieving requested data at the same time instead of relying on just one disk to do the work.

Several different RAID approaches can be considered:

- **RAID 0** (Striped disks) simply spreads the data that would be kept on the one disk across several disks. This decreases the time it takes to retrieve data, because the data is read from multiple drives at the same time, but it does not improve reliability as the loss of any single drive will result in the loss of all the data (since portions of files are spread out among the different disks). With RAID 0, the data is split across all the drives with no redundancy offered.

- **RAID 1** (Mirrored disks) is the opposite of RAID 0. RAID 1 copies the data from one disk onto two or more disks. If any one disk is lost, the data is not lost since it is also copied onto the other disk(s). This method can be used to improve reliability and retrieval speed, but it is relatively expensive when compared to other RAID techniques.

- **RAID 2** (Bit-level error-correcting code) is not typically used, as it stripes data across the drives at the bit level as opposed to the block level. It is designed to be able to recover the loss of any single disk through the use of error-correcting techniques.

- **RAID 3** (Byte-striped with error check) spreads the data across multiple disks at the byte level with one disk dedicated to parity bits. This technique is not commonly implemented because input/output operations can't be overlapped due to the need for all to access the same disk (the disk with the parity bits).

- **RAID 4** (Dedicated parity drive) stripes data across several disks but in larger stripes than in RAID 3, and it uses a single drive for parity-based error checking. RAID 4 has the disadvantage of not improving data retrieval speeds, since all retrievals still need to access the single parity drive.

- **RAID 5** (Block-striped with error check) is a commonly used method that stripes the data at the block level and spreads the parity data across the drives. This provides both reliability and increased speed performance.

RAID 0 through 5 are the original techniques, with RAID 5 being the most common method used, as it provides both the reliability and speed improvements. Additional methods have been implemented, such as duplicating the parity data across the disks (RAID 6), a stripe of mirrors (RAID 10), and a commercial trademarked technique using caching to improved other methods (RAID 7).

Spare Parts and Redundant Services   RAID increases reliability through the use of *redundancy*. When developing plans for ensuring that an organization has what it needs to keep operating, even if hardware or software fails or if security is breached, you should consider other measures involving redundancy and spare parts. Some common applications of redundancy include the use of redundant servers, redundant connections, and redundant ISPs. The need for redundant servers and connections may be fairly obvious, but redundant ISPs may not be so, at least initially. Many ISPs already have multiple accesses to the Internet on their own, but by having additional ISP connections, an organization can reduce the chance that an interruption of one ISP will negatively impact the organization. Ensuring uninterrupted access to the Internet by employees or access to the organization's e-commerce site for customers is becoming increasingly important.

Many organizations don't see the need for maintaining a supply of spare parts. After all, with the price of storage dropping and the speed of processors increasing, why replace a broken part with older technology? However, a ready supply of spare parts can ease the process of bringing the system back online. Replacing hardware and software with newer versions can sometimes lead to problems with compatibility. An older version of some piece of critical software may not work with newer hardware, which may be more capable in a variety of ways. Having critical hardware (or software) spares for critical functions in the organization can greatly facilitate maintaining business continuity in the event of software or hardware failures.

EXAM TIP   Redundancy is an important factor in both security and reliability. Make sure you understand the many different areas that can benefit from redundant components.

Single Point of Failure   A common thread in previous discussions is the attempt to avoid a *single point of failure* in critical functions within an organization. When developing your BCP, you should be on the lookout for areas in which a critical function relies on a single item (such as switches, routers, firewalls, power supplies, software, or data) that if lost would stop this critical function. When these points are identified, think about how this possible single point of failure can be eliminated (or mitigated). The use of the techniques discussed in the preceding sections can be used to address these issues.

Look beyond hardware, software, and data to consider how the loss of various critical infrastructures can also impact business operations. The type of infrastructures you should consider in your BCP is the subject of the next section.

Utilities

The interruption of power is a common issue during a disaster. Computers and networks obviously require power to operate, so emergency power must be available in the event of any disruption of operations. For short-term interruptions, such as what might occur as the result of an electrical storm, uninterruptible power supplies (UPSs) may suffice. These devices contain a battery that provides steady power for short periods of time—enough to keep a system running should power be lost for only a few minutes, or enough to allow administrators to halt the system or network gracefully. For continued operations that extend beyond a few minutes, another source of power will be required, such as a backup emergency generator.

While backup generators are frequently used to provide power during an emergency, they are not a simple, maintenance-free solution. Generators need to be tested on a regular basis, and they can easily become strained if they are required to power too much equipment. If your organization relies on an emergency generator for backup power, you must ensure that the system has reserve capacity beyond the anticipated load for the unanticipated loads that will undoubtedly be placed on it.

Generators also take time to start up, so power will most likely be lost, even if only for a brief second, until they come on. This means that a UPS should also be used for a smooth transition to backup power. Generators are also expensive and require fuel—when looking for a place to locate your generator, don't forget the need to deliver fuel to it or you may find yourself hauling cans of gasoline up a number of stairs.

When determining the need for backup power, don't forget to factor in environmental conditions. Power to computer systems in a room with no air conditioning in the middle of the summer in the Southwest will result in an extremely uncomfortable environment for all to work in. Mobile backup sites, generally using trailers, often rely on generators for their power but also factor in the requirement for environmental controls.

Power is not the only essential utility for operations. Depending on the type of disaster that has occurred, telephone and Internet communication may also be lost, and wireless services may not be available. Planning for redundant means of communication (such as using both land lines and wireless) can help with most outages, but for large disasters, your backup plans should include the option to continue operations from a completely different location while waiting for communications in your area to be restored. Telecommunication carriers have their own emergency equipment and are fairly efficient at restoring communications, but it may take a few days.

Secure Recovery

Several companies offer recovery services, including power, communications, and technical support that could be needed if your organization's operations are disrupted.

These companies advertise secure recovery sites or offices from which your organization can again begin to operate in a secure environment. Secure recovery is also advertised by other organizations that provide services that can remotely (over the Internet, for example) provide restoration services for critical files and data.

In both cases—the actual physical suites and the remote service—security is an important element. During a disaster, your data does not become any less important, and you should make sure that you maintain the security (in terms of confidentiality and integrity, for example) of your data. As in other aspects of security, the decision to employ these services should be made based on a calculation of the benefits weighed against the potential loss if alternative means are used.

High Availability and Fault Tolerance

Some other terms that are often used in discussions of continuity of operations in the face of a disruption of some sort are *high availability* and *fault tolerance.*

One of the objectives of security is the availability of data and processing power when an authorized user desires it. High availability refers to the ability to maintain availability of data and operational processing (services) despite a disrupting event. Generally this requires redundant systems, both in terms of power and processing, so that should one system fail, the other can take over operations without any break in service. High availability is more than data redundancy; it requires that both data and services be available.

Fault tolerance basically has the same goal as high availability—the uninterrupted access to data and services. It is accomplished by the mirroring of data and systems. Should a "fault" occur, causing disruption in a device such as a disk controller, the mirrored system provides the requested data with no apparent interruption in service to the user.

Obviously, providing redundant systems for data and services and redundant equipment comes with a price. The need to provide this level of continuous, uninterrupted operation needs to be carefully evaluated.

Chapter Review

Every organization should have a plan to address the interruption of normal operations. The first step in developing such a plan is creating a business impact assessment, which helps the organization determine the critical systems and processes needed in order to function. A disaster recovery plan must also be created to outline how the organization will address various disasters that can affect operations. A business continuity plan should be created to address long-term disruptions of the organization's operations, and it should be focused on reestablishing those functions essential for the continued operation of the organization.

A key point in developing a BCP is the identification of single points of failure in an organization's operations. These can involve hardware, software, data, or critical infrastructures. Organizations need to consider the multiple methods practiced in industry such as the periodic creation of system backups, the use of RAID technology, and areas where redundant products or services should be considered.

Questions

1. A business impact assessment is designed to do which of the following?

   A. Determine the impact your business has on other organizations.

   B. Determine the impact your business has on local, regional, and national economies.

   C. Determine the effect your corporate security strategy has on the way you conduct your operations.

   D. Determine which processes, systems, and people are critical to the operation of your organization.

2. A good backup plan will include which of the following?

   A. The critical data needed for the organization to operate

   B. Any software that is required to process the organization's data

   C. Specific hardware to run the software or to process the data

   D. All of the above

3. Which backup strategy backs up only the files and software that have changed since the last full backup?

   A. Full

   B. Differential

   C. Incremental

   D. Delta

4. Which of the following is *not* a consideration in calculating the cost of a backup strategy?

   A. The cost of the backup media

   B. The storage costs for the backup media

   C. The probability that the backup will be needed

   D. The frequency with which backups are created

5. Which of the following is the name for a fully configured environment similar to the normal operating environment that can be operational immediately to within a few hours?

   A. Hot site

   B. Warm site

   C. Online storage system

   D. Backup storage facility

PART V

6. Which of the following is considered an issue with long-term storage of magnetic media, as discussed in the chapter?

   A. Tape media can be used a limited number of times before it degrades.

   B. Software and hardware evolve, and the media stored may no longer be compatible with current technology.

   C. Both of the above.

   D. None of the above.

7. Which of the following is the best approach to take for potential short-term loss of electrical power?

   A. Don't worry about it. If it is short term, the systems will be back up in at most a few minutes, and processing can resume.

   B. Install an uninterruptible power supply (UPS) to allow processing to continue while you wait for power to be restored. If it will take longer than a few minutes, the supply will allow you to gracefully bring the system down so no loss of information is suffered.

   C. Install a backup power generator and maintain a supply of fuel for it.

   D. Have the power company install a backup power line into your facility.

8. What other common utility is it important to consider when developing your recovery plans?

   A. Water

   B. Gas

   C. Communications

   D. Television/cable

9. RAID stands for

   A. Replacement Array of Identical Disks

   B. Replacement Array of Inexpensive Disks

   C. Redundant Array of Identical Devices

   D. Redundant Array of Inexpensive Disks

10. Which RAID technique uses an array of identical disks with all data copied to each of the disks?

    A. RAID 0

    B. RAID 1

    C. RAID 4

    D. RAID 5

11. Which of the following is a reason to maintain a supply of spare parts (hardware and software)?

    A. Products fail but newer versions may not be compatible with older versions.

    B. Buying multiple copies of products will reduce the overall cost.

    C. Insurance companies that provide insurance against data loss require it.

    D. In the case of a security incident, law enforcement agencies can seize your original equipment so you'll need to have extra copies to maintain business continuity.

12. Developing a DRP, BCP, and backup policy is just one step in preparing for a disaster. What other step needs to be taken?

    A. Once developed, the plans should be exercised to make sure that they are complete and that all individuals know their responsibilities.

    B. The plans need to be provided to the organization's insurance provider to ensure that they are sufficient to cover the needs of the organization.

    C. The plans should be published on the Internet to share with others who can learn from the organization's experience.

    D. An independent contractor should be consulted to ensure that the plans are complete and adequate.

Answers

1. D. This is the description of what a business impact assessment is supposed to accomplish. It is important to emphasize that the BIA not only includes the systems (hardware and software) needed by the organization, but any supplies or specific individuals that are critical for the operation of the organization.

2. D. All of these are important. Having copies of your data will not be useful if specialized software is required to process it and if specialized hardware is needed to run the special software. You must consider all of these in your backup plan.

3. B. This is the definition of a differential backup. In an incremental backup, the data and software that has changed since the last full or incremental backup is saved. A delta backup saves only those portions of the files that have changed, instead of the entire file.

4. C. This was a tricky question. The probability that the backup will be needed is a factor in determining the optimal backup frequency, but it was not discussed as part of the cost of the backup strategy. It is also a figure that can be used in a risk analysis to determine the optimum strategy.

5. **A.** This is the definition of a hot site.

6. **C.** Both **A** and **B** were identified as issues that must be considered when planning your long-term storage strategy.

7. **B.** Purchasing and using a UPS is the best strategy to address short-term power loss. It allows for continued operation if the loss is brief or lets you bring the system down without loss of data. Generators are expensive to purchase and maintain and are not appropriate for short-term power loss. They may be essential for long-term loss of power in installations where this is likely and processing is critical. Ignoring the issue (answer **A**) is not a good approach as even a brief loss in power can disrupt processing and cause loss of data. Installing a second power line is also not a reasonable answer.

8. **C.** Communications (whether telephone or wireless) is critical for organizations today. Water and gas may be important, especially for long-term utility interruption, but they are generally not considered as important as communications, where even a short-term loss can be disastrous. While loss of television or cable may result in you missing your favorite show, it generally is not considered as crucial to business (unless the cable also supplies your Internet connectivity and is relied on for business operations).

9. **D.** This is the original definition for this acronym, but Redundant Array of Independent Disks is also now used.

10. **B.** This is the description for RAID 1. This technique is more expensive than other techniques as the total capacity for the entire RAID implementation is the capacity of a single disk.

11. **A.** Older equipment and software may not be compatible with newer versions, which could mean that business continuity is lost if a product fails. Having spare parts enables you to bring systems back up more quickly without problems associated with compatibility issues.

12. **A.** This is the best answer. Every plan should be tested to ensure that it is complete and so that key individuals in the plan know their parts and can accomplish assigned tasks. Exercising a plan can also identify items that are required in the event of a disaster but that are not required during normal business operations. The other answers may all have elements that could be partially correct but are not the best answer. Insurance companies may indeed want to know that the organization has a BCP, DRP, and backup plan, but this is not the best answer. Sharing information between organizations certainly is a practice that can help raise the level of preparedness across an industry, but sharing specifics about your plan is not advisable and could lead to a security breach. Contractors might be able to help develop a plan and can provide valuable assistance, but they are not required in the process if your organization has sufficient expertise.

Risk Management

In this chapter you will

- Discover the purpose of risk management and an approach to manage risk effectively
- Learn the differences between qualitative and quantitative risk assessment
- See, by example, how both approaches are necessary to manage risk effectively
- Review important definitions and tools

Risk management can best be described as a decision-making process. In the simplest terms, when you manage risk, you determine what could happen to your business, you assess the impact if it were to happen, and you decide what you could do to control that impact as much as you or your management deems necessary. You then decide to act or not to act, and, finally, you evaluate the results of your decision. The process may be iterative, as industry best practices clearly indicate that an important aspect of effectively managing risk is to consider it an ongoing process.

An Overview of Risk Management

Risk management is an essential element of management from the enterprise level down to the individual project. Risk management encompasses all the actions taken to reduce complexity, increase objectivity, and identify important decision factors. There has been, and will continue to be, discussion about the complexity of risk management and whether or not it is worth the effort. Businesses must take risks to retain their competitive edge, however, and as a result, risk management must occur as part of managing any business, program, or project.

Risk management is both a skill and a task that is performed by all managers, either deliberately or intuitively. It can be simple or complex, depending on the size of the project or business and the amount of risk inherent in an activity. Every manager, at all levels, must learn to manage risk. The required skills can be learned.

 EXAM TIP This chapter contains several bulleted lists. These are designed for easy memorization in preparation for taking the Security+ exam.

Example of Risk Management at the International Banking Level

The Basel Committee on Banking Supervision comprises government central-bank governors from around the world. This body created a basic, global risk management framework for market and credit risk. It implemented internationally a flat 8 percent capital charge to banks to manage bank risks. In layman's terms, this means that for every $100 a bank makes in loans, it must possess $8 in reserve to be used in the event of financial difficulties. However, if banks can show they have very strong risk mitigation procedures and controls in place, that capital charge can be reduced to as low as $0.37 (0.37 percent). If a bank has poor procedures and controls, that capital charge can be as high as $45 (45 percent) for every $100 the bank makes.

This example shows that risk management can be and is used at very high levels—the remainder of this chapter will focus on smaller implementations. It will be shown that risk management is used in many aspects of business conduct.

Key Terms for Understanding Risk Management

You need to understand a number of key terms to manage risk successfully. Some of these terms are defined here because they are used throughout the chapter. This list is somewhat ordered according to the organization of this chapter. More comprehensive definitions and other pertinent terms are listed alphabetically in the glossary at the end of this book.

Risk   The possibility of suffering harm or loss.

Risk management   The overall decision-making process of identifying threats and vulnerabilities and their potential impacts, determining the costs to mitigate such events, and deciding what actions are cost effective for controlling these risks.

Risk assessment (or risk analysis)   The process of analyzing an environment to identify the risks (threats and vulnerabilities), and mitigating actions to determine (either quantitatively or qualitatively) the impact of an event that would affect a project, program, or business.

Asset   Resource or information an organization needs to conduct its business.

Threat   Any circumstance or event with the potential to cause harm to an asset. For example, a malicious hacker might choose to hack your system by using readily available hacking tools.

Vulnerability   Characteristic of an asset that can be exploited by a threat to cause harm. Your system has a security vulnerability, for example, if you have not installed patches to fix a cross-site scripting (XSS) error on your web site.

Impact   The loss resulting when a threat exploits a vulnerability. A malicious hacker (the threat) uses an XSS tool to hack your unpatched web site (the vulnerability), stealing credit card information that is used fraudulently. The credit card company pursues legal recourse against your company to recover the losses from the credit card fraud (the impact).

Control (also called countermeasure or safeguard) A measure taken to detect, prevent, or mitigate the risk associated with a threat.

Qualitative risk assessment The process of subjectively determining the impact of an event that affects a project, program, or business. Qualitative risk assessment usually involves the use of expert judgment, experience, or group consensus to complete the assessment.

Quantitative risk assessment The process of objectively determining the impact of an event that affects a project, program, or business. Quantitative risk assessment usually involves the use of metrics and models to complete the assessment.

NOTE The distinction between qualitative and quantitative risk assessment will be more apparent as you read the section, "Qualitative vs. Quantitative Risk Assessment," later in the chapter that describes them in detail.

Mitigate Action taken to reduce the likelihood of a threat occurring.

Single loss expectancy (SLE) The monetary loss or impact of each occurrence of a threat.

Exposure factor A measure of the magnitude of loss of an asset. Used in the calculation of single loss expectancy.

Annualized rate of occurrence (ARO) On an annualized basis, the frequency with which an event is expected to occur.

Annualized loss expectancy (ALE) How much an event is expected to cost per year.

EXAM TIP These terms are important, and you should completely memorize their meanings before taking the Security+ exam.

What Is Risk Management?

Three definitions relating to risk management reveal why it is sometimes considered difficult to understand. (See Figure 17-1.)

- The dictionary defines *risk* as the possibility of suffering harm or loss.
- Carnegie Mellon University's Software Engineering Institute (SEI) defines *continuous risk management* as "processes, methods, and tools for managing

risks in a project. It provides a disciplined environment for proactive decision-making to 1) assess continuously what could go wrong (risks); 2) determine which risks are important to deal with; and 3) implement strategies to deal with those risks" (SEI, *Continuous Risk Management Guidebook* [Pittsburgh, PA: Carnegie Mellon University, 1996], 22).

- The Information Systems Audit and Control Association (ISACA) says, "In modern business terms, risk management is the process of identifying vulnerabilities and threats to an organization's resources and assets and deciding what countermeasures, if any, to take to reduce the level of risk to an acceptable level based on the value of the asset to the organization" (ISACA, *Certified Information Systems Auditor (CISA) Review Manual, 2002* [Rolling Meadows, IL: ISACA, 2002], 344).

These three definitions show that risk management is based on what can go wrong and what action should be taken, if any. Figure 17-1 provides a macro-level view of how to manage risk.

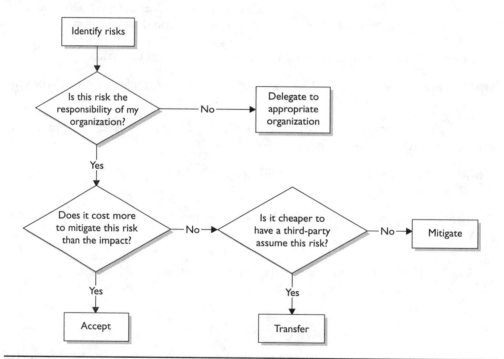

Figure 17-1   A planning decision flowchart for risk management

> ## Transferring Risk
> One possible action to manage risk is to transfer that risk. The most common method of transferring risk is to purchase insurance. Insurance allows risk to be transferred to a third party that manages specific types of risk for multiple parties, thus reducing the individual cost.

Business Risks

No comprehensive identification of all risks in a business environment is possible. In today's technology-dependent business environment, risk is often simplistically divided into two areas: business risk and a major subset, technology risk.

Examples of Business Risks

Following are some of the most common business risks:

- **Treasury management**   Management of company holdings in bonds, futures, currencies, and so on.
- **Revenue management**   Management of consumer behavior and the generation of revenue.
- **Contract management**   Management of contracts with customers, vendors, partners, and so on.
- **Fraud**   Deliberate deception made for personal gain, obtain property or services, and so on.
- **Environmental risk management**   Management of risks associated with factors that affect the environment.
- **Regulatory risk management**   Management of risks arising from new or existing regulations.
- **Business continuity management**   Management of risks associated with recovering and restoring business functions after a disaster or major disruption occurs.
- **Technology**   Management of risks associated with technology in its many forms.

NOTE   It is important that you understand that technology, itself, is a business risk. Hence, it must be managed along with other risks. Today, technology risks are so important they should be considered separately.

Examples of Technology Risks

Following are some of the most common technology risks:

- **Security and privacy**   The risks associated with protecting personal, private, or confidential information.

- **Information technology operations**   The risks associated with the day-to-day operation of information technology systems.

- **Business systems control and effectiveness**   The risks associated with manual and automated controls that safeguard company assets and resources.

- **Business continuity management**   The risks associated with the technology and processes to be used in event of a disaster or major disruption.

- **Information systems testing**   The risks associated with testing processes and procedures of information systems.

- **Reliability and performance management**   The risks associated with meeting reliability and performance agreements and measures.

- **Information technology asset management**   The risks associated with safeguarding information technology physical assets.

- **Project risk management**   The risks associated with managing information technology projects.

- **Change management**   The risks associated with managing configurations and changes (see Chapter 18).

Risk According to the Basel Committee
The Basel Committee referenced at the beginning of this chapter defined three types of risk specifically to address international banking:

- **Market Risk**   Risk of losses due to fluctuation of market prices
- **Credit Risk**   Risk of default of outstanding loans
- **Operational Risk**   Risk from disruption by people, systems, processes, or disasters

---

Risk Management Models

Risk management concepts are fundamentally the same despite their definitions, and they require similar skills, tools, and methodologies. Several models can be used for managing risk through its various phases. Two models are presented here: the first can be applied to managing risks in general, and the second is tailored for managing risk in software projects.

General Risk Management Model

The following steps can be used in virtually any risk management process. Following these steps will lead to an orderly process of analyzing and mitigating risks.

Asset Identification

Identify and classify the assets, systems, and processes that need protection because they are vulnerable to threats. This classification leads to the ability to prioritize assets, systems, and processes and to evaluate the costs of addressing the associated risks. Assets can include

- Inventory
- Buildings
- Cash
- Information and data
- Hardware
- Software
- Services
- Documents
- Personnel
- Brand recognition
- Organization reputation
- Goodwill

Threat Assessment

After identifying the assets, you identify the possible threats and vulnerabilities associated with each asset and the likelihood of their occurrence. Threats can be defined as any circumstance or event with the potential to cause harm to an asset. Common classes of threats (with examples) include

- **Natural disasters** Hurricane, earthquake, lightning, and so on.
- **Man-made disasters** Earthen dam failure, such as the 1976 Teton Dam failure in Idaho; car accident that destroys a municipal power distribution transformer; the 1973 explosion of a railcar containing propane gas in Kingman, Arizona.
- **Terrorism** The 2001 destruction of the World Trade Center, the 1995 gas attack on the Shinjuku train station in Tokyo.
- **Errors** Employee not following safety or configuration management procedures.

- **Malicious damage or attacks**   A disgruntled employee purposely corrupting data files.
- **Fraud**   An employee falsifying travel expenses or vendor invoices and payments.
- **Theft**   An employee stealing a laptop computer from the loading dock after it has been inventoried but not properly secured.
- **Equipment or software failure**   An error in the calculation of a company-wide bonus overpaying employees.

Vulnerabilities are characteristics of resources that can be exploited by a threat to cause harm. Examples of vulnerabilities include

- **Unprotected facilities**   Company offices with no security officer present or no card-entry system.
- **Unprotected computer systems**   A web-facing server temporarily connected to the network before being properly configured/secured.
- **Unprotected data**   Not installing critical security patches to eliminate application security vulnerabilities.
- **Insufficient procedures and controls**   Allowing an accounts payable clerk to create vendors in the accounting system, enter invoices, and authorize check payments.
- **Insufficient or unqualified personnel**   A junior employee not sufficiently securing a server due to a lack of training.

Impact Definition and Quantification

An impact is the loss created when a threat exploits a vulnerability. When a threat is realized, it turns risk into impact. Impacts can be either tangible or intangible. Tangible impacts result in financial loss or physical damage. For intangible impacts, assigning a financial value of the impact can be difficult. For example, in a manufacturing facility, storing and using flammable chemicals creates a risk of fire to the facility. The vulnerability is that flammable chemicals are stored there. The threat would be that a person could cause a fire by mishandling the chemicals (either intentionally or unintentionally). A tangible impact would be the loss incurred (say $500,000) if a person ignites the chemicals and fire then destroys part of the facility. An intangible impact would be the loss of goodwill or brand damage caused by the impression that the company doesn't safely protect its employees or the surrounding geographic area.

Tangible impacts include

- Direct loss of money
- Endangerment of staff or customers
- Loss of business opportunity

- Reduction in operational efficiency or performance
- Interruption of a business activity

Intangible impacts include

- Breach of legislation or regulatory requirements
- Loss of reputation or goodwill (brand damage)
- Breach of confidence

 EXAM TIP You should be able to distinguish between tangible and intangible impacts as you prepare for the Security+ exam.

Control Design and Evaluation

In this phase, you determine which controls to put in place to mitigate the risks. Controls (also called countermeasures or safeguards) are designed to control risk by reducing vulnerabilities to an acceptable level. (For use in this text, the terms *control, countermeasure*, and *safeguard* are considered synonymous and are used interchangeably.)

Controls, countermeasures, or safeguards can be actions, devices, or procedures. They can be preventive or detective. *Preventive controls* are designed to prevent the vulnerability from causing an impact. *Detective controls* are those that detect a vulnerability that has been exploited so that action can be taken.

> ### Business Dependencies
> An area often overlooked in risk assessment is the need to address business dependencies—each organization must assess risks caused by other organizations with which it interacts. This occurs when the organization is either a consumer of, or a supplier to, other organizations (or both). For example, if a company is dependent on products produced by a laboratory, then the company must determine the impact of the laboratory not delivering the product when needed. Likewise, an organization must assess risks that can occur when it is the supplier to some other company dependent on its products.

Residual Risk Management

Understand that risk cannot be completely eliminated. Any risks that remain after implementing controls are termed *residual risks*. Residual risks can be further evaluated to identify where additional controls are required to reduce risk even more. This leads us to the earlier statement that the risk management process is iterative.

 EXAM TIP The steps in the general risk management model should allow you to identify the steps in any risk management process.

> ## Can All Risks Be Identified?
> It is important to note that not all risks need to be mitigated or controlled; however, as many risks as possible should be identified and reviewed. Those deemed to have potential impact should be mitigated by countermeasures.

Software Engineering Institute Model

In an approach tailored for managing risk in software projects, SEI uses the following paradigm (SEI, *Continuous Risk Management Guidebook* [Pittsburgh, PA: Carnegie Mellon University, 1996], 23). Although the terminology varies slightly from the previous model, the relationships are apparent, and either model can be applied wherever risk management is used.

1. **Identify**   Look for risks before they become problems.
2. **Analyze**   Convert the data gathered into information that can be used to make decisions. Evaluate the impact, probability, and timeframe of the risks. Classify and prioritize each of the risks.
3. **Plan**   Review and evaluate the risks and decide what actions to take to mitigate them. Implement those mitigating actions.
4. **Track**   Monitor the risks and the mitigation plans. Trends may provide information to activate plans and contingencies. Review periodically to measure progress and identify new risks.
5. **Control**   Make corrections for deviations from the risk mitigation plans. Correct products and processes as required. Changes in business procedures may require adjustments in plans or actions, as do faulty plans and risks that become problems.

Model Application

The two model examples define steps that can be used in any general or software risk management process. These risk management principles can be applied to any project, program, or business activity, no matter how simple or complex. Figure 17-2 shows how risk management can be applied across the continuum and that the complexity of risk management generally increases with the size of the project, program, or business to be managed.

Qualitatively Assessing Risk

Qualitative risk analysis allows expert judgment and experience to assume a prominent role. To assess risk qualitatively, you compare the impact of the threat with the probability of occurrence. For example, if a threat has a high impact and a high probability of

Figure 17-2
Risk complexity
versus project size

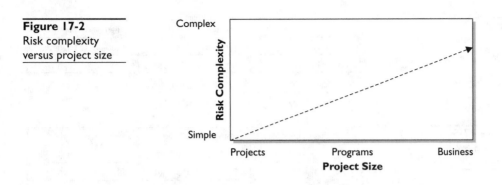

occurring, the risk exposure is high and probably requires some action to reduce this threat (see darkest box in Figure 17-3). Conversely, if the impact is low with a low probability, the risk exposure is low and no action may be required to reduce this threat (see white box in Figure 17-3). Figure 17-3 shows an example of a *binary assessment*, where only two outcomes are possible each for impact and probability. Either it will have an impact or it will not (or it will have a low or high impact), and it can occur or it will not (or it will have a high probability of occurring or a low probability of occurring).

In reality, a few threats can usually be identified as presenting high-risk exposure and a few threats present low-risk exposure. The threats that fall somewhere between (light gray boxes in Figure 17-3) will have to be evaluated by judgment and management experience.

If the analysis is more complex, requiring three levels of analysis, such as low-medium-high or red-green-yellow, nine combinations are possible, as shown in Figure 17-4. Again, the darkest boxes probably require action, the white boxes may or may not require action, and the gray boxes require judgment. (Note that for brevity, in Figures 17-4 and 17-5, the first term in each box refers to the magnitude of the impact, and the second term refers to the probability of the threat occurring.)

Other levels of complexity are possible. With five levels of analysis, 25 values of risk exposure are possible. In this case, the possible values of impact and probability could take on the values: very low, low, medium, high, or very high. Also, note that the matrix does not have to be symmetrical. For example, if the probability is assessed with three values (low, medium, high) and the impact has five values (very low, low, medium, high, very high), the analysis would be as shown in Figure 17-5. (Again, note that the first term in each box refers to the impact, and the second term in each box refers to the probability of occurrence.)

So far, the examples have focused on assessing probability versus impact. Qualitative risk assessment can be adapted to a variety of attributes and situations in combination

Figure 17-3
Binary assessment

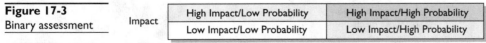

Probability

Figure 17-4
Three levels of
analysis

Impact

High	Low	High	Medium	High	High
Medium	Low	Medium	Medium	Medium	High
Low	Low	Low	Medium	Low	High

Probability

Figure 17-5
A 3-by-5 level
analysis

Impact

Very high	Low	Very high	Medium	Very high	High
High	Low	High	Medium	High	High
Medium	Low	Medium	Medium	Medium	High
Low	Low	Low	Medium	Low	High
Very low	Low	Very low	Medium	Very low	High

Probability

with each other. For example, Figure 17-6 shows the comparison of some specific risks that have been identified during a security assessment. The assessment identified the risk areas listed in the first column (weak intranet security, high number of modems, Internet attack vulnerabilities, and weak incident detection and response mechanisms). The assessment also identified various potential impacts listed across the top (business impact, probability of attack, cost to fix, and difficulty to fix). Each of the impacts has been assessed as low, moderate, or high—depicted using green (G), yellow (Y), and

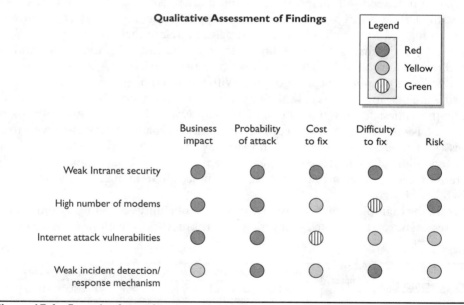

Figure 17-6 Example of a combination assessment

red (R), respectively. Each of the risk areas has been assessed with respect to each of the potential impacts, and an overall risk assessment has been determined in the last column.

Quantitatively Assessing Risk

Whereas qualitative risk assessment relies on judgment and experience, quantitative risk assessment applies historical information and trends to attempt to predict future performance. This type of risk assessment is highly dependent on historical data, and gathering such data can be difficult. Quantitative risk assessment can also rely heavily on models that provide decision-making information in the form of quantitative metrics, which attempt to measure risk levels across a common scale.

It is important to understand that key assumptions underlie any model, and different models will produce different results even when given the same input data. Although significant research and development have been invested in improving and refining the various risk analysis models, expert judgment and experience must still be considered an essential part of any risk-assessment process. Models can never replace judgment and experience, but they can significantly enhance the decision-making process.

Adding Objectivity to a QualitativeAssessment

Making a Qualitative assessment more objective can be as simple as assigning numeric values to one of the tables shown in Figures 17-3 through 17-6. For example, the impacts listed in Figure 17-6 can be prioritized from highest to lowest and then weighted, as shown in Table 17-1, with business impact weighted the most and difficulty to fix weighted least.

Next, values can be assigned to reflect how each risk was assessed. Figure 17-6 can thus be made more objective by assigning a value to each color that represents an assessment. For example, a red assessment indicates many critical, unresolved issues, and this will be given an assessment value of 3. Green means few issues are unresolved, so it is given a value of 1. Table 17-2 shows values that can be assigned for an assessment using red, yellow, and green.

<table>
<tr><td>

Table 17-1

Adding Weights and Definitions to the Potential Impacts
</td><td>

Impact	Explanation	Weight
Business impact	If exploited, would this have a material business impact?	4
Probability of attack	How likely is a potential attacker to try this technique or attack?	3
Cost to fix	How much will it cost in dollars and resources to correct this vulnerability?	2
Difficulty to fix	How hard is this to fix from a technical standpoint?	1

</td></tr>
</table>

Table 17-2 Adding Values to Assessments	Assessment	Explanation	Value
	Red	Many critical, unresolved issues	3
	Yellow	Some critical, unresolved issues	2
	Green	Few unresolved issues	1

The last step is to calculate an overall risk value for each risk area (each row in Figure 17-6) by multiplying the weights depicted in Table 17-1 times the assessed values from Table 17-2 and summing the products:

$$Risk = W_1 * V_1 + W_2 * V_2 + \dots W_4 * V_4$$

The risk calculation and final risk value for each risk area listed in Figure 17-6 have been incorporated into Figure 17-7. The assessed areas can then be ordered from highest to lowest based on the calculated risk value to aid management in focusing on the risk areas with the greatest potential impact.

A Common Objective Approach

More complex models permit a variety of analyses based on statistical and mathematical models. A common method is the calculation of the annualized loss expectancy (ALE).

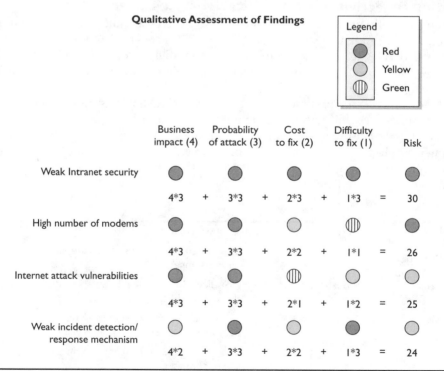

Figure 17-7 Final quantitative assessment of the findings

This calculation begins by calculating a single loss expectancy (SLE) with the following formula:

SLE = *asset value * exposure factor*

By example, to calculate the exposure factor, assume the asset value of a small office building and its contents is $2 million. Also assume that this building houses the call center for a business, and the complete loss of the center would take away about half of the capability of the company. Therefore, the exposure factor is 50 percent. The SLE is

$2 million * 0.5 = $1 million

The ALE is then calculated simply by multiplying the SLE by the number of times the event is expected to occur in a year, which is called the annualized rate of occurrence (ARO):

ALE = SLE * ARO

If the event is expected to occur once in 20 years, then the annualized rate of occurrence is 1/20. Typically the ARO is defined by historical data, either from a company's own experience or from industry surveys. Continuing our example, assume that a fire at this business's location is expected to occur about once in 20 years. Given this information, the ALE is

$1 million * 1/20 = $50,000

The ALE determines a threshold for evaluating the cost/benefit ratio of a given countermeasure. Therefore, a countermeasure to protect this business adequately should cost no more than the calculated ALE of $50,000 per year.

EXAM TIP It is always advisable to memorize these fundamental equations for certifications such as Security+.

The examples in this chapter have been simplistic, but they demonstrate the concepts of both qualitative and quantitative risk analysis. More complex algorithms and software packages are available for accomplishing risk analyses, but these examples suffice for the purposes of this text.

Qualitative vs. Quantitative Risk Assessment

It is recognized throughout industry that it is *impossible* to conduct risk management that is purely *quantitative*. Usually risk management includes both qualitative and quantitative elements, requiring both analysis and judgment or experience. In contrast to quantitative assessment, it is *possible* to accomplish *purely qualitative* risk management. It is easy to see that it is impossible to define and quantitatively measure all factors that exist in a given risk assessment. It is also easy to see that a risk assessment that measures no factors quantitatively but measures them all qualitatively is possible.

The decision of whether to use qualitative versus quantitative risk management depends on the criticality of the project, the resources available, and the management style. The decision will be influenced by the degree to which the fundamental risk management metrics, such as asset value, exposure factor, and threat frequency, can be quantitatively defined.

Accepting Risk

In addition to mitigating risk or transferring risk, it may be acceptable for a manager to accept risk in that despite the potential cost of a given risk and its associated probability, the manager of the organization will accept responsibility for the risk if it does happen. For example, a manager may choose to allow a programmer to make "emergency" changes to a production system (in violation of good segregation of duties) because the system cannot go down during a given period of time. The manager accepts the risk that the programmer could possibly make unauthorized changes because of the high-availability requirement of that system. However, there should always be some additional controls such as a management review or a standardized approval process to ensure the assumed risk is adequately managed.

Tools

Many tools can be used to enhance the risk management process. The following tools can be used during the various phases of risk assessment to add objectivity and structure to the process. Understanding the details of each of these tools is not necessary for the Security+ exam, but understanding what they can be used for is important. More information on these tools can be found in any good project-management text.

Affinity grouping   A method of identifying items that are related and then identifying the principle that ties them together.

Baseline identification and analysis   The process of establishing a baseline set of risks. It produces a "snapshot" of all the identified risks at a given point in time.

Cause and effect analysis   Identifying relationships between a risk and the factors that can cause it. This is usually accomplished using *fishbone diagrams* developed by Dr. Kaoru Ishikawa, former professor of engineering at the Science University of Tokyo.

Cost/benefit analysis   A straightforward method for comparing cost estimates with the benefits of a mitigation strategy.

Gantt charts   A management tool for diagramming schedules, events, and activity duration.

Interrelationship digraphs   A method for identifying cause-and-effect relationships by clearly defining the problem to be solved, identifying the key elements of the problem, and then describing the relationships between each of the key elements.

Pareto charts   A histogram that ranks the categories in a chart from most frequent to least frequent, thus facilitating risk prioritization.

PERT (program evaluation and review technique) charts   A diagram depicting interdependencies between project activities, showing the sequence and duration of each activity. When complete, the chart shows the time necessary to complete the project and the activities that determine that time (the critical path). The earliest and latest start and stop times for each activity and available slack times can also be shown.

Risk management plan   A comprehensive plan documenting how risks will be managed on a given project. It contains processes, activities, milestones, organizations, responsibilities, and details of each major risk management activity and how it is to be accomplished. It is an integral part of the project management plan.

Risks Really Don't Change, But They Can Be Mitigated
One final thought to keep in mind is that the risk itself doesn't really change, no matter what actions are taken to mitigate that risk. A high risk will always be a high risk. However, actions can be taken to reduce the impact of that risk if it occurs.

Chapter Review

Risk management is a key management process that must be used at every level, whether managing a project, a program, or an enterprise. Managing risk is important in keeping a business competitive and must be done by managers at all levels. Both qualitative and quantitative risk assessment approaches must be used to manage risk effectively, and a number of approaches were presented in this chapter. Understand that it is impossible to conduct a purely quantitative risk assessment, but it is possible to conduct a purely qualitative risk assessment.

Questions

1. Which of the following correctly defines qualitative risk management?
    A. The loss resulting when a vulnerability is exploited by a threat
    B. To reduce the likelihood of a threat occurring

    C. The process of subjectively determining the impact of an event that affects a project, program, or business

    D. The process of objectively determining the impact of an event that affects a project, program, or business

2. Which of the following correctly defines risk?

    A. The risks still remaining after an iteration of risk management

    B. The possibility of suffering harm or loss

    C. The loss resulting when a vulnerability is exploited by a threat

    D. Any circumstance or event with the potential to cause harm to an asset

3. Single loss expectancy (SLE) can best be defined by which of the following equations?

    A. SLE = asset value * exposure factor

    B. SLE = annualized loss expectancy * annualized rate of occurrence

    C. SLE = asset value * annualized rate of occurrence

    D. SLE = annualized loss expectancy * exposure factor

4. Which of the following correctly defines annualized rate of occurrence?

    A. On an annualized basis, the frequency with which an event is expected to occur

    B. How much an event is expected to cost per year

    C. A measure of the magnitude of loss of an asset

    D. Resources or information an organization needs to conduct its business

5. Which of the following are business risks?

    A. Business continuity management

    B. Fraud

    C. Contract management

    D. Treasury management

    E. All of the above

    F. None of the above

6. The Basel Committee defines operational risk as which of the following?

    A. Risk of default of outstanding loans

    B. Risk of losses due to fluctuations of market prices

    C. The possibility of suffering harm or loss

    D. Risk from disruption by people, systems, processes, or disasters

7. Which of the following are *not* assets?

    A. Hardware

B. Inventory

C. Equipment or software failure

D. Cash

E. All of the above

F. None of the above

For questions 8 and 9, assume the following: The asset value of a small distribution warehouse is $5 million, and this warehouse serves as a backup facility. Its complete destruction by a disaster would take away about 1/5 of the capability of the business. Also assume that this sort of disaster is expected to occur about once every 50 years.

8. Which of the following is the calculated single loss expectancy (SLE)?

    A. SLE = $25 million

    B. SLE = $1 million

    C. SLE = $2.5 million

    D. SLE = $5 million

9. Which of the following is the calculated annualized loss expectancy (ALE)?

    A. ALE = $50,000

    B. ALE = $20,000

    C. ALE = $1 million

    D. ALE = $50 million

10. When discussing qualitative risk assessment versus quantitative risk assessment, which of the following is true?

    A. It is impossible to conduct a purely quantitative risk assessment, and it is impossible to conduct a purely qualitative risk assessment.

    B. It is possible to conduct a purely quantitative risk assessment, but it is impossible to conduct a purely qualitative risk assessment.

    C. It is possible to conduct a purely quantitative risk assessment, and it is possible to conduct a purely qualitative risk assessment.

    D. It is impossible to conduct a purely quantitative risk assessment, but it is possible to conduct a purely qualitative risk assessment.

Answers

1. C. Qualitative risk management is the process of *subjectively* determining the impact of an event that affects a project, program, or business. A defines impact, B defines mitigation, and D defines quantitative risk assessment.

2. B. Risk is the possibility of suffering harm or loss. A defines residual risk, C defines impact, and D defines threat.

3. **A.** SLE is the value of the asset multiplied by the exposure factor.

4. **A.** Annualized rate of occurrence is defined as the frequency with which an event is expected to occur on an annual basis. Answer **B** defines annualized loss expectancy. Answer **C** defines exposure factor. Answer **D** defines asset.

5. **E.** All listed items are business risks.

6. **D.** The Basel Committee defines operational risk as risk from disruption by people, systems, processes, or disasters. Answer **A** defines credit risk. Answer **B** defines market risk. Answer **C** defines risk.

7. **C.** Equipment or software failure *is* a threat. All other answers are examples of assets.

8. **B.** SLE = asset value ($5 million) * exposure factor (1/5) = $1 million.

9. **B.** ALE = SLE ($1 million) * annualized rate of occurrence (1/50) = $20,000.

10. **D.** A purely quantitative risk assessment is not achievable because it is impossible to define and quantitatively measure all factors. On the other hand, a risk assessment that qualitatively evaluates risk is possible.

CHAPTER 18

Change Management

In this chapter, you will

- Learn why change management is an important enterprise management tool
- Understand the key concept of segregation of duties
- Review the essential elements of change management
- Learn a process for implementing change management
- Study the concepts of the Capability Maturity Model Integration

It is well recognized that today's computer systems are extremely complex, and it is obvious that inventory management systems for large international enterprises such as Walmart and Home Depot are probably as complex as an aircraft or skyscraper. Prominent operating systems such as Windows or UNIX are also very complex, as are computer processors on a chip. Many of today's web-based applications are relatively complex as well.

You wouldn't think of constructing an aircraft, large building, computer chip, or automobile in the informal manner sometimes used to develop and operate computer systems of equal complexity. Computer systems have grown to be so complex and mission-critical that enterprises cannot afford to develop and maintain them in an ad hoc manner.

Change management procedures can add structure and control to the development and management of large software systems as they move from development to operation and during operation. In this chapter, *change management* refers to a standard methodology for performing and recording changes during software development and system operation. The methodology defines steps that ensure that system changes are required by the organization and are properly authorized, documented, tested, and approved by management. In this chapter, the term *configuration management* is considered synonymous with *change management* and, in a more limited manner, *version* or *release control*.

The term *change management* is often applied to the management of changes in the business environment, typically as a result of business process reengineering or quality enhancement efforts. The term *change management* as used in this chapter is directly related to managing and controlling software development, maintenance, and system operation.

Why Change Management?

Chapter 17 presented risk management as an essential decision-making process. In much the same way, change management is an essential practice for managing a system during its entire lifecycle, from development through deployment and operation, until it is taken out of service. To manage the system development and maintenance processes effectively, you need discipline and structure to help conserve resources and enhance effectiveness. Change management, like risk management, is often considered expensive, nonproductive, unnecessary, and confusing—an impediment to progress. However, like risk management, change management can be scaled to control and manage the development and maintenance of systems effectively. Recent legislation in the U.S. aimed at regulating how firms manage their information, such as Sarbanes-Oxley (SOX), have had an indirect effect on change management. Although SOX does not mandate a specific change management methodology, it does mandate that IT processes be under the control of management, and change management is a crucial element in achieving the required level of control.

Change management should be used in all phases of a system's life: development, testing, quality assurance (QA), and production. Short development cycles have not changed the need for an appropriate amount of management control over software development, maintenance, and operation. In fact, short turnaround times make change management more necessary, because once a system goes active in today's web-based environment, it often cannot be taken offline to correct errors—it must stay up and online or business will be lost and brand recognition damaged. In today's volatile stock market, for example, even small indicators of lagging performance can have dramatic impacts on a company's stock value.

The following scenarios exemplify the need for appropriate change management policy and for procedures over software, hardware, and data:

- The developers can't find the latest version of the production source code.
- A bug corrected a few months ago mysteriously reappears.
- Fielded software was working fine yesterday but does not work properly today.
- Development team members overwrote each other's changes.
- A programmer spent several hours changing the wrong version of the software.
- A customer record corrected by the call center yesterday, shows the old, incorrect information today.
- New tax rates stored in a table have been overwritten with last year's tax rates.
- An application runs fine at some overseas locations but not at other locations.
- A network administrator inadvertently brings down a server as he incorrectly punched down the wrong wires.
- A newly installed server is hacked soon after installation because it is improperly configured.

Just about anyone with more than a year's experience in software development or system operations can relate to at least one of the preceding scenarios. However, each of these scenarios can be controlled, and impacts mitigated, through proper change management procedures.

The Sarbanes-Oxley Act of 2002, officially entitled the Public Company Accounting Reform and Investor Protection Act of 2002, was enacted on July 30, 2002, to help ensure management establishes viable governance environments and control structures to ensure the accuracy of financial reporting. Section 404 outlines the requirements most applicable to information technology. Change management is an essential part of creating a viable governance and control structure and critical to compliance with the Sarbanes-Oxley Act.

> **NOTE** All software can be placed under an appropriate software change management process, including:
> Web pages
> Service packs
> Security patches
> Third-party software releases
> Test data and test scripts
> Parameter files
> Scripts, stored procedures, or job control language–type programs
> Customized vendor code
> Source code of any kind
> Applications

The Key Concept: Separation (Segregation) of Duties

A foundation for change management is the recognition that involving more than one individual in a process can reduce risk. Good business control practices require that duties be assigned to individuals in such a way that no one individual can control all phases of a process or the processing and recording of a transaction. This is called *separation of duties* (also called *segregation of duties*). It is an important means by which errors and fraudulent or malicious acts can be discouraged and prevented. Separation of duties can be applied in many organizational scenarios because it establishes a basis for accountability and control. Proper separation of duties can safeguard enterprise assets and protect against risks. They should be documented, monitored, and enforced.

A well-understood business example of separation of duties is in the management and payment of vendor invoices. If a person can create a vendor in the finance system, enter invoices to payment, and then authorize a payment check to be written, it is apparent that fraud could be perpetrated because the person could write a check to him/ herself for services never performed. Separating duties by requiring one person to create the vendors and another person to enter invoices and write checks makes it more difficult for someone to defraud an employer.

Information technology (IT) organizations should design, implement, monitor, and enforce appropriate separation of duties for the enterprise's information systems and processes. Today's computer systems are rapidly evolving into an increasingly decentralized and networked computer infrastructure. In the absence of adequate IT controls, such rapid growth may allow exploitation of large amounts of enterprise information in a short time. Further, the knowledge of computer operations held by IT staff is significantly greater than that of an average user, and this knowledge could be abused for malicious purposes.

Some of the best practices for ensuring proper separation of duties in an IT organization are as follows:

- Separation of duties between development, testing, QA, and production should be documented in written procedures and implemented by software or manual processes.

- Program developers' and program testers' activities should be conducted on "test" data only. They should be restricted from accessing "live" production data. This will assist in ensuring an independent and objective testing environment without jeopardizing the confidentiality and integrity of production data.

- End users or computer operations personnel should not have direct access to program source code. This control helps lessen the opportunity of exploiting software weaknesses or introducing malicious code (or code that has not been properly tested) into the production environment either intentionally or unintentionally.

- Functions of creating, installing, and administrating software programs should be assigned to different individuals. For example, since developers create and enhance programs, they should not be able to install them on the production system. Likewise, database administrators should not be program developers on database systems they administer.

- All accesses and privileges to systems, software, or data should be granted based on the principle of least privilege, which gives users no more privileges than are necessary to perform their jobs. Access privileges should be reviewed regularly to ensure that individuals who no longer require access have had their privileges removed.

- Formal change management policy and procedures should be enforced throughout the enterprise. Any changes in hardware and software components (including emergency changes) that are implemented after the system has been placed into production must go through the approved formal change management mechanism.

Managers at all levels should review existing and planned processes and systems to ensure proper separation of duties. Smaller business entities may not have the resources to implement all of the preceding practices fully, but other control mechanisms, including hiring qualified personnel, bonding contractors, and using training, monitoring, and evaluation practices, can reduce any organization's exposure to risk. The establishment of such practices can ensure that enterprise assets are properly safeguarded and can also greatly reduce error and the potential for fraudulent or malicious activities.

Change management practices implement and enforce separation of duties by adding structure and management oversight to the software development and system operation processes. Change management techniques can ensure that only correct and authorized changes, as approved by management or other authorities, are allowed to be made, following a defined process.

Elements of Change Management

Change management has its roots in system engineering, where it is commonly referred to as *configuration management*. Most of today's software and hardware change management practices derive from long-standing system engineering configuration management practices. For example, automakers know that a certain amount of configuration management is necessary to build safe cars efficiently and effectively. Bolts and screws with proper strengths and qualities are used on every car, in specific places—employees don't just reach into a barrel of bolts, pull one out that looks about right, and bolt it on. The same applies to aircraft—for an aircraft to fly safely, it must be built of parts of the right size, shape, strength, and so on. Computer hardware and software development have also evolved to the point that proper management structure and controls must exist to ensure the products operate as planned.

Change management and configuration management use different terms for their various phases, but they all fit into the four general phases defined under configuration management:

- Configuration identification
- Configuration control
- Configuration status accounting
- Configuration auditing

Configuration identification is the process of identifying which assets need to be managed and controlled. These assets could be software modules, test cases or scripts, table or parameter values, servers, major subsystems, or entire systems. The idea is that, depending on the size and complexity of the system, an appropriate set of data and software (or other assets) must be identified and properly managed. These identified assets are called *configuration items* or *computer software configuration items*.

Related to configuration identification, and the result of it, is the definition of a baseline. A *baseline* serves as a foundation for comparison or measurement. It provides the necessary visibility to control change. For example, a software baseline defines the software system as it is built and running at a point in time. As another example, network security best practices clearly state that any large organization should build its servers to a standard build configuration to enhance overall network security. The servers are the configuration items, and the standard build is the server baseline.

Configuration control is the process of controlling changes to items that have been baselined. Configuration control ensures that only approved changes to a baseline are allowed to be implemented. It is easy to understand why a software system, such as a web-based order entry system, should not be changed without proper testing and control—otherwise, the system might stop functioning at a critical time. Configuration control is a key step that provides valuable insight to managers. If a system is being changed, and configuration control is being observed, managers and others concerned will be better informed. This ensures proper use of assets and avoids unnecessary downtime due to the installation of unapproved changes.

Configuration status accounting consists of the procedures for tracking and maintaining data relative to each configuration item in the baseline. It is closely related to configuration control. Status accounting involves gathering and maintaining information relative to each configuration item. For example, it documents what changes have been requested; what changes have been made, when, and for what reason; who authorized the change; who performed the change; and what other configuration items or systems were affected by the change.

Returning to our example of servers being baselined, if the operating system of those servers is found to have a security flaw, then the baseline can be consulted to determine which servers are vulnerable to this particular security flaw. Those systems with this weakness can be updated (and only those that need to be updated). Configuration control and configuration status accounting help ensure systems are more consistently managed and, ultimately in this case, the organization's network security is maintained. It is easy to imagine the state of an organization that has not built all servers to a common baseline and has not properly controlled their systems' configurations. It would be very difficult to know the configuration of individual servers, and security could quickly become weak.

NOTE It is important that you understand that even though all servers may be initially configured to the same baseline, individual applications might require a system-specific configuration to run properly. Change management actually facilitates system-specific configuration in that all exceptions from the standard configuration are documented. All people involved in managing and operating these systems will have documentation to help them quickly understand why a particular system is configured in a unique way.

Configuration auditing is the process of verifying that the configuration items are built and maintained according to the requirements, standards, or contractual agreements. It is similar to how audits in the financial world are used to ensure that generally accepted accounting principles and practices are adhered to and that financial statements properly reflect the financial status of the enterprise. Configuration audits ensure that policies and procedures are being followed, that all configuration items (including hardware and software) are being properly maintained, and that existing documentation accurately reflects the status of the systems in operation.

Configuration auditing takes on two forms: functional and physical. A *functional configuration audit* verifies that the configuration item performs as defined by the documentation of the system requirements. A *physical configuration audit* confirms that all configuration items to be included in a release, install, change, or upgrade are actually included, and that no additional items are included—no more, no less.

Implementing Change Management

Change management requires some structure and discipline in order to be effective. The change management function is scalable from small to enterprise-level projects. Figure 18-1 illustrates a sample software change management flow appropriate for medium to large projects. It can be adapted to small organizations by having the developer perform work only on his/her workstation (never on the production system) and having the system administrator serve in the buildmaster function. The buildmaster is usually an independent person responsible for compiling and incorporating changed software into an executable image.

Figure 18-1 shows that developers never have access to the production system or data. It also demonstrates proper separation of duties between developers, QA and test personnel, and production. It implies that a distinct separation exists between development, testing and QA, and production environments. This workflow is for changes that have a major impact on production or the customer's business process. For minor changes that have minimal risk or impact on business processes, some of the steps may be omitted.

The change management workflow proceeds as follows:

1. The developer checks out source code from the code-control tool archive to the development system.

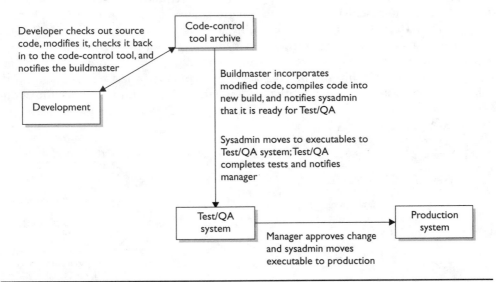

Figure 18-1 Software change control workflow

2. The developer modifies the code and conducts unit testing.

3. The developer checks the modified code into the code-control tool archive.

4. The developer notifies the buildmaster that changes are ready for a new build and testing/QA.

5. The buildmaster creates a build incorporating the modified code and compiles the code.

6. The buildmaster notifies the system administrator that the executable image is ready for testing/QA.

7. The system administrator moves the executables to the test/QA system.

8. QA tests the new executables. If tests are passed, test/QA notifies the manager. If tests fail, the process starts over.

9. Upon manager approval, the system administrator moves the executable to the production system.

 NOTE Observe the separation of duties between development, test/QA, and production. The functions of creating, installing, and administrating are assigned to different individuals. Note also appropriate management review and approval. This implementation also ensures that no compiler is necessary on the production system. Indeed, compilers should not be allowed to exist on the production system.

The Purpose of a Change Control Board

To oversee the change management process, most organizations establish a change control board (CCB). In practice, a CCB not only facilitates adequate management oversight, but it also facilitates better coordination between projects. The CCB convenes on a regular basis, usually weekly or monthly, and can be convened on an emergency or as-needed basis as well. Figure 18-2 shows the process for implementing and properly controlling hardware or software during changes.

The CCB's membership should consist of development project managers, network administrators, system administrators, test/QA managers, an information security man-

Figure 18-2
Change control
board process

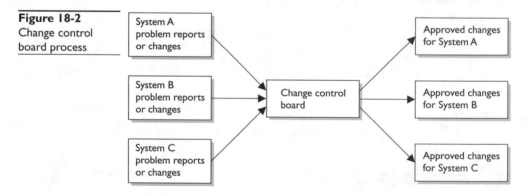

ager, an operations center manager, and a help desk manager. Others can be added as necessary, depending on the size and complexity of the organization.

A system problem report (SPR) is used to track changes through the CCB. The SPR documents changes or corrections to a system. It reflects who requested the change and why, what analysis must be done and by whom, and how the change was corrected or implemented. Figure 18-3 shows a sample SPR. A large enterprise probably cannot rely on a paper-based SPR process, so many software systems can be used to perform change

SYSTEM PROBLEM REPORT (SPR)

☐ Error   SPR Number:_____

☐ Improvement   Originator:_____

----------------------------------- **Problem** -----------------------------------

System Affected:_____

Related Systems:_____

Classification: Problem Description:_____

❑ Software   _____

❑ Hardware   _____

❑ Documentation   _____

❑ Comment   _____

Analysis Assigned to:_____

----------------------------------- **Analysis** -----------------------------------

(Prepared by responsible software design organization)   Date Received:_____

Classification: Explanation:

❑ Design   _____

❑ Coding   _____

❑ Documentation   _____

❑ Environment   _____

Signatures

Analyst:_____ Date:_____ Originator:_____ Date:_____

----------------------------------- **Correction** -----------------------------------

Brief Description of Work and List of Modules Changed:

_____

_____

Documentation Changed:

_____

_____

Signatures

Developer:_____ Date:_____ Manager:_____ Date:_____

Figure 18-3 Sample system problem report

PART V

management functions. While this example shows a paper-based SPR, it contains all the elements of change management: it describes the problem and who reported it, it outlines resolution of the problem, and it documents approval of the change.

Code Integrity

One key benefit of adequate change management is the assurance of code consistency and integrity. Whenever a modified program is moved to the production source-code library, the executable version should also be moved to the production system. Automated change management systems greatly simplify this process and are therefore better controls for ensuring executable and source-code integrity. Remember that at no time should the user or application developer have access to production source and executable code libraries in the production environment.

Finally, in today's networked environment, the integrity of the executable code is critical. A common hacking technique is to replace key system executable code with modified code that contains backdoors, allowing unauthorized access or functions to be performed. Executable code integrity can be verified using host-based intrusion detection systems. These systems create and maintain a database of the size and content of executable modules. Conceptually, this is usually done by performing some kind of hashing or sophisticated checksum operation on the executable modules and storing the results in a database. The operation is performed on a regular schedule against the executable modules, and the results are compared to the database to identify any unauthorized changes that may have occurred to the executable modules.

The Capability Maturity Model Integration

One area that is likely to be covered on the Security+ test is the Capability Maturity Model Integration (CMMI) developed at Carnegie Mellon University's Software Engineering Institute (SEI). The CMMI replaces the older Capability Maturity Model (CMM). Configuration or change management is one of the fundamental concepts of CMMI, which provides organizations with the ability to improve their software and other processes by providing an evolutionary path from ad hoc processes to disciplined management processes.

The SEI's web page defines six capability levels:

- **Level 0: Incomplete**   The software process is partially performed or not performed.
- **Level 1: Performed**   The process satisfies the goals of the process area but may not be sustainable because it is not institutionalized.
- **Level 2: Managed**   The process is a performed process (as defined in level 1) and has a supporting infrastructure in place, such as policies and qualified personnel, and it is monitored, controlled, reviewed, and evaluated. Most important, the processes are disciplined enough to remain intact during times of stress.

- **Level 3: Defined** The process is managed (as defined in level 2) but is tailored from the organization's standard set of processes, according to the organization's tailoring guidelines.

- **Level 4: Quantitatively Managed** The process is a defined process (see level 3) and uses statistical evaluation and quantitative objectives to control and manage the process.

- **Level 5: Optimizing** Key business processes are quantitatively managed (level 4) and improved by understanding root causes of variation. Improvements can be both incremental and innovative.

 EXAM TIP To complete your preparations for the Security+ exam, it is recommended that you consult SEI's web site (www.sei.cmu.edu/cmmi) for specific CMMI definitions. Be sure that you understand the differences between capability levels and maturity levels as defined in CMMI.

Change management is a key process to implementing the CMMI in an organization. For example, if an organization is at CMMI level 0, it probably has no formal change management processes in place. At level 3, an organization has a defined change management process that is followed and tailored to the specific project needs. At level 5, the change management process is a routine, quantitatively evaluated part of improving software products and implementing innovative ideas. In order for an organization to effectively manage software development, operation, and maintenance, it should have effective change management processes in place.

Chapter Review

Change management is an essential management tool and control mechanism. The key concept of segregation of duties ensures that no single individual or organization possesses too much control in a process. Therefore, it helps prevent errors and fraudulent or malicious acts. The elements of change management (configuration identification, configuration control, configuration status accounting, and configuration auditing), coupled with a defined process and a change control board, will provide management with proper oversight of the software lifecycle. Once such a process and management oversight exists, the company will be able to use CMMI to move from ad hoc activities to a disciplined software management process.

Questions

1. An upgrade to a software package resulted in errors that had been corrected in the previously released upgrade. This type of problem could have been prevented by

    A. The system administrator making the changes instead of the developer

     B. Proper change management procedures being used when changing the object code

     C. The use of an object-oriented design approach rather than a rapid prototyping design approach

     D. Proper change management procedures when changing the source code

2. Change management procedures are established to

     A. Ensure continuity of business operations in the event of a major disruption

     B. Ensure that changes in business operations caused by a major disruption are properly controlled

     C. Add structure and control to the development of software systems

     D. Identify threats, vulnerabilities, and mitigating actions that could impact an organization

3. Which of the following is *not* a principle of separation of duties?

     A. Software development, testing, quality assurance, and production should be assigned to different individuals.

     B. Software developers should have access to production data and source code files.

     C. Software developers and testers should be restricted from accessing "live" production data.

     D. The functions of creating, installing, and administrating software programs should be assigned to different individuals.

4. Why should end users not be given access to program source code?

     A. It could allow an end user to implement the principle of least privilege.

     B. It helps lessen the opportunity of exploiting software weaknesses.

     C. It assists in ensuring an independent and objective testing environment.

     D. It ensures testing and quality assurance perform their proper functions.

5. Configuration status accounting consists of

     A. The process of controlling changes to items that have been baselined

     B. The process of identifying which assets need to be managed and controlled

     C. The process of verifying that the configuration items are built and maintained properly

     D. The procedures for tracking and maintaining data relative to each configuration item in the baseline

6. Configuration identification consists of

     A. The process of controlling changes to items that have been baselined

    B. The process of identifying which assets need to be managed and controlled

    C. The process of verifying that the configuration items are built and maintained properly

    D. The procedures for tracking and maintaining data relative to each configuration item in the baseline

7. Which position is responsible for moving executable code to the test/QA or production systems?

    A. System administrator

    B. Developer

    C. Manager

    D. Quality assurance

8. Which computer security technology is used to ensure the integrity of executable code?

    A. Host-based intrusion detection systems

    B. Firewalls

    C. Gateways

    D. Network-based intrusion detection systems

9. In the Software Engineering Institute's Capability Maturity Model Integration (CMMI), which of the following correctly defines Level 3, Defined?

    A. Statistical evaluation and quantitative objectives are used to control and manage the process.

    B. The process satisfies process area goals but is not institutionalized.

    C. The process is managed but is tailored from the organization's standard set of processes.

    D. The process has a supporting infrastructure and is monitored, controlled, reviewed, and evaluated.

10. In the Software Engineering Institute's Capability Maturity Model Integration (CMMI), which of the following correctly defines Level 2, Managed?

    A. Statistical evaluation and quantitative objectives are used to control and manage the process.

    B. Key business processes are quantitatively managed and improved by understanding root causes of variation.

    C. The process is managed but is tailored from the organization's standard set of processes.

    D. The process has a supporting infrastructure and is monitored, controlled, reviewed, and evaluated.

Answers

1. **D.** Reappearing errors are likely caused by a developer not using the most recent version of the source code. Answer **A** is wrong because proper segregation of duties states that the developer is responsible for changing software programs, not the system administrator. Answer **B** is wrong because the source code will be recompiled, not the object code. Answer **C** is wrong because the design approach would not have caused this problem.

2. **C.** The fundamental purpose of software change management is to add structure and control to the software development process. Answers **A** and **B** are incorrect because software change management does not apply directly to ensuring business continuity. Answer **D** is incorrect; this is the definition of risk management.

3. **B.** Programmers should not be given direct access to production data or files. All the other answers are principles of segregation of duties, as outlined in the chapter.

4. **B.** If end users have access to source code, they could possibly view, identify, and abuse errors or weaknesses in the source code. Answer **A** is incorrect because the principle of least privilege does not directly apply here. Answer **C** is incorrect because end user access to program source code is not directly related to the testing environment. Answer **D** is incorrect because end user access to program source code is not directly related to the testing and quality assurance functions.

5. **D.** Configuration status accounting consists of the procedures for tracking and maintaining data relative to each configuration item in the baseline. Answers **A**, **B**, and **C** are the definitions of configuration control, configuration identification, and configuration auditing, respectively.

6. **B.** Configuration identification consists of the process of identifying which assets need to be managed and controlled. Answers **A**, **C**, and **D** are the definitions of configuration control, configuration auditing, and configuration status accounting, respectively.

7. **A.** The system administrator should be the only person allowed to move executables. The developer modifies the source code, the manager approves moving the executable to the production system, and quality assurance tests the executables.

8. **A.** Host-based intrusion detection systems create and maintain a database of the size and content of executable modules. Firewalls filter IP traffic; gateways also filter traffic, and network-based intrusion detection systems monitor IP traffic.

9. **C.** Level 3, Defined means that the process is managed but is tailored from the organization's standard set of processes. Answers **A**, **B**, and **D** are the definitions of Level 4, Quantitatively Managed; Level 1, Performed; and Level 2, Managed, respectively.

10. **D.** Level 2, Managed means the process has a supporting infrastructure and is monitored, controlled, reviewed, and evaluated. Answers **A**, **B**, and **C** are the definitions of Level 4, Quantitatively Managed; Level 5, Optimizing; and Level 3, Defined, respectively.

Privilege Management

In this chapter, you will

- Learn the differences between user, group, and role management
- Explore password policies
- Discover the advantage of single sign-ons
- Understand the pros and cons of centralized versus decentralized privilege management
- Learn about different auditing types (privilege, usage, and escalation)
- Explore methods of managing access (MAC, DAC, and RBAC)
- Discuss rights and privileges under Windows operating systems

Computer systems are in such wide use now that they touch almost every facet of our lives: they process credit card transactions, handle airline reservations, store a vast amount of personal information, and manage car engines to ensure optimal fuel efficiency. Most of the time, computers—particularly the more complicated systems, such as PCs, servers, and mainframes—require interaction from a human user. The user interacts with the applications and operating system to complete tasks and perform specific functions.

On single-user systems such as PCs, the individual user typically has access to most of the system's resources, processing capability, and stored data. On multiuser systems, such as servers and mainframes, an individual user may have very limited access to the system and the data stored on that system. An administrator responsible for managing and maintaining the multiuser system may have much greater access. So how does the computer system know which users should have access to what data? How does the operating system know what applications a user is allowed to use?

On early computer systems, anyone with physical access had fairly significant rights to the system and could typically access any file or execute any application. As computers became more popular and it became obvious that some way of separating and restricting users was needed, the concepts of *users*, *groups*, and *privileges* came into being. These concepts continue to be developed and refined and are now part of what we call *privilege management*.

Though privilege management has become a crucial part of modern operating systems and computer operations, it's really quite a simple concept. Privilege management is the process of restricting a user's ability to interact with the computer system. A user's interaction with a computer system covers a fairly broad area and includes viewing, modifying, and deleting data; running applications; stopping and starting processes; and controlling computer resources. Essentially, everything a user can do to or with a computer system falls into the realm of privilege management.

Privilege management occurs at many different points within an operating system or even within applications running on a particular operating system. While UNIX and Windows operating systems have a slightly different approach to privilege management, they share some similar approaches and concepts that are covered in this chapter.

User, Group, and Role Management

To manage the privileges of many different people effectively on the same system, a mechanism for separating people into distinct entities (*users*) is required, so you can control access on an individual level. At the same time, it's convenient and efficient to be able to lump users together when granting many different people (*groups*) access to a resource at the same time. At other times, it's useful to be able to grant or restrict access based on a person's job or function within the organization (*role*). While you can manage privileges on the basis of users alone, managing user, group, and role assignments together is far more convenient and efficient.

User

The term *user* generally applies to any person accessing a computer system. In privilege management, a user is a single individual, such as "John Forthright" or "Sally Jenkins." This is generally the lowest level addressed by privilege management and the most common area for addressing access, rights, and capabilities. When accessing a computer system, each user is generally given a *user ID*—a unique alphanumeric identifier he or she will use to identify himself or herself when logging in or accessing the system. User IDs are often based on some combination of the user's first, middle, and last name and often include numbers as well. When developing a scheme for selecting user IDs, you should keep in mind that user IDs must be unique to each user, but they must also be fairly easy for the user to remember and use.

With some notable exceptions, in general a user wanting to access a computer system must first have a user ID created for him on the system he wishes to use. This is usually done by a system administrator, security administrator, or other privileged user, and this is the first step in privilege management—a user should not be allowed to create his own account.

Once the account is created and a user ID is selected, the administrator can assign specific permissions to that user. *Permissions* control what the user is allowed to do on the system—which files he may access, which programs he may execute, and so on. While PCs typically have only one or two user accounts, larger systems such as servers and mainframes can have hundreds of accounts on the same system. Figure 19-1 shows the Users management tab from the Computer Management utility on a Windows 2003

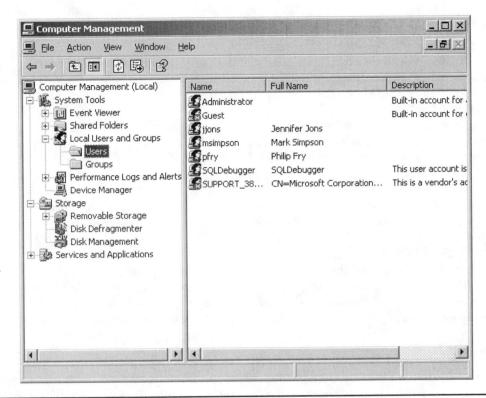

Figure 19-1 Computer Management utility showing list of user accounts

system. Note that several user accounts have been created on this system, each identified by a unique user ID.

A few "special" user accounts don't typically match up one-to-one with a real person. These accounts are reserved for special functions and typically have much more access and control over the computer system than the average user account. Two such accounts are the *administrator* account under Windows and the *root* account under UNIX. The administrator and root accounts are known as *superusers*—if something can be done on the system, the superuser has the power to do it. These accounts are not typically assigned to a specific individual and are often shared, accessed only when the full capabilities of that account are required.

Due to the power possessed by these accounts, and the few, if any, restrictions placed on them, they must be protected with strong passwords that are not easily guessed or obtained. These accounts are also the most common targets of attackers—if the attacker can gain root access or assume the privilege level associated with the root account, she can bypass most access controls and accomplish anything she wants on that system.

Groups

Under privilege management, a *group* is a collection of users with some common criteria, such as a need for access to a particular dataset or group of applications. A group can consist of one user or hundreds of users, and each user can belong to one or more groups. Figure 19-2 shows a common approach to grouping users—building groups based on job function.

By assigning a user membership in a specific group, you make it much easier to control that user's access and privileges. For example, if every member of the engineering department needs access to product development documents, administrators can place all the users in the engineering department in a single group and allow that group to access the necessary documents. Once a group is assigned permissions to access a particular resource, adding a new user to that group will automatically allow that user to access that resource. In effect, the user "inherits" the permissions of the group as soon as she is placed in that group. As Figure 19-3 shows, a computer system can have many different groups, each with its own rights and privileges.

As you can see from the description for the Administrators group in Figure 19-3, this group has complete and unrestricted access to the system. This includes access to all files, applications, and datasets. Anyone who belongs to the Administrators group or is placed in this group will have a great deal of access and control over the system.

Role

Another common method of managing access and privileges is by roles. A role is usually synonymous with a job or set of functions. For example, the role of "backup operator" may be applied to someone who is responsible for making sure that the system and any data residing on the system is regularly and successfully saved (usually to some sort of removable media, such as tapes). Backup operators need to accomplish specific functions and will need access to certain resources—for example, they may need to be able to read files on the system and save them to tape. In general, anyone serving in the role of backup operator will need the same rights and privileges as every other backup

Figure 19-2
Logical
representation
of groups

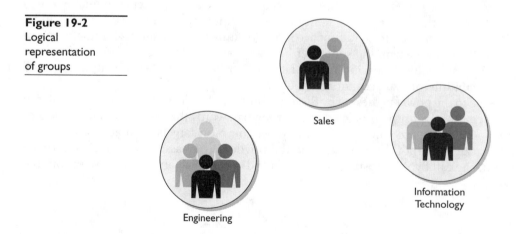

Sales

Engineering

Information
Technology

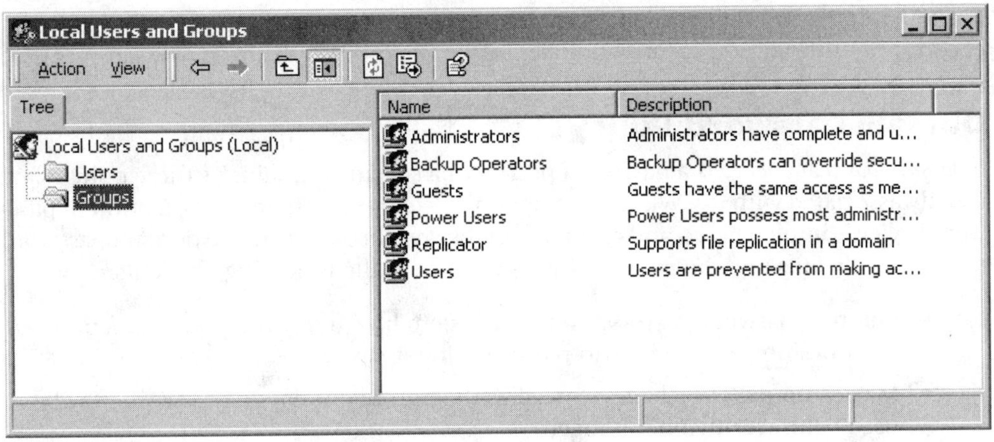

Figure 19-3   Group management screen from a Windows 2000 system

operator. For simplicity and efficiency, rights and privileges can be assigned to the role backup operator, and anyone assigned to fulfill that role will automatically have the correct rights and privileges to perform the required tasks.

Password Policies

The user ID/password combination is by far the most common means of controlling access to applications, web sites, and computer systems. The average user may have a dozen or more user ID and password combinations between school, work, and personal use. To help users select a good, difficult-to-guess password, most organizations implement and enforce a *password policy*, which typically has the following components:

- **Password construction**   How many characters a password should have, the use of capitalization/numbers/special characters, not basing the password on a dictionary word, not basing the password on personal information, not making the password a slight modification of an existing password, and so on

- **Reuse restrictions**   Whether or not passwords can be reused, and, if so, with what frequency (how many different passwords must you use before you can use one you've used before)

- **Duration**   The minimum and maximum number of days a password can be used before it can be changed or must be changed

- **Protection of passwords**   Not writing down passwords where others can find them, not saving passwords and not allowing automated logins, not sharing passwords with other users, and so on

- **Consequences**   Consequences associated with violation of or noncompliance with the policy

The SANS Institute offers several examples of password policies (along with many other common information security policies) available on its web site (www.sans.org).

Domain Password Policy

A *domain password policy* is a password policy for a specific domain. As these policies are usually associated with the Windows operating system (see Figure 19-4), a domain password policy is implemented and enforced on the *domain controller*. The domain password policy usually falls under a *group policy object* and has the following elements:

- **Enforce password history** Tells the system how many passwords to remember and does not allow a user to reuse an old password

- **Maximum password age** Specifies the number of days a password may be used before it must be changed

- **Minimum password age** Specifies the number of days a password must be used before it can be changed again

- **Minimum password length** Specifies the minimum number of characters that must be used in a password

- **Password must meet complexity requirements** Specifies that the password must meet the minimum length requirement and have characters from at least three of the following four groups: English uppercase characters (A through Z), English lowercase characters (a through z), Numerals (0 through 9), and nonalphabetic characters (such as !, $, #, %)

- **Store passwords using reversible encryption** Essentially the same as storing a plaintext version of the password; should be used only when applications use

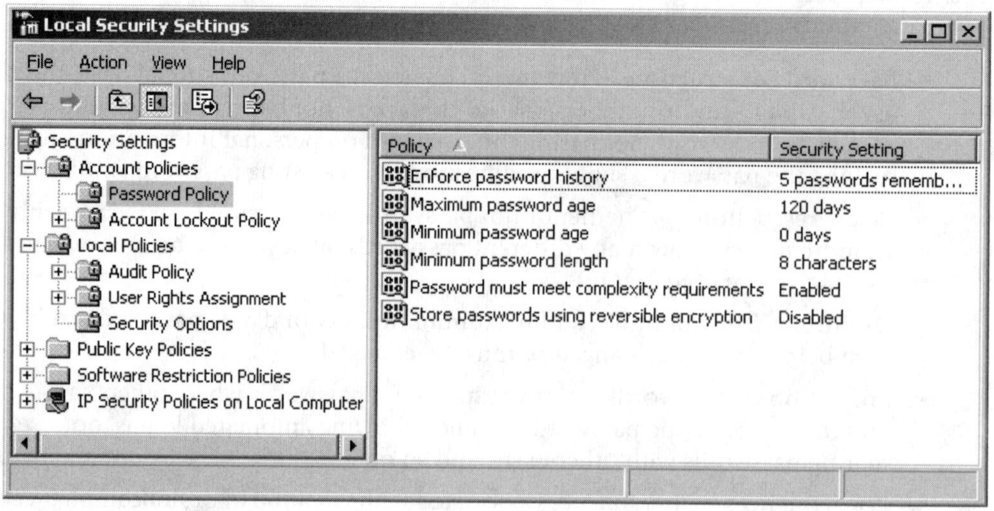

Figure 19-4 Password policy options in Windows Local Security Settings

protocols that require the user's password for authentication (such as Challenge-Handshake Authentication Protocol, or CHAP)

Single Sign-On

To use a system, users must be able to access it, which they usually do by supplying their user IDs and corresponding passwords. As any security administrator knows, the more systems a particular user has access to, the more passwords that user must have and remember. The natural tendency for users is to select passwords that are easy to remember, or even the same password for use on the multiple systems they access. Invariably, users will forget the passwords they chose for infrequently accessed systems, which creates more work for system administrators who must assist users with password changes or password recovery efforts. Wouldn't it be easier for the user simply to log in once and have to remember only a single, good password? This is made possible with a technology called *single sign-on*.

Single sign-on (SSO) is an authentication process in which the user can enter a single user ID and password and then be able to move from application to application or resource to resource without having to supply further authentication information. Put simply, you supply the right user ID and password once and you have access to all the applications and data you need, without having to log in multiple times and remember many different passwords. From a user standpoint, SSO means you need to remember only one user ID and one password. From an administration standpoint, SSO can be easier to manage and maintain. From a security standpoint, SSO can be even more secure, as users who need to remember only one password are less likely to choose something too simple or something so complex they need to write it down. Figure 19-5 shows a logical depiction of the SSO process:

1. The user signs in once, providing a user ID and password to the SSO server.

2. The SSO server then provides authentication information to any resource the user accesses during that session. The server interfaces with the other applications and systems—the user does not need to log in to each system individually.

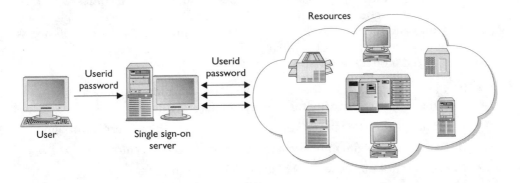

Figure 19-5   Single sign-on process

In reality, SSO is usually a little more difficult to implement than vendors would lead you to believe. To be effective and useful, all your applications need to be able to access and use the authentication provided by the SSO process. The more diverse your network, the less likely this is to be the case. If your network, like most, contains multiple operating systems, custom applications, and a diverse user base, SSO may not even be a viable option.

 EXAM TIP   The Security+ certification exams will very likely contain questions regarding single sign-on because it is such a prevalent topic and a very common approach to multisystem authentication.

Centralized vs. Decentralized Management

In the world of telecommunications and computers, there is almost always more than one way to accomplish a goal. Coincidentally, several schools of thought exist as to why one method is better than the other. This is especially true of security and privilege management. Regardless of how vast or minute your computer deployment, you will have to manage the rights and privileges of the users and processes using those systems. The two main approaches to rights and privilege management are *centralized* and *decentralized*.

Centralized Management

Centralized management brings the authority and responsibility for managing and maintaining rights and privileges into a single group, location, or area. To illustrate, consider the employees of a bank: The bank tellers have certain rights and privileges: they can process withdrawals and deposits, count money, and process a specific set of transactions. But bank tellers can't approve your car loan, and they don't have unrestricted access to the bank vault. Even if they wanted to, bank tellers can't expand their privileges or give additional access to other tellers. In a bank, the bank manager is the central management authority—she decides who can approve loans, access the vault, and give away free toasters. To get elevated rights and privileges, a teller must go through the central authority: the bank manager. In a similar fashion, when it comes to managing and maintaining rights and privileges under the centralized model, a single group or person creates and manages users, assigns rights and privileges, and controls access to information systems for the entire organization.

The centralized model has certain advantages:

- It can be more efficient, especially for large organizations, to have a specialized, central capacity for privilege management.
- Fewer people must be trained on tasks associated with privilege management.
- It is easier to implement new capabilities and processes centrally.
- Central control makes systems easier to audit and manage.
- A more consistent approach is ensured, as everyone "does it the same way."

And it has some disadvantages:

- Central management makes it more difficult to implement changes quickly.
- Functions at remote offices may be slowed down.
- It adds bureaucracy and is less flexible.
- Central control usually requires dedicated personnel and resources.

Most large corporations will use some form of centralized management, particularly with sensitive or business critical systems. For example, if a company has offices in Dallas, Phoenix, and Seattle, with a headquarters in New York, the IT department in New York may handle the creation of user and e-mail accounts for the entire company. Centralizing the creation of user and e-mail accounts gives a single group control over the process to ensure that standards and procedures are followed.

Decentralized Management

Decentralized management spreads out the authority and ability to manage privileges and rights. While this might sound like a recipe for anarchy to some, it can be an effective model for the right organization. To illustrate, reconsider our company with offices in Dallas, Phoenix, Seattle, and New York. Each office has a network perimeter with a firewall controlling what traffic comes into and leaves the local network. If each office has control over its own firewall with an administrator in each office responsible for that local firewall, then the company is using decentralized management with its firewall infrastructure. No central authority manages and maintains the firewalls—each office manages its own firewall.

The decentralized model has certain advantages:.

- It is highly flexible, as changes can be made whenever they are needed.
- It does not require a dedicated set of personnel and resources.
- Bureaucracy is reduced.

And it has some disadvantages:

- It can produce very different approaches in each department and office.
- It is more difficult to manage, audit, and maintain.
- It increases the risk of security breaches and corruption.
- More users must be trained on the same tasks.

A decentralized model works well for rapidly changing environments in which the tasks are constantly changing and the personnel are highly skilled and motivated. An academic research lab is a good example: in this environment, each researcher may need the capability to modify, manage, and maintain his own information systems without having to rely on a centralized authority.

The Decentralized, Centralized Model

In reality, most companies, and particularly large ones, use a combination approach. Imagine a company with 100,000 employees and offices in 52 locations around the world. It's not feasible for a single person or group to manage the rights and privileges of every user in an organization that large. It's much more efficient to decentralize control away from the main corporate office and let each office location handle its own privilege management tasks. Within each office, privilege management is usually centralized to a specific group of individuals (often the system administrators or security personnel). On a macro scale, the company as a whole is decentralized, while on a micro scale each office is centralized—it just depends on the level at which you're examining the organization.

Auditing (Privilege, Usage, and Escalation)

If you go through the trouble and effort of restricting access to certain resources and datasets, you will likely want to make sure only authorized individuals are able to gain access to those resources. Chances are, you'll also want to know who accessed what resources, when they accessed the resources, and what they did. When dealing with privilege management, *auditing* includes any actions or processes used to verify the assigned privileges and rights of a user, as well as any capabilities used to create and maintain a record showing who accessed a particular system and what actions they performed. Records showing which users accessed a computer system and what actions they performed are called *audit trails*. This section covers auditing as it pertains to three specific areas: privilege, usage, and escalation.

Privilege Auditing

Privilege auditing is the process of checking the rights and privileges assigned to a specific account or group of accounts. Each user account, group, and role is checked to see what rights and privileges are assigned to it. These results are then compared to the "expected" results to see where the actual results and expected results differ. Privilege auditing helps to find accounts that have been granted more privileges than they need, as well as accounts that have fewer privileges than they require. By comparing expected to actual results, the auditor can determine which changes need to be made (such as the removal of certain accounts, putting users into new groups, taking them out of other groups, and so on) and which rights and privileges need to be adjusted. Most organizations perform some type of privilege auditing, either formally or informally, on a regular basis.

How does privilege auditing enhance security? Privilege auditing helps ensure that users have been granted the correct privileges and rights required to perform their jobs—not too much access and not too little access. Privilege auditing follows the "trust but verify" philosophy of double-checking each account, group, and role to ensure that administrators have performed their jobs correctly. This is particularly important in large corporations or positions with a high rate of turnover or employee movement. As an employee leaves or changes positions, her privileges and rights must be revoked or modified to ensure that her account is properly disabled (if she is leaving) or that her account has been adjusted to reflect her new position (if she is changing positions).

Usage Auditing

Usage auditing is the process of recording *who* did *what* and *when*. Usage auditing creates a record showing who has accessed specific computer systems and what actions that user performed during a given period of time. Usage auditing can also be applied to datasets, specific applications, or databases, and it is very commonly used in accounting systems, transaction-based systems, and database management systems.

Usage auditing is usually performed by a process that records actions and stores them in a file for later analysis. These files can be in plaintext or custom formats, or they can even be encrypted to prevent unauthorized access. Figure 19-6 shows an example of the usage-auditing process on a Red Hat Linux system.

In Figure 19-6, you can see various processes starting, a user logging in, and actions being performed. Each of these pieces of information can help a system administrator determine what happened on that system during that period of time. In this example, we see an entry indicating the root user logged in on January 3 at 16:21:48 (4:21 P.M.). This tells us several things:

- Someone with knowledge of the password for the root account has accessed the system.

- The login from 127.0.0.1 tells us that the user logged in on the system's console, so he or she had physical access to the system.

- The time of 4:21 P.M. tells us that the access occurred during business hours.

Usage auditing is very common in both UNIX and Windows operating systems. Depending on the operating system and logging utility, the administrator can have a great deal of flexibility in what types of information are logged. Figure 19-7 shows the Audit Policy options available in the Windows 2008 operating system. As you can see, several audit policies can be enabled with success and failure criteria. For example, you

```
Jan  3 15:48:03 donald sshd[729]: Server listening on 0.0.0.0 port 22.
Jan  3 16:20:22 donald webmin[4086]: Webmin starting
Jan  3 16:20:40 donald xinetd[743]: START: sgi_fam pid=4142 from=<no address>
Jan  3 16:21:48 donald webmin[4212]: Successful login as root from 127.0.0.1
Jan  3 16:29:19 donald useradd[4323]: new group: name=mysql, gid=101
Jan  3 16:29:19 donald useradd[4323]: new user: name=mysql, uid=100, gid=101,
home=/var/lib/mysql, shell=/bin/bash
Jan  3 16:57:02 donald sshd[729]: Received signal 15; terminating.
Jan  3 16:58:03 donald sshd[728]: Server listening on 0.0.0.0 port 22.
Jan  3 16:58:14 donald webmin[917]: Webmin starting
Jan  3 16:58:40 donald xinetd[742]: START: sgi_fam pid=1024 from=<no address>
Jan  3 17:08:52 donald sshd[728]: Received signal 15; terminating.
```

Figure 19-6 Sample of usage-auditing log from a Red Hat Linux system

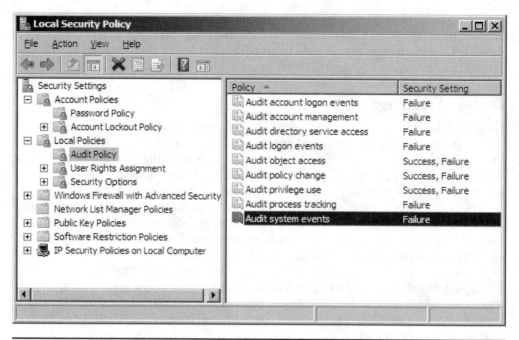

Figure 19-7 Auditing options available in Windows 2008

can audit the successful access to a particular file, or you can audit a logon failure. This type of customizable auditing allows the administrator to adjust the auditing process to suit his or her particular concerns and environment.

This type of information can be very useful when performing any kind of security investigation or incident response activities. With usage-auditing information, if a security incident occurs, you can attempt to re-create the event: which accounts were compromised, what actions were performed, and so on. Having this type of information may enable you to spot the incident, correct any problems, address any issues, and return the machine to operational status. Without this type of information, you might be forced to rebuild the system completely as you would have no way of knowing what the attacker did or what he accessed on the system.

Escalation Auditing

Escalation auditing is the process of looking for an increase in privileges—a normal user suddenly switches to the administrator or root account or obtains admin-level access. Administrators normally operate using their own accounts and switch to the administrator or root account only when they need to perform specific operations that require that level of privilege. So in the normal course of operations, you will see certain users elevating their privilege level, and this is acceptable behavior. However, this is usually a small subset of the overall user community, and any privilege escalation by someone outside the administrator group likely indicates a security breach. Escalation auditing looks for those unexpected or unauthorized increases in rights or privileges and can help security administrators determine when they have happened.

Figure 19-8 shows a good example of escalation auditing. In this section of the auditing log file, you see the user Zack log in to the system and attempt to switch to the root account. Zack fails once and then succeeds, becoming root and assuming all the rights and privileges associated with that account. As a security administrator, you would need to make sure Zack had legitimate access to the root account and is authorized to elevate his privileges accordingly.

Logging and Auditing of Log Files

Log files are records of activity: what happened, when it happened, who did it, where it came from, and so on. Although many administrators dread the auditing and analysis of log files, the simple truth is that effective logging and analysis of log files can be excellent tools for maintaining and securing a network. The first and most critical step is to enable logging on systems and network devices and ensure that the correct activities are logged. Logging failed logins is good, but logging each time a common file is successfully accessed by a legitimate user may be overkill. Determining what to log, how to log it, and how long to maintain audit logs are topics of lengthy discussions among system administrators.

One of the key determinants for deciding what should be logged is an examination of what information needs to be kept as part of a forensic record. Logging events as they happen allows investigators to examine activity after the fact by consulting the log. Logs by themselves are not a panacea, for they need to be examined and interpreted to be useful, and this requires an ongoing effort and resources to examine the logs. This is the second key determinant of what should be logged—logging items that are never reviewed is a common problem.

Common Logs

Many events in a computer system can be logged. Events from different levels of the OSI model can all be logged in a common logging scheme. Maintaining logs on a remote

```
Jan 26 15:17:21 donald (pam_unix)[16605]: session opened for user zack
Jan 26 15:17:45 donald su(pam_unix)[16650]: authentication failure; logname=
uid=500 euid=0 tty= ruser=zack rhost=  user=root
Jan 26 15:17:51 donald su(pam_unix)[16651]: session opened for user root by
(uid=500)
Jan 26 15:17:53 donald su(pam_unix)[16651]: session closed for user root
Jan 26 15:17:54 donald su(pam_unix)[16605]: session closed for user zack
```

Figure 19-8 Escalation auditing example

server offers security and simplicity in maintaining a centralized log monitoring solution. Following are examples of some areas where logging is effective and necessary:

- **Security applications** Generically a "security application" can be anything that helps assess or secure the network. Any security application that has the ability to generate a log file should be configured to do so, and the resulting logs should be analyzed on a regular basis.

- **DNS** A DNS server can be configured to log transactions—resolution requests, updates made or attempted, requests forwarded for resolution, and so on. DNS log files should be audited to help identify attempted intrusions, attacks, fraudulent updates, poisoning attempts, and so on.

- **System** System logs track events on the system—failures, program crashes, system shutdowns and restarts, process start and stop times, and so on. System logs can be valuable tools in identifying suspicious, undesirable, or malicious activity.

- **Performance** Performance logs track items such as memory usage, CPU usage, disk usage, network traffic, and so on. Performance logs can be another good indicator of malicious activity as the system may be either unusually "busy" or unusually "quiet" when compared to normal levels.

- **Access** Tracking what user accessed a certain resource, how they used it, what they did to or with that resource, and when the access occurred is a crucial logging activity. Auditing access logs can be an excellent method of detecting malicious activity, lapses in proper user management, and other activities.

- **Firewall** Firewall activity logs will track attempted connections, network volume, source addresses, destination address, ports used, and so on. Firewall logs should be audited periodically to ensure that the firewall is functioning as intended, to help identify common sources of attack traffic, to identify commonly targeted systems and services, and so on.

- **Antivirus** Antivirus logs will often track infected e-mails or files, the sources of offending mail or files, update status, scanning activity, and so on. Periodic auditing is required to ensure the antivirus program is providing the desired level of protection and is effectively scanning e-mail traffic and systems.

- **IDS/IPS** Intrusion detection system and intrusion prevention system logs are also excellent sources of suspicious, undesirable, or malicious activities. These logs can identify attack traffic, sources of attack traffic, targeted resources, possible and actual compromises, data loss, and other information.

Periodic Audits of Security Settings

As part of any good security program, administrators must perform periodic audits to ensure things "are as they should be" with regard to users, systems, policies, and procedures. Installing and configuring security mechanisms is important, but they must be reviewed on a regularly scheduled basis to ensure they are effective, up-to-date, and serving their intended function. Here are some examples, but by no means a complete list, of items that should be audited on a regular basis:

- **User access**   Administrators should review which users are accessing the systems, when they are doing so, what resources they are using, and so on. Administrators should look closely for users accessing resources improperly or accessing legitimate resources at unusual times.

- **User rights**   When a user changes jobs or responsibilities, she will likely need to be assigned different access permissions; she may gain access to new resources and lose access to others. To ensure that users have access only to the resources and capabilities they need for their current positions, all user rights should be audited periodically.

- **Storage**   Many organizations have policies governing what can be stored on "company" resources and how much space can be used by a given user or group. Periodic audits help to ensure that no undesirable or illegal materials exist on organizational resources.

- **Retention**   How long a particular document or record is stored can be as important as what is being stored in some organizations. A records retention policy helps to define what is stored, how it is stored, how long it is stored, and how it is disposed of when the time comes. Periodic audits help to ensure that records or documents are removed when they are no longer needed.

- **Firewall rules**   Periodic audits of firewall rules are important to ensure the firewall is filtering traffic as desired and helps ensure that "temporary" rules do not end up as permanent additions to the rule set.

Handling Access Control (MAC, DAC, and RBAC)

The last area of privilege management we will discuss deals with four methods for handling access control:

- **MAC**   Mandatory Access Control
- **DAC**   Discretionary Access Control
- **RBAC**   Role-based Access Control
- **RBAC**   Rule-based Access Control

Mandatory Access Control (MAC)

Mandatory access control is the process of controlling access to information based on the sensitivity of that information and whether or not the user is operating at the appropriate sensitivity level and has the authority to access that information. Under a MAC system, each piece of information and every system resource (files, devices, networks, and so on) is labeled with its sensitivity level (such as Public, Engineering Private, Jones Secret). Users are assigned a clearance level that sets the upper boundary of the information and devices that they are allowed to access. For example, if the administrator defines a file as having an Engineering Private sensitivity level, only the members of the engineering group with access to private information currently operating at a Private sensitivity level can access that file and its contents. A file with a Public sensitivity label would be available to anyone on the system.

The access control and sensitivity labels are required in a MAC system. Administrators define the labels and assign them to users and resources. Users must then operate within their assigned sensitivity and clearance levels—they don't have the option to modify their own sensitivity levels or the levels of the information resources they create. Due to the complexity involved, MAC is typically run only on systems and operating systems such as Trusted Solaris and OpenBSD where security is a top priority.

Figure 19-9 illustrates MAC in operation. The information resource on the right has been labeled "Engineering Secret," meaning only users in the Engineering group operating at the Secret sensitivity level or above can access that resource. The top user is operating at the Secret level but is not a member of Engineering and is denied access to the resource. The middle user is a member of Engineering but is operating at a Public sensitivity level and is therefore denied access to the resource. The bottom user is a member of Engineering, is operating at a Secret sensitivity level, and is allowed to access the information resource.

In the U.S. government, the following security labels are used to classify information and information resources for MAC systems:

- **Top Secret**   The highest security level that is publicly disclosed and is defined as information that would cause "exceptionally grave damage" to national security if disclosed to the public.

- **Secret**   The second highest level and is defined as information that would cause "serious damage" to national security if disclosed to the public.

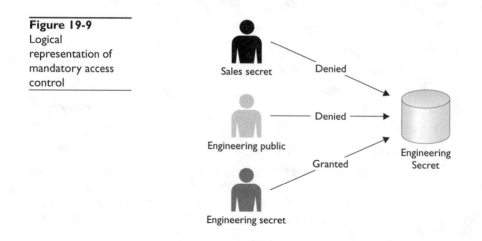

Figure 19-9
Logical representation of mandatory access control

- **Confidential**   The lowest level of classified information and is defined as information which would "damage" national security if disclosed.

- **Unclassified**   Any of this information can be released to individuals without a clearance.

The labels work in a top-down fashion so that an individual holding a Secret clearance would have access to information at the Secret, Confidential, and Unclassified levels. An individual with a Secret clearance would not have access to Top Secret resources, as that label is above the highest level of the individual's clearance.

Discretionary Access Control (DAC)

Discretionary access control is the process of using file permissions and optional access control lists (ACLs) to restrict access to information based on a user's identity or group membership. DAC is the most common access control system and is commonly used in both UNIX and Windows operating systems. The "discretionary" part of DAC means that a file or resource owner has the ability to change the permissions on that file or resource.

Under UNIX operating systems, file permissions consist of three distinct parts:

- **Owner permissions (read, write, and execute)**   The owner of the file
- **Group permissions (read, write, and execute)**   The group to which the owner of the file belongs
- **World permissions (read, write, and execute)**   Anyone else who is not the owner and does not belong to the group to which the owner of the file belongs

For example, suppose a file called *secretdata* has been created by the owner of the file, Luke, who is part of the Engineering group. The owner permissions on the file would reflect Luke's access to the file (as the owner). The group permissions would reflect the access granted to anyone who is part of the Engineering group. The world permissions would represent the access granted to anyone who is not Luke and is not part of the Engineering group.

In a simplified view, a file's permissions are usually displayed as a series of nine characters, with the first three characters representing the owner's permissions, the second three characters representing the group permissions, and the last three characters representing the permissions for everyone else, or for the world. This concept is illustrated in Figure 19-10.

	Owner	Group	World
Figure 19-10 Discretionary file permissions in the UNIX environment	**rwx**	**rw-**	**---**

PART V

Suppose the file *secretdata* is owned by Luke with group permissions for Engineering (because Luke is part of the Engineering group), and the permissions on that file are rwx, rw-, and ---, as shown in Figure 19-10. This would mean that:

- Luke can read, write, and execute the file (rwx)
- Members of the Engineering group can read and write the file but not execute it (rw-)
- The world has no access to the file and can't read, write, or execute it (---)

Remember that under the discretionary model, the file's owner, Luke, can change the file's permissions any time he wants.

Role-based Access Control (RBAC)

Role-based access control is the process of managing access and privileges based on the user's assigned roles. RBAC is the access control model that most closely resembles an organization's structure. Under RBAC, you must first determine the activities that must be performed and the resources that must be accessed by specific roles. For example, the role of "backup operator" must be able to mount and write to removable media and must be able to read every file (in order to save it to tape). Once all the roles are created and the rights and privileges associated with those roles are determined, users can then be assigned one or more roles based on their job functions. When a role is assigned to a specific user, the user gets all the rights and privileges assigned to that role.

Rule-based Access Control (RBAC)

Rule-based access control is yet another method of managing access and privileges (and unfortunately shares the same acronym as role-based). In this method, access is either allowed or denied based on a set of predefined rules. Each object has an associated ACL (much like DAC), and when a particular user or group attempts to access the object, the appropriate rule is applied.

A good example is permitted logon hours. Many operating systems give administrators the ability to control the hours during which users can log in. For example, a bank may allow its employees to log in only between the hours of 8 A.M. and 6 P.M. Monday through Saturday. If a user attempts to log in during these hours, the rule will allow the user to attempt the login. If a user attempts to log in outside of these hours, 3 A.M. on Sunday for example, then the rule will reject the login attempt whether or not the user supplies valid login credentials. Another good example of RBAC would be an ACL on a router. The ACL defines what traffic is allowed to pass through the router based on the rules established and maintained by the administrator—users cannot change access rules.

 EXAM TIP   The Security+ certification exams will very likely expect you to be able to differentiate between the four major forms of access control we've discussed: Mandatory Access Control, Discretionary Access Control, Role-based Access Control, and Rule-based Access Control.

Account Expiration

In addition to all the other methods of controlling and restricting access, most modern operating systems allow administrators to specify the length of time an account is valid and when it "expires." This is a great method for controlling temporary accounts, guest accounts, or accounts for contractors or contract employees. When creating the account, the administrator can specify an expiration date; when the date is reached, the account automatically becomes locked out and cannot be logged into without administrator intervention. A similar action can be taken with accounts that never expire: they can automatically be marked "inactive" and locked out if they have been unused for a specified number of days.

Permissions and Rights in Windows Operating Systems

The Windows operating systems use the concepts of *permissions* and *rights* to control access to files, folders, and information resources. When using the NTFS file system, administrators can grant users and groups permission to perform certain tasks as they relate to files, folders, and registry keys. The basic categories of NTFS permissions are as follows:

- **Full Control**   A user/group can change permissions on the folder/file, take ownership if someone else owns the folder/file, delete subfolders and files, and perform actions permitted by all other NTFS folder permissions.

- **Modify**   Users/groups can view and modify files/folders and their properties, can delete and add files/folders, and can delete or add properties to a file/ folder.

- **Read & Execute**   Users/groups can view the file/folder and can execute scripts and executables but cannot make any changes (files/folders are read-only).

- **List Folder Contents**   A user/group can list only what is inside the folder (applies to folders only).

- **Read**   Users/groups can view the contents of the file/folder and the file/ folder properties.

- **Write**   Users/groups can write to the file or folder.

Figure 19-11 shows the permissions on a folder called Data from a Windows 2008 system. In the top half of the Permissions window are the users and groups that have permissions for this folder. In the bottom half of the window are the permissions assigned to the highlighted user or group.

Figure 19-11
Permissions for the
"Data" folder

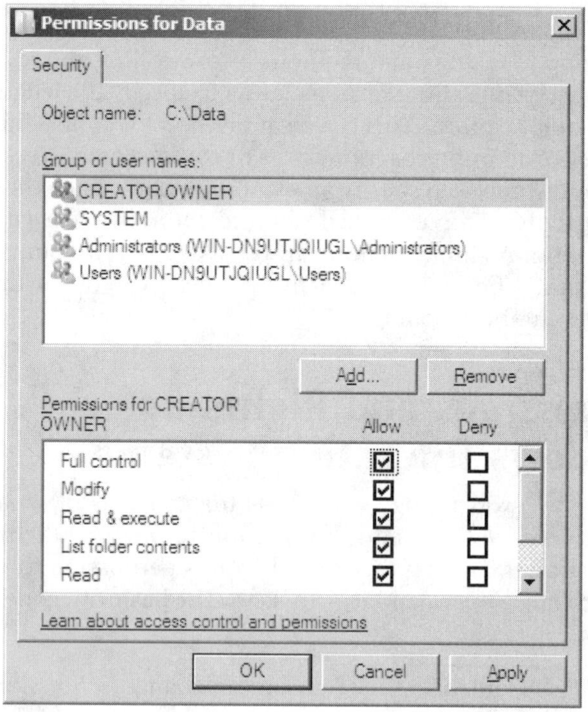

The Windows operating system also uses user rights or privileges to determine what actions a user or group is allowed to perform or access. These user rights are typically assigned to groups, as it is easier to deal with a few groups than to assign rights to individual users, and they are usually defined in either a group or a local security policy. The list of user rights is quite extensive but a few examples of user rights are

- **Log on locally**   Users/groups can attempt to log on to the local system itself.
- **Access this computer from the network**   Users/groups can attempt to access this system through the network connection.
- **Manage auditing and security log**   Users/groups can view, modify, and delete auditing and security log information.

Rights tend to be actions that deal with accessing the system itself, process control, logging, and so on. Figure 19-12 shows the user rights contained in the local security policy on a Windows XP system. The user rights within Windows XP, 2003, Vista, and 2008 are very similar.

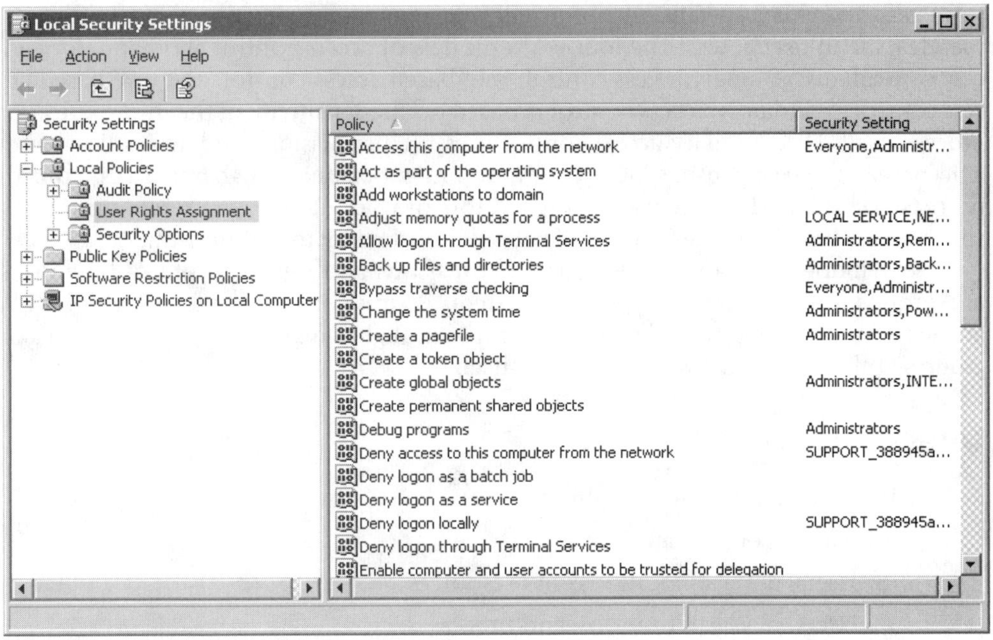

Figure 19-12 User Rights Assignment options from Windows Local Security Settings

Chapter Review

Privilege management is the process of restricting a user's ability to interact with the computer system. Privilege management can be based on an individual user basis, on membership in a specific group or groups, or on a function/role. Regardless of the method chosen, the key concepts are the ability to restrict and control access to information and information systems. One of the methods used to simplify privilege management is single sign-on, which requires a user to authenticate successfully once. The validated credentials and associated rights and privileges are then automatically carried forward when the user accesses other systems or applications.

Privilege management can be performed in a centralized or decentralized mode. In a centralized mode, control, along with modifications, updates, and maintenance, are performed from a central entity. In a decentralized mode, control is pushed down to a much lower and more distributed level. Tracking the effectiveness of privilege management and any suspected violations can be accomplished through the use of auditing. *Auditing* is the process of tracking logons, logoffs, file access, and process start or stop events, for example. Auditing can be performed on a privilege level, usage, or escalation basis.

Access control is a specific part of privilege management, more specifically the part that deals with user access. The four main models of access control are mandatory access control, discretionary access control, role-based access control, and rule-based access control. Mandatory access control is based on the sensitivity of the information or process itself. Discretionary access control uses file permissions and access lists to restrict access based on a user's identity or group membership. Role-based access control restricts access based on the user's assigned role or roles. Rule-based access control restricts access based on a defined set of rules established by the administrator.

The Windows operating system uses permissions and rights to control how users and groups interact with the operating system. Permissions are used to control what actions a user or group can take on a file or folder. Rights are used to control a user's or group's ability to interact with the system itself.

Questions

1. Privilege management applies to

    A. Files, resources, and users

    B. Users, physical locations, and resources

    C. Users, physical locations, and processes

    D. Applications, systems, and security

2. A user ID is

    A. A unique identifier assigned to each user

    B. A form of privilege management

    C. A unique identifier given to each process

    D. A type of system command

3. Role management is based on

    A. The user ID

    B. The group to which a user is assigned

    C. A job or function

    D. The rights associated with the root user

4. Single sign-on

    A. Works for only one user

    B. Requires only one user ID and password

    C. Groups like users together

    D. Requires the user to log in to each resource one time

5. Compared to decentralized management, centralized management

    A. Typically requires less training and fewer resources

    B. Brings control to a central location

    C. Is easier to audit and manage

    D. All of the above

6. Records showing which users accessed a computer system and what actions they performed are called

    A. User rights

    B. System and event logs

    C. Audit trails

    D. Permissions

7. Minimum password age is

    A. The number of days a password must be used before it can be changed

    B. The number of days a password can be used

    C. The number of days before the password becomes inactive

    D. The number of days before a password must be changed

8. The three types of auditing are

    A. Privilege, usage, and escalation

    B. User, system, and application

    C. File, process, and media

    D. None of the above

9. In the context of privilege management, MAC stands for

    A. Media access control

    B. Monetary audit control

    C. Mandatory access control

    D. None of the above

10. Under discretionary access control,

    A. File access is controlled by permissions.

    B. Owners can change permissions of their own files.

    C. File permissions may consist of owner, group, and world.

    D. All of the above.

11. In role-based access control

    A. Resources are assigned to individual user IDs

    B. Access is granted based on job function

    C. Files are labeled with sensitivity levels

    D. Users are divided into groups

12. A domain password policy

    A. Tells users how to safeguard their passwords

    B. Specifies the minimum length of a password

    C. Determines when passwords should be used

    D. Controls access to resources based on time of day

Answers

1. **A.** Privilege management is the process of restricting a user's ability to interact with the computer system, including files and resources.

2. **A.** A user ID is a unique identifier assigned to each user of a computer system. It allows the system to distinguish one user from another as well as determine what information, applications, and resources a particular user can access.

3. **C.** Role management is based on jobs and functions, not specific groups or users.

4. **B.** Single sign-on requires only one user ID and password. The user logs on to the SSO server once, and the SSO server then performs any additional authentication tasks for the user.

5. **D.** When compared to decentralized management, centralized management typically requires less training and fewer resources, brings control to a central location, and is easier to audit and manage.

6. **C.** Records showing which users accessed a computer system and what actions they performed are called audit trails.

7. **A.** Minimum password age is the number of days that must pass before a password can be changed.

8. **A.** The three main types of auditing discussed were privilege, usage, and escalation.

9. **C.** MAC stands for mandatory access control, which is the process of controlling access to information based on the sensitivity of that information and whether or not the user is operating at the appropriate sensitivity level and has the authority to access that information.

10. **D.** Under discretionary access control, file access is controlled by permissions, Owners can change their files' permissions when they want to, and file permissions in UNIX operating systems consist of different privileges for owner, group, and world.

11. **B.** In role-based access control, access to files and resources is usually assigned by job function. For example, a person with a "backup operator" role would be assigned the rights and privileges needed to perform that function.

12. **B.** A domain password policy specifies the minimum length of a password. Answers A and C should be part of the organizational password policy.

Computer Forensics

In this chapter, you will

- Learn the rules and types of evidence
- Review the collection of evidence
- Study the preservation of evidence
- Discover the importance of a viable chain of custody
- Explore the steps to investigating a computer crime or policy violation

Computer forensics is certainly a popular buzzword in computer security. This chapter addresses the key aspects of computer forensics in preparation for the Security+ certification exam. It is not intended to be a legal tutorial regarding the presentation of evidence in a court of law. These principles are of value in conducting any investigative processes, including internal or external audit procedures, but many nuances of handling legal cases are far beyond the scope of this text.

The term *forensics* relates to the application of scientific knowledge to legal problems. Specifically, computer forensics involves the preservation, identification, documentation, and interpretation of computer data, as explained in Warren G. Kruse and Jay Heiser's *Computer Forensics: Incident Response Essentials* (Addison-Wesley, 2002). In today's practice, computer forensics can be performed for three purposes:

- Investigating and analyzing computer systems as related to a violation of laws
- Investigating and analyzing computer systems for compliance with an organization's policies
- Investigating computer systems that have been remotely attacked

This last point is often referred to as *incident response* and can be a subset of the first two points. If an unauthorized person is remotely attacking a system, laws may indeed have been violated. However, a company employee performing similar acts may or may not violate laws and corporate policies. Any of these three purposes could ultimately result in legal actions and may require legal disclosure. Therefore, it is important to note that computer forensics actions may, at some point in time, deal with legal violations, and investigations could go to court proceedings. As a potential first responder, you should always seek legal counsel. Consult legal counsel ahead of time as you develop and implement corporate policies and procedures. It is extremely important to understand that even minor procedural missteps can have significant legal consequences.

Evidence

Evidence consists of the documents, verbal statements, and material objects admissible in a court of law. Evidence is critical to convincing management, juries, judges, or other authorities that some kind of violation has occurred. The submission of evidence is challenging, but it is even more challenging when computers are used because the people involved may not be technically educated and thus may not fully understand what's happened.

Computer evidence presents yet more challenges because the data itself cannot be sensed with the physical senses—that is, you can see printed characters, but you can't see the bits where that data is stored. Bits of data are merely magnetic pulses on a disk or some other storage technology. Therefore, data must always be evaluated through some kind of "filter" rather than sensed directly by human senses. This is often of concern to auditors, because good auditing techniques recommend accessing the original data or a version as close as possible to the original data.

Standards for Evidence

To be credible, especially if evidence will be used in court proceedings or in corporate disciplinary actions that could be challenged legally, evidence must meet three standards:

- **Sufficient**   The evidence must be convincing or measure up without question.
- **Competent**   The evidence must be legally qualified and reliable.
- **Relevant**   The evidence must be material to the case or have a bearing on the matter at hand.

Types of Evidence

All evidence is not created equal. Some evidence is stronger and better than other, weaker evidence. Several types of evidence can be germane:

- **Direct evidence**   Oral testimony that proves a specific fact (such as an eyewitness's statement). The knowledge of the facts is obtained through the five senses of the witness, with no inferences or presumptions.
- **Real evidence**   Also known as associative or physical evidence, this includes tangible objects that prove or disprove a fact. Physical evidence links the suspect to the scene of a crime.

- **Documentary evidence**   Evidence in the form of business records, printouts, manuals, and the like. Much of the evidence relating to computer crimes is documentary evidence.

- **Demonstrative evidence**   Used to aid the jury and can be in the form of a model, experiment, chart, and so on, offered to prove that an event occurred.

Three Rules Regarding Evidence

Three rules guide the use of evidence, especially if it could result in court proceedings:

- **Best evidence rule**   Courts prefer original evidence rather than a copy to ensure that no alteration of the evidence (whether intentional or unintentional) has occurred. In some instances, an evidence duplicate can be accepted, such as when the original is lost or destroyed by acts of God or in the normal course of business. A duplicate is also acceptable when a third party beyond the court's subpoena power possesses the original.

- **Exclusionary rule**   The Fourth Amendment to the U.S. Constitution precludes illegal search and seizure. Therefore, any evidence collected in violation of the Fourth Amendment is not admissible as evidence. Additionally, if evidence is collected in violation of the Electronic Communications Privacy Act (ECPA) or other related violations of the U.S. Code, it may not be admissible to a court. For example, if no policy exists regarding the company's intent to monitor network traffic or systems electronically, and the employee has not acknowledged this policy by signing an agreement, sniffing network traffic could be a violation of the ECPA.

- **Hearsay rule**   Hearsay is second-hand evidence—evidence not gathered from the personal knowledge of the witness. Computer-generated evidence is considered hearsay evidence.

 NOTE   The laws mentioned here are U.S. laws. Other countries and jurisdictions may have similar laws that would need to be considered in a similar manner.

Collecting Evidence

When information or objects are presented to management or admitted to court to support a claim, that information or those objects can be considered as evidence or documentation supporting your investigative efforts. Senior management will always ask a lot of questions—second- and third-order questions that you need to be able to answer quickly. Likewise, in a court, credibility is critical. Therefore, evidence must be properly acquired, identified, protected against tampering, transported, and stored.

Acquiring Evidence

When an incident occurs, you will need to collect data and information to facilitate your investigation. If someone is committing a crime or intentionally violating a company policy, he or she will likely try to hide his/her tracks. Therefore, you should collect as much information as soon as you can. In today's highly networked world, evidence can be found not only on the workstation or laptop computer, but also on company-owned file servers, security appliances, and servers located with the Internet service provider (ISP).

A first responder must do as much as possible to control damage or loss of evidence. Obviously, as time passes, evidence can be tampered with or destroyed. Look around on the desk, on the Rolodex, under the keyboard, in desktop storage areas, and on cubicle bulletin boards for any information that might be relevant. Secure floppy disks, CDs, flash memory cards, USB drives, tapes, and other removable media. Request copies of logs as soon as possible. Most ISPs will protect logs that could be subpoenaed. Take photos (some localities require use of Polaroid photos, as they are more difficult to modify without obvious tampering) or video tapes. Include photos of operating computer screens and hardware components from multiple angles. Be sure to photograph internal components before removing them for analysis.

When an incident occurs and the computer being used is going to be secured, you must consider two questions: should it be turned off, and should it be disconnected from the network? Forensics professionals debate the reasons for turning a computer on or turning it off. Some state that the plug should be pulled in order to freeze the current state of the computer. However, this results in the loss of any data associated with an attack in progress from the machine. Any data in RAM will also be lost. Further, it may corrupt the computer's file system and could call into question the validity of your findings.

Imaging or dumping the physical memory of a computer system can help identify evidence not available on a hard drive. This is especially appropriate for rootkits, where evidence on the hard drive is hard to find. Once the memory is imaged, you can use a hex editor to analyze the image offline on another system. (Tools for dumping memory and hex editors are available on the Internet.) Note that dumping memory is more applicable for investigative work where court proceedings will not be pursued. If a case is likely to end up in court, be sure to seek legal advice that live analysis of the memory is acceptable before proceeding, as it would be easy to dispute the claim that evidence was not tampered with.

On the other hand, it is possible for the computer criminal to leave behind a software bomb that you don't know about, and any commands you execute, including shutting down or restarting the system, could destroy or modify files, information, or evidence. The criminal may have anticipated such an investigation and altered some of the system's binary files. While teaching at the University of Texas, Austin, Dr. Larry Leibrock led a research project to quantify how many files are changed when turning off and on a Windows workstation. The research documents that approximately 0.6 percent of the operating system files are changed each time a Windows XP system is shut down and restarted.

Examine suspect system using its software without verification	Verify software on suspect system and use that software for investigation	Examine suspect system using external media with verified software	Build a new system that completely images suspect system	Boot suspect system with verified floppy, CD, kernel and tools	Use dedicated forensic workstation

Simple ←————————————————————————————————————→ Rigorous

Figure 20-1 Investigative method rigor

Further, if the computer being analyzed is a server, it is unlikely management will support taking it offline and shutting it down for investigation. So, from an investigative perspective, either course may be correct or incorrect, depending on the circumstances surrounding the incident. What is most important is that you are deliberate in your work, you document your actions, and you can explain why you took the actions you did.

EXAM TIP For Security+ testing purposes, remember this: the memory should be dumped, the system powered down cleanly, and an image should be made and used as you work.

Many investigative methods are used. Figure 20-1 shows the continuum of investigative methods from simple to more rigorous.

Figure 20-2 shows the relationship between the complexity of your investigation and both the reliability of your forensic data and the difficulty of investigation.

CAUTION You should never examine a system with the utilities provided by that system. You should always use utilities that have been verified as correct and uncorrupted. Do not open any files or start any applications. If possible, document the current memory and swap files, running processes, and open files. Disconnect the system from the network and immediately contact senior management. If your organization has Computer Incidence Response Team (CIRT) procedures, follow them. Capture and secure mail, Domain Name Service (DNS), and other network service logs on supporting hosts. Unless you have appropriate forensic training and experience, consider calling in a professional.

Figure 20-2
Rigor of the investigative method versus both data reliability and the difficulty of investigation

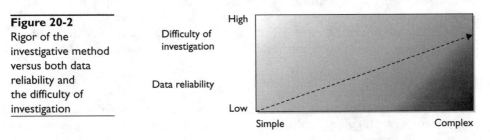

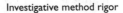
Investigative method rigor

Identifying Evidence

Evidence must be properly marked as it is collected so that it can be identified as a particular piece of evidence gathered at the scene. Properly label and store evidence, and make sure the labels can't be easily removed. Keep a log book identifying each piece of evidence (in case the label is removed); the persons who discovered it; the case number; the date, time, and location of the discovery; and the reason for collection. This information should be specific enough for recollection later in court. It is important to log other identifying marks, such as device make, model, serial number, cable configuration or type, and so on. Note any type of damage to the piece of evidence.

Being methodical is extremely important while identifying evidence. Do not collect evidence by yourself—have a second person who can serve as a witness to your actions. Keep logs of your actions during both seizure and during analysis and storage. A sample log is shown here:

Item Description	Investigator	Case #	Date	Time	Location	Reason
Dell Latitude laptop computer, D630, Serial number: 6RKC1G0	Smith	C-25	30 Jan 2008	1325 MST	Room 312 safe	Safekeeping

Protecting Evidence

Protect evidence from electromagnetic or mechanical damage. Ensure that evidence is not tampered with, damaged, or compromised by the procedures used during the investigation. Be careful not to damage the evidence to avoid potential liability problems later. Protect evidence from extremes in heat and cold, humidity, water, magnetic fields, and vibration. Use static-free evidence protection gloves as opposed to standard latex gloves. Seal the evidence in a proper container with evidence tape, and mark it with your initials, date, and case number. For example, if a mobile phone with advanced capabilities is seized, it should be properly secured in a hard container designed to prevent accidentally pressing the keys during transit and storage. If the phone is to remain turned on for analysis, radio frequency isolation bags that attenuate the device's radio signal should be used. This will prevent remote locking or disabling of the device.

Transporting Evidence

Properly log all evidence in and out of controlled storage. Use proper packing techniques, such as placing components in static-free bags, using foam packing material, and using cardboard boxes. Be especially cautious during transport of evidence to ensure custody of evidence is maintained and it isn't damaged or tampered with.

Storing Evidence

Store the evidence in an evidence room that has low traffic, restricted access, camera monitoring, and entry logging capabilities. Store components in static-free bags, foam packing material, and cardboard boxes.

Conducting the Investigation

When analyzing computer storage components, you must use extreme caution. A copy of the system should be analyzed—never the original system, as that will have to serve as evidence. A system specially designed for forensics examination should be used. Conduct analysis in a controlled environment with strong physical security, minimal traffic, controlled access, and so on.

 EXAM TIP   Never analyze the seized system directly. Always make multiple copies of the device and analyze a copy.

Remember that witness credibility is extremely important. It is easy to imagine how quickly credibility can be damaged if the witness is asked, "Did you lock the file system?" and can't answer affirmatively. Or, when asked, "When you imaged this disk drive, did you use a new system?" the witness can't answer that the destination disk was new or had been completely formatted using a low-level format before data was copied to it.

Unless you have tools specifically designed to take forensic images under Windows, your imaging process should use a live CD which executes upon booting the system without installing anything to the hard drive. Only the minimal amount of software should be installed to preclude propagation of a virus or the inadvertent execution of a Trojan horse or other malicious program. Windows can then be used when examining copies of the system. The Helix LiveCD contains many forensic tools.

Although each investigation will be different, the following image backup process is a good example of a comprehensive investigation:

1. Remove or image only one component at a time to avoid corrupting data or inadvertently contaminating evidence by dealing with too many aspects of the investigation at one time.

2. Remove the hard disk and label it. Be sure to use an anti-static or static-dissipative wristband and mat before conducting forensic analysis.

3. Identify the disk type (IDE, SCSI, or other type). Log the disk capacity, cylinders, heads, and sectors.

4. Image the disk by using a bit-level copy, sector by sector. This will retain deleted files, unallocated clusters, and slack space.

5. Make either three or four copies of the drive: one replaces the drive removed if the system is to be returned to its owner and you don't want to divulge that the drive has been exchanged; a second is marked, sealed, logged, and stored with the original, unmodified disk as evidence; a third will be used for file authentication; and the last is for analysis.

6. Check the disk image to make sure no errors occurred during the imaging process.

7. Before analyzing the suspect disk, generate a message digest for all system directories, files, disk sectors, and partitions. MD5 and SHA are suitable and

are superior to the older CRC32 or weaker hashing algorithms. Remember that even creating the message digest can change file access times, so it is important that you lock the files and use the image, not the original evidence. Keep a good log of the hash values.

8. Inventory all files on the system.

9. Document the system date and time.

 TIP Although this text describes the process and provides specific steps to be performed, they should be used as guidelines. Any notes or record of results you make can end up being evidence in a court. Therefore, using a checklist and making notes on it could result in those lists and notes becoming evidence. Your credibility could be damaged if you create specific checklists and skip a step or two because they aren't applicable—remember that you may need to explain why you skipped certain steps. While following the checklist, keep a log of all commands you issued on the system between the time you identified the incident and the time you imaged the disk. That way, if you are questioned in court about whether you changed anything on the disk, you can say, in effect, "Yes, but here is exactly what I did and here is how it would have changed things."

Chain of Custody

Evidence, once collected, must be properly controlled to prevent tampering. The chain of custody accounts for all persons who handled or had access to the evidence. The chain of custody shows who obtained the evidence, when and where it was obtained, where it was stored, and who had control or possession of the evidence.

The following shows critical steps in a chain of custody:

1. Record each item collected as evidence.

2. Record who collected the evidence along with the date and time.

3. Write a description of the evidence in the documentation.

4. Put the evidence in containers and tag the containers with the case number, the name of the person who collected it, and the date and time.

5. Record all message digest (hash) values in the documentation.

6. Securely transport the evidence to a protected storage facility.

7. Obtain a signature from the person who accepts the evidence at this storage facility.

8. Provide controls to prevent access to and compromise of the evidence while it is being stored.

9. Securely transport it to court for proceedings.

Free Space vs. Slack Space

When a user deletes a file, the file is not actually deleted. Instead, a pointer in a file allocation table is deleted. This pointer was used by the operating system to track down the file when it was referenced, and the act of "deleting" the file merely removes the pointer and marks the cluster(s) holding the file as available for the operating system to use. The actual data originally stored on the disk remains on the disk (until that space is used again); it just isn't recognized as a coherent file by the operating system.

Free Space

Since a deleted file is not actually completely erased or overwritten, it sits on the hard disk until the operating system needs to use that space for another file or application. Sometimes the second file that is saved in the same area does not occupy as many clusters as the first file, so a fragment of the original file is left over.

The cluster that holds the fragment of this file is referred to as *free space* because the operating system has marked it as usable when needed. As soon as the operating system stores something else in this cluster, it is considered *allocated*. The unallocated clusters still contain the original data until the operating system overwrites them. Looking at the free space might reveal information left over from files the user thought were deleted from the drive.

Slack Space

Another place that should be reviewed is *slack space*, which is different from free space. When a file is saved to a storage media, such as a hard drive, the operating system allocates space in blocks of a predefined size, called *clusters*. The size of all sectors is the same on a given system or hard drive. Even if your file contains only 10 characters, the operating system will allocate a full sector of 512 bytes—with space left over in the cluster. This is slack space.

It is possible for a user to hide malicious code, tools, or clues in slack space, as well as in the free space. You may also find information in slack space from files that previously occupied that same physical sector on the drive. Therefore, an investigator should review slack space using utilities that can display the information stored in these areas.

Message Digest and Hash

If files, logs, and other information are going to be captured and used for evidence, you need to ensure that the data isn't modified. In most cases, a tool that implements a hashing algorithm to create message digests is used.

A *hashing algorithm* performs a function similar to the familiar parity bits, checksum, or cyclical redundancy check (CRC). It applies mathematical operations to a data stream (or file) to calculate some number that is unique based on the information contained in the data stream (or file). If a subsequent hash created on the same data stream results in a different hash value, it usually means that the data stream was changed.

NOTE The mathematics behind hashing algorithms has been researched extensively, and although it is possible that two different data streams could produce the same message digest, it is very, very improbable. This is an area of cryptography that has been rigorously reviewed, and the mathematics behind Message Digest 5 (MD5) and Secure Hash Algorithm (SHA) are very sound. In 2005, weaknesses were discovered in the MD5 and SHA algorithms leading the National Institute of Standards and Technology (NIST) to announce in November 2007, a competition to find a new cryptographic hashing algorithm to be named SHA-3 (entries are due October 2008). These algorithms are still strong and are the best available—the discovered weaknesses show they aren't as strong as originally calculated. (For more information about hashing and algorithms, see Chapter 4.)

The hash tool is applied to each file or log and the message digest value is noted in the investigation documentation. When the case actually goes to trial, the investigator may need to run the tool on the files or logs again to show that they have not been altered in any way. The logs may also need to be written to a write-once media, such as a CD-ROM.

NOTE The number of files stored on today's hard drives can be very large, with literally hundreds of thousands of files. Obviously this is far too many for the investigator to analyze. However, if it were possible to know the message digests for most of the files installed by the most popular software products, and those message digests matched the message digests of the files on the drive being analyzed, approximately 90 percent of the files would not need to be analyzed by the investigator because they can be assumed to be unmodified. The National Software Reference Library (NSRL) collects software from various sources and incorporates file profiles into a Reference Data Set available for download as a service. See www.nsrl.nist.gov.

Analysis

After successfully imaging the drives to be analyzed and calculating and storing the message digests, the investigator can begin the analysis. The details of the investigation will depend on the particulars of the incident being investigated. However, in general, the following steps will be involved:

1. Check the Recycle Bin for deleted files.
2. Check the web browser history files and address bar histories.

3. Check the web browser cookie files. Each web browser stores cookies in different places. Browsers not listed here will require individual research. Internet Explorer stores cookies in two places:

   - In the Temporary Internet Files folder on Windows 98/ME, c:\windows\ temporary internet files; in Windows XP/2000, c:\documents and settings\<user name>\local settings\temporary internet files; on Windows Vista, C:\Users\<user name>\AppData\Local\Microsoft\Windows\ Temporary Internet Files.

   - In the Cookies folder on Windows 98/ME, c:\windows\cookies; on Windows XP/2000, c:\documents and settings\<user name>\cookies; on Windows Vista, C:\Users\<user name>\AppData\Roaming\Microsoft\ Windows\Cookies and C:\Users\<user name>\AppData\Roaming\ Microsoft\Windows\Cookies\low.

4. In Netscape for Mac, click the hard drive icon and open the System folder. Double click Preferences | Netscape Users Folder | Your Profile Folder.

5. Netscape for UNIX stores them in $HOME/netscape. A handy tool for viewing Internet Explorer cookies is IECookiesView available by searching the web.

6. Check the Temporary Internet Files folders. Usually these are found in the Windows directory C:\Documents and Settings\<username>\Local Settings\ Temporary Internet Files. This location can be changed, so be sure to check where Internet Explorer is storing those files. In Internet Explorer, choose Tools | Internet Options | General | Browsing History | Settings. The current location will be indicated on that screen.

7. Search files for suspect character strings. To conserve valuable time, be wise in the choice of words you search for, choosing "confidential," "sensitive," "sex," or other explicit words and phrases related to your investigation.

8. Search the slack and free space for suspect character strings as described previously.

NOTE The Helix LiveCD or Knoppix Live Linux CD are just two examples of the many tools you can use to perform computer forensics activities.

Chapter Review

This chapter provided information essential to understanding the role of forensic analysis. The topics covered help you understand that certain rules must be followed when dealing with evidence and why evidence must be properly collected, protected, and controlled to be of value during court or disciplinary activities. The terms discussed and concepts presented are essential to understand in your preparation for the Security+ certification exam. Understanding the process of conducting an investigation will not only assist the reader during Security+ exam preparations but will also help in the discovery of potential violations of laws or corporate policies.

Questions

1. Which of the following correctly defines evidence as being sufficient?

    A. The evidence is material to the case or has a bearing to the matter at hand.

    B. The evidence is presented in the form of business records, printouts, and so on.

    C. The evidence is convincing or measures up without question.

    D. The evidence is legally qualified and reliable.

2. Which of the following correctly defines direct evidence?

    A. The knowledge of the facts is obtained through the five senses of the witness.

    B. The evidence consists of tangible objects that prove or disprove a fact.

    C. The evidence is used to aid the jury and may be in the form of a model, experiment, chart, or the like, offered to prove an event occurred.

    D. It is physical evidence that links the suspect to the scene of a crime.

3. Which of the following correctly defines demonstrative evidence?

    A. The evidence is legally qualified and reliable.

    B. The evidence consists of tangible objects that prove or disprove a fact.

    C. The evidence is used to aid the jury and may be in the form of a model, experiment, chart, or the like, offered to prove an event occurred.

    D. The evidence is in the form of business records, printouts, manuals, and so on.

4. Which of the following correctly defines the best evidence rule?

    A. The evidence is legally qualified and reliable.

    B. Courts prefer original evidence rather than a copy to ensure that no alteration of the evidence (intentional or unintentional) has occurred.

    C. The evidence is used to aid the jury and may be in the form of a model, experiment, chart, or the like, offered to prove an event occurred.

    D. Physical evidence that links the suspect to the scene of a crime.

5. Which of the following correctly defines the exclusionary rule?

    A. The knowledge of the facts is obtained through the five senses of the witness.

    B. The evidence consists of tangible objects that prove or disprove a fact.

C. The evidence is used to aid the jury and may be in the form of a model, experiment, chart, or the like, offered to prove an event occurred.

D. Any evidence collected in violation of the Fourth Amendment is not admissible as evidence.

6. Which of the following is the *most* rigorous investigative method?

A. Build a new system that completely images the suspect system.

B. Verify software on the suspect system and use that software for investigation.

C. Examine the suspect system using its software without verification.

D. Use a dedicated forensic workstation.

7. Which of the following correctly defines slack space?

A. The space on a disk drive that is occupied by the boot sector

B. The space located at the beginning of a partition

C. The remaining clusters of a previously allocated file that are available for the operating system to use

D. The unused space on a disk drive when a file is smaller than the allocated unit of storage (such as a cluster)

8. Which of the following correctly defines the process of acquiring evidence?

A. Dump the memory, power down the system, create an image of the system, and analyze the image.

B. Power down the system, dump the memory, create an image of the system, and analyze the image.

C. Create an image of the system, analyze the image, dump the memory, and power down the system.

D. Dump the memory, analyze the image, power down the system, and create an image of the system.

9. If you are investigating a computer incident, and you need to remove the disk drive from a computer and replace it with a copy so the user doesn't know it has been exchanged, how many copies of the disk should you make, and how should they be used?

A. Three copies: One to replace the drive removed, one to be used for file authentication, and one for analysis.

B. Four copies: One to replace the drive removed; one is marked, sealed, logged, and stored with the original, unmodified disk as evidence; one is for file authentication; and one is for analysis.

C. Five copies: One to replace the drive removed; one is marked, sealed, logged, and stored with the original, unmodified disk as evidence; one is for file authentication; one is for analysis; and one is for holding message digests.

    D. Four copies: One to replace the drive removed; one is marked, sealed, logged, and stored with the original, unmodified disk as evidence; one is for file authentication; and one is for holding message digests.

10. Which of the following correctly describes the hashing concept?

    A. A method of verifying that data has been completely deleted from a disk

    B. A method of overwriting data with a specified pattern of 1s and 0s on a disk

    C. An algorithm that applies mathematical operations to a data stream to calculate a unique number based on the information contained in the data stream

    D. A method used to keep an index of all files on a disk

Answers

1. **C** is the correct definition. Answer **A** defines relevant evidence. Answer **B** defines documentary evidence. Answer **D** defines competent evidence.

2. **A** is the correct definition. Answer **B** defines real evidence. Answer **C** defines demonstrative evidence. Answer **D** defines real evidence.

3. **C** is the correct definition. Answer **A** defines competent evidence. Answer **B** defines real evidence. Answer **D** defines documentary evidence.

4. **B** is the correct definition. Answer **A** defines competent evidence. Answer **C** defines demonstrative evidence. Answer **D** defines real evidence.

5. **D** is the correct definition. Answer **A** defines direct evidence. Answer **B** defines real evidence. Answer **C** defines demonstrative evidence.

6. **D.** Answers **A** and **B** are other methods on the rigor spectrum. Answer **C** is the least rigorous method.

7. **D.** Answers **A** and **B** are contrived definitions. Answer **C** defines free space.

8. **A.** The other answers are not in the correct order.

9. **B.** The other answers are contrived responses.

10. **C** is the correct definition. The other answers are contrived responses.

PART VI

Appendixes

■ **Appendix A** About the CD
■ **Appendix B** OSI Model and Internet Protocols

About the CD

The CD-ROM included with this book comes complete with MasterExam, the electronic version of the book, and Session #1 of LearnKey's online training. The software is easy to install on any Windows 2000/XP/Vista computer and must be installed to access the MasterExam feature. You may, however, browse the electronic book directly from the CD without installing the software. To register for LearnKey's online training, simply click the Online Training link on the Main Page and follow the directions to the free online registration.

System Requirements

The software requires Windows 2000 or higher and Internet Explorer 6.0 or above and 20MB of hard disk space for full installation. The electronic book requires Adobe Reader. To access the Online Training from LearnKey, you must have Windows Media Player 9 or higher and Adobe Flash Player 9 or higher.

LearnKey Online Training

The **LearnKey Online Training** link will allow you to access online training from Osborne.Onlineexpert.com. The first session of this course is provided at no charge. Additional sessions for this course and other courses may be purchased directly from www.LearnKey.com or by calling 800-865-0165.

The first time that you run the Training software, you will be required to register the product online. Follow the instructions for a first-time user. Please make sure to use a valid e-mail address.

Installing and Running MasterExam

If your computer CD-ROM drive is configured to auto run, the CD-ROM will automatically start up when you insert the disk. From the opening screen, you may install MasterExam by pressing the MasterExam button. This will begin the installation process and create a program group named "LearnKey." To run MasterExam, select Start | All Programs | LearnKey | MasterExam. If the auto-run feature did not launch your CD, browse to the CD drive and click the LaunchTraining.exe icon.

MasterExam

MasterExam provides you with a simulation of the actual exam. The number of questions, the type of questions, and the time allowed are intended to be an accurate representation of the exam environment. You have the option to take an open book exam, including hints, references, and answers, a closed book exam, or the timed MasterExam simulation.

When you launch MasterExam, a digital clock display will appear in the bottom-right-hand corner of your screen. The clock will continue to count down to zero unless you choose to end the exam before the time expires.

Electronic Book

The entire contents of the Study Guide are provided as a PDF. Adobe Reader has been included on the CD.

Help

A help file is provided through the Help button on the main page in the lower-left-hand corner. Individual Help features are also available through MasterExam and LearnKey's Online Training.

Removing Installation(s)

MasterExam is installed to your hard drive. For best results removing the program, select the Start | All Programs | LearnKey | Uninstall option to remove MasterExam.

Technical Support

For questions regarding the technical contents of the electronic book or MasterExam, please visit www.mhprofessional.com or e-mail customer.service@mcgraw-hill.com. For customers outside the 50 United States, e-mail international_cs@mcgraw-hill.com.

LearnKey Technical Support

For technical problems with the software (installation, operation, removing installations) and for questions regarding LearnKey Online Training content, please visit www.learnkey.com, e-mail techsupport@learnkey.com, or call toll free 1-800-482-8244.

OSI Model and Internet Protocols

B

In this appendix, you will

- Learn about the OSI model
- Review the network protocols associated with the Internet

Networks are interconnected groups of computers and specialty hardware designed to facilitate the transmission of data from one device to another. The basic function of the network is to allow machines and devices to communicate with each other in an orderly fashion.

Networking Frameworks and Protocols

Today's networks consist of a wide variety of types and sizes of equipment from multiple vendors. To ensure an effective and efficient transfer of information between devices, agreements as to how the transfer should proceed between vendors are required.

The term *protocol* refers to a standard set of rules developed to facilitate a specific level of functionality. In networking, a wide range of protocols have been developed, some proprietary and some public, to facilitate communication between machines. Just as speakers need a common language to communicate, or they must at least understand each other's language, computers and networks must agree on a common protocol.

Communication requires that all parties have a common understanding of the object under discussion. If the object is intangible or not present, each party needs some method of referencing items in such a way that the other party understands. A *model* is a tool used as a framework to give people common points of reference when discussing items. Mathematical models are common in science, because they give people the ability to compare answers and results. In much the same way, models are used in many disciplines to facilitate communication. Network models have been developed by many companies as ways to communicate among engineers what specific functionality is occurring when and where in a network.

As the Internet took shape, a series of protocols was needed to ensure interoperability across this universal network structure. The Transmission Control Protocol (TCP),

User Datagram Protocol (UDP), and Internet Protocol (IP) are three of the commonly used protocols that enable data movement across the Internet. As these protocols work in concert with one another, you typically see TCP/IP or UDP/IP as pairs in use. A basic understanding of the terms and of the usage of protocols and models is essential to discuss networking functionality, for it provides the necessary points of reference to understand what is happening where and when in the complex stream of operations that are involved in networking.

OSI Model

To facilitate cross-vendor and multicompany communication, in 1984 the International Organization for Standardization (ISO) created the Open Systems Interconnection (OSI) model for networking. The OSI model is probably the most referenced and widely discussed model in networking. Although it never fully caught on in North America, portions of it have been adopted as reference points, even to the extent of being incorporated into company names. Layer 2, layer 3, network layer, level 3—these are all references to portions of the OSI model. These references allow people to communicate in a clear and unambiguous fashion when speaking of abstract and out of context issues. These references provide context to detail in the complex arena of networking. The terms *level* and *layer* have been used interchangeably to describe the sections of the OSI model, although *layer* is the more common term.

The OSI model is composed of seven layers stacked in a linear fashion. These layers are, from top to bottom, application, presentation, session, transport, network, datalink, and physical. You can use a mnemonic to remember them: All People Seem To Need Data Processing. Each layer has defined functionality and separation designed to allow multiple protocols to work together in a coordinated fashion.

Although the OSI model is probably the most referenced, standardized network model, a more common model, the Internet model, has risen to dominate the Internet. The OSI model enjoys the status of being a formal, defined international standard, while the Internet model has never been formally defined. The Internet model is basically the same as the OSI model, with the top three OSI layers combined into a single application layer, leaving a total of five layers in the Internet model. Both models are shown in Figure B-1.

One aspect of these models is that they allow specific levels of functionality to be broken apart and performed in sequence. This delineation also determines which layers can communicate with others. At each layer, specific data forms and protocols can exist, which makes them compatible with similar protocols and data forms on other machines at the same layer. This makes it seem as if each layer is communicating with its counterpart on the same layer in another computer, although this is just a virtual connection. The only real connection between boxes is at the physical layer of these models. All other connections are virtual—although they appear real to a user, they do not actually exist in reality.

The true communication between layers occurs vertically, up and down—each layer can communicate only with its immediate neighbor above and below. In Figure B-2,

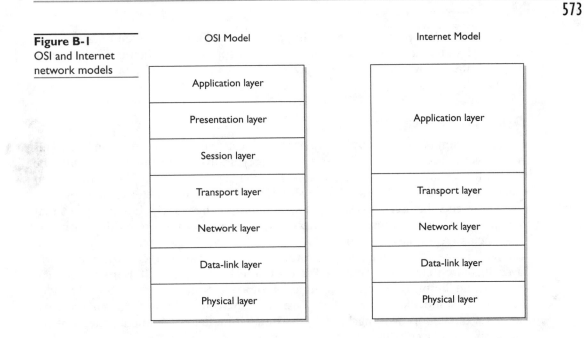

the direct communication path is shown as a bold line between the two physical layers. All data between the boxes traverses this line. The dotted lines between higher layers represent virtual connections, and the associated activities and protocols are also listed

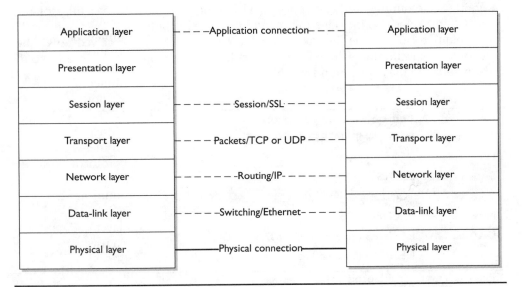

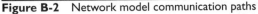

Figure B-2 Network model communication paths

for most layers (the protocols are also listed in Table B-1). These dotted lines are virtual—data does not actually cross them, although it appears as though it does. The true path of data is down to the physical layer and back up to the same layer on another machine.

Application Layer

The application layer is the typical interface to the actual application being used. This is the layer of the communication stack that is typically responsible for initiating the request for communication. For example, Internet Explorer is an application program that operates in the application layer using HTTP to move data between systems. This layer represents the user's access to the system and the network. While it appears that the application is communicating directly with an application on another machine, this is actually a *virtual* connection. The application layer is also sometimes referred to as layer 7 in the OSI model. Several protocols are commonly found in the application layer, including Hypertext Transfer Protocol (HTTP), Simple Mail Transfer Protocol (SMTP), and Simple Network Management Protocol (SNMP).

In the OSI model, the application layer actually communicates with the presentation layer only on its own machine. In the Internet model, the immediate level below the application layer is the transport layer, and this is the only layer directly called by the application layer in this model. As a result of the "missing" presentation and session layers in the Internet model, the functionality of these OSI layers is performed by the application layer.

The session layer functionality present in the Internet model's application layer includes the initiation, maintenance, and termination of logical sessions between endpoints in the network communication. The session layer functionality also includes session level accounting and encryption services. The presentation layer functionality of the OSI model is also included in the Internet model's application layer, specifically functionality to format the display parameters of the data being received. Any other functions not specifically included in the lower layers of the Internet model are specifically included in the application layer.

Layer	Commonly Used Protocols
Application	HTTP, SNMP, SMTP, FTP, Telnet
Presentation	XDR
Session	SSL, TLS
Transport	TCP, UCP
Network	IP, ICMP
Data-link	IEEE 802.3 (Ethernet), IEEE 802.5 (Token Ring), ARP, RARP
Physical	IEEE 802.3 (Ethernet) hardware, IEEE 802.5 (Token Ring) hardware

Table B-1   Common Protocols by OSI Layer

Presentation Layer

The presentation layer gets its name from its primary function: preparing for the presentation of data. It is responsible for preparing the data for different interfaces on different types of terminals or displays so the application does not have to deal with this task. Data compression, character set translation, and encryption are found in this layer.

The presentation layer communicates with only two layers—the application layer above it and the session layer below it. The presentation layer is also known as layer 6 of the OSI model.

Session Layer

The primary responsibility of the session layer is the managing of communication sessions between machines. The management functions include initiating, maintaining, and terminating sessions. Managing a session can be compared to making an ordinary phone call. When you dial, you initiate a session. The session must be maintained in an open state during the call. At the completion of the call, you hang up and the circuit must be terminated. As each session can have its own parameters, the session layer is responsible for setting them up, including security, encryption, and billing or accounting functions.

The session layer communicates exclusively with the presentation layer above it and the transport layer below it. The session layer is also known as layer 5 of the OSI model.

Transport Layer

The transport layer is responsible for dealing with the end-to-end transport of data across the network connection. To perform this task, the transport layer handles data entering and leaving the network through logical connections. It can add and use address-specific information, such as ports, to accomplish this task. A *port* is an address-specific extension that enables multiple simultaneous communications between machines. Should the data transmission be too large for a single-packet transport, the transport layer manages breaking up the data stream into chunks and reassembling it. It ensures that all packets are transmitted and received, and it can request lost packets and eliminate duplicate packets. Error checking can also be performed at this level, although this function is usually performed at the data-link layer.

Protocols can be either connection oriented or connectionless. If the protocol is connection oriented, the transport layer manages the connection information. In the case of TCP, the transport layer manages missing packet retransmission requests via the sliding window algorithm.

The transport layer communicates exclusively with the session layer above it and the network layer below it. The transport layer is also known as layer 4 of the OSI model.

PART VI

Network Layer

The network layer is responsible for routing packets across the network. Routing functions determine the next best destination for a packet and will determine the full address of the target computer if necessary. Common protocols at this level include IP and Internet Control Message Protocol (ICMP).

The network layer communicates exclusively with the transport layer above it and the data-link layer below it. The network layer is also known as layer 3 of the OSI model.

Data-Link Layer

The data-link layer is responsible for the delivery and receipt of data from the hardware in layer 1, the physical layer. Layer 1 only manipulates a stream of bits, so the data-link layer must convert the packets from the network layer into bit streams in a form that can be understood by the physical layer. To ensure accurate transmission, the data-link layer adds end-of-message markers onto each packet and also manages error detection, correction, and retransmission functions. This layer also performs the media-access function, determining when to send and receive data based on network traffic. At this layer, the data packets are technically known as *frames*, although many practitioners use *packet* in a generic sense.

The data-link layer communicates exclusively with the network layer above it and the physical layer below it. The data-link layer is also known as layer 2 of the OSI model, and it is where LAN switching based on machine address functionality occurs.

Physical Layer

The physical layer is the realm of communication hardware and software, where 1s and 0s become waves of light, voltage levels, phase shifts, and other physical entities as defined by the particular transmission standard. This layer defines the physical method of signal transmission between machines in terms of electrical and optical characteristics. The physical layer is the point of connection to the outside world via standard connectors, again determined by signal type and protocol.

The physical layer communicates with the physical layer on other machines via wire, fiber-optics, or radio waves. The physical layer also communicates with the data-link layer above it. The physical layer is also referred to as OSI layer 1.

Internet Protocols

To facilitate cross-vendor product communication, protocols have been adopted to standardize methods. The Internet brought several new protocols into existence, a few of which are commonly used in routing of information. Two protocols used at the transport layer are TCP and UDP, whereas IP is used at the network layer. In each session, one transport layer protocol and one network layer protocol is used, making the pairs TCP/IP and UDP/IP.

TCP

TCP is the primary transport protocol used on the Internet today, accounting for more than 80 percent of packets on the Internet.

TCP begins by establishing a virtual connection through a mechanism known as the TCP *handshake*. This handshake involves three signals: a SYN signal sent to the target, a SYN/ACK returned in response, and then an ACK sent back to the target to complete the circuit. This establishes a virtual connection between machines over which the data will be transported, and that is why TCP is referred to as being *connection oriented*.

TCP is classified as a reliable protocol and will ensure that packets are sent, received, and ordered using sequence numbers. Some overhead is associated with the sequencing of packets and maintaining this order, but for many communications, this is essential, such as in e-mail transmissions, HTTP, and the like.

TCP has facilities to perform all the required functions of the transport layer. TCP has congestion- and flow-control mechanisms to report congestion and other traffic-related information back to the sender to assist in traffic-level management. Multiple TCP connections can be established between machines through a mechanism known as *ports*. TCP ports are numbered from 0 to 65,535, although ports below 1024 are typically reserved for specific functions. TCP ports are separate entities from UDP ports and can be used at the same time.

UDP

UDP is a simpler form of transport protocol than TCP. UDP performs all of the required functionality of the transport layer, but it does not perform the maintenance and checking functions of TCP. UDP does not establish a connection and does not use sequence numbers. UDP packets are sent via the "best effort" method, often referred to as "fire and forget," because the packets either reach their destination or they are lost forever. It offers no retransmission mechanism, which is why UDP is called an unreliable protocol.

UDP does not have traffic-management or flow-control functions as TCP does. This results in much lower overhead and makes UDP ideal for streaming data sources, such as audio and video traffic, where latency between packets can be an issue. Essential services such as Dynamic Host Configuration Protocol (DHCP) and Domain Name Service (DNS) use UDP, primarily because of the low overhead. When packets do get lost, which is rare in modern networks, they can be resent.

Multiple UDP connections can be established between machines via ports. UDP ports are numbered from 0 to 65,535, although ports below 1024 are typically reserved for specific functionality. UDP ports are separate entities from TCP ports and can be used at the same time.

IP

IP is a connectionless protocol used for routing messages across the Internet. Its primary purpose is to address packets with IP addresses, both destination and source, and to use these addresses to determine the next hop to which the packet will be transmitted. As IP is *connectionless*, IP packets can take different routes at different times between the same hosts, depending on traffic conditions. IP also maintains some traffic-management information, such as time-to-live (a function to give packets a limited lifetime) and fragmentation control (a mechanism to split packets en route if necessary).

The current version of IP is version 4, referred to as IPv4, and it uses a 32-bit address space. The newer IPv6 protocol adds significant levels of functionality, such as security, improved address space, 128 bits, and a whole host of sophisticated traffic-management options. IPv4 addresses are written as four sets of numbers in the form v.x.y.z, with each of these values ranging from 0 to 255. As this would be difficult to remember, a naming system for hosts was developed around domains, and DNS servers convert the host names, such as www.ietf.org, to IP addresses, such as 4.17.168.6.

Message Encapsulation

As a message traverses a network from one application on one host, down through the OSI model, out through the physical layer, and up another machine's OSI model, the data is encapsulated at each layer. This can be viewed as an envelope inside an envelope scheme. As only specific envelopes are handled at each layer, only the necessary information for that layer is presented on the envelope. At each layer, the information inside the envelope is not relevant and previous envelopes have been discarded—only the information on the current envelope is used. This offers efficient separation of functionality between layers. This concept is illustrated in Figure B-3.

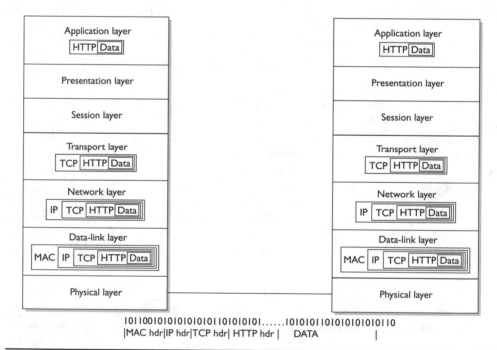

Figure B-3 OSI message encapsulation

As a message traverses the OSI model from the application layer to the physical layer, envelopes are placed inside bigger envelopes. This increases the packet size, but this increase is known and taken into account by the higher-level protocols. At each level, a header is added to the front end, and it acts to encapsulate the previous layer as data. At the physical level, the bits are turned into the physical signal and are transmitted to the next station.

At the receiving station, the bits are turned into one large packet, which represents the original envelope-within-envelope concept. Then each envelope is handled at the appropriate level. This encapsulation exists at the transport layer and lower, as this is the domain of a packet within a session.

Review

To help variable systems understand the functions performed in network communication, a common framework is necessary. This framework is provided by the OSI and Internet network models, which specify which functions occur, and in what order, in the transmission of data from one application to another across a network.

An understanding of the OSI model and thus the state in which the data exists as it transits a network enables a deeper understanding of issues related to security. Understanding that SSL occurs before TCP and IP allows you to understand how SSL protects TCP and IP from outside sniffing. Understanding the different protocols and what happens with data loss gives you a better understanding of how certain types of attacks are performed.

The essence of a framework is to allow enhanced understanding of relationships, and these network models perform this function for network professionals.

3DES Triple DES encryption—three rounds of DES encryption used to improve security.

802.11 A family of standards that describe network protocols for wireless devices.

802.1X An IEEE standard for performing authentication over networks.

acceptable use policy (AUP) A policy that communicates to users what specific uses of computer resources is permitted.

access A subject's ability to perform specific operations on an object, such as a file. Typical access levels include read, write, execute, and delete.

access control Mechanisms or methods used to determine what access permissions subjects (such as users) have for specific objects (such as files).

access control list (ACL) A list associated with an object (such as a file) that identifies what level of access each subject (such as a user) has—what they can do to the object (such as read, write, or execute).

Active Directory The directory service portion of the Windows operating system that stores information about network-based entities (such as applications, files, printers, and people) and provides a structured, consistent way to name, describe, locate, access, and manage these resources.

ActiveX A Microsoft technology that facilitates rich Internet applications, and therefore extends and enhances the functionality of Microsoft Internet Explorer. Like Java, ActiveX enables the development of interactive content. When an ActiveX-aware browser encounters a web page that includes an unsupported feature, it can automatically install the appropriate application so the feature can be used.

Address Resolution Protocol (ARP)   A protocol in the TCP/IP suite specification used to map an IP address to a Media Access Control (MAC) address.

adware   Advertising-supported software that automatically plays, displays, or downloads advertisements after the software is installed or while the application is being used.

algorithm   A step-by-step procedure—typically an established computation for solving a problem within a set number of steps.

annualized loss expectancy (ALE)   How much an event is expected to cost the business per year, given the dollar cost of the loss and how often it is likely to occur. ALE = single loss expectancy * annualized rate of occurrence.

annualized rate of occurrence (ARO)   The frequency with which an event is expected to occur on an annualized basis.

anomaly   Something that does not fit into an expected pattern.

application   A program or group of programs designed to provide specific user functions, such as a word processor or web server.

ARP   *See* Address Resolution Protocol.

asset   Resources and information an organization needs to conduct its business.

asymmetric encryption   Also called public key cryptography, this is a system for encrypting data that uses two mathematically derived keys to encrypt and decrypt a message—a public key, available to everyone, and a private key, available only to the owner of the key.

audit trail   A set of records or events, generally organized chronologically, that record what activity has occurred on a system. These records (often computer files) are often used in an attempt to re-create what took place when a security incident occurred, and they can also be used to detect possible intruders.

auditing   Actions or processes used to verify the assigned privileges and rights of a user, or any capabilities used to create and maintain a record showing who accessed a particular system and what actions they performed.

authentication   The process by which a subject's (such as a user's) identity is verified.

authentication, authorization, and accounting (AAA)   Three common functions performed upon system login. Authentication and authorization almost always occur, with accounting being somewhat less common.

Authentication Header (AH)   A portion of the IPsec security protocol that provides authentication services and replay-detection ability. AH can be used either by itself or with Encapsulating Security Payload (ESP). Refer to RFC 2402.

availability   Part of the "CIA" of security. Availability applies to hardware, software, and data, specifically meaning that each of these should be present and accessible when the subject (the user) wants to access or use them.

backdoor   A hidden method used to gain access to a computer system, network, or application. Often used by software developers to ensure unrestricted access to the systems they create. Synonymous with trapdoor.

backup   Refers to copying and storing data in a secondary location, separate from the original, to preserve the data in the event that the original is lost, corrupted, or destroyed.

baseline   A system or software as it is built and functioning at a specific point in time. Serves as a foundation for comparison or measurement, providing the necessary visibility to control change.

BGP   *See* Border Gateway Protocol.

biometrics   Used to verify an individual's identity to the system or network using something unique about the individual, such as a fingerprint, for the verification process. Examples include fingerprints, retinal scans, hand and facial geometry, and voice analysis.

BIOS   The part of the operating system that links specific hardware devices to the operating system software.

Blowfish   A free implementation of a symmetric block cipher developed by Bruce Schneier as a drop-in replacement for DES and IDEA. It has a variable bit-length scheme from 32 to 448 bits, resulting in varying levels of security.

bluebugging   The use of a Bluetooth-enabled device to eavesdrop on another person's conversation using that person's Bluetooth phone as a transmitter. The bluebug application silently causes a Bluetooth device to make a phone call to another device, causing the phone to act as a transmitter and allowing the listener to eavesdrop on the victim's conversation in real life.

bluejacking   The sending of unsolicited messages over Bluetooth to Bluetooth-enabled devices such as mobile phones, PDAs, or laptop computers.

bluesnarfing   The unauthorized access of information from a Bluetooth-enabled device through a Bluetooth connection, often between phones, desktops, laptops, and PDAs.

Border Gateway Protocol (BGP)   The interdomain routing protocol implemented in Internet Protocol (IP) networks to enable routing between autonomous systems.

botnet   A term for a collection of software robots, or bots, that run autonomously and automatically and commonly invisibly in the background. The term is most often associated with malicious software, but it can also refer to the network of computers using distributed computing software.

buffer overflow   A specific type of software coding error that enables user input to overflow the allocated storage area and corrupt a running program.

Bureau of Industry and Security (BIS)   In the U.S. Department of Commerce, the department responsible for export administration regulations that cover encryption technology in the United States.

cache   The temporary storage of information before use, typically used to speed up systems. In an Internet context, refers to the storage of commonly accessed web pages, graphic files, and other content locally on a user's PC or a web server. The cache helps to minimize download time and preserve bandwidth for frequently accessed web sites, and it helps reduce the load on a web server.

Capability Maturity Model (CMM)   A structured methodology helping organizations improve the maturity of their software processes by providing an evolutionary path from ad hoc processes to disciplined software management processes. Developed at Carnegie Mellon University's Software Engineering Institute.

centralized management   A type of privilege management that brings the authority and responsibility for managing and maintaining rights and privileges into a single group, location, or area.

CERT   *See* Computer Emergency Response Team.

certificate   A cryptographically signed object that contains an identity and a public key associated with this identity. The certificate can be used to establish identity, analogous to a notarized written document.

certificate revocation list (CRL)   A digitally signed object that lists all of the current but revoked certificates issued by a given certification authority. This allows users to verify whether a certificate is currently valid even if it has not expired. CRL is analogous to a list of stolen charge card numbers that allows stores to reject bad credit cards.

certification authority (CA)   An entity responsible for issuing and revoking certificates. CAs are typically not associated with the company requiring the certificate, although they exist for internal company use as well (such as Microsoft). This term is also applied to server software that provides these services. The term *certificate authority* is used interchangeably with *certification authority*.

chain of custody   Rules for documenting, handling, and safeguarding evidence to ensure no unanticipated changes are made to the evidence.

Challenge Handshake Authentication Protocol (CHAP)   Used to provide authentication across point-to-point links using the Point-to-Point Protocol (PPP).

change (configuration) management A standard methodology for performing and recording changes during software development and operation.

change control board (CCB) A body that oversees the change management process and enables management to oversee and coordinate projects.

CHAP *See* Challenge Handshake Authentication Protocol.

CIA of security Refers to confidentiality, integrity, and authorization, the basic functions of any security system.

cipher A cryptographic system that accepts plaintext input and then outputs ciphertext according to its internal algorithm and key.

ciphertext Used to denote the output of an encryption algorithm. Ciphertext is the encrypted data.

CIRT *See* Computer Emergency Response Team.

cold site An inexpensive form of backup site that does not include a current set of data at all times. A cold site takes longer to get your operational system back up, but it is considerably less expensive than a warm or hot site.

collisions Used in the analysis of hashing cryptography, it is the property by which an algorithm will produce the same hash from two different sets of data.

Computer Emergency Response Team (CERT) Also known as a computer incident response team, this group is responsible for investigating and responding to security breaches, viruses, and other potentially catastrophic incidents.

computer security In general terms, the methods, techniques, and tools used to ensure that a computer system is secure.

computer software configuration item *See* configuration item.

confidentiality Part of the CIA of security. Refers to the security principle that states that information should not be disclosed to unauthorized individuals.

configuration auditing The process of verifying that configuration items are built and maintained according to requirements, standards, or contractual agreements.

configuration control The process of controlling changes to items that have been baselined.

configuration identification The process of identifying which assets need to be managed and controlled.

configuration item   Data and software (or other assets) that are identified and managed as part of the software change management process. Also known as computer software configuration item.

configuration status accounting   Procedures for tracking and maintaining data relative to each configuration item in the baseline.

control   A measure taken to detect, prevent, or mitigate the risk associated with a threat.

cookie   Information stored on a user's computer by a web server to maintain the state of the connection to the web server. Used primarily so preferences or previously used information can be recalled on future requests to the server.

countermeasure   *See* control.

cracking   A term used by some to refer to malicious hacking, in which an individual attempts to gain unauthorized access to computer systems or networks. *See also* hacking.

CRC   *See* Cyclic Redundancy Check.

CRL   *See* Certificate Revocation List

cryptanalysis   The process of attempting to break a cryptographic system.

cryptography   The art of secret writing that enables an individual to hide the contents of a message or file from all but the intended recipient.

Cyclic Redundancy Check (CRC)   An error detection technique that uses a series of two, 8-bit block check characters to represent an entire block of data. These block check characters are incorporated into the transmission frame and then checked at the receiving end.

DAC   *See* Discretionary Access Control.

Data Encryption Standard (DES)   A private key encryption algorithm adopted by the government as a standard for the protection of sensitive but unclassified information. Commonly used in triple DES, where three rounds are applied to provide greater security.

datagram   A packet of data that can be transmitted over a packet-switched system in a connectionless mode.

decision tree   A data structure in which each element in the structure is attached to one or more structures directly beneath it.

demilitarized zone (DMZ)   A network segment that exists in a semi-protected zone between the Internet and the inner secure trusted network.

denial-of-service (DoS) attack   An attack in which actions are taken to deprive authorized individuals from accessing a system, its resources, the data it stores or processes, or the network to which it is connected.

DES   *See* Data Encryption Standard.

DHCP   *See* Dynamic Host Configuration Protocol.

DIAMETER   The DIAMETER base protocol is intended to provide an authentication, authorization, and accounting (AAA) framework for applications such as network access or IP mobility. DIAMETER is a draft IETF proposal.

Diffie-Hellman   A cryptographic method of establishing a shared key over an insecure medium in a secure fashion.

digital signature   A cryptography-based artifact that is a key component of a public key infrastructure (PKI) implementation. A digital signature can be used to prove identity because it is created with the private key portion of a public/private key pair. A recipient can decrypt the signature and, by doing so, receive the assurance that the data must have come from the sender and that the data has not changed.

direct-sequence spread spectrum (DSSS)   A method of distributing a communication over multiple frequencies to avoid interference and detection.

disaster recovery plan (DRP)   A written plan developed to address how an organization will react to a natural or manmade disaster in order to ensure business continuity. Related to the concept of a business continuity plan (BCP).

discretionary access control (DAC)   An access control mechanism in which the owner of an object (such as a file) can decide which other subjects (such as other users) may have access to the object, and what access (read, write, execute) these objects can have.

distributed denial-of-service (DDoS) attack   A special type of DoS attack in which the attacker elicits the generally unwilling support of other systems to launch a many-against-one attack.

diversity of defense   The approach of creating dissimilar security layers so that an intruder who is able to breach one layer will be faced with an entirely different set of defenses at the next layer.

Domain Name Service (DNS)   The service that translates an Internet domain name (such as www.mcgraw-hill.com) into IP addresses.

DRP   *See* disaster recovery plan.

DSSS   *See* direct-sequence spread spectrum.

dumpster diving   The practice of searching through trash to discover material that has been thrown away that is sensitive, yet not destroyed or shredded.

Dynamic Host Configuration Protocol (DHCP)   An Internet Engineering Task Force (IETF) Internet Protocol (IP) specification for automatically allocating IP addresses and other configuration information based on network adapter addresses. It enables address pooling and allocation and simplifies TCP/IP installation and administration.

EAP   *See* Extensible Authentication Protocol.

elliptic curve cryptography (ECC)   A method of public-key cryptography based on the algebraic structure of elliptic curves over finite fields.

Encapsulating Security Payload (ESP)   A portion of the IPsec implementation that provides for data confidentiality with optional authentication and replay-detection services. ESP completely encapsulates user data in the datagram and can be used either by itself or in conjunction with Authentication Headers for varying degrees of IPsec services.

escalation auditing   The process of looking for an increase in privileges, such as when an ordinary user obtains administrator-level privileges.

evidence   The documents, verbal statements, and material objects admissible in a court of law.

exposure factor   A measure of the magnitude of loss of an asset. Used in the calculation of single loss expectancy (SLE).

Extensible Authentication Protocol (EAP)   A universal authentication framework used in wireless networks and Point-to-Point connections. It is defined in RFC 3748 and has been updated by RFC 5247.

false positive   Term used when a security system makes an error and incorrectly reports the existence of a searched-for object. Examples include an intrusion detection system that misidentifies benign traffic as hostile, an antivirus program that reports the existence of a virus in software that actually is not infected, or a biometric system that allows access to a system to an unauthorized individual.

FHSS   *See* frequency-hopping spread spectrum.

File Transfer Protocol (FTP)   An application level protocol used to transfer files over a network connection.

firewall   A network device used to segregate traffic based on rules.

forensics (or computer forensics)   The preservation, identification, documentation, and interpretation of computer data for use in legal proceedings.

free space   Sectors on a storage medium that are available for the operating system to use.

frequency-hopping spread spectrum (FHSS)   A method of distributing a communication over multiple frequencies over time to avoid interference and detection.

Generic Routing Encapsulation (GRE)   A tunneling protocol designed to encapsulate a wide variety of network layer packets inside IP tunneling packets.

hacking   The term used by the media to refer to the process of gaining unauthorized access to computer systems and networks. The term has also been used to refer to the process of delving deep into the code and protocols used in computer systems and networks. *See also* cracking.

hash   Form of encryption that creates a digest of the data put into the algorithm. These algorithms are referred to as one-way algorithms because there is no feasible way to decrypt what has been encrypted.

hash value   *See* message digest.

HIDS   *See* host-based intrusion detection system.

HIPS   *See* host-based intrusion prevention system.

honeypot   A computer system or portion of a network that has been set up to attract potential intruders, in the hope that they will leave the other systems alone. Since there are no legitimate users of this system, any attempt to access it is an indication of unauthorized activity and provides an easy mechanism to spot attacks.

host-based intrusion detection system (HIDS)   A system that looks for computer intrusions by monitoring activity on one or more individual PCs or servers.

host-based intrusion prevention system (HIPS)   A system that automatically responds to computer intrusions by monitoring activity on one or more individual PCs or servers and with the response being based on a rule set.

hot site   A backup site that is fully configured with equipment and data and is ready to immediately accept transfer of operational processing in the event of failure on operational system.

Hypertext Transfer Protocol (HTTP)   A protocol for transfer of material across the Internet that contains links to additional material.

ICMP   *See* Internet Control Message Protocol.

IDEA   *See* International Data Encryption Algorithm.

IEEE   *See* Institute for Electrical and Electronics Engineers.

PART VI

IETF   *See* Internet Engineering Task Force.

IKE   *See* Internet Key Exchange.

impact   The result of a vulnerability being exploited by a threat, resulting in a loss.

incident response   The process of responding to, containing, analyzing, and recovering from a computer-related incident.

information security   Often used synonymously with computer security but places the emphasis on the protection of the information that the system processes and stores, instead of on the hardware and software that constitute the system.

Institute for Electrical and Electronics Engineers (IEEE)   A nonprofit, technical, professional institute associated with computer research, standards, and conferences.

intangible asset   An asset for which a monetary equivalent is difficult or impossible to determine. Examples are brand recognition and goodwill.

integrity   Part of the CIA of security, the security principle that requires that information is not modified except by individuals authorized to do so.

International Data Encryption Algorithm (IDEA)   A symmetric encryption algorithm used in a variety of systems for bulk encryption services.

Internet Assigned Numbers Authority (IANA)   The central coordinator for the assignment of unique parameter values for Internet protocols. The IANA is chartered by the Internet Society (ISOC) to act as the clearinghouse to assign and coordinate the use of numerous Internet protocol parameters.

Internet Control Message Protocol (ICMP)   One of the core protocols of the TCP/IP protocol suite, used for error reporting and status messages.

Internet Engineering Task Force (IETF)   A large international community of network designers, operators, vendors, and researchers, open to any interested individual concerned with the evolution of the Internet architecture and the smooth operation of the Internet. The actual technical work of the IETF is done in its working groups, which are organized by topic into several areas (such as routing, transport, and security). Much of the work is handled via mailing lists, with meetings held three times per year.

Internet Key Exchange (IKE)   The protocol formerly known as ISAKMP/Oakley, defined in RFC 2409. A hybrid protocol that uses part Oakley and part of Secure Key Exchange Mechanism for Internet (SKEMI) protocol suites inside the Internet Security Association and Key Management Protocol (ISAKMP) framework. IKE is used to establish a shared security policy and authenticated keys for services that require keys (such as IPsec).

Internet Message Access Protocol version 4 (IMAP4)   One of two common Internet standard protocols for e-mail retrieval.

Internet Protocol (IP)   The network layer protocol used by the Internet for routing packets across a network.

Internet Protocol Security (IPsec)   A protocol used to secure IP packets during transmission across a network. IPsec offers authentication, integrity, and confidentiality services and uses Authentication Headers (AH) and Encapsulating Security Payload (ESP) to accomplish this functionality.

Internet Security Association and Key Management Protocol (ISAKMP)   A protocol framework that defines the mechanics of implementing a key exchange protocol and negotiation of a security policy.

Internet service provider (ISP)   A telecommunications firm that provides access to the Internet.

intrusion detection system (IDS)   A system to identify suspicious, malicious, or undesirable activity that indicates a breach in computer security.

IPsec   *See* Internet Protocol Security.

ISAKMP/Oakley   *See* Internet Key Exchange.

Kerberos   A network authentication protocol designed by MIT for use in client/server environments.

key   In cryptography, a sequence of characters or bits used by an algorithm to encrypt or decrypt a message.

keyspace   The entire set of all possible keys for a specific encryption algorithm.

LDAP   *See* Lightweight Directory Access Protocol.

least privilege   A security principle in which a user is provided with the minimum set of rights and privileges that he or she needs to perform required functions. The goal is to limit the potential damage that any user can cause.

Level Two Tunneling Protocol (L2TP)   A Cisco switching protocol that operates at the data-link layer.

Lightweight Directory Access Protocol (LDAP)   An application protocol used to access directory services across a TCP/IP network.

local area network (LAN)   A grouping of computers in a network structure confined to a limited area and using specific protocols, such as Ethernet for OSI layer 2 traffic addressing.

logic bomb A form of malicious code or software that is triggered by a specific event or condition. *See also* time bomb.

MAC *See* mandatory access control or Media Access Control.

man-in-the-middle attack Any attack that attempts to use a network node as the intermediary between two other nodes. Each of the endpoint nodes thinks it is talking directly to the other, but each is actually talking to the intermediary.

mandatory access control (MAC) An access control mechanism in which the security mechanism controls access to all objects (files), and individual subjects (processes or users) cannot change that access.

MD5 Message Digest 5, a hashing algorithm and a specific method of producing a message digest.

Media Access Control (MAC) A protocol used in the data-link layer for local network addressing.

message digest The result of applying a hash function to data. Sometimes also called a hash value. *See* hash.

metropolitan area network (MAN) A collection of networks interconnected in a metropolitan area and usually connected to the Internet.

Microsoft Challenge Handshake Authentication Protocol (MSCHAP) A Microsoft developed variant of the Challenge Handshake Authentication Protocol (CHAP).

mitigate Action taken to reduce the likelihood of a threat occurring.

MSCHAP *See* Microsoft Challenge Handshake Authentication Protocol.

NAC *See* Network Access Control.

NAP *See* Network Access Protection.

NAT *See* Network Address Translation.

Network Access Control (NAC) An approach to endpoint security that involves monitoring and remediating end point security issues before allowing an object to connect to a network.

Network Access Protection (NAP) A Microsoft approach to Network Access Control.

Network Address Translation (NAT)   A method of readdressing packets in a network at a gateway point to enable the use of local nonroutable IP addresses over a public network such as the Internet.

network-based intrusion detection system (NIDS)   A system for examining network traffic to identify suspicious, malicious, or undesirable behavior.

network-based intrusion prevention system (NIPS)   A system that examines network traffic and automatically responds to computer intrusions.

network operating system (NOS)   An operating system that includes additional functions and capabilities to assist in connecting computers and devices, such as printers, to a local area network.

nonrepudiation   The ability to verify that an operation has been performed by a particular person or account. This is a system property that prevents the parties to a transaction from subsequently denying involvement in the transaction.

Oakley protocol   A key exchange protocol that defines how to acquire authenticated keying material based on the Diffie-Hellman key exchange algorithm.

object reuse   Assignment of a previously used medium to a subject. The security implication is that before it is provided to the subject, any data present from a previous user must be cleared.

one-time pad   An unbreakable encryption scheme in which a series of nonrepeating, random bits are used once as a key to encrypt a message. Since each pad is used only once, no pattern can be established and traditional cryptanalysis techniques are not effective.

Open Vulnerability and Assessment Language (OVAL)   An XML-based standard for the communication of security information between tools and services.

operating system (OS)   The basic software that handles input, output, display, memory management, and all the other highly detailed tasks required to support the user environment and associated applications.

Orange Book   The name commonly used to refer to the now outdated Department of Defense Trusted Computer Security Evaluation Criteria (TCSEC).

OVAL   *See* Open Vulnerability and Assessment Language.

P2P   *See* peer-to-peer.

PAP   *See* Password Authentication Protocol.

PART VI

password   A string of characters used to prove an individual's identity to a system or object. Used in conjunction with a user ID, it is the most common method of authentication. The password should be kept secret by the individual who owns it.

Password Authentication Protocol (PAP)   A simple protocol used to authenticate a user to a network access server.

patch   A replacement set of code designed to correct problems or vulnerabilities in existing software.

PBX   *See* private branch exchange.

peer-to-peer (P2P)   A network connection methodology involving direct connection from peer to peer.

penetration testing   A security test in which an attempt is made to circumvent security controls in order to discover vulnerabilities and weaknesses. Also called a pen test.

permissions   Authorized actions a subject can perform on an object. *See also* access controls.

personally identifiable information (PII)   Information that can be used to identify a single person.

phreaking   Used in the media to refer to the hacking of computer systems and networks associated with the phone company. *See also* cracking.

PII   *See* personally identifiable information.

plaintext   In cryptography, a piece of data that is not encrypted. It can also mean the data input into a encryption algorithm that would output ciphertext.

Point-to-Point Protocol (PPP)   The Internet standard for transmission of IP packets over a serial line, as in a dial-up connection to an ISP.

Point-to-Point Protocol Extensible Authentication Protocol (PPP EAP)   EAP is a PPP extension that provides support for additional authentication methods within PPP.

Point-to-Point Protocol Password Authentication Protocol (PPP PAP)   PAP is a PPP extension that provides support for password authentication methods over PPP.

Pretty Good Privacy (PGP)   A popular encryption program that has the ability to encrypt and digitally sign e-mail and files.

preventative intrusion detection   A system that detects hostile actions or network activity and prevents them from impacting information systems.

privacy   Protecting an individual's personal information from those not authorized to see it.

private branch exchange (PBX)   A telephone exchange that serves a specific business or entity.

privilege auditing   The process of checking the rights and privileges assigned to a specific account or group of accounts.

privilege management   The process of restricting a user's ability to interact with the computer system.

public key cryptography   *See* asymmetric encryption.

public key infrastructure (PKI)   Infrastructure for binding a public key to a known user through a trusted intermediary, typically a certificate authority.

qualitative risk assessment   The process of subjectively determining the impact of an event that affects a project, program, or business. It involves the use of expert judgment, experience, or group consensus to complete the assessment.

quantitative risk assessment   The process of objectively determining the impact of an event that affects a project, program, or business. It usually involves the use of metrics and models to complete the assessment.

RADIUS   Remote Authentication Dial-In User Service is a standard protocol for providing authentication services. It is commonly used in dial-up, wireless, and PPP environments.

RAS   *See* Remote Access Service.

RBAC   *See* rule-based access control or role-based access control.

Remote Access Service (RAS)   A combination of hardware and software used to enable remote access to a network.

repudiation   The act of denying that a message was either sent or received.

residual risk   Risks remaining after an iteration of risk management.

risk   The possibility of suffering a loss.

risk assessment or risk analysis   The process of analyzing an environment to identify the threats, vulnerabilities, and mitigating actions to determine (either quantitatively or qualitatively) the impact of an event affecting a project, program, or business.

risk management   Overall decision-making process of identifying threats and vulnerabilities and their potential impacts, determining the costs to mitigate such events, and deciding what actions are cost effective to take to control these risks.

role-based access control (RBAC)   An access control mechanism in which, instead of the users being assigned specific access permissions for the objects associated with the computer system or network, a set of roles that the user may perform is assigned to each user.

rule-based access control (RBAC)   An access control mechanism based on rules.

safeguard   *See* control.

Secure Hash Algorithm (SHA)   A hash algorithm used to hash block data. The first version is SHA1, with subsequent versions detailing hash digest length: SHA256, SHA384, and SHA512.

Secure/Multipurpose Internet Mail Extensions (S/MIME)   An encrypted implementation of the MIME (Multipurpose Internet Mail Extensions) protocol specification.

Secure Shell (SSH)   A set of protocols for establishing a secure remote connection to a computer. This protocol requires a client on each end of the connection and can use a variety of encryption protocols.

Secure Sockets Layer (SSL)   An encrypting layer between the session and transport layer of the OSI model designed to encrypt above the transport layer, enabling secure sessions between hosts.

security association (SA)   An instance of security policy and keying material applied to a specific data flow. Both IKE and IPsec use SAs, although these SAs are independent of one another. IPsec SAs are unidirectional and are unique in each security protocol, whereas IKE SAs are bidirectional. A set of SAs are needed for a protected data pipe, one per direction per protocol. SAs are uniquely identified by destination (IPsec endpoint) address, security protocol (AH or ESP), and security parameter index (SPI).

security baseline   The end result of the process of establishing an information system's security state. It is a known good configuration resistant to attacks and information theft.

segregation or separation of duties   A basic control that prevents or detects errors and irregularities by assigning responsibilities to different individuals so that no single individual can commit fraudulent or malicious actions.

service set identifier (SSID)   Identifies a specific 802.11 wireless network. It transmits information about the access point to which the wireless client is connecting.

signature database   A collection of activity patterns that have already been identified and categorized and that typically indicate suspicious or malicious activity.

Simple Mail Transfer Protocol (SMTP)   The standard Internet protocol used to transfer e-mail between hosts.

single loss expectancy (SLE)   Monetary loss or impact of each occurrence of a threat. SLE = asset value * exposure factor.

single sign-on (SSO)   An authentication process by which the user can enter a single user ID and password and then move from application to application or resource to resource without having to supply further authentication information.

slack space   Unused space on a disk drive created when a file is smaller than the allocated unit of storage (such as a sector).

sniffer   A software or hardware device used to observe network traffic as it passes through a network on a shared broadcast media.

social engineering   The art of deceiving another person so that he or she reveals confidential information. This is often accomplished by posing as an individual who should be entitled to have access to the information.

spam   E-mail that is not requested by the recipient and is typically of a commercial nature. Also known as unsolicited commercial e-mail (UCE).

spoofing   Making data appear to have originated from another source so as to hide the true origin from the recipient.

symmetric encryption   Encryption that needs all parties to have a copy of the key, sometimes called a shared secret. The single key is used for both encryption and decryption.

tangible asset   An asset for which a monetary equivalent can be determined. Examples are inventory, buildings, cash, hardware, software, and so on.

Tempest   The U.S. military's name for the field associated with electromagnetic eavesdropping on signals emitted by electronic equipment. *See also* van Eck phenomenon.

Temporal Key Integrity Protocol (TKIP)   A security protocol used in 802.11 wireless networks.

threat   Any circumstance or event with the potential to cause harm to an asset.

time bomb   A form of logic bomb in which the triggering event is a date or specific time. *See also* logic bomb.

TKIP   *See* Temporal Key Integrity Protocol.

token A hardware device that can be used in a challenge-response authentication process.

Transmission Control Protocol (TCP) The transport layer protocol for use on the Internet that allows packet-level tracking of a conversation.

Transport Layer Security (TLS) A newer form of SSL being proposed as an Internet standard.

trapdoor *See* backdoor.

Trojan horse A form of malicious code that appears to provide one service (and may indeed provide that service) but that also hides another purpose. This hidden purpose often has a malicious intent. This code may also be referred to as simply a Trojan.

Trusted Platform Module (TPM) A hardware chip to enable trusted computing platform operations.

uninterruptible power supply (UPS) A source of power (generally a battery) designed to provide uninterrupted power to a computer system in the event of a temporary loss of power.

usage auditing The process of recording who did what and when on an information system.

User Datagram Protocol (UDP) A protocol in the TCP/IP protocol suite for the transport layer that does not sequence packets—it is "fire and forget" in nature.

User ID A unique alphanumeric identifier that identifies individuals when logging in or accessing a system.

vampire taps A tap that connects to a network line without cutting the connection.

Van Eck phenomenon Electromagnetic eavesdropping through the interception of electronic signals emitted by electrical equipment. *See also* Tempest.

virtual local area network (VLAN) A broadcast domain inside a switched system.

virtual private network (VPN) An encrypted network connection across another network, offering a private communication channel across a public medium.

virus A form of malicious code or software that attaches itself to other pieces of code in order to replicate. Viruses may contain a payload, which is a portion of the code that is designed to execute when a certain condition is met (such as on a certain date). This payload is often malicious in nature.

vulnerability   A weakness in an asset that can be exploited by a threat to cause harm.

WAP   *See* Wireless Application Protocol.

war-dialing   An attacker's attempt to gain unauthorized access to a computer system or network by discovering unprotected connections to the system through the telephone system and modems.

war-driving   The attempt by an attacker to discover unprotected wireless networks by wandering (or driving) around with a wireless device, looking for available wireless access points.

WEP   *See* Wired Equivalent Privacy.

wide area network (WAN)   A network that spans a large geographic region.

Wi-Fi Protected Access (WPA/WPA2)   A protocol to secure wireless communications using a subset of 802.11i standard.

Wired Equivalent Privacy (WEP)   The encryption scheme used to attempt to provide confidentiality and data integrity on 802.11 networks.

Wireless Application Protocol (WAP)   A protocol for transmitting data to small handheld devices such as cellular phones.

Wireless Transport Layer Security (WTLS)   The encryption protocol used on WAP networks.

worm   An independent piece of malicious code or software that self-replicates. Unlike a virus, it does not need to be attached to another piece of code. A worm replicates by breaking into another system and making a copy of itself on this new system. A worm can contain a destructive payload but does not have to.

X.509   The standard format for digital certificates.

XOR   Bitwise exclusive OR, an operation commonly used in cryptography.

PART VI

1G mobile networks, 277
2G mobile networks, 277
3DES (Triple DES), 89–90
3G mobile networks, 276, 277, 279
4G mobile networks, 276, 277
9/11 attack, 58–59
128-bit hash, 85
802.1x standard, 247
802.11 protocol, 281–289
    overview, 247, 260, 281–283
    security issues, 283–289
    versions, 275–276, 281–282, 287
    WEP and, 177

A

AAA (authentication, authorization, and
    accounting), 242, 248
acceptable use policy (AUP), 39–40
access, described, 16
access cards, 192
access control, 16–19. *See also* permissions;
    remote access
    basics, 191–193
    confidential security level, 545
    described, 12, 16–17, 19, 191
    discretionary, 18, 545–546
    electronic systems for, 192–193
    elements of, 242–247
    group policy, 30–31
    implicit deny, 11–12
    logical, 30–34
    mandatory, 18–19, 543–545
    methods for, 17–20
    need-to-know principle, 18–19, 42
    privilege management, 543–547
    role-based, 19, 546
    rule-based, 19, 546–548
    secret security level, 544
    top secret security level, 544
    unclassified security level, 545
    vs. authentication, 16

Access Control knowledge domain, 3, 5
access control lists. *See* ACLs
access control matrix, 17
access logs, 542
access points (APs)
    rogue, 285
    wireless, 212–213, 281, 283, 285
access tokens, 192, 194–195
accounting, described, 242
ACK packets, 395–396, 403
ACLs (access control lists)
    described, 17, 30
    discretionary access control, 545
    IIS, 373–374
    logical access controls, 30–34
    routers, 208–209
    rule-based access, 19, 546–548
    traffic filtering, 368–370
ACs (Attribute Certificates), 157, 159
Active Directory (AD), 381–382
active HIDS, 306
active NIDSs, 320
ActiveX, 459–461
ActiveX controls, 459, 460
AD. *See* Active Directory
Adams, Carlisle, 91
address system attacks, 406–407
administrative law, 56
administrator accounts, 531. *See also* user
    accounts
Advanced Encryption Standard (AES), 87,
    90–91
AES (Advanced Encryption Standard), 87,
    90–91
affinity grouping, 508
AH (Authentication Header), 175, 265–268
AirSnort program, 285, 286
ALE (annualized loss expectancy), 495, 506–507
alert message truncation attack, 278
algorithms, 78. *See also* encryption algorithms
analysis engine, 299, 303, 316
Anderson, James, 298

Anderson, Ross, 90
annualized loss expectancy (ALE), 495, 506–507
annualized rate of occurrence (ARO), 495, 507
anomaly detection, 322–323, 360
anonymizing proxies, 327
anonymous FTP, 454
anti-spam solutions, 331–333
antivirus logs, 542
antivirus products, 307–310. *See also* viruses
    considerations, 427–428
    encryption and, 308–309
    features, 309
    heuristic scanning, 308
    history of, 308–309
    overview, 308–309
    servers, 205
    signature-based scanning, 308
    workstations, 202–203
Apache web server, 376–377
APIs (application programming interfaces), 115
applets, signed, 465–466
appliances, 317
application layer, 574
application layer proxies, 212
application programming interfaces (APIs), 115
application servers, 205
application-level attacks, 415–416
applications. *See also* software
    bugs, 268
    cryptographic, 103–104
    hardening, 370–382
    malware, 54, 426, 427
    patches, 371, 416
    rogue, 437
    security issues, 10–11
    security programs, 542
    Trojan horse, 412, 427, 451
    upgrades, 371
    viruses, 410
    vulnerabilities, 467–468
APs. *See* access points
ARL (authority revocation list), 129
ARO (annualized rate of occurrence), 495, 507
AS (authentication server), 244
assessments, security, 502–508
Assessments & Audits knowledge domain, 3, 4, 6
assets
    change management, 517, 518
    defined, 494

hiding, 15
identifying, 499
risks associated with, 498
asymmetric encryption, 95–103, 173
ATM cards, 20
attacks, 391–424
    address system, 406–407
    application-level, 415–416
    avenues of, 391–394
    backdoors, 398
    birthday, 409
    brute-force, 81, 342, 343, 365, 408–409
    buffer overflow, 409, 456
    collision, 82, 84, 85
    DDoS, 396–398, 427
    dictionary, 342, 408
    DNS system, 406–407
    DoS, 187–188, 394–398
    on encryption, 405–406
    hacking, 6–7
    "hacktivist," 391
    hijack, 405
    hybrid, 409
    indirect, 406
    logic bombs, 413
    malicious code, 409–416, 426–428
    man-in-the-middle, 110, 403–404
    minimizing, 394
    null sessions, 398
    password guessing, 407–409
    performing, 393–394
    ping of death, 318–319, 396
    reasons for, 391–392
    reconnaissance, 392
    replay, 404–405
    researching vulnerabilities, 393
    rootkits, 398, 413–414
    scanning. *See* scanning
    security audits and, 417–418
    smurf, 401
    sniffing. *See* sniffers/sniffing
    social engineering. *See* social engineering
    software exploitation, 409
    spoofing. *See* spoofing
    spyware, 307, 313–314, 412–413
    steps in, 392–394
    SYN flooding, 395–396, 402
    targeted, 391, 392
    TCP/IP hijacking, 405

time bombs, 413
trapdoors, 96, 398
Trojan horses, 412
viruses. *See* viruses
war-dialing, 416–417
war-driving, 416–417
worms. *See* worms
Attribute Certificates (ACs), 157, 159
audit logs, 134
audit trails, 301, 538
auditing, 538–541
    considerations, 417–418
    escalation, 540–541
    firewall rules, 543
    log files, 541–543
    overview, 538
    privilege, 538–539
    records retention, 543
    security settings, 542–543
    storage, 543
    usage, 539–540
    user access, 543
    user rights, 543
AUP (acceptable use policy), 39–40
authentication, 243–247. *See also* passwords;
  privileges
    802.1x standard, 247
    access tokens, 194–195
    basics, 19–20, 101–102, 194
    biometric systems, 20, 195–197, 244
    certificates, 245
    challenge/response, 245–246, 256–257
    CHAP, 256–257
    cryptographic algorithms, 101–102
    described, 16, 101, 194, 241, 242, 243
    DIAMETER, 248, 250
    EAP, 257
    examples of, 16–17, 101
    Kerberos, 244–245
    L2TP, 254, 257
    lock/key systems, 20, 243
    m of n, 134
    methods for, 19–20
    multifactor, 246
    multiple-factor, 195, 196–197
    mutual, 246–247
    NTLM, 258
    one-way, 101–102
    overview, 19–20

PAP, 257
passwords. *See* passwords
physical security, 194–197
PPP, 256
PPTP, 254–256
RADIUS, 248–250
remote access, 243–266
single sign-on, 246, 535–536
TACACS+, 251–253
tokens. *See* tokens
two-way, 101–102
user IDs, 20
vs. access control, 16
authentication, authorization, and accounting
  (AAA), 242, 248
Authentication Header (AH), 175, 265–268
authentication server (AS), 244
Authenticode, 460, 461
authority revocation list (ARL), 129
authorization
    described, 242, 247
    DIAMETER, 248, 250
    RADIUS, 250
    remote access, 247
    TACACS+, 253
autorun feature, 189–190
availability, 7, 8, 201

B

Back Orifice (BO), 398, 411
    configuration, 364–366
backdoors, 398
backup generators, 487
backups, 478–487
    alternative sites for, 483, 484–485
    data retention, 482–483
    delta, 481
    differential, 480, 481
    frequency of, 482
    full, 480, 481
    incremental, 481
    online storage, 483–484
    overview, 478–479
    RAID techniques, 485–486
    single points of failure, 486–487
    storage of, 483–484
    strategies, 479–487

transactional, 481
what to back up, 479
badges, security, 191, 193
banking transactions, 8
banner grabbing, 393
Basel Committee on Banking Supervision, 494, 498
baseline identification/analysis, 508
baselines. *See* security baselines
batch mode, 300
BCPs (business continuity plans), 478
Berkeley Internet Name Domain (BIND), 380
Berners-Lee, Tim, 443
BIA (business impact statement), 476
Biham, Eli, 90
Bill of Rights, 41
binary assessment, 503
BIND (Berkeley Internet Name Domain), 380
biometric systems, 20, 101, 196–197
biometrics, 20, 195–197, 244
BIOS passwords, 190
birthday attacks, 409
birthday paradox, 409
BIS (Bureau of Industry and Security), 61
Bitlocker encryption, 80, 103–104, 346
black hats, 418
blacklist services, 430
blacklisting, 332
blind FTP, 454
block ciphers, 87, 90, 92
Blowfish cipher, 94
Blue Pill rootkit, 414
blue screen of death, 457
bluebugging, 280–281
bluejacking, 280
Blue-ray format, 228
bluesnarfing, 280
Bluetooth technology, 276, 279–281
BO (Back Orifice), 60, 411
boot sector viruses, 410
bootable CDs/DVDs, 186–187
bootdisks, 186–187, 189
botnets, 54
branches, 302
bridge CAs, 144
bridges, 206
browsers. *See* web browsers
brute-force attacks, 81, 342, 343, 365, 408–409
buffer overflow attacks, 409, 456

buffer overflows, 378, 379, 409
bugs, 268
buildings. *See* physical security
bump key, 192
Bureau of Industry and Security (BIS), 61
business continuity management risks, 497, 498
business continuity plans (BCPs), 478
business dependencies, 501
business functions, 477–478
business impact statement (BIA), 476
business system controls, 498

C

cable modems, 214–215
cables, 219–222
cache, web, 328
caching proxies, 327–328
Caesar's cipher, 78–79
Cain & Able tool, 341
California Senate Bill 1386 (SB 1386), 67
callback verification, 332
cameras, security, 193
Canadian laws/regulations, 64
CAN-SPAM Act of 2003, 331
Capability Maturity Model (CMM), 522–523
Capability Maturity Model Integration (CMMI), 522–523
CAPI (Crypto API) interface, 115
Carlisle Adams and Stafford Tavares. *See* CAST
Carnivore program, 58–59
CAs. *See* certificate authorities
CAST (Carlisle Adams and Stafford Tavares) algorithm, 173–174
CAST-128 algorithm, 91
CAST-256 algorithm, 91
cause/effect analysis, 508
CC (Common Criteria), 176
CCB (change control board), 520–522
CCMP (Cipher Block Chaining-Message Authentication Coded Protocol), 287
CCTV (closed circuit television) systems, 193
CD Universe hack, 455
CD-R discs, 228
CD-R drives, 226
CD-ROM drives, 190
CD-RW discs, 228
CDs
bootable, 186–187
deleting data on, 43

included with book, 569–570
live, 559, 563
security issuesk, 227–228
cell phones, 276–279
centralized infrastructures, 130–131
centralized management, 536–537
CEP (Certificate Enrollment Protocol), 175
CERN (European Laboratory for Particle
Physics), 443
CERT (Computer Emergency Response Team),
415
certificate authorities (CAs). *See also* certificates;
digital certificates
basics, 112–113
bridge CAs, 144
certificate revocation lists, 126–129
certificate server, 112
certification practices statement, 112
classes, 113–114
described, 122
examples of, 110–111
hierarchical model, 122
in-house, 136, 137
internal, 117, 136, 137
outsourced, 138–139
overview, 112–113
private, 136
public, 136
registration authorities, 113–116
revoked certificates, 119, 126–128
root, 122, 131, 142–144
self-signed, 122
subordinate, 142
superior, 122
trust in, 113, 116–120
trust models, 140–146
validating, 143–144
verifying certificates, 116–120, 140–144
web browsers and, 117, 136
Certificate Enrollment Protocol (CEP), 175
Certificate Management Protocol (CMP),
168–169
certificate path, 143–144
certificate policy (CP), 136
certificate revocation lists. *See* CRLs
certificate server, 112
certificates. *See also* certificate authorities; digital
certificates
Attribute Certificates, 157, 159

described, 164, 245, 448
destruction of, 129–130
establishing authenticity with, 245
extensions, 123–124
lifecycles, 124–130
lifetimes, 129
PKI, 157
repositories, 116
revoked, 126–128
self-certifying, 164
self-signed, 142, 143
suspended, 129
use of, 448–450
verifying, 116–120, 140–144
certification practices statement (CPS), 112,
128, 158
CFAA (Computer Fraud and Abuse Act), 56, 58
CGI (Common Gateway Interface), 461–462
CGI scripts, 462
chain of custody, 560
Challenge Handshake Authentication Protocol
(CHAP), 256–257
challenge/response authentication, 245–246,
256–257
challenge/response system, 430
change control board (CCB), 520–522
change management, 513–527
basics, 38–39
Capability Maturity Model Integration,
522–523
code integrity, 522
described, 498, 513
elements of, 517–519
implementing, 519–522
need for, 514–515
separation of duties, 11, 42, 134, 515–517
CHAP (Challenge Handshake Authentication
Protocol), 256–257
chmod command, 351, 354
chosen plaintext attack, 278
chown command, 351, 354
CIA (confidentiality, integrity, and availability),
7–8
Cipher Block Chaining-Message Authentication
Coded Protocol (CCMP), 287
ciphertext, 86, 89, 405
CIRT (Computer Incidence Response Team), 557
Cisco NAC (network access control) system,
216–217

classification of information, 39
clear text, 268
click fraud, 54
client-side extensions (CSEs), 382
client-to-server ticket, 244
Clipper Chip, 135
closed circuit television (CCTV) systems, 193
CMM (Capability Maturity Model), 522–523
CMMI (Capability Maturity Model Integration), 522–523
CMP (Certificate Management Protocol), 168–169
CMS (Cryptographic Message Syntax), 172–173
coaxial cables, 219
code
    HTML, 312, 427, 451
    integrity of, 522
    malicious, 409–416, 426–428
    vulnerabilities, 455–467
code of ethics, 46, 69–71
Code Red II worm, 414
Code Red worm, 414
code signing, 465–466
cold sites, 484
collision attacks, 82, 84, 85
collision domains, 206
collisions, 206
combination assessments, 503–504
Common Criteria (CC), 176
Common Gateway Interface (CGI), 461–462
common law, 56
Common Vulnerability and Exposures (CVE) list, 416, 468
compact discs. See CDs
CompTIA (Computing Technology Industry Association) Security+ exam, 3–6
CompTIA web site, 4
computer crime. See cybercrime
Computer Emergency Response Team (CERT), 415
computer forensics. See forensics
Computer Fraud and Abuse Act (CFAA), 56, 58
computer IDs, 242
Computer Incidence Response Team (CIRT), 557
computer mischief, 57
computer readers, 228–229
computer rooms, 187, 188–189, 192
computer security. See security
computer software configuration items. See assets

computer trespass, 56–57
computer-assisted crime, 54
computer-incidental crime, 54, 55
computers
    dependence on, 7
    disabling unnecessary services, 16, 204
    disposal of, 42
    as evidence, 554–558
    laptop. See laptop computers
    locking, 191
    terminated employees, 46
    theft of, 187, 191, 500
    unprotected, 500
computer-targeted crime, 54
Computing Technology Industry Association (CompTIA) Security+ exam, 3–6
Concept virus, 411
confidential security level, 545
confidentiality, 7–8, 100
confidentiality, integrity, and availability (CIA), 7–8
configuration
    devices, 364–366
    ports, 366–368
    services, 366–368
configuration auditing, 518
configuration control, 518
configuration identification, 517
configuration items. See assets
configuration management, 513, 517. See also change management
configuration status accounting, 518
conflicts of interest, 46
Constitution, 41
contactless access cards, 192
content filtering proxies, 328
content protection, 262
content-based signatures, 320–321
content-filtering systems, 328–329, 332
context-based signatures, 321
contract management risks, 497
controls
    described, 495, 501
    design/evaluation, 501
    detective, 501
    insufficient, 500
    preventive, 501
Convention on Cybercrime, 57
cookies, 285, 462–465

corporate LAN, 29–30
cost/benefit analysis, 508
countermeasures. *See* controls
CP (certificate policy), 136
CPS (certification practices statement), 112,
128, 158
Crack (UNIX) utility, 341
crackers/cracking, 7
credit card transactions, 59–60, 455
credit risks, 498
creditcards.com hack, 455
crime, computer. *See* cybercrime
critical files, 301, 302
CRL distribution, 128–129
CRL files, 128–129
CRLs (certificate revocation lists), 126–129
cross certification, 144
cross-certificates, 122
cross-scripting (XSS) worm, 415
cross-site–scripting attacks, 329
cryptanalysis, 77–78, 405
Crypto API (CAPI) interface, 115
cryptographic applications, 103–104
cryptographic keys, 87
Cryptographic Message Syntax (CMS), 172–173
cryptography, 77–107. *See also* encryption;
encryption algorithms
asymmetric encryption, 95–103
described, 405
hashing, 81–86
overview, 77–78
symmetric encryption, 86–95, 100–103
vs. steganography, 99–100
Cryptography knowledge domain, 3, 4, 6
CSEs (client-side extensions), 382
CVE (Common Vulnerability and Exposures)
list, 416, 468
cybercrime, 54–66. *See also* forensics
click fraud, 54
computer trespass, 56–57
computer-assisted crime, 54
computer-incidental crime, 54, 55
computer-targeted crime, 54
Convention on Cybercrime, 57
Digital Rights Management, 65–66
digital signature laws, 63–64
e-mail. *See* e-mail
identity theft, 37, 44, 66–67

import/export encryption restrictions,
60–63
Internet crime schemes, 55–56
laws/regulations. *See* laws/regulations
overview, 54–55
Payment Card Industry Data Security
Standards, 59–60
social engineering. *See* social engineering
types of, 54
cyber-law environment, 53

D

DAC (discretionary access control), 18, 545–546
Daemen, John, 90
DAP (Directory Access Protocol), 452–454
DAT (digital audio tape), 227
data. *See also* information
attacks on, 13
availability, 7, 8
categories, 39
classification of, 39
confidentiality, 7–8
destruction of, 37, 42–43
encrypted, 13
hiding in other data, 99–100
integrity, 8
layered security and, 13
personally identifiable information, 37,
43–44
privacy issues, 7
retention policies, 543
shredding, 37, 43
storage of, 225
unprotected, 500
data aggregation, 35
Data Encryption Standard (DES), 87–90
Data Over Cable Service Interface Specification
(DOCSIS), 214
Data Protection Directive, 68
data protection laws, 67–68
data-link layer, 576
DDoS (distributed denial-of-service) attacks,
396–398, 427
decentralized, centralized model, 538
decentralized infrastructures, 130–131
decentralized management, 537
decision tree, 302
decryption keys, 78

degaussers, 43
degaussing media, 43
delay-based filtering, 332
delegation, 381
deleted files, 43, 559, 561, 562
demilitarized zone (DMZ), 14–15, 230–231
deniable volumes, 103
denial-of-service (DoS) attacks, 187–188,
    394–398
Denning, Dorothy, 298
Department of Defense, 18
Department of Justice, 331
dependencies, business, 501
DES (Data Encryption Standard), 87–90
detection, 8
detective controls, 501
devices, 201–218. *See also* hardware
    bridges, 206
    configuration, 364–366
    failure, 500
    firewalls. *See* firewalls
    hubs, 206
    mobile, 218
    modems, 214–215
    network interface cards, 205–206
    overview, 201–202
    passwords, 364–365
    routers, 208–209
    switches, 206–208
    Telecom/PBX systems, 215
    tokens, 33–34, 245–246
    wireless, 212–213
    workstations, 202–204
DHCP (Dynamic Host Configuration Protocol),
    214
DIAMETER protocol, 248, 250
dictionary attacks, 342, 408
differential cryptanalysis, 78
Diffie, Whitfield, 95, 97
Diffie-Hellman algorithm, 95, 97, 173–174
digital audio tape (DAT), 227
digital certificates, 120–130. *See also* certificate
    authorities; certificates
    certificate extensions, 123–124
    certificate lifecycles, 124–130
    cross-certificates, 122
    described, 101–102, 120–121, 245
    end-entity certificates, 122
    key destruction, 129–130

lifetimes, 129
    network addresses, 121
    obtaining, 113–114
    policy certificates, 123
    revoked, 119, 126–128
    self-signed, 142, 143
    signed applets, 465–466
    subject of, 121
    suspended, 129
    types of, 121–123
    verifying, 116–120
    X.509 certificate, 120–121
digital linear tape (DLT), 227
Digital Millennium Copyright Act (DMCA),
    65–66
Digital Rights Management, 65–66
digital sandbox, 325
Digital Signature Algorithm (DSA), 83
Digital Signature Standard (DSS), 83
digital signatures. *See also* certificates; signatures
    certificate revocation lists, 126–128
    certificate server, 112
    cryptographic algorithms, 83, 102
    decrypting, 119–120
    described, 102
    laws/regulations, 63–64
    signed applets, 465–466
digital video discs. *See* DVDs
digraphs, 509
directories, 116, 452
Directory Access Protocol (DAP), 452–454
directory services, 452–454
disaster recovery, 475–492. *See also* disasters;
    risk management
    backup plans. *See* backups
    business continuity plans, 478
    business functions, 477–478
    communications, 487
    emergency generators, 487
    exercises, 476–477
    fault tolerance, 488
    high availability, 488
    personnel, 476
    physical resources, 476
    plans/process, 476–478
    recovery services, 487–488
    single point of failure, 486–487
    terrorist attacks, 58–59, 499
    utilities, 487

disaster recovery plans (DRPs), 476–478

disasters, 475–476, 499

discretionary access control (DAC), 18, 545–546

discs. *See* CDs; DVDs

diskettes, 43, 225, 226, 410, 426

disks. *See also* drives
  bootdisks, 186–187, 189
  floppy, 43, 225, 226, 410, 426
  hard. *See* hard drives
  Zip, 226

disposal and destruction policy, 42–43

distinguished names, 117

distributed denial-of-service (DDoS) attacks, 396–398, 427

diversity of defense, 14–15

DLT (digital linear tape), 227

DMCA (Digital Millennium Copyright Act), 65–66

DMZ (demilitarized zone), 14–15, 230–231

DNS (Domain Name Service), 379–380, 406–408

DNS checks, 332

DNS kiting, 407

DNS log files, 542

DNS poisoning, 407

DNS servers, 379–380

Dobbertin, Hans, 85

DOCSIS (Data Over Cable Service Interface Specification), 214

documents. *See also* files
  critical, 301, 302
  deleted files, 43, 559, 561, 562
  destruction of, 42–43
  shredding, 37, 43
  "undeleting," 43

domain controllers, 534

Domain Name Service. *See* DNS

domain password policy, 31–32, 534–535

domains, 31–32, 381

DoS (denial-of-service) attacks, 187–188, 394–398

drive imaging, 187

drives. *See also* disks
  CD-R, 226
  CD-ROM, 190
  DVD, 190
  floppy, 189, 190
  hard. *See* hard drives

DRPs (disaster recovery plans), 476–478

DSA (Digital Signature Algorithm), 83

DSL modems, 214–215

DSS (Digital Signature Standard), 83

due care, 41

due diligence, 41

due process, 41

dumpster diving, 37, 42

DVD drives, 190

DVD formats, 228

DVDs
  bootable, 186–187
  deleting data on, 43
  security issues, 227–228

Dynamic Host Configuration Protocol (DHCP), 214

Dynamic HTML, 312

E

EAP (Extensible Authentication Protocol), 257

EAP messages, 247

EAPOL (Extensible Authentication Protocol over LAN), 247

EAR (Export Administration Regulations), 61

eavesdropping, 58–59

eBay, 54

ECC (elliptic curve cryptography), 98–99

e-commerce, 61–64

ECPA (Electronic Communications Privacy Act), 58, 555

EDGAR site, 392

EFF (Electronic Freedom Foundation), 65

EFS (encrypting file system), 103–104

egghead.com credit card hack, 455

egress filtering, 333

electromagnetic waves, 222

electronic book, 570

Electronic Communications Privacy Act (ECPA), 58, 555

Electronic Freedom Foundation (EFF), 65

electronic key exchange, 97

electronic media, 228–229

Electronic Signatures in Global and National Commerce Act (E-Sign law), 63

ElGamal, Taher, 98

ElGamal algorithm, 98

elliptic curve cryptography (ECC), 98–99

e-mail
  early years, 425
  encryption, 431–435

filtering, 332
forged "from" addresses, 332
headers, 321
hoaxes, 37, 411–412, 426, 428–429
HTML in, 427
phishing attacks, 35–36
popularity of, 425
privacy issues, 41, 431–435
security issues, 425–426
spam. *See* spam
spoofed addresses, 332
spoofing, 400
usage policy, 40
viruses, 309, 411, 425, 426–428
worms, 415, 425, 426–428
e-mail servers, 205
emergency generators, 487
employees. *See also* users
background checks, 44
code of ethics, 46
conflicts of interest, 46
disaster recovery and, 476
disgruntled, 30, 44, 45–46, 500
drug tests, 44, 45
hiring of, 44
ID badges, 191, 193
Internet use and, 40
job rotation, 12
leaving company, 45–46
legal issues/rights, 41
mandatory vacation policy, 46
monitoring activity of, 39–40
need-to-know principle, 18–19, 42
privacy issues, 39–40, 41
productivity, 39, 40
promotions, 45
retirement, 45
separation of duties, 11, 42, 134, 515–517
social engineering and. *See* social
engineering
"tailgating," 193
terminated, 45–46
time of day restrictions, 32–33
unqualified, 500
Encapsulating Security Payload (ESP), 175,
265–268
encrypted data, 13
encrypted traffic, 319, 324, 404
encrypting file system (EFS), 103–104

encryption
Advanced Encryption Standard, 87, 90–91
algorithms. *See* encryption algorithms
antivirus products and, 308–309
asymmetric, 95–103, 173
attacks on, 405–406
Bitlocker, 80, 103–104, 346
Data Encryption Standard, 87–90
described, 405
elliptic curve cryptography, 98–99
e-mail, 431–435
file systems, 103–104
hard drives, 226
hashing functions, 81–86
import/export encryption restrictions,
60–63
instant messaging and, 437
layered security and, 13
in malware, 308
multiple, 89–90
one-way, 81
passwords, 534–535
PGP, 173–174, 432–435
public-key, 404
reversible, 534–535
RFID, 78
steganography, 99–100
symmetric, 86–95, 100–103, 173
Triple DES, 89–90
in viruses, 308–309
encryption algorithms. *See also* algorithms;
encryption
authentication, 101–102
block ciphers, 87, 90, 92
Blowfish cipher, 94
broken, 81
Caesar's cipher, 78–79
CAST-128 algorithm, 91
confidentiality, 100
cryptographic algorithms, 100–104
Diffie-Hellman algorithm, 95, 97,
173–174
digital certificates. *See* digital certificates
digital signatures. *See* digital signatures
ElGamal algorithm, 98
hashing, 82
integrity, 101
International Data Encryption Algorithm,
94–95

key escrow, 102–103
MARS cipher, 90
nonrepudiation, 101
obsolete, 81
one-time pad ciphers, 81, 86
overview, 78–81
polyalphabetic substitution cipher, 79–80
Proposed Encryption Cipher, 94
public, 78
RC ciphers, 91–94
Rijndael cipher, 90
ROT13 cipher, 77
RSA algorithm, 96–97, 173
Serpent cipher, 90
shift ciphers, 77
stream ciphers, 93
substitution ciphers, 79
transposition ciphers, 77
Twofish cipher, 90
use of, 100–104
Vigenère cipher, 79, 80
encryption export regulations, 60–63
encryption keys, 78
encryption machine, 77
end-entities, 157
end-entity certificates, 122
Enigma machine, 77
enterprise assets. See assets
Entrust, 3
environmental controls, 193–194
environmental management risks, 497
equipment. See computers; devices
escalation auditing, 540–541
E-Sign law (Electronic Signatures in Global and National Commerce Act), 63
ESP (Encapsulating Security Payload), 175, 265–268
ethics, 46, 68–71
European Commission, 64, 68
European Laboratory for Particle Physics (CERN), 443
European laws/regulations, 64, 67–68
EVDO (Evolution Data Optimized), 277
evidence, computer crime, 554–559
Evolution Data Optimized (EVDO), 277
Exchange mail server, 378
exclusive-OR (XOR), 81
expn command, 377–378
Export Administration Regulations (EAR), 61

export/import encryption restrictions, 60–63
exposure factor, 495
Extended Terminal Access Controller Access Control System (XTACACS), 251
Extensible Authentication Protocol (EAP), 247, 257
Extensible Authentication Protocol over LAN (EAPOL), 247
Extensible Markup Language. See XML
extranets, 232, 233
Exxon Mobil SpeedPass RFID encryption, 78

F

facilities. See physical security
false negatives, 322
false positives, 304–305, 322, 323
Family Education Records and Privacy Act of 1974, 67
fault tolerance, 488
FBI (Federal Bureau of Investigation), 3, 55
FCC (Federal Communications Commission), 56
Federal Bureau of Investigation (FBI), 3, 55
Federal Communications Commission (FCC), 56
Federal Information Processing Standards (FIPS), 82, 175–176
Federal Trade Commission (FTC), 56, 68, 331
fees, Security+ exam, 4
Ferguson, Niels, 90
fiber-optic cables, 221–222
file permissions. See permissions
file resources, 33
file servers, 205
file services, 380–381
file sharing, 33
file systems, 103–104, 381, 547
File Transfer Protocol. See FTP
files. See also documents
    critical, 301, 302
    CRL, 128–129
    deleted, 43, 559, 561, 562
    free space vs. slack space, 561
    log. See log files
    shadow, 349
    "undeleting," 43
filters/filtering
    e-mail, 332
    Internet content, 328–329, 332

keywords, 332
traffic, 368–370
financial information, 7, 59–60
fingerprint scans, 195, 196
FIPS (Federal Information Processing Standards),
    82, 175–176
fire suppression, 194
Firefox browser. *See also* web browsers
    ActiveX and, 461
    certificate options, 450
    cookies, 463, 464
    pop-up ads, 312
    secure connections, 451, 452
    security options, 445, 446–447
firewall activity logs, 542
firewall rules, 543
firewalls
    cable/DSL modems and, 214–215
    demilitarized zones, 14–15
    from different vendors, 15
    DMZ and, 14–15, 230–231
    importance of, 327
    Internet Connection Firewall, 310
    IP addresses, 211
    Linux systems, 356
    Mac OS, 357–358
    Network Address Translation, 211, 235
    overview, 209–212, 327
    personal, 310–312
    security features, 209–211
    security policies and, 209–210
    software, 310–312
    telecommunications, 215
    telephone, 416
    traffic filtering, 369–370
    UNIX, 310–312
    Windows Firewall, 310, 311
    workstations, 203
firmware updates, 364
Fix, Bernt, 307–308
flags, 320–321
Flash plug-in, 467
floppy disks, 43, 225, 226, 410, 426
floppy drives, 189, 190
forensics, 553–566. *See also* cybercrime
    analysis procedures, 562–563
    chain of custody, 560
    conducting investigation, 557, 559–560
    evidence, computer crime, 554–559

first responders, 553–554, 556
free space vs. slack space, 561
hashing algorithms, 451–452
incident response, 553–554
laws/legal actions, 553–554, 555
message digests, 559, 560, 561–562
overview, 553–554
frames, 576. *See also* packets
fraud risks, 497, 500
free space, 561
FreeOTFE application, 103
FTC (Federal Trade Commission), 56, 68, 331
FTP (File Transfer Protocol), 158, 379, 454–455
FTP clients, 454–455
FTP servers, 158, 379, 454–455

G

Gantt charts, 508
gateways, 327
generators, 487
Generic Routing Encapsulation (GRE), 255
German Enigma machine, 77
GLB (Gramm-Leach-Bliley Act), 59, 67
global catalog, 381–382
Global Learning Consortium, 64
globalization, 68–69
globally unique identifier (GUID), 382
glossary, 581–599
Gnu Privacy Guard, 103
GnuPG application, 103
Good Times virus, 411
government agencies, 56
GPMC (Group Policy Management Console),
    382
GPOs (group policy objects), 382–384, 534
Gramm-Leach-Bliley Act (GLB), 59, 67
GRE (Generic Routing Encapsulation), 255
greylisting, 430
group policies, 30–31, 382–385
Group Policy Management Console (GPMC),
    382
group policy objects (GPOs), 382–384, 534
groups
    access levels, 31
    advantages of, 30
    described, 532
    examples of, 30–31
    logical representation of, 532

privileges, 532
security considerations, 31
guards, security, 189
GUID (globally unique identifier), 382
guidelines, defined, 28

H

hackers/hacking, 6–7. *See also* attacks
"hacktivist" attacks, 391
Hall, Chris, 90
hard drives
boot sector virus, 410
data destruction, 42–43
drive imaging, 187
encryption, 226
portable, 226
RAID, 485–486
security issues, 226
hardening
applications, 370–382
described, 339, 345
Linux systems, 352–357
Mac OS–based systems, 357–360
network, 363–370
operating systems, 230, 344–360
Solaris systems, 349–352
UNIX systems, 347–352
Windows 2003, 345–346
Windows 2008, 346–347
hardware. *See also* computers; devices
disposal of, 42
redundant, 486
storage devices, 131
hardware tokens, 33–34
hash functions, 82, 84, 85, 101
hash values, 204–205
hashes/hashing, 81–86, 342
hashing algorithms, 82, 451–452
hashing functions, 81–86
HD-DVD formats, 228
health information, 67
Health Insurance Portability & Accountability
Act (HIPAA), 67
heating, ventilating, and air conditioning
(HVAC) systems, 194
Helix LiveCD, 559, 563
Hellman, Martin, 95, 97
heuristic scanning, 308
HIDS (host-based IDS), 299, 300–307

hierarchical trust model, 142–143
high availability, 488
High Speed Packet Access (HSPA), 277
hijack attacks, 405
HIPAA (Health Insurance Portability &
Accountability Act), 67
history, password, 33
hoaxes, 37, 411–412, 426, 428–429
honeynets, 325, 327
honeypots, 325–327
host security, 9
host-based IDS (HIDS), 299, 300–307
hosts.allow file, 350, 370
hosts.deny file, 350, 370
hot sites, 484
hotfixes, 361, 371. *See also* patches; service
packs; updates
hover ads, 312
HSPA (High Speed Packet Access), 277
HTML (Hypertext Markup Language), 312,
427, 451
HTTP (HyperText Transfer Protocol), 158,
174, 451–452
HTTP connections, 451–452
HTTP protocol, 323
HTTP servers, 323, 376–377
HTTP traffic, 323
HTTPS (HyperText Transfer Protocol - Secure),
174–175, 451, 453
hubs, 206
human resources policies, 44–46
HVAC (heating, ventilating, and air
conditioning) systems, 194
hybrid attacks, 342, 409
hybrid filtering, 333
hybrid trust model, 144–145, 146
Hypertext Markup Language (HTML), 312, 427,
451
HyperText Transfer Protocol (HTTP), 158, 174
HyperText Transfer Protocol - Secure (HTTPS),
174–175, 451, 453

I

ICMP (Internet Control Message Protocol),
318–319
ICMP packets
address spoofing, 401
DoS attacks, 396, 398
not responding to, 383

ping flood attack, 321
Ping of Death and, 318–319
ID badges, 191, 193
IDEA (International Data Encryption
Algorithm), 94–95, 173
identification, 242–243
identity theft, 37, 44, 66–67
Identity Theft and Assumption Deterrence Act,
66–67
IDES (Intrusion Detection Expert System), 298
IDS (intrusion detection system), 297–338.
See also IPS
components, 299–300
described, 216
false positives/negatives, 304–305,
322, 323
firewalls. *See* firewalls
history of, 298–299
honeynets, 325, 327
honeypots, 325–327
host-based, 299, 300–307
Internet content filters, 328–329
log files, 301, 542
malware. *See* malware; malware
protection
network mappers, 331, 366, 393
network-based, 299, 315–320
overview, 216, 297, 299–300
protocol analyzers, 329–331
proxy servers, 327–328
signatures, 320–322
IDS models, 298, 322–323
IDS sensors, 317–318, 319
IE. *See* Internet Explorer (IE)
IETF (Internet Engineering Task Force),
172–173, 445
IIS (Internet Information Server), 345, 374–376
IIS LockDown tool, 375–376
IKE (Internet Key Exchange), 265, 268
IKMP (Internet Key Management Protocol), 265
IM (instant messaging), 426
images, hiding information in, 99–100
impact, 494–495, 500–501
implicit deny principle, 11–12
import/export encryption restrictions, 60–63
incident response, 553–554
inetd service, 352
inetd.conf file, 349–350

information. *See also* data
categories, 39
classification of, 39
health, 67
medical, 67
personally identifiable, 37, 43–44
sensitive. *See* sensitive information
information assurance, 7
information discovery, 377
information security, 7
Information Systems Audit and Control
Association (ISACA), 3, 496
Information Systems Security Association
(ISSA), 3
information systems testing, 498
information technology (IT) organizations,
498, 516
infrared (IR) transmissions, 222, 223
infrastructure, 38–39, 112, 130–131
infrastructure security, 201–240
devices. *See* devices
media. *See* media
NAT, 235
overview, 201
security topologies, 229–235
security zones, 229–233
tunneling, 235, 236
VLANs, 207–208, 233–234
initialization vectors (IVs), 278, 286
inlining, 466
instant messaging (IM), 426, 435–438
intangible impacts, 501
integrity
certificate revocation lists, 127–128
code, 522
cryptographic algorithms, 101
described, 101
message, 101
intellectual property, 69
International Data Encryption Algorithm
(IDEA), 94–95, 173
international laws, 62–63. *See also* laws/
regulations
International Organization for Standardization
(ISO), 164
International Telecommunication Union (ITU),
120, 164, 453
Internet. *See also* web entries
criminal activities on. *See* cybercrime

described, 231
electronic wiretaps on, 58–59
inappropriate use of, 40
pornography on, 55, 329, 400
security issues, 28–29, 231–232
Internet Connection Firewall, 310
Internet content filters, 328–329
Internet Control Message Protocol. *See* ICMP
Internet Crime Complaint Center, 55–56
Internet crime schemes, 55–56. *See also* cybercrime
Internet Engineering Task Force (IETF), 172–173, 445
Internet Explorer (IE). *See also* web browsers
certificate options, 449
cookies, 463, 464–465, 563
pop-up ads, 312, 313
secure connections, 451
security options, 445, 446
Internet Information Server (IIS), 345, 374–376
Internet Key Exchange (IKE), 265, 268
Internet Key Management Protocol (IKMP), 265
Internet Protocol. *See* IP
Internet Security Association and Key Management Protocol (ISAKMP), 167–168
Internet Service Providers (ISPs), 486
Internet usage policy, 40
Internet-based protocols, 444–455, 576–579
Internetwork Operating System (IOS), 364
interrelationship digraphs, 509
intranets, 232–233
Intrusion Detection Expert System (IDES), 298
intrusion prevention system (IPS), 305–306, 323–325. *See also* IDS
IOS (Internetwork Operating System), 364
IP (Internet Protocol), 577–578
IP addresses
DNS servers and, 379–380
firewalls and, 211
intranets, 232–233
purpose of, 577–578
spoofing, 401
static, 214
IP Payload Compression Protocol (IPcomp), 175
IP-based cameras, 193
ipchains, 310–312
IPcomp (IP Payload Compression Protocol), 175

IPS (intrusion protection system), 305–306, 323–325. *See also* IDS
IPS logs, 542
IPSec (Internet Protocol Security), 175, 261–268
IPsec protocol, 216
iptables, 312
IPv4 protocol, 175, 216, 266, 578
IPv6 protocol, 175, 211, 216, 266, 578
IR (infrared) transmissions, 222, 223
ISACA (Information Systems Audit and Control Association), 3, 496
ISAKMP (Internet Security Association and Key Management Protocol), 167–168
ISO (International Organization for Standardization), 164
ISO 17799 standard, 177–178
ISO/IEC 27002 standard, 177–178
ISPs (Internet Service Providers), 486
ISSA (Information Systems Security Association), 3
IT Code of Ethics, 69–71
IT infrastructure. *See* infrastructure
IT (information technology) organizations, 498, 516
ITU (International Telecommunication Union), 120, 164, 453
IVs (initialization vectors), 278, 286

J

Java language, 457–459
Java Virtual Machine (JVM), 457
JavaScript, 457, 458–459
job rotation, 12
John the Ripper program, 341
JVM (Java Virtual Machine), 457

K

KASUMI standard, 279
KDC (Key Distribution Center), 244
KDS (Key Distribution Server), 245
Kelsey, John, 90
Kerberos authentication, 244–245
Kerberos realms, 244–245
key archiving system, 134
Key Distribution Center (KDC), 244
Key Distribution Server (KDS), 245
key escrow, 102–103, 135

key pairs
    generating, 124–125
    lifecycles, 124
    lifetimes, 129
    multiple, 124–125
    public/private, 111, 125
    recovery of, 133–134
    registering, 125
key recovery, 133–134
key stores, 115, 132
key usage extensions, 123
key/lock authentication, 20
keylogging, 412
keys
    complexity of, 80
    cryptographic, 87
    decryption, 78
    DES, 87–89
    described, 78
    destruction of, 129–130
    encryption, 78
    escrowed, 135
    limitations, 194
    lock/key systems, 20, 243
    managing, 80, 87
    private. See private keys
    public. See public keys
    random, 81
    recovery of, 133–134
    reusing, 81
    semi-weak, 88
    splitting, 135
    weak, 88, 89, 405–406
keyspace, 80, 81, 406
keyword filtering, 332
kill command, 348
Kim, Gene, 205
Klíma, Vlastimil, 86
Knoppix Live CD, 563
knowledge domains, 3–6
Knudsen, Lars, 90

L

L2F (Layer 2 Forwarding) protocol, 257
L2TP (Layer Two Tunneling Protocol), 254, 257
languages, Security+ exam, 4
LANs (local area networks), 29–30
laptop computers
    network attacks via, 186
    theft of, 187, 191, 500
    war-driving, 224
"last mile" problem, 223
laws/regulations. See also legal issues; U.S. laws
    evidence, 555
    forensics, 553–554, 555
    import/export, 62–63
    against piracy, 65–66
    privacy (Europe), 67–68
    privacy (U.S.), 58–59, 66–67, 555
    sources of, 56
    statutory laws, 56
Layer 2 Forwarding (L2F) protocol, 257
Layer Two Tunneling Protocol. See L2TP
layered access, 192
layered security, 12–14
LDAP (Lightweight Directory Access Protocol), 116, 382, 452–454
LDAP directories, 116
LDAP servers, 453–454
LearnKey Online Training, 569, 570
least privilege, 10–11, 42
Least Significant Bit (LSB) encoding, 100
leaves, 302
legal issues. See also laws/regulations
    child pornography, 55
    employee issues, 41
    employee rights, 41
    forensics and, 553–554, 555
    overview, 55
    piracy, 65–66
legal rights, 41
Leibrock, Larry, 556
Lightweight Directory Access Protocol (LDAP), 116, 382, 452–454
linear cryptanalysis, 78
Linux systems
    described, 352–353
    hardening, 352–357
    passwords, 341
    patches, 355
    permissions, 354–355
    Red Hat Linux, 353–357
    removing unnecessary programs, 355
    turning services on/off, 353–354
    updates, 355, 362–363
    user accounts, 355–356
LiveCDs, 186–187, 190
local area networks (LANs), 29–30

local key store, 115
local registration authority (LRA), 116
lock/key systems, 20, 243. *See also* keys
locks, computer room, 192
log files, 541–543
    access logs, 542
    antivirus logs, 542
    auditing of, 541–543
    common logs, 541–542
    DNS logs, 542
    failed logins, 541
    firewall activity logs, 542
    HIDS, 301
    IDS/IPS logs, 542
    performance logs, 542
    security applications, 542
    system logs, 542
logic bombs, 413
logical access controls, 30–34
logical tokens, 33–34
logins
    failed, 541
    mutual authentication, 246–247
    rlogin command, 258–259
    single sign-on, 246
logon IDs, 243
LRA (local registration authority), 116
LSB (Least Significant Bit) encoding, 100
Lucifer algorithm, 87

M

m of n authentication, 134
MAC (Media Access Control), 330
MAC (mandatory access control), 18–19,
    543–545
MAC (message authentication code), 82
MAC addresses, 206, 330, 407
MAC algorithms, 277
Mac OS–based systems, 357–360
    file permissions, 358–359
    firewalls, 357–358
    malware, 203
    removing unnecessary programs,
        359–360
    turning services on/off, 357–358
    user accounts, 359–360
macro viruses, 410–411
magnetic media, 43, 225–827
mail relaying, 430

mail servers, 377–378
malicious code, 409–416, 426–428
malware, 54, 308, 426, 427
malware protection, 307–314
    antivirus products, 307–310
    personal firewalls, 310–312
    pop-up blockers, 312–313
    Windows Defender, 313–314
mandatory access control. *See* MAC
man-in-the-middle attacks, 110, 403–404
man-made disasters, 499
mantrap, 193
market risks, 498
MARS cipher, 90
Master Boot Record (MBR), 410
MasterExam, 569–570
MBR (Master Boot Record), 410
MBSA (Microsoft Baseline Security Analyzer),
    378
MD (Message Digest), 84–86, 559, 560,
    561–562
MD2 (Message Digest 2), 84–85
MD4 (Message Digest 4), 85
MD5 (Message Digest 5), 85–86, 562
MD5 hash, 86
MD5 hash values, 204–205
media
    degaussing, 43
    electronic, 228–229
    magnetic, 43, 225–827
    optical, 227–228
    removable. *See* removable media
    transmission. *See* transmission media
    unguided, 222–223
Media Access Control. *See* MAC
medical information, 7, 67
mesh architecture, 144
message authentication code (MAC), 82
Message Digest. *See* MD
message encapsulation, 578–579
message integrity, 101
Microsoft Baseline Security Analyzer (MBSA),
    378
Microsoft Corporation, 3
Microsoft NAP (Network Access Protection)
    system, 216–217
Microsoft Point-to-Point Encryption (MPPE),
    256
microwave communications, 222, 223

military security classifications, 18, 39
MIME (Multipurpose Internet Mail Extension),
    171–173, 431–432
misuse detection, 323
mitigating risks, 495, 509
Mitnick, Kevin, 34
Mitre Corporation, 468
mks_vir program, 307
mobile devices, 218
mobile networks, 276–279
mobile phones, 276–279
modems, 30, 214–215, 416
monitoring employees, 39–40
monitoring systems, 192, 193
Morris, Robert, 415
Morris Internet worm, 415
Motion Picture Association of America
    (MPAA), 65
Motorola, 3
MPAA (Motion Picture Association of
    America), 65
MPPE (Microsoft Point-to-Point
    Encryption), 256
multifactor authentication, 246
multilevel security, 18, 19
multiple encryption, 89–90
multiple-factor authentication, 195, 196–197
Multipurpose Internet Mail Extension.
    See MIME
mutual aid agreements, 484–485
mutual authentication, 246–247
MySpace worm, 415

N

NAC (network access control), 216–217
nameservers, 380
NAP (Network Access Protection), 216–217,
    346
NAT (Network Address Translation), 211, 235
National Bureau of Standards (NBS), 87
National Conference of Commissioners on
    Uniform State Laws (NCCUSL), 63
National Institute of Standards and Technology
    (NIST), 3, 82, 87, 175–176, 562
National Security Agency (NSA), 82, 87
National Software Reference Library
    (NSRL), 562
National White Collar Crime Center
    (NW3C), 55

natural disasters, 499
NBS (National Bureau of Standards), 87
NCCUSL (National Conference of
    Commissioners on Uniform State Laws), 63
Needham-Schroeder protocol, 244
need-to-know principle, 18–19, 42
Nessus scans, 321
NetBus, 398
NetRanger IDS, 298, 323
Netscape, 444, 465
Netscape web server product, 444–445
netstat program, 366, 367, 368
NetStumbler, 284
network access control (NAC), 216–217
Network Access Protection (NAP), 216–217, 346
Network Address Translation (NAT), 211, 235
network analyzers, 329
network diagnostics, 217–218
network diagrams, 29
Network File System (NFS), 381
network hardening, 363–370
Network Infrastructure knowledge domain,
    3, 4, 5
network interface cards (NICs), 205–206,
    316, 330
network layer, 576
network mapper (nmap) utility, 366, 393
network mappers, 331, 366, 393
network operating system (NOS), 344
network operations centers (NOCs), 217–218
network security. *See also* networks; security
    described, 7, 9
    implicit deny, 11–12
    least privilege, 10–11
    security zones, 229–233
network sniffers
    activities detected by, 35–36
    described, 224, 399
    use of, 284–285, 399–400
network taps, 330
network-based IDSs (NIDS), 299, 315–320
NetworkICE, 323
networking frameworks, 571–572
networks
    bridges, 206
    extranets, 232, 233
    firewalls. *See* firewalls
    honeynets, 325, 327
    hubs, 206

intranets, 232–233
LANs, 29–30
layered security, 13–14
mobile, 276–279
monitoring, 217–218
PANs, 279
physical security, 224–225
routers, 208–209
security. *See* network security
security perimeter, 28–30
security zones, 229–233
switches, 206–208
telephone, 29–30, 36
topologies. *See* security topologies
virtual, 326
VLANs, 207–208, 233–234
VPNs. *See* VPNs
wireless. *See* wireless networks
Neumann, Peter, 298
NFS (Network File System), 381
NICs (network interface cards), 205–206,
316, 330
NIDS (network-based IDSs), 299, 315–320
NIDS sensors, 317–318, 319
Nimba worm, 414
NIST (National Institute of Standards and
Technology), 3, 82, 87, 175–176, 562
nmap (network mapper) utility, 366, 393
NOCs (network operations centers), 217–218
nonrepudiation, 8, 101, 123
nonrepudiation services, 123
nonvolatile RAM (NVRAM), 364
NOS (network operating system), 344
NoScript plug-in, 461
Novell, 3
npasswd, 341
NSA (National Security Agency), 82, 87
NSRL (National Software Reference
Library), 562
NT File System (NTFS), 547
NT LAN Manager (NTLM), 86, 258
NTFS (NT File System), 547
NTLM (NT LAN Manager), 86, 258
null sessions, 398
number generators, 131
NVRAM (nonvolatile RAM), 364
NW3C (National White Collar Crime
Center), 55

O

OCSP (Online Certificate Status Protocol),
119, 129
one-time pad ciphers, 81, 86
one-way encryption, 81
online banking transactions, 8
Online Certificate Status Protocol (OCSP),
119, 129
open proxies, 328
open relay, 430
Open System Interconnection. *See* OSI
Open Vulnerability and Assessment Language
(OVAL), 468
Open Web Application Security Project
(OWASP), 468
operating systems (OS). *See also specific operating
systems*
hardening, 230, 344–360
host security and, 9
updates, 360–363
operational model, 28
operational risks, 498
optical media, 227–228
"Orange Book," 18
organizational policies/procedures, 37–46
Organizational Security knowledge domain,
3, 4, 6
OS. *See* operating systems
OSI message encapsulation, 578–579
OSI (Open System Interconnection) model,
445, 572–576
OVAL (Open Vulnerability and Assessment
Language), 468
OWASP (Open Web Application Security
Project), 468

P

packet filtering, 211–212
packet sniffers, 329
packets
described, 576
ICMP. *See* ICMP packets
SSL, 13
SYN/ACK, 395–396, 402–403, 577
TCP, 320–321, 402
PAM (Pluggable Authentication Modules), 341
PANs (personal area networks), 279

PAP (Password Authentication Protocol), 256, 257
Pareto charts, 509
passcodes, 243
PASSFILT.DLL, 341
passing scores, Security+ exam, 4
passive HIDS, 306
passive NIDSs, 320
passphrases, 342–343
passwd command, 352
passwd file, 320, 348–349
Password Authentication Protocol (PAP), 256, 257
password generation utility, 32
password guessing, 407–409
password policies
    complexity requirements, 534
    components, 533
    domain passwords, 31–32, 534–535
    examples of, 533
    guidelines for, 340–342
    overview, 31–32
    password duration/aging, 533, 534
password strings, 342
password-cracking utilities, 341–342, 408
passwords
    aging, 343–344, 533, 534
    as authentication mechanism, 20, 243
    BIOS, 190
    brute-force attacks, 81, 342, 343, 365, 408–409
    changing, 343–344
    clear text, 268
    complexity requirements, 534
    devices, 364–365
    dictionary attacks, 342, 408
    domain, 31–32, 534–535
    duration of, 343–344, 533, 534
    encrypted, 534–535
    expired, 33
    guessing, 407–409
    guidelines, 31, 32, 341, 342–344, 534
    history, 33, 534
    hybrid attacks, 409
    key stores, 132
    length of, 534
    Linux-based systems, 341
    lock/key authentication, 20
    policies. See password policies

polyalphabetic substitution cipher, 79–80
    problems with, 20
    protection of, 533
    recycling, 344
    reuse restrictions, 533
    selecting, 340, 342–343
    single sign-on, 535–536
    SNMP, 365–366
    Solaris systems, 341, 351–352
    storing, 534–535
    superusers, 531
    verifying, 16
    weak, 31, 407–408
    Windows-based systems, 341, 534–535
patchadd command, 351
patches, 371–374. See also hotfixes; service packs; updates
    Apache servers, 377
    applications, 371, 416
    described, 361
    importance of keeping up on, 393, 394, 397
    Linux systems, 355
    managing, 371–374
    Solaris systems, 349, 351
    UNIX systems, 349
    Windows-based systems, 347
    worms and, 415
patchrm command, 351
Patriot Act, 58–59
Payment Card Industry Data Security Standards (PCI DSS), 59–60
PayPal, 54
PBXs (private branch exchanges), 215
PC-based malware. See malware
PCI DSS (Payment Card Industry Data Security Standards), 59–60
PDAs (personal digital assistants), 186, 218
peer-to-peer trust model, 144
penetration testing, 28, 418
performance logs, 542
performance management, 498
perimeter security, 315
permission bits, 18
permissions. See also privileges
    described, 530
    discretionary access control, 18
    Linux systems, 354–355
    Mac OS–based systems, 358–359

NTFS, 547
Solaris systems, 350–351
UNIX systems, 545–546
Windows systems, 545, 547–549
permutation, 88
personal area networks (PANs), 279
personal digital assistants (PDAs), 186, 218
personal firewalls, 310–312
personal identification numbers (PINs), 20, 37, 246
personally identifiable information (PII), 37
PERT (program evaluation and review technique) charts, 509
PES (Proposed Encryption Cipher), 94
PGP (Pretty Good Privacy), 103, 173–174, 432–435
phishing attacks, 35–36
phone calls, spoofed, 36
phone company, 29–30
phone connectors, 205
phones, wireless, 276–279
phreaking, 7
physical layer, 219, 576
physical security, 185–200
    barriers, 188
    computer room, 187, 188–189
    computer theft, 187, 191, 500
    considerations, 30
    denial-of-service attacks, 187–188
    environmental controls, 193–194
    guards, 189
    ID badges, 191, 193
    importance of, 185
    "insiders" and, 30
    networks, 224–225
    overview, 185–188
    safeguards, 188–197
    transmission media, 224–225
    unprotected facilities, 500
PID (process identifier), 348
PII (personally identifiable information), 37, 43–44
ping flood attacks, 321
ping of death (POD) attacks, 318–319, 396
ping sweeps, 392, 393
PINs (personal identification numbers), 20, 36, 246
piracy, 65–66
PKC certificates, 159

PKC (Public Key Certificate) format, 157
PKCS (Public Key Cryptography Standards), 157, 162–164
PKCS #1 attack, 278
PKCS #11 interface, 115
pkg utilities, 349
pkgadd command, 349
pkgparam command, 351
pkgrm command, 349
PKI certificates, 157, 163
PKI service providers, 138–139
PKI X.509 (PKIX), 120, 157–164
PKIs (Public Key Infrastructures), 109–154
    audit logs, 134
    basics, 109–112
    centralized infrastructures, 130–131
    certificate authorities, 110, 111, 112–113
    certificate repositories, 116
    certificate verification, 116–120, 140–144
    decentralized infrastructures, 130–131
    described, 109
    digital certificates. See digital certificates
    intercommunications, 139–146
    PKIX, 120, 157–164
    plaintext, 86
    private key protection, 132–135
    registration authorities, 110, 113–116
    trust and, 109–112, 116–119
    trust models, 140–146
PKIX (PKI X.509), 120, 157–164
plaintext, 277, 278, 405
plaintext alert messages, 277
Plato, Andrew, 323
Pluggable Authentication Modules (PAM), 341
plug-ins, 456, 466–467
PMI (privilege management infrastructure), 159
POD (ping of death) attacks, 318–319, 396
Point-to-Point Protocol (PPP), 256
Point-to-Point Tunneling Protocol (PPTP), 254–256
poisoning attacks, 407
policies. See also procedures; security policies
    acceptable use, 39–40
    change management, 38–39
    data disposal/destruction, 42–43
    data retention, 543
    data storage, 543
    described, 28, 37
    due care, 41

due diligence, 41
due process, 41
e-mail usage, 40
group, 30–31, 382–385
human resources, 44–46
Internet usage, 40
least privilege, 10–11, 42
mandatory vacations, 46
need-to-know principle, 18–19, 42
organizational, 37–46
password, 31–32, 340–342
physical security, 30
privacy, 43–44
security, 189–191
separation of duties, 11, 42, 134, 515–517
service level agreements, 44
time of day restrictions, 32–33
updating, 38
usernames, 32
policy certificates, 123
polyalphabetic substitution cipher, 79–80
polymorphic viruses, 411
pop-under ads, 312
pop-up blockers, 312–313
pornography, 55, 329, 400
port mirroring, 330
port scans/scanners, 318, 321, 392–393, 430
ports
blocking traffic to, 210–211
configuring, 366–368
open, 366–368
scanning, 318, 321, 392–393, 430
TCP, 251
threats to, 366
UDP, 251
USB, 190, 229
PPP (Point-to-Point Protocol), 256
PPTP (Point-to-Point Tunneling Protocol),
254–256
presentation layer, 575
Pretty Good Privacy (PGP), 103, 173–174,
432–435
preventative measures, 8
preventive controls, 501
print resources, 33
print services, 380–381
printer sharing, 33
privacy, 66–68
considerations, 7, 66

defined, 66
e-mail, 431–435
employee, 39–40, 41
financial information, 59–60
Gnu Privacy Guard, 103
laws (Europe), 67–68
laws (U.S.), 58–59, 66–67, 555
Patriot Act and, 58–59
Pretty Good Privacy, 103, 173–174,
432–435
risks, 498
privacy policy, 43–44
private branch exchanges (PBXs), 215
private keys, 95–103
certificate authority, 133
certificate verification, 119–120
compromised, 126–128
key escrow, 102–103
PGP and, 173–174
protection of, 132–135
storage of, 132
private/public keys, 121, 125. See also private
keys; public keys
privilege auditing, 538–539
privilege management, 529–552. See also
privileges
access control, 543–547
centralized management, 536–537
decentralized, centralized model, 538
decentralized management, 537
overview, 529–530
users, 530–531
privilege management infrastructure (PMI), 159
privileges. See also permissions
auditing, 538–541
groups, 532
least, 10–11, 42
managing. See privilege management
roles, 532–533
users, 530–531
procedures. See also organizational policies/
procedures
described, 28, 37
insufficient, 500
organizational, 37–46
process identifier (PID), 348
program evaluation and review technique
(PERT) charts, 509
program viruses, 410

programs. *See* applications; software
project risk management, 498
promiscuous mode, 316, 330
proof of possession, 125
Proposed Encryption Cipher (PES), 94
proprietary systems, 78
protection mechanisms, 8, 9
protocol analyzers, 329–331
protocols. *See also* standards
    802.11. *See 802.11 entries*
    CCMP, 287
    CEP, 175
    CHAP, 256–257
    CMP, 168–169
    DAP, 452–454
    described, 444, 571
    DHCP, 214
    DIAMETER, 248, 250
    EAP, 257
    EAPOL, 247
    eliminating unnecessary, 16
    FIPS, 82, 175–176
    FTP, 158, 379, 454–455
    HTTP, 158, 174, 451–452
    HTTPS, 174–175, 451, 453
    ICMP, 318–319
    IKMP, 265
    Internet-based, 444–455, 576–579
    IP. *See* IP
    IPSec, 175
    IPv4, 175, 216, 266, 578
    IPv6, 175, 211, 216, 266, 578
    ISAKMP, 167–168
    L2F, 257
    L2TP, 254, 257
    LDAP, 116, 382, 452–454
    Needham-Schroeder, 244
    OCSP, 119, 129
    OSI layers, 574–576
    overview, 155–156
    PAP, 256, 257
    PGP, 103, 173–174
    PPP, 256
    PPTP, 254–256
    SMTP. *See* SMTP
    SNMP, 217, 218, 365–366
    SSL. *See SSL entries*
    SSL/TLS, 445–451
    TACACS+, 251–253
    TCP, 445, 576, 577
    TCP/IP, 258
    Telnet, 258
    TKIP, 287
    TLS, 165–167, 445, 453–455
    UDP, 576, 577
    VPNs, 254–261
    vulnerabilities, 455
    WAP, 176, 276, 277–279
    web components, 444–455
    WEP, 177, 225, 281–287
    WTLS, 157–158, 176
proxy servers, 232–233, 327–328
ps command, 348, 349
PSTN (public switched telephone network),
    29–30, 254
PTR checks, 332
public algorithms, 78
public certificate authorities, 136
Public Key Certificate. *See* PKC
public key cryptography, 95–99
Public Key Cryptography Standards (PKCS),
    157, 162–164
Public Key Infrastructure. *See* PKI
public keys, 95–103
    certificate verification, 116–120
    encryption, 404
    PGP and, 173–174
    repositories for, 116
public switched telephone network (PSTN),
    29–30, 254
public/private key pairs, 111
public/private keys, 111, 125. *See also* private
    keys; public keys
pull model, 382

Q

QC (Qualified Certificate), 159
Qualified Certificate (QC), 159
qualitative risk analysis, 495, 502–508
quantitative risk analysis, 495, 505–508
QuickTime plug-in, 467

R

RA (registration authority), 110, 113–116,
    157, 158
radio frequency (RF) waves, 222, 223

RADIUS (Remote Authentication Dial-In User Service), 248–250
RADIUS accounting, 250
RADIUS clients, 248–250
RADIUS servers, 247–250
RAID (Redundant Array of Independent Disks), 485–486
rainbow tables, 342
random number generators, 131
RAS (Remote Access Service), 215–216
RAS (remote access servers), 216, 217, 231, 241
rate-based monitoring, 324
RAW format, 78
RBAC (role-based access control), 19, 546
RBAC (rule-based access control), 19, 546
RBL (Realtime Blackhole List), 430
RC (Rivest Cipher), 91–94
RC2 cipher, 91–92
RC4 cipher, 93–94
RC5 cipher, 92
RC6 cipher, 90, 93
real time, 300
RealOne Player, 466–467
RealSecure IDS, 298
Realtime Blackhole List (RBL), 430
reconnaissance, 377, 392
Recording Industry Association of America (RIAA), 65
records retention, 543
recovery, disaster. *See* disaster recovery
recovery services, 487–488
Red Hat Linux, 353–357
redundancy, 486
Redundant Array of Independent Disks (RAID), 485–486
redundant services, 486
Reference Data Set, 562
registration authority (RA), 110, 113–116, 157, 158
registry key, 190
regulations. *See* laws/regulations
regulatory management risks, 497
relaying, 378
release control, 513
reliability management, 498
remote access
    802.11 protocol. *See* 802.11 protocol
    authentication, 243–266
    authorization, 247

    connection process, 241–247
    described, 241
    identification, 242–243
    IEEE 802.1x standard, 247
    IPSec, 175, 261–268
    NTLM, 258
    Secure Shell, 258–259
    Telnet protocol, 258
    VPNs, 260–261
    vulnerabilities, 268
remote access servers (RAS), 216, 217, 231, 241
Remote Access Service (RAS), 215–216
Remote Authentication Dial-In User Service. *See* RADIUS
removable media, 225–229
    CDs. *See* CDs
    DVDs. *See* DVDs
    electronic media, 228–229
    floppy disks, 43, 225, 226, 410, 426
    hard drives. *See* hard drives
    magnetic media, 225–827
    optical media, 227–228
    tapes, 227
    Zip disks, 226
replay attacks, 404–405
Requests for Comment (RFCs), 159–162
reset messages (RSTs), 320
residual risk management, 501
residual risks, 501
resources
    disaster recovery and, 476
    file, 33
    implicit deny policy, 11–12
    physical, 476
    print, 33
    time of day restrictions, 32–33
response, 8
retina/iris scans, 195, 196
revenue management risks, 497
reverse DNS checks, 332
reverse proxies, 328
RF (radio frequency) waves, 222, 223
RFCs (Requests for Comment), 159–162
RFID encryption, 78
RIAA (Recording Industry Association of America), 65
Rijmen, Vincent, 90
Rijndael algorithm, 91

Rijndael cipher, 90
risk analysis, 494
risk assessment, 494
risk management, 493–511. *See also* disaster
    recovery; risks
        business risks, 497
        continuous, 495–496
        defined, 494
        general risk management model, 499–502
        overview, 493–497
        planning decision flowchart, 496
        qualitative risk analysis, 495, 502–508
        quantitative risk analysis, 495, 505–508
        residual, 501
        technology risks, 498
        terminology, 494–495
        terrorist attacks, 58–59, 499
        tools for, 508–509
        transferring risk, 497
risk management models, 498–502
risk management plan, 509
risks. *See also* threats; vulnerabilities
        accepting, 508
        assets, 498
        Basel Committee, 498
        binary assessment, 503
        business continuity, 497, 498
        color-coding risk levels, 504–505
        contract management, 497
        credit, 498
        defined, 494
        environmental management, 497
        examples of, 498
        fraud, 497, 500
        identified, 502
        managing. *See* risk management
        market, 498
        mitigating, 495, 509
        operational, 498
        privacy, 498
        regulatory management, 497
        residual, 501
        revenue management, 497
Rivest, Ron, 91
Rivest Cipher. *See* RC
Rivest-Shamir-Adleman (RSA) algorithm,
    96–97, 173
RJ-45 connectors, 205, 221
rlogin command, 258–259

rogue access points, 285
rogue modems, 416
role-based access control (RBAC), 19, 546
roles
        privileges, 532–533
        users, 19, 530
root account, 531
root CAs, 122, 131, 142–144
rootkits, 398, 413–414
ROT13 cipher, 77
round, 88
routers, 208–209, 364
RSA (Rivest-Shamir-Adleman) algorithm,
    96–97, 173
RSA Security, 3
RSTs (reset messages), 320
rule-based access control (RBAC), 19, 546
rule-based filtering, 332–333
run levels, 348

S

SAD (security association database), 262
sadmind worm, 414
Safe Harbor Provision, 68
safeguards. *See* controls
Samy worm, 415
SANS Institute IT Code of Ethics, 69–71
SANS Internet Storm Center, 307
Sarbanes-Oxley (SOX) Act, 59, 514
SAs (security associations), 167–168, 262
scanning
        ports, 318, 321, 392–393, 430
        process for, 392–393
schema, 381
Schneier, Bruce, 90, 94
screensavers, 191
Secret clearance, 544–545
secret security level, 544
Secure FTP (SFTP), 455
Secure Hash Algorithm. *See* SHA
Secure MIME (S/MIME), 171–173, 426, 431–433
Secure Shell (SSH), 258–259
Secure Sockets Layer. *See* SSL
security
        applications, 10–11
        basics, 7
        "CIA" of, 7–8
        defined, 7
        detection, 8

diversity of defense, 14–15
encryption. *See* encryption
environmental controls, 193–194
firewalls. *See* firewalls
host, 9
infrastructure. *See* infrastructure security
IPsec, 265–268
layered, 12–14
measurable, 468
military classifications, 18, 39
multilevel, 18, 19
network. *See* network security; networks
operational model, 8
passwords. *See* passwords
physical, 30
policies. *See* policies
preventative measures, 8
principles of, 8–9
procedures. *See* procedures
protection mechanisms, 8, 9
response, 8
risks. *See* risk management; risks
separation of duties, 11, 42, 134, 515–517
simple vs. complex systems, 16
terminology, 6–20
threats to. *See* threats
wireless. *See* wireless networks
security applications, 542
security assessments, 502–508
security association database (SAD), 262
security associations (SAs), 167–168, 262
security audits, 417–418. *See also* auditing
security baselines, 339–389
configuration control, 518
described, 10, 517–518
detecting anomalies with, 360
group policies, 382–385
hardening applications, 370–382
hardening networks, 363–370
hardening operating systems, 230, 344–360
overview, 339–340
password selection, 340–344
Security+ Exam, 3–6
fees, 4
languages for, 4
passing scores, 4
preparing for, 3–6
retaking, 4

security guards, 189
security perimeter, 28–30, 315
security policies, 38–43. *See also* policies
data destruction, 42–43
described, 209
firewalls and, 209–210
implicit deny, 11–12
need-to-know principle, 18–19, 42
security templates, 384–385
security through obscurity, 15
security topologies, 229–235
security zones, 229–233
SEI (Software Engineering Institute), 495–496, 502, 522–523
self-signed certificates, 142, 143
Sender ID Framework (SIDF), 431
Sender Policy Framework (SPF), 431
sensitive information. *See also* information
destruction of, 42–43
financial information, 7, 59–60
lost/stolen, 67
shredding, 37, 43
sensors, 317–318, 319
separation of duties, 11, 42, 134, 515–517
September 11 attack, 58–59
sequence numbers, 402–404
Serpent cipher, 90
servers
antivirus software for, 205
Apache web server, 376–377
application, 205
authentication, 244
certificate, 112
described, 204
DNS, 379–380
e-mail, 205
Exchange mail server, 378
file, 205
FTP, 158, 379, 454–455
HTTP, 323, 376–377
Internet Information Server, 345, 374–376
Key Distribution Server, 245
LDAP, 453–454
mail, 377–378
MD5 hash values, 204–205
nameservers, 380
proxy, 232–233, 327–328
RADIUS, 247–250
redundant, 486

remote access, 216, 217, 231
security considerations, 204–205
SMTP, 333, 430
ticket granting, 244
trusted, 332
web, 374–380, 443
server-side scripting, 462
service level agreements (SLAs), 44
service packs, 361, 375. *See also* hotfixes;
patches; updates
service set identifiers (SSIDs), 285–286
services
blacklist, 430
configuring, 366–368
disabling unnecessary, 16, 204
file, 380–381
hiding, 15
inetd, 352
nonrepudiation, 123
print, 380–381
recovery, 487–488
redundant, 486
restricting access to, 15
telephony, 7
Telnet, 353–354
VPN, 259, 261
xinetd, 352
XKMS, 169–171
session hijacking, 405
session layer, 575
SFTP (Secure FTP), 455
SHA (Secure Hash Algorithm), 82–84, 562
SHA-1 algorithm, 83–84
SHA-256 algorithm, 84
SHA-384 algorithm, 84
SHA-512 algorithm, 84
shadow files, 349
shared items, 33, 115
shared secret principle, 86, 97, 99
shielded twisted-pair (STP) cables, 220–221
shift ciphers, 77, 86
Shockwave plug-in, 467
shoulder surfing, 36
shredders, 37, 43
shredding sensitive data, 37, 43
SIDF (Sender ID Framework), 431
signature database, 300, 303, 316
signature sets, 306, 320, 322, 323
signature-based scanning, 308

signatures, 320–322. *See also* digital signatures
signed applets, 465–466
SIIA (Software & Information Industry
Association), 65
Simple Mail Transfer Protocol. *See* SMTP
Simple Network Management Protocol.
See SNMP
single loss expectancy (SLE), 495, 507
single points of failure, 486–487
single sign-on authentication, 246
single sign-on (SSO) authentication, 535–536
slack space, 561
Slammer worm, 456
SLAs (service level agreements), 44
SLE (single loss expectancy), 495, 507
smart cards, 131, 195
S/MIME (Secure MIME), 171–173, 426,
431–433
smpatch command, 351
SMTP (Simple Mail Transfer Protocol), 430
SMTP servers, 332, 333, 430
smurf attacks, 401
sniffers/sniffing, 224, 399–400. *See also*
eavesdropping
described, 224, 399
network. *See* network sniffers
packet, 329
SNMP (Simple Network Management
Protocol), 217, 218, 365–366
SNMP passwords, 365–366
Sobig worm, 414
social engineering, 34–37
data aggregation, 35
described, 34, 417
dumpster diving, 37, 42
goal of, 35
hoaxes, 37
phishing, 35–36
shoulder surfing, 36
vishing, 36
social norms, 68
software. *See also* applications
bugs, 268
exploitation, 409
failures, 500
Trojan horse, 412, 427, 451
updates, 364
Software & Information Industry Association
(SIIA), 65

Software Engineering Institute (SEI), 495–496, 502, 522–523
software firewalls, 310–312
software tokens, 34
Solaris systems
    baselines, 349
    file permissions, 350–351
    hardening, 349–352
    passwords, 341, 351–352
    patches, 349, 351
    removing software, 349, 350
    turning services on/off, 349, 350
    user accounts, 351–352
Sony BMG Corporation, 413
sources of laws/regulations, 56
SOX (Sarbanes-Oxley) Act, 59, 514
Spafford, Eugene, 205
spam, 429–431
    anti-spam solutions, 331–333
    CAN-SPAM Act of 2003, 331
    described, 331
    e-mail, 332
    protecting against, 331–333
spam filtering, 332–333
spammers, 331, 332
SPAN (Switched Port Analyzer) port, 330
spare parts, 486
SpeedPass RFID encryption, 78
SPF (Sender Policy Framework), 431
spoofed addresses, 332
spoofed telephone calls, 36
spoofing, 400–403
    described, 400
    e-mail, 400
    IP addresses, 401
    sequence numbers and, 402–404
    trusted relationships and, 401–402
    web sites, 400
SPR (system problem report), 521–522
spyware, 307, 313–314, 412–413
SQL Slammer worm, 414, 416
SSH (Secure Shell), 258–259
SSIDs (service set identifiers), 285–286
SSL (Secure Sockets Layer), 97, 165–167, 444–445
SSL connections, 452
SSL handshake, 447–448
SSL packets, 13
SSL sessions, 324, 447–448

SSL/TLS, 445–455
SSL/TLS LDAP, 453–454
SSO (single sign-on) authentication, 535–536
Stalker IDS, 298
standards. See also protocols
    802.11. See 802.11 protocol
    Common Criteria, 176
    described, 28
    digital signatures, 83
    encryption, 87–91
    federal information processing, 82
    IEEE 802.1x, 247
    ISO 17799, 177–178
    ISO/IEC 27002, 177–178
    overview, 155–156
    payment cards, 59–60
    PKCS, 157, 162–164
    PKIX, 120, 157–164
    public key cryptography, 157–164
    S/MIME, 171–173, 426, 431–433
    X.500, 117
    X.509, 120–121, 164–165
    XKMS, 169–171
stateful packet filtering, 211–212
stateless web traffic, 448, 462–463
static IPs, 214
statutory laws, 56
stealth mode, 324
stealthy viruses, 411
steganography, 99–100
Stoned virus, 410
storage auditing, 543
store preferences, 7
STP (shielded twisted-pair) cables, 220–221
stream ciphers, 93
student records, 67
substitution ciphers, 79
SubVirt rootkit, 414
Sun Microsystems, 3, 457
SuperScan tool, 393
superusers, 531
Switched Port Analyzer (SPAN) port, 330
switches, 206–208
symmetric encryption, 86–95, 100–103, 173
SYN flooding attacks, 395–396, 402
SYN packets, 395–396, 402
SYN/ACK packets, 395–396, 402–403, 577
system logs, 542
system problem report (SPR), 521–522

system requirements, CD-ROM, 569
Systems Security knowledge domain, 3, 4, 5

T

TACACS+ accounting, 253
TACACS+ (Terminal Access Controller Access
    Control System+) protocol, 251–253
"tailgating," 193
tangible impacts, 500–501
tape media, 227
Tavares, Stafford, 91
TCI (Trustworthy Computing Initiative), 345
TCP (Transmission Control Protocol), 445,
    576, 577
TCP handshake, 577
TCP packets, 320–321, 402
TCP ports, 251
TCP reset messages, 320
TCP streams, 331
TCP wrappers, 310, 350, 356, 370
TCP/IP hijacking, 405
TCP/IP protocol, 258
technical support, LearnKey, 570
technology risks, 497
Telecom/PBX systems, 215
telephone firewalls, 416
telephone networks, 29–30, 36
telephony services, 7
Telnet protocol, 258
Telnet service, 353–354
Telnet sessions, 320
templates, security, 384–385
Temporal Key Integrity Protocol (TKIP), 287
Terminal Access Controller Access Control
    System+. See TACACS+
terminology
        basic, 6–20
        glossary, 581–599
terrorist attacks, 58–59, 499
text
        clear, 268
        plaintext, 277, 278, 405
TGS (ticket granting server), 244
TGT (ticket granting ticket), 244, 245
theft, 187, 191, 500
third-party trust model, 110
threats, 494, 499–500. See also risk
    management; vulnerabilities
three-way handshake, 256, 395, 402–403

ticket granting server (TGS), 244
ticket granting ticket (TGT), 244, 245
tickets, 244–245
time bombs, 413
time of day restrictions, 32–33
time stamp authority (TSA), 123–124, 159
TKIP (Temporal Key Integrity Protocol), 287
TLS (Transport Layer Security), 165–167, 445.
        See also SSL/TLS
tokens. See also access tokens; authorization
        access, 192
        described, 33, 101
        hardware, 33–34
        logical, 33–34
        overview, 245–246
        remote access, 245–246
        software, 34
top secret security level, 544
topologies. See security topologies
Torvalds, Linus, 352
TPM (Trusted Platform Module), 80
traffic
        blocking for ports, 210–211
        encrypted, 319, 324, 404
        filtering, 368–370
        HTTP, 323
        stateless, 448, 462–463
        web, 448, 462–463
traffic collector, 299, 301, 316
Transmission Control Protocol. See TCP
transmission media, 219–225
        coaxial cables, 219
        degaussing, 43
        fiber-optic cables, 221–222
        floppy, 43, 225, 226, 410, 426
        magnetic, 43
        physical security, 224–225
        removable, 225–229
        security concerns, 224–225
        twisted-pair cables, 219–221
        unguided, 222–223
transport layer, 575
Transport Layer Security (TLS), 165–167
transport method, 262
transposition ciphers, 77
trapdoors, 96, 398
treasury management risks, 497
trees, 302
Triple DES (3DES), 89–90

Tripwire, 205
Trojan horse programs, 412, 427, 451
TrueCrypt application, 103
trunking, 233
trunks, 234
trust
    bidirectional, 141–142, 144
    certificate authorities, 113, 116–120
    level of, 109–112
    Public Key Infrastructure, 109–112,
      116–119
    unidirectional, 141, 142
trust anchors, 141, 142, 143, 145
trust domains, 140, 142, 143, 145
trust models, 140–146
trust relationships, 10, 141–142
Trusted Platform Module (TPM), 80
trusted relationships, 10, 401–402
trusted servers, 332
Trustworthy Computing Initiative (TCI), 345
TSA (time stamp authority), 123–124, 159
tunneling
    described, 236, 254
    example of, 236
    IPSec and, 262, 263–264
    PPTP, 254–256
tunneling proxies, 327
tunnels, 254, 255
twisted-pair cables, 219–221
Twofish cipher, 90

U

UDP (User Datagram Protocol), 576, 577
UDP ports, 251
UECA (Uniform Electronic Commerce Act), 64
UETA (Uniform Electronic Transactions Act), 63
UNCITRAL (United Nations Commission on
    International Trade Law), 63–64
unclassified security level, 545
unguided media, 222–223
Uniform Electronic Commerce Act (UECA), 64
Uniform Electronic Transactions Act (UETA), 63
uniform resource locators (URLs), 451
uninterruptible power supply (UPS), 487
United Nations, 63–64
United Nations Commission on International
    Trade Law (UNCITRAL), 63–64
UNIX firewalls, 310–312

UNIX systems
    baselines, 347–357
    discretionary access control, 545
    file permissions, 545
    hardening, 347–352
    patches, 349
    removing unnecessary programs, 347–348
    root account, 531
    turning services on/off, 348
    usage auditing, 539
    user accounts, 348–349
unshielded twisted-pair (UTP) cables, 220–221
updates. *See also* hotfixes; patches; service packs
    automatic, 361, 371, 372
    firmware, 364
    operating system, 360–363
    virus signatures, 309
upgrades, application, 371
UPS (uninterruptible power supply), 487
urban legends, 37, 426, 428
URLs (uniform resource locators), 451
U.S. Air Force, 298
U.S. Department of Defense, 298
U.S. laws. *See also* laws/regulations; legal issues
    administrative law, 56
    common law, 56
    cybercrime, 57–59
    encryption regulations, 60–63
    import/export, 61–62
    legislative laws, 56
    privacy, 58–59, 66–67, 555
    sources of, 56
    statutory laws, 56
usage auditing, 539–540
USB devices, 190–191
USB drive keys, 190
USB ports, 190, 229
USB sticks, 229
user access auditing, 543
user accounts. *See also* administrator accounts;
   users
    administrator, 531
    expired, 33, 547
    Linux systems, 355–356
    Mac OS–based systems, 359–360
    privileges, 530–531
    Solaris systems, 351–352
    UNIX systems, 348–349
    Windows, 376, 377

User Datagram Protocol. *See* UDP
user IDs, 242–243
    as authentication mechanism, 20
    described, 530
    schemes for, 530
    single sign-on authentication, 535–536
    verifying, 16–17
user interface, IDS, 300, 303
user rights auditing, 543
useradd command, 356
useradd tool, 351
userdel command, 356
usernames, 32
users. *See also* employees; user accounts
    chain of custody, 560
    described, 530
    end-entities, 157
    file sharing, 33
    groups, 530
    implicit deny policy, 11–12
    job rotation, 12
    need-to-know principle, 18–19, 42
    permitted logon hours, 546
    privileges, 530–531
    roles, 19, 530
    shoulder surfing, 36
    superusers, 531
    time of day restrictions, 32–33
utilities, 487
UTP (unshielded twisted-pair) cables, 220–221

V

vacations, mandatory, 46
VeriSign, 3
version control, 513
Vigenère cipher, 79, 80
virtual LANs (VLANs), 207–208, 233–234
virtual networks, 326
virtual private networks. *See* VPNs
virus signatures, 309
viruses, 410–412. *See also anti-virus entries;*
  worms
    boot sector, 410
    Concept virus, 411
    e-mail, 309, 411, 425, 426–428
    encryption in, 308–309
    Good Times virus, 411
    hoaxes, 411–412

    instant messaging programs, 436–437
    macro, 410–411
    malicious code and, 426–428
    overview, 203, 410, 426–428
    polymorphic, 411
    program, 410
    protection against, 411
    stealthy, 411
    Stoned virus, 410
    vs. worms, 414
vishing, 36
VLANs (virtual LANs), 207–208, 233–234
Voice over IP (VoIP), 36
VoIP (Voice over IP), 36
VPN endpoints, 288–289
VPN services, 259, 261
VPNs (virtual private networks), 216, 254–261
vrfy command, 377–378
vulnerabilities. *See also* risks; threats
    code-based, 455–467
    defined, 494
    examples of, 500
    remote access, 268
    researching, 393
vulnerability assessment, 28

W

Wagner, David, 90
WAP (Wireless Application Protocol), 176, 276,
    277–279
war-chalking, 284
war-dialing, 284, 416–417
war-driving, 224, 416–417
warm sites, 484
WASC (Web Application Security Consortium),
    467–468
Wassenaar Arrangement, 62
Web Application Security Consortium (WASC),
    467–468
web browsers, 443–444. *See also specific browsers*
    ActiveX and, 459–461
    browser extensions, 461
    certificate authorities, 117, 136
    cookies, 462–465, 563
    development of, 443
    functionality, 455–456, 461
    JavaScript and, 457–459
    plug-ins, 456, 466–467

pop-up ads, 312–313
security and, 461
SSL/TLS options, 445, 451
web cache, 328
web components, 443–472
code-based vulnerabilities, 455–467
overview, 443–444
protocols, 444–455
security concerns, 444
web proxies, 328
web servers, 374–380, 443
web sites. See also Internet
access to, 12
CompTIA, 4
EDGAR, 392
Internet crime information, 55
LearnKey Online Training, 569
McGraw-Hill, 570
Mitre Corporation, 468
offensive, 40
phishing attacks, 35–36
pop-up ads, 312–313
pornographic, 55, 329, 400
spoofing, 400
web-based vulnerabilities, 467–468
WEP (Wired Equivalent Privacy), 177, 225,
281–287
white balance encryption, 78
white-hat hacking, 418
Whiting, Doug, 90
Whois.Net, 392
Wi-Fi Protected Access (WPA), 281
Windows 2003 systems, 345–346
Windows 2008 systems, 346–347
Windows Defender, 313–314
Windows Firewall, 310, 311
Windows Media Player, 467
Windows Update, 361
Windows Update Services (WSUS), 373–374
Windows-based systems
administrator account, 531
discretionary access control, 545
hardening, 345–347
passwords, 341, 534–535
permissions, 545, 547–549
updates, 361–362
usage auditing, 539–540
user accounts, 376, 377

wire speed, 324
Wired Equivalent Privacy (WEP), 177, 225,
281–287
wireless access points, 212–213
Wireless Application Protocol (WAP), 176, 276,
277–279
wireless bridge, 186
wireless devices, 212–213
wireless networks, 275–293
802.11 protocol. See 802.11 protocol
Bluetooth technology, 276, 279–281
mobile phones, 276–279
overview, 275–289
security issues, 283–289
threats to, 225, 226–227
wireless phones, 276–279
Wireless Transaction Layer Security (WTLS),
157–158, 176
Wireshark protocol analyzer, 331
wiretaps, 58–59
workstations, 202–204
World Wide Web (WWW), 232, 443–444.
See also Internet
worms, 414–415. See also viruses
Code Red II worm, 414
Code Red worm, 414
cross-scripting worm, 415
e-mail, 415
instant messaging programs, 436–437
malicious code and, 426–428
Morris Internet worm, 415
MySpace worm, 415
Nimba worm, 414
overview, 203, 414
protection against, 415
sadmind worm, 414
Samy worm, 415
Slammer worm, 456
Sobig worm, 414
SQL Slammer worm, 414, 416
vs. viruses, 414
Zotob worm, 414
WPA (Wi-Fi Protected Access), 281
WSUS (Windows Update Services), 373–374
WTLS (Wireless Transaction Layer Security),
157–158, 176
WWW (World Wide Web), 232, 443–444

X

X.500 standard, 117, 164, 453
X.509 certificate, 164–165
X.509 Public Key Certificate (PKC) format, 157
X.509 standard, 120–121, 164–165
xinetd service, 352
XKMS (XML Key Management Specification), 169–171
XKMS services, 169–171
XML (Extensible Markup Language), 169–170
XML Key Management Specification (XKMS), 169–171

XOR (exclusive-OR), 81
XSS (cross-scripting) worm, 415
XTACACS (Extended Terminal Access Controller Access Control System), 251

Z

Zimmerman, Philip, 103, 173
Zip disks, 226
zombies, 396, 397
zone transfers, 380
zones, security, 229–233
Zotob worm, 414

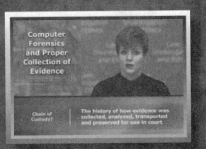